James McCosh

The Scottish Philosophy

Biographical, expository, critical. From Hutcheson to Hamilton.

James McCosh

The Scottish Philosophy
Biographical, expository, critical. From Hutcheson to Hamilton.

ISBN/EAN: 9783337236786

Printed in Europe, USA, Canada, Australia, Japan

Cover: Foto ©Thomas Meinert / pixelio.de

More available books at **www.hansebooks.com**

THE

SCOTTISH PHILOSOPHY,

𝔅iographical, 𝔈xpository, 𝔆ritical,

FROM HUTCHESON TO HAMILTON.

BY

JAMES McCOSH, LL.D., D.D.,

PRESIDENT OF THE COLLEGE OF NEW JERSEY, PRINCETON.

NEW YORK:

ROBERT CARTER AND BROTHERS,

530 BROADWAY.

1875.

PREFATORY NOTE.

THIS work has been with me a labor of love. The gathering of materials for it, and the writing of it, as carrying me into what I feel to be interesting scenes, have afforded me great pleasure, which is the only reward I am likely to get. I publish it, as the last, and to me the only remaining, means of testifying my regard for my country — loved all the more because I am now far from it — and my country's philosophy, which has been the means of stimulating thought in so many of Scotland's sons.

The English-speaking public, British and American, has of late been listening to divers forms of philosophy, — to Coleridge, to Kant, to Cousin, to Hegel, to Comte, to Berkeley, — and is now inclined to a materialistic psychology. Not finding permanent satisfaction in any of these, it is surely possible that it may grant a hearing to the sober philosophy of Scotland.

M. Cousin has remarked that the philosophy of Scotland is part of the history of the country. I have treated it as such; and I claim to have one qualification for the work: I am in thorough sympathy with the characteristic sentiments of my native land. I have farther tried to make my work a contribution to what may be regarded as a new department of science, the history of thought, which is quite as important as the history of wars, of commerce, of literature, or of civilization.

Some of these articles have appeared in the " North British Review," the " British and Foreign Evangelical Review," and the " Dublin University Magazine; " but the greater number are now given to the public for the first time, and all of them have been rewritten.

J. McC.

PRINCETON, New Jersey,
    October, 1874.

CONTENTS.

APPENDIX.

THE SCOTTISH PHILOSOPHY.

I. — *CHARACTERISTICS OF THE SCHOOL.*

THE Germans have histories without number of their philosophy from Kant to Hegel, with not a few historical reviews
of the later speculations. The French, too, have numerous
sketches of the philosophy of their country generally, and of
individual systems, such as that of Descartes. It is no way
to the credit of British thought, and least of all to that of the
Scotch metaphysicians, that we have not in our language a history of the Scottish school of philosophy. There are valuable
notices of it, it is true, in Dugald Stewart's Historical Dissertation, and in his Eloges of Reid and Adam Smith ; but Stewart
is far too dignified and general in his style to be able to give an
articulate account of the special doctrines of the different masters of the school, or a vivid picture of the times, with many of
the marked characteristics of which he had no sympathy. The
best history of the Scottish Philosophy is by a Frenchman, and
has not been translated into English. We look on " Philosophie Ecossaise," the volume in which M. Cousin treats of the
Scottish school, as containing upon the whole the most fault-
less of all his historical disquisitions. In his other volumes he
scarcely does justice to Locke, whom he always judges from
the evil consequences which have flowed from his philosophy
on the continent, and he is not able to wrestle successfully with
the powerful logical intellect of Kant ; but he has a thorough
appreciation of the excellencies of the Scottish metaphysicians,
and, when he finds fault, his criticisms are always worthy of
being considered. But it could not be expected of a foreigner,

1

that he should thoroughly comprehend the state of Scotland when its peculiar philosophy arose, nor be able to estimate its relation to the national character; and the account given by M. Cousin is fragmentary, and critical rather than expository.

The Scottish Philosophy possesses a unity, not only in the circumstance that its expounders have been Scotchmen, but also and more specially in its method, its doctrines, and its spirit. It is distinguished by very marked and decided features, which we may represent as determined by the bones rather than the flesh or muscles.

I. It proceeds on the method of observation, professedly and really. In this respect it is different from nearly all the philosophies which went before, from many of those which were contemporary, and from some of those which still linger among us. The method pursued in Eastern countries, in ancient Greece and Rome, in the scholastic times, and in the earlier ages of modern European speculation, had not been that of induction, either avowedly or truly. No doubt, speculators have been obliged in all ages and countries to make some use of facts, in the investigation both of mind and matter. But in the earlier theosophies, physiologies, and philosophies, they looked at the phenomena of nature merely as furnishing a starting-point to their systems, or a corroboration of them; and their inquiries were conducted in the dogmatic, or deductive, or analytic manner, explaining phenomena by assumed principles, or bringing facts to support theories, or resolving the complexities of the universe by refined mental distinctions. This spirit had been banished from physical science, first, by the great realistic awakening of the sixteenth century; then by the profound wisdom and far-sighted sagacity of Bacon; and, finally, by the discoveries of Newton and the establishment of the Royal Society of London. But it lingered for some ages longer in mental science, from which it has not even yet been finally expelled. Bacon had declared, that his method was applicable to all other sciences as well as to the investigation of the material universe. " Does any one doubt (rather than object)," says he, " whether we speak merely of natural philosophy or of other sciences also, such as logics, ethics, politics, as about to be perfected by our method?" "We certainly," he replies, "understand all these things which have been referred to; and like as the vulgar logic, which regulates things by the syllogism, pertains not to the natural but all sciences, so ours, which proceeds by induction, embraces them all. For thus we would form a history and tables concerning anger, fear, modesty, and the like, as also examples of civil affairs, not omitting the mental emotions of memory, composition, division, judgment, and the rest, just as we form such of heat and cold, of light, vegetation, and such like." Sir Isaac Newton had said in his Optics : " And if natural philosophy in all its parts, by pursuing this method, shall at length be perfected, the bounds of moral philosophy will also be enlarged." But the employment of the method of induction in the study of the human mind was for ages slow, wavering, and uncertain. It has been asserted, that Descartes proceeded on the method of induction ; but the statement has been made by metaphysicians who have never correctly apprehended the mode of procedure recommended by Bacon. Descartes does indeed appeal to profound ideas, which may be regarded as mental facts ; but it is not by them to arrive at laws by a gradual generalization ; it is rather to employ them as foundation-stones of his structure, which is reared high above them by the joint dogmatic and deductive method, and on the geometric and not the inductive plan. It has been averred that Hobbes proceeded on the method of his friend Bacon ; but Hobbes nowhere professes to do so: his doctrine of the origin of civil government is a mere theory, his system of the human mind and of morals is obtained by a very defective analysis, and, in fact, is mainly borrowed from Aristotle, whose profounder principles he was incapable of appreciating. It cannot be denied that Locke does proceed very largely in the way of observation ; but it is a curious circumstance that he nowhere professes to follow the method of induction ; and his great work may be summarily represented as an attempt to establish by internal facts the preconceived theory, that all our ideas are derived from sensation and reflection. To the Scottish school belongs the merit of being the first, avowedly and knowingly, to follow the inductive method, and to employ it systematically in psychological investigation. As the masters of the school were the first to adopt it, so they, and those who have borrowed from them, are almost the only persons who have studiously adhered to it. The school of Condillac in France, and its followers in England

and Germany, do indeed profess to attend to observation, but it is after the manner of the empiricists, described by Bacon as beginning with experience, but immediately abandoning it for premature hypotheses. It will be seen, as we advance, that Kant followed the critical and not the inductive method. Hutcheson and Turnbull, and especially Reid and Stewart, have the credit of announcing unambiguously, that the human mind is to be studied exclusively by the method of observation, and of consistently employing this mode of procedure in all their investigations.

II. It employs self-consciousness as the instrument of observation. It may thus be distinguished from some other schools with which it has been confounded. Bacon, we have seen, did believe in the applicability of his method to all the mental sciences. But he had no clear apprehension of the agency by which the observation is to be accomplished ; he supposed it to be by "the history and tables concerning anger, fear, modesty, the memory, composition, division, judgment, and the like." In respect of the means of observation, philosophy is greatly indebted to Descartes, who taught men, in studying the human mind, to seize on great internal ideas. The questions started by Locke, and his mode of settling them, tend towards the same issue ; he dwells fondly on reflection as the alone source of the ideas which we have of the workings of the human mind, and ever appeals to the internal sense as an arbiter in discussions as to the origin of ideas. But the Scottish philosophers took a step in advance of any of their predecessors, inasmuch as they professed to draw all the laws of mental philosophy — indeed, their whole systems — from the observations of consciousness. .

By this feature they are at once distinguished from those who would construct a science of the human mind from the observation of the brain or nerves, or generally from animal physiology. Not indeed that the Scottish philosophy is required, by its manner or its principles, to reject the investigation of the functions of the bodily frame, as fitted to throw light on mental action. Certain of the masters of the school, such as Reid, Brown, and Hamilton, were well acquainted with physiology in its latest discoveries in their day, and carefully employed their knowledge to illustrate the operations of the human mind.

There is nothing in the method, or the spirit, or the cherished doctrines of the school tending to discountenance or disparage a painstaking experimental investigation of the parts of the bodily frame most intimately connected with mental action. Possibly the next great addition may be made to psychology, when internal observation of the thoughts and feelings, and external observation of the brain and nerves and vital forces, are—in circumstances to combine their lights. But in the days of the great masters of the Scottish school, physiology was not in a state, nor is it yet in a position, to furnish much aid in explaining mental phenomena. The instrument employed by them was the internal sense; and they always maintained that it is only by it that we can reach an acquaintance with mind proper and its various operations, and that the knowledge acquired otherwise must ever be regarded as subordinate and subsidiary. They might have admitted that the occasion of the production, and the modifications of our mental states, could so far be influenced by the cerebro-spinal mass, or the forces operating in it; but they strenuously maintained that we can know what our perceptions, and judgments, and feelings, and wishes, and resolves, and moral appreciations are, not by the senses or the microscope, not by chemical analysis, or the estimation of the vital forces, but solely through our inward experience revealed by consciousness.

But let us properly understand what the Scottish school intend when they maintain that a science of the human mind can be constructed only by immediate consciousness. They do not mean that the study of the mind can be prosecuted in no other way than by looking in for ever on the stream of thought as it flows on without interruption. The operation of introspection is felt to be irksome in the extreme if continued for any length of time, and will certainly be abandoned when thought is rapid or feeling is intense; and those who trust to it exclusively are apt to fix their attention on a few favorite mental states, and omit many others no less characteristic of the human mind. He who would obtain an adequate and comprehensive view of our complex mental nature must not be satisfied with occasional glances at the workings of his own soul: he must take a survey of the thoughts and feelings of others so far as he can gather them from their deeds and from their words; from the acts of mankind generally, and of individual men, women, and children ; from universal language as the expression of human cogitation and sentiment ; and from the commerce we hold with our fellow-men by conversation, by writing, or by books. Reid in particular is ever appealing to men's actions and language, as a proof that there must be certain principles, beliefs, and affections in the mind. Still this evidence ever carries us back to consciousness, as after all both the primary witness and the final judge of appeal ; as it is only by it, and by what has passed through our own minds, that we can come to discern and appreciate the feelings of our brother men.[1]

III. By the observations of consciousness, principles are reached which are prior to and independent of experience. This is another grand characteristic of the school, distinguishing it, on the one hand, from empiricism and sensationalism ; and, on the other hand, from the dogmatism and *a priori* speculation of all ages and countries. It agrees with the former in holding that we can construct a science of mind only by observation, and out of the facts of experience ; but then it separates from them, inasmuch as it resolutely maintains that we can discover principles which are not the product of observation and experience, and which are in the very constitution of the mind, and have there the sanction of the Author of our nature. These are somewhat differently apprehended and described by the masters of the school, some taking a deeper and others a more superficial view of them. Hutcheson calls them senses, and finds them in the very constitution of the mind. Reid designates them principles of common sense, and represents them as being natural, original, and necessary. Stewart characterizes them as fundamental laws of human thought and belief. Brown makes them intuitions simple and original. Hamilton views them under a great many aspects, but seems

---

[1] Mr. Buckle, in his "History of Civilization," vol. ii., professes a deep acquaintance with the Scottish metaphysicians of last century, who are represented by him as proceeding in the deductive, and not in the inductive, method. He adds, that in Scotland "men have always been deductive." But Mr. B. was never able to understand the difference between the method of deduction on the one hand, and the method of induction with consciousness as the agent of observation, on the other : the former derives consequences by reasoning from principles, the latter reaches principles by internal observation. That his whole views on this subject were confused is evident, from the circumstance that he represents women as proceeding (like Scotchmen) by deduction !

to contemplate them most frequently and fondly after the manner of Kant, as *a priori* forms or conditions.   But whatever
minor or major differences there may be in the fulness of their
exposition, or in the favorite views which they individually
prefer, all who are truly of the Scottish school agree in maintaining that there are laws, principles, or powers in the mind
anterior to any reflex observation of them, and acting independently of the philosophers' classification or explanation of them.
While the Scottish school thus far agrees with the rational and
a priori systems, it differs from them most essentially, in refusing to admit any philosophic maxims except such laws or principles as can be shown by self-inspection to be in the very
constitution of the mind.   It has always looked with doubt, if
not suspicion, on all purely abstract and rational discussions,
such as that by which Samuel Clarke demonstrated the existence of God ; and its adherents have commonly discountenanced or opposed all ambitious *a priori* systems, such as those
which were reared in imposing forms in Germany in the end
of last, and the beginning of the present, century.
    These three characters are found, in a more or less decided
form, in the works of the great masters of the school.   I am not
sure indeed whether they have been formally announced by
all, nor whether they have always been consistently followed
out.   I allow that the relation of the three principles one to
another, and their perfect congruity and consistency, have not
always been clearly discerned or accurately expressed.   In particular, I am convinced that most of the Scottish metaphysicians have not clearly seen how it is that we must ever proceed
in mental science by observation, while there are at the same
time in the mind laws superior to and independent of observation ; how it is that while there are *a priori* principles in the
mind, it is yet true that we cannot construct a philosophy by *a
priori* speculation.   But with these explanations and deductions,
it may be maintained that the characters specified are to be
found, either announced or acted on, in the pages of all the
writers of the school, from Hutcheson to Hamilton.   Whenever
they are discovered in the works of persons connected with
Scotland, the writers are to be placed among the adherents of
the school.   Wherever there is the total absence of any one of
them, we cannot allow the author a place in the fraternity.

The Scottish metaphysicians and moralists have left their impress on their own land, not only on the ministers of religion, and through them upon the body of the people, but also on the whole thinking mind of the country.   The chairs of mental science in the Scottish colleges have had more influence than any others in germinating thought in the minds of Scottish youth, and in giving a permanent bias and direction to their intellectual growth.   We have the express testimony of a succession of illustrious men for more than a century, to the effect that it was Hutcheson, or Smith, or Reid, or Beattie, or Stewart, or Jardine, or Mylne, or Brown, or Chalmers, or Wilson, or Hamilton, who first made them feel that they had a mind, and stimulated them to independent thought.   We owe it to the lectures and writings of the professors of mental science, acting always along with the theological training and preaching of the country, that men of ability in Scotland have commonly been more distinguished by their tendency to inward reflection than inclination to sensuous observation.   Nor is it to be omitted that the Scottish metaphysicians have written the English language, if not with absolute purity, yet with propriety and taste, — some of them, indeed, with elegance and eloquence, — and have thus helped to advance the literary cultivation of the country.   All of them have not been men of learning in the technical sense of the term, but they have all been well informed in various branches of knowledge (it is to a Scottish metaphysician we owe the "Wealth of Nations") ; several of them have had very accurate scholarship ; and the last great man among them was not surpassed in erudition by any scholar of his age.   Nor has the influence of the Scottish philosophy been confined to its native soil.   The Irish province of Ulster has felt it quite as much as Scotland, in consequence of so many youths from the north of Ireland having been educated at Glasgow University.   Though Scotch metaphysics are often spoken of with contempt in the southern part of Great Britain, yet they have had their share in fashioning the thought of England, and, in particular, did much good in preserving it, for two or three ages towards the end of last century and the beginning of this, from falling altogether into low materialistic and utilitarian views ; and in this last age Mr. J. S. Mill got some of his views through his father from Hume, Stewart, and Brown,

and an active philosophic school at Oxford has built on the
foundation laid by Hamilton. The United States of America,
especially the writers connected with the Presbyterian and
Congregational Churches, have felt pleasure in acknowledging
their obligations to the Scottish thinkers. It is a most interesting circumstance, that when the higher metaphysicians of
France undertook, in the beginning of this century, the laborious work of throwing back the tide of materialism, scepticism,
and atheism which had swept over the land, they called to their
aid the sober and well-grounded philosophy of Scotland. Nor
is it an unimportant fact in the history of philosophy, that the
great German metaphysician, Emmanuel Kant, was roused, as
he acknowledges, from his dogmatic slumbers by the scepticism
of David Hume.

But the great merit of the Scottish philosophy lies in the
large body of truth which it has — if not discovered — at least —
settled on a foundation which can never be moved. It has
added very considerably to our knowledge of the human mind,
bringing out to view the characteristics of mental as distinguished from material action ; throwing light on perception
through the senses ; offering valuable observations on the intellectual powers, and on the association of ideas ; furnishing, if
not ultimate, yet very useful provisional classifications of the
mental faculties ; unfolding many of the peculiarities of man's
moral and emotional nature, of his conscience, and of his taste
for the beautiful ; resolving many complex mental phenomena
into their elements ; throwing aside by its independent research
a host of traditional errors which had been accumulating for
ages ; and, above all, establishing certain primary truths as a
foundation on which to rear other truths, and as a breakwater
to resist the assaults of scepticism.

In comparing it with other schools, we find that the transcendental speculators of Germany have started discussions
which they cannot settle, and followed out their principles to
extravagant consequences, which are a *reductio ad absurdum*
of the whole method on which they proceed. Again, the physiologists have failed to furnish any explanation of consciousness, of thought, of moral approbation, or of any other peculiar
mental quality. Meanwhile, the philosophy of consciousness
has co-ordinated many facts, ascertained many mental laws,

explained many curious phenomena of our inward experience, and established a body of intuitive truths. By its method of careful observation, and by it alone, can the problems agitated in the rival *a priori* schools be solved, so far as they can be solved by the human faculties. Whatever aid physiological research as it advances may furnish to psychology, it must always be by the study, not of the brain, and nerves, and vital forces, but of our conscious operations, that a philosophy of the human mind is to be constructed. Whether the Scottish philosophy is to proceed exclusively in its old method, and go on co-ordinating facts with ever-increasing care, and expressing them with greater and greater precision, or whether it is to borrow from other schools, — say to resolve in its own way the questions started by Schelling and Hegel, or to call in physiology to account for the rise of mental states, — it is at least desirable that we should now have a combined view of what has been accomplished by the philosophy of consciousness. This is what is attempted in this work.

It should be freely admitted that the Scottish school has not discovered all truth, nor even all discoverable truth, in philosophy; that it does not pretend to have done so is one of its excellencies, proceeding from the propriety of its method and the modesty of its character. Among the writings of the Scottish school, it is only in those of Sir William Hamilton that we find some of the profoundest problems of philosophy, such as the conditions of human knowledge and the idea of the infinite discussed; and the majority of the genuine adherents of the school are inclined to think that on these subjects his conclusions are too bare and negative, and that he has not reached the full truth. Reid and Stewart are ever telling us that they have obtained only partial glimpses of truth, and that a complete science of the human mind is to be achieved solely by a succession of inquirers prosecuting the investigation through a series of ages. Brown and Hamilton make greater pretensions to success in erecting complete systems, but this is one of the defects of these great men, arising, as we shall see, from their departing from the genuine Scottish method, and adopting, so far, other and continental modes of philosophizing, the one betaking himself to the empirical analysis of the French sensational school, and the other adopting the critical method

of Kant ; and it is to be said in behalf of Brown, that he never
mounts into a region of cloudy speculation ; and in favor of
Hamilton, that his most vigorous efforts were employed in showing how little can be known by man.   All the great masters
of the school not only admit, but are at pains to show, that
there are mysteries in the mind of man, and in every department of human speculation, which they cannot clear up.   This
feature has tempted some to speak of the whole school with
contempt, as doing little because attempting little.   They have
been charged with their country's sin of caution, and the
national reproach of poverty has been unsparingly cast upon
them.   Let them not deny, let them avow, that the charge is
just.   Let them acknowledge that they have proceeded in time
past in the patient method of induction, and announce openly,
and without shame, that they mean to do so in time to come.
Let it be their claim, that if they have not discovered all truth,
they have discovered and settled some truth ; while they have
not promulgated much error, or wasted their strength in rearing
showy fabrics, admired in one age and taken down the next.
It is the true merit of Scotchmen that, without any natural
advantages of soil or climate, they have carefully cultivated
their land, and made it yield a liberal produce, and that they
have been roused to activity, and stimulated to industry, by
their very poverty.   Let it, in like manner, be the boast of the
Scottish philosophy, that it has made profitable use of the
materials at its disposal, and that it has by patience and shrewdness succeeded in establishing a body of fundamental truth,
which can never be shaken, but which shall stand as a bulwark
in philosophy, morals, and theology, as long as time endures.

II. — *STATE OF SCOTLAND.*

DURING the seventeenth century, the three kingdoms had
passed through a series of political and religious convulsions,
and in the opening of the following century the Protestant people were seeking to enjoy and improve the seasonable — as
they reckoned it the providential — rest which was brought by
the Revolution Settlement.   The floods had swept over the

country, partly to destroy and partly to fertilize, and men are busily employed in removing the evils (as they reckon them) which had been left, and in sowing, planting, and building on the now dry and undisturbed territory.   In particular, there is a strong desire on the part of the great body of the people to make the best use of the peace which they now possess, and to employ it to draw forth the material resources of the country. As a consequence of the intellectual stimulus which had been called forth mainly by the previous great contests, and of the liberty achieved, and the industry in active exercise, the riches of the nation are increasing, agriculture begins to make progress, great commercial cities are aggregating, household and social elegance and comfort are sought after and in a great measure secured, refinement of manners is cultivated, and civilization is advancing.   In the eager pursuit of these worldly ends, the generation then springing up scarcely set sufficient value on the higher blessings which had been secured by the struggles of their forefathers.   By the profound discussions of the seventeenth century, the great body of the people had been made to read their Bibles, and to inquire into the foundation and functions of political government.   By the deeds done, by the sufferings endured, and the principles enunciated, the great questions of civil and religious liberty had been started, and opinions set afloat which were ultimately to settle them theoretically and practically.   But the race now reared did not sufficiently appreciate the advantages thence accruing.   They were kept from doing so by two impressions left by the terrible battles which had been fought on their soil.

Every one who has read the history of the period knows that a large amount of profligacy had prevailed among certain classes in the latter reigns of the Stuarts.   The rampant vice led naturally to religious infidelity, and the two continued to act and react on each other.   Self-indulgent men were little inclined to value the truths of spiritual religion, and lent their ears to plausible systems of belief or unbelief which left them undisturbed in their worldly enjoyments ; while youths who had broken loose from the old religious trammels were often tempted to break through moral restraints likewise, and to rush into vice, as exhibiting spirit and courage.   The great cavalier party, composed largely of the upper classes, and of those who aspired to rise to them, had been all along in the habit of ridiculing the fervor and strictness of the puritan movement, which had sprung up chiefly among the middle and better portion of the lower classes, and of describing all who made solemn pretensions to religion as being either knaves or fools.   Many of those who had originally brought the charge did not believe it in their hearts, as they had been constrained to respect the great and good qualities of their opponents ; but they succeeded in instilling their sentiments into the minds of their children, who were taught to regard it as a mark of a gentleman to swear and to scoff at all religion.   From whatever causes it may have proceeded, it is certain that in the first half of the eighteenth century there is a frequent and loud complaint on the part of theologians, both within and beyond the Established Churches, of the rapid increase and wide prevalence of infidelity, and even of secret or avowed atheism.

The struggles of the seventeenth century had left another very deep sentiment.   The sects had contended so much about minor points, that now, in the reaction, there was a strong disposition, both among the professedly religious and irreligious, to set little or no value on doctrinal differences, and to turn away with distaste from all disputes among ecclesiastical bodies.   The indifference thence ensuing tended, equally with the mistaken zeal of the previous age, to prevent the principles of toleration from being thoroughly carried out.   Those who stood up for what were esteemed small peculiarities were reckoned pragmatical and obstinate.   Their attempts to secure full liberty of worship and of propagation met with little sympathy, and were supposed to be fitted to bring back needlessly the battles and the sufferings of the previous ages.

The two sentiments combined, the desire to have a liberal or a loose creed, and the aversion to the discussion of lesser differences, issued in a result which it is more to our present purpose to contemplate.   It led the great thinkers of the age, such as Samuel Clarke, Berkeley, and Butler, to spend their strength, not so much in discussing doctrines disputed among Christians, as in defending religion in general, and in laying a deep foundation on which to rest the essential principles of morality and the eternal truths of religion, natural and revealed. The first age of the eighteenth century, as it was the period in which the first serious attacks were made on Christianity, so it was also the time in which were produced the first great modern defences of religion, natural and supernatural. Men of inferior philosophical breadth, but of eminent literary power, such as Addison, were also employing their gifts and accomplishments and contributing to what they reckoned the same good end, by writing apologies in behalf of religion, and laboring to make it appear amiable, reasonable, and refined.

These same causes led preachers of the new school to assume a sort of apologetic air in their discourses, to cultivate a refined language, moulded on the French, and not the old English model, to avoid all extravagance of statement and appeal, to decline doctrinal controversy, and to dwell much on truths, such as the immortality of the soul, common to Christianity and to natural religion, and to enlarge on the loveliness of the Bible morality. The manner and spirit were highly pleasing to many in the upper and refined classes ; were acceptable to those who disliked earnest religion, as they had nothing of "the offence of the cross ;" and were commended by some who valued religion, as it seemed to present piety in so attractive a light to their young men, about whom they were so anxious in those times, and of whom they hoped that they would thus be led to imbibe its elements, and thereby acquire a taste for its higher truths. But all this was powerless on the great body of the people, who were perfectly prepared to believe the preacher when he told them that they were sinners, and that God had provided a Saviour, but felt little interest in refined apologies in behalf of God and Christ and duty ; and they gradually slipped away from a religion and a religious worship which had nothing to interest, because they had nothing to move them. All this was offensive in the extreme to those who had been taught to value a deeper doctrine and a warmer piety. They complained that when they needed food they were presented with flowers ; and, discontented with the present state of things, they were praying for a better era.

To complete the picture of the times, it should be added that there was little vital piety among the clergy to counteract the tendency to religious indifference. The appointments to the livings in England and Ireland lay in the hands of the government and the upper classes, who preferred men of refine-

ment and prudence, inclined to political moderation or subserviency, to men of spiritual warmth and religious independence.
The Nonconformists themselves felt the somnolent influence
creeping over them, after the excitement of the battle in which
they had been engaged was over. Their pastors were restrained
in their ministrations, and consequently in their activities, by
laws which were a plain violation of the principles of toleration, but which, as they did not issue in any overt act of bitter
persecution, were not resented with keenness by the higher
class of Dissenters, who, to tell the truth, after what they had
come through in the previous age, were not much inclined to
provoke anew the enmity from which they had suffered, but
were rather disposed, provided only their individual convictions
were not interfered with, to take advantage of what liberty they
had, to proclaim peace with others, and to embrace the opportunities thrown open to them in the growing cities and manu-
factories, of promoting the temporal interests of themselves
and their families. In these circumstances, the younger ministers were often allured (as Butler was) to go over to the
Established Church ; and those who remained were infected
with the spirit which prevailed around them, and sought to
appear as elegant and as liberal as the clergy of the church,
who were beginning to steal from them the more genteel portion of the younger members of their flocks. The design of
those who favored this movement was no doubt to make
religion attractive and respected. The result did not realize
the expectation. The upper classes were certainly not scan-
dalized by a religion which was so inoffensive, but they never
thought of heartily embracing what they knew had no earnestness ; and, paying only a distant and respectful obeisance to
religion in the general, they gave themselves up to the fashionable vices, or, at best, practised only the fashionable moralities
of their times. The common people, little cared for by the
clergy, and caring nothing for the refined emptiness presented
to them instead of a living religion, went through their daily
toils with diligence, but in most districts, both of town and
country, viewed religion with indifference, and relieved their
manual labor with low indulgences. England is rapidly growing in wealth and civilization, and even in industry, mainly from
the intellectual stimulus imparted by moral causes acting in the

previous ages ; but it is fast descending to the most unbelieving condition to which it has ever been reduced. From this
state of religious apathy it is roused, so far as the masses of
the people are concerned, in the next age, and ere the life had
altogether died out, by the trumpet voices of Whitfield and
Wesley. It was in a later age, and after the earthquake convulsions of the French Revolution had shaken society to its
foundation, that the upper classes were made to know and feel
that when "the salt has lost its savor," it is good for nothing
but to be cast out and trodden under foot of men, and that a
dead religion is of no use either to rich or poor, either for political ends or for personal comfort.

An analogous, but by no means identical, process begins and
goes on, and is consummated in Scotland about half an age or
an age later in point of time. All throughout the seventeenth
century, Scotland, like England, had been ploughed by religious contests. But the penetrating observer notices a difference between the shape taken by the struggle in the two
countries. In England, the war had been a purely internal one
between opposing principles, the prelatic and puritan ; whereas,
in Scotland, the battle had been mainly against an external foe,
that is, an English power, which sought to impose a prelatic
church on the people contrary to their wishes. Again, in
England the contest had been against an ecclesiastical power,
which sought to crush civil liberty ; whereas, in Scotland, the
power of the Church of Scotland had been exerted in behalf of
the people, and against a foreign domination. This difference
in the struggle was followed by a difference in the state of feeling resulting when the contest was terminated by the accession
of William and Mary.

The great body of the people, at least in the Lowlands,
acquiesced in the Revolution Settlement, and clung round the
Government and the Presbyterian Church as by law established.
But there soon arose antagonisms, which, though they did not
break out into open wars, as in the previous century, did yet
range the country into sections and parties with widely differ-
ing sympathies and aims. In fact, Scotland was quite as much
divided in opinion and sentiment in the eighteenth, as it ever
was in the seventeenth century. In saying so, I do not refer
to the strong prelatic feeling which existed all over the north-

east coast of Scotland, or to the attachment to the house of Stuart which prevailed in the Highlands, — for these, though they led to the uprisings of 1715 and 1745, were only the backward beatings of the retreating tide, — but to other and stronger currents which have been flowing and coming into more or less violent collision with one another from that day till ours.

At the close of the seventeenth and beginning of the eighteenth century, the Church of Scotland was composed of a somewhat heterogeneous mixture of covenanting ministers, who had lived in the times of persecution ; of prelatic clergy whose convictions in favor of Episcopacy were not sufficiently deep to induce them to abandon their livings, and to suffer the annoyances and persecutions to which the more sincere nonjurors were exposed ; and of a race of young men zealous for the Presbyterian establishment, but "only half educated and superficially accomplished." The conforming " curates " were commonly indifferent to religion of every kind, and it was hoped that they would soon die out, and that the heritors and elders, with whom the election of pastors lay, would fill the churches with a learned and zealous ministry. But, in 1711, the Jacobite government of Queen Anne took the power of election from the parish authorities, and vested it in the ancient patrons, being the Crown for above five hundred and fifty livings, and noblemen, gentlemen of landed property, and town-councils, for the remaining four hundred.[1] The effect of this new law became visible in the course of years, in the appointment of persons to the churches who, for good reasons or bad, were acceptable to the government of the day, or were able to secure the favor of the private patrons.

Forced upon the people in the first instance, there was a public feeling ready to gather round this law of patronage. From bad motives and from good — like those which we have traced in England — there was a desire among the upper, and a portion of the middle and educated, classes to have a clergy suited to the new age which had come in. As the result, there was formed a type of ministers which has continued till nearly our time in Scotland, called " new light " by the people, and designating themselves " moderates," as claiming the virtue of being moderate in all things, though, as Witherspoon charges

---

[1] See " Considerations on Patronage, by Francis Hutcheson," 1735.

them, they became very immoderate for moderation, when they rose to be the dominant party. Most of them refrained in their preaching from uttering a very decided sound on disputed doctrinal points ; some of them were suspected of Arianism or Socinianism, which, however, they kept to themselves out of respect for, or fear of, the Confession of Faith, which they had sworn to adhere to ; the more highly educated of them cultivated a refinement and elegance of diction, and dwelt much on the truths common to both natural and revealed religion ; and all of them were fond of depicting the high morality of the New Testament, and of recommending the example of Jesus. It is scarcely necessary to remark, that this style of preaching did not gain, as it did not warm, the hearts of the common people, who either became callous to all religion, without any zealous efforts being made to stir them up, or longed and prayed for a better state of things. The enforcement of the law of patronage, and the settlement of ministers against the wishes of the people, led to the separation of the Erskines and the Secession Body in 1733, and of Gillespie and the Relief Body in 1753. In the Established Church there still remained a number of men of evangelical views and popular sympathies, such as Willison and Boston, who hoped that they might stem and ultimately turn the tide which was for the time against them. The boast of the moderate party was, that they were introducing into Scotland a greater liberality of sentiment on religious topics, and a greater refinement of taste. The charge against them is, that they abandoned the peculiar doctrines of the gospel, that they could not draw towards them the affections of the people who, in rural districts, sank into a stupid ignorance of religious truth, and, in the crowded lanes of the rising cities, into utter ungodliness and criminality, — except, indeed, in so far as they were drawn out by the rapidly increasing dissenters, or by the evangelical minority within the Established Church.

The collisions of the century took various forms. After the Union with England, dancing assemblies, theatres, and wandering players (with Allan Ramsay to patronize them), dancing on the tight-rope, cock-fighting, gambling, and horse-racing make their appearance, and receive considerable countenance and patronage from various classes, upper and lower ; while ineffectual attempts are made to put them down by civil penalties inflicted by burgher magistrates, and by public ecclesiastical censures, which the zealous clergy rigidly enforce, but which the new-light clergy are anxious to relax. In the turmoil of opinions which sprang up in this new state of things, there are rumors of deism, and even of atheism, being secretly entertained or openly avowed, and of the establishment here and there, in town and country, of "hell-fire clubs," where bold men met to discuss new opinions, and even, it is said, to act mock ceremonies, intended to ridicule the sacraments, and all that is awful in religion. Worse than all, and without being much noticed, or meeting with much opposition on the part of the clergy of either party, there is the commencement of those drinking customs, which have ever since exercised so prejudicial an influence on the Scottish character.

If we look to the common people in the first quarter of the century, we find them in a state of great rudeness in respect of the comforts and elegancies of life. In the Highlands, they are scarcely removed above the lowest state of barbarism; and in the borders between the Highlands and Lowlands, the Celts are lifting cattle and exacting black-mail from the Lowlanders. Even in the more favored districts in the south of Scotland, the ground is unfenced; roads are very rare; and goods are carried on the backs of horses. The clothing of the people in the same region is of undyed black and white plaiding, and neither men nor women have shoes or stockings. Their ordinary food is oatmeal, pease, or beer, with kail groats and milk, and they rarely partake of flesh meat. The houses have only the bare ground as floors, with a fireplace in the midst, and the smoke escaping out of a hole in the roof, and with seats and the very beds of turf; even in the dwellings of the farmers there are seldom more than two apartments; not unfrequently, however, in the south-west of Scotland, there is in addition a closet, to which the head of the house would retire at set times for devotion.

Superstitious beliefs are still entertained in all ranks of life, and are only beginning to disappear among the educated classes. In the Highlands and Islands, second-sight is as firmly believed by the chieftain as by the clansmen. In the Lowlands, mysterious diseases, arising from a deranged nervous system, are ascribed to demoniacal possessions; and witches, supposed to have sold themselves to the Evil One, and accomplishing his purposes in inflicting direful evils on the persons and properties of neighbors, are being punished by the magistrates, who are always incited on by the people, and often by the more zealous ministers of religion. Toleration is not understood or acknowledged by any of the great parties, political or religious.

What, it may be asked, is there in the condition of this people fitted to raise any hope that they are ever to occupy a high place among the nations of the earth? I am sure that a worldly-minded traveller, or an admirer of mere refinement and art, in visiting the country at those times, and comparing it with France or Italy, would have discovered nothing in it to lead him to think that it was to have a glorious future before it. But a deeper and more spiritually-minded observer might have discovered already the seeds of its coming intelligence and love of freedom: — in the schools and colleges planted throughout the land; in the love of education instilled into the minds of the people; and, above all, in their acquaintance with the Bible, and in their determined adherence to what they believed to be the truth of God.[1]

Before the first age of the century has passed, there are unmistakable signs of industrial and intellectual activity. The Union has connected the upper classes with the metropolis and the Court of England, from which they are receiving a new refinement and some mental stimulus. The middle classes, and even the lower orders, are obtaining instruction from a very different quarter, from their parochial schools and churches,

[1] Mr. Buckle is reported to have expressed, in his dying days, his regret that he could not see moral causes operating in the promotion of civilization. Of course intellectual power must always be the immediate agent in producing civilization; but did it never occur to Mr. Buckle to ask what stirred up the intellectual power in a country so unfavorably situated as Scotland? It is all true that steam power is the main agent in producing manufactures in our country; but how contracted would be the vision of one who can see only the steam power, and not the intellectual power which called the steam into operation! Equally narrow is the view of the man who discerns the intellectual power which effected the peculiar civilization of Scotland, but cannot discover the moral power which awoke the intelligence. It should be added, that just as the steam power, invented by intellectual skill, may be devoted to very unintellectual uses, so the intelligence aroused by moral or religious causes may be turned (as Scotland shows) to very immoral and irreligious ends.

from their burgh academies and their universities. The towns
are hastening to take advantage of the new channels of trade
and commerce; manufactures are springing up in various
places, and already there is a considerable trading intercourse
between the west of Scotland and America. The proprietors
of the soil, in need of money to support their English life and
to buy luxuries, are beginning to subdivide and enclose their
lands, and to grant better dwellings and leases to their tenantry,
who, being thereby placed in circumstances fitted to encourage
and reward industry, are prepared to reclaim waste lands, to
manure their grounds, to improve their stock of sheep and cattle, and introduce improved agricultural implements.

This imperfect sketch may help the reader to comprehend
the circumstances in which the Scottish philosophy sprang up
and grew to maturity, and the part which its expounders acted
in the national history. It could have appeared only in a time
of peace and temporal prosperity, but there had been a preparation for it in the prior struggles. The stream which had
risen in a higher region, and long pursued its course in rugged-
ness, — like the rivers of the country, — is now flowing through
more level ground, and raising up plenty on its banks. It is a
collegiate, and therefore a somewhat isolated, element among
the agencies which were forming the national character and
directing the national destiny ; but it had its sphere. Through
the students at the universities, it fostered a taste for literature
and art ; it promoted a spirit of toleration, and softened the
national asperities in religious and other discussions ; it is identified with the liberalism of Scotland, and through Adam Smith,
D. Stewart, Mackintosh, Horner, Brougham, Jeffrey, Sydney
Smith, Lord John Russell, and Palmerston, with the liberalism
of the three kingdoms ; and, above all, it has trained the educated portion of the inhabitants of North Britain to habits of
reflection and of independent thought. The Scottish metaphysicians, with the exception of Chalmers, have never identified themselves very deeply with the more earnest spiritual
life of the country ; but they defended the fundamental truths
of natural religion, and they ever spoke respectfully of the
Bible. The Scottish philosophy, so far as it is a co-ordination
of the facts of consciousness, never can be antagonistic to a
true theology ; I believe indeed it may help to establish some

of the vital truths of religion, by means, for instance, of the moral faculty, the existence of which has been so resolutely maintained by the Scottish school. Some of the moderate clergy did at times preach the Scottish moral philosophy instead of scriptural truth ; but they did so in opposition to the counsel of the metaphysicians, at least of Hutcheson, who recommended his students to avoid the discussion of philosophic topics in the pulpit. Some of those who have been the most influential expounders of the Scottish theology, such as Chalmers and Welsh, have also been supporters of the Scottish philosophy, and have drawn from its established doctrines arguments in favor of evangelical religion.

III. — *PRECURSORS OF THE SCHOOL.*

In the Libraries of some of the Scotch Colleges are collected a number of the theses which had been defended in the Scottish Universities in the seventeenth century. These seem to fall under the heads of Theses Logicæ, Theses Ethicæ, Theses Physicæ, Theses Sphericæ. Aristotle still rules both in logic and ethics. In logic, there is much abstract enunciation, and there are many acute distinctions in regard to Ens and unity, singulars and universals; and in ethics, the discussions are about virtue and vice, and choice. In physics, there are rational and deductive investigations of the nature of motion and resistance. During the century, the courses of study differ somewhat in the different universities, but still there is a general correspondence. In the course of Philosophy the Regents use Aristotle *De Anima*, Porphyry's Introduction, the Categories of Aristotle, the Dialectics of Ramus, and the Rhetoric of Vossius, with the works of such writers as Crassotus, Reas, Burgersdicius, Ariaga, Oviedo, &c. The ethics include politics and economics, and there are discussions about the nature of habits. It is scarcely necessary to say that all topics are treated in a logical and rational, and not in an observational, manner and spirit.

The Parliamentary Commission for visiting the universities, appointed in 1690, and following years, directed, in 1695, the professors of philosophy in St. Andrews to prepare the heads of a system of logic, and the corresponding professors in Edinburgh to prepare a course of metaphysics. The compends drawn up in consequence were passed from one college to another for revision ; there is no evidence that they were finally sanctioned, but they may be accepted as giving a fair idea of the instructions in philosophy conveyed in the universities of Scotland at the close of the eighteenth century, — at the very time when Locke's Essay was finding its way so rapidly over the three kingdoms.[1] Logic is called the instrument to acquire other sciences, inasmuch as it prescribes rules for rightly apprehending, judging, and arguing. It is said to be defined by others as the science which directs the operations of the mind for finding out truth in every other science. It is represented as treating of the three operations of apprehension, judgment, and discourse, to which some add a fourth part, on method, under which analysis and synthesis are explained. In all this there is nothing but the commonplace of by-gone ages. But in this same text-book of logic we have the distinction drawn in the Port Royal Logic, between the extension and comprehension of the notion, adopted and stated. "We must distinguish betwixt the extension and comprehension of an idea. All the essential attributes of an idea are called its comprehension, as being, substance, vegetative, sensitive, and rational are the comprehension of man ; but Peter, Paul, &c., contained under man, are called the extent of man." It can be shown that this distinction comes down in an unbroken historical chain in Glasgow to Sir W. Hamilton, who has so profitably amplified and applied it. It is found in the Introduction to Logic by Carmichael, and in the Logical Compend of Hutcheson ; and the latter continued to be used in Glasgow till towards the time when Hamilton was a student there.

Metaphysics are said to be defined by some, as a science of being as being ; by others as a speculative science, which considers being in general, and its properties and kinds, as abstracted from matter. The benefits arising from the study of metaphysics are said to be, that treating of undoubted truths and axioms, we are enabled by their assistance the better to discover truths generally, and avoid errors ; that as dividing

[1] There is a copy in the Edinburgh University Library.

beings into classes it keeps us from confusion; that giving general names to common and abstracted beings, it aids the understanding in every kind of learning, and specially in theology, in which use is made of metaphysical terms. The first part of metaphysics treats of the principles of being, and of the various species of beings. The second part treats of the properties of being, such as unity, verity, goodness; and under this head we have abstract discussions as to the finite and infinite, the necessary and contingent, the absolute and relative, cause and effect, means and end, substance and quality. Such was the pabulum on which college youths fed during the century. This was the learning which helped to sharpen the intellects of such men as Henderson, Rutherford, Leighton, Gillespie, Baillie, Dickson, Burnet (Bishop), Stair (Lord), and Carstairs, who acted so important a part in the affairs of their country.

But in order to appreciate fully the philosophic tastes and capacities of Scotchmen, we must follow them into France. From a very old date, certainly from the thirteenth century, there had been a close connection between that country and Scotland, arising from the jealousy entertained by both nations of the power and ambition of England. The Scottish youth who had a love of adventure, or a thirst for military glory, had a splendid opening provided for them in the Scottish Guard, which protected the person of the king of France, while those who had a taste for letters found means of instruction and employment in the numerous French colleges.[1] The Scotch scholars who returned to their own land brought back the French learning with them. Bishop Elphinston, who was the founder, and Hector Boece, who was the first principal of King's College, Aberdeen, had both taught in the University of Paris; and they set up the Scottish University on the model of the French one. John Major or Mair, who taught scholastic theology in Glasgow and St. Andrews, and who was the preceptor of Knox and Buchanan, had been for some time in the University of Paris. During the sixteenth, and the early part of the seventeenth century, there was a perpetual stream of Scottish scholars flowing into France. Some of these were Catho-

---

[1] The reader curious on this subject will find ample information in "Les Écossais en France," by Michel.

lics, to whom toleration was denied at home, and who betook themselves to a country where they had scope for the free exercise of their gifts. But quite as many were Protestants, who finding (as Scotchmen in later ages have done) their own land too narrow, or thirsting for farther knowledge or learned employment, connected themselves with one or other of the reformed colleges of Saumur, Montauban, Sedan, Montpellier, and Nismes, where some of them remained all their lives, while others returned to their own country. Some of these emigrants were lawyers or physicians; but by far the greater number of them were devoted to literature, philosophy, or theology. George Buchanan, Thomas Ricalton, three Blackwoods, Thomas Dempster, two Barclays, Andrew Melville, John Cameron, Walter Donaldson, and William Chalmers are only a few of the Scotchmen who occupied important offices in France. Two deserve to be specially named, as they wrote able logical works, — the one, Robert Balfour, a Catholic, and Principal of Guienne College, Bourdeaux, and an erudite commentator on Aristotle; and the other, Mark Duncan, a Protestant, and Principal of the University of Saumur, and author of Institutes of Logic. There must have been some reality as the ground of the extravagant statement of Sir Thomas Urquhart in his " Discovery of a Most Exquisite Jewel," that " the most of the Scottish nation, never having restricted themselves so much to the propriety of words as to the knowledge of things, where there was one preceptor of languages among them, there was above forty professors of philosophy." " The French conceived the Scots to have above all nations in matter of their subtlety in philosophical disputations, that there have not been till of late for these several years together any lord, gentleman, or other in all that country, who, being desirous to have his son instructed in the principles of philosophy, would entrust him to the discipline of any other than a Scottish master." He adds, that " if a Frenchman entered into competition, a Scotchman would be preferred."

By such teaching at home, and by such foreign intercourse, a considerable amount of narrow but intense intellectual life was produced and fostered in Scotland. But youths were beginning to feel that the air was too close, too confined, and too monastic for them, and were longing for greater freedom and

expansion. While Aristotle and the scholastic method still
hold their place in the cloisters of the colleges, there is a more
bracing atmosphere in the regions without and beyond ; and
this is now to rush into Scotland.

From the time of the revival of letters in the sixteenth century, almost every great and original thinker had thought it
necessary to protest against the authority of Aristotle and the
schoolmen. Bacon left Cambridge with a thorough contempt
for the scholastic studies pursued there; and the grand end
aimed at in his "Novum Organum," was to carry away men's
regards from words and notions, to which they had paid too
exclusive attention, and to fix them on things. In respect of a
disposition to rebel against Aristotle and the schoolmen, Descartes was of the same spirit as Bacon ; and Gassendi and
Hobbes agreed with Descartes, with whom they differed in
almost every thing else. It would be easy to produce a succession of strong testimonies against the Stagyrite and the Mediæ-
vals, spread over the whole of the seventeenth century. The
rising sentiment is graphically expressed by Glanvil in his
"Scepsis Scientifica," published in 1665. He declares that
the "ingenious world is grown quite weary of qualities and
forms ;" he declaims against "dry spinosities, lean notions,
endless altercations about things of nothing ;" and he recommends a "knowledge of nature, without which our hypotheses
are but dreams and romances, and our science mere conjecture
and opinion ; for, while we have schemes of things without consulting the phenomena, we do but build in the air, and describe
an imaginary world of our own making, that is but little akin
to the real one that God made."

The realistic reaction took two different but not totally diver-
gent directions in the seventeenth century, and both the streams
reached Scotland in the following century. In the works of
Grotius and Puffendorf, an elaborate attempt was made to
determine the laws of nature in regard to man's political and
social conditions, and apply the same to the examination and
rectification of national and international laws. This was
thought by many to be a more profitable and promising theme
than the perpetual discussion of the nature of being and universals. This school had undoubtedly its influence in Scotland,
where Carmichael, in 1718, edited and annotated Puffendorf,

and where Hutcheson, and Hume, and A. Smith, and Ferguson, and D. Stewart, combined juridical and political with moral
inquiries, and became the most influential writers of the century on all questions of what has since been called social science.

But a stronger and deeper current was setting in about the
same time, — a determination to have the experimental mode
of investigation applied to every department of knowledge.
This method had already been applied to physical science with
brilliant results. And now there was a strong desire felt to
have the new manner adopted in the investigation of the
human mind. In 1670, John Locke and five or six friends are
conversing in his chamber in Oxford on a knotty topic, and
quickly they find themselves at a stand ; and it occurred to
Locke that, before entering " on inquiries of that nature, it was
necessary to examine our own abilities, and see what objects
our understandings were or were not fitted to deal with." He
pondered and wrote on this subject for twenty years, at the
close of which (in 1690) he published his immortal " Essay on
the Human Understanding." In this work he would banish
for ever those innate ideas which had offered such obstacles to
the progress of thought ; and, by an inquiry into the actual
operations of the human mind, he would trace the ways in
which mankind attain ideas and knowledge, and settle the
bounds imposed on the human understanding. Locke's Essay
was hailed with acclamation by all who were wearied of the old
scholastic abstractions and distinctions, and who had caught
the new spirit that was abroad.

Still Locke's Essay was not allowed to take possession of the
thinking minds of the country without a vigorous opposition.
Locke was met in his own day by Stillingfleet, the Bishop
of Worcester, who argued resolutely that the view given in
the Essay of our idea of substance was not sufficiently deep to
enable it to bear up the great truths of religion, especially the
doctrine of the Trinity. The great Leibnitz severely blamed
Locke for overlooking necessary truth, and reviewed his work,
book by book and chapter by chapter, in his " Nouveaux Essais
sur l'Entendement Humain ;" which, however, in consequence
of Locke's death taking place in the mean time, was not published for many years after. It was felt by many otherwise

favorable to the new spirit, that Locke had not laid a sufficiently deep foundation for morality in his account of our idea
of virtue, which he derived from mere sensations of pleasure
and pain, with the law of God superadded in utter inconsistency
with his theory. There were still in England adherents of the
great English moralists, More and Cudworth, who had opposed
Hobbes with learning and ability; and these maintained that
there was need of deeper principles than those laid down by
Locke to oppose the all-devouring pantheistic fatalism of Spinoza on the one hand, and the rising materialistic spirit on the
other.

In the early part of the eighteenth century, there appeared
several works which were not conceived at least wholly in the
spirit of Locke. I do not refer to such works as Norris's
"Ideal World," in which we have an able defence of the Aristotelian analysis of reasoning, and an exposition of Platonism,
more ideal far than that presented in Plato's own dialectic; nor
to Collier's "Clavis," "being a demonstration of the non-exist-
ence or impossibility of an external world:" I allude to works
which left a far deeper impression on their age. Samuel
Clarke, with vast erudition and great logical power, was establishing, in a mathematical manner, the existence and attributes
of God, giving virtue a place among the eternal relations of
things perceived by reason, and defending the doctrine of
human freedom and responsibility against those who were
reducing men to the condition of brutes or machines. Berkeley
did adopt the theory of Locke as to the mind being percipient
only of ideas, but the view which he took of human knowledge
was very different; for while Locke, consistently or inconsis-
tently, was a sober realist, Berkeley labored to show that
there was no substantial reality except spirit, and thought in
this way to arrest the swelling tide of materialism and scepticism. A more accurate thinker than either, Bishop Butler,
was establishing the supremacy of conscience, and showing that
there was a moral government in the world; and that revealed
religion was suited to the constitution of the mind, and to the
position in which man is placed.

It was while philosophic thought was in this state that the
Scottish Philosophy sprang up. The Scottish metaphysicians
largely imbibed the spirit of Locke; all of them speak of him

with profound respect; and they never differ from him without expressing a regret or offering an apology. Still the Scottish school never adopted the full theory of Locke ; on the contrary, they opposed it in some of its most essential points ; and this while they never gave in to the mathematical method of Clarke, and while they opposed the ingenuities of Berkeley. Hutcheson, the founder of the Scottish school, was a rather earlier author than Butler, to whom therefore he was not indebted for the peculiarities of his method and system. But there was a writer to whom both Butler and Hutcheson, and the early Scottish school generally, were under deeper obligation than to any other author, or all other authors, and who deserves in consequence a more special notice.

IV. — *SHAFTESBURY.*

THE author who exercised the most influence on the earlier philosophic school of Scotland was not Locke, but Lord Shaftesbury (born 1671, died 1713), the grandson of the Lord Chancellor Shaftesbury, who had been the friend of Locke. " Peace," says he, " be with the soul of that charitable and courteous author, who, for the common benefit of his fellow-authors, introduced the way of miscellaneous writing." He follows this miscellaneous method. The pieces which were afterwards combined in his " Characteristics of Men, Manners, and Times," were written at various times, from 1707 to 1712. They consist of a " Letter Concerning Enthusiasm," " Sensus Communis, an Essay on the Freedom of Wit and Humor," " Soliloquy, or, Advice to an Author," " An Inquiry Concerning Virtue and Merit," " The Moralists, a Philosophical Rhapsody," " Miscellaneous Reflections on the said Treatises, and other Critical Subjects," " A Notion of the Historical Draught or Tablature of the Judgment of Hercules, with a Letter concerning Design." He tells us that the miscellaneous manner was in the highest esteem in his day, that the old plan of subdividing into firsts and seconds had grown out of fashion, and that the " elegant court divine exhorts in miscellany, and is ashamed to bring his twos and threes before a fashionable assembly." " Ragouts and fricassees are the reigning dishes ; so authors, in order to become fashionable, have run into the more savory way of learned ragout and medley." His style is evidently after the French, and not the old English, model. It has the jaunty air of one who affects to be a man of elegance and fashion. Undoubtedly he was extensively read in the Greek and Roman philosophy, especially in Plato, Aristotle, Cicero, and the Roman Stoics, and he has many just and profound views, but these are ever made to appear as the ornaments of a modern nobleman, who studies philosophy as an accomplishment.

His "Characteristics" open with remarks on " Enthusiasm," and on " Wit and Humor." He tells us that "vapors naturally rise," and he would dispel them by ridicule. " The melancholy way of treating religion is that which, according to my apprehension, renders it so tragical, and is the occasion of its acting in reality such dismal tragedies in the world." He would "recommend wisdom and virtue in the way of pleasantry and mirth," and tells us that "good-humor is not only the best security against enthusiasm, but the best foundation of piety and true religion." It does not appear very clearly what is the nature of the piety and religion which he would recommend. Sometimes he seems to scoff at the Scriptures, and at all their spiritual verities and holy mysteries ; at other times he would make it appear as if he wished to be thought a believer in Christianity. There is, I suspect, much of latent levity in the profession he makes : "We may in a proper sense be said faithfully and dutifully to embrace those holy mysteries even in their minutest particulars, and without the least exception on account of their amazing depth," " being," he adds, "fully assured of our own steady orthodoxy, resignation, and entire submission to the truly Christian and catholic doctrines of our holy church, as by law established."

But he reckons these pleasantries merely as an introduction to graver subjects. He has largely caught the spirit of Locke, but he by no means follows him, especially in his rejection of innate ideas. " No one," says he, " has done more than Locke towards recalling of true philosophy from barbarity into the use and practice of the world, and into the company of the better and politer sort, who might well be ashamed of it in its

other dress. No one has opened a better and clearer way to
reason." But he qualifies his praise. " 'Twas Mr. Locke that
struck at all fundamentals, threw all order and virtue out of
the world, and made the ideas of these, which are the same with
those of God, unnatural, and without foundation in our minds.
Innate is a word he poorly plays upon : the right word, though
less used, is *connatural.*" He shows that there are many of
our mental qualities natural to us. " Life, and the sensations
which accompany life, come when they will, are from mere
nature and nothing else. Therefore, if you dislike the word
innate, let us change it, if you will, for instinct, and call instinct
that which nature teaches, exclusive of art, culture, or discipline." Beginning with these lower affections, he goes on to
show that "preconceptions of a higher kind have place in
human kind, preconceptions' of the 'fair and beautiful.'" [1]

He reviews the famous argument of Descartes, "We think,
therefore we are." "Nothing more certain : for the Ego or I
being established in the first part of the proposition, the Ergo,
no doubt, must hold it good in the latter." " For my own part,"
he adds, " I take my being upon trust." He everywhere appeals
to the " Sensus Communis," or Common Sense. His general
doctrine is thus expressed : " Some moral and philosophical
truths there are withal so evident in themselves, that it would
be easier to imagine half mankind to have run mad, and joined
precisely in one and the same species of folly, than to admit
any thing as truth which should be advanced against such *natural knowledge, fundamental reason,* and *common sense.*" [2] He
allows that what is natural to us may require labor and pains
to bring it out. " Whatever materials or principles of this kind
we may possibly bring with us, whatever good faculties, senses,
or anticipating sensations and imaginations may be of nature's
growth, and arise properly of themselves without our art, promotion, or assistance, the general *idea* which is formed of all
this management, and the clear notion we attain of what is
preferable and principal in all these subjects of choice and estimation, will not, as I imagine, by any person be taken for

---

[1] Letters to a student at the University.

[2] It was owing, I doubt not, to the influence, direct or indirect, of Shaftesbury
that the phrase "common sense" came to be so much used by the Scottish
School.

innate. Use, practice, and culture must precede the understanding and wit of such an advanced size and growth as this."
These surely are the very views which were developed more
fully and articulately by Reid, in his opposition to the scepticism of Hume.

The object of his works is to carry out these principles to
taste and morals. "Nor do I ask more when I undertake to
prove the reality of virtue and morals. If I be certain that I
am, it is certain and demonstrable who and what I should be."
"Should one who had the countenance of a gentleman ask me
'why I would avoid being nasty when nobody was present?' in
the first place, I should be fully satisfied that he himself was
a very nasty gentleman who could ask this question, and that
it would be a hard matter for me to make him ever conceive
what true cleanliness was. However, I might, notwithstanding this, be contented to give him a slight answer, and say, 'It
was because I had a nose.' Should he trouble me further, and
ask again, 'What if I had a cold? or what if naturally I had no
such nice smell?' I might answer perhaps, 'That I cared as
little to see myself nasty as that others should see me in that
condition.' 'But what if it were in the dark?' 'Why, even
then, though I had neither nose nor eyes, my *sense* of the matter
would still be the same: my nature would rise at the thought
of what was sordid.'" He thus reaches a sense of beauty.
"Much in the same manner have I heard it asked, 'Why should
a man be honest in the dark?'" The answer to this question
brings him to a moral sense.

He speaks of nature in general, and human nature in particular, as an "economy," and as having a "constitution" and
a "frame." In examining the nature of the soul, he finds
(1) self-affections, which lead only to "the good of the private."
He enumerates, as belonging to this class, "love of life, resentment of injury, pleasure, or appetite towards nourishment and
the means of generation ; interest, or the desire of those conveniences by which we are well provided for or maintained ; emula-
tion, or love of praise and honor ; indolence, or love of ease
and rest." But he finds also (2) natural affections, which lead
to the good of the public. He takes great pains to establish
the existence of disinterested affections, and opposes the views
of those who, like Rochefoucauld, would resolve all human action

into a refined selfishness. Referring to the common saying, that interest governs the world, he remarks shrewdly : " Whoever looks narrowly into the affairs of it, will find that passion, humor, caprice, zeal, faction, and a thousand other springs which are counter to self-interest, have as considerable a part in the movements of this machine. There are more wheels and counterpoises in this engine than are easily imagined." With such affections, " man is naturally social, and society is natural to him ; " and in illustrating this position, he sets himself vigorously against the social theory of Hobbes, who represents the original state of man as one of war.

Virtue consists in the proper exercise of these two classes of affections. Vice arises when the public affections are weak and deficient, when the private affections are too strong, or affections spring up which do not tend to the support of the public or private system. He shows that virtue, as consisting in these affections, is natural to man, and that he who practises it is obeying the ancient Stoic maxim, and living according to nature. The virtues which he recommends fall far beneath the stern standard of the Stoics, and leave out all the peculiar graces of Christianity : they consist of, — "a mind subordinate to reason, a temper humanized and fitted to all natural affection, an exercise of friendship uninterrupted, thorough candor, benignity, and good-nature, with constant security, tranquillity, equanimity."

He would establish a morality on grounds independent of religion. " Whoever thinks that there is a God, and pretends formally to believe that he is just and good, must suppose that there is, independently, such a thing as justice, truth, and falsehood, right and wrong, according to which he pronounces that God is just, righteous, and true." " If virtue be not really estimable in itself, I can see nothing estimable in following it for the sake of a bargain ; " and he complains of those who "speak so much of the rewards and punishments, and so little of the worth or value of the thing itself." He remarks very justly : " By building a future state on the ruins of virtue, religion in general, and the cause of a deity, is betrayed ; and by making rewards and punishments the principal motives to duty, the Christian religion in particular is overthrown, and its greatest principle, that of love, rejected and exposed." He admits, however, that a good God, as a model, has an effect on our views of morals and conduct ; and allows that "fear of future punishment and hope of future reward, how mercenary and servile however it may be accounted, is yet, in many circumstances, a great advantage, security, and support to virtue."

Such is his view of the nature of virtue. But Shaftesbury is quite aware that the question of the character of the virtuous act is not the same as that of the mental faculty which looks at it and appreciates it. This faculty he represents as being of the nature of a sense. Locke had allowed the existence of two senses, an external and an internal ; and had labored in vain to derive all men's ideas from these two sources. Hutcheson, perceiving that the inlets to the mind were too few according to the theory of Locke, calls in other senses. These senses become very numerous in the systems of some of the Scottish metaphysicians, such as Gerard. In the writings of Shaftesbury, two occupy an important place, — the sense of beauty and the moral sense.

"No sooner," he says, "does the eye open upon figures, the ear to sounds, than straight the Beautiful results, and grace and harmony are known and acknowledged. No sooner are actions viewed, no sooner the human affections and passions discerned (and they are most of them as soon discerned as felt), than straight an *inward* eye distinguishes and sees the *fair* and *shapely*, the *amiable* and *admirable*, apart from the *deformed*, the *foul*, the *odious*, or the *despicable*." Though in all this advancing quite beyond the "Essay on the Human Understanding," yet he seems to be anxious to connect his view of the moral sense with the reflection or inward sense of Locke. "In a creature capable of forming general notions of things, not only the outward beings which offer themselves to the sense are the objects of the affections, but the very actions themselves, and the affections of pity, kindness, gratitude, and their contraries, being brought into the mind by reflection, become objects. So that by means of this reflected sense, there arises another kind of affection towards these very affections themselves, which have been already felt, and are now become the subject of a new liking or dislike." Conscience is represented by him "as the reflection in the mind of any unjust action or behavior, which he knows to be naturally odious and ill-deserv-

ing.   No creature can maliciously and intentionally do ill, without being sensible, at the same time, that he deserves ill.   And
in this respect, every sensible creature may be said to have a
conscience." [1]

He has evidently been smitten with some of the Platonic
views of beauty. "We have," he says, "a sense of order and
proportion ; and having a sensation, reason can give this account
of it, that whatever things have order, the same have unity of
design and concur in one, are parts constituent of one whole,
or are in themselves one system.   Such is a tree with all its
branches, an animal with all its members, an edifice with all
exterior and interior ornaments."   He is fond of connecting or
identifying the beautiful and the good ; in fact, virtue is represented by him as a higher kind of beauty.   "It is, I must own,
on certain relations or respective proportions, that all natural
affection does in some measure depend."   "The same numbers,
harmony, and proportions have a place in morals."   He evidently clings fondly to the idea that "beauty and good are one
and the same."

We have given so full an account of the philosophy of Shaftesbury, because of the influence which it exercised on the
Scottish Philosophy.   Francis Hutcheson did little more than
expound these views, with less versatility, but in a more equable, thorough, and systematic manner.   Turnbull, who founded
the Aberdeen branch of the school, and influenced greatly the
mind of Reid, avowedly drew largely from Hutcheson in his
theories of taste and virtue.   Reid and Beattie got their favorite phrase, "common sense," I have no doubt, directly or indirectly from the treatise so entitled in the "Characteristics."
Hume was evidently well acquainted with the writings of

[1] The intelligent reader will see how much indebted Bishop Butler was to
Shaftesbury, for the views propounded in his "Sermons on Human Nature."
Shaftesbury, before Butler, had spoken of human nature as a "constitution," and
had shown that to live according to nature implies a respect to the conscience.
He complains of those who speak much of nature, without explaining its meaning
("Wit and Humor," iii. 2).   He had divided our affections into personal and public and the moral power, and represented that power as a principle of reflection.
Butler goes beyond Shaftesbury in showing that our personal affections are not
in themselves selfish, and that the moral faculty is not only in our soul, but
claims supremacy there.   Butler declines to say whether the moral faculty is a
a sense, or what else ; and he will not say that moral good consists in benevolence.

Shaftesbury; and I am inclined to think that they may have
helped to form his style, and to suggest some of his essays.
We have an anticipation of the spirit of Hume in the miscellany entitled, " Philocles to Palemon : " " You know that in
this Academic Philosophy I am to present you with, there is a
certain way of questioning and doubting, which in no way suits
the genius of our age. Men love to take party instantly. They
can't bear being kept in suspense. The examination torments
them." Theocles observes, that "if there be so much disorder
in the present state of things, he would not be disposed to think
better of the future." Lord Monboddo declares that " Shaftesbury's Inquiry is the best book in English on the subject of
morals." His Draught or Tablature of the Judgment of Hercules, and his Disquisitions on Taste, originated the theories of
Beauty which formed an essential part of Scottish metaphysics
for more than a century.

V. — *GERSHOM CARMICHAEL.*

Sir William Hamilton says that Gershom Carmichael "may
be regarded, on good grounds, as the real founder of the Scottish
school of philosophy." (" Reid's Works," p. 30.) I am disposed to retain the honor for Francis Hutcheson, to whom it
is usually ascribed. Carmichael does not possess the full characteristics of the school. He seems to me to be the bond which
connects the old philosophy with the new in Scotland.

He was descended from a genuine covenanting stock. His
father was Alexander Carmichael, the son of Frederick Carmichael, who had been minister in various places in Fifeshire,
and who died in 1667 ; his mother was relict (she had been
the second wife) of Fraser of Bray. Alexander was minister
at Pittenain, and had at one time been attached to prelacy, but
abandoned it to join the suffering ministers. Early in 1672,
he is in the tolbooth of Edinburgh. On February 22, he is
before the Council, charged with keeping conventicles, and is
ordered to depart the kingdom, never to return without license ;
and February 26, he is transported in a ship to London, where

he was useful as a minister, and died about the year 1676 or
1677. In 1677, shortly after his death, there was published,
from the copy which he had left, a treatise, entitled, "The Believer's Mortification of Sin by the Spirit," edited by Thomas
Lye, who says in the preface, "As for that flesh of his flesh,
and the fruit of his loins, as for that Ruth and Gershom he
hath left behind him, I question not but as long as the saints
among you continue to bear your old name, Philadelphia (so
the old Puritans of England have used to style you), you will
not, you cannot, forget to show kindness to Mephibosheth for
Jonathan's sake." Gershom, so called by his father because
he was "a stranger in a strange land," seems to have been born
in London about 1672. It may be supposed that the family
returned to Scotland after the father's death. We certainly
find Gershom enrolled a Master of Arts in the University of
Edinburgh, July 31, 1691. He afterwards became Regent at
St. Andrews, where he took the oath of allegiance, and subscribed the Assurance. On November 22, 1694, he is elected
and admitted Master in the University of Glasgow, having been
brought in by public dispute, that is, by disputation on comparative trial, through the influence of Lord Carmichael, afterwards the first Earl of Hyndford. About the same time he
lost his mother, and "married a good woman, the daughter of
Mr. John Inglis." Wodrow, who tells us this (" Letters "), was
his pupil, and describes him as at that time possessed of little
reading, as dictating several sheets of peripatetic physics *de
materia prima*, as teaching Rohault, and being very much a Car-
tesian,—this seven years after the publication of Newton's
" Principia." Afterwards he made himself master of the mathematics and the new philosophy, and Wodrow used to jest with
him on this matter of his juvenile teaching. From these notices it appears that, by parentage and birth and training and
ancestral prepossessions, he belongs to the seventeenth, but
catches the spirit of the eighteenth century. He exhibits in
his own personal history the transition from the old to the new
thought of Scotland.

He is represented as a hard student, a thinking, poring man,
his favorite study being moral philosophy. At the commencement of his professorial life, a Master took up the batch of students as they entered on the study of philosophy, and carried

them in successive years through all the branches, including
logic, pneumatology, moral philosophy, and natural philosophy.
This system required the teacher to be a well-informed man
in various departments, but was a hinderance to eminence in
any one branch of learning. But from 1727 the Masters are
restricted to their several classes, and to Carmichael is consigned moral philosophy. It appears that, in 1726, there were
thirty-six students in the third year's class, and nineteen in that
of the fourth year ; in the latter days of Carmichael the numbers were larger. The classes were swelled by non-conforming
students from England, who, shut out from the English universities by their tests and their churchified influence, betook
themselves to the Scottish colleges. Many of these were
attracted to Glasgow by the fame of Carmichael. The college
session lasted from the beginning of November to the end of
May. On the Lord's day, the Masters met with their classes,
to take an account of the sermons, and this was a work in which
Carmichael felt a special interest.

Carmichael was a most affectionate, friendly man, but withal
a little warm in his temper, and became involved in consequence in scenes which seem somewhat inconsistent with the
supposed calm of an academic life. The college corporation
was evidently much agitated by internal feuds, and Carmichael
takes his part in them, commonly siding with the party of independence against the Principal. In 1704, joined by Mr. Loudon, he protests that several things minuted as Acts of Faculty
were written and signed privately by the Principal. The Faculty finds the charge unfounded, and suspends the two from
their functions. Subsequently they ask forgiveness, and are
restored. In 1705, Mr. Law, one of the Regents, complains
that some expressions had been uttered against him by Mr.
Carmichael, who is gravely admonished, and exhorted to avoid
every thing irritating towards his colleagues in time to come.
In 1717, there are hot disputes as to who should elect the Rector. The Masters combine against the Principal, call the students to the common hall, and choose their man. But, in 1718,
the Commission for the Visitation of the College finds some
of the Masters, including Carmichael, guilty of great disorder in
the election of the Rector ; and they are discharged for a time
from exercising any part of their office (such as choosing pro-

fessors), except the ordinary discipline in the class.   In 1722, a bonfire was kindled by the students on a decision in favor of the election of Lord Molesworth (we shall meet with him again in these articles) to Parliament, and Carmichael rushes into the heart of the mob, and gets into trouble in extinguishing the flames.   In November, 1728, we find him joining in a protest against the claim of the Chancellor to sit and vote.   It was by such disputes that the constitution of the Scottish colleges came to be settled.

Patriotic exertions helped to relieve the sameness of the college life, and in these the collegiate body in Glasgow (it was different in Aberdeen) are of one mind.   In 1708, the kingdom is threatened with "an invasion of French and Irish papists," and the Masters agree each to maintain a number of foot soldiers ; and Carmichael signs for five men.   In September, 1715, the rising in the north of Scotland in favor of the pretender becomes known.   The Faculty agrees to raise fifty men at sixpence a day ; the Principal provides eight, the professor of divinity five, and Carmichael subscribes for four.   It was by such active exertions in the south of Scotland that the progress of the Rebellion was so speedily arrested.

In his later years, as he became known, Carmichael carried on a correspondence with Barbeyrac and other learned men. He had a numerous family, "who were all a comfort to him, except one, who was a cause of great distress."   Wodrow says, that " in his advanced years he was singularly religious.   I know he was under great depths of soul exercise, and much the worse that he did not communicate his distress to anybody almost."   This is the only record we have of a Scottish metaphysician having had his "soul exercises ;" but surely there must have been others who had their conflicts as they dived into the depths of the human soul.   For the last two or three years of his life, he had a cancerous wart, which spread over one eye and across his nose to the other eye, and at last carried him off.   During all his illness he remained a hard student and serious Christian.   He died, November 25, 1729.   On his death the English students leave the university, the attendance at which is reported by Wodrow as very thin in December ; and it does not seem to improve till Hutcheson commences his lectures in the following October.

Carmichael published "Breviuscula Introductio ad Logicam," which reached a second edition in 1722. He defines logic as the science which shows the method of discovering truth, and of expounding it to others. He represents it as having to do with judgment, but then it also treats of apprehension as necessary to judgment. Under apprehension he speaks of the doctrine of the difference of the comprehension and extension of a notion, and of the former being evolved by definition, and the latter by division, as being quite commonplace. He distinguishes between immediate and mediate judgment. Immediate is between two ideas immediately compared ; mediate, in which the comparison is by means of a third judgment, is called discourse. He says all knowledge may ultimately be resolved into immediate judgments, known in their own light ; and he divides immediate judgments into two classes : one abstract, in which there is no direction of the mind to the thing itself as really existing, *e. g.*, the whole is greater than a part ; and the other intuitive, when the mind has a consciousness of the thing as present, as, for example, the proposition, *Ego cogitans existo.* Coming to mediate judgment, he gives as the supreme rule of affirmative syllogism the axiom, "Things which are the same with one and the same third are the same with one another ; " and of negative syllogisms the axiom, " Things of which one is the same with a third, and the other not the same, are not the same with one another." These statements show a " thinking, poring," man, and will be valued most by those who have thought longest on these subjects. We see a new historical step in the transmission of the distinction between the extension and comprehension of a notion ; we see that the difference between immediate and mediate judgments was known in these times ; and that there was an attempt to find a supreme rule of mediate reasoning in the sameness (here lies the looseness) of two things with a third. Carmichael is aware that there are propositions seen to be true in their own light ; and that there is an intuitive apprehension, in which the thing is known as present ; and many will think that the *ego cogitans existo* is a preferable form to the *cogito ergo sum* of Descartes.

Carmichael published an edition of Puffendorf, " De Officio Hominis et Civis," with Notes and Supplements, for the use of students, described by Hutcheson as more valuable than the original work.   In the notes he offers many acute observations, and gives extracts from De Vries, Titius, and Grotius.   In the first supplement he speaks of a divine law, to which all morality has reference, which alone obliges, and to which all obligation of human laws is ultimately to be referred.   The law may be made known either by means of signs, oral or written, or by the constitution of human nature, and other things which offer themselves to the observation of men.   What is known by the latter is called *natural law*, which has two meanings, — one the faculty of reason itself as given to man by God, and the other such a power of intelligence as can discover what is in nature by ordinary diligence.   He takes far higher grounds of religion than those adopted by Shaftesbury and Hutcheson.   He declares that no one can be said to obey the law who does not know what the law enjoins, or who acts without reference to God and his law.   At the same time, he seems to be a eudaimonist, and inclined to look on God as having an ultimate respect to happiness in his law.   He has a second supplement, calm, moderate, and sensible, on the "Duties of Man towards his own Mind," and a third on "Quasi-Contracts."

His latest work, published in 1729, shortly before his death, is "Synopsis Theologiæ Naturalis."   In his preface he tells us that, in teaching pneumatology, he had used two Belgian textbooks.   He advises that the forms of the Aristotelian school be avoided, as obscure and artificial, but declares at the same time that the doctrines of the scholastics, at least of the older, are more agreeable to reason and holy Scripture than those opposed to them in his day, especially in their finding a foundation for morality and obligation in God ; and he denounces some who, of late years, with a showy appearance of genius and eloquence, would separate morality from religion, referring, I should suppose, to the school of Shaftesbury, against which, therefore, he thus gives his dying testimony, as it were in the name of the old philosophy.

In establishing the existence and perfections of God, he draws arguments from a variety of sources.   He would call in metaphysical principles.   Thus he urges that there must be *ens aliquod independens*, otherwise we are landed in an infinite series of causes, which he declares (with Aristotle) self-evidently impossible.   He appeals, with the French theologian Abbadie, to universal consent. But he reckons the arguments of Descartes and De Vries, and that by Samuel Clarke, as unsatisfactory. He maintains that we can argue that what we attribute to a thing in idea exists, only after we have shown that the thing exists. He maintains that the existence of God as an existing being is to be established, not *a priori*, but *a posteriori*, and appeals to the traces of order, beauty, and design in the universe, and to the illustrations to be found in the writings of Ray, Pelling, Cheyne, Derham, Niewentite, and in Pitcairn on the Circulation of the Blood. He refers to the properties of matter, as established by Newton ; and argues, as Baxter did so resolutely afterwards, that matter cannot move of itself, but needs a new force impressed on it. In regard to the dependence of creature on created power, he holds that things spiritual and corporeal exist so long as they have being from the creative efficacy of God, and speaks of the need of a divine *precursus* or *concursus*. He admits, however, that created spirits have efficacy in themselves. He refers to Leibnitz, and shows that he was well acquainted with his theory of possible worlds. It is surely interesting to observe a modest and retiring Scottish writer so thoroughly acquainted with the highest philosophy of his time, British and Continental, and yet retaining his own independence in the midst of his learning. If he cannot be regarded as the founder of the new school, he has the credit of judiciously combining some of the best properties of the old and new philosophy.

VI. — *ANDREW BAXTER.*

BAXTER cannot be justly described as a leader or a follower of the Scottish school. His method is not really nor professedly that of inductive observation. He belongs rather to the school of Samuel Clarke, to whom he often refers, and always with admiration. But he was a Scotchman, and an independent thinker : he does not belong to the old philosophy ; but he was a contemporary of the men who founded the Scottish school, and treated of many of the same topics. He had readers both in England and Scotland in his own day, and for some years after his death ; and he deserves a passing notice as the representative of a style of thought which met with considerable favor in his time, but had to give way before the new school.

We have a life of him in Kippis's " Biographia Britannica," drawn up from materials supplied by his son. He was the son of a merchant in Old Aberdeen, where he was born in 1686 or 1687. His mother was Elizabeth Frazer, descended from a considerable family in the north. He was educated at King's College, Aberdeen, where, at the beginning of last century, he would be trained in the old logic and metaphysics. But, as we shall see more fully in future articles, a considerable amount of a fresh literary taste, and of a spirit of philosophical inquiry, began to spring up in Aberdeen in connection with the two Universities pretty early in that century. Baxter, besides being a good mathematician, was well acquainted with the discoveries of Sir Isaac Newton, and with the theories of Leibnitz as to matter and motion. He was familiar with the Essay on the Human Understanding, but had a deeper appreciation of the speculations of Clarke.

The chief professional employment of his life was that of tutor to young men of good family. The boys who, in our days, would be sent to the great public schools of England taught by Oxford or Cambridge masters, were very often, in the seventeenth and eighteenth centuries, put under tutors, who went about with them to the colleges at home, or travelled with them abroad. The occupation of teaching and travelling tutor was one coveted by young men of limited means and of a reading taste, who did not wish officially to enter the church, and had no other office open to them than that referred to, fitted to furnish them with means of study. When the tutor had trained and travelled with the heir of a good estate, the family felt bound to make provision for him for life. It was thus that, in the seventeenth century, Hobbes had been tutor to two successive Earls of Devonshire ; that, in the eighteenth century, Thomson the poet became tutor to the Lord Chancellor Talbot's son on the Grand Tour ; that Hume coveted the office of travelling tutor to Murray of Broughton ; and Turnbull and A. Smith gave up chairs in the Scottish colleges to become tutors, — the one to the Wauchopes of Niddrie (?) and the other to the Duke of Buccleuch. Baxter was tutor, among others, to Lord John Gray, Lord Blantyre, and Mr. Hay of Drummelzier.

In the spring of 1741, he went abroad with Mr. Hay, having also Lord Blantyre under his care. He resided some years at Utrecht, and thence made excursions into Flanders, France, and Germany. Carlyle met him — " Immateriality Baxter," as he calls him — at Utrecht in 1745, and says of him, " though he was a profound philosopher and a hard student, he was at the same time a man of the world, and of such pleasing conversation as attracted the young." His son had described him as being at polite assemblies in Holland, and a favorite of ladies ; but a writer in the Corrigenda of the following volume of the " Biographia," after mentioning that he saw him daily for more than two years at Utrecht, declares : " His dress was plain and simple, — not that of a priggish Frenchman, but of a mathematician who was not a sloven. I am pretty well persuaded that, while in the Low Countries, he never had any conversation with women of higher or lower degree, unless it were to ask for the bill at an ordinary, or desire the servant-maid to bring up the turf for his chimney." The same writer describes him as a " plain, decent, good-humored man, who passed all his time, but what was bestowed at his meals, in meditation and study." His son describes him as social and cheerful, and extremely studious, sometimes sitting up whole nights reading and writing.

In 1724, he had married the daughter of Mr. Mebane, a minister in Berwickshire; and, while he was abroad, his wife and family seem to have resided at Berwick-on-Tweed. In 1747, he returned to Scotland, and resided till his death at Whittingham, in East Lothian, where he employed himself in country affairs, and in his philosophic studies. In his latter years, he was much afflicted with gout and gravel. In January 29, 1750, he wrote to (the afterwards notorious) John Wilkes, with whom he had formed a friendship in Holland, " I am a trouble to all about me, especially my poor wife, who has the life of a slave night and day in helping to take care of a diseased carcass." He had long, he states, considered the advantages of a separate state, but " I shall soon know more than all men I leave behind me." He died April 13, 1750, and was buried in the family vault of Mr. Hay at Whittingham.

He wrote a book in two volumes entitled " Matho," being a compend of the universal scientific knowledge of the day. He published his principal work, " An Inquiry into the Nature of the Human Soul," in 1733,[1] and it reached a second edition in 1737. In 1750, shortly after his death, was published, " An Appendix to his Inquiry into the Nature of the Human Soul." He had taken a great body of manuscripts with him to Holland; in the letter referred to, he speaks fondly of his unfinished manuscripts, in which he had discussed "a great many miscellaneous subjects in philosophy of a very serious nature, few of them ever considered before, as I know of." In 1779, the Rev. Dr. Duncan of South Warnborough published from his manuscripts, after correcting the style, " The Evidence of Reason in proof of the Immortality of the Soul," and at the close is his letter to Wilkes. Another work of his, entitled " Histor," discussing, on the English side, the controversy between the British and Continental writers as to force, and on the side of Clarke, the controversy between Clarke and Leibnitz, was offered to Millar the bookseller; but the new generation did not appreciate his life-labors; his day was over, and the offer was declined.

The avowed design of Baxter, in all his works, is to establish the existence of an immaterial power. Such a defence seemed to him to be required, in consequence of the new views of the powers of matter founded on the discoveries of Sir Isaac Newton; by the equivocal language of Locke, frequently quoted about our not being "able to know whether any material being thinks or not;" and by the materialistic spirit abroad. The new doctrine of all matter attracting other matter seemed to show that we must be prepared to modify the old doctrine, that body is altogether passive. Leibnitz, on metaphysical grounds, and in opposition to the accepted Carte-

---

[1] Stewart was not "able to discover the date of the first edition," and others have been as unsuccessful. It is criticised in Jackson's "Dissertation on Matter and Spirit," 1735, and referred to in " Bibliothèque Raisonnée des Ouvrages des Savans," for April, May, and June, 1735. But the question is settled by its appearing (as a friend has shown us) in the "Gentleman's Magazine," in the register of books published October, 1733.

sian doctrine, had maintained that matter has an essential potency. Baxter proceeds on the doctrine of Clarke, the friend of Newton, and quotes his language. "All things that are done in the world are done either immediately by God himself, or by created intelligent beings ; matter being evidently not at all capable of any laws or powers whatsoever, any more than it is capable of intelligence, excepting only this one negative power, that every part of it will always and necessarily continue in that state, whether of rest or motion, wherein it at present is. So that all those things which we commonly say are the effects of the natural powers of matter and laws of motion, of gravitation, attraction, or the like, are indeed (if one will speak strictly and properly) the effects of God's acting continually and every moment, either immediately by himself, or mediately by some created intelligent being." The first volume of Baxter's work on the "Nature of the Soul," his "Appendix," and a large part of his "Evidence," are mainly occupied with a full elucidation and elaborate defence of the views summarily expressed in this passage.

He labors to prove that a *vis inertiæ*, or resistance to a change of present state of rest or motion, is essential to matter ; that matter hath this and nothing else ; that it cannot have any sort of active power ; that what are called the powers of matter is force impressed upon it *ab extra.* He maintains that matter is "liable to but one change or casualty, viz., to be annihilated, or to be destroyed by a Being to whose power that effect is competent," and he denies that Infinite Power may "superadd a property to a substance incapable of receiving it." He maintains this doctrine as resolutely as if it were the foundation of religion, which must stand or fall with it. The questions which he has taken up had been discussed in a profound manner by Descartes and Leibnitz, and they cannot be regarded as settled at this day. But from his dogma of the impotency of matter he argues the necessity of an immaterial powerful being who first made the dead substance, matter, who originally impressed, and still continues to impress, motion upon it. "I am of opinion, and think it would be easy to show it, if one had leisure to run through the several particulars, that unless an immaterial power continually re-excited motion in the material universe, all would stop in it in a very short time, perhaps in half an hour, except that the planets would run out in straight-lined directions"!! "To say that Deity interposes when he sees that matter would go wrong, is the same thing, in other words, as owning that he interposes always if that were proper. Every particle of matter resists a change of its present state, and therefore could not effect a change of state in itself nor in other particles." He would thus establish his conclusion, that the "Deity, who can be excluded from no place, but is active and present everywhere, acts immediately on all the parts of matter," and that his governing is only his creating power constantly repeated. "Our philosophy can only be consistent when we take in the immediate power of the Creator as the efficient cause in all the works of nature." He looks on his own position as being very much superior, in its religious aspects, to the doctrines which had been entertained by many others. "Low and pitiful are the shifts we are put to when we would remove the Deity to the head of nature, and the head of nature out of sight."

" It is not right to exalt the Deity in words and derogate from his perfections in facts. This is only paying him a compliment, and then setting aside his government in whole or in part, — a state artifice. Cicero objects this low cunning to Epicurus, when he says, it is "verbis ponere re tollere." "Descartes, before Spinoza, had given the government of the universe to matter and motion ; and Leibnitz, under a pretence of extolling the original contrivance of things, leaves the execution of all this to dead substance. According to all these schemes, we see nothing that the Deity does now : we behold only the operations of matter. This fills the mind with anxious doubts. If matter performs all that is wonderful, it catches our first admiration ; and we know not where to search for the being who contrived that which we see matter executes with such dexterity." Much may be said in favor of the doctrine, that God acts in all physical action ; but it is wiser not to found it on the peculiar dogma of Baxter, that matter is inactive.

But the grand aim of Baxter, in depriving matter of its powers, is to establish the immateriality, and consequent immortality, of the soul. It is a fundamental position with him, that "a power always belongs to something living." He is thus able to establish the existence of a human soul active and immortal. He maintains that "no substance or being can have a natural tendency to annihilation or become nothing," and argues that the "soul must endlessly abide an active perceptive substance, without either fear or hopes of dying, through all eternity." When we find such positions coolly assumed, one almost feels justified in rejoicing that in that very age David Hume rose up to dispute all such dogmas ; and that in the following age Emmanuel Kant examined narrowly the foundations both of rational theology and of rational psychology. We are certainly warranted in feeling a high gratification that Thomas Reid, a wiser man than any of these, did immediately after the time of Hume, and before the time of Kant, set about establishing natural religion and philosophy upon a safer foundation.

Baxter is prepared to follow out his principles to all their consequences, however preposterous they might appear. The phenomena of dreaming came in his way, and he gives an explanation of them. He cannot refer these dreams to dead matter, nor can it be the soul that forms the scenes present to it. His theory is, that separate immaterial beings act upon the matter of our bodies, and produce on the sensory a φάντασμα or vision, which is perceived by the active and recipient mind. He acknowledges that he knows nothing of the conditions and circumstances of these separate agencies, but he evidently clings to the idea that there is no scarcity of living immaterial beings, and asks triumphantly : "Why so much dead matter, without living immaterial substance in proportion ?" "Hath not the most despicable reptile animalcule an immaterial soul joined to it ?"

It ought to be added, that in his " Evidence " he adduces stronger arguments, than those derived from his favorite view of matter, in favor of the soul's immortality. He shows that if there be no state beyond the grave, our existence is incomplete, without design, irrelative ; and he calls in the divine perfections as furnishing " a certain ground of confidence that our existence will not be finally broken off in the midst of divine purposes thus visibly unfinished here," and securing that beings "becoming good for something should not instantly become nothing." In arguing thus, he shows his besetting tendency to take up extreme positions ; for he maintains that in our world pain is much more extensive in its nature than pleasure, and that all bodily pleasures are merely instigations of pains. He argues that as in this world reason may often be disobeyed with no evil consequences and obeyed without any good ones, so there must be a future world to make every thing consistent with reason. He shows that the prepossessions of mankind are in favor of this tenet. " In the very dawnings of reason, let a child be told what is death, having no idea of any way of existing beside the present, amazement seizes him : he is perplexed, uneasy, dismayed." He is met, as so many others have been, by the objection, that most of these arguments would prove that brutes are immortal. In answering it, he is obliged to allow that immortality does not depend solely on immateriality, and to throw himself on the moral argument, which does not apply to brutes, which, not being moral agents, are not capable of rewards and punishments. But it is clear that he cherishes the idea that the immaterial part of brutes, while not constituting the same conscious being, may not perish ultimately when separated from the material frame.

In treating of these favorite topics, he discusses a great many important philosophic questions, and always gives a clear and decided opinion. He evidently favors the arguments derived from "abstract reason and the nature of things" in behalf of the divine existence. He argues the necessity of an infinitely perfect intelligent being, — not only from space and time, as Clarke did, but from " the necessity of eternal truth in geometry or in other abstract sciences." " Truth is not a being existing by itself, and therefore the immutable necessary nature of truth must be referred to some being existing of itself, and existing immutably and eternally." We have only to define truth as the conformity of our ideas to things, to see the fallacy lurking in this argument.

His view of space and time is taken from Newton and Clarke. He represents them as not beings, but the affections of beings : " And as time and space are not existences, so their correlate infinites (if I may say so), that is, eternity and immensity, are not existences, but the properties of necessary existence." In some other of his statements, he goes back to some of the mystic statements of the schoolmen, and anticipates some of the doctrines of Kant. " God's existence is unsuccessive." He says, " *Nunc stans* implies opposite ideas, if applied to our existence ; but if we allow an eternal and immutable mind, the distinction of past and future vanishes with respect to such a mind, and the phrase has propriety." But surely there is an inconsistency in first arguing the divine existence from our ideas of space and time, and then declaring that our ideas in regard to space and time do not apply to Deity.

In maintaining that mind is ever active, he has to consider its seeming dormancy in sleep. " The soul in sleep seems to suffer something like what happens to a live coal covered up under ashes ; which is alive all the while, but only appears so when disencumbered and exposed to open air." As to what has since been called unconscious mental action, his theory of it is the same as that defended in after years by D. Stewart ; he supposes that the mind was conscious of its action at the time, but that the memory could not recall it. "There is certainly a great deal of our past consciousness which we retain no memory of afterwards. It is a particular part of our finite and imperfect nature, that we cannot become conscious of all our past consciousness at pleasure. But no man at night would infer that he was not in a state of consciousness and thinking at such a certain minute, about twelve o'clock of the day, because now perhaps he hath no memory what particular thought he had at that minute. And it is no better argument, considered in itself, that a man was not conscious at such a minute in his sleep because next morning he hath no memory of what ideas were in his mind then."

Baxter was most earnest in restricting the properties of matter, but he was equally resolute in maintaining its existence. In his work on the soul he has a long section on "Dean Berkeley's scheme." He was one of the first who examined systematically the new theory. He takes the obvious and vulgar view of it, and not the refined one ascribed to the ingenious author by his admirers : for those who have opposed Berkeley have usually given one account of his system, while those who have defended him have usually given another ; and some have thence come to the conclusion, that his whole theory is so ethereal that it is not capable of definite expression. Baxter maintains that "we perceive, besides our sensations themselves, the objects of them ; " that "we are conscious not only of sensation excited, but that it is excited by some cause beside ourselves," and that "such objects as rivers, houses, mountains, are the very things we perceive by sense." He endeavors to prove that the system of Berkeley carried out consistently would land us in a solitary egoism, for "we only collect concerning the souls of other men from the spontaneous motions and actions of their bodies ; these, according to him, belong to nothing." Berkeley had boasted that, by expelling matter out of nature, he had dragged with it so many sceptical and impious notions ; Baxter replies that this "puts us into a way of denying all things, that we may get rid of the absurdity of those who deny some things," — "as if one should advance that the best way for a woman who may silence those who attack her reputation is to turn a common prostitute." He thinks that the doctrine may tend to remove the checks to immorality ; for "he who thinks theft, murder, or adultery nothing real beyond bare idea, and that for aught we know he injures nobody, will be surely under less restraint to satisfy his inclinations of any kind." The mathematician is evidently annoyed and vexed at the attacks which Berkeley had made on his science, and shows "that if there be no such thing as quantity, we have a large body of immutable truths conversant about an impossible object."

In examining Berkeley, he gives his views of sense-perception, which are not so clear and satisfactory as those of Reid : but are vastly juster than those of his contemporaries. He distinctly separates himself from those who hold that the mind can perceive nothing but its own states. "If our ideas have no parts, and yet if we perceive parts, it is plain we perceive something more than our own perceptions." He adds "We are as conscious that we perceive parts as that we have perceptions at all." "The existence of matter in general, or at least of material sensories to which the soul is united, seems to me to be nearer intuitive than demonstrative knowledge." He declares that the "same perception of parts proves to us both the spirit and a material agency." This is so far an anticipation of the doctrine of Hamilton as an advance upon that of Reid. As to the manner of the action of matter on spirit, and spirit on matter, he says, in the very spirit of Reid, "We are certain this is matter of fact in many instances, whether we conceive it or not." He adds, in his own manner: "The Deity himself moves matter in almost all the phenomena of nature, and the soul of man perhaps moves some matter of the body, though in an infinitely less degree."

<hr />

VII. — *FRANCIS HUTCHESON.*[1]

DURING the greater part of the seventeenth century there was a constant immigration into the north-east of Ireland of Scotchmen, who carried with them their hardy mode of life and persevering habits ; their love of education and their anxiety to have an educated ministry ; their attachment to the Bible and the simple Presbyterian worship. This movement commenced with the attempt of the first James of England to civilize Ireland by the Plantation of Ulster, and was continued during the period of the prelatic persecution in Scotland, whereby not a few sturdy adherents of the Solemn League and Covenant were driven for refuge to the sister isle. The Scottish Church kept a watchful guardianship over her scattered children, and sent after them a succession of ministers to preach the gospel, for a time in the Established Church, and, when churchmen from England (such as Jeremy Taylor) would not tolerate this any longer, to set up a Presbyterian organization. Among these was the Rev. Alexander Hutcheson, the second son of an old and respectable family at Monkwood, in Ayrshire, who became minister at Saintfield, in the heart of county Down, and purchased the townland of Drumalig. His second son, John, was settled at Ballyrea, within two miles of Armagh, and ministered to a Presbyterian congregation in the archiepis.opal city, where he

[1] "Account of the Life, Writings, and Character of Francis Hutcheson," by William Leechman, D.D., prefixed to Hutcheson's "Moral Philosophy ;" Carlyle's "Autobiography ;" MSS. Letters from Hutcheson to Dr. Drennan, &c.

was known by his church as a man of retiring habits and of superior abilities, and a firm supporter of Calvinistic doctrine. His second son, Francis, was born Aug. 8, 1694, it is said in his grandfather's house in Drumalig.[1] When about eight years of age, he (with his elder brother, Hans) was put under the care of the same grandfather, and attended a classical school kept by Mr. Hamilton in the "meeting-house" at Saintfield. He was afterwards sent to Killyleagh, in the same county, to an academy kept by the Rev. James Macalpin, said to be a man of virtue and ability, and who taught the future metaphysician the scholastic philosophy. We have it on record, that the Presbyterian Church of Ireland — seeking now, after coming through a long period of harassment and trouble, to work out its full educational system — did about this time set up several such schools for philosophy and theology. However, the great body of the young men intending for the ministry did then, and for more than a century after, resort to the University of Glasgow for their higher education. Of this college Hutcheson became a student about 1710 (he does not seem to have matriculated till 1711). During his residence with his grandfather he became such a favorite with the old man, that when he died in 1711, it was found that he had altered a prior settlement of his family affairs, and, passing by the older grandson, had left all his landed property to the second. Francis, though a cautious, was a generous youth : he had all along taken pains, even by means of innocent artifices, to uphold his brother in the old man's esteem ; and now he refused to accept the bequest, while Hans, with equal liberality, declined to receive what had been destined for another ; and the friendly dispute had at last to be settled by a partition of the lands, which again became united when Hans, dying without issue, left his share to the son of Francis.

Francis Hutcheson thus sprang, like Gershom Carmichael (and we shall afterwards see George Turnbull), from the old

---

[1] Sir James Mackintosh says in his "Dissertation:" "The place of Hutcheson's birth is not mentioned in any account known to me. Ireland may be truly said to be *incuriosa suorum*." Had Sir James made inquiries in the likely quarter, he would have found the place of his birth and the leading incidents of his life mentioned in an article signed "M." in the "Belfast Magazine" (for August, 1813), edited by Dr. Drennan, a man of superior literary ability, and son of the Rev. Thomas Drennan, one of Hutcheson's most intimate friends.

orthodox Presbyterian Church and its educated pastors ; and both were early nurtured in the scholastic logic, from which they received much benefit.   But Hutcheson comes an age later than Carmichael, and falls more thoroughly under the new spirit which has gone abroad.

At Glasgow the youth followed the usual course of study in the classical languages and philosophy, and enjoyed the privilege of sitting under the prelections of Carmichael. In after years, when called back to be a professor in the college, he gives in his Introductory Lecture a glimpse of the books and branches in which he fe t most interest in his student life.   After referring to the pleasure which he experienced in seeing once more the buildings, gardens, fields, suburbs, and rivers' banks (more pleasant then than now), which had been so dear to him, he expresses the peculiar gratification which he felt in revisiting the place where he had drunk the first elements of the quest for truth ; where Homer and Virgil, where Xenophon, Aristophanes, and Terence, where the philosophy of Cicero and the discussions of the Fathers, had been opened to him ; and where he had first been taught to inquire into the nature and reasons (*rationes*) of virtue, the eternal relations of number and figures, and the character of God.   Having taken the Master's degree in 1712, he entered, the following year, on the study of theology under Professor John Simson.   This professor was at that time, and, indeed, for the greater part of the period from 1712 to 1729, under prosecution before the ecclesiastical courts for teaching doctrines inconsistent with the Confession of Faith. It appears from the charges brought against him, and from his shuffling and vacillating explanations (he was often in a shattered state of health), that he too'; a favorable view of the state of the heathen ; that he was inclined to the doctrine of free-will ; he maintained that punishment for original sin alone was not just ; he held that rational creatures must necessarily seek their chief good, — always under subserviency to the glory of God, who cannot impose a law contrary to his own nature and to theirs, and who cannot condemn any except those who seek their chief good in something else, and in a different way than God has prescribed : but the special charge against him was, that he denied that Jesus Christ is a necessarily existent being in the same sense as the Father is.   The lengthened process concluded with the General Assembly declaring, in 1729, that Mr. Simson was not fit to be intrusted with the training of students for the ministry. It does not appear that young Mr. Hutcheson ever threw himself into this agitation on the one side or other, but it doubtless left its impression on his mind ; and this, I rather think, was to lead him to adopt, if not the doctrine, at least some of the liberal sentiments of Simson ; to keep him from engaging in religious controversy ; and to throw him back for certainty on the fundamental truths of natural theology and the lofty morality of the New Testament.

To the teaching of Simson the historians of the Church of Scotland are accustomed to trace the introduction of the " New Light " theology into the pulpits both of Scotland and Ulster. But there were other and deeper causes also at work, producing simultaneously very much the same results all over the Protestant Continent of Europe, and in England both in the Church and among Non-conformists. It was a period of growing liberality of opinion, according to the view of the rising literary men of the country. It was a time of doctrinal deterioration, followed rapidly by a declension of living piety, and in the age after of a high morality, according to the view of the great body of earnest Christians. In the preceding age, Milton, Newton, and Locke had abandoned the belief in the divinity of Christ, and the great Church of England divine of that age, Samuel Clarke, was defending the Arian creed, and setting aside the Reformation doctrine of grace. Francis Hutcheson, by this time a preacher, writes from Ireland to a friend in Scotland, in 1718, of the younger ministers in Ulster: " I find by the conversation I have had with some ministers and comrades, that there is a perfect Hoadley mania among our younger ministers in the north ; and, what is really ridiculous, it does not serve them to be of his opinions, but their pulpits are ringing with them, as if their hearers were all absolute princes going to impose tests and confessions in their several territories, and not a set of people entirely excluded from the smallest hand in the government anywhere, and entirely incapable of bearing any other part in the prosecution but as sufferers. I have reason, however, to apprehend that the antipathy to confessions is upon other grounds than a new spirit of charity. Dr. Clarke's work (on the Trinity), I'm sufficiently informed, has made several

unfixed in their old principles, if not entirely altered them."
Hutcheson never utters any more certain sound than this on
the religious controversies of his day. It is evident that his
mind is all along more inclined towards ethical philosophy and
natural theology.

It is interesting to notice that, in 1717, he wrote a letter to
S. Clarke stating objections to his famous "Demonstration of
the Being and Attributes of God," and that he received a reply,
both of which are lost. We are reminded that, about four
years before this, Joseph Butler, then a youth of twenty-one, at
a dissenting academy, had written Clarke, taking exception to
certain points in his "Demonstration," and had received answers
to his letters. The objections of Hutcheson must have been
more fundamental as to method than those of Butler. He was
convinced that, as some subjects from their nature are capable
of demonstration, so others admit only of probable proof, and
he had great doubts of the validity of all metaphysical arguments in behalf of the existence of Deity. Dr. Leechman tells
us : " This opinion of the various degrees of evidence adapted
to various subjects first led Dr. Hutcheson to treat morals as a
matter of fact, and not as founded on the abstract relation of
things."

During his student life he was tutor for a time to the Earl of
Kilmarnock. Leaving college about 1716, he was licensed to
preach the gospel by the Presbyterian Church in Ireland. His
preaching does not seem to have been acceptable to the people,
who were alarmed at the New Light doctrine which was creeping in among them, and felt that the young preacher's discourses were scarcely in the spirit of the Scriptures, as they
were not after the model of the ministers and divines whom
they reverenced.[1] However, he received a call from a country

---

[1] "His father, laboring under a slight rheumatic affection, deputed him to
preach in his place on a cold and rainy sabbath. About two hours after Francis
had left Ballyrea, the rain abated and the sun shone forth, the day became serene
and warm, and Mr. Hutcheson, feeling anxious to collect the opinions of his congregation on the merits of his favorite son, proceeded directly to the city. But
how was he astonished and chagrined when he met almost the whole of his flock
coming from the meeting-house, with strong marks of disappointment and disgust
visible in their countenance. One of the elders, a native of Scotland, addressed
the surprised and mortified father thus : ' We a' feel muckle wae for your mis-
hap, reverend sir ; but it canna be concealed. Your silly loon Frank has fashed
a' the congregation wi' his idle cackle ; for he has been babbling this oor about a

congregation at Magherally, in his native county, but was easily
persuaded to accept instead an invitation to open an academy
in Dublin, to give instruction in the higher branches. About
the time he settled there the Protestant Non-conformists, aided
by the government, but after a keen opposition from the Irish
bishops, had succeeded in obtaining a parliamentary repeal of
the Acts which required all persons to resort to their parish
church every Sunday, and imposed a fine of £100 upon the
dissenting minister who officiated in any congregation. But
the young teacher had to suffer two prosecutions in the archbishop's court for daring to teach youth without subscribing
the canons and obtaining a license. These attacks upon him
came to nothing, as they were discouraged by the Archbishop.
Dr. King, author of the metaphysical work on the " Origin of
Evil," who, though he had been a determined opponent of the
relaxation allowed by law to dissenters, was unwilling to oppress
so accomplished a man and well-disposed a citizen as Hutcheson. In Dublin he had laborious duties to discharge, which
left him, he complained, little time for literature and mental
culture ; but he seems to have met with congenial society. The
Presbyterians and Independents were the representatives of the
English Non-conformists, who had been a considerable body
there when Henry Cromwell was vice-regent, and when Winter
and Charnock preached to them in Christ's Church Cathedral ;
and they had among them families of standing and influence.
His literary accomplishments opened other circles to him.
There seems to have been at that time a considerable taste for
learning and philosophy in the metropolis of Ireland. From a
very early date after its publication, the " Essay on the Human

---

gude and benevolent God, and that the sauls o' the heathens themsels will gang
to heeven, if they follow the light of their own consciences. Not a word does
the daft boy ken, speer, nor say, about the gude auld comfortable doctrine of election, reprobation, original sin, and faith. Hoot, mon, awa' wi' sic a fellow !' "
The only members who waited for the end of the sermon were Mr. Johnson of
Knappa, Mr. M'Geough, and the clerk. (Stuart's " History of Armagh.") This
story may be made somewhat more pointed in the telling, but is, we have no
doubt, substantially correct. It will be remembered that Professor Simson held
similar views in regard to the heathen ; and, in the Introduction to the Translation of Antoninus by Hutcheson and Moor, the authors maintain : " 'Tis but a
late doctrine in the Christian church that the grace of God and all divine influences were confined to such as knew the Christian history, and were by profession in the Christian church."

Understanding," had been most enthusiastically welcomed by
Molyneux, who corresponded with Locke, and expressed his
excessive admiration of him.   Berkeley, the tutor of Molyneux's
son, began in 1707 to give to the world his ingenious speculations on mathematical and philosophical subjects.   It does not
appear that Hutcheson was acquainted with Berkeley, who, we
rather think, would not appreciate the views of Hutcheson:
he has certainly condemned the opinions of Shaftesbury.   But
he enjoyed the friendship of a number of eminent men, including Viscount Molesworth and Dr. Synge afterwards Bishop of
Elphin ; both of whom encouraged him to publish his first work,
and assisted him in preparing it for the press.   The former
connects him historically with Shaftesbury, who had written
letters to Molesworth, which were published in 1721.   When
in Dublin, Hutcheson and some others formed a club in which
papers were read by the members on philosophic themes.   It is
an interesting circumstance, that in the next age some of the
more important works of Gerard, Reid, Beattie, and Campbell
sprang out of a similar society in Aberdeen.

It was in 1725 that he published in London his first work,
" An Inquiry into the Original of our Ideas of Beauty and Virtue."   The treatise was published anonymously, as (so he tells
us in the second edition) he had so little confidence of success
that he was unwilling to own it.   The subject, the thoughts,
and the style were suited to the age ; and the work was favorably received from the first.   Lord Granville (afterwards Lord
Carteret), the Lord Lieutenant of Ireland, sent his private secretary to inquire at the bookseller's for the author ; and when
he could not learn his name he left a letter to be conveyed to
him, in consequence of which Hutcheson became acquainted
with his Excellency and was treated by him with distinguished
marks of esteem.   A second edition, corrected and enlarged,
was called for in 1726.

This was the age of serial literary essays which had commenced in England with the " Tatler " and " Spectator."   There
was such a periodical set up in the metropolis of Ireland called
the " Dublin Journal " conducted by Hibernicus (Dr. Arbucle),
and to this paper Hutcheson sent two letters, of date June 5th
and June 12th, 1725, on " Laughter," in opposition to the views
of Hobbes, who attributed men's actions to selfish motives, and

represented laughter as nothing else but sudden glory arising
from some sudden conception of some eminency in ourselves,
by comparison with the infirmity of others or our own formerly.
He characterizes Hobbes as "having fallen into a way of speaking which was much more intelligible than that of the Schoolmen," and "so becoming agreeable to many wits of his age;"
and as "assuming positive, solemn airs, which he uses most
when he is going to assert some solemn absurdity or some ill-
natured nonsense." He finds it difficult to treat the subject of
laughter "gravely," but gives his theory of the cause of laughter, which is "the bringing together of images which have
contrary additional ideas, as well as some resemblance in the
principal idea; this contrast between ideas of grandeur, dignity,
sanctity, perfection, and ideas of meanness, baseness, profanity,
seems to be the very spirit of burlesque, and the greater part
of our raillery and jest are founded on it." Some such view
as this has ever since been given of wit. Samuel Johnson
describes it as a sort of *concordia discors* or *concors discordia.*
Hutcheson ventures to specify the use of laughter: "Our passions are apt to lead us into foolish apprehensions of objects
both in the way of admiration and honor, and ridicule comes
in to temper our minds." This moderate view falls considerably short of that given by Shaftesbury, who represents ridicule as a test of truth.

Mandeville, in "The Fable of the Bees," had advanced some
curious and doubtful speculations as to private vices being public benefits; showing that the power and grandeur of any nation
depend much upon the number of people and their industry,
which cannot be procured unless there be consumption of manufactures; and that the intemperance, luxury, and pride of men
consume manufactures, and promote industry. The author has
here caught hold of a positive and important truth, the explanation of which carries us into some of the deepest mysteries of
Providence, in which we see good springing out of vice, and
God ruling this world in spite of its wickedness, and by means
of its wickedness, but without identifying himself with it. But
Mandeville was not able to solve the profound problem, and in
dealing with it he uses expressions which look as if he intended
to justify, or at least to palliate vice. Hutcheson hastens to
save morality, and writes letters on the subject to Hibernicus,

and easily shows that virtue tends to private and public happiness, and vice to private and public misery ; and that there
" would be an equal consumption of manufactures without these
vices and the evils which flow from them."

Hutcheson had now tasted the draught of authorship, and
must drink on.   In the " London Journal " for 1728, there appeared some Letters signed " Philaretus," containing objections
to the doctrine of the " Inquiry into the Ideas of Beauty and
Virtue," which is represented as not giving a sufficiently deep
view of virtue as founded on the nature of things and perceived
by reason.   Hutcheson replies in the same journal.   In that
same year he published his second great work, being " An Essay
on the Nature and Conduct of the Passions and Affections,
with illustrations of the Moral Sense."   In the Preface he says,
" Some Letters in the ' London Journal,' in 1728, subscribed
' Philaretus,' gave occasion to the Fourth Treatise (on the
Moral Sense) ; the answer given to them in these weekly papers
bore too visible marks of the hurry in which they were wrote,
and therefore the author declined to continue the debate that
way, choosing to send a private letter to Philaretus to desire a
more private correspondence on the subject of our debate.   He
was soon after informed that his death disappointed the author's
great expectations from so ingenious a correspondent."   Philaretus turned out to be Gilbert Burnet (second son, I believe,
of the bishop), and the correspondence was published in 1735,
with a postscript written by Burnet shortly before his death.
Burnet examines Hutcheson from the stand-point of Clarke,
and fixes on some of the weak points of the new theory.

At this time there was a keen controversy in Ulster as to
whether the Presbyterian Church should require an implicit
subscription to the Westminster Confession of Faith, and this
issued in those who refused to subscribe forming themselves
into a separate body called the Antrim Presbytery, the members of which published a " Narrative of the Proceedings of the
Seven Synods," which led to their separation.   The work of
replying to this document was committed to Mr. Hutcheson, of
Armagh, whose paper, however, was not published till after his
decease, which took place in February, 1729.   The old man had
anxieties about his son, lest he should be tempted by the flattering attentions paid him in Dublin to conform to the Estab-

lished Church, and wrote a letter expressing his fears. We have the reply of the son, of date Aug. 4, 1726. In this he avows that he did not regard the "government or externals of worship so determined in the gospel as to oblige men to one particular way in either:" that he looks upon the established form as an "inconvenient one;" that he reckons the dissenters' cause "in most disputed points the better;" that he believes the original of both civil and ecclesiastical power is from God; he denounces those religious penal laws which "no magistrate can have a right to make;" but he would not blame any man of his own principles who did conform, if the "ends proposed were such as would over-balance the damage which the more just cause would sustain by his leaving, particularly if he had any prospect of an unjust establishment being altered," of which, he confesses, he does not see the least probability. He says, that both Lord Cathcart and the Bishop of Elphin had professed their desire to have him brought over "to the Church, to a good living;" that he kept his mind "very much to himself in these matters, and resolved to do;" but that he had no intention whatever to depart from his present position, and that he would feel it his duty continually to promote the cause of dissenters. I rather think that this frank but expediency letter would not altogether satisfy the good old father, who had stood firm on principle in trying times. I have referred to these transactions, because they exhibit the struggles which were passing in many a bosom in those times of transition from one state of things to another. Hutcheson never conformed, as his contemporary Butler did, to the Church. His Presbyterian friends were soon relieved from all anxieties in this direction by his being appointed, after he had been seven or eight years in Dublin, to an office altogether congenial to his tastes, in Glasgow University, where, however, he exercised a religious influence which his father, provided he had been spared to witness it, would have viewed with apprehension and disapproval.

He was chosen to succeed Carmichael, Dec. 19, 1729, by a majority of the Faculty, over Mr. Warner, favored at first by the principal, and over Mr. Frederick Carmichael, son of Gershom, supported by five of the professors. His appointment could be justified on the ground of merit; but he owed it mainly

to family connections, who gained Lord Isla, the great government patron of the day, before whom the principal had to give
way.[1] In October, 1730, twenty English students have come
to the college, expecting Mr. Hutcheson — whose " Inquiry " and
work on the " Passions " were already well known — to " teach
morality ; " Professor Loudon, however, insisted that he had a
right to take the chair of Moral Philosophy, whereupon the
English students gave in a paper declaring that, if Mr. Hutcheson, who had not yet come over from Ireland, did not teach
them morality, they would set off to Edinburgh, and Mr. Loudon had to yield.   On November 30, he was publicly admitted,
and delivered, in a low tone and hurried manner, as if awed and
bashful, an inaugural discourse, " De Naturali Hominum Socia-
litate," in which he expounds, in a clear and pleasant manner,
and in good Latin, his favorite doctrine as to man having in his
nature disinterested affections.   He maintains, in opposition to
the " very celebrated " Locke, that man has something natural,
but admits that it requires time and circumstances to bring it
forth ; and in opposition to Hobbes and Puffendorff, that man
can be swayed by other motives than self-love.   He represents
the conscience as the $\tau\grave{o}$ $\eta\gamma\epsilon\mu o\nu\iota\kappa\acute{o}\nu$ to which all our nature ought
to be subjected, and to which it had been subjected in our
entire state ; but admits that our nature is fallen, weakened,
and corrupted, in many ways.   Hutcheson lectured five days
a week on his proper course, which embraced Natural Religion,
Morals, Jurisprudence, and Government ; and at another hour
he read three days of the week, with his students, some of the
finest writers of antiquity, Greek and Latin, on the subject of
morals ; interpreting both the language and sentiment.   This
practice of combining reading with lectures was followed by
his successors in the moral chair in Glasgow, and is vastly
superior to the plan of the Edinburgh professors of a later date,
who instructed their pupils only by reading lectures.   His prelections were at first, after the manner of the times, in Latin ;
but he had the courage to break off from the ancient custom,
and to speak in the English tongue, no doubt to the great joy
and benefit of the students, who might lose somewhat in not
being familiarized with the ancient learned language ; but would
gain vastly more in being brought into close sympathy with the

---

[1] Wodrow's " Analecta."

speaker, in listening from day to day to elegant English, and in the mastery which they would thereby acquire over their own tongue. Dr. Carlyle has left us a picture of the lecturer: "I attended Hutcheson's class this year (1743–44) with great satis- faction and improvement. He was a good-looking man, of engaging countenance. He delivered his lectures without notes, walking backwards and forwards in the area of his room. As his elocution was good, and his voice and manner pleasing, he raised the attention of his hearers at all times ; and when the subject led him to explain and enforce the moral virtues, he displayed a fervent and persuasive eloquence which was irresistible." A like account is given of him by his professed biographer Leechman : "A stature above middle size, a gesture and manner negligent and easy, but decent and manly, gave a dignity to his appearance. His complexion was fair and san- guine, and his features regular. His countenance and look bespoke sense, spirit, kindness and joy of heart." It may be added that this is the very impression left as we gaze on his portrait, with wig and gown, with florid face, and easy but dig- nified air, in the common hall of Glasgow College. Leechman represents him as dwelling in his lectures in a more diffuse manner on such moral considerations as are suited to touch the heart, and excite a relish for what is truthful and noble ; and by his vivacity of thought, and sensibility of temper, com- manding the attention of his students, and leaving strong impressions on their minds.

In the college he had an eminent colleague in Mr. Robert Simson (nephew of the theological professor), and a congenial one in Mr. Alexander Dunlop, the professor of Greek. Mr. Simson was an eccentric man, who spent his time between severe geometrical studies in the morning, and social meetings in the tavern at which he lived, or in his club, in the evening. Hutcheson and Dunlop — who was a man of strong sense and capacity for business — got the credit of managing all the affairs of the university, and both exerted themselves to main- tain the discipline of the college and foster its literary tastes. In particular, Hutcheson had great success in reviving the study of ancient literature, particularly the Greek, which had been much neglected in the university before his time. At a later date, he had associates of a kindred spirit in the elegant

and grave Dr. Leechman, professor of theology (afterwards .. –
principal) ; in the lively and learned Dr. Moor, first the librarian of the college, and in 1746 made professor of Greek ; and
in the two eminent printers, Robert and Andrew Foulis, who
published a multitude of learned works, including many of
Hutcheson's.   With such a spirit reigning in the college, and
a great thirst for education on the part of the Scottish youth,
fostered by the parish and burgh schools, the class-rooms were
filled with students.   Carlyle, who had just come in 1743 to
Glasgow, after having been at Edinburgh College, describes
the spirit that reigned among the youths : "Although at the
time there appeared to be a marked superiority in the best
scholars and most diligent students of Edinburgh, yet in Glasgow learning seemed to be an object of more importance, and
the habit of application was much more general," — a description which applies equally to Glasgow in after years.   He mentions that among the students there were sundry young
gentlemen from Ireland, with their tutors ; and he names,
among young men of station attending, Walter Lord Blantyre,
Sir —— Kennedy and his brother David, afterwards Lord
Cassilis, Walter Scott of Harden, James Murray of Broughton,
and Dunbar Hamilton, afterwards Earl of Selkirk.   The Scotch
colleges were quite competent at that time to educate the
nobility of the country, who had not yet fallen into the way of
going to the great English schools and colleges, there to lose
their national predilections and become separated, as they did
in succeeding ages, from the sympathies, social, political, and
religious, of the middle classes and common people of Scotland, to the great injury of the church and the nation generally.

   Hutcheson exercised a special influence in drawing students,
Scottish, Irish Presbyterian, and English Non-conformist, to
the college.   His own class was so large that he had to employ
an assistant.   The Calvinistic creed of the south-west of Scotland, the theological preaching of the old-school ministers, and
the training of the young in the Shorter Catechism, all inclined
the students to mental philosophy ; and in Hutcheson they had
much to attract, and little to offend.   When he set before them
wide fields of knowledge ; when, in his lectures on natural theology, he pointed out evidences of the wisest contrivance and

most beneficent intention ; when he led them from the external
world into the still greater wonders of the internal, and traced
the parts of man's moral constitution, and described the virtues
in their loveliest form, and enlarged on the elevated enjoyments
furnished by them ; when he quoted, with glowing zest, the
noblest passages of Greek and Roman literature ; when he
inculcated, with immense enthusiasm, the importance of civil
and religious liberty, — the students felt as if a new world were
thrown open to them, and a new life kindled within them. Following the custom of his predecessor, he lectured on the sabbath evenings on the truth and excellence of Christianity, and
the students of all the classes eagerly rushed to his prelections.
The conversation of the youths in their social walks and visits
often turned on the literary and philosophic themes which he
discussed, and some of them chose to attend his lectures for
four or five successive years. Among his pupils were Mr.
Millar, afterwards President of the Court of Session ; Archibald
Maclaine, who in future years translated Mosheim's " Ecclesiastical History ;" Matthew Stewart, famous for his Mathematical
Tracts, and father of Dugald Stewart ; and a youth, specially
appreciated by Hutcheson, with a vast capacity for learning of
every kind, and destined in future years to be so famous in
Hutcheson's own department, — Adam Smith, author of "The
Theory of Moral Sentiments," and of "The Wealth of Nations."
All of these ever spoke of Hutcheson in terms of high admira-
tion and gratitude.

Defoe describes the city of Glasgow, with its four principal
streets meeting in a cruciform manner at a point, as being, in
1726, one of the cleanliest, most beautiful, and best built cities
in Great Britain. On the street that ran toward the north
stood the college, completed in 1656, with quadrangles, arcade,
and spire, built after the style of Louis XIII. and Louis XIV.
The population, when Hutcheson was a professor, might be
upwards of twenty thousand. At the summit of the social
scale were the foreign merchants engaged in the American
trade, in which they carried out linen and brought back tobacco ;
"the tobacco merchants, with their scarlet cloaks and gold-
headed canes, and cocked hats, perched on powdered hair or
wig, with dangling clubtie or pigtail." Next to them, but at a
considerable distance, were the ordinary shopkeepers ; and far-

ther down, the tradesmen and servants ; while at the base were
the Highlandmen, with their tartan jacket and kilts, driven
from their native hills by starvation, and ready to perform the
most servile work.   All classes made a solemn religious profession ; but Wodrow mourns over degenerate customs which
wealth and luxury were introducing.   The better citizens dined
early in their own homes, without show ; and many of them
spent their evenings in social meetings at taverns, — a practice
which gendered those drinking customs which, beginning with
the upper classes about this time, went down to the peasant
class in the days of Burns, and by the end of the century infected the whole of Scottish society, which has not yet recovered from the evil influence.   But Hutcheson does not seem to
have been much mixed up with the citizen life of Glasgow ; we
do not hear of his spending his evenings in the tavern, or being
a member of any of the social clubs which began to spring up
in Glasgow at this time.   He had experience of the evil effects
of the new habits (which were coming in with the new theology), in the lives of some of the Irish students who were committed to his care, and over whom he watched with the most
friendly interest.   "The wretched turn their minds take is to
the silly manliness of taverns."   He satisfies himself with keeping personally free from the evil.   He presses his friend Tom
Drennan, from Belfast, to pay him a visit for a month or six
weeks, and promises : "Robert Simson, with you and Charles
Moor, would be wondrous happy till three in the morning ; I
would be with you from five to ten."

His sphere was within the walls of the college ; whence, however, his influence spread over the educated mind of the south-
west of Scotland and of Ulster, and over not a few of the
Non-conformists in England.   Carlyle tells us that he was
believed by the students to be a Socinian.   There is no evidence of this, nor of his expressing any positive opinion on any
doctrinal subject.   Even in his Sabbath evening lectures he kept
to Grotius "De Veritate Christianæ Religionis," and avoided,
Leechman tells us, "the party tenets or scholastic system of
modern ages."   He seems to have maintained a friendly communication with the non-subscribing Presbyterian ministers in
Ireland, some of whom (such as Abernethy and Leland, and
Bruce and Boyce) were as accomplished men as any theolo-

gians of their age, and of whom it may be said to their credit, that they suffered in their temporal interests rather than subscribe articles which they did not believe. In particular, Hutcheson carried on a very genial correspondence with the Rev. Thomas Drennan, a non-subscribing minister at Belfast.[1] The ministers of this communion, more especially as they were often abandoned by the people when their views became known, were at times in very poor circumstances. On hearing this, Hutcheson writes to his friend (May 31, 1742): "I am concerned that in my prosperous circumstances I did not think of it sooner. If you have any little contributions made towards such as are more distressed than the rest, you may mark me as a subscriber for £5 *per annum*, and take the above ten pounds as my payment for two years past. . . . I think it altogether proper you should not mention my name to your brethren, but conceal it. I am already called New Light here. I don't value it for myself, but I see it hurts some ministers who are most intimate with me. I have been these ten days in great hurry and perplexity, as I have for that time foreseen the death of our professor, who died last Wednesday, and some of my colleagues join me in laboring for Mr. Leechman to succeed. We are not yet certain of the event, but have good hopes. If he succeed, it will put a new face upon theology in Scotland."

This was no doubt one of the ends for which Hutcheson lived and labored, "*to put a new face upon theology in Scotland.*"[2] Discouraging all doctrinal exposition, and all rousing appeals to the conscience, he would have the preachers recommend the Christian religion as embracing a pure morality, and holding out the hope of a blessed immortality; but meanwhile providing no pardon to the poor sinner anxious about the past, nor gracious aid to help him in his struggles to deliver himself from sin in the future. Never avowing any doctrinal belief, his stu-

[1] The valuable letters of Hutcheson have been kindly placed at the disposal of the author of this work by Dr. Drennan, grandson of the Rev. Thomas Drennan, and have been used in this Memoir.

[2] There is evidently an analogous (not identical) movement going on in Scotland at this present time. There is an understood combination of persons in and beyond the universities, laboring in reviews, in books, and from the pulpits "to put a new face upon theology in Scotland," just as Hutcheson and Leechman did.

dents looked upon him as a Socinian, and so his influence went
in that direction. The crop that sprang up may be taken as
represented by such men as Carlyle, elegant and accommodating,
but dreadfully rankled by a Calvinistic creed which they had to
swear, and by the opposition of the people, who could not be
made to feel that the New Light was suited to them, or to
believe that it had any title to be called a religion. But all
this was in the future, and was not the precise result expected
by Hutcheson. Meanwhile he rejoices in Leechman, and describes him as one "who sees all I do." It seems that the
Scotch divine received a call from a non-subscribing congregation in Belfast, and Hutcheson is rather inclined that he should
go; he is so anxious to have him out of "that obscure place
where he was so much lost," and where he was "preaching to a
pack of horse-copers and smugglers of the rudest sort," who,
we venture to say, would not profit much by that calm, abstract,
elegant style which so pleased the professor of moral philosophy. Hutcheson uses every means to secure Leechman's
appointment to the chair of theology in Glasgow, and brings
influence of a very unscrupulous character (as I reckon it) to
carry his point. He writes Mr. Mure of Caldwell (Nov. 23,
1743) that he wants a letter from the Duke of Montrose, the
Chancellor of the University, in behalf of Leechman to Morth-
land, professor of Oriental languages, to be shown to others,
and he malignantly mentions that Professor Anderson, the chief
opponent of Leechman, "made himself ridiculous to all men of
sense by dangling after Whitefield and M'Cullogh" ("Caldwell
Papers"); and he wants this to be specially known to Tweeddale,
who was Secretary of State for Scotland, and to Andrew Mitchell, his private secretary. It seems that the advocates of liberality could not tolerate that a man should be favorable to a
revival of religion. It was by such means that "a new face was
to be put upon the theology of Scotland." He writes to his
Belfast friend (Feb. 20, 1743–44): "I could tell you a good deal
of news upon the unexpected election of a professor of divinity,
and the furious indignation of our zealots." He had written
previously (March 5, 1738–39): "I hope Jack Smith has sent
down to your town a 'Serious Address to the Kirk of Scotland,'
lately published in London; it has run like lightning here, and
is producing some effect; the author is unknown; 'tis wrote

5

with anger and contempt of the Kirk and Confession, but it
has a set of objections against the Confession which I imagine
few will have the brow to answer." The moderate party in the
Church of Scotland is being crystallized by coldness out of the
floating elements ; and already there is a felt polar antipathy
between them and those whom they choose to call "zealots."
Hutcheson writes (April 16, 1746), "I would as soon speak to
the Roman conclave as our presbytery."

The professor of theology introduced by him to the college,
had signed the Confession of Faith, and professed his willingness to sign it at any time. He accomplished the end of
Hutcheson. The subjects represented by him as suitable to
be dwelt on by the preacher from the pulpit, were the perfections of God ; the excellence of virtue, and the perfection of the
divine law ; the truth of the Christian religion, and the important purposes for which Jesus came into the world ; the great
doctrines he taught ; the interesting scenes of providence he
has displayed to men ; the dignity and immortality of the soul,
and the inconceivable happiness of the heavenly state. In the
social circle he was grave and silent, but is represented by Carlyle as having a lively wife, who entertained the students that
came to his house in the evening, and was anxious to hear
about the new plays and novels which were coming into Scotland. He set out a body of young preachers, who unfortunately
lost the common people, and the pious of all ranks, without
gaining the worldly and unbelieving. He published a sermon
in which he thought to recommend prayer as fitted to have an
influence on the mind of the person praying, and submitted a
copy to Hume, who told him plainly that the person praying
must believe that his prayers have an influence on God and
bring an answer.

It should be allowed that Hutcheson was most anxious to
impart a taste for learning and refinement to the ministers of
the Church of Scotland. He was deeply impressed with the
evils which were springing from the law of patronage being
now put in operation with a high hand. In 1735, he published
"Considerations on Patronage, addressed to the Gentlemen of
Scotland." In this pamphlet he predicts that, "instead of
studying sobriety of manners, piety, diligence, or literature, one
or other of which qualities are now necessary to recommend

the candidates to the favor of heritors, elders or presbytery, the candidate's sole study will be to stand right in politics, to make his zeal for the *ministry of state* conspicuous ; or by all servile compliance with the humor of some great lord who has many churches in his gift, whether that humor be virtuous or vicious, to secure a presentation." He fears the mischiefs of patronage were but beginning to appear, and that gentlemen's sons will no longer devote themselves to the ministerial office, which will be sought by lads of mean parentage and circumstances. It is quite certain that, owing to the law of patronage, combined with the smallness of the livings, estimated by Hutcheson as at that time about £80 a year, and the influence of London court life, the upper classes (from which so many ministers had sprung in the previous century) ceased from this time to encourage their sons to enter the sacred office.

The recorded incidents of his person and family life are not numerous. He seems to have been engrossed in lecturing to his students, in managing college matters, and in preparing text-books. He published a "Compend of Logic," a "Synopsis of Metaphysics," and "Institutes of Philosophy," all in clear and graceful Latin (referred to with commendation by Dr. Parr in his "Spital Sermon"). He joined Dr. Moor in publishing a translation of the "Meditations" of Antoninus, with a life of Antoninus, an introduction and notes in English, the last showing a considerable acquaintance with the Stoic philosophy.

When in Dublin, he had married Mary Wilson, daughter of Francis Wilson, a gentleman of property, and belonging to a Presbyterian family in Longford. In a letter to a friend, Feb. 12, 1740, he speaks of himself as "having been married now fifteen years and having only one boy surviving, of seven children borne to me by a very agreeable woman. I bless God for the one he has spared to me, and that he has no bad genius. If he proves a wise and good man, I am very well in this world. Since my settlement in this college I have had an agreeable and I hope not an useless life, pretty much hurried with study and business, but such as is not unpleasant. I hope I am contributing to promote the more moderate and charitable sentiments in religious matters in this country, where yet there remains too much warmth, and commonly about matters of no great consequence to real religion. We must make allowance for the power of education in all places, and have indulgence to the weakness of our brethren."[1]

So early as June, 1741, he writes to his Belfast friend: "In short, Tom, I find old age, not in gray hairs and other trifles, but in an incapacity of mind for such close thinking and composition as I once had, and have pretty much dropped the thoughts of some great designs I had once sketched out." On April 3, 1745, he was nominated to the chair of moral philosophy in Edinburgh by the Town Council, but declined the honor, in consequence of not feeling strong enough to engage in new labors. He writes, April 16, 1746: "I am in a great deal of private distresses about Jo. Wilson and his sister, the latter in the utmost danger, the other scarce recovered from death ; my wife, too, very tender ; but, by a set of most intricate business, upon which the soul of this college depends, and all may be ruined by the want of one vote, I cannot leave this till after 26th June, and we go to Dublin first." He had been for some months in an uncertain state of health : he went to Dublin about the time mentioned in the letter quoted ; and there, after a few days' fever, he was cut off, Aug. 8,. 1746. His remains were buried in the old graveyard of Knockmark, East Meath, among his wife's kindred, the Wilsons and Stanhopes. He left one son, who became a physician, and rose to be professor of chemistry in Dublin College. That son published, in 1754, his "System of Moral Philosophy," to which is prefixed an account of the father's life by Dr. Leechman.

Hutcheson has nowhere explained very fully or formally the method on which he proceeds. But he everywhere appeals to facts ; he brings all theories to the test of the actual operations of the human mind as disclosed to consciousness (a word frequently employed by him) ; he sets no value on speculations built up in any other way ; and he everywhere speaks doubtfully or disparagingly of the logical distinctions and verbal subtleties of the schoolmen, and of the rational deductions of Descartes and Samuel Clarke. Proceeding on the method of observation, he discovers certain cognitive powers, which he

[1] MS. letter to Rev. T. Steward, minister at St. Edmundsbury, in possession of Mr. Reid in Londonderry.

calls, perhaps unhappily, senses, which have a place in our very
nature and constitution, and operate independent of any notice
we may take of them.   These features show that he belongs to
the Scottish school, of which he is entitled to be regarded as
the founder, inasmuch as no philosopher connected with North
Britain had previously combined these characters, and as he in
fact gave the modern stimulus to philosophic speculation in
Scotland.

He does not dwell at great length, nor very minutely, on the
intellectual powers.   He says that "late inquiries have been
very much employed about our understanding, and the several
methods of obtaining truth ;" and so he would rather investigate "the various pleasures which human nature is capable of
receiving," and our various internal senses, perceptions, and
affections, specially the sense of beauty and the moral sense.
Still he intimates very clearly what views he takes of man's
intellectual nature.   And first, as to the senses, he says, " It is
not easy to divide distinctly our several sensations into classes.
The division of our external senses into the five common
classes seems very imperfect.   Some sensations received without any previous idea, can either be reduced to none of them,
such as the sensations of hunger, thirst, weariness, sickness ;
or, if we reduce them to the sense of feeling, they are perceptions as different from the other ideas of touch, such as cold,
heat, hardness, softness, as the ideas of taste or smell.
Others have hinted at an external sense different from all of
these.   The following general account may possibly be useful :
(1) That certain motions raised in our bodies are by a general law constituted the occasion of perceptions in the mind.
(2) These perceptions never come alone, but have some other
perceptions joined with them.   Thus every sensation is accompanied with the idea of duration, and yet duration is not a
sensible idea, since it also accompanies ideas of internal consciousness or reflection ; so the idea of number may accompany
any sensible ideas, and yet may also accompany any other ideas
as well as external senses.   Brutes, when several objects are
before them, have probably all the proper ideas of sight which
we have without the idea of number.   (3) Some ideas are
found accompanying the most different sensations, which yet
are not to be perceived separately from some sensible quality,

such as extension, figure, motion, and rest, which accompany
the ideas of sight or colors, and yet may be perceived without
them, as in the ideas of touch, at least if we move our organs
along the parts of the body touched.   Extension, figure,
motion, or rest, seem therefore to be more properly called
ideas accompanying the sensations of sight and touch than
the sensations of either of these senses, since they can be
received sometimes without the ideas of color, and sometimes
without those of touching, though never without the one or
other.   The perceptions which are purely sensible, received
each by its proper sense, are tastes, smells, colors, sound,
cold, heat, &c.   The universal concomitant ideas which may
attend any idea whatsoever are duration and number.   The
ideas which accompany the most different sensations are extension, figure, motion, rest.   These all arise without any previous ideas assembled or compared ; the concomitant ideas are
reputed images of something external.   From all these we may
justly distinguish those pleasures perceived upon the previous
reception and comparison of various sensible perceptions with
their concomitant ideas, or intellectual ideas, when we find
uniformity or resemblance among them.   These are meant by
the perceptions of the internal sense." (" Nature and Conduct of the Passions," Sect. I.)

  This note comprises the result and the sum of much reading
and much reflection.   The principal thoughts, more especially
as to the separation of the ideas of number and duration, and
of extension, figure, motion, and rest from our common sensations, are taken, directly or indirectly, from Aristotle's " Psyche,"
B. II. c. vi. (which is not referred to, however), where there is
a distinction drawn between common and proper percepts.
But he seems to take a step beyond Aristotle when he tells us
here, and still more expressly in his " Logic," that number and
duration can be perceived both by the external and internal
sense.   It has been felt by all profound thinkers, that in order
to account for the phenomena, and to save the senses from
deceiving us, there must be distinctions of some sort drawn
between different kinds of sensations or perceptions.   Adopting the distinction of Aristotle, we find him in his " Logic " identifying it with that of Locke, between the primary and secondary
qualities of bodies. · It may be doubted whether we can so

absolutely divide, as Aristotle and Hutcheson did, the accompanying ideas from the sensations or perceptions. The sensations and ideas are in every case wrapped up in one concrete cognitive act, while, however, they may come up in a different concretion in our next experience, and may be separated into elements by an analytic process. I rather think, too, that the perception of extension (as has been shown by Hamilton) is involved in all our sense-perceptions, for we seem to know our organism as in space and localized by every one of the senses. The language about the motions of bodies constituting the *occasion* of the perceptions in the mind, proceeds upon the inadequate distinction between efficient and occasional cause, drawn by the disciples of Descartes, — a distinction adopted by Reid as well as Hutcheson. I suspect that it still remains true, that the common division of our external senses is very imperfect, and that it is not easy to arrange our sensations into classes.

In regard to the question started in the next age by Reid, as to whether we perceive by the senses the external object, or an idea of it, it is certain that he accepts the view and the language of the great body of philosophers prior to his time, and speaks of our perceiving by ideas "as images of something external."

Formal logic has been taught, I believe, in Glasgow University from its establishment in 1451 to this present time. Hutcheson has a "Logical Compendium" which was used as a text-book in Glasgow and elsewhere. In this treatise, after a meagre dissertation on the rise of philosophy, he defines logic as "the art of guiding the mind in the knowledge of things;" adding, that it may also be considered a science, and that others define it "the art of discovering and declaring truth." These definitions will be regarded as too loose and vague by the rigid logicians of our time. In treating of the concept, notion, or idea, he represents ideas as being divided into sensations, imaginations, and pure intellections, — a theory adopted by Gassendi, and favorably received by not a few for an age or two after the time of Descartes and Gassendi, as seeming to reconcile these two eminent men. Hutcheson had previously represented all sensation as external and internal, and declared, with Locke, that all our ideas arise either from the external sense or from reflection. The intellections he defines as "any ideas not reached or comprehended by any bodily sense;" they are chiefly "suggested by the internal sense, and include our actions, passions, judgments, doubts, and the like, and also abstract ideas." There is an incongruous mixture here of the Lockian with an older theory. The ideas derived from reflection, which are all singular and concrete, should not be put in the same class with those abstract and general ideas which are formed by the intellect from the materials got from sensation and reflection, and, we may add, from those furnished by the faculties of the mind in their exercise, such as those we have of the beautiful and the good. This confusion long lingered in the Scottish psychology, from which it has scarcely yet been expelled.

Hutcheson represents complex (concrete would be the better phrase) ideas as having comprehension, and universal ideas as having extension; and announces the rule that extension and comprehension stand to each other in a reverse order. He distinguishes between a logical whole, which is a universal in respect of its species, which are spread out in division; and a metaphysical whole, which is the comprehension of a complex idea, and is declared by definition. He distinguishes between noetic and dianoetic judgment, in the former of which the two ideas are compared immediately (*proxime*), and in the latter by means of a third. The subject, predicate, and copula are said to be in the proposition either expressed or suppressed and involved. He does give the dictum of Aristotle as the regulating principle of reasoning, but derives all the force of syllogism from these three axioms, in which, we think, there is a very unsatisfactory vagueness in the phrase *agree:* "(1) Things which agree in one third agree with one another; (2) Things of which the one agrees and the other does not agree with one and the same third do not agree with one another; (3) Things which agree in no third do not agree with each other; (4) Things which disagree in no third do not disagree among themselves. Hence are deduced the general rules of syllogisms." This "Compend" continued to be printed and used down to at least the close of the third quarter of the eighteenth century. One is inclined to think that these phrases and distinctions must have been introduced to the notice, and inscribed on the memory, of William Hamilton during his collegiate life at Glasgow, and that they may have helped as they recurred, consciously or unconsciously, to suggest to him certain of the essential principles of the " New Analytic of Logical Forms."

He has a separate treatise on metaphysics (" Metaphysical Synopsis," 1742) which he divides into ontology, or the science of being, and pneumatology, or the science of spirit (divine and human). " It appears from his treatise on metaphysics," says his admiring biographer, "that he was well acquainted with the logomachies, meaningless questions, and trivial debates of the old scholastics, which had thrown a thick darkness on that part of philosophy : he has set that branch of knowledge in a clear light, and rendered it instructive and entertaining." The sneer at the scholastics is a symptom of the age. The alleged "meaningless questions" are still put, and must be put, by profound thinkers who would go down to the foundations of truth. Even Hutcheson was obliged to put them and to answer them. The answers which he gives, if not so profound in fact or in appearance as those given by the ancient Greek philosophers, by the scholastics, or by Descartes and Leibnitz, are always clear and sensible, and often just and satisfactory. He discusses, and this by no means in a superficial manner, topics which the Scottish metaphysicians between him and Hamilton carefully avoided. His scholastic training at Killyleagh, and the spirit of the older teaching, had still a hold upon him for good.

He treats of being, declaring it to be undefinable, and showing that it involves existence and essence, and that potency and action are the principles of being. He refers the conviction of our identity of being to consciousness. As to the much agitated question of the principle of individuation he comes to the sound conclusion that it is to be ascribed to the nature of the thing existing.

He discusses the question whether metaphysical axioms are innate. He denies that they are innate in the sense of their being known or observed by the mind from its birth, and affirms that in their general form they are not reached till after many comparisons of singular ideas. He shows that the mind assents to them in their singular form, even when a sensible object is presented. He stands up for axioms, self-evident and immuta-

ble, — with him, as with Locke, self-evidence being their prominent feature and their mark ; but he also declares them to be
eternal and unchangeable, — the mind perceiving at once the
agreement or disagreement of the subject or predicate. He
denies that there is any principle entitled to be regarded as the
first of all, and maintains that it is vain to seek any other criterion of truth than the faculty of reason itself, and the native
power of the mind.   These views are surely more profound than
those of Locke, less extravagant than those of Descartes, Leibnitz, or Wolf (he refers to Wolf).   They do not exhaust the
subject ; in particular, while he says truly (with Aristotle) that
the singulars and the less general are first known, he does not
enter on the question, which neither the Scottish nor any other
metaphysicians have yet settled, of the relation of self-evident
truths in their singular to their generalized form.

In regard to space and time, he avoids the extreme positions both of Clarke, who represents them as modes of the
divine being, and of Leibnitz, who describes them as mere
relations perceived by the mind.   He represents them as things
or realities, and declares modestly and truly that we are ignorant of the relation in which they stand towards the divine
nature.   These judicious views were followed by the Scottish
metaphysicians generally down to the time of Hamilton.

This leads him into the investigation of the infinite. He
regards the following propositions as probable : that it is
scarcely possible that there should be a number of infinite things
of the same kind ; that the infinite, because it is infinite, cannot
be greater ; that infinites, so far as infinites, cannot be multiplied ; nor can have any finite relation (*rationem*) to finite parts,
although things by one reason infinite and by another finite
may be divided and multiplied, if only there are other things of
the same description.   But after enunciating these bold propositions he cautiously adds that these questions may well be held
to surpass human capacity.

He declares that, properly speaking, there is only one sort of
cause, the efficient. He says that in the impulse and motion
of bodies, and in the effort to change the idea in our minds,
and to produce motions in our bodily members, we not only
see change, but perceive some energy or efficacy. This view
is not thoroughly carried out ; it certainly is the truth so far as

it goes. He cautions us, in the very spirit of Reid, against dogmatizing too minutely as to the power of the mind over the body.

Substance is that which remains when the affections change. He agrees with Locke that the nature of substance is unknown, except that we have an obscure idea of something as the substratum of qualities. His views on this whole subject are meagre and unsatisfactory.

Still it is in the discussion of these questions that he passes beyond Shaftesbury, and shows the clearness, the judiciousness, and the independence of his thinking. I am not sure whether these metaphysical topics have been discussed in a profounder manner by any thinker of the Scottish school except Sir W. Hamilton ; and he has not shown the same amount of speculative caution and good sense as Hutcheson.

But Hutcheson dwells far more on the motive and moral parts of man's nature than on logical and metaphysical subjects. We have seen that he brings in many other senses besides the external ones. He defines sense, " every determination of our minds to receive ideas independently on our will, and to have perceptions of pleasure and pain." The following is his classification of them : " 1. In the first class are the external senses, universally known. 2. In the second, the pleasant perceptions arising from regular harmonious uniform objects, as also from grandeur and novelty. These we may call, after Mr. Addison, the 'pleasures of the imagination,' or we may call the power of receiving them an internal sense. Whoever dislikes this name may substitute another. 3. The next class of perceptions we may call a public sense ; viz., our determination to be pleased with the happiness of others, and to be uneasy at their misery. This is found in some degree in all men, and was sometimes called Κοινονοημοσύνη, or *sensus communis*, by the ancients ; this inward pain or compassion cannot be called a sensation of sight. It solely arises from an opinion of misery felt by another, and not immediately from a visible form. The same form presented to the eye by the exactest painting, or the action of a player, gives no pain to those who remember that there is no misery felt. When men by imagination conceive real pain felt by an actor, without recollecting that it is merely feigned, or when they think of the real story represented, then, as there is a confused opinion of real misery, there is also pain in compassion. 4. The fourth class we may call the moral sense, by which we perceive virtue or vice in ourselves or others. This is plainly distinct from the former class of perceptions, since many are strongly affected with the fortunes of others who seldom reflect upon virtue or vice in themselves or others as an object ; as we may find in natural affection, compassion, friendship, or even general benevolence to mankind, which connect our happiness or pleasure with that of others, even when we are not reflecting upon our own temper, nor delighted with the perception of our own virtue. 5. The fifth class is a sense of honor which makes the approbation or gratitude of others, for any good actions we have done, the necessary occasion of pleasure, and then dislike, condemnation, or resentment of injuries done by us, the occasion of that uneasy sensation called shame, even when we fear no further evil from them." He adds that this enumeration may not be sufficient, and says that "there may be others, such as some ideas of decency, dignity, suitableness to human nature in certain actions and circumstances."

He then shows that the objects gratifying these senses call forth desires, which fall into five corresponding classes, those of the bodily senses, of the imagination or internal sense, of public happiness, of virtue, and honor. We are yet (so I am inclined to think) without a thoroughly exhaustive classification of the natural appetencies which lead to emotion, and desire, and action. That of Hutcheson is one of the best which we yet have, and should be looked to by those who would draw out a scheme of the categories of man's motive principles. I am disposed to think, however, that the sense of honor may be resolved into the moral sense combined with some other principles. ("Moral Philosophy," Book I.)

He shows how secondary grow upon these original desires. " Since we are capable of reflection, memory, observation, and reasoning about the distant tendencies of objects and actions, and not confined to things present, there must arise, in consequence of our *original desires, secondary desires* of every thing imagined useful to gratify any of the primary desires, and that

with strength proportioned to the several original desires and
the imagined usefulness or necessity of the advantageous
object. Thus, as soon as we come to apprehend the use of
wealth or power to gratify any of our original desires we must
also desire them. Hence arises the universality of these desires
of wealth and power, since they are the means of gratifying
all other desires." Mackintosh says, "He seems to have been
the first who entertained just notions of the formation of
the secondary desires which had been overlooked by Butler."
(" Passions," Sect. I. Mackintosh's " Diss.," Sect. V.)

He also shows how the association of ideas, which he characterizes as the "disposition in our nature to associate any
ideas together for the future which once presented themselves
jointly," has an influence upon our desires, primary and secondary, and specially on our sense of beauty. " Some objects
which, of themselves, are indifferent to any sense, yet by reason
of some additional grateful idea may become very desirable, or
by like addition of an ungrateful idea may raise the strongest
aversion. When any circumstance, dress, state, posture, is constituted as a mark of infamy, it may become, in like manner,
the object of aversion, though in itself most inoffensive to our
senses. If a certain way of living, of receiving company, of
showing courtesy, is once received among those who are honored, they who cannot bear the expense of all this may be made
uneasy at their condition, though much freer from trouble than
that of higher stations. Thus dress, retinue, equipage, furniture, behavior, and diversions, are made matters of considerable
importance by additional ideas." " The beauty of trees, their
cool shades and their aptness to conceal from observation, have
made groves and woods the usual retreat to those who love solitude, especially to the religious, the pensive, the melancholy,
and the amorous. And do not we find that we have so joined
the ideas of these dispositions of mind with those external objects, that they always recur to us along with them." He thus
started those views regarding the influence of association of
ideas on our perceptions of beauty and moral good which were
prosecuted by Turnbull, Beattie, and others, till they culminated
in the ingenious but extravagant theories of Alison and Jeffrey
in regard to the beautiful, and of Adam Smith and Mackintosh
as to virtue. Hutcheson certainly has not developed the full

influence of asssociation of ideas, but the account which he gives is just, so far as it goes.[1]

He dwells at great length on the sense of beauty. The feeling is raised at once on the perception of certain objects. He does not stand up for beauty supposed to be in the nature of things without relation to any mind perceiving it. On the contrary, all beauty implies the perception of some mind. Still there may be a distinction drawn between original or absolute beauty on the one hand, and relative or comparative beauty on the other. By the former he understands the beauty which we perceive in objects without comparison with any thing external, such as that observed in the works of nature, artificial forms, figures, theorems ; by the latter, the beauty founded on uniformity, or a kind of unity between the original and the copy. In determining what the beautiful is, he propounds the theory that it is a compound ratio of uniformity and variety, so that where the uniformity of bodies is equal, the beauty is as the variety ; and where the variety is equal, the beauty is as the uniformity. He seeks to establish this view by examples, dwelling on beautiful objects in nature and art, showing how there is in all of them uniformity or unity, proportion or harmony. This doctrine may not be the full theory of beauty ; but there must surely be some truth in it ; for in some modification or other it has cast up among profound thinkers in all ages, from Plato and Augustine in ancient times, to Cousin, Macvicar, and Ruskin in our day.

He stands up resolutely for the existence of disinterested and social affections. He earnestly opposes those who, like the Cyrenaics, and probably the Epicureans, would make pleasure the end of existence, and who would make us desire the good of others or of societies merely as the means of our own safety and prosperity, or as the means of some subtler

---

[1] There is a curious book, " An Introduction towards an Essay on the Origin of the Passions, in which it is endeavored to be shown how they are all acquired, and that they are no other than Associations of Ideas of our own making, or what we learn of others," London, printed for R. Dodsley, at Tully's Head in Pall Mall, and sold by T. Cooper, at the Globe in Paternoster Row, 1741. It is a mere fragment of thirty-two pages. The author says that the arguments made use of by Locke in order to prove that there are no innate ideas will, I think, hold fully as strong against all implanted appetites, or whatsoever "actions which we style moral or immoral, virtuous or vicious, are approved and disapproved, not by nature and constitution, but by habit and association."

pleasures of our own by sympathy with others in their happiness ; or who would make our end to be the pleasure we
enjoy in being honored, or some reward we expect for our services, and these either from God or man. He opposes also
that more refined system which makes our aim the joys proceeding from generous motions and moral approbation. He
shows, with great acuteness, that in all our desires, whether
benevolent or selfish, there is some motive, some end intended
distinct from the joy of success, or the removal of the pain of
desire ; and that there is first the motive operating, and then
the joy or pain following, according as the motive is gratified or
thwarted. He proves that men have affections, such as the
love of offspring and of relatives, which fit them for a state of
society ; he takes pains to show that in this respect he differs
from Puffendorf, who constructs his theory of society on the
principle that self-love is the spring of all our actions ; and he
offers a most determined opposition to Hobbes when he makes
the natural state of man to be one of war.

A considerable portion of all his works is occupied in demonstrating that man is possessed of a moral sense. In his
" Inquiry," published before Butler's " Sermons on Human
Nature," he declares, " that from the very frame of our nature
we are determined to perceive pleasure in the practice of virtue,
and to approve of it when practised by ourselves or others."
He declares that the vast diversity of moral principles in various ages and nations " is indeed a good argument against
innate ideas or principles, but will not evidence mankind to be
void of 'a moral sense to perceive virtue or vice in actions."
He ever kindles into a gentle warmth when he speaks of the
joys derived from this sense, which he represents as purer and
more elevated than those which can be had from any other
source. The conscience, though often unable to govern our
inferior nature, is yet in its own nature born for government ;
it is the ruling principle (τὸ ἡγεμονικόν) to which all things had
been subjected in the entire (*integro*) state of our nature, and
to which they ought to be subjected. His views on the subject
of the supremacy of conscience are not so thoroughly wrought
out as those of Butler ; but they are explicitly stated, and
become more decisive in his later works.

But what is the quality in actions looked at, appreciated, and

approved by the moral sense ?　To this question Hutcheson
gives, if not a satisfactory, a very decisive reply.　He represents this quality as good-will or benevolence.　"All those
kind affections which incline us to make others happy, and all
actions which flow from such affections, appear morally good,
if while they are benevolent towards some persons they be not
pernicious to others."　Advancing a step farther, he discovers
that "the several affections which are approved, though in very
different degrees, yet all agree in one general character of
tendency to the happiness of others," and the most perfectly
virtuous actions are such "as appear to have the most unlimited tendency to the greatest and most extensive happiness of
all the rational agents to whom our influence can reach."　He
is evidently inclined to reckon the moral sense as planted in
our nature to lead us to commend at once those actions which
tend towards the general happiness.　His theory of virtue thus
comes to be an exalted kind of eudaimonism, with God giving
us a moral sense to approve of the promotion of happiness
without our discovering the consequences of actions.　Hume
required only to leave out the divine sanction (he retained
some sort of moral sense) in order to reach his theory of virtue
consisting in the useful and agreeable.　Hutcheson opposes
very resolutely all those moralists who seek to give morality a
deeper foundation in the nature of things.　The function of
reason in morals is simply to show what external actions are
laudable or censurable, according as they evidence good or evil
affections of soul.[1]

Proceeding on these principles, derived mainly from Shaftesbury, but more systematically expounded, he builds up a
system of moral philosophy.　He gives a division of the
virtues, and treats of the duties we owe toward God, toward
mankind, and toward ourselves.　In proving the existence of
God, he appeals to the structure of the world.　He reaches the
divine perfections by a set of metaphysical principles surreptitiously introduced, and scarcely consistent with his philosophy.

[1] There is a work, "An Examination of the Scheme of Morality advanced by
Dr. Hutcheson, late Professor of Morality in the University of Glasgow," 1759,
in which the author criticises Hutcheson's whole doctrine of senses, instincts,
affections; and objects to his attempts to reduce all virtue and religion to
benevolence or good-will to others, and also to his doctrine of moral sense as
a faculty.

He answers the objections derived from the existence of evil
in a commonplace way, by showing how particular evils are
necessary to superior good.   He seeks to establish the immortality of the soul by an appeal to the nature of the soul as
being different from the body, and to the hopes of a future
state.

IIe enters at great length into the discussion of the ages
which preceded him, as to the law of nature.   He shows that
there are rights antecedent to the institution of civil government.   He establishes the right of property, first, on the principle that " things fit for present use the first occupier should
enjoy undisturbed ; " and on the farther principle, that each
has a right to the fruits of his own labor, and that it is the
common interest of society, and tends towards the furtherance
of industry, that mankind should be secured in their possessions.

He says that "civil power is most naturally founded by these
three different acts of a whole people : 1. An agreement or
contract of each one with all the rest, that they will unite into
one society or body, to be governed in all their common interests by one council ; 2. A decree or designation made by the
whole people of the form or plan of power and of the persons
to be intrusted with it ; 3. A mutual agreement or contract
between the governors thus constituted and the people, the
former obliging themselves to a faithful administration of the
powers vested in them for the common interest, and the latter
obliging themselves to obedience.   Though it is not probable
that, in the constitution of the several states, men have generally taken these three regular steps ; yet it is plain that, in
every just constitution of power, there is some such transaction
as implicitly contains the whole force of all the three." He
argues that the people have a right of resistance, and of
dethroning a prince who is grossly perfidious to his trust.

He thinks that the senate of the country should create a
censorial power, " that by it the manners of the people may
be regulated, and luxury, voluptuous debauchery, and other
private vices prevented or made infamous."   He holds that the
" magistrate should provide proper instruction for all, especially for young minds, about the existence, goodness, and
providence of God, and all the social duties of life and motives

6

to them." But he particularly maintains that "every rational creature has a right to judge for itself in these matters." While an earnest supporter of liberty of thought and action, he yet holds "as to those who support atheism, or deny a moral providence, or the obligation of the moral law, or social virtues, that the state may justly restrain them by force, as hurting it in its most important interests."

When Calamy heard of Hutcheson's call to Glasgow, he smiled, and said he was not for Scotland, and that he would be reckoned there as unorthodox as Simson. But Hutcheson lived an age later than Simson; he was much more prudent, and was personally liked; he was professor of philosophy and not of theology; and so he passed through life with very little public opposition. Still the stone which he had set a-moving could not go on without meeting with some little ruffling. About the beginning of the session 1737-38, a paper was printed and published anonymously by one who professed to have been lately in the college, charging Hutcheson with teaching dangerous views. I have not seen this attack; but the reply prepared by a body of his favorite students is preserved. There seems to be force in some of the objections taken; others entirely fail. It is objected to him that he taught that we could have the knowledge of moral good and evil, although we knew nothing of the being of a God; it is replied that Hutcheson's doctrine was that we might have knowledge of some virtues, though we had not known God, and that a notion of moral good must come prior to any notion of the will or law of God. It is objected that he taught that the tendency to promote the happiness of others is the standard of moral goodness; it is acknowledged in the answer that benevolent affections towards others are our primary notion of moral goodness, and the primary object of our approbation. It is objected that he taught that it is sometimes lawful to tell a lie; it is answered that Hutcheson's doctrine was very much against lying, but did imply that there might be cases in which lying was justifiable.

Throughout Scotland there was an impression among the scholars who had been trained in the previous generation that he was sensualizing and degrading the old philosophy. The friends of evangelical truth perceived that the young preachers who admired him addressed them in a very different speech from that of their old divines and from that of the inspired writers. The description given of the new style of preaching by the clerical satirist Witherspoon, in his " Characteristics," was found to have point and edge : " It is quite necessary in a moderate man, because his moderation teaches him, to avoid all the high flights of evangelic enthusiasm and the mysteries of grace of which the common people are so fond. It may be observed, nay, it is observed, that all our stamp avoid the word grace as much as possible, and have agreed to substitute the ' moral virtues' in the room of the 'graces of the Spirit.' Where an old preacher would have said a great degree of sanctification, a man of moderation and politeness will say a high pitch of virtue." In the advice to a good preacher the following counsels are given : " 1. His subjects must be confined to the social duties. 2. He must recommend them only from rational considerations ; viz., the beauty and comely proportions of virtue, and its advantages in the present life, without any regard to a future state of more extended self-interest. 3. His authorities must be drawn from heathen writers ; none, or as few as possible, from Scripture. 4. He must be very unacceptable to the common people." " The scattering a few phrases in their sermons, as harmony, order, proportion, taste, sense of beauty, balance of the affections, will easily persuade the people that they are learned ; and this persuasion is to all intents and purposes the same thing as if it were true. It is one of those deceitful feelings which Mr. H—— in his essays has shown to be beautiful and useful." In illustrating the third counsel he says : " It is well known there are multitudes in our island who reckon Socrates and Plato to have been much greater men than any of the apostles, although (as the moderate preacher I mentioned lately told his hearers) the apostle Paul had a university education and was instructed in logic by Gamaliel. Therefore let religion be constantly and uniformly called virtue, and let the heathen philosophers be set up as great patterns and promoters of it. Upon this head most particularly recommend M. Antoninus by name, because an eminent person of the moderate character says his ' Meditations' are the best book that ever was written for forming the heart." The effect of this accommodation of religion to the world is graphically and truly described: "The necessity of such a conduct cannot be denied when it is considered what effect the length and frequency of public devotion have had in driving most of the fashionable gentry from our churches altogether." "Now the only way to regain them to the church is to accommodate the worship as much as may be to their taste." "I confess there has sometimes been an ugly objection thrown up against this part of my argument; viz., that this desertion of public worship by those in high life seems, in fact, to be contemporary with, and to increase in a pretty exact proportion to, the attempts that have been made and are made to suit it to their taste."

Hutcheson's works got fit audience in his own day, but did not continue to be much read after his death. In his mode and manner of writing he is evidently indebted to the wits of Queen Anne, such as Shaftesbury, Bolingbroke, Pope, and Swift, who were Frenchifying the English tongue, polishing away at once its roughness and its vigor, introducing the French clearness of expression, and, we may add, the French morals. Hutcheson has their clearness, but is without their liveliness and wit. His style is like a well-fenced, level country, in which we weary walking for any length of time; it is not relished by those who prefer elevations and depressions, and is disliked by those who have a passion for mountains and passes. He ever maintains a high moral tone; but it is doubtful whether he has retained for morality a sufficiently deep foundation.

His philosophy is undoubtedly an advance upon that of Locke, and rises immeasurably above that of those professed followers of Locke in England and France, who in the days of Hutcheson were leaving out Locke's reflection, and deriving all man's ideas from sensation, and all his motives from pleasures and pains. His view of the moral faculty is correct so far as it goes. He represents it as natural to man, and in his very constitution and nature. There may even be a propriety in calling it a *sense* with the qualifying phrase *moral*, inasmuch as, like the senses, it is a source of knowledge, revealing to us certain qualities of voluntary acts or agents, and inasmuch as it has always feeling or sensibility attached to its exercises.

But, on the other hand, his view of the moral power falls greatly beneath that of the great English moralists of the previous century, and below that of the school of Clarke in his own day. The word sense allies the conscience too much with the animal organism, and the whole account given of it separates it from the reason or higher intelligence. On this point he was met, immediately on the publication of his views, by Gilbert Burnet, who maintains that moral good and evil are discerned by reason ; that there is first reason, or an internal sense of truth and falsehood, moral good and evil, right and wrong, which is accompanied by another succeeding internal sense of beauty and pleasure ; and that reason is the judge of the goodness and badness of our affections and of the moral sense itself. Hutcheson does speak of the moral sense as being superior in its nature to the other senses, but he does not bring out so prominently and decisively as Butler did its supremacy and its right to govern.

If his theory of the moral power is superficial and defective, his account of that to which the conscience looks is positively erroneous. He represents virtue as consisting in benevolence, by which he means good-will. This view cannot be made to embrace love to God, except by stretching it so wide as to make it another doctrine altogether ; for surely it is not as a mere exercise of good-will that to love God can be described as excellent. His theory is especially faulty in that it overlooks justice, which has ever been regarded by our higher moralists as among the most essential of the virtues. Nor is it to be omitted that his moral system is self-righteous in its injunctions, and pagan in its spirit. No doubt he speaks everywhere with deep admiration of the morality of the New Testament ; but the precepts which he inculcates, are derived fully as much from Antoninus and the Stoics as from the discourses of our Lord, and the epistles of the apostles ; and we look in vain for a recommendation of such graces as repentance and humility, meekness and long-suffering.

By bringing down morality from the height at which the great ethical writers, of ancient and modern times, had placed it, he prepared the way for the system of Adam Smith, and even for that of Hume. Smith was a pupil of his own, and Hutcheson was brought into contact with Hume. Hume submitted to Hutcheson in manuscript the "Third Part of his Treatise of Human Nature," that on morals, before giving it to the world. The remarks which Hutcheson offered have been lost, but we can gather what they were from the letter which Hume sent him on receiving them, and which has been preserved. Hutcheson most characteristically objects to Hume, that he had not expressed a sufficient warmth in the cause of virtue, and that he was defective in point of prudence. Was this all that the high moralist Hutcheson had to object to the founder of modern utilitarianism? On the publication of his "Institutes of Moral Philosophy," Hutcheson sends a copy of it to Hume, who remarks upon it, specially objecting to it as adopting Butler's opinion, that our moral sense has an authority distinct from its force and desirableness; but confessing his delight "to see such just philosophy, and such instructive morals, to have once set their foot in the schools. I hope they will next get into the world, and then into the churches." Yes, this was what the rationalists wished in that day, and what they wish in ours, to get their views *into the churches*. Hutcheson, though disapproving of the philosophy of Hume, and refusing to support him as a candidate for the chair of moral philosophy in Edinburgh, which he himself declined, had not retained sufficiently deep principles to enable him successfully to resist the great sceptic who had now appeared. Error has been committed, God's law has been lowered, and the avenger has come.

VIII. — *RELIGIOUS CONFLICTS.* — *RALPH ERSKINE.*

WE are now in the heart of the Scottish conflicts of the century. It is the crisis of the contest between Cavalier and Whig. On one point the philosophers and the evangelicals agree: they are defenders of the House of Hanover and opponents of the Pretender and the Stuarts, of whom they could not expect that they would be supporters of culture on the one hand, or of Protestantism on the other. The last formidable contest between Jacobite and Whig, was decided in behalf of the latter in 1746, at Culloden; and henceforth the former is sinking into a state of complaining and garrulous, though often lively, old age. The religious conflicts are deeper, and continue for a longer period. From the time of Hutcheson, there is a felt and known feud, not always avowed, between the new philosophy and the old theology. It would have been greatly for the benefit of both, had there been one to reconcile and unite them. In the absence of such, each ran its own

course and did its own work, being good so far as it went, and evil only in
its narrowness and exclusiveness, in what it overlooked or denied. The
philosophers were laudably engaged when they were unfolding man's intellectual, esthetic, and moral nature ; but they missed the deepest properties
of human nature, when, in the fear of the ghosts of fanaticism, they took no
notice of man's feelings of want, his sense of sin, and his longing after God
and immortality; and the views of theologians would have been more just
and profound, had they observed — always in the inductive manner of the
Scottish school — those nascent ideas of good and evil and infinity which
are at the basis of all religious knowledge and belief. The evangelical
preachers were only faithful to their great Master when they declined to
allow the doctrines of grace to sink out of sight; but they erred so far as
they opposed the refinement and liberal sentiments which the moral philosophers were introducing, and showed that they were incapable of fully
appreciating the apostolic command, "Whatsoever things are true, whatsoever things are honest, whatsoever things are just, whatsoever things are
pure, whatsoever things are lovely, whatsoever things are of good report, if
there be any virtue, and if there be any praise, think on these things."
Pity it is that it should be so, but it is only by vibrations that the world
moves on, only by breezes that its atmosphere is kept pure ; and when the
church errs by cowardice, it has to be rebuked by the unbelieving as — an
old Covenanter might have said — the father of the faithful was rebuked by
a pagan Egyptian. It was only in a later age, and mainly through the influence of Chalmers, that the church was prepared heartily to accept what was
true in the Scottish philosophy, and to acknowledge its compatibility with
the doctrine of salvation by grace.

Three distinct religious parties are being formed in Scotland, not including the covenanting "remnant," who never submitted to the Revolution
settlement, and whose vocation was on the mountains, rather than the colleges of their country. First, in the Church of Scotland there is the
"Moderate" type of minister crystallized by coldness out of the floating
elements. He is or he affects to be elegant and tolerant, and he is terribly
afraid of a zealous religious life. He wishes to produce among the people
a morality without religion, or at least without any of the peculiar dogmas
of Christianity. As yet he himself is a moral man, and the people are
moral, for they believe in the old theology ; in the next age both pastors and
people, retaining little faith, become considerably immoral, showing that, if
we would have the fruit good, we must make the tree good. This party,
preaching moral sermons without doctrine, is the genuine product of the
Scottish philosophy in the Church of Scotland.

Secondly, the Evangelical party, called by their opponents 'zealots' and
'highflyers,' were placed in an ambiguous position and shorn of much of
their strength since the enforcement of the law of patronage. They are fast
becoming a minority, and a small minority, in the church ; and they have to
submit to much that they abhor, as, for example, to the settlement of pastors
contrary to the will of the people. But they labor earnestly to keep alive
the fire all through the dark and wild night ; they cherish fellowship with
other evangelical churches, and anticipate the missionary spirit of a later

age by countenancing the "Society for the Propagation of Christian Knowledge." They come into collision with the philosophic moralists, by maintaining so resolutely the doctrines of grace ; and they carry their antagonism to the "legal" system to the very verge of Antinomianism, as shown in their favor for the "Marrow of Divinity," this by a reaction prompting the moral divines to preach a morality without an atonement for immorality.

Thirdly, beyond the Established Church, the Seceding body, encompassed with hardships as fierce as the storms, but breathing a spirit as free as the air of their country, are rallying around them the old-fashioned and more determined religious life of Scotland. At this stage of its history it serves itself heir to the Covenants of the previous century, blames the Church of Scotland for being too indulgent, is intolerant of toleration, and has little sympathy with other churches. This body is beneath the notice of the philosophers ; and in return it shows its utter distrust of them by declining to allow its students to attend the classes of moral philosophy, and appointing a professor of its own to give instruction in that branch, on which, as on other high departments of learning, it continued to set a high value.

The event of that period which agitated lowland Scotland more than even the inroad of the Pretender was the preaching of Whitefield, which moved the common people as the winds do the trees of the forest. The moderate party affected to despise and actually hated the preacher and his doctrine. The evangelicals in the Established Church rejoiced in his labors and their fruits. The seceders might have triumphed in his success ; but they expected him to identify himself with their peculiar ecclesiastical constitution, and stand by them in the fight for the old cause of the Covenant. Upon Whitefield declining to do this, they became jealous of his influence, and were in doubts about the sound character of the revivals which he was the means of awakening. Out of this arose a very curious controversy, forgotten by all but a few antiquarians, but not unworthy of being noticed.

Mr. Robe, belonging to the evangelical party in the Church of Scotland, and a promoter of revivals and of the lively feeling manifested in them, declared that "our senses and imagination are greatly helpful to bring us to the knowledge of the divine nature and perfections ; " and in defending this he asked : "Can you or any man else think upon Christ really as he is, God-man, without an imaginary idea of it ?" To this Ralph Erskine, the seceder, replies in a treatise of 372 closely printed pages, entitled "Faith no Fancy ; or a Treatise of Mental Images, discovering the Vain Philosophy and Vile Divinity of a late Pamphlet entitled ' Mr. Robe's Fourth Letter to Mr. Fisher,' and showing that an Imaginary Idea of Christ as Man (when supposed to belong to Saving Faith, whether in its Act or Object) imports nothing but Ignorance, Atheism, Idolatry, great Falsehood, or gross Delusion " (1745). He says of Mr. Robe : "This way of speaking appears indeed new and strange divinity to me, and makes the object of faith truly a sensible object ; not the object of faith, but of sense." This leads him to criticise various philosophies. He refers to Tertullian (as quoted by Jerome), who in regard to Platonic ideas said, "Hæreticorum patriarchæ philosophi." He shows him that the learned De Vries, Mastricht, and other eminent doctors and divines abroad, had noticed how the ideal doctrine of Cartesius and his followers had led to imagery and idolatry. He also criticises Locke with considerable skill. "There seems nothing more common in the experience of mankind than that a man who hath the greatest stock of habitual knowledge and understanding relating to many truths, yet while his body sleeps, or his mind is in a muse about other things, he perceives none of these truths." So "I see no greater absurdity in saying one may have a stock of seminal or habitual knowledge, though he have no actual knowledge, than to say one may have a stock of senses, though he hath no actual sensation, or consciousness of the acts or exercise of any of his senses, as a child not born or a man in a deep sleep; or a natural store of affections subjectively in him, and yet affected with nothing till occasions and objects appear. One may have a good pair of eyes, and yet see nothing till light be given and objects be presented. Nor is it an improper way of speaking to say a man hath not his eyes or sight, though he be not actually seeing. And as little is it improper to say a man hath understanding and knowledge, though he be not actually knowing or perceiving the truths he has the impress of in his understanding." This is a wonderfully clear statement of the distinctions between the seminal capacity and the actual ideas, between a laid-up stock and occasions, by which philosophers have sought to overthrow the theory of Locke. In regard to the special question discussed, Mr. Robe had quoted the received rule, "Oportet intelligentem phantasmata speculari." Erskine quotes against him Hieroboord, "Mens non indiget semper phantasmata ad suas perceptiones." "The object of that idea is only corporeal things as corporeal; but the object of rational knowledge is not only corporeal things, but spiritual and corporeal things, not as corporeal, but as intelligible." "It is reason, and not sense, that is the only help to attain the natural knowledge of God and his perfections." Above reason he places faith. "True faith differs as much from, and is as far above, mere intellectual ideas as intellectual ideas are above corporeal and imaginary ideas: yea, much farther than human reason is above sense; even as far as what is above human and supernatural, is above merely natural." It is evident that there are curious questions started, though not precisely settled, as to the place which the phantasm has in thought, and the imagination in religion. We feel that we are in the society of men of reflection and of reading. The evangelical and the seceding ministers of these days are quite as erudite as the academic men who despised them, and are holding firmly by old truths which the new philosophy is overlooking.

IX. —*ARCHIBALD CAMPBELL.*

He was a pupil of Professor Simson's, in Glasgow, and became minister of Tarbert in Stirlingshire. I have been able to collect few notices of him. He is worthy of being mentioned, as having had played upon him one of the basest tricks mentioned in literary history. He wrote a treatise on

"Moral Virtue," and sent it up to London to his friend, Alexander Innes, D.D., assistant at St. Margaret's, Westminster, to have it published; and Innes published it in his own name, with the date, Tothill Fields, Jan. 20, 1727–28. In 1730, Campbell went to London and exposed Innes's imposture. It seems that the Lord Chancellor, believing that Innes was the author of the work, presented him to a living. The Chancellor, being convinced of the deceit, sought to make amends by offering a living to Campbell, who declined the offer, saying that he preferred his own country; and he becomes professor of ecclesiastical history in St. Andrews. In 1733, he published the work in his own name, dating it St. Andrews, and disowning the "Prefatory Introduction" and "some little marginal notes of Innes." "An Inquiry into the Original of Moral Virtue, wherein is shown, against the Author of the Fable of the Bees, that Virtue is founded in the Nature of Things, is unalterable and eternal, and the great Means of Private and Public Happiness, with some Reflections on a late Book entitled 'An Inquiry into the Original of our Ideas of Beauty and Virtue.'" Hutcheson, whom he thus assailed, spoke of him as no better than a disciple of Epicurus. His system is the baldest form of self-love. "Human nature is originally formed to pleasure and pain." "There is, indeed, a distinction of goodness into natural and moral, but the latter as well as the former lies wholly in pleasure." "God and all mankind are governed by one common principle, viz., self-love." "They can favor or esteem no other beings but as they gratify this principle." "The affections and actions that correspond to the self-love of our own species are likewise agreeable to the self-love of the Deity." "From self-love we desire the love and esteem of other intelligent beings." There is a passage in which there is an anticipation of Smith's theory of sympathy: "Whatever tenderness we conceive in favor of other people, it comes from putting ourselves in their circumstances, and must therefore be resolved into self-love." He also wrote a treatise on the "Necessity of Revelation," 1730; and another, "Oratio de Vanitate Luminis Naturæ." He thinks it impossible that mankind, left to themselves, should 'discover' the great truths and articles of natural religion, or should be capable of giving a system to natural religion." He died in April, 1756. A posthumous work, "The Authenticity of the Gospel History," was published 1759. He was opposed by

———•———

X. — *ALEXANDER MONCRIEFF.*[1]

ALEXANDER MONCRIEFF of Culfergie in the parish of Abernethy was educated at the grammar school of Perth and St. Andrews University, and became minister of his native parish. He was favorable to the Marrow school of divinity, and took part with the Erskines in defending the popular rights and in seceding from the Church of Scotland, being one of the four fathers of the secession. In 1724, he was made their professor of divinity. He

[1] "Memorials of Alexander Moncrieff and James Fisher," by Dr. Young and Dr. Brown.

died in 1761. He wrote "An Inquiry into the Principle, Rule, and End of Moral Actions, wherein the Scheme of Selfish Love laid down by Mr. Archibald Campbell . . . is examined, and the received Doctrine vindicated." To quote the summary supplied by his biographers, he establishes the following propositions : " (1) To show that self-love is not, or ought not to be, the leading principle of moral virtue ; (2) That self-interest or pleasure is not the only standard by which we can and should judge of the virtue of our own and others' actions, or that actions are not to be called virtuous on account of their correspondency to self-interest ; (3) That self-love, as it exerts itself in the desire of universal, unlimited esteem, ought not to be the great remaining motive to virtuous actions," &c.

XI. — *RISE OF THE ABERDEEN BRANCH.*

The north-east of Scotland, — embracing Aberdeen, Banff, Murray, Mearns, and a large portion of Angus, — though now very much amalgamated with the rest of Scotland, had a character of its own in the seventeenth century.   The people had a large Scandinavian element in their composition, had a shrill intonation, and a marked idiom, and a harder aspect (though probably with quite as much feeling within) than the people of the south and west.   When Samuel Johnson lumbered through the region in 1773, and visited Lord Monboddo, he found it miserably bare of trees ; but, had he travelled a century or two earlier, he would have had to pass through wide-spread forests. These were cut down in the seventeenth century ; and in the stead of the deer and wild animals a more industrious people substituted sheep and cattle, ranging over high mountains and large undulating plains, on which you would have seen patches of oats or bear here and there around the clay or turf dwellings of the tenants, but few fences or enclosures of any kind, except in the immediate neighborhood of the proprietors, whose castles and gardens, on the French model, relieved the wildness of the scene.   On to the eighteenth century the rural population consisted of landlords, with rather small farmers absolutely dependent on them, and who paid their rent in the service, on certain occasions, of men and horses, and in such articles as oats, bear, mutton, salmon, geese, poultry, and peats.   In these regions the peasantry had not been taught to think and act for themselves, as they had been in the south-west by the plough-

ing up of the soil effected by the great covenanting movement.
But in some of the towns, particularly in Aberdeen, which was
looked up to as a capital by a considerably wide district, there
was not a little refinement, which spread its influence over the
landlords, the ministers of religion, and the other professional
men : in particular, there had been in the city named a gifted
painter, Jameson, a disciple of Rubens ; and a very superior
printer, Raban, who put in type the works of the Aberdeen doctors.   The two universities, King's and Marischal's, trained and
sent forth a large body of educated men, some of whom found
their proper field on the Continent ; while the great body of them
remaining at home, were the special instruments — as teachers,
clergymen, doctors, lawyers, or country gentlemen — of spreading a civilizing influence in these regions.   For ten years after
the Restoration, seventy students entered annually at King's,
and a considerable number, though not so large, at Marischal :
some of these rose to eminence, and all of them helped to
create a taste for learning and an appreciation for it, on the
southern slope of the Grampians, and in the wide region lying
north of that range of mountains, which was never crossed
by the Roman legions, but was now conquered by the Roman
literature.

The Calvinistic and covenanting principles which had determined the Scottish character in the south and west, and so far
north as Fife, Perth, and some parts of Angus, had not generally permeated the region beyond.   No doubt, the common
people in the northern counties gladly listened to the evangelical preachers from the west, when they had the opportunity ;
and some of the covenanting ministers, banished in the times
of persecution from their own people in the south, gathered
around them in the places of their exile — as Samuel Rutherford in Aberdeen, David Dickson in Turriff — bodies of
devoted adherents attached to the Presbyterian preaching and
organization.   Still these were as yet merely fermenting, but
leavening, centres in the midst of influences which were resisting their extension.   In the wide country held by the Gordon
family, the Roman Catholic religion still held its sway.   In the
other parts, the landlords, the college regents, and the clergy
were mostly Cavalier in politics and High Church in religion ;
and the mass of the people had not learned to claim the pre-

rogative of thinking and acting for themselves. When a deputation from the General Assembly of the Presbyterian Church of Scotland — consisting of Alexander Henderson, Samuel Rutherford, and Andrew Cant — went north to Aberdeen to proclaim the Covenant in 1638, they were met by " Replies and Duplies " on the part of the Aberdeen doctors, and the landlords discouraged their tenantry from following the new zeal imported from the south. The divines of Aberdeen, during that century, such as Baron and John Forbes (author of " Irenicum "), were adherents of Episcopacy ; their studies were in the later fathers of the church, and their sympathies with the Laudean divines of England ; and like them they wrote against Popery on the one hand, and Puritanism on the other. It was years after the Revolution before the Presbyterian Church could put its legal rights in execution in the north-east of Scotland. Almost all the old Presbyterian ministers had disappeared ; and, in 1694, the Synod of Aberdeen consisted of six clerical members, most of them brought from the south. It was not till 1703 that John Willison was settled as first Presbyterian minister at Brechin in Angus ; it was not till 1708 that he was in a position to dispense the sacrament of the Lord's Supper. When he intimated that he was to do so next Lord's day, Mr. Skinner, the Episcopalian minister who preached in the same church in the after part of the day, announced that he would dispense the communion on the same day in the afternoon to his supporters ; and the ecclesiastical records report that 1500 communicated with Mr. Skinner. When Mr. Gray was appointed minister of Edzell, in the same district, the Presbytery had to conduct the services at his ordination in a neighboring parish ; and they then passed into the parish to " lay hands on him " and return immediately ; and, on the following sabbath when he rode to Edzell for the purpose of preaching, the people, hounded on by the landlords, took him off his horse, flung him into the West Water, and kept him there till he was nearly drowned, " to their eternal disgrace," as he causes it to be written in the parish records. During the Rebellion of 1715 the Presbyterian ministers were *rabbled* from their churches, which were occupied by the nonjuring clergy praying for the Pretender. A considerable body of the students in both the Aberdeen colleges sympathized

with the banished king ; and, after the battle of Sheriffmuir,
several of the professors had to retire in consequence of the
part which they had taken against the government. It was
not till after the suppression of the Rebellion of 1715, — indeed,
not fully till after the crushing of the chieftain power after
1745, — that the north-east of Scotland became one with the
south of Scotland in religion and in national feeling.

In the universities, both under Prelatic and Presbyterian
domination, the philosophy taught had been to a great extent
Aristotelian and scholastic. The university commissioners
appointed, in 1643, a *cursus* for Aberdeen ; and in it the student
is required, after taking Greek the first year, to go on the
second year to the dialectics of Ramus, to Aristotle's categories, interpretation, and prior analytics, and in the third year
to the rest of logics and portions of the ethics of Aristotle,
&c. In the "Metaphysics" of Robert Baron, who lectured in
Marischal College in the first half of the seventeenth century,
he treats of being, unity, and goodness ; enters fully into the
controversy between the Thomists and Scotists ; gives the divisions of *ens* and of cause, and treats of necessity and contin-
gency, of sameness and diversity, of absolute and relative, of
whole and parts. In the university library of Aberdeen we
have theses occupying 121 pages by Andrew Cant, the
younger, of date 1658 ; in these he shows that he knew the
Copernican theory of the heavens and Harvey's discovery of
the circulation of the blood : but the whole discussions are
conducted in a formal manner ; and he dwells fondly on the
scholastic logic, in the treatment of which he shows some
independence of thought. In 1710 there was published a work
by Thomas Blackwell, who had come from Paisley, in 1700, to
be minister at Aberdeen in the Presbyterian interest, and who
was made professor in 1711, and principal in 1717 : his work is
entitled " Schema Sacrum, or a Sacred Scheme of Natural and
Revealed Religion ; " and in it the common orthodox theology
is defended by the old distinctions, and there are no traces of a
new spirit or a new school.

But, after the year 1715, Aberdeen was prepared for a new
style of thought. The High Church theology was no longer
encouraged, except among a scattered nonjuring clergy subjected to poverty and privation. The Calvinistic divinity had

never struck its roots deep into the soil ; but the literature and physical science of England were known to and relished by the educated classes, and there must be a fresh philosophy to meet the awakened intelligence and new tastes of the country.   The first to gratify this feeling was a young graduate of Edinburgh, appointed as one of the rectors in Marischal by the Crown, which had seized the patronage of the college, vacated by the attainder of Earl Marischal, who had been out in the rebellion.

XII. — *GEORGE TURNBULL.*[1]

THE celebrated Hogarth, in his " Beer Street," has a graphic picture of a porter drinking barley wine, after depositing on the ground a load, directed to the trunk-maker, of five enormous folios ; one of which has on the back, " Turnbull on Ancient Paintings."   Turnbull was one of the most voluminous writers of his age.   I have read many thousand pages written by him ; but I fear the greater part of the copies of his works have gone to the destiny indicated by Hogarth.   It is disappointing to find that this author, who was both an able and a graceful writer, has passed away from the public view so effectively that it is difficult now to procure materials for his biography, or even to get a sight of most of his works.   It may be doubted whether any one, except the writer of this history, has been at pains to peruse his works as a whole, for the last hundred years.   Dugald Stewart, so well informed on British philosophy, had only looked into one of his volumes ; and Sir William Hamilton, in his multifarious researches among obscure writers, does not seem to have thought it worth his while making any inquiries about him.   Yet it can be shown that he exercised a greater influence than all other masters and writers put together on his pupil Thomas Reid, — the true representative of the Scottish philosophy.   He seems to have been the son of the Rev. George Turnbull (his mother's name was Elizabeth Glass), of whom we

---

[1] Parish records of Alloa in Register Office, Edinburgh ; " Catalogue of Graduates in Edinburgh," edited by Laing (Bannatyne Club) ; " Presentation Book " of Marischal College, Aberdeen.

can gather a few scattered notices : as that he was born about 1656 ; that he graduated in Edinburgh University in 1675 ; that he became minister of Alloa in 1689, when the Episcopal clergyman was ejected ; that he was translated to Tyningham in 1699 ; that he was nominated but not carried as moderator of the General Assembly in 1711 ; that he preached before that body in 1713 ; that his name appears among the members of "The Society for Propagating Christian Knowledge," in 1720 ; and that he died in June, 1744, at the age of eighty-eight. His son was born in 1698 (he was baptized July 15) ; graduated in Edinburgh in April, 1721 ; and in November of the same year he was appointed, by a presentation from the Crown, regent of Marischal College ; and is taken on trial in philosophy and the Greek language, and declares his willingness to sign the Confession of Faith. He comes to have among his colleagues Thomas Blackwell, son of the principal, admitted regent in 1723, who did much to create a taste for Greek in the college, and who is still known to antiquarian scholars by his learned but uninteresting works, "Inquiry into the Life and Writings of Homer," "Letters concerning Mythology," and "Memoirs of the Court of Augustus." In Aberdeen at that time there was — as we have seen there was in Glasgow — a principal's party and an opposition party ; and there were disputes about the election of the rector. The majority of the masters, including Mr. Turnbull, in opposition to the principal, Blackwell the elder, wish the society to make up a list of persons recommended for the office of rector, to be submitted to the procurators chosen by the students in their nations ; and, upon the principal refusing, they elect a preses in his roòm, and choose a rector, who holds a court and summons the principal to appear before them ; but they are stayed in their career by a suit from "the Lords of Council and Session." On April 14, 1726, he has carried a batch of thirty-nine students through a course of philosophy on to graduation ; and the last name on the list is Thomas Reid. As having to preside on this occasion, he prepares a thesis, afterwards published, to be discussed by the candidates, — "De Pulcherrima Mundi Materialis tum Rationalis Constitutione," — in which the new physics are employed to furnish proofs of the existence of God, and in which he declares that natural science (physiology) is to be taught before moral philosophy, and inclines to censure Socrates because he discouraged inquiries into the structure of nature. He also printed, when at Aberdeen, a " Thesis on the Connection of Natural and Moral Philosophy." In his lectures on pneumatology he delivered to his students those views which, after being rewritten, were given to the world in his treatise on moral philosophy. In his later writings he frequently quotes Hutcheson and Butler ; but his own philosophic opinions seem to have been formed, and delivered in lectures, before either of these influential writers had published any of their works.

In 1726, he published " A Philosophical Inquiry concerning the Connection between the Doctrines and Miracles of Jesus Christ." In it he treats of subjects in which there is a revived interest and which are anxiously discussed in our day, and advances principles which would be favorably received by many in these times. He argues that the works of Jesus were natural proper samples of his doctrines. That he had abandoned the old theology of Scotland is evident, from his declaring that the Scripture way of talking about the Spirit of God and his operations means simply assistance to the virtuous. It is interesting to notice, that in this treatise he refers once and again to common-sense as settling certain moral questions ; in this, as in other matters, anticipating and probably guiding Dr. Reid.

In the spring of 1727, Turnbull resigned his office in Marischal College ; and for the next twelve years we have little record of him. There is reason to believe that he became a travelling tutor, — it is said, to the family of the Wauchopes, of Niddry, near Edinburgh. It is certain that he must have travelled extensively on the Continent, and made himself conversant with the treasures of art in Italy. In 1732, he received the honorary degree of doctor of laws from the University of Edinburgh. He seems to have mingled in the literary circles of London,[1] and acquired friends among persons of eminence. During these years he prepared an immense store of literary works, which were issued in rapid succession, — more rapidly, I suspect, than the public were prepared to receive them. In

---

[1] In the Preface to his "Moral Philosophy," he refers to a certain poet, " universally confessed to have shown a most extraordinary genius for descriptive poetry in some of his works, and in all of them a heart deeply impregnated with the warmest love of virtue and mankind," as likely from friendship to cast his eye on that Preface ; from which we may argue that he had contracted a friendship with James Thomson.

October, 1739, he advertises, at four guineas, in sheets, his " Treatise on Ancient Painting ;" in which he has observations on the rise, progress, and decline of that art among the Greeks and Romans, comments on the genius of Raphael, Michael Angelo, Nicholas Poussin, and others, and illustrates the work with engravings of fifty pieces of ancient painting. It will be remembered that Shaftesbury had " Disquisitions on Taste ;" and we shall see most of the Scottish metaphysicians speculate on taste and beauty. The work was not of such an original or daring character as to recommend it to the genius of Hogarth ; yet it seems to have had a considerable roll of subscribers. His style is pleasant, and the remarks judicious and highly appreciative of the classical painters. In February, 1740, there appeared his most important work, and the only one that continues to be read, " The Principles of Moral Philosophy." At the close he promises, as soon as his health admits, a work on " Christian Philosophy," which was actually published before the close of the year ; and in it he treats of the Christian doctrines concerning God, providence, virtue, and a future state, and recommends the Word of God because it embraces and illustrates such doctrines. He dates October, 1740, a preface and appendix to Heineccius's " Methodical System of Universal Law."[1] In 1742, he published " Observations upon Liberal Education ;" and in it he speaks as having long been engaged in the work of education. He subscribes himself as Chaplain to the Prince of Wales, and dedicates the treatise to the " Right Reverend Father in God," Thomas, Lord Bishop of Derry ; in whose esteem, he says, " he had long had a share."[2] It appears that before

---

[1] I cannot find that this work was published till 1763, the date of the copy in W. S. Library, Edinburgh. In 1740, he published a translation of " Vertot, Three Dissertations."

[2] This was Thomas Rundle (born 1686, died 1743). Strong objections were taken to his getting the see of Gloucester, and so he went to Derry, when Thomson writes of him in a poem to the memory of Talbot : —

> " Though from native sunshine driven,
> Driven from your friends, the sunshine of the soul,
> By slanderous zeal and politics' infern,
> Jealous of worth."

In these times, men were sent to Ireland who would not be tolerated in the Church of England. Pope says of him : " Rundle has a heart ;" and Swift : —

> " Rundle a bishop, well he may,
> He's still a Christian more than they."

He was the author of " Letters to the late Mrs. Barbara Landis," in which he

this time he had left the communion of the Presbyterian Church of Scotland, and entered into orders in the Episcopal Church of England, which was doubtless more congenial to his tastes. Through the bishop, to whom he dedicated his work, he was appointed Rector of Drumachose, in the diocese of Derry. I cannot find that he left any mark behind him in that parish : there is no remembrance of him in the popular tradition of the district, and no record of him in the diocese. In consequence of failing health, he went to the Continent, and died at the Hague, Jan. 31, 1748.[1]

Turnbull was the first metaphysician of the Scottish — I believe of any — school to announce unambiguously and categorically that we ought to proceed in the method of induction in investigating the human mind. He takes as the motto of his "Moral Philosophy" the passage from Newton about the method of natural philosophy being applicable to moral subjects, and the line of Pope, "Account for moral as for natural things." His enunciations on this subject are as clear and decided as those of Reid and Stewart in after ages. "If a fact be certain, there is no reasoning against it ; but every reasoning, however specious it may be, — or rather however subtle and confounding, — if it be repugnant to fact, must be sophistical." It must have been from Turnbull that Reid learned, even as it was from Reid that Stewart learned, to appeal to common language as built on fact or universal feeling. "Language not being invented by philosophers, but contrived to express common sentiments or what every one perceives, we may be morally sure that where universally all languages make a distinction there is really in nature a difference." Reid only catches the spirit of his old master, who speaks of "philosophers who, seeking the knowledge of human nature not from experience, but from I know not what subtle theories of their own invention, depart from common language, and therefore are

speaks in favor of theatres, gives a high place to reason, says a word in behalf of Chubb, praises Shaftesbury, though he regrets his opposition to Christianity. He says of those who would destroy the foundation of virtue : "That they turn, as the elephants did of old, and trample down those that brought them to the war." The following has often been uttered since : "Christianity is so amiable in itself, that what Plato says of virtue is true of it, that if it is beheld in its native charms every man would be in love with it."

[1] See "London Magazine," for that year.

not understood by others, and sadly perplex and involve themselves." In some respects, his exposition of the method is more
comprehensive and correct (so I believe) than that given Ly
Reid and Stewart; inasmuch as he awows distinctly that, having
got facts and ideas from experience, we may reason deductively
from them, in what Mr. J. S. Mill calls the deductive method,
but which is in fact a joint inductive and deductive method.
He sees clearly that in natural philosophy there is a mixture
of experiments with reasonings from experiments; and he asserts that reasonings from experiments may have the same
relation to moral philosophy that mathematical truths have to
natural philosophy. "In both cases equally, as soon as certain
powers or laws of nature are inferred from experience, we may
consider them, reason about them, and compare them with
other properties, powers, or laws." He instances among the
moral ideas which we may compare, and from which we may
draw deductions, those of intelligence, volition, affection, and
habit. Moral philosophy is described by him as a mixed science of observations, and reasonings from principles known by
experience to take place in or to belong to human nature. In
his preface to Heineccius, he says that the appended "discourse upon the nature and origin of laws is an attempt to
introduce the experimental way of reasoning into morals, or
to deduce human duties from internal principles and dispositions in the human mind." In following this method, he
claims to be superior to Puffendorf, to Grotius, and the older
jurists.

Proceeding in this method he discovers, both in matter and
mind, an established order and excellent general laws, and on
this subject quotes largely from his contemporaries Berkeley
and Pope. He constantly appeals to these laws as illustrating
the divine wisdom; and to the excellence of laws as justifying
the divine procedure, despite certain incidental acts which may
flow from them. As inquirers discover these laws, science is
advanced; and he dwells as fondly on the progressiveness of
knowledge as Bacon had done and as Stewart has done.

In particular, he shows that if we look at human nature as
a whole, and at its several parts, we shall find beneficent general laws. He discovers in our constitution means to moral
ends, and the science of these means and ends is prop-

erly called moral philosophy. He shows that by such a study
we can discover what are natural laws ; and that, in all
well-regulated states, the sum and substance of what is called
its civil laws are really laws of natural and universal obligation ; " adding that "civil law adopts only those laws of nature
on which the quiet of mankind entirely depends, and that
there are other duties to which men must attend out of reverence to their Creator and sincere love to mankind, without
regard to the fear of human penalties." He shows that mankind are not left indifferent to virtue and to beauty: "As
we are capable of distinguishing truth from falsehood, so we
are capable of distinguishing good and approvable actions,
affections, and characters, from bad and disapprovable ones."
He would call this capacity moral sense, moral taste, moral
discernment, or moral conscience.   Like Shaftesbury (" who
must live forever in the esteem of all who delight in moral
inquiries"), and Hutcheson, whom he often approvingly quotes,
he represents the virtues as capable of being reduced into
benevolence.

In unfolding the elements of human nature, he dwells with
evident fondness on the "association of ideas." He does not
seem to attempt an ultimate resolution of the laws ; but he considers association as " a league or cohesion formed by frequent
conjunction in the mind," and says that "any appearance
immediately suggests its concomitants and consequents to
us." He adds, "that association is more easily engendered
between ideas that have some affinity or likeness." It may
be doubted whether we have a better account at this day of
the law of association as a whole. In regard to what Brown
calls " secondary laws," and Hamilton the " law of preference,"
he prescribes two rules from Cicero for helping the memory :
one is to attend to the things we would wish to recall ; and
the other is to consider its analogies, relations, and oppositions
to other objects which will thus call it up. He accounts (as
Stewart does) by the association of ideas for the law of habit,
which he represents as a " propension to do, and a facility and
readiness in doing, what we have often done." He shows truly
and ingeniously how association influences the senses, by connecting the qualities perceived by one sense with those perceived by the others (a subject much dwelt on in a later age

by Brown) ; and, in particular, how, according to the theory of Berkeley, it aids the eye in discovering distance, not itself an idea of sight.   He shows how our ideas have other ideas so associated with them that they make one perception, and how difficult it is to separate ideas that have thus been associated, and to find out precisely and philosophically what is involved in any particular idea, and how apt we are in consequence to confound qualities that are different.   He is particularly successful in showing that desires and volitions are prompted by associations.   " Ideas, as often as they return, must excite certain affections ; and the affections which lead to action must, as often as they are revived, dispose and excite to act, or, in other words, produce will to act."   He remarks that " very few, if any, of the ideas which excite our warmest and keenest affections are quite free from associated parts." He insists that " various associations must produce various tempers and dispositions of mind ; since every idea, as often as it is repeated, must move the affection it naturally tends to excite, and ideas with their correspondent affections often returning must naturally form inclinations, propensions, and tempers."   He would account in this way for much of our feeling of beauty, and for propensity to imitate passing into custom.   His exposition of the association of ideas is more satisfactory and accurate than the one, so much commended, published by Hume at the same time ; and is far more philosophical than that given by Reid, who, in this respect, fell behind his master.   I am acquainted with no exposition of this part of our constitution published prior to his time which seems to me so full and correct.

His ideas on education are liberal and advanced.   He is opposed to corporal punishment, and declares that the grand aim of education should be to foster good habits.   Giving a high place to the study of the mind, he maintains, as did all the great masters of the Aberdeen school who came after him, that mental science should not be taught to young men till their minds have been otherwise well furnished.   He gives logic a somewhat large and wide field ; in this respect, too, like the Scottish metaphysicians who came after him.   Its province is to " examine the power and faculties of our minds (favorite phrases of Reid's), their objects, and operations ; to inquire into the foundations, the causes of error, deceit, and false taste ; and, for that effect, to compare the several arts and sciences with one another, and to observe how each of them may derive light and assistance from all the rest. Its business is to give a full view of the natural union, connection, and dependence of all the sciences." Like Reid, and Stewart after him, he sets a high value on the study of "the nature and degrees of moral, probable, or historical evidence," and complains that it is left out in the logical treatises. The teacher should aim to make his pupil look at things, instead of words. At the same time, he recommends the study of languages with the study of things ; employing language in an enlarged sense, as embracing the different methods of expressing, embellishing, or enforcing and recommending truth, such as oratory, poetry, design, sculpture, and painting. He complains that in education the arts of design are quite severed, not only from philosophy, but from classical studies. The object contemplated by him in his work on " Painting " was to bring these various branches into union : he thinks that paintings may teach moral philosophy. The essential elements of painting are represented by him as being truth, beauty, unity, greatness, and grace, in composition. He dwells fondly on the analogy between the sense of beauty and moral sense ; and on the inseparable connection between beauty and truth. His works on " education " and on the fine arts are clear and judicious, written in a pleasant and equable, but at the same time a commonplace style ; and they seem never to have attracted the attention which they deserved, and which would have been freely given to works of greater pretension, eccentricity, or extravagance.

But, after all, we are most interested in noticing the points in which Turnbull seems to have influenced Reid. We have already had some of these before us. We have seen that Turnbull announces as clearly as Reid that the human mind is to be studied by careful observation. Both are averse to abstruse scholastic distinctions and recondite ratiocinations on moral subjects. Turnbull ever appeals, as Reid did after him, to consciousness as the instrument of observation. Both are fond of designating mental attributes by the terms "powers" and "faculties." Both would give a wide, and I may add a loose, field to logic, and include in it the inquiry into the nature of probable evi-

dence. In proceeding in the way of observation, both discover
natural laws or principles, and both call them by the name of
"common-sense." "Common-sense is certainly sufficient to
teach those who think of the matter with tolerable seriousness
and attention, all the duties and offices of human life ; all our
obligations to God and our fellow-creatures ; all that is morally
fit and binding. And there is no need of words to prove that
to be morally fit and obligatory, which common-sense and reason clearly show to be so." Reid holds that all active power
implies mind. This was the expressed doctrine of Turnbull
before him. "It is, therefore, will alone that produces both
power and productive energy." "To speak of any other activity and power, is to speak without any meaning at all ; because
experience, the only source of all our ideas (and of the materials of our knowledge), does not lead us to any other conception or idea of power." Nor should it be omitted that both — in
this respect, however, like all the other Scotch metaphysicians —
ever speak with profound reverence of Scripture ; ever, however,
dwelling most fondly on those doctrines of the word which are
also truths of natural religion ; such as the existence of God, the
obligations of morality, and the immortality of the soul.

I have been at pains to trace these agreements, not with the
view of depreciating the originality and still less the independence of Reid, who may have had some of these views suggested to him by his teacher, but who may have afterwards
found them in other writers, and who no doubt thought them
all for himself, and adopted them because they seemed to him
to be sound.[1] We have seen that in one or two points, Reid
fell behind his master, who had clearer apprehensions than his
pupil of mingling deductive with inductive observation, and
of the laws of the association of ideas. But in other and more
important philosophic doctrines, Reid passed far beyond his
teacher. Reid claims to be original in rejecting the ideal theory of sense perception ; which had been the received one for
two thousand years, which had been adopted by Locke, and
pursued to its logical consequences by Berkeley. But Turnbull evidently adheres to the old view. "Properly speaking, what
we call matter and space are but certain orders of sensible

---

[1] It does seem rather strange that Reid should nowhere have acknowledged
what he owed to Turnbull.

ideas produced in us, according to established rules of nature, by some external cause; for when we speak of material effects and of space, we only mean, and can indeed only mean, certain sensible perceptions excited in our mind according to a certain order, which are experienced to be absolutely inert and passive, and to have no productive force." He speaks of the "external material world" as unperceived by us, and in itself absolutely unperceivable, as all philosophers acknowledge." When, in speaking of the material world, he says it may be called the "external cause or occasion of those sensible ideas, and their connections, which make to each of us what we call the sensible world," we see that this is the doctrine which Reid set aside; and yet we may notice that the phrase "occasion" is used by Turnbull, as by Reid, to designate the relation of the external action to the internal perception. In another point, Reid made a more important advance upon Turnbull. Living at a later age, Reid had to meet the objections of the great modern revolutionist, and had in consequence to dive down into profounder depths of the human constitution. The scepticism of Hume brought out to view the superficialities of the philosophy of Shaftesbury, partly by following its principles to their legitimate consequences, but mainly by making all men feel that it is nothing wherewith to meet the assaults of the new and formidable enemy. Shaftesbury, Hutcheson, and Turnbull had all appealed to common-sense; but Reid behoved to take a deeper and more searching view of the principles which constitute common-sense, in order to meet the exigencies of the new era.

Turnbull's works had no great circulation in their own day, and they speedily disappeared from public view. It might have been different had he continued in Aberdeen, and gathered around him a body of young men ready to receive and to propagate the lessons he taught them. But he departed into other fields, — into the literary circle of England, and a church which set more value on liturgy than on abstract doctrine, — and there he met with few to appreciate his gifts. A Presbyterian Scot might have urged, with some plausibility, that his name has perished because he forsook the country and the church in which his philosophic labors would have been valued. It might even have been different, had he published his meta-

physical treatises a dozen of years earlier; for then they might
have run their course with those of Hutcheson and Butler.
But at the very time that Turnbull advertised his work on
"Moral Philosophy," Hume published his "Treatise of Human
Nature," which, as it forced its way to the front, required philosophy to deepen its foundations and give a new facing to its
buttresses. Turnbull is remembered because he had, for three
years, when he was himself a very young man, a diligent and
thoughtful pupil, who in due time wrestled with the great sceptic, and is acknowledged by Scotland as the representative of
its native philosophy.

-----•-----

XIII. — *DAVID FORDYCE.*[1]

HE was born in Aberdeen in 1711, entered Marischal College in 1742, and
was drowned at sea, as he was returning from travel, in September, 1751.
During that age and the next there was a strong disposition towards the
study of mental philosophy. In 1748, R. Dodsley began the publication of
the "Preceptor," in London, and Fordyce wrote the article on "Moral Philosophy." He was appointed professor of moral philosophy in the college
in which he had been educated, in 1742. In 1745, he published "Dialogues
concerning Education," a very pleasantly written book. He discusses the
question whether nature or training does most, and inquires whether the
Socratic method is fitted to bring forth what is in our nature. He dwells
fondly, like most of the philosophers of the Scottish school, on the influence of the association of ideas. The religion he recommends was evidently the moderate type: "As the religion of Christ was designed as a
plain, consistent rule of life, and not a system of abstracted reasonings and
speculations, — to influence the heart more than fill the head, — I would endeavor above all things a high spirit of disinterested and extensive virtue."
He was author also of an essay on "Action of the Pulpit." After his
death there was published a work of his, "Theodorus, a Dialogue concerning the Art of Preaching," to which was added "A discourse on the Eloquence of the Pulpit, by James Fordyce." His "Elements of Moral
Philosophy" was published in 1754. There is little that is original in his
works, but much that is judicious and useful. It is evident that he was
acquainted with the works of Butler and Hutcheson. "Moral philosophy
contemplates human nature, its moral powers and connections, and deduces
the laws of action." "Moral philosophy has this in common with natural

[1] "Preceptor," vol. ii., 1748; Darling's "Cyclopædia;" Mackie's "Index
Funererius;" Kennedy's "Annals of Aberdeen."

philosophy that it appeals to nature or to fact." He finds passions or affections, some private, some public, and above these ; (1) reason or reflection ; (2) conscience, by which we denominate some actions and principles of conduct honest and good, and others wrong, dishonest, or ill." " We came by the idea of moral obligation or duty in the same way as our other original and primary perceptions : we receive them from the Author of our nature." We employ reason in moral cases, in "examining the condition, relations, and other circumstances of the agent, and patient." " Therefore, when we use these terms, obligation, duty, ought, and the like, they stand for a simple idea." He opposes those who establish morals on the divine will, and those who place it in the natures and reasons, truths and fitnesses, of things."

XIV. — *WILLIAM DUNCAN.*[1]

HE was born in Aberdeen, July, 1717, and was the son of a respectable tradesman. He received his education partly at Aberdeen and partly at Foveran. He entered Marischal College in 1733, and took his degree in 1737. Originally, he was designed for the gospel ministry ; but not finding an inclination for the work, he went, as so many Scottish youths have done in like circumstances, to London (in 1739), and devoted himself to literature ; translating "Select Orations of Cicero " and " Cæsar's Commentaries," which were long found useful by youths averse to turn over the leaves of a dictionary. He wrote for Dodsley's " Preceptor" the article on " Logic ; " and this was afterwards published in a separate volume, and continued for an age or two to furnish, not very philosophical but very useful, instruction to Scottish and other youths. The work is partly psychological partly logical. In Book First he treats of the origin and division of ideas, and of language ; in the Second, of judgment, self-evident and demonstrable ; in the Third, of reasoning and demonstration ; and in the Fourth, of invention, science, and the parts of knowledge. He was appointed professor of philosophy in Marischal College, May 18, 1752, and entered the professorship, Aug. 21, 1753. He was drowned when bathing, May, 1760.

XV. — *JOHN STEVENSON.*[2]

FROM the date at which we have now arrived, we have a succession of distinguished men testifying to the benefit they received from the instruction imparted in the departments of logic and moral philosophy in the Scotch colleges. As being among the eminently successful teachers of his age, we have to give a place to John Stevenson, professor of Logic or

1 "Scottish Register," January, February, March, 1794.
2 "Scot's Magazine," August, 1841 ; Somerville's " Life and Times."

"Rational and Instrumental philosophy" in the University of Edinburgh. Dugald Stewart says of him that to his "valuable prelections, particularly to his illustrations of Aristotle's "Poetics," and of Longinus on the "Sublime," Dr. Robertson has been often heard to say, that he considered himself as more deeply indebted than to any other circumstance in his academic studies." "I derived," says Dr. Somerville, "more substantial benefit from these exercises and lectures than from all the public classes I attended at the university." Similar testimony is borne by the famous leader of the evangelical party in the Church of Scotland, Dr. Erskine (see Life by Sir Henry W. Moncreiff). The course of instruction followed by Stevenson is given in the Scots Magazine, and is well worthy of being quoted as an exhibition of the highest style of education imparted in the age. He gives lectures upon "Heineccii Elementa Philosophiæ Rationalis," and Wynne's abridgment of Locke's "Essay upon the Human Understanding:" in which he explains all the different forms of reasoning, the nature of certainty both mathematical and moral, with the different degrees of probability; and shows how the understanding is to be conducted in our inquiries after truth of all kinds. He likewise explains the fundamental rules to be observed in the interpretation of the texts of very ancient authors. He teaches metaphysics in lectures upon De Vries's "Ontologia," in which he explains the several terms and distinctions which frequently occur in the writings of the learned. He also lectures upon Longinus, περὶ ὕψους, in which he illustrates the several precepts of oratory given by Cicero and Quintilian; and also, upon Aristotle, περὶ ποιητικῆς, in which he illustrates his rules by examples from ancient and modern poets, and explains the grounds of criticism in eloquence and poetry. He gives likewise a course upon "Heineccii Historia Philosophica," in which he gives an account of the most famous philosophers ancient and modern, and the several opinions by which the different sects were distinguished. Each of his students is required to make a discourse upon a subject assigned him, and to impugn and defend a thesis, for his improvement in the art of reasoning. These exercises are performed before the principal and some of the professors with open doors. The students met him two hours daily; one of them was devoted to lectures on logic, delivered in the Latin tongue. It is stated that the college opens about the 10th of October, and rises about the end of May. The shortening of the length of the session in the colleges of Scotland, in later years, has done much to lower the standard of attainment.

John Stevenson was appointed professor in Edinburgh, in 1730, and died Sept. 12th, 1775, in the eighty-first year of his age. It is mentioned to his credit, by Stewart, that at the age of seventy he gave a candid reception to the philosophy of Reid, which was subversive of the theories which he had taught for forty years; and that "his zeal for the advancement of knowledge prompted him, when his career was almost finished, to undertake the laborious task of new-modelling that useful compilation of elementary instruction to which a singular diffidence of his powers limited his literary exertions." (Stewart's "Life and Writings of Reid.")

HE was for a time "professor of pneumatology and ethical philosophy" in Edinburgh University. The pneumatics are divided into the following parts : 1. A physical inquiry into the nature of such subtle and material substances as are imperceptible to the senses, and known only from their operations ; 2. The nature of immaterial substances connected with matter, in which is demonstrated, by natural evidence, the immortality of the human soul ;[1] 3. The nature of immaterial created beings not connected with matter ; 4. Natural theology, or the existence and attributes of God demonstrated from the light of nature. Ethics or moral philosophy is divided into the theoretical and practical parts, in treating of which the authors he chiefly uses are Cicero, Marcus Antoninus, Puffendorf, and Lord Bacon. He had lectures explaining the origin and principles of civil government, illustrated with an account of the rise and fall of the ancient governments of Greece and Rome, and a view of that form of government which took its rise from the irruptions of the northern nations. His students have also discourses presented to them upon some important heads of pneumatical or moral philosophy, which are delivered before the principal with open doors. Pringle was by no means so thorough an instructor as Stevenson. Carlyle describes him "as an agreeable lecturer, though no great master of the science he taught." "His lectures were chiefly a compilation from Lord Bacon's works, and had it not been for Puffendorf's small book, which he made his text, we should not have been instructed in the rudiments of the science." Nevertheless, we see that he discussed topics which must issue, sooner or later, in a scientific jurisprudence and political economy. We see, in the case both of Stevenson and Pringle, how much attention was paid in the Scottish universities to the practice of English composition.

Pringle's taste did not lie specially in metaphysics. He was born in Roxburghshire, in 1707, and became a physician. He settled in Edinburgh about 1734 ; and after 1748, resided in London, where he was elected president of the Royal Society in 1773. He died in 1782.

----•----

XVII. — *THOMAS BOSTON.*

WE wish our readers to transport themselves to the eastern border country of Scotland, and to try to realize its condition in the first half of last century. People are apt to take their views of that district from Sir Walter Scott, who passed the most interesting portion of his boyhood there, and picking up the dim traditions of the past ere they were finally lost, and tingeing them with the romantic hues of his own imagination, has presented to us such a picture as a man of the nineteenth century, in love with chivalry, would be

1 "Scot's Magazine," 1747, 1749 ; Chambers's "Biographical Dictionary."

likely to furnish of the ages of border strife. But the truth is, Sir Walter has given us only one side of the Scottish character; he never thoroughly sympathized with the more earnest features of the national mind, and he did not appreciate the attempts which were made in the seventeenth century to deliver the country from violence and superstition, and to promote education and a scriptural religion. The people of the eighteenth century had such traditions of the earlier ages as to be glad that the days of the border raids had passed away. At the time we wish to sketch, two classes of people were to be found in the district. There were landed proprietors, disposed to allow no opposition to their not very generous or enlightened will, but who were already catching the taste for improving the land, which has made Berwickshire one of the most advanced agricultural districts in the three kingdoms. Under them were small farmers and their servants, with the ignorance and much of the rudeness of the previous ages, and not yet awakened to independent thought and action. Between them there was scarcely any middle class, except the parish ministers, who, in the early part of the century, if not highly cultivated, were zealous preachers of the doctrines of grace, and actively seeking to raise their people to church-going habits and a decent morality; and who, at a later date, as patrons began to assert their legal rights, and colleges adopted the new philosophy, became the most vehement opponents of the evangelical party: so that, in the days of Carlyle, the Synod of Merse and Teviotdale turned the vote against popular rights, and the ministers of it, coming to the General Assembly, rushed to the theatre to hear Mrs. Siddons when she happened to be in Edinburgh. Believing that there was nothing suited to them in such a religion, the common people set up in the towns and large villages seceding congregations, which drew towards them the more earnest of the inhabitants. Out of one of these congregations sprang Thomas M'Crie, who has given us the other phase of the Scottish character.

At the beginning of the century, the most remarkable man in the district was undoubtedly Thomas Boston. Born at Dunse in the previous century, he remembered his going, when a boy, to the prison of his native place to keep his father company when he was incarcerated for resisting the imposition of Prelacy. All his life he is most sedulous and consistent in discountenancing the system of church patronage, which is being steadily introduced. Settled as a minister first in Simprin, and then in Ettrick, he is consumingly earnest in visiting once a year, in catechising twice a year, and in preaching on Sabbath-day and week-day to, an ignorant and careless people just rising out of barbarism. But he contrived to retain a literary taste amidst his active parochial employments. With a difficulty in getting books, and rejoicing so when a good one came in his way, he was able, by his own independent study, to develop views in regard to the importance of Hebrew points which were far in advance of those attained in his time by any British scholar. Endowed with a clear, logical mind, he has, in his "Fourfold State" and "Covenant of Grace," given us perhaps the best exposition we have of the old Scotch theology in its excellencies, — some would add, in its exclusiveness. Living and breathing in the doctrine of free grace, he seized with avidity and valued excessively the "Marrow of Modern Divinity,"

which he found in the cottage of one of his people, and he vigorously
opposed the moral or legal preaching which was fast coming in with the
new literature and philosophy. Singularly single-minded, earnest, and fervent in his piety, this man becomes a favorite and a power, first in his district, and, in the end, by his theological works all over Scotland. In
reading his Memoirs, we observe that he was painfully careful in watching
his moods of mind, often referring to spiritual interposition what arose from
wretched health ; and that he was ever looking on events occurring in
God's providence as *signs* indicating that he should pursue a particular
line of conduct. It needed a philosophy — we regret that it should have
been an infidel one which did the work — to correct these errors of a narrow theology.[1]

----◆----

XVIII. — DAVID DUDGEON.

ALREADY the old orthodoxy was being troubled. Mr. David Dudgeon
published, in 1732, a work entitled "The Moral World." We have no
record of the early history of this man, and we do not know whether he
received a college education. When he comes under our notice, he is
tenant of a large farm called Lennel Hill, in the parish of Coldstream.
In the work referred to he maintains, with clearness and ability, a doctrine
like that of Anthony Collins, whom he had read. He asserts "that there
is no evil in the moral world but what necessarily ariseth from the nature
of imperfect creatures, who always pursue their good, but cannot but be
liable to error or mistake," and "that evil or sin is inseparable in some
degree from all created beings, and most consistent with the designs of a
perfect Creator." On account of the errors in this work, he was summoned
before the Presbytery, where two charges are brought against him : 1st,
That he denies and destroys all distinction and difference between moral
good and evil, or else makes God the author of evil, and refers all evil to
the imperfection of creatures ; 2d, That he denies the punishment of another
life, or that God punishes men for sin in this life, — yea, that man is accountable. He appears before the court, and holds it to be contrary to Scripture
that man has free-will in the Arminian sense, but holds that man is accountable and punishable for practising contrary to the divine precepts of our
Saviour, the practice of which tends to make all men happy. The case
goes up from presbytery to synod, and from synod to General Assembly,
which remits it to the Commission of Assembly in 1733, again in 1734, again
in 1735, and again in 1736, with no evidence that the commission ever vent-

----

[1] The representative book of the age then passing away was "Natural Religion Insufficient, and Revealed Necessary to Man's Happiness in his Present
State" by the late Rev. Thomas Halyburton, professor of divinity in the University of St. Andrews (born 1674, died 1712). It is a clearly written, respectably
learned work, and establishes its point. It was superseded by the deeper discussions raised by Hume. ("Life and Writings," by Burns.)

ured to take it up.[1] In 1734, he published a vindication of the "Moral World," in reply to a pamphlet against him, said to be written by Andrew Baxter; and therein he maintains that when a rogue is hanged he is set free to enter a state where he may be reformed. His most important work is "Philosophical Letters concerning the Being and Attributes of God," first printed in 1737. These letters were written, in the midst of pressing agricultural cares, to the Rev. Mr. Jackson, author of a work written in the spirit of Clarke, "The Existence and Unity of God." In these letters, Dudgeon reaches a species of refined Spinozism, mingled with Berkeleyanism. He denies the distinction of substances into spiritual and material, maintains that there is no substance distinct from God, and that "all our knowledge but of God is about ideas; they exist only in the mind, and their essence and modes consist only in their being perceived." In 1739, he published a "Catechism founded upon Experience and Reason, collected by a Father for the use of his Children;" and, in an introductory letter, he wishes that natural religion alone was embraced by all men, and states that, though he believes there was an extraordinary man sent into our world seventeen hundred years ago to instruct mankind, yet he doubts whether he "ever commanded any of those things to be written concerning him which we have." The same year, he published "A View of the Necessitarian or Best Scheme, freed from the Objections of M. Crousaz, in his Examination of Pope's 'Essay on Man.'"

Dudgeon died at Upsettlington, on the borders of England, January, 1743, at the age of thirty-seven. His works were published in a combined form in 1765, in a volume without a printer's name attached, showing that there was not as yet thorough freedom of thought in Scotland. His writings had for a time a name in the district (the "Catechism" reached a third edition), but afterwards passed away completely from public notice. The late Principal Lee was most anxious to know more of his history, and in particular whether he could have influenced David Hume in personal intercourse or by his writings. As they lived in the same district, Hume must have heard of the case, which appeared when Hume was cogitating his own system. There are points in which Dudgeon anticipated Hume. Thus, Dudgeon maintains that all knowledge is about ideas, the essence of which is that they are perceived. He says that the words "just, unjust, desert, &c., are necessarily relative to society;" and that if we allow that there is not justice in the government of this world, we cannot argue that there is justice in the world to come. Dudgeon, too, is a stern necessarian. But in all these points Dudgeon had himself been anticipated by others. In other respects the two widely differ. Dudgeon assumes throughout a much higher moral tone than Hume ever did. Dudgeon had evidently abandoned a belief in Christianity, but he stood up resolutely for a rational demonstration of the existence of God as the cause of the ideas which come under our experience; and he has a whole system of natural religion: whereas Hume undermines all religion, natural as well as revealed.

---

[1] The author of this work has been aided in his researches on this subject by the great kindness of the Rev. Alexander Christison, clerk to the Presbytery of Chirnside.

Dudgeon had superior philosophic abilities; and in other circumstances might have had a chance of becoming the head of a new philosophic heresy. But there was a young man in his own neighborhood being trained to supersede and eclipse him in his own line, and to go beyond deism to atheism. It is thus that error advances till it corrects itself.

———•———

XIX. — *DAVID HUME.*[1]

DAVID HUME was born at Edinburgh, on April 26, 1711. He was the second son of Joseph Home or Hume, of Ninewells, so called from a number of springs which may still be seen as fresh as when the name was given. The mansion is in the parish of Chirnside, in Berwickshire, and is situated on the green slope of a hill which rises from the river Whitadder, immediately in front. The situation is remarkably pleasant, and from the heights above there are extensive views of the whole eastern border country, now associated in the minds of all reading people with tales of romance. Here David Hume passed the greater portion of his younger years, and much of the quieter and more studious parts of his middle age. But he never refers to the scenes of his native place, not even (as Mr. Burton has remarked) when he has occasion in his " History of England " to relate events which might have led him to do so. It is clear that his taste for the beauties of nature was never very keen ; the time had not come when all people rave about natural scenery ; he was in no way disposed to expose himself to English prejudice by betraying Scottish predilections, and I rather think that he was glad that the time of border raids had for ever passed away.

His father was a member of the Faculty of Advocates, but passed his life as a country gentleman. His mother was a daughter of Sir D. Falconer of Newton, who had been a lawyer in the times of the Stuarts, and had filled the office of president of the Court of Session from 1682 to 1685. So far as the youth was exposed to hereditary predilections, they were those of Scotch landlords, who ruled supreme in their own estates, of hard-headed Edinburgh lawyers, and of old families

[1] "My own Life," by David Hume; "Life and Correspondence of David Hume," by John Hill Burton, &c.

S

opposed to the great Whig or covenanting struggle of the previous century. His father having died when the second son was yet an infant, the education of the children devolved on their mother, who is represented as training them with great care, — in what way or form in respect of religion we are not told.

David became an entrant of the class of William Scott, professor of Greek in the Edinburgh University, February 27, 1723, being still under twelve years of age. What his precise college course was is not recorded ; but we know generally that in those times, and for many years after, boys who should have been at school, after getting an imperfect acquaintance with Latin and Greek, were introduced in the classes of logic, pneumatics, and moral philosophy, to subjects fitted only for men of mature powers and enlarged knowledge. I suspect there was no ruling mind among his teachers to sway him, and he was left to follow the bent of his own mind. Already he has a taste for literature, and a tendency to speculative philosophy. " I was seized very early," he says in " My Own Life," " with a passion for literature, which has been the ruling passion of my life, and a great source of my enjoyments." In writing to a friend, July 4, 1727, he mentions having by him written papers which he will not make known till he has polished them, and these evidently contain the germs of a system of mental philosophy. " All the progress I have made is but drawing the outlines on loose bits of paper : here a hint of a passion ; there a phenomenon in the mind accounted for ; in another an alteration of these accounts." Mr. Burton publishes part of a paper of his early years, being " An Historical Essay on Chivalry and Modern Honor." In it we have no appreciation of chivalry, but we have the germs of the historical, political, and ethical speculations which he afterwards developed. He inquires why courage is the principal virtue of barbarous nations, and why chastity is the point of honor with women (always a favorite topic with him), and is evidently in the direction of his utilitarian theory of virtue. About his seventeenth year he began, but speedily relinquished, the study of the law. " My studious disposition, my sobriety, and my industry, gave my family a notion that the law was a proper profession for me ; but I found an unsurmountable aversion to every thing but the pursuits of philosophy and general learning ; and while they fancied I was poring upon Voet and Vinnius, Cicero and Virgil were the authors I was secretly devouring."

We have two admirable accounts of Hume's life : the one, "My Own Life," calm as philosophy itself ; the other by Mr. Hill Burton, who had access to the papers collected by Baron Hume, and deposited with the Royal Society of Edinburgh ; and who has collected all other available information, and put it together in a clear and systematic manner. But there is much that we should like to know not communicated. The autobiography, though honest enough, is not open or communicative. We may rest assured that in that great lake which spreads itself so calmly before us, there were depths, and movements in these depths, which have been kept from our view. Though so skilled in psychological analysis, he gives no account of the steps by which he was led to that deadly scepticism in philosophy and theology which he held by so firmly, and propounded so perseveringly. Mr. Burton has, however, published a remarkable document, which lets us see what we should never have learned from " My Own Life," that there had been an awful struggle and a crisis.

It is a letter written to a physician with great care, but possibly never sent. He begins with stating that he "had always a strong inclination to books and letters," and that, after fifteen years, he had been left to his own choice in reading: "I found it to incline almost equally to books of reasoning and philosophy, and to poetry and the polite authors. Every one who is acquainted either with the philosophers or critics, knows that there is nothing yet established in either of these sciences, and that they contain little more than endless disputes, even in the most fundamental articles. Upon examination of these, I found a certain boldness of temper growing in me, which was not inclined to submit to any authority on these subjects, but led me to seek out some new medium by which truth might be established. After much study and reflection on this, at last, when I was about eighteen years of age, there seemed to be opened up to me a new source of thought, which transported me beyond measure, and made me, with an ardor natural to young men, throw up every other pleasure or business to apply actively to it. The law, which was the business I designed to follow, appeared nauseous to me ; and I could think of no other way of pushing my fortune in the world but that of scholar and philosopher. I was infinitely happy in this course of life for some months, till at last, about the beginning of September, 1729, all my ardor seemed in a moment to be extinguished, and I could no longer raise my mind to that pitch which formerly gave me such excessive pleasure. I felt no uneasiness or want of spirits when I laid aside my book ; and therefore never imagined there was any bodily distemper in the case, but that my coldness proceeded from a laziness of temper which must be overcome by redoubling my application. In this condition I remained for nine months, very uneasy to myself, but without growing any worse, which was a miracle. There was another particular which contributed more than any thing to waste my spirits, and bring on me this distemper, which was, that, having read many books of morality, — such as Cicero, Seneca, and Plutarch, — and being smit with their beautiful representations of virtue and philosophy, I undertook the improvement of my temper and will, along with my reason and understanding. I was continually fortifying myself with reflections against death and poverty and shame and pain, and all the other calamities of life. These no doubt are exceeding useful when joined with an active life, because the occasion being presented, along with the reflection, works it into the soul, and makes it take a deep impression ; but in solitude they serve to little other purpose than to waste the spirits, the force of the mind meeting with no resistance, but wasting itself in the air, like our arm when it misses the aim. This, however, I did not learn but by experience, and till I had already ruined my health, though I was not sensible of it." He then describes the symptoms : scurvy spots breaking out on his fingers the first winter, then a wateriness in the mouth. Next year, about May, 1731, there grew upon him a ravenous appetite, and a palpitation of heart. In six weeks, from " being tall, lean, and rawboned, he became on a sudden the most sturdy, robust, healthful-like fellow you have seen, with a ruddy complexion and a cheerful countenance." He goes on to say, that " having now time and leisure to cool my inflamed imagination, I began to consider seriously how I should proceed with my philosophical studies. I found that the moral philosophy transmitted to us by antiquity labored under the same inconvenience that has been found in their natural philosophy, of being entirely hypothetical, and depending more upon invention than experience ; every one consulted his fancy in erecting schemes of virtue and happiness, without regarding human nature, upon which every moral conclusion must depend. This, therefore, I resolved to make my principal study, and the source from which I would derive every truth in criticism as well as morality." He tells how he had read most of the celebrated books in Latin, French, and English ; how "within these three years I find I have scribbled many a quire of paper, in which there is nothing contained but my own inventions ;" how he "had collected the rude materials for many volumes ;" but he adds, " I had no hopes of delivering my opinions with such elegance and neatness as to draw to me the attention of the world, and I would rather live and die in obscurity than produce them maimed and imperfect." "It is a weakness rather than lowness of spirits which troubles me ;" and he traces an analogy between what he had passed through and recorded religious experiences. "I have noticed in the writings of the French mystics, and in those of our fanatics here, that when they give a history of the situation of their souls, they mention a coldness and desertion of the spirit, which frequently returns." But, "however this may be, I have not come out of the cloud so well as they commonly tell us they have done, or rather began to despair of ever recovering. To keep myself from being melancholy on so dismal a prospect, my only security was in peevish reflections on the vanity of the world, and of all human glory, which, however just sentiments they may be esteemed, I have found can never be sincere, except in those who are possessed of them. Being sensible that all my philosophy would never make me contented in my present situation, I began to rouse up myself." He found these two things very bad for this distemper, study and idleness, and so he wishes to betake himself to active life. His choice was confined to two kinds of life, that of a travelling governor, and that of a merchant. The first not being fit for him he says he is now on his way to Bristol, to engage in business till he is able to "leave this distemper behind me." He says, that "all the physicians

I have consulted, though very able, could never enter into my distemper," and so he now applies to this eminent doctor.

In this remarkable document Hume unbosoms himself for the first time, and, I may add, for the last time. He had endeavored to act the self-righteous and self-sufficient stoic. We have other evidence of this. In the letter already extracted from, written when he was sixteen, he says. "I hate task-reading, and I diversify them at pleasure; sometimes a philosopher, sometimes a poet." "The philosopher's wise man and the poet's husbandman agree in peace of mind in a liberty and independence on fortune, and contempt of riches, power, and glory. Every thing is placid and quiet in both, nothing perturbed or in disorder." "A perfectly wise man that outbraves fortune is surely greater than the husbandman who slips by her; and indeed this pastoral and Saturnian happiness I have in a great measure come at just now. I live a king, pretty much by myself, neither full of action nor perturbation, — *molles somnos.* This state, however, I can foresee, is not to be relied on. My peace of mind is not sufficiently confirmed by philosophy to withstand the blows of fortune. This greatness and elevation of soul is to be found only in study and contemplation; this can alone teach us to look down on human accidents. You must allow me to talk thus like a philosopher; 'tis a subject I think much on, and could talk all day long of." But the attempt had turned out a miserable failure, as he acknowledges in his letter to the physician. Doubts had crept in, and the stoic was tempted to turn sceptic. Writing long after to Sir Gilbert Elliott in regard to his "Dialogues on Natural Religion," which sap all religion, he mentions a manuscript, afterwards destroyed, which he had written before twenty. "It began with an anxious search after arguments to confirm the common opinion, doubts stole in, dissipated, returned, were again dissipated, returned again; and it was a perpetual struggle of a restless imagination against inclination, perhaps against reason."

The letter is supposed by Mr. Burton, on good grounds, to have been written to the celebrated Dr. Cheyne, author of the "Philosophical Principles of Natural Religion" (1705), and "The English Malady; or a Treatise of Nervous Diseases of all kinds, Spleens, Vapours, Lowness of Spirits, Hypochondriacal

Distempers," &c.   It is doubtful whether the letter ever reached
Dr. Cheyne, and it may be doubted whether that eminent physician had in all his pharmacopœa a medicine to cure the
malady of this remarkable youth.   Dr. Cheyne defends with
the common arguments the "great fundamental principles of
all virtue and all morality : viz., the existence of a supreme and
infinitely perfect Being ; the freedom of the will, the immortality of the spirits of all intellectual beings, and the certainty
of future rewards or punishments."   But the youth who proposed to address him had already a system evolved which undermined all these.   One could have wished that there had
been a friend at hand to direct him away from Cicero, Seneca,
and Plutarch, to a better teacher who is never mentioned.   Not
that we should have expected him in his then state to be drawn
to the character of Jesus, but he might have found something
in His work fitted to give peace and satisfaction to his dis-
tracted soul.   But it is useless to speculate on these possibilities.   All he says himself is : "In 1734 I went to Bristol with
some recommendations to eminent merchants, but in a few
months found that scene totally unsuitable to me.   I went over
to France, with a view of prosecuting my studies in a country
retreat, and I there laid that plan of life which I have steadily
and successfully pursued." [1]

We can easily picture the youth of twenty-three as he set
out for France.   By nature he is one of a class of persons to be
found in all countries, but quite as frequently in Scotland as
anywhere else, who are endowed with a powerful intellect, conjoined with a heavy animal temperament, and who, with no
high aspirations, ideal, ethereal, or spiritual, have a tendency

[1] For some years past it has been well known in literary circles in Edinburgh,
that there was a scandal about David Hume in his younger years.   Having been
kindly allowed to look into the ecclesiastical records which bear upon it, I find
that there was a charge brought, but no evidence to support it.   A woman did,
March 5, 1734, charge "Mr. David Home, brother to Ninewells, as being the
father of her child."   But this woman had previously had three illegitimate children ; she had refused to say who was the father of her child when David Hume
was in the country, though it was known he was leaving, and she brought the
charge after he was gone.   The Presbytery of Chirnside, when the case was
brought before them, rebuked the woman for her conduct, and there is no other
record of the matter.   It is a curious circumstance that this incident should have
happened at the time when the youth was leaving his home in so singular a frame
of mind.

to look with suspicion on all kinds of enthusiasm and high-flown zeal. With an understanding keen and searching, he could not be contented with the appearances of things, and was ever bent on penetrating beneath the surface ; and his native shrewdness, his hereditary predilections, and the reaction against the heats of the previous century, all combined to lead him to question common impressions and popular opinions. He saw the difficulties which beset philosophical and theological investigations, and was unable to deliver himself from them, being without the high sentiments which might have lifted him above the low philosophy of his own day in England and France, and the sophistries suggested by a restless intellect. He knew only the ancient Stoic philosophy in the pages of Roman authors, and the modern philosophy of Locke, as modified by such men as Shaftesbury and Hutcheson, and driven to its logical consequences by Berkeley : he had tried the one in his practical conduct, and the other by his sifting intellect, and having found both wanting, he is prepared to abandon himself to scepticism, which is the miserable desert resorted to by those who despair of truth. Meanwhile his great intellectual powers find employment in constructing theories of the mind, in which he himself perhaps had no great faith, but which seemed the logical conclusion of the acknowledged philosophical principles of his time, and quite as plausible as any that had been devised by others, and brought such fame to their authors.

With these predilections, France was the country which had most attractions to him, but was at the same time the most unfortunate country he could have gone to, and the middle of the eighteenth century the most unfortunate period for visiting it. In philosophy, the age had outgrown Descartes and Malebranche, Arnauld and Pascal, and the grave and earnest thinkers of the previous century, and was embracing the most superficial parts of Locke's philosophy, which had been introduced by Voltaire to the knowledge of Frenchmen, who turned it to a wretched sensationalism. In religion he saw around him, among the great mass of the people, a very corrupted and degenerate form of Christianity, while, among the educated classes, infidelity was privately cherished, and was ready to burst out. Voltaire had issued his first attack on Christianity, in his "Epitre à Uranie," published in 1728, and the fire spread with a rapidity which showed that there were materials ready to catch it and propagate it. Sixty years later, one so fond of order and peace would have been scared by the effects produced by scepticism, so powerful in overthrowing old abuses, and so weak in constructing any thing new or better ; but at this time infidelity was full of hope, and promising an era of liberty and peace. The very section of the Catholic Church which retained the highest faith and the purest moral- ity, had unfortunately been involved in a transaction which favored the sceptical tendency among shrewd minds. Only a few years before, the people believed that the sick were healed, and the blind made to see at the tomb of the famous Jansenist, the Abbé Paris ; the noise made by the occurrences, and the discussions created by them, had not passed away when Hume arrived in Paris ; and the youth pondered the event, to bring it out years after in his " Essay on Miracles." While he lived at La Flêche, a Jesuit plied him with some "nonsensical miracle," performed lately in their convent, and then and there occurred to him the famous argument which he afterwards published against miracles. " As my head was full of the topics of the ' Treatise of Human Nature,' which I was at that time composing, the argument immediately occurred to me, and I thought it very much gravelled my companion ; but at last he observed to me that it was impossible for that argument to have any validity, because it operated equally against the gospel as the Catholic miracles, which observation I thought fit to admit as a sufficient answer."

After living a short time in Paris, he retired to Rheims, and afterwards went to La Flêche, where he passed two of the three years he spent in France. We know nothing of his em- ployments these years, except that he devoted himself most earnestly to the composition of his " Treatise on Human Nature." In 1737 he brought it over with him to London, where he published the two first books the end of the following year.

This treatise is by far the most important of all his philo- sophical works. If we except certain speculations in history and political economy, it contains nearly all his favorite ideas. He devoted to it all the resources of his mighty intellect. He had read extensively, pondered deeply, and taken immense pains in polishing his style. He could scarcely, indeed, be called a learned man, in the technical sense of the term, but he was well informed. We could have wished that he had possessed wider sympathies with earnest seekers after truth in all ages, but this was not in the nature of the man. His knowledge of Greek was very imperfect at this time (he afterwards renewed his acquaintance with that language) ; what he knew of Greek philosophy was chiefly through Cicero (his very pictures of the Stoics and Epicureans are Roman rather than Grecian), and he never entered into the spirit of such deep and earnest thinkers as Socrates, Plato, and Aristotle, — he tells us somewhere that the fame of Aristotle is utterly decayed. In respect even of modern writers, he never comprehended the profundity of such men as Cudworth and Descartes in the previous century ; and he had no appreciation of the speculations of Clarke and Leibnitz, who lived in the age immediately preceding his own. He belongs to the cold, elegant, doubting, and secular eighteenth century ; and, setting little value on antiquity, he builds for the present and the future on the philosophy of his own time.

As to style, which he greatly cultivated, the models which he set before him were the Roman prose writers, the French authors of his own day, and the Englishmen who were introducing the French clearness and point, such as Shaftesbury, Bolingbroke, and Pope, — he says : "The first polite prose we have was writ by Swift." Though he took great pains, he never altogether succeeded in weeding out his Scotticisms, nor in acquiring a genuine English idiom ; but his style is always clear, manly, and elegant, and worthy of his weighty thoughts. When he broke down his elaborate treatise into smaller ones, he endeavored to catch the ease and freedom of the lighter French literature ; but neither the subjects discussed nor the ideas of the author admit of such treatment ; and though the essays are more ornate, and have more attempts at smartness and repartee, the student will ever betake himself to the treatise, as containing the only systematic, and by far the most satisfactory statement of his views.

He is now publicly committed to a theory, and he adheres to it resolutely and doggedly. In after years he said : "So great an undertaking, planned before I was one-and-twenty, and composed before twenty-five, must necessarily be very defective. I have repented my haste a hundred and a hundred times." But this refers to the form and style, not the matter. He never abandoned nor modified the scepticism advanced in the early work. When he failed in obtaining a hearing for his views in the more elaborate treatise, he set them forth in " Essays," which might be more attractive to the general reader. He had instituted an inquiry, and satisfied himself that speculative truth was unattainable, either in philosophy or theology, owing to the weakness of the human intellect, and he did not wish to be disturbed with questionings. He seems to have studiously abstained from speaking on such subjects in social intercourse, except at times, in a tone of playful humor, not meant to be offensive ; and on becoming an author he formed the resolution " never to reply to anybody." He rather delighted to associate with ministers of religion, such as Robertson, Blair, and Carlyle, whom he reckoned moderate and tolerant, and helpful in producing a religious indifference ; but he never allowed them to try to convert him to the truths of natural and revealed religion which they held by ; and when Dr. Blair ventured on one occasion to make the attempt, he received such a reply as prevented the repetition of it on any future occasion. There are traditions of him and Adam Smith conversing familiarly on such subjects on the sands of Kirkcaldy, and of Hume succeeding in bringing his friend over to infidelity ; but we have no authenticated record of Hume ever opening to any human being the religious or irreligious convictions of his soul. A good-natured and sociable man, kind and indulgent to those with whom he came in contact, he passed through life a solitary being, certainly with no God, and apparently with no human being to whom to unbosom himself.

Having set the matured and confirmed man before our readers, we have no intention of detailing minutely the events of his future life. Having published his work, he retired to Ninewells to wait the result. " Never literary attempt was more unfortunate than my ' Treatise of Human Nature.' It fell deadborn from the press without reaching such distinction as even to create a murmur among the zealots." He evidently felt the disappointment. "I am out of humor with myself." He was amazed that the liberty he had taken with all established truth had not created a sensation. But he was conscious of intellectual power: he had laid his plan for life ; and he indomitably persevered in his literary career. Next year he published the third volume of his treatise, that on ethics, with no better success. In 1741 he printed at Edinburgh the first, and in 1742 the second, of his "Essays Moral and Political." The work was favorably received and he was encouraged. In 1744 he was anxious to be appointed Professor of Moral Philosophy in the University of Edinburgh, but public sentiment could not bear the idea of one so sceptical being appointed a teacher of youth. He was a younger brother without a profession, and he wished to have a competency ; and so in 1745, the year of the rebellion of Prince Charles, he became the companion and guide of the weak-minded Marquis of Annandale. The engagement brought him some accession of fortune, but terminated abruptly from the caprice of the Marquis. In 1747 he attended General St. Clair in his military embassy to the Courts of Vienna and Turin. There he saw a variety of life ; and he congratulates himself that when the engagement closed, he was "master of near a thousand pounds." In 1748 he cast the first part of his unfortunate treatise in a new form, in the "Inquiry concerning Human Understanding," but the work failed to excite any interest. His brother at Ninewells having married in 1751, his place of residence was now Edinburgh, where he was appointed to, and held for five years, the office of librarian to the advocates' library, a situation which brought him little or no emolument. In 1752 he published in Edinburgh the second part of his essays, being his "Political Discourses." This work was immediately received with acclamation ; and, being translated into French, it procured him a high reputation, and in fact awakened those discussions which issued in making political economy a science in the "Wealth of Nations." Whatever merit Hume may have in demolishing error, he has, I believe, established very little positive truth : what he effected in this way was done in political economy. The same year he published his "Inquiry concerning the Principles of Morals," being an improved version of the third part of his treatise. "Meanwhile my bookseller, A. Millar, informed me that my former publications (all but the unfortunate treatise) were beginning to be the subject of conversation, that the sale of them was gradually increasing, and that new editions were demanded. Answers by reverends and right reverends came out two or three in a year ; and I found, by Dr. Warburton's railing, that the books were beginning to be esteemed in good company."   He had long had the idea of writing some historical work, and from the time of his being appointed librarian to the well-stored advocates' collection of books, he formed the plan of writing the " History of England."   The first volume commenced with the accession of the house of Stuart, but was received so coldly that in a twelvemonth the publisher sold only forty-five copies.   Nevertheless he persevered, bringing out volume after volume, till at last the great merits of the work were acknowledged.   This perseverance in his life plan, in spite of discouragements, I reckon as the noblest feature in Hume's character.   It does not concern us here to speak of the excellencies and defects of the history.   It could be shown that the prejudices running throughout it were his constitutional and hereditary ones, and that the work, as a whole, is an illustration of his metaphysical and ethical theory.

In 1763 he received from the Earl of Hertford an invitation to attend him on his embassy to Paris.   His visit to the capital of France on this occasion deserves a special notice.   It may be doubted whether there ever were such compliments paid to any literary man.   Dukes, mareschals, foreign ambassadors, vied with each other in honoring him.   The famous men, whose persons and conversations he liked best, were D'Alembert, Marmontel, Diderot, Duclos, Helvetius, and old President Henault ; and he writes to Dr. Blair, and bids him tell Dr. Robertson that there was not a single deist among them, meaning that there was none of them but went farther.   He met also with Buffon, Malesherbes, Crebillon, Holbach, Renauld, Suard, and Turgot.

But he was the special favorite of the ladies, who at that time ruled the fashion in Paris.   In particular, he was flattered and adored by the Countess de Boufflers.   His correspondence with that lady had commenced in 1761.   She addressed him first, declaring the admiration which "your sublime work (the ' History of England ') has awakened in me."   " I know no terms

capable of expressing what I felt in reading the work. I was
moved, transported ; and the emotion which it caused me, is in
some measure painful by its continuance. It elevates the soul ;
it fills the heart with sentiments of humanity and benevolence ;
it enlightens the intellect, by showing that true happiness is
closely connected with virtue ; and discovers, by the same light,
what is the end, the sole end, of every reasonable being"! "In
truth, I believed I had before my eyes the work of some celestial being, free from the passions of humanity, who, for the
benefit of the human race, has designed to write the events of
these latter times"! The philosopher is evidently gratified.
"What new wonder is this which your letter presents to me?
I not only find a lady, who, in the bloom of beauty and height
of reputation, can withdraw herself from the pleasures of a gay
court, and find leisure to cultivate the sciences, but deigns to
support a correspondence with a man of letters, in a remote
country, and to reward his labors by a suffrage the most agreeable of all others to a man who has any spark of generous sentiment or taste for true glory." This lady, it is proper to say
in plain terms, was the wife of the Comte de Boufflers, still
alive, but the mistress of the Prince of Conti, who superintended
for the king that mean diplomatic correspondence which he
carried on unknown to his ministers. Hume might also be
seen attending the evening *salons* of Madame Geoffrin, who
had been the daughter of a *valet de chambre*, and was now the
centre of a circle of artists and men of letters. He also waited
on the entertainments of the famous Mademoiselle de l'Espi-
nasse, who, originally an illegitimate child, had raised herself
by being, first, the humble companion, and then the rival of
Madame Du Deffaud, and was well known to have been the
mistress of a number of successive or contemporaneous lovers.
There must have been something in the philosophy of Hume
which recommended him to so many ladies of this description.
We believe they were glad to find so eminent a philosopher,
with a system which did not seem to bear hard upon them.
The courtiers told him that Madame de Pompadour "was never
heard to say so much to any man."

He says of himself : "I eat nothing but ambrosia, drink nothing but nectar, breathe nothing but incense, and tread on nothing but flowers. Every man I meet, and still more every lady,

would think they were wanting in the most indispensable duty if they did not make a long and elaborate harangue in my praise." Lord Charlemont has given us a picture, or rather a caricature, of his person as he met him at Turin some years before this. "His face was broad and flat, his mouth wide, and without any other expression than that of imbecility. His eyes vacant and spiritless, and the corpulence of his whole person was far better fitted to communicate the idea of a turtle-eating alderman than of a refined philosopher. His speech in English was rendered ridiculous by the broadest Scotch accent, and his French was, if possible, still more laughable." This was the man who was made by the Parisian ladies to take the part, in an acted tableau, of a sultan assailed by two female slaves : "On le place sur un sopha entre les deux plus jolies femmes de Paris, il les regarde attentivement, il se frappe le ventre et les genoux à plusieurs reprises, et ne trouve jamais autre chose à leur dire que, — ' Eh bien ! mes demoiselles. . . . Eh bien ! nous voilà donc. . . . Eh bien ! vous voilà. . . . vous voilà ici.'" His good sense led him to see the vanity of all this : but he was pleased with it ; and he often expresses a wish to settle in Paris, or somewhere in France.

When he was introduced to the Dauphin, his son, afterwards the unfortunate Louis XVI., but then a boy of nine, stepped forth, evidently by instruction, and told him how many friends and admirers he had in the country, and that he reckoned himself among the number from the reading of many passages in his works. The Comte de Provence (who, after his long exile, became Louis XVIII.), a year or so younger, now approached Hume, and told him he had been long and impatiently expected in France, and that he anticipated great pleasure from reading his fine history. Even the Comte d'Artois, afterwards Charles X., but then a boy of six, had to mumble a panegyric. A wise man learned in providence might have seen that awful miseries must issue from a state of things in which, as Horace Walpole pointedly expresses it, "There is a God and the king to be pulled down first, and men and women are devoutly employed in the demolition," while princes were taught to cherish the viper that was to sting them. It would have been an appropriate punishment to have got Hume placed, half a century later, in the scenes of the French Revolution, to let him eat the fruit of the seed he had helped to sow.

But what, it may be asked, did he think of the state of society in which he had to mingle? It is evident that he was horrified at times with the proclaimed atheism of men and women. But what did he think of the morality of the circles in which he moved, more especially of the loose relationship of the marriage tie? Did his utilitarian theory of morals, of which he surely knew the bearing and tendency, allow of such a state of things? It is certain that Hume uttered no protest at the time, and he has left behind no condemnation of the morality of France, while he was fond of making sly and contemptuous allusions to the manifestations of religious zeal in his own country. The tone of morality in France could never have been amended by him, nor, we venture to say, by any utilitarian. When the husband of Madame Boufflers dies, he writes to her as a person now within reach of honor and felicity; that is, as likely to be married to the Prince de Conti. However, the prince declines, and Hume gives her wise enough counsel: gradually to diminish her connection with the prince, and at last to separate from him; and, he says: "If I could dispose of my fate, nothing would be so much my choice as to live where I might cultivate your friendship. Your taste for travelling might also afford you a plausible pretence for putting this plan in execution; a journey to Italy would loosen your connections here; and, if it were delayed, I would, with some probability, expect to have the felicity of attending you thither." One can picture the scene; the countess travelling with Hume attending her. But the prospect had not such attractions as to induce her to leave the prince. Hume continued his correspondence with her; and, on hearing of the death of the Prince of Conti, wrote her within a few days of his own death, knowing he was dying, and expresses no condemnation of her past conduct. The question arises whether this would be the moral tone allowed in a community in which the word of God is discarded, and utilitarian principles are adopted?

We do not mean to discuss the miserable quarrel between him and Rousseau. His attention was called to the alleged ill-usage of Rousseau by Madame de Boufflers, who described him as a noble and disinterested soul, "flying from intercourse with the world," and "feeling pleasure only in solitude." Hume, believing him to be persecuted, exerted himself to help him.

But his morbid vanity and intolerable habits (he insisted in taking his disgusting governante with him when he visited a family) rendered it impossible to befriend him. Unwilling to allow himself to think, or let others conclude, that he was indebted to any one, he repaid Hume's manly and delicate kindness with suspicion ; and Hume, who began by describing him as a man " whose modesty proceeded from ignorance of his own excellence," ended by declaring him to be "the blackest and most atrocious villain beyond comparison that now exists in the world." It is justice to Hume to say that he was always kind to persons of literary ability. Thus, he interested himself much in Thomas Blacklock, a blind man, of some poetical talent, when the people of Kirkcudbright declined to accept him as their minister. He also did all in his power to bring into notice the publications of Robertson, Adam Smith, and Ferguson.

By his connection with the embassy and the sale of his works, which had become great, he now attained a competency which made him feel independent. He had many temptations to settle in France, but old associations drew him back to Scotland. It was proposed by Lord Hertford to send him to Ireland as Secretary ; but the Irish would not receive him, because he was a Scotchman. It was on this occasion that the Princess Amelia said that she thought the affair might be easily accommodated. " Why may not Lord Hertford give a bishopric to Mr. Hume ?" In 1767–68 he was appointed by Lord Conway Under-Secretary of State, and had charge of Scottish affairs, including the patronage of churches ! But his residence was now mainly in Edinburgh, first in the old town, afterwards in a house which he built in the new town, in St. David Street, so called as the name had been chalked on the wall by a witty young lady as she passed. Here he was the acknowledged chief of a literary circle, embracing men of considerable eminence, such as Robertson, Blair, Lord Kames, Adam Ferguson, and Adam Smith at Kirkcaldy, who all looked up to him with respect. He rather enjoyed being an object of wonder to the multitude beyond the favored circle in which he mingled, and made many jocular remarks about the unpopularity of his opinions. Good-natured, sociable, and avoiding controversy, he suffered few annoyances because of his scepticism — certainly none that deserved to be called persecution. For we suppose it will be scarcely reckoned as such, that, on one occasion, in picking his steps from his lodging in the old town to the house he was building in the new, he fell into a swamp, and, observing some Newhaven fishwives passing, he called to them for help, but on learning that it was Hume the unbeliever who was in such a plight, they refused to aid him till he said the Lord's prayer. He carried on a pleasant correspondence with Sir Gilbert Elliott of Minto, with Mure of Caldwell, and others of a literary or philosophic taste. He lived on familiar terms with several of the moderate clergy, such as Robertson and Blair, and at times mingled in their ecclesiastical counsels. Many of the younger ministers reckoned it an honor to be admitted to his society, and he encouraged them to associate with him. These circumstances have led some to think that the leading moderate ministers of that period must have been infidels in secret, and acting hypocritically in professing Christianity ; but there is no ground for such a charge : they believed sincerely in the doctrines of natural religion, and in the Word of God as inspired to teach a pure morality and the immortality of the soul. But it is equally clear, that they had no faith in the peculiar Bible doctrines of grace ; and Hume was delighted to find them frowning on all religious earnestness, and advancing so rapidly on the road to deism and philosophic indifference.

By April, 1776, Hume knew that he would not recover from the disease with which he had been afflicted for two years, being a disorder in the bowels. He bought a piece of ground in the new church-yard in the Calton Hill as a burying-place, and left money for the erection of a small monument, with the simple inscription, " David Hume." He wrote " My Own Life," giving an account of his literary career. In his will Adam Smith had been appointed his literary executor, and two hundred pounds had been bequeathed to him for the pains he might take in correcting and publishing his " Dialogues on Natural Religion," a work written before 1751, but not yet given to the world. But he had ground for fearing that Smith might be unwilling to take the odium of editing such a work, and so he took effectual steps to guard against its suppression. He came to

an understanding with Smith on the subject, and in a codicil
to his will, dated August 7, he left the manuscripts to Strahan
the publisher, ordaining " that if my ' Dialogues ' from whatever cause be not published within two years and a half after
my death, as also the account of my life, the property shall return to my nephew David, whose duty in publishing them, as
the last request of his uncle, must be approved of by all the
world." Strahan was as indisposed as Smith to undertake the
responsibility of publishing so offensive a work. The truth is,
Hume's Scottish friends, though they had abandoned Christianity, were most anxious to have left to them a natural religion, in which they might find a refuge and some comfort ; and
in the "Dialogues" Hume had undermined this last support. The
" Dialogues " were published in 1779 by the author's nephew.

In April he took a journey to Bath for the benefit of his
health, but with no hope of ultimate recovery. John Home,
the author of " Douglas, a Tragedy," travelled with him, and has
preserved a diary. He talked cheerfully of the topics of the
day, and of his favorite subjects, lamenting over the state of
the nation, and predicting that the national debt must be the
ruin of Britain. He returned to Edinburgh about the beginning of July. Dr. Cullen reports : " He passed most part of the
day in his drawing-room : admitted the visits of his friends, and
with his usual spirits conversed with them upon literature, politics, or whatever was accidentally started." Colonel Edmonstoune had come to take leave of him ; Hume said he had been
reading a few days before, Lucian's " Dialogues of the Dead,"
and, among all the reasons for not entering readily into Charon's boat, he could not find one that fitted him, and he invented
several peculiar ones to give the boatman. " I might urge,
' Have a little patience, good Charon : I have been endeavoring
to open the eyes of the public. If I live a few years longer, I
may have the satisfaction of seeing the downfall of some of the
prevailing systems of superstition.' But Charon would then
lose all temper and decency : ' You loitering rogue, that will
not happen these many hundred years. Do you fancy I will
grant you a lease for so long a term ? Get into the boat this
instant, you lazy, loitering rogue.' " All this is evidently very
gratifying to the colonel. Dr. Black reports that he " passes
his time very well with the assistance of amusing books."

Dr. Cullen continues: "For a few days before his death, he became more averse to receive visits; speaking became more and more difficult to him; and for twelve hours before his death his speech failed him altogether. His senses and judgment did not fail till the last hour of his life. He constantly discovered a strong sensibility to the attention and care of his friends, and, amidst great uneasiness and languor, never betrayed any peevishness or impatience."

This was the account left by his literary friends, and it was matter of triumph to them that he betrayed no signs of fear in his hour of weakness. Are we to allow, that, as in the early ages of the world's history, those who did not like to retain God in their knowledge continued all their lives in the most abject superstition; so in these last days, under other influences, there may be persons so bewildered that they die as they live, without any fixed religious belief? The fact, if it be a fact, is not flattering to the race; nor is the prospect encouraging. Good Christians had hoped, that ere he left the world there might be a change of sentiment, and an acknowledgment of the existence of God, and the need of a Saviour. Many of them maintained that it was impossible for an infidel to die in peace, and it was reported among religious circles, that, though he was cheerful when his unbelieving friends visited him, he had terrible uneasiness when left alone. Some of these rumors utterly break down when we try to trace them to their original sources. The statement, however, of Mr. Robert Haldane of Airthrey, as to what he learned from his neighbor, Mr. Abercromby of Tullibody, must contain some truth. Mr. Abercromby was travelling to Haddington in a lumbering stage-coach. "The conversation during the tedious journey turned on the death-bed of the great philosopher, and as Mr. Abercromby's son-in-law, Colonel Edmonstoune of Newton, was one of Hume's intimate friends, he had heard from him much of the buoyant cheerfulness which had enlivened the sick room of the dying man. Whilst the conversation was running on in this strain, a respectable-looking female, dressed in black, who made a fourth in the coach, begged permission to offer a remark: 'Gentlemen,' she said, 'I attended Mr. Hume on his death-bed, but, I can assure you, I hope never again to attend the death-bed of a *philosopher.*'

They then cross-examined her as to her meaning ; and she told them that, when his friends were with him, Mr. Hume was cheerful even to frivolity, but that when alone he was often overwhelmed with unutterable gloom, and had in his hours of depression declared that he had been in search of light all his life, but was now in greater darkness than ever." This is Mr. Haldane's statement, as taken from Mr. Abercromby.[1] We confess we should like to know more of this woman in black, and to have taken part in the cross-questioning. The question is left in that region of doubt where Hume himself left all religion. He died on Monday, August 26, 1776, at four o'clock in the afternoon.

Everybody knows that Hume was a sceptic. It is not so generally known that he has developed a full system of the human mind. Students of philosophy should make themselves acquainted with it. It has in fact been the stimulating cause of all later European philosophy : of that of Reid and his school ; of that of Kant, and the powerful thinkers influenced by him ; and of that of M. Cousin, and his numerous followers in France, in their attempt to combine Reid and Kant. Nor is it to be omitted that Mr. J. S. Mill, in his "Examination of Hamilton," has reproduced to a large extent the theory of Hume, but without so clearly seeing or candidly avowing the consequences. I rather think that Mr. Mill himself is scarcely aware of the extent of the resemblance between his doctrines and those of the Scottish sceptic ; as he seems to have wrought out his conclusions from data supplied him by his own father, Mr. James Mill, who, however, has evidently drawn much from Hume. The circumstance that Mr. Mill's work was welcomed by such acclamations by the chief literary organs in London is a proof, either that the would-be leaders of opinion are so ignorant of philosophy that they do not see the consequences ; or that the writers, being chiefly young men bred at Oxford or Cambridge, are fully prepared to accept them in the reaction against the revived mediævalism which was sought to be imposed upon them. In no history of philosophy that we are acquainted with is there a good account of the system of Hume. As few persons now read, or in fact ever did read, through his weighty

[1] "Memoirs of R. and J. A. Haldane," chap. xxv.

volumes, we are in hopes that some may feel grateful to us, if in short space we give them an expository and critical account of his philosophy, with a special facing towards the philosophy which has been introduced among us by the British section of the nescient school of Comte.

Hume begins thus his famous "Treatise of Human Nature:" "All the perceptions of the human mind resolve themselves into two distinct kinds, which I call *impressions* and *ideas*. The difference betwixt them consists in the degrees of force and liveliness with which they strike upon the mind, and make their way into our thought or consciousness. Those perceptions which enter with most force and violence, we may name *impressions*, and under this name I comprehend all our sensations, passions, and emotions, as they make their first appearance in the soul. By *ideas*, I mean the faint images of these in thinking and reasoning ; such, for instance, are all the perceptions excited by the present discourse, excepting only those which arise from the sight and touch, and excepting the immediate pleasure or uneasiness it may occasion." He tells us, that, in the use of terms, "I rather restore the word *idea* to its original sense, from which Mr. Locke had perverted it, in making it stand for all our perceptions." This theory is certainly very simple, but surely it is lamentably scanty. It will not do to place under the same head, and call by the one name of impressions, two such things as the affections of the senses on the one hand, and the mental emotions of hope, fear, joy, and sorrow, on the other. Nor can we allow him to describe all our sense-perceptions by the vague name of *impressions*. What is meant by impressions? If the word has any proper meaning, it must signify that there is something impressing, without which there would be no impression, and also something impressed. If Hume admits all this to be in the impression we ask him to go on with us to inquire what is in the thing impressed and in the thing that impresses, and we are at once in the region of existences, internal and external. "I never," he says, "catch myself at any time without a perception, and never can observe any thing but the perception." His very language contradicts itself. He talks of catching *himself*. What is this *self* that he catches? But he may say it is only a perception. I reply that there is more. We never observe a perception alone. We always observe self as perceiving. It is true that I never can catch myself at any time without a perception ; but it is quite as certain, and we have the same evidence for it, that we never observe a perception except when we observe self perceiving. Let us unfold what is in this self, and we shall find that it no way resembles an impression, like that left by a seal upon wax.[1] In regard to certain of our perceptions, those through the senses, we observe not only the self perceiving, but an object perceived.

He now explains the way in which *ideas* appear. By memory the impressions come forth in their original order and position as ideas. This is a defective account of memory, consciousness being the witness. In memory, we have not only a reproduction of a sensation, or, it may be, a mental affection, we recognize it as *having been before us in time past.* Of all this we have as clear evidence as we have of the presence of the idea.[2] In imagination the ideas are more strong and lively, and are transposed and changed. This, he says, is effected by an associating quality ; and he here develops his account of the laws of association, which has been so commended. But the truth is, his views on this subject, so far from being an advance on those of Hutcheson, are rather a retrogression : they are certainly far behind those of his contemporary Turnbull. He seems to confine the operation of association to the exercise of imagination : he does not see that our very memories are regulated by the same principle ; nay, he allows that the imagination can join two ideas without it. The associating qualities are said by him to be three in number : resemblance, contiguity in time or place, and cause or effect. " I do not find," he says, " that

---

[1] J. S. Mill labors to derive all our ideas and convictions from sensations. He is to be met by showing that we never have a sensation without knowing *a self* as sentient.

[2] Mr. Mill is in difficulties at this point, and avows it in a foot-note, p. 174 : "Our belief in the veracity of memory is evidently ultimate ; no reason can be given for it which does not presuppose the belief, and assume it to be well grounded." The full facts of the recognitive power of memory are not embraced in this brief enunciation, but there is much stated, and more implied ; he should have inquired how much is involved, and he would have seen that there is truth admitted fatal to his system. He should also have shown on what ground he proclaims this belief to be "evidently ultimate," and then we might have shown that on the same ground, that is self-evidence, we are entitled to call in the other ultimate beliefs.

any philosopher has attempted to enumerate all the principles of association." But the classification propounded by him bears so close a resemblance to that of Aristotle, that we must believe that the one given by the Stagyrite had, in the course of his reading, fallen under his notice, though he had forgotten the circumstance. The difference between the two lies in Hume giving us cause and effect, instead of contrast as proposed by the Greek philosopher. It has often been remarked that Hume's arrangement is redundant, inasmuch as cause and effect, according to him, are nothing but contiguity in time and place.

He now shows how our complex ideas are formed. Following Locke, he represents these as consisting of substances, modes, and relations. He dismisses substance very summarily. He proceeds on the view of substance given by Locke, one of the most defective and unsatisfactory parts of his philosophy. Locke stood up for some unknown thing, called substance, behind the qualities. Berkeley had shown that there is no evidence of the existence of such a substratum. Hume assumes that we have no idea of external substance different from the qualities, and he proceeds to show that we have no notion of the substance mind distinct from particular perceptions. " I believe none will assert that substance is either a color, or a sound, or a taste. The idea of substance must therefore be derived from an impression of reflection, if it really exist. But the impressions of reflection resolve themselves into our passions and emotions, none of which can possibly represent a substance." A substance is thus nothing else than a collection of particular qualities united by the imagination. He thus suits the idea to his preconceived theory, instead of looking at the peculiar idea, and suiting his theory to the facts. I give up the idea of an unknown substratum behind the qualities. I stand up only for what we know. In consciousness, we know self, and in sense-perception we know the external objects as *existing things exercising qualities.* In this is involved what I reckon the true idea of substance. We can as little know the qualities apart from an object exercising them, as we can an object apart from qualities. We know both in one concrete act, and we have the same evidence of the one as the other.

When he comes to modes, he examines them by the doctrine

of abstract or general ideas propounded by Berkeley, which he characterizes "as one of the greatest and most valuable discoveries that has been made of late years in the republic of letters." According to this very defective theory (as it appears to us), all abstract or general ideas are nothing but particular ones annexed to a certain term. Like Locke, Hume confounds abstract and general ideas, which should be carefully distinguished : the former meaning the notion of the part of an object as a part, more particularly an attribute ; the other, the notion of objects possessing common attributes, the notion being such that it embraces all the objects possessing the common attributes. Abstraction and generalization are most important intellectual operations, the one bringing specially to view what is involved in the concrete knowledge (not impression) of the individual, and the other exhibiting the qualities in respect of which objects agree. Without such elaborative processes, we should never know all that is involved in our original perceptions by sense and consciousness. Nor is it to be forgotten, that when the concrete is a real object, the abstract is a real quality existing in the object ; and that when the singulars are real, the universal is also real, that is, a class all the objects in which possess common qualities. Here again we find Hume overlooking one of the most essential of our mental attributes, and thus degrading human intelligence. In relation to the particular end for which he introduces his doctrine, I hold that substance and mode are known in one concrete act and that we can separate them by abstraction for more particular consideration ; the one having quite as real an existence as the other, and both having their reality in the singular object known by sense and consciousness.

He goes on to a very subtle discussion as to our ideas of space and time. He says, that " it is from the disposition of visible and tangible objects we receive the idea of space, and from the succession of ideas and impressions we form the idea of time." The statement requires to be amended. It is not from the disposition of separate objects we have the idea of space, but in the very perception of material objects we know them as extended, that is, occupying space ; and in the very remembrance of events we have time in the concrete, that is, events happening in time past. He is therefore wrong in the sceptical conclusion which he draws, that the ideas of space and time are no distinct ideas ; for they are ideas formed by a high intellectual process from things immediately known. Taking a defective view of the nature and function of abstraction, he denies that we can form any idea of a vacuum or extension without matter. He maintains that the idea we form of any finite quality is not infinitely divisible. The dispute, he says, should not be about the nature of mathematical points, but about our ideas of them ; and that, in the division of our ideas, we come to a minimum, to an indivisible idea. This whole controversy seems to me to arise from a misapprehension. Our *idea* of space, it is evident, is neither divisible nor indivisible ; and as to space, it is not divisible either finitely or infinitely ; for while we can divide matter, that is, have a space between, we cannot separate any portion of space from all other space : space is and must be continuous. He is evidently jealous of the alleged certainty of mathematics, which seemed to be opposed to his universal scepticism. He maintains that the objects of geometry are mere ideas in the mind. I admit that surfaces, lines, points, have no independent existence, but they have all an existence in solid bodies. By an excess of ingenuities and subtleties, he would drive us to the conclusion that space and time are mere ideas, for which we need not seek a corresponding reality ; a conclusion unfortunately accepted by Kant, who thus opened the way to the empty idealism which so long reigned in the German philosophy.[1]

[1] J. S. Mill's treatment of space and time is superficial. He brings in time quietly without noticing it, or giving any account of it. He does not see that the idea of it in the concrete is involved in memory ; we remember the event as happening *in time past.* He derives our idea of space from that of the time occupied by our muscular sensations : " When we say that there is a space between A and B, we mean that some amount of these muscular sensations must intervene." " Resisting points " are said to be " at different distances from one another, because the series of intervening muscular sensations is longer in some cases than in others " (pp. 228, 229). He thus avowedly makes, p. 227, an "identification" of length in time and length in space " as one ; " whereas our consciousness declares them to be as different as it is possible for ideas to be. The hypothesis on which he and Professor Bain build their whole theory of the origin of our idea of extension, viz., the sensations of our muscles, is doubted by some. The conclusion of E. H. Weber, from numerous and careful observations, is : "Of the voluntary motion of our limbs, we know originally nothing. We do not perceive the motion of our muscles by their own sensations, but attain a knowledge of them only when perceived by another sense " (see Abbot on "Sight and Touch," p. 71).

The result reached is summed up in the statement: "As long as we confine our speculations to the *appearances* of objects to our senses, without entering into disquisitions concerning their real nature and operations, we are safe from all difficulties, and can never be embarrassed by any question;" but, "if we carry our inquiry beyond the appearances of objects to the senses, I am afraid that most of our conclusions will be full of scepticism and uncertainty." The intelligent reader will here perceive the source whence Kant derived his doctrine that the senses give us, not things, but *phenomena*, that is appearances, and that we are involved in contradiction when we suppose that they furnish more. However great the logical power of the German metaphysician, it is clear that he did not possess the shrewdness of the common-sense philosopher of Scotland, when he adopted the conclusion of the sceptic as his starting-point.

He has now to face the important subjects of existence and knowledge. Proceeding on his assumption that nothing is present to the mind but perceptions, he argues, I think logically (if the premises be allowed), that we can never advance a step beyond ourselves, and that it is "impossible for us so much as to conceive or form an idea of any thing specifically different from ideas or impressions." As knowledge had been represented by Locke as consisting in comparison (I reckon this a false and dangerous doctrine), Hume has to consider the relations which the mind of man can discover.

These he represents as being seven: those of resemblance, identity, space and time, quantity, degree, contrariety, cause and effect. This is a very good enumeration of the relations perceivable by man: it is certainly very much superior to that of many later metaphysicians, British and Continental. "These relations may be divided into two classes, into such as depend entirely on the ideas which we compare together, and such as may be changed without any change in the ideas." In the first class he places resemblance, contrariety, degree, proportion. These depend solely on our ideas. These only can be the objects of knowledge and certainty, but they can never go beyond our ideas, which can never go beyond our impressions. The other four do not depend on our ideas, and might seem to carry us beyond them; but this he shows is an illusion. In identity, and time and space, we can never "go beyond what is immediately present to the senses," and thus can never discover the real existence or the relations of objects. And so "'tis only causation which produces such a connection as to give us assurance, from the existence or action of one object, that 'twas followed or preceded by any other existence or action." He devotes the whole energy of his intellect to the task of showing that we know nothing of the nature of the relation between cause and effect ; that we know their conjunction within our experience, but not their connection.

In discussing this question, and kindred ones, he finds it necessary to explain the nature of belief. " The belief of the existence of an object joins no new ideas to those which compose the idea of the object." What then is the difference between belief and incredulity ? It consists solely in the liveliness of the former. " We must not be contented with saying that the vividness of the idea produces the belief, we must maintain that they are individually the same." " The belief or assent which always attends the memory and senses is nothing but the vivacity of those perceptions they represent, and this alone distinguishes them from imagination." The theory is surely palpably false here, for our imaginations, in which there is no faith, are often livelier than our memories, in which there is belief. But, by this theory, he would account for all our beliefs. He would establish it as a general maxim in the science of human nature, that when any impression becomes present to us, it not only transports the mind to such ideas as are related to it, but likewise communicates to them a share of its force and vivacity. " A present impression being vivid, conveys its vividness to all the ideas which are associated with it by such general laws as those of resemblance, contiguity, and causation." " A person that has lost a leg or an arm by amputation, endeavors, for a long time afterwards, to serve himself with them. After the death of any one, 'tis a common remark of the whole family, but especially the servants, that they can scarce believe him to be dead, but still imagine him to be in his chamber, or in any other place where they were accustomed to find him." The explanation may seem a very ingenious, but it is a very feeble one. We may believe that we saw a particular person yesterday, though we have no lively impression or idea regarding him ; and we do not believe in the existence of Achilles, though the reading of Homer has given us a vivid conception of him.[1]

But this theory is employed to give an explanation of our

[1] J. S. Mill has made a most unwarrantable application of the laws of association, in accounting for the formation of our higher ideas. He labors to derive all our ideas from sensation through association. But sensations — say of sounds, smells, colors, and forms, or of pleasure and pain — can never be any thing else than sensations, — that is sounds, smells, colors, forms, pleasures or pains, — and never can of themselves yield such ideas as those of space and time, cause and effect, moral good and moral obligation. But then he gives to association a sort of chemical power, by which it changes a series of successive or contemporaneous ideas into something different from any of the ideas, just as oxygen and hydrogen by their union form a third substance, water. He is to be met here by showing that the laws of the association are merely the laws of the succession of our ideas, and they do not generate a new idea. Repeated association may quicken the flow of our ideas, and make several, as it were, coalesce into one, or it may weaken some and intensify others, but it cannot yield a new element. Even on the supposition that there is (which there is not) a chemical power in association to transmute one thing into another, this would be a new and different capacity, not in the sensations and associations, but superinduced upon them. Mr. Mill's professed evolution of our higher ideas out of sensation by association, is a mere jugglery, in which he changes the elements without perceiving it, and overlooks the peculiarities of the composites he would explain.

He has been guilty of an equal error in very much overlooking the relations which the mind of man can discover ; and, so far as he does notice them, in giving a very inadequate account of them. In this respect he is far behind Hume, who, we have seen, gives a very comprehensive summary of them. So far as Mr. Mill treats of them, he (followed by Professor Bain) seems to give the mind no other power of comparison than that of observing resemblances and differences. Nor is this his worst error. He confounds the judgments of the mind with associations, and thus endeavors, in a plausible but superficial way to account for that conviction of necessity which is appealed to as a test of fundamental truth. " If we find it," he says, "impossible by any trial to separate two ideas, we have all the feeling of necessity the mind is capable of " (p. 264). Now there is here the confounding of two things that are very different, the association of two ideas, so that the one always calls up the other, with the judgment which declares that two things are necessarily related. The letter A suggests the letter B; this is one mental phenomenon : we decide that two plus two makes four, and that it cannot be otherwise ; this is an entirely different phenomenon. Now it is this necessity of judgment, and not the invariable association, that is the test of first truths. When we thus show that association cannot produce a new idea, and that judgment, especially necessary judgments, are something different from associations, we deprive Mr. Mill's theory of the plausibility which has so deceived the London critics bred at the English universities, — where, I may take the liberty of saying, they would be very much the better of instruction in a sound and sober philosophy.

belief in the relation of cause and effect. The one having always been with the other in our experience, we are led by habit, and proceeding on the principle of association, when we find the one to look for the other, and thus, too, the effect being present, that is an impression, gives its vividness to the cause as an associating idea. "The idea of cause and effect is derived from experience, which, presenting us with certain objects constantly conjoined with each other, produces such a habit of surveying them in that relation, that we cannot, without a sensible violence, survey them in any other." This is his explanation of what is implied in efficacy, agency, power, force, energy, connection, productive quality. The essence of necessity is "the propensity which custom produces to pass from an object to the idea of its usual attendant." "When any object is presented to it, it immediately conveys to the mind a lively idea of that object which is usually found to attend it, and this determination forms the necessary connection of these objects." His definition of cause is "an object precedent and contiguous to another, and so united with it that the idea of the one determines the mind to form the idea of the other, and the impression of the one to form a more lively idea of the other."

Hume's doctrine is founded on his favorite principle, "that all our ideas are copied from our impressions;" but the necessary connection of cause and effect cannot be in the impression, for "when I cast my eye on the known qualities of objects, I immediately discover that the relation of cause and effect depends not the least on them." Not being in the impression, it cannot be found in the idea. Now it is here, I apprehend, that Hume is to be met. I have disputed his theory that the mind begins with mere impressions; it commences with the perception or knowledge of objects within itself, and without itself. Now, in its primitive perception of objects, it knows them as having power; it knows self as a power, and it knows the not-self as a power, — as a power in resisting and impressing the self. Here is the *impression*, if any one will call it so (I call it knowledge), that gives rise to the idea which may be separated in thought by abstraction, and put in the form of a maxim by generalization.

Unfortunately, as I think, the opponents of Hume have

not always met him at the proper point. They have allowed him that we have no original knowledge of power in the objects, and having given this entrance to the sceptic, they find great difficulty in resisting his farther ravages. Sometimes they have endeavored to discover a *nexus* of some kind *between* the cause and its effect, but have always failed to tell what the bond is. Causation is not to be regarded as a *connection between* cause and effect, but a power in the object, that is, substance (or objects and substances), acting as the cause to produce the effect. Kant labored to oppose the scepticism of the Scotchman by supposing that the mind, by its own forms, bound together events in its contemplation of them. But when he allowed that the power was not in the objects, he introduced a more subtle and perilous scepticism than that which he sought to overthrow. We avoid this subjective idealism by insisting that it is on the bare contemplation of a thing becoming, and not by the mere association of ideas and custom (which may aid), that we declare that it must have had a cause.

He is now prepared to discuss two questions: "Why we attribute a continued existence to objects even when they are not present to the senses, and why we suppose them to have an existence distinct from the mind and perception?" He shows, as to the first, the senses give us nothing but a present perception; and, as to the second, that our perceptions being of ourselves, can never give us the least intimation of any thing beyond. He dwells in the usual manner on the acknowledged unreality of what have been called the secondary qualities of matter, and as we naturally look upon the primary qualities, such as motion and solidity, and the secondary qualities, such as colors, sound, heat and cold, as alike real, so we must philosophically consider them as alike unreal. After the manner of the times, he rejects the notion that we can immediately perceive our bodily frame, and not mere impressions, and that we can know both the "objects and ourselves." But whence, it is asked, the coherence and constancy of certain impressions? He accounts for it on the principle that the thought, according to the laws of association, slides from one impression to others with which it has been joined, and reckons them the same, and mistakes the succession of images for an identity of objects.

The result reached by him is, " All our distinct perceptions are distinct existences," and " the mind never perceives any real connection among distinct existences." "What we call mind is nothing but a heap or collection of different impressions united together by certain relations, and supposed, though falsely, to be endowed with a perfect simplicity and identity." He gives the same account of what we call matter. He shows that having nothing but impressions, we can never, on the mere ground of a conjunction which we have never witnessed, argue from our perceptions to the existence of external continued objects ; and he proves (very conclusively, I think, on his assumption), that we could never have any reason to infer that the supposed objects resemble our sensations.[1] He now draws his sceptical conclusion : "There is a direct and total opposition betwixt our reason and our senses, or, more properly speaking, betwixt those conclusions which we form from cause and effect, and those that persuade us of the continued and independent existence of body. When we reason from cause and effect, we conclude that neither color, sound, taste, nor smell have a continued and independent existence. When we exclude these sensible qualities, there remains nothing in the universe which has such an existence."

The question is : How is such a scepticism to be met ? Reid opposed it by showing that the sensation leads us intuitively to believe in the existence of the external thing, and that the states of self, known by consciousness, imply a thinking sub-

---

[1] Here again, from like premises, J. S. Mill has arrived at much the same conclusions. Mind, according to him, is "a series of feelings," with "a belief of the permanent possibility of the feelings." He is to be met by showing that in every conscious act we know self as existing ; that when we remember, we remember self as in some state ; and that, on comparing the former self with the present, we declare them to be the same. This implies more than a mere series of feelings, or a belief (he does not well know what to make of this belief) in possibilities ; it implies a self existing and feeling, now and in time past. Again : "Matter may be defined the permanent possibility of sensation." He is to be met here by showing that we apprehend matter as an existence external and extended, and that we cannot get this idea of extension from mere sensations which are not extended. As to the contradiction between the senses and the reason, which Hume maintains, Mr. Mill makes the reason and senses say the same thing, that we can know nothing whatever of matter except as the "possibility of sensation," and that it "may be but a mode in which the mind represents to itself the possible modifications of the Ego" (p. 189), which Ego is but a series of feelings. This conclusion is quite as blank as that reached by Hume.

stance.   The more correct statement seems to me to be, that we know at once the external objects; that intuitively we know our own frame and objects affecting it; that we are conscious, not of states arguing a self, but of self in a certain state; and that, on comparing a former self recalled by memory and a present self known by consciousness, we declare them to be the same.   Kant certainly did not meet the scepticism of Hume in a wise or in an effective manner, when he supposed that the unity was given to the scattered phenomena by forms in the mind.

It is clear that all the usual psychological arguments for the immateriality and immortality of the soul are cut up and destroyed by this theory.   We cannot speak of the soul as either material or spiritual, for we know nothing either of matter or spirit except as momentary impressions.   " The identity which we ascribe to the mind of man is only a fictitious one." Identity is nothing really belonging to these different perceptions, but is merely a quality which we attribute to them because of the union of their ideas in the imagination, when we reflect upon them.

His theory of causation undermines the argument for the divine existence.   He carefully abstains from dwelling on this in his great philosophic work, but he expounds it at great length, and with all his intellectual power, in his " Dialogues on Natural Religion."   We know nothing of cause, except that it has been observed to be the antecedent of its effect; when we have noticed an occurrence usually preceded by another occurrence, we may on discovering the one look for the other.   But when we have never seen the events together, we have really nothing to guide us in arguing from the one to the other.   We can argue that a watch implies a watchmaker, for we have observed them together; but never having had any experience of the making of a world, we cannot argue that the existence of a world implies the existence of a world maker.   There is no effective way of answering this objection, but by maintaining that an effect necessarily implies a cause.   It was on this ground that he was met by Reid, who argues that traces of design in God's works argue an intelligent cause.   Kant deprived himself of the right to argue in this way, by making the mind itself impose the relation of causation on events, so that we cannot argue that there is a corresponding law in the things themselves. Hume urges with great force and ingenuity, as Kant did after him, that if we are compelled to seek for a cause of every object, we must also seek for a cause of the Divine Being. This is to be met by showing that our intuitive conviction simply requires us to seek for a cause of a new occurrence. He argues, as Kant also did after him, that the existence of order in the universe could at best prove merely a finite and not an infinite cause. The reply is, that we must seek for the evidence of the infinity of God in the peculiar conviction of the mind in regard to the infinite and the perfect.[1]

This may be the most expedient place for stating and examining his famous argument against miracles, as advanced in his essay on the subject. It is clear that he could not argue, as some have done, that a miracle is an impossibility, or that it is contrary to the nature of things. He assails not the possibility of the occurrence of a miraculous event, but the proof of it. Experience being with him the only criterion of truth, it is to experience he appeals. He maintains that there has been an invariable experience in favor of the uniformity of nature, and that a miracle being a violation of a law of nature, can never be established by as strong proof as what can be urged against it. He then exerts his ingenuity in disparaging the evidence usually urged in behalf of miraculous occurrences, by showing how apt mankind are to be swayed on these subjects by such principles as fear, wonder, and fancy. We are not

---

[1] Mr. Mill has adopted Hume's doctrine of causation with a few modifications. The question is : Has he left to himself or to his followers an argument for the divine existence ? He advises the defenders of theism to stick by the argument from design, but does not say that it has convinced himself. The advice is a sound one ; we should not give up the argument from design because of the objections of Kant, which derive their force from the errors of his philosophy. Mr. Mill says, that we can "find no difficulty in conceiving that in some one of the many firmaments into which sidereal astronomy now divides the universe, events may succeed one another at random, without any fixed law" ("Logic," b. iii. c. 21). I should like to see an attempt made to construct an argument for the divine existence by those who accept this view. Mr. Mill shows that our belief in the uniformity of nature is the result of experience. But the uniformity of nature is one thing and causation is a different thing. He should be met by showing that we have a necessary conviction that every thing that begins to be has a cause, and that he has utterly failed in deriving this conviction from sensations and associations.

sure whether Hume has always been opposed in a wise or judicious manner by his opponents on this subject. It is of little use showing that there is some sort of original instinct leading us to believe in testimony ; for this instinct, if it exists, often leads us astray, and we must still go to experience to indicate what we are to trust in and what we are to discard. But the opponents of Hume were perfectly right when they showed, that in maintaining that nature always acted according to certain mundane laws, he was assuming the point in dispute. Let us admit that the whole question is to be decided by experiential evidence. Let us concede that in the present advanced state of science there is ample evidence that there is a uniformity in nature ; but then let us place alongside of this a counterpart fact, that there is a sufficient body of evidence in favor of there being a supernatural system. For this purpose let the cumulative proofs in behalf of Christianity, external and internal, be adduced ; those derived from testimony and from prophecy, and those drawn from the unity of design in the revelation of doctrine and morality, and from the character of Jesus ; and we shall find that in their consistency and congruity they are not unlike those which can be advanced in behalf of the existence of a natural system.

In Book Second of his Treatise, Hume treats of the passions. It is the most uninteresting part of his writings. The reading of it is like travelling over an immense plain, which looks inviting at the distance, but in which we find no spots of fertility or of historical interest. It looks as if the good-humored but phlegmatic man were incapable of discussing the nature of the passions. The composition, though clear and sustained, is never elevated by bursts of feeling or irradiated by gleams of genius. He has a theory to support, and he defends it by wiredrawn ingenuity. When he treats of the understanding, if he does not establish much truth, he at least overthrows venerable error, and we are constrained to admire his intellectual energy and courage ; but, in dealing with the feelings of our nature, he wastes his strength in rearing a baseless fabric, which, so far as I know, no one has ever adopted, and no one has been at the trouble to assail. He has no proper analysis of man's original springs of action. He says only in a general way, that " the chief spring or actuating

principle of the human mind is pleasure and pain." He gives
no psychological account of the place which the idea or apprehension of an object as good or evil, or rather as appetible or
inappetible, has in all feeling. Of course, all passions are
according to him impressions, only he calls them reflective
impressions, to distinguish them from sensations. The reflective impressions are of two kinds, the calm and the violent;
the first including beauty and deformity, and the latter such
passions as love and hatred, grief and joy, pride and humility.
He connects his theory of the passions throughout with his
theory of the understanding. There are associations among
the passions, as there are associations among ideas ; only he
says, that while ideas are associated by resemblance, contiguity,
and causation, impressions are associated only by resemblance.
There has as yet been no thorough examination, so it appears
to me, of the laws of succession of feeling, as distinguished
from that of ideas ; I am not convinced that the theory of
Hume, that feelings are associated only by resemblance, is the
correct one. He draws a distinction between the cause and
the object of passion. Thus if a man has made a beautiful
house, the object of the passion is himself, and the cause is
the beautiful house. The idea of ourselves is always present
with, and conveys a sensible degree of vivacity to the idea of
any other object to which we are related ; in short, turns the
idea into an impression. Some other person is the object of
love, but the cause of that passion is the relation of that person to self. Out of this may proceed the desire of happiness
or misery of others, which he describes "*as an arbitrary and
original instinct implanted in our nature*," — I put the language in italics, as I may have occasion again to refer to it.
In this way he constructs an elaborate, but by no means clear,
theory of the passions. He divides them into direct and
indirect. By direct, he understands such as arise immediately
from good or evil, that is, from pain or pleasure. He says of
them : " The direct passions frequently arise from a natural
impulse or instinct, which is perfectly unaccountable. Of this
kind is the desire of punishment to our enemies and of happiness to our friends, hunger, lust, and a few other bodily appetites." Under the direct, he includes desire, aversion, grief,
joy, hope, fear, despair, and security. The indirect proceed

from the same principles, but by conjunction with other qualities; and he comprehends under them pride, humility, ambition,
vanity, love, hatred, envy, pity, malice, generosity, with their
dependents.   It may be said of his exposition of the passions
generally, that he has often seized on important circumstances
which modify their action, but has altogether failed in his
explanation of their nature.   Thus he has some just remarks
upon the transition of one idea to another, upon the effects
thus produced, and upon the predominant passion swallowing
up the inferior; but after all we have no proper evolution of
the psychological process.

He occasionally refers to beauty, but the account he gives of
it is very inadequate.   "Beauty is such an order and construction of parts, as either by the primary constitution of our nature, or by custom, or by caprice, is fitted to give a pleasure
and satisfaction to our souls."   "The conveniency of a house,
the fertility of a field, the strength of a horse, the capacity, security, and swift-sailing of a vessel, form the principal beauty
of these several objects."   It is clear that the æsthetic tastes
of one satisfied with such a theory could not have been keen,
and we do not wonder to find that in the letters written during
his travels, he never makes a single allusion to a fine statue or
painting.

The account which he gives of the will is still more defective.   "The will is the internal impression we feel and are
conscious of, when we knowingly give rise to any new motion
of our body."   Surely we may have will in regard to our mental operations as well as in regard to our bodily motions.   The
will, he says, is an impression, but surely it is an impression of
a very peculiar kind; and he should have inquired, which he
has not done, into its nature, when he would have seen that it
possesses an essential freedom.   As not perceiving this, he has
left nothing to save man from being driven on by an iron necessity.

In Book Third, he treats of morals, and starts his utilitarian
theory, which, however, he develops more fully, and in a livelier,
more pointed, and ornate manner, in his essay, "An Inquiry
concerning the Principles of Morals."   He says of this work,
that it is "of all my writings, historical, philosophical, or literary, incomparably the best."   In respect of practical influ-

ence, it has certainly been the most important. By his speculative doubts in regard to the operations of the understanding, he has furnished a gymnastic to metaphysicians ever since his time ; but by his theory of virtue he has swayed belief and practice.

He shows that we cannot distinguish between good and evil by reason alone, defining reason as the discovery of truth or falsehood, and truth and falsehood as consisting in the agreement or disagreement, either to the real relation of ideas, or to real existence and matter of fact. Taking reason in this sense, it certainly cannot be said to discern the morally good. But then it may be maintained that the mind has a power of discerning moral good and evil analogous to the reason which distinguishes truth and falsehood, and all that he could urge in opposition would be, that such a view is inconsistent with his theory of impressions and ideas. It is by no means clear what is the faculty or feeling to which he allots the function of perceiving and approving the morally good. Sometimes he seems to make man a selfish being, swayed only by motives of pleasure or pain ; and in this view virtue is to be regarded as good, because associated directly or indirectly with the pleasure it would bring to ourselves. But in other places he calls in a "benevolent sentiment, leading us to approve what is useful." Hume's general theory might certainly seem opposed to every thing *innate*, and yet, in criticising Locke, he is obliged to say: "I should desire to know what can be meant by asserting that self-love or resentment of injuries, or passion between the sexes, is not innate." We have already quoted passages in which he appeals to instincts. He says elsewhere, " The mind, by an *original* instinct, tends to unite itself with the good, and avoid the evil." At times he seems to adhere to the theory of Shaftesbury and Hutcheson, as to the existence of a moral sense. "The mind of man is so formed by nature, that upon the appearance of certain characters, dispositions, and actions, it immediately feels the sentiment of approbation or blame." He tells us expressly that he is inclined to think it probable that the final sentence in regard to moral excellence "depends on some internal sense or feeling which nature has made universal in the whole species." I believe that we cannot account for the ideas in the mind except by calling in such a faculty or feeling; and it was his business, as an experimental inquirer, to ascertain all that is in this power, and to determine its mode of operation and its laws. But such an investigation would have overthrown his whole theory, metaphysical as well as ethical.

According to Hume, virtue consists in the agreeable and useful. "Vice and virtue may be compared to sounds, colors, heat and cold, which, according to modern philosophy, are not qualities in objects, but perceptions in the mind." "Virtue is distinguished by the pleasure, and vice by the pain, that any action, sentiment, or character gives us by the mere view and contemplation." This theory goes a step farther than that of Hutcheson in the same direction. Hutcheson placed virtue in benevolence, thereby making the intention of the agent necessary to virtue; whereas Hume does not regard it as necessary that it should be voluntary, and requires us to look merely to the act and its tendency. His definition might lead one to think that an easy road or a pleasant carriage should be regarded as virtuous. But he will not admit that because an inanimate object may be useful as well as a man, that therefore it ought also to merit the appellation of virtuous; for he says: "The sentiments excited by utility are in the two cases very different, and the one is mixed with affection, esteem, approbation, and not the other." This language, more particularly the phrases "esteem" and "approbation," might have led him to discover that there is a peculiar judgment or sentiment attached to virtuous action not produced by mere utility.

He easily satisfies himself that he can show that benevolence is a virtue because it is so agreeable and useful; but he never faces the real difficulty, which is to account for the sense of obligation which we feel, and the obligation actually lying upon us, to do good to others.[1] He strives to show that justice is commended by us because of its beneficial tendency. Justice can have a meaning, he maintains, only in regard to society and arrangements made with others. True, the giving to every one his due, implies beings to whom the due is to be

---

[1] In his "Utilitarianism," Mr. Mill has endeavored to defend the theory from the objections commonly taken to it. But he has utterly failed in his attempt to derive our idea and conviction of moral good from mere sensations and associations of sensation.

given ; but the due arises from the relation in which we stand to these beings. Thus the first man and woman having children, had duties to discharge towards them as soon as they were born, and independent of any promise. He labors to prove that our obligation to keep a promise arises from utility. "Fidelity is no natural virtue, and promises have no force antecedent to human conventions." True, a promise implies a person to whom it is made, but, once made, the obligation is complete.

This leads us at once to the fundamental objections which may be taken to the utilitarian theory. Whence the obligation lying on us to promote the happiness of others ? to give others their due ? to keep our promises ? From their utility, it is answered. But why are we bound to attend to what is useful ? is the question that immediately occurs ; why the reproach that follows, and which justifies itself when we have failed to keep our word ? These questionings bring us to a justice which guards conventions, to a law which enjoins love.

The practical morality sanctioned by the system, and actually recommended by Hume, excludes all the higher virtues and loftier graces. The adoration of a Supreme Being, and love to him, are represented as superstition. He has no God to sanction the moral law, and no judgment day at which men have to give in an account. Repentance has and can have no place in a system which has no fixed law and no conscience. Humility, of which he treats at great length, is disparaged. The stern virtues of justice, of self-sacrifice, of zeal in a good cause, of faithfulness in denouncing evil, and of courage in stemming the tide of error and corruption, these are often so immediately disagreeable, that their ultimate utility will never be perceived except by those who are swayed by a higher principle. It is certain that they were not valued by Hume, who speaks of them as superstition and bigotry, and characterizes those who practise them as zealots and fanatics. His view of the marriage relation was of a loose and flexible character, and did not profess to discountenance the evil practices of his time. "A man in conjoining himself to a woman is bound to her according to the terms of his engagement : in begetting children, he is bound by all the ties of nature and humanity to provide for their sustenance and education. When he has performed these two parts of duty, no one can reproach him with injustice or injury." Not acknowledging a God bestowing the gift of life, and requiring us to give an account of the use we make of it, and setting no value on courage in difficulties, he argues that a man may take away his life when it is no longer useful.

The state of society which he aimed at producing is thus described : " But what philosophical truths can be more advantageous to society than those here delivered, which represent virtue in all her genuine and most engaging charms, and make us approach her with ease, familiarity, and affection ? The dismal dress falls off with which many divines, and some philosophers, have covered her, and nothing appears but gentleness, humanity, beneficence, affability ; nay, even at proper intervals play, frolic, and gayety. She talks not of useless austerities and rigors, suffering and self-denial." People have often speculated as to what Hume would have taught had he been elected professor of moral philosophy in Edinburgh. I believe he would have expounded a utilitarian theory, ending in the recommendation of the pleasant social virtues ; speaking always respectfully of the Divine Being, but leaving his existence an unsettled question.

And what, it may be asked, is the conclusion to which he wishes to bring us by his whole philosophy ? I am not sure that he has confessed this to himself. Sometimes it looks as if his sublime aim was to expose the unsatisfactory condition of philosophy, in order to impel thinkers to conduct their researches in a new and more satisfactory manner. " If, in order to answer the doubts started, new principles of philosophy must be laid, are not these doubts themselves very useful ? Are they not preferable to blind and ignorant assent ? I hope I can answer my own doubts ; but, if I could not, is it to be wondered at ? " I verily believe that this was one of the alternatives he loved to place before him to justify his scepticism. " I am apt," he says, in writing to Hutcheson, " to suspect in general that most of my reasonings will be more useful in furnishing hints, and exciting people's curiosity, than as containing any principles that will augment the stock of knowledge that must pass to future ages." But I suspect that the settled conviction reached by him was that no certainty could be attained in speculative philosophy ; he was sure that it had not been attained in time past. The tone of the introduction to his great work is : " There is nothing which is not the subject of debate, and in which men of learning are not of contrary opinions. If truth be at all within the reach of human capacity, it is certain it must be very deep and abstruse ; and to hope we shall arrive at it without pains, while the greatest geniuses have failed with the utmost pains, must certainly be esteemed sufficiently vain and presumptuous." As being thus deep, he feels as if the great body of mankind need not trouble themselves much about it. He seems at times complacently to contemplate this as the issue to which he would drive mankind ; for he sees at once that if men become convinced that they cannot reach certainty in such speculations, they will give up inquiry. "For nothing is more certain than that despair has almost the same effect upon us as enjoyment, and that we are no sooner acquainted with the impossibility of satisfying any desire than the desire itself vanishes ;" and he thinks it a satisfactory condition of things when men discover the impossibility of making any farther progress, and make a free confession of their ignorance. Considered in this light, Hume's philosophy, in its results, may be considered as an anticipation of the positive school of M. Comte, which in the British section of it approaches much nearer the position of Hume than most people are aware of.

He allows that man should, as indeed he must, follow his natural impulses, and the lessons of experience, as far as this world is concerned. But he will grant nothing more. He thus closes his inquiry into the understanding : " When we trace up the human understanding to its first principles, we find it to lead us into such sentiments as seem to turn into ridicule all our past pains and industry, and to discourage us from future inquiries." " The understanding, when it acts alone, and according to its general principles, entirely subverts itself, and leaves not the lowest degree of confidence in any proposition, either in philosophy or common life." In common life this scepticism meets with insuperable barriers, which we should not try to overcome. But it is different with philosophical, and, we may add, theological truths, which are supported solely by speculative considerations. In these departments we may discuss and doubt as we please, without doing any injury. "What injury can ever come from ingenious reasoning and inquiry ? The worst speculative sceptic I ever knew was a much better man than the best superstitious devotee." Those who think they can reach truth in these matters are at liberty to cherish their conviction, provided always that they do not thereby disturb their neighbors. But the time is coming, and already wise men see that it is coming, when mankind will not concern themselves with such speculative questions, or will engage in them only as a gymnastic to the intellect, or as a means of showing that ultimate truth is unattainable by man.

It was, I believe, on such grounds as these that Hume justified himself in his sceptical doubts, and his sceptical solution of these doubts. He thought they might stir up inquiry on subjects on which no truth had been reached ; and tend to confound the dogmatism and restrain the disputations in philosophy, and the fanaticism and superstition in religion, which had wrought such mischief ; and prepare the way for a reign of universal toleration. As to religious belief, it could be supported only by speculative arguments, derived from an absolute causation, or from miracles which cannot stand a searching investigation. So far as men follow a moderate and tolerant religion, Hume was rather pleased with them, and he evidently shrank from the fanatical atheism avowed by some of the more advanced followers of the system in France. If there be a world to come, it will clear up itself when it comes ; and, meanwhile, there are duties which we must perform, from a regard to ourselves and our relation to others. There had hitherto been no science of metaphysics ; but there could be a science of ethics (and also of politics) founded on the circumstance, that certain acts are found to be agreeable and useful to ourselves and others.

It is in this way we are to reconcile certain seeming inconsistencies in his character. He had no settled faith in any religion, yet he went to church, at least at times ; he wished his servant to go to church, and he mingled in the counsels of the Church of Scotland. He never committed himself to deism or atheism. He wrapped up his thoughts on these subjects in his bosom, perhaps with some feeble hope that he might get light ; but the cloud seems only to have settled more deeply upon him. When the pert Mrs. Mallet met him one night at an assembly, and boldly accosted him, " Mr. Hume, give me leave to introduce myself to you: we deists ought to know each other," " Madam," replied he, " I am no deist : I do not style myself so, neither do I desire to be known by that appellation." He did not avow himself an atheist in Paris. Sir Samuel Romilly has detailed a characteristic anecdote told of him by Diderot. He dined with a large company at the house of Baron D'Holbach. " As for atheists," said Hume, " I do not believe one exists : I have never seen one." " You have been a little unfortunate," said the baron : " here you are with seventeen of them at the table for the first time." We may suppose there was some sincerity in the statement he made : " I have surely endeavored to refute the sceptic with all the force of which I am master, and my refutation must be allowed to be sincere because drawn from the capital principles of my system," only he was not prepared to review his system. In writing to Elliott, he says he wishes to make Cleanthes, the theist, the hero of the dialogue. Adam Ferguson told his son, who reports the incident, that one clear and beautiful night, when they were walking home together, Hume suddenly stopped, looked up to the starry sky, and said, " O Adam, can any one contemplate the wonders of that firmament, and not believe there is a God ! " Dr. Carlyle tells us, that when his mother died he was found in deepest affliction and a flood of tears, upon which Mr. Boyle said to him that his uncommon grief arose from his having thrown off the principles of religion ; to which he replied : " Though I throw out my speculations to entertain the learned and metaphysical world, yet in other things I do not think so differently from the rest of the world as you imagine." In whatever way we may account for it, there was evidently a consistency in the character of Hume which made him respected by his worldly friends, who thought a man might be good, though he had no godliness.

The all-important question is, How is this spirit to be corrected, this error to be met ?

First. It must be firmly maintained that an honest mind can spontaneously attain such truth, secular, moral, and religious,

as is needful to its peace and progress.   This truth does not lie
deep down in some pit, which can be reached only by deep
digging, or whence it can be drawn only by the cords of lengthened ratiocination ; it lies on the surface, and may be seen by immediate perception, or picked up by brief discursive processes.
By this spontaneous exercise of our faculties and common
observation, we reach the existence of God, the accountability
of man, and a day of judgment.   By such an easy method we
rise to a belief in the Word of God, and in the spiritual verities
there set forth.   We should hold that man reaches all this by
as natural a procedure as that by which he comes to know
what path he should take in the common affairs of this life.
No doubt he will at times meet with difficulties, but this only
as he may be beset by perplexities in the affairs of this world ;
and in the one case, as in the other, the sincere mind has commonly enough of light to guide it.

Secondly. It should be held that he who undermines the
fundamental truth spontaneously discovered, is doing an injury
to humanity. Scepticism, as Hume delights to show, can
produce no mischief in the common secular affairs of life,
because there are circumstances which keep men right in
spite of their principles, or want of principles. But it is very
different in respect of those questions which fall to be discussed in higher ethics and theology. A man will not be
tempted by any sophistry to doubt the connection of cause and
effect when he is thirsty and sees a cup of water before him ;
in such a case he will put forth his hand and take it, knowing
that the beverage will refresh him. But he may be led by a
wretched sophistry to deny the necessary relation of cause and
effect when it would lead him upward from God's works to
God himself, or induce him to seek peace in Him. Hence the
importance of not allowing fundamental truth to be assailed ;
not because the attack will have any influence on the practical affairs of this life, but because it may hold back and
damp our higher aspirations, moral and religious. Hume
hoped that his scepticism might soften asperities, but he
did not wish to think that any bad influences could follow
from it. On one occasion he was told of a banker's clerk in
Edinburgh, of good reputation, who had eloped with a sum
of money ; and the philosopher wondered greatly what could

induce such a man thus to incur, for an inconsiderable sum, such an amount of guilt and infamy. "I can easily account for it," said John Home, "from the nature of his studies, and the kind of books he was in the habit of reading." "What were they," said the philosopher. He was greatly annoyed when told, Boston's "Fourfold State," and Hume's "Essays." Certainly the youth must have been in a perplexed state who had been converted from a belief in the "Fourfold State" by Hume's "Essays," or who was hesitating between them.

Thirdly. The philosopher must undertake a more important work. He must inquire into the nature of fundamental truth; he must endeavor to unfold the mental powers that discover it, and to expound their mode of operation, and their laws. He cannot indeed prove first truths by mediate evidence, for if they were capable of probation they could not be first truths; but he can show that they are first truths perceived by immediate cognition of the objects, and in no need of external support. He must as far as possible clear up the difficulties and perplexities in which the discussions in regard to them have become involved. In particular, he must show that while the reflex consideration of the ultimate principles of knowledge often lands us in difficulties, the principles themselves never lead us into positive contradictions; and that, therefore, while we allow that the human faculties are limited, we cannot admit that they are deceptive. This is what has been attempted by one philosopher after another since the days of Hume.

In fact, all later philosophy springs directly or indirectly from the thorough-going examination to which the Scotch sceptic had subjected received truths. It has been the aim of the Scottish school, as modified and developed by Reid, to throw back the scepticism of Hume. Reid tells us that he once believed the received doctrine of ideas so firmly as to embrace the whole of Berkeley's system along with it, till, on discovering the consequences to which it had been driven by Hume, he was led to review the whole theory and abandon it. Kant declares that he was roused from his dogmatic slumbers by the assaults of the Scottish sceptic, and was thus impelled to the task of repelling the attack. It is scarcely necessary to say that all other philosophies, deserving the name, which have originated within the last hundred years, have ramified directly or indirectly from the Scottish and the German schools; one school, the French school of M. Cousin, seeking to combine the two.

It is interesting to observe the respective ways in which the Scottish and the German metaphysician sought to meet the great sceptic. It is evident that his assaults might be repelled at one or other of two places : either where the foe has entered, or after he has made certain advances. That the mind begins with impressions and goes on to ideas, which are mere reproductions of impressions, — this is the fundamental principle of Hume. Now this may be denied, I think should be denied. On what ground, we ask, does he allow the existence of impressions and ideas? When he answers, we can show him that on the same ground he must admit more; that he must allow that the mind has convictions in regard to its own existence, and the existence of external objects, and perceptions of moral goodness. But again, he may be met at the farther stages of his progress. He asserts that the mind can reach no truth except such as it gets from experience. It may be shown in opposition that it has an original furniture in the shape of tendencies and laws which lead to and guarantee necessary and eternal truth.

It is interesting to observe that Reid met him at both these points. Reid made a very careful inquiry into the nature of the senses as inlets of knowledge ; and showed that accompanying the sensation there is always an intuitive perception of an external world. He showed too, though he did not make so much of it as he might, that consciousness is a mental faculty and a source of knowledge. He farther met the sceptic at the more advanced point, and proved that the mind has a primitive reason or common-sense which decides at once that things are so and so ; that every effect, for instance, must have a cause. I am not of opinion that Reid has thoroughly cleared up these subjects, that he has detected all that is in the senses, that he has unfolded fully the laws of intuition and its mode of operation ; but he has established enough to repel the assaults of the sceptic.

Reid possessed many of the best qualities of his countrymen ; in particular, he was shrewd and independent : but he was not

endowed with great powers of logical analysis. On the other
hand, Kant was strong where Reid was weak ; that is, in power
of dissection and construction : but was deficient where Reid
excelled, in patient observation. He neglected, as I think
most unfortunately, to oppose the fundamental principle of
Hume. He allows that the mind begins with *phenomena* in
the sense of appearances, and these phenomena are just the
impressions of Hume. But if it be allowed that in the original
inlet we have only impressions or phenomena, it never can be
satisfactorily shown how we can reach reality by any composition or decomposition of these. Kant exercised his vast
powers in meeting Hume at the other point ; that is, in showing that there is an *a priori* furniture in the mind, independent
of all experience. But what he built with the one hand he
took down with the other. For these *a priori* forms could not,
in his theory, guarantee any objective reality. He accepts
the conclusion of Hume, and allows that the speculative reason could not guide to truth ; he goes so far as to maintain
that it lands us in contradictions. This philosophy, intended
to overthrow the scepticism of Hume, has thus led to a scepticism which has had a more extensive sway than that of the
cold Scotchman ever had. He endeavored to save himself
from such an issue by calling in a practical reason, which
guaranteed as its corollaries the freedom and immortality of
the soul, and the Divine existence. But it was immediately
asked how it could be shown that the practical reason does
not deceive, after it has been conceded that the speculative
reason leads to illusion? Thus the insecure mound, raised
with such labor to stem the flood, only aggravated the outburst
and overflow as it gave way.

Sir W. Hamilton sought to unite Reid and Kant, but was
never able to weld thoroughly together the principles which
he took from two such different sources. His doctrines of
the relativity of knowledge, and of causation as a mere impotency of the mind, have prepared the way for a doctrine
of nescience now largely espoused. Some of his pupils have
betaken themselves to a sort of confused Berkeleyanism mingled with Kantism, which will furnish an easy passage to the
nescient theory in so shrewd a nation as Scotland, and among
so practical a people as the English. Mr. Mill, in his examina-

tion of Hamilton's Philosophy, has brought us to a *Humism* joined to Comtism.   This is the dismal creed provided for those who choose to follow the negative criticisms of the day in philosophy and theology.   What we need in these circumstances is a new Thomas Reid, not to do over again the work which the common-sense philosopher did, but a corresponding service in this age to what he did in his time.

XX.—*BOOKS ADVERTISED IN "SCOT'S MAGAZINE."*

THE "SCOT'S MAGAZINE" begins in 1739. The works mentioned and the topics discussed will give us a better idea of the times, than any thing else that can be produced. In January is advertised " A Treatise of Human Nature," the work that revolutionized all modern philosophy. For years, we have papers about Whitefield, who revolutionized religion in England, and had a mighty influence in Scotland and America. The magazine has a series of papers, lasting for years, under the head of "Common Sense." In March, there is an advertisement of a "Second Volume of Common-Sense Letters collected," showing that we have no need to go to remote quarters to find the source from which Reid and the Aberdeen school got the phrase, "common sense," which had been in constant use since the time of Shaftesbury (p. 31). It is curious to notice that, in January, comedians are prosecuted before the Court of Session, and, in February, are found guilty, and "decerned for the penalties in the late Act against strollers."   In March, there is an advertisement, "A View of the Necessitarian or Best Scheme, freed from the Objections of M. Crouzaz in his Examinations of Pope's 'Essay on Man.'"   In June, "The Necessity of Revelation," by Archibald Campbell, pp. 45. 3*d*. in sheets, showing that revelation needed to be defended. In October, an attack on Campbell's book, and, in December, a reply by Campbell. In October, "A Treatise of Ancient Painting," by Dr. Turnbull, 4*l*. 4*s*. in sheets. In February, 1740, "The Principles of Moral Philosophy;" in December, "A Methodical System of Universal Law;" and, in May, "A Curious Collection of fifty Ancient Paintings," 1*l*. 8*s*., all by Turnbull, showing that there was a taste in the country for ethical and æsthetic discussions, — the failure of Turnbull's works proving that it was not to be gratified by the excellent commonplace of that author. In 1740, Simson, whose views in regard to the Trinity raised such discussion, passes away from this world, after having lived in retirement since his suspension in 1728. In May, we have "The Principles and Connection of Natural and Revealed Religion," by A. Ashley Sykes; and "The Divine Authority of the Old and New Testament asserted," by J. Leland, D.D., 25*s*.; and, in July, "Discourses concerning the Being and Natural Perfections of God," by J. Abernethy, M.A., 5*s*. 6*d*.; all showing that there were men ready to defend natural and revealed religion on sound, sensible principles.   That deism is alive, appears from May, when " Physico, Theologico, Philosophico, Moral Disquisition concerning Human Nature, Free Agency, Moral Government, and Divine Providence," by T. Morgan, M.D., 5*s*. 6*d*., appears.   In June, " Remarks on the Inquiry into the Nature of the Human Soul," 1*s*.   In December, among preferments, Adam Smith, Comptroller of the Customs at Kirkcaldy, Inspector-General of the Customs ; showing that a competent man was being prepared to discuss political economy.   In April, 1741, " The Temper, Character, and Duty of a Minister of the Gospel," a sermon by William Leechman, M.A., 6*d*. ; indicating the introduction of Moderatism into the Church of Scotland in its most plausible form, denying no orthodox doctrine, and yet recommending, in graceful language, only the truths of natural religion, and the common moralities of life, — an evidence that the attacks of deistical writers had made many ashamed of the deeper doctrines of Scripture.   In January, 1744, there is an abstract of the associate presbytery for renewing the Covenants, dated at Stirling, Dec. 23, 1743, "complaining of several immoralities, and the repealing of the penal statutes against witches.   The penal statutes against witches have been repealed by the parliament, contrary to the express law of God : by which a holy God may be provoked in a way of righteous judgment, to leave those who are already ensnared to be hardened more and more, and to permit Satan to tempt and seduce others to the same wicked and dangerous snares."   The above list shows clearly an age of great intellectual activity, a strong tendency to philosophical discussion among Scotchmen, a vigorous attack on Christianity, a respectable defence of it and of natural religion, a revival of evangelical religion under Whitefield, and a strong love of it on the part of the common people, along with the appearance of intemperance and strolling players.   It was in the midst of this ferment that Hume's work appeared, to shake all that was thought to be established in philosophy and in natural religion.

XXI. — *ADAM SMITH.*[1]

His is perhaps the most illustrious name appearing in these sketches.   But he has a higher reputation in political economy than in metaphysics, in which latter department he comes before us as the author of a theory of moral sentiments, and of very interesting fragmentary histories of certain departments of philosophy.

[1] "Account of the Life and Writings of Adam Smith," by Dugald Stewart ; "Life and Writings of Adam Smith," anonymous, but understood to be by J. R. M'Culloch ; " Literary and Characteristical Lives," by William Smellie, &c.

He was born June 5, 1723, in the "lang toun" of Kirkcaldy, which lies on the opposite side of the Frith of Forth from Edinburgh. His father was comptroller of the customs there; and his mother, a benignant Christian lady, watched over his sickly childhood with tenderness, which he repaid her by a corresponding kindness for the long period of sixty years, for the greater part of which the two lived together. When about three years old he was stolen by a party of tinkers, who took him to the woods, but was fortunately rescued. We should have liked to hear him, in his later years, speculating as to what might have been his place in the gypsy camp had he been brought up among them. We can conceive that, while fashioning spoons out of horns and mending tin dishes, his comprehensive head would have been spinning a theory of the organization of the tribe. But it would have been beyond the capacity even of the explorer of the nature and causes of national wealth to determine what he himself or any other might have become if trained in such different circumstances. He seems to have received an excellent education in his native place, at a school which reared a number of eminent men. Unable from his weak bodily constitution to join in active amusements, he gave himself to reading, and, even at that early age, was noted for speaking to himself when alone, and falling into absent fits in company. At the premature age of fourteen, he went to the University of Glasgow, where his favorite studies seem to have been mathematics and natural philosophy. But before he left he attended the lectures of Hutcheson, whom he greatly admired, and who, no doubt, helped to direct him to philosophic pursuits. From Glasgow he went, on a salary provided by the Snell Foundation, to Baliol College, Oxford, where he resided for seven years, and seems to have given himself specially to the studies of polite literature. " He employed himself frequently in the practice of translation (particularly from the French), with a view to the improvement of his own style." Every one knows that the French authors were the models to which the greater part of the Scottish writers looked at that time. Hume and Smith entertained a feeling of admiration for French prose and poetry, but had no appreciation (as Adam Ferguson remarked) of Shakespeare or Milton.

His original destination had been to the Church of England, but he did not find the profession to suit him. When at Oxford, the heads of the college found him reading Hume's "Treatise of Human Nature," and they seized the work, and reprimanded the youth. ("Life," by M'Culloch.) On leaving Oxford he spent two years at Kirkcaldy, uncertain as to what he might do. In 1748 he removed to Edinburgh, where he delivered lectures on rhetoric and belles-lettres ; the commencement, I believe, of that instruction in polite literature and English composition which has ever since been a distinguishing feature of the collegiate education in Scotland. In 1751 he was elected professor of logic, and in 1752 professor of moral philosophy, in the University of Glasgow. In the former, after an exposition, apparently brief (as we might expect from the spirit of the times), of the ancient logic, he devoted the rest of his time to rhetoric and belles-lettres. In the latter he divided his course into four parts : 1. Natural theology ; 2. Ethics, unfolding the views he afterwards published in his "Theory of Moral Sentiments ; " 3. Justice, that part of morality which can be expressed in precise rules ; 4. Political science in which he delivered the thoughts and observations which were afterwards embodied in his great work, "The Wealth of Nations." In the later years of his Glasgow life, he expanded this last part more and more. An eminent pupil, Dr. Millar, afterwards professor of law in the university, describes him as a lecturer. "In delivering his lectures, he trusted almost entirely to extemporary elocution. His manner, though not graceful, was plain and unaffected ; and, as he seemed to be always interested in the subject, he never failed to interest his hearers. Each discourse consisted commonly of several distinct propositions, which he successively endeavored to prove and illustrate. These propositions, when announced in general terms, had, from their extent, not unfrequently something of the air of a paradox. In his attempts to explain them, he often appeared at first not to be sufficiently possessed of the subject, and spoke with some hesitation. As he advanced, however, the matter seemed to crowd upon him : his manner became warm and animated, and his expression easy and fluent. In points susceptible of controversy, you could easily discover that he secretly conceived an opposition to his opinions, and that he was led upon this account to support them with greater energy and vehemence. By the fulness and variety of his illustrations, the subject gradually swelled in his hands, and acquired a dimension which, without a tedious repetition of the same views, was calculated to seize the attention of his audience, and to afford them pleasure, as well as instruction, in following the same object through all the diversity of shades and aspects in which it was presented, and afterwards in tracing it backwards to that original proposition or general truth from which this beautiful train of speculation had proceeded."

The thirteen years he spent in this office, he looked back upon as the happiest in his life. He published, in 1759, his "Theory of Moral Sentiments," to which was appended an article on Johnson's Dictionary for the then "Edinburgh Review." While in Glasgow he collected a large body of the observations and facts which he afterwards embodied in his immortal work. He was stimulated and aided in these studies by his attending a weekly club founded by Provost Cochran, a Glasgow merchant, who furnished him with much valuable information on mercantile subjects.

In 1763 he gave up his chair in Glasgow, and, at the invitation of Mr. Charles Townsend, became travelling tutor to the young Duke of Buccleuch. One wonders, in these times, at so intellectual a man abandoning the influential position he held in Glasgow to become the teacher of a single youth, however eminent in station. But it was undoubtedly a great advantage to Smith that he was thus enabled to see more of mankind and of the world, and was brought into immediate contact with eminent men of kindred tastes and pursuits in France. Proceeding to France in the spring of 1764, he and his pupil spent eighteen months at Toulouse, and lived on terms of intimacy with some of the principal members of their parliament, and is supposed to have gathered there further materials for his great projected work. On leaving this place, he took an extensive tour in the south of France ; spent two months at Geneva ; and then went to Paris, and, having recommendations from Hume, he enjoyed the society of such men as Turgot, Quesnay, Morellet, Necker, D'Alembert, Helvetius, Marmontel, and Madame Riccoboni. He is supposed to have derived special benefit from his intercourse with Turgot and Ques-

nay, who were engaged in political studies similar to his own.
In October, 1766, he returned to Great Britain, and spent the
next ten years with the mother whom he so much loved, in Kirkcaldy.   There are traditions of David Hume visiting him there
from time to time, and of their holding earnest conversations
on questions of political economy, and, it is supposed, of religion, as they walked on the sands of the Frith of Forth.   From
this retreat issued, in 1776, his "Inquiry into the Nature and
Causes of the Wealth of Nations," — the work which made
political economy a science.

In 1778 he was appointed, at the request of the Duke of
Buccleuch, one of the commissioners of his majesty's customs
in Scotland, and removed to Edinburgh, taking his mother
with him : it is scarcely necessary to mention that he continued all his life a bachelor.   Here he spent the last twelve
years of his life.   Henceforth he became an object of curiosity
to all people of literary culture ; and his person was scrutinized,
as he walked the streets, by the curious, and his peculiar habits
reported.   Many a youth, studying in Edinburgh, was proud to
relate in after years that he had seen him, — a fine gentleman of
the old school, a little above the ordinary size, with a manly countenance lighted by large gray eyes, wearing a cap, a long, wide
great-coat, breeches, and shoebuckles ; and they remarked that,
when " he walked, his head had a gentle motion from side
to side, and his body, at every step, a rolling or vermicular
motion, as if he meant to alter his direction, or even turn back.
In the street, or elsewhere, he always carried his cane on his
shoulder, as a soldier does his musket." (" Lives," by Smellie.)
Dr. Carlyle gives a graphic picture of his manner in company.   "Adam Smith was far superior to Hume in conversa-
tional talents.   In that of public speaking they were equal.
David never tried it ; and I never heard Adam but once, which
was at the first meeting of the Select Society, when he
opened up the design of the meeting.   His voice was harsh,
and enunciation thick, approaching to stammering.   His conversation was not colloquial, but like lecturing, in which, I
have been told, he was not deficient, especially when he grew
warm.   He was the most absent man in company that I ever saw ;
moving his lips, and talking with himself, and smiling, in the
midst of large companies.   If you awaked him from his rev-

erie and made him attend to the subject of conversation, he immediately began to harangue, and never stopped till he told you all he knew about it, with the utmost philosophical ingenuity. He knew nothing of characters, and yet was ready to draw them on the slightest invitation. But when you checked him, or doubted, he retracted with the utmost ease, and contradicted all he had been saying." Carlyle tells us that "David Hume, like Smith, had no discernment at all of character."

Dugald Stewart mentions it as an interesting circumstance that all Hume's works were written with his own hands, whereas Smith dictated to a secretary as he walked up and down his apartment, and hints that we may perceive, in the different styles of these two classical writers, the effects of these different modes of study: as he wrote with his own pen, Hume gave a greater terseness and compactness to his style, whereas Smith, in dictating to an amanuensis, kept himself more in sympathy with his reader, and was more disposed, like a speaker, to flow and fluency. It may have been from the same circumstance that Hume wrote with great rapidity, whereas Smith composed as slowly, and with as great difficulty, at last as at first.

In Edinburgh, his studies were much interrupted by his official duties, and often — as he mentions in a letter written on his being elected by the students lord rector of his old University — did he cast a longing eye back upon the academic leisure he enjoyed in Glasgow. Like most men of high aims, he regretted, when he saw death approaching, that he had done so little. " I meant to have done more, and there are materials in my papers of which I could have made a great deal. But that is now out of the question." Shortly before his death, he gave orders to destroy all his manuscripts, which were supposed to contain his lectures on rhetoric, on natural religion, and on jurisprudence. He died in July, 1790.

Let us turn to his philosophy. His mind was essentially a reflecting one, a self-revolving one. He was always thinking, and talking to himself, gathering facts, forming theories, and seeking out events to confirm them ; thus building up a system which was always ingenious, sometimes too ingenious, but

ever worthy of being weighed. His "Theory of Moral Sentiments" has commonly been a favorite with students, because
of the eloquence of its language, modelled after the best philosophic writers of ancient Rome and modern France, and of
the fertility of his resources in confirming his positions from
his varied observation and reading. But his theory has gained
the assent of few, and has often been prescribed by professors
as a subject on which to exercise the critical acumen of their
pupils. Adam Smith is always a discursive writer, and in the
work now before us he wanders like a river amidst luxuriant
banks, and it is not easy to define his course. Dugald Stewart
in his "Memoir" has given the clearest account of it I have
seen ; and I mean to make free use of what he has written, in
the shorter abstract which I submit.

According to the common moral theories, men first judge
of their own actions, and then those of their neighbors. Smith
reverses this, and maintains that the primary objects of our
moral perceptions are the actions of other men. We put ourselves in their position, and partake with them in their affections by what he calls *sympathy* or fellow-feeling, which is the
grand principle of his system. We thus judge of their conduct, and then apply to ourselves the decisions which we have
passed on our neighbors, and which we may conceive they
would pronounce on us. Our moral judgments, both with respect to others and ourselves, include two perceptions : first,
of conduct as right or wrong ; and, secondly, of the merit or
demerit of the agent. When the spectator of another man's
situation, upon bringing home to himself all its various circumstances, feels himself affected in the same manner with the
person principally concerned, he approves of the affection or
passion of this person as just, proper, and suitable to its object.
We judge of the propriety of the affection of another only by
its coincidence with that which we feel when we put ourselves
in the same circumstances, and the perception of this coincidence is the foundation of the perception of moral obligation.
Now this is a very circuitous way of gendering our moral ideas
and judgments. Whether we look to ourselves or others, the
mind pronounces a judgment upon the act, — say a deed of
benevolence or cruelty, — and must do so according to some law
which is the true basis of morality. We are more likely to

pronounce first upon ourselves. But it may be acknowledged that it does help us in forming a correct judgment, to put ourselves in the position of others, and inquire how they would view us ; and hence the important rule : " Whatsoever ye would that men should do unto you, do ye even so unto them." This is the element of truth in Smith's theory. In illustrating his views, he is particularly happy in showing how circumstances affect our moral judgments ; that, for example, when there is no envy in the case, our sympathy with joy is much stronger than our sympathy with sorrow, and that in consequence it is more easy to obtain the approbation of mankind in prosperity than in adversity. From the same principle he traces the origin of ambition, or of the desire of rank and pre-eminence ; the great object of which passion is to attain that situation which sets a man most in view of general sympathy and attention, and gives an easy empire over the affections of others.

Having thus shown how we come to a sense of propriety (as he calls moral excellence), he proceeds to analyze our sense of merit and demerit, which have always a respect to the effect which the affection tends to produce. The only actions which appear to us deserving of reward are actions of a beneficial tendency, proceeding from proper motives, with which we can sympathize; the only actions which seem to us to deserve punishment are actions of a hurtful tendency, proceeding from improper motives. He accounts for our sense of justice by the circumstance that, if I wish to secure the sympathy and approbation of my fellow-men, — represented by Smith as the strongest desire of our natures, — it is necessary for me to regard my happiness not in that light in which it appears to myself, but that in which it appears to mankind in general, — as if in all justice there was not an inflexible rule for judging of the conduct both of ourselves and others.

He then shows how our sense of duty comes to be formed in consequence of an application to ourselves of the judgments we have previously passed on others. In doing this we lay down rules of morality which become universally applicable. He allows to Hume that every thing approved of by the mind is useful and agreeable ; but he insists that it is not the view of this utility which is either the first or principal source of moral approbation.

Most people have felt that this theory is too artificial, — is too ingenious to be true. It contains some elements of truth, but they are not put in their proper place ; and the fabric is left without a sure foundation, — virtue has no other foundation than the sympathy and approbation of men. The beauty of the building lies not in the structure as a whole, but in portions, often subordinate portions of it. His illustrations are abundant, and always felicitous ; and many of them show a very nice and delicate perception of the peculiarities of human nature. We see this very specially in his chapter " Of the Influence of Custom and Fashion upon our Notions of Beauty and Deformity," — perhaps the most valuable part of his work, as being that in which he sketches the various moral systems, such as those of the Stoics and Epicureans. Here he shows erudition, and enters thoroughly into the spirit of the authors and their times. The work will continue to be read for its style and these adjuncts, by persons who set no value on the theory which he expounds.

Smith intended to write a connected history of the liberal sciences and elegant arts, but found the plan far too extensive. He has left us only a few fragments, which were published posthumously by Joseph Black and James Hutton. In these he discusses, always ingeniously, such topics as the nature of the imitation which takes place in what are called the imitative arts ; the affinity between music, dancing, and poetry ; the affinity between English and Italian verses. But the most valuable of these papers, are three on the principles which lead and direct philosophical inquiries, illustrated by the history of astronomy, of ancient physics, of ancient logic and metaphysics, and one on the external senses.

The three philosophico-historical essays exhibit all the peculiarities of his mind : they are theoretical, they inquire into causes, and display an enlarged acquaintance with the sciences. He begins with showing that wonder called forth by the new and singular, surprise excited by what is unexpected, and admiration raised by what is great and beautiful, these — and not any expectation of advantage, or the love of truth for its own sake — are the principles which prompt mankind to try to discover the concealed connections that unite the various appearances of nature, which give rise to the study of philosophy, which is defined as the science of the connecting principles of nature. " Nature, after the largest expenditure that common observation can acquire, seems to abound with events which appear solitary and incoherent with all that go before them, which therefore disturb the easy movement of the imagination ; and philosophy aims at discovering the invisible chains which bind together all the disjointed objects. Hence, in astronomy, the invention of eccentric spheres, of epicycles, and of the revolution of the centres of the eccentric spheres ; in physics, the four elements ; and in metaphysics and logic, species, essence, and ideas, — all these give the imagination something to rest on." These motives have no doubt helped to create a taste for science, and often given it a particular direction ; but many other causes have been in operation. It appears to me that, had Smith been able to devote as much time to a history of philosophy as he did to the " Wealth of Nations," and been in circumstances to review his theories from time to time, he might have written a better work than any produced in that century. No doubt he would at times have added a thought of his own to the account given of a philosophic opinion ; but, following out his favorite principle of sympathy, he would always have put himself *en rapport* with the authors and their times.

His paper "Of the External Senses" is characterized by much sound sense and a profound study of the subject. He goes over the senses one by one. He has a glimpse of the important distinction — afterwards carefully elaborated by Sir William Hamilton, and Müller the physiologist — between the perception of the organ and of objects beyond the body. Tasting, smelling, hearing, and certain sensations of touch, are altogether in the organ, and nowhere else but in the organ. But in regard to touching, " the thing which presses and resists I feel as something altogether different from these affections, — as external to my hand, and as altogether independent of it." He represents the objects of touch as solidity, and those modifications of solidity which we consider as essential to it and inseparable from it, — solid extension, figure, divisibility, and mobility." He defines the impenetrability of matter as " the absolute impossibility that two solid, resisting substances should occupy the same place at the same time." He ex-

pounds a doctrine in regard to the so-called secondary qualities of matter; " or, to speak more properly, these four classes,
of sensations: heat and cold, taste, smell, and sound being felt
not as resisting or pressing on the organ, but as in the organ."
He says that they "are not naturally perceived as external and
independent substances, but as mere affections of the organ,
and what can exist nowhere but in the organ." This is perhaps a more philosophical account than that given by Locke,
Reid, or Hamilton, who proceed on the distinction drawn
between the primary and secondary qualities of matter. In
regard to sight, he says the objects of it are color, and those
modifications of color which in the same manner we consider as essential to it and inseparable from it, — colored extension, figure, divisibility, and mobility." The tangible world
has three dimensions, — length, breadth, and depth; the visible
world, only two, — length and breadth. He recognizes Berkeley's theory of vision as "one of the finest examples of philosophical analysis that is to be found either in our own or in any
other language;" and he quotes the Chiselden case. He notices
the fact that, antecedent to all experience, the young of at
least the greater part of animals possess some instinctive
perception of distance. "The young partridge, almost as soon
as it comes from the shell, runs about among the long grass
and corn." He is inclined to think that the young of the
human race may have some instinctive perception of the same
kind, which does not come forth or manifest itself so strongly
as in the lower animals, because mankind have greater aids
from intelligence and education. He thinks that other senses,
"antecedently to all observation and experience, may obscurely
suggest a vague notion of some external thing which excites
it. The smell not only excites the appetite, but directs to the
object which can alone gratify that appetite. But, by suggesting the direction towards that object, the smell must necessarily
give some notion of distance and externality, which are necessarily involved in the idea of direction." These hints are worthy of being carried out: they will certainly not be despised by
those who in our day are studying hereditary instinct.

It does not consist with our purpose to give an account of
his labors in political economy. I may remark, however, that
in his work, and in every other, there is an omitted chapter,

which will require to be written by some one before the science is completed. In speaking of soil, labor, money, rent, and other external agents, there is no searching estimate of the internal motives which impel men to the acquisition and distribution of wealth. Some writers, such as James Mill, represent all men as swayed only by self-love ; others dwell fondly on such principles as a taste for literature or the fine arts : but there has been no discriminating computation of the springs of action, general and special, which lead men to make acquisitions, and which have produced different results in different ages and nations ; for instance, to one form of civilization in Italy or in France, to others in Germany or in Scotland. Smith might have been tempted to set too high a value on certain influences which were favorites with him, but he was eminently fitted to begin the undertaking ; and had he done so, he would have left us admirable illustrations of the power of motives actually swaying mankind.

XXII. — *HENRY HOME (LORD KAMES)*.[1]

HE was the son of George Home, of Kames, a country gentleman of small fortune, in Berwickshire, married to a granddaughter of Principal Baillie. He was born in 1696, and was educated at home, under a private tutor. It was in after life that he devoted himself to the study of Greek and Latin, to which he added mathematics, natural philosophy, logic, ethics, and metaphysics. He was never at any university. He showed an early taste for philosophical speculation. It seems that he came in contact with Andrew Baxter, who was tutor to a son of Mr. Hay, of Drumelzier, and lived at that time at Dunse Castle, within a few miles of Kames, and the two had a correspondence ; Home arguing that motion was not a single effect, but a continued succession of effects, each requiring a new or a successive repetition of the cause to produce it. Like so many others in the same age, he had a thrust at Clarke's "Demonstra-

[1] "Memoirs of the Life and Writings of the Hon. Henry Home, of Kames," by Alex. Fraser Tytler, Lord Woodhouselee, 2 vols., 1807.

tion of the Existence of God," and wrote, in 1723, a letter to the doctor. Already he is drawing up arguments against liberty of will. Having chosen the law as his profession, he was called to the bar 1723-24. As a pleader he began with a very short and distinct statement of the facts of the cause and a plain enunciation of the question of law thence arising, abandoning all the weaker points of the case. He excelled more in making an opening statement than in reply. We have a picture of his habits. He rose at five or six, and spent his morning in preparation for the business of the court. In the forenoon he was at the Court of Session, which, at that time, rose soon after mid-day. He did not go much out to dinner, as he needed all his time for business and study. In the evening, if he had leisure, he joined the ladies in the drawing-room, or took part in a game of cards, or might be seen at the concert or the assembly room. "The evening was generally closed by a small domestic party, where a few of his intimate friends assembled, for the most part without invitation ; found a plain but elegant little supper ; and where, enlivened often by some of Mrs. Home's female acquaintance, the hours were passed in the most rational enjoyment of sensible and spirited conversation, and easy social mirth, till after midnight."

Throughout his life he published various works on law and jurisprudence ; beginning, in 1728, with a folio volume of " Remarkable Decisions of the Court of Session " from 1716 down to that period. In 1752 he was appointed a judge of the Court of Session, by the title of Lord Kames.

But his tastes ever led him towards metaphysical speculation From 1727 he had been acquainted with David Hume, and he carefully studied his writings as they were published. It seems he had dissuaded the sceptic from publishing his " Philosophical Essays," and he felt himself called to oppose what he believed to be the extreme views there propounded. This gave rise, in 1751, to a work which produced a great noise in his own day, " Essays on the Principles of Morality and Natural Religion." It was published under the name of " Sopho." He shows that man is influenced by a great number and variety of principles, such as self-love, benevolence, sympathy, and utility, consonance to the divine will ; and that his actions are most frequently the combined result of the op-

posite springs, tempering and restraining each other's powers.
He shows that man has, as a separate principle, in his nature and constitution, a moral feeling or conscience, the function of which is to judge with unerring rectitude of all his
motives to action, and direct his conduct to one great and
beautiful end, — the utmost happiness of his nature.   In expounding these views, he examines Hume's theory, and shows
that it annihilates all real distinction between right and wrong
in human actions, and makes our preference of one or other
depend on the fluctuating opinions of men in respect to the
general good.   In particular, he opposes Hume's view of justice,
and shows that the idea of property is coeval with society, and
that its violation is universally attended with a feeling of a
breach of duty, which is the sentiment of justice.   He sets
himself specially to oppose Hume's attempt to undermine the
arguments in behalf of the Divine Existence.

In developing his moral and esthetic views, in this and in
other works, he enunciates his metaphysical principles.   He
maintains that man can acquire intuitive knowledge from a single
act of perception.   " It is an undoubted truth that man has an
original feeling or consciousness of himself and of his existence."   He maintains (" History of Man,") that there is a
sense ·by which we perceive the truth of many propositions :
such as that every thing which begins to exist must have a
cause ; that every effect adapted to some end or purpose proceeds from a designing cause ; and that every effect adapted to
a good end or purpose proceeds from a designing and benevolent
cause.   A multitude of axioms in every science, particularly
in mathematics, are equally perceived to be true.   By a peculiar sense we know that there is a Deity.   From all this it is
evident that he stood up for intuitive principles.

There must surely be truth in the account he gives of
power ; so different from that of Locke on the one hand, and
that of the high *a priori* philosophers on the other.   " Every
action we perceive gives a notion of power ; for a productive
cause is implied in every action or event, and the very idea
of a cause comprehends the power of producing its effects.
Let us only reflect on the perception we have when we see a
stone thrown into the air out of one's hand."   "As I discover
power in external objects by the eye, so I discover power in

my mind by an internal sense." " This feeling is involved in the very perception of the action, without taking in either reason or experience." " We cannot discover power in any object as we discover the object itself, merely by intuition ; but the moment an alteration is produced by any object, we perceive that the object has a power to produce that alteration, which leads us to denominate the one a cause and the other an effect." It is generally acknowledged that we know objects within and without us only by their properties ; but what are properties but powers, which must thus be known intuitively with the objects that possess them.

But the doctrine which startled the public was that of philosophical necessity, as expounded and defended by him. It is a circumstance worthy of being noted that this doctrine was upheld by three men, who arose about the same period and in much the same district of country, — David Dudgeon, David Hume, and Henry Home ; it looks as if it were the residuum left by the doctrine of predestination, when the flowing waters of the stream have been dried up by an arid period. " With respect to instinctive actions, no person, I presume, thinks that there is any freedom ; an infant applies to the nipple, and a bird builds a nest, no less necessarily than a stone falls to the ground. With respect to voluntary actions done in order to produce some effect, the necessity is the same, though less apparent at first view. The external action is determined by the will ; the will is determined by desire ; and desire, by what is agreeable or disagreeable. Here is a chain of causes and effects, not one link of which is arbitrary, or under command of the agent. He cannot will but according to his desire ; he cannot desire but according to what is agreeable or disagreeable in the objects perceived. Nor do these qualities depend on the inclination or fancy : he has no power to make a beautiful woman appear ugly, nor to make a rotten carcase smell sweetly." " Thus, with regard to human conduct, there is a chain of laws established by nature, no one link of which is left arbitrary. By that wise system man is made accountable ; by it he is made a fit subject for divine and human government ; by it persons of sagacity foresee the conduct of others ; and by it the presence of the Deity with respect to human actions is clearly established." He founds the responsibility of man upon this very doctrine.

"The final cause of this branch of our nature is admirable. If the necessary influence of motives had the effect either to lessen the merit of a virtuous action, or the demerit of a crime, morality would be totally unhinged." In regard to liberty, man acts with the conviction of his being a free agent, and is quite as much accountable as if he were truly free. The answer to all this is, that man has an intuition in regard to his possessing freedom quite as deep and ineradicable as his intuition about cause and effect. If we attend to the latter of these, and adhere to it, as Home does, we should equally hold by the other.

The friends of religion, unenlightened and enlightened, felt at once that there was something here repugnant to all that they had been led to believe about God and man ; and Henry Home came to be put in the same class with David Hume, to whom he was in many respects opposed. In 1753, there appeared " An Estimate of the Profit and Loss of Religion, illustrated with References to Essays on Morality and Natural Religion." The author was Rev. George Anderson, who had been an army officer, and was now chaplain to Watson's Hospital in Edinburgh, and who wrote some tracts against the stage, and a " Remonstrance against Bolingbroke's Philosophical Religion." He is described, by Home's biographer, as " a man of a bold spirit and irascible temperament, and considerable learning." This gave rise to other pamphlets, as " A Letter to the Author of a late Book entitled an ' Estimate of the Profit and Loss of Religion.' " Anderson sets himself in opposition to those who say that Christianity is not founded on argument, and to Sopho, Hume, and Hutcheson. " Feelings being so uncertain and variable, it is most ridiculous to found upon them a law so important and extensive as is the law of nature." He prefers the ground taken by Clarke and Cumberland. As to the scheme of necessity, it is no other than that of Collins. " That Sopho's (Home's) principles serve the cause of atheism will be plain enough to any who duly consider the consequences of his scheme of necessity, which excludes a providence and binds up the Almighty in the same chain of fate with all other intelligent beings." [1] There appeared in 1755 "An An-

---

1 There appeared " Some late Opinions concerning the Foundation of Morality examined, in a Letter to a Friend," London, 1753. The author says of Home : " His merit is great, were it only in stating so clearly the sentiment of duty or

alysis of the Moral and Religious Sentiments contained in
the Writings of Sopho and David Hume, Esq., addressed to the
Consideration of the Reverend and Honorable Members of the
General Assembly.[1] The author denounces Home as maintaining that man is a mere machine, under an irresistible necessity
in all his actions, and yet, " though man be thus necessarily determined in all his actions, yet does he believe himself free, God
having planted in his nature this deceitful feeling of liberty,"—
this deceitful feeling being the only foundation of virtue. He
argues that from this doctrine it follows, as a necessary consequence, that there can be no sin or moral evil in the world.[2] As
to Hume, he is charged with making all distinction betwixt virtue and vice as merely imaginary : "Adultery is very lawful, but
sometimes not expedient." This letter was met by a pamphlet,
" Observations on the Analysis," generally attributed to Blair,
" who is believed likewise to have lent his aid to the composition of a formal reply made by Mr. Home himself, under the
title of "Objections against the 'Essays on Morality and Natural
Religion ' examined, 1756."

moral obligation, and distinguishing it from the sentiment of simple moral obligation." The peculiarity of this sentiment, as expressed by the words "ought"
and "should," our author distinctly explains, and shows how it is "to be distinguished from simple approbation by the sanction of self-condemnation or
remorse." He says of Hume, that it is "his error from the beginning to the end
to have overlooked the innate feelings of duty, — that authority which conscience
carries in itself, prescribing certain virtues as a law or rule upon which alone
morality can be founded and ascertained." "Mr. Hutcheson led the way, by resolving all the several virtues into benevolence, as our author has done into utility, which, in his sense of it, is much the same."

[1] It is said that Home has been confuted by "the smart and sensible author of
the 'Estimate of the Profit and Loss of Religion,' and in the modest and elegant
'Delineation of Morality' (Balfour). Two other authors have distinguished
themselves against the particular parts of the scheme ; viz., Rev. Mr. Adams, a
clergyman of the Church of England, in his answer to the 'Essay on Miracles,'
and Dr. John Stewart in his very masterly reply to the 'Essay on Motion.' "

[2] It is proper to state that in his third edition (1779) Home says, on farther
reflection he has modified some of his opinions. He gives up the position that
"some of our moral feelings and emotions must be founded on a delusion." He
now asserts that the notion we have of being able to act against motives "is suggested by the irregular influence of passion, and that we never have it in our cool
moments ; consequently it is not a delusion of nature, but of passion only." He
thinks that he thus escapes the position that virtue in any measure rests on the
foundation of any natural feelings being a delusion. But, in avoiding one difficulty, he only falls into another ; for it is in our moments of cool reflection that
we adhere most resolutely to the conviction that we have an essential freedom.

In all this we have an able and legitimate discussion. But the opponents of the rising scepticism resorted to other and more doubtful steps. Henry Home, it is presumed, was a member of the Church of Scotland, and it would have been quite within the province of that church to summon him before it, and inquire into the opinions which he was believed to be propagating. Over David Hume, it is clear that the church had no jurisdiction. But the Church of Scotland claimed to be the guardian of religion in the country, and to have an authority to prevent the circulation of error. So a motion was made in the committee of overtures of the General Assembly that the body should take into their consideration how far it was proper to call before them and censure the authors of infidel books. "There is one person, styling himself David Hume, Esq., hath arrived at such a degree of boldness as publicly to avow himself the author of books containing the most rude and open attacks on the glorious gospel of Christ, and principles evidently subversive even of natural religion and the foundations of morality, if not establishing direct atheism : therefore, the Assembly appoint the following persons as a committee to inquire into the writings of this author, to call him before them, and prepare the matter for the next General Assembly." There was a keen debate in the committee for two days. It was moved in opposition, " that although all the members have a just abhorrence of any principles tending to infidelity or to the prejudice of our holy religion ; yet, on account of certain circumstances in this case, they drop the overture, because it would not, in their judgment, serve the purpose of edification." The question being put, "transmit the overture to the Assembly or not," it passed in the negative by a majority of fifty to seventeen votes. After this, Mr. Anderson gave in a petition and complaint to the Presbytery of Edinburgh against the printer and publisher of the " Essays on the Principles of Morality and Natural Religion," requiring that the presbytery should summon them to appear before them and declare the name of the author of that work, that he might be censured according to the law of the gospel and the practice of this and all other well-governed churches." The defenders appeared by counsel. Meanwhile Mr. Anderson was summoned away by death from the scene. The case, however, goes on to a decision on the merits, and the complaint is rejected. These incidents give us a more vivid picture of the times than any generalized statements. It is evidently the good function of the rising Moderate party in the church to restrain the intemperate zeal of those who would lay restraint on liberty of thought and writing, who would claim for the church a power not committed to it, and meet error with other weapons than argument.

Meanwhile there are able thinkers preparing to meet the scepticism both of Hume and Home, by well-established philosophic principles. We shall see that Reid and James Gregory, in particular, came forth to defend the doctrine of the freedom of the will. A curious cross-fight was produced at this stage by the introduction into Scotland of Edwards' "Treatise on the Will." In the pamphlet published in defence of Home, it is urged that, "among the list of subscribers to Edwards' book are many members of this church ; and it was dispersed last year in this city by the most zealous friends to religion and true Calvinism." It is clear that Home and his friends wished to shelter themselves under the Calvinism of the Church of Scotland ; and the pamphlet quotes Calvin, Turretin, and Pictet. It might have been urged in reply that Calvin stands up for an essential freedom of the will, possessed by all responsible beings ; and that the reformers generally, in holding by a slavery of the will, meant a slavery produced by the fall of man and by sin. As to Edwards' doctrine, it is a metaphysical one not before the mind of the reformers ; and it is so explained and illustrated by the author as to make it have a very different aspect and practical tendency from that propounded by the Scottish necessarians.

The "Essays on Morality" was the work of Home that produced the greatest sensation. It was followed by other philosophical works. In 1761, he published his "Introduction to the Art of Thinking," in which shrewd metaphysics and practical remarks are grafted on the old logic. For several years he had meditated an extensive work on the principles of criticism, which would inquire into the causes of that pleasure which is derived from the production of poetry, painting, sculpture, music, and architecture. The work appeared in 1762, under the title of "Elements of Criticism." It is grace-

fully written : it treats of all the subjects usually discussed in
books of rhetoric, and shows an extensive reading in the great
classical writers of ancient and modern times.   He professes
to found the whole upon a philosophic basis.   But his analysis
of the mental principles involved does not seem to me to be
very searching or profound.   What is the use of telling us,
" What is now said about the production of emotion or passion
resolves into a very simple proposition, that we love what is
agreeable and hate what is disagreeable " ?   He does not follow
the Scottish metaphysicians in resolving beauty into association
of ideas.   He discovers a beauty that is intrinsic as well as a
relative beauty.

For years he was collecting materials for a work on man,
which appeared in 1774 under the title of " Sketches of the
History of Man."   This work is meant to describe the progress made by man, in respect of language, food, commerce, the
arts, science, government, morality, and religion.   He is
inclined to think that, as there are different climates, so there
are different species of men fitted for these climates, and
argues that we cannot account for the differences of mankind
by climate or by external agencies.   He would believe that
there must have been an original difference of languages ; but,
yielding to the Scriptures, he accounts for the diversities by the
confusion of tongues at Babel.   He is fond of discovering everywhere a final cause on the part of God, and a progress on the
part of man.   He has collected what seems a wide induction
of facts ; but there is a great want of what Bacon insists on as
a necessary part of all legitimate induction, — " the necessary
rejections and exclusions."

He was married to Miss Drummond, by whom he became
possessed of one of the most beautiful places in Scotland, Blair
Drummond, — on the banks of the Teith, half way between hill
and dale, — in the south of Perthshire.   Home was one of the
earliest of those agricultural improvers who became very
numerous, from this time onward, for an age or two among
those lawyers of Edinburgh who possessed landed estates.
He took a lead first at Kames, and then at Blair Drummond,
in summer-fallow, and in raising green crops and sown grass.
His great agricultural work, which made him famous all over
Scotland, consisted in clearing the moss of Kincardine, which

extended four miles in length and one or two miles in breadth, and was covered with turf, eight or nine feet in thickness, and underneath which was a rich soil. He effected this by giving the land for a time to moss-planters, who floated away the turf by means of ditches which he dug. He was a leading member of the Board of Trustees for the Encouragement of the Fisheries, Arts, and Manufactures of Scotland, and of the Commission for the Management of Forfeited Estates, the rents of which were to be applied to the improvement of the highlands and islands of Scotland. By means of these boards he did much to stimulate the industry of Scotland. It is asserted that he did more than any man in his time in encouraging the introduction of "new modes and instruments of industry, the enclosure and culture of wastes and moors, the rearing of forest timber, the draining and cultivation of moss lands, the raising and spinning of flax, the growth and storing of winter fodder for cattle, the improvement of the breed of sheep, and the manufacture of coarse woollen stuffs."

In his old age he published "Loose Hints on Education." He thought that religion should form a main branch of education even in the earliest period of infancy, and that the parents or preceptor should acquaint the child with the fundamental doctrines of revealed religion. The common opinion of him was, that he must be a man devoid of all religion. But a clergyman writes "I have heard him mention the light of immortality as an excellence peculiar to the doctrine of Christ. He gave unqualified praise to Butler's 'Analogy,' which is a defence of revealed as well as of natural religion. He was regular in his attendance upon public worship; and during my abode with him he had divine worship in his family every evening." It is interesting to notice that he defends the Scottish view of the sabbath. "This consideration leads me necessarily to condemn a practice authorized among Christians, with very few exceptions; that of abandoning to diversion and merriment what remains of Sunday after public worship, parties of pleasure, dancing, gaming, any thing that trifles away the time without a serious thought; as if the purpose were to cancel every virtuous impression made at public worship." ("Sketches of the History of Man," B. III.)

In his person he was tall and of a thin and slender make. His portrait shows a high, marked brow ; a long nose ; and a shrewd, humorous face, — altogether a strong-marked countenance. "In his manners there was a frankness amounting to bluntness, and in his conversation a humorous playfulness." He died Dec. 27, 1782, in the eighty-seventh year of his age.

XXIII. — *AMERICAN PHILOSOPHY.* — *JOHN WITHERSPOON.*

AMERICA was now reaching such a settled condition that reflective thought could make its appearance. Underneath the Puritan action and self-sacrifice, there was a Puritan faith which required men to judge and reason. American philosophy put forth at that time its greatest representative. Jonathan Edwards was born in Connecticut, in 1703 ; was a tutor in Yale in 1724 ; was pastor and missionary from 1726 to 1757 ; and died President of Princeton College, in 1758. From his very childhood he pondered the profoundest subjects, and penetrated as far as — at times farther, some think, than — human thought could carry him. Possessed of no great variety of reading, he reached his very definite opinions, by revolving every subject in his own mind. I am inclined to think that his opinions might have been modified, had he been brought more fully into contact and collision with other thinkers. His "Freedom of the Will" is the acutest work ever written on that perplexing subject ; but many think that he has overlooked an essential freedom in the mind, acknowledged by Calvin, Owen, and the great Calvinistic divines, and revealed by consciousness. He is known more as a theologian than a philosopher ; but the fact is, his metaphysics, always along with his deep spiritual insight, are the valuable element in his divinity. Contemporaneously with Berkeley, he arrives at a doctrine of power and of body, — not the same with that of the ideal bishop, but coming close to it, and perhaps of a more consistently philosophic structure. Cause he explains to be "that, after or upon the existence of which, or its existence after such a manner, the existence of another thing follows. The connection between these two existences, or between the cause and effect, is what is called power." "When we say that grass is green, all that we can mean is, that, in a constant course, when we see grass, the idea of green is excited by it." "What idea is that which we call by the name of body? I find color has the chief share in it. 'Tis nothing but color, and figure, which is the termination of this figure, together with some powers, such as the power of resisting and motion, that wholly takes up what we call body, and if that which we principally mean by the thing itself cannot be said to be in the thing itself, I think

nothing can be. If color exists not out of the mind, then nothing belonging to body exists out of the mind, but resistance, which is solidity,
and the termination of this resistance with its relations, which is figure, and
the communication of this resistance from place to place, which is motion ;
though the latter are nothing but modes of the former. Therefore, there
is nothing out of the mind but resistance ; and not that either, when nothing
is actively resisted. Then there is nothing but the power of resistance.
And, as resistance is nothing but the actual exertion of God's power, so the
power can be nothing else but the constant law or method of that actual
exercise." (Notes on Mind, in Dwight's " Life of Edwards.")

It could be shown that, at this time, there was everywhere a tendency
towards idealism among the higher minds, which had been trained under the
philosophy of Locke. The Rev. Samuel Johnson, the tutor of Edwards in
Yale, who afterwards wrote " Elementa Philosophica," welcomed Berkeley
on his coming to Rhode Island, and adopted his philosophy. Berkeley was
personally beloved by all who came in contact with him, and gained some
devoted adherents to his theory. In Princeton College, Mr. Meriam, a
tutor, defended the system. But idealism has never struck deep into the
American soil. The " Scottish Philosophy," coming in with the great
Scotch and Scotch-Irish migration, which, next to the Puritan, has had the
greatest power for good on the American character, has had much greater
influence. Edwards was acquainted with the moral theory of Hutcheson,
which makes virtue consist in benevolence ; but propounded one of his
own, somewhat akin to it, but much more profound, making virtue consist
in love to being as being. I feel that I must take a passing notice of
the energetic man who actually introduced Scottish thought into the new
world.

John Witherspoon [1] was the son of a minister of the Church of Scotland,
and was born February 5, 1722, in the parish of Yester, in East Lothian,
the probable birthplace of Knox. He entered the university of Edinburgh,
at the age of fourteen, and pursued his studies there for seven years, with
such fellow-students as Blair, Robertson, and John Erskine. Carlyle, who
could not have been specially inclined towards him, is obliged to say that
" he was open, frank, and generous, pretending to what he was, and supporting his title with spirit." " At the time I speak of, he was a good
scholar, far advanced for his age, very sensible and shrewd, but of a disagreeable temper, which was irritated by a flat voice and awkward manner,
which prevented his making an impression on his contemporaries at all
adequate to his abilities." Descended from Knox, through his heroic
daughter, Mrs. Welch, who told King James that she would rather " kep
his head in her lap" than have him submit to the king's supremacy in

---

[1] MS. " Life of Witherspoon," by Ashbel Green (formerly President of Princeton College), in the Library of the New Jersey Historical Society MS. " Life
of Witherspoon," in a History of the College, by Ex-President Maclean, who has
kindly allowed me to use it. " Funeral Sermon," by Rev. Dr. Rodgers, of New
York, in edition of Witherspoon's " Works," Philadelphia, 1800.

religion," young Witherspoon inherited the spirit of the reformer,[1] — his
devoted piety, his keen perception of abounding evil, his undaunted courage, his unflinching perseverance, and, I may add, his vigorous sense and
his broad humor. He was settled as minister, first in Beith in Ayrshire,
famous for its cheese, and then in Paisley, famous for its shawls and for
the piety of its older inhabitants ; and in both places was an effective,
popular preacher, and wrote works — such as his Treatises on Justification,
and on Regeneration — which continue to be read with profit to this day.
    He perceived clearly and felt keenly the great change which was coming
over the Church of Scotland : he watched carefully the rise and progress
of moderatism, tracing it to the restoration of church patronage, and to
the philosophy of Shaftesbury and Hutcheson, favored by a young race of
divines, who seemed to him to be addicted to levity in their whole character, to be ready to abandon the old truths, and to trample on the spiritual
rights of the people.   He did not scruple to satirize. it in a work, published anonymously, and distinguished for its plain speaking and its humor,
scarcely inferior in power to the sarcasm of Swift, and having a much
higher aim, — " Ecclesiastical Characteristics, or the Arcana of Church
Policy : Being an humble attempt to open the mystery of moderation,
wherein is shown a plain and easy way of attaining to the character of a
moderate man, as at present in repute in the Church of Scotland," " Oh,
yes ! fierce for moderation."   " When any man is charged with loose practices or tendencies to immoralities, he is to be screened and protected as
much as possible ; especially if the faults laid to his charge be — as they are
incomparably termed in a sermon, preached by a hopeful youth, that made
some noise lately — ' good-humored vices.' "   " It will serve further for the
support of this maxim, that, according to modern discoveries, there is a
great analogy between the moral virtues, or, if you will, the science of-
morals, and the fine arts : and it is on account of this analogy that most
of the present reigning expressions upon the subject of morals are borrowed from the arts ; as, beauty, order, proportion, harmony."   " Another
thing strongly pleads for gentlemen having the chief hand in settling kirks,
that nowadays very few of our principal gentry attend ordinances, or
receive any benefit by a minister after he is settled, unless perhaps talking
of the news at a private visit or playing a game at backgammon."   " As for
logic, it is well known this part of education is fallen into great contempt,
and it is not to be expected that such brisk and lively spirits, who have
always hated every thing that looked scholastic-like, can bear to be tied
down to the strict rules of argumentation."   " It illustrates the truth of
Mr. H ———'s doctrine : that virtue is founded upon instinct and affection, and not upon reason ; that benevolence is its source, support, and
perfection ; and that all the particular rules of conduct are to be suspended
when they seem to interfere with the general good."   This satire cut deep,
and he was attacked on all hands, for resorting to such a weapon.   He

---

[1] The genealogy seems to have been : — John Knox ; Mrs. Welch ; her
daughter married to Mr. Witherspoon ; Rev. James Witherspoon, their son :
Rev. John Witherspsoon.

defended himself in a "Serious Apology for the 'Ecclesiastical Character-istics,' by the real author of that performance." "One other reason I shall mention for making choice of this way of writing was drawn from the mod-ern notions of philosophy, which had so greatly contributed to the cor-ruption of the clergy. The great patron and advocate for these was Lord Shaftesbury, one of whose leading principles it is, that 'ridicule is the test of truth.' This principle of his had been adopted by many of the clergy; and there is hardly any man conversant in the literary world, who has not heard it a thousand times defended in conversation. I was there-fore willing to try how they themselves could stand the edge of this weapon." Taking his part in the controversy raised by the publication of Home's "Douglas," he published "A Serious Inquiry into the Nature and Effects of the Stage." Robertson, now acknowledged as the consummately able leader of the moderate party, found at times a powerful opponent in With-erspoon. Dr. Robertson had remarked that, with a real minority, the mod-erate party had been able to carry their measures; whereupon Witherspoon said: 'We allow you whatever merit you may be entitled to for your skill, but remember the authority which says, 'the children of this world are wiser in their generation than the children of light.'" One day after Witherspoon had carried some important questions in the General Assembly, Dr. Robertson said to him in a pleasant and easy manner: "I think you have your men better disciplined than formerly," a remark showing how much value he set on skilful leadership. "Yes," replied Witherspoon, "by urging your politics too far, you have compelled us to beat you with your own weapons." He acts in character throughout, and as if he still lived in the seventeenth century. On the night before the communion sab-bath, it is reported that a set of youths, following the example set in the "hell-fire clubs," to which I have referred (p. 19), held a meeting for mock preaching and praying. This was an awful scene to be enacted, in so godly a town as Paisley, where, on a sabbath morning, family praise might be heard rising from every dwelling; and Witherspoon a fortnight after, Feb. 21, 1762, preaches "a seasonable advice to young persons," and publishes it with the names of the offenders. But he is living in the eight-eenth and not the seventeenth century, and a lawyer started an action and got costs, which greatly embarrassed the doctor. All these things — the enemies raised up by the "Characteristics," and these local troubles — must have made Scotland somewhat too hot for him, the more so that the law was against him, and the church party opposed to him was increasing in power and in imperiousness. He had a brave heart and could have stood it all. But it was at this juncture that there came an invitation to him to become president of the college of New Jersey, Princeton. He did not listen to that call when it was first made in 1766; but he accepted it in 1768, and was inducted as president, Sept. 28 of that year. He had now a far wider field opened to him than ever he could have had in his own country, where all the civil patronage and the literature of the age were against him. He has evidently fallen into his predestined sphere, and feels that he has a fitness, a taste, and a talent for the work.

The course of instruction followed in the college during his administra-

tion was a good one. " In the first year, they read Latin and Greek, with
the Roman and Grecian antiquities and rhetoric. In the second, continuing the study of languages, they learn a complete system of geography
with the use of the globes, the first principles of philosophy, and the elements of mathematical knowledge. The third, though the languages are
not wholly omitted, is chiefly employed in mathematics and natural philosophy, and the senior year is employed in reading the higher classics, proceeding in the mathematics and natural philosophy, and going through a
course of moral philosophy." In addition, Dr. Witherspoon delivered lectures to the juniors and seniors upon chronology and history, and upon
composition and criticism, and taught Hebrew and French to those who
wished it. During the whole course of their studies, the three younger
classes, two or three every evening, were called to pronounce an oration on
a stage erected for the purpose, immediately after prayers, "that they may
learn, by early habit, presence of mind and proper pronunciation and gesture in public speaking." " The senior scholars, every five or six weeks,
pronounce orations of their own composition, to which all persons of any
note in the neighborhood are invited or admitted." ("Address by Witherspoon in behalf of the College of New Jersey.") It will be observed that in
this last provision, that for public speaking, there is something not found
in the European colleges. The course as a whole is good ; but the State
of New Jersey would not furnish funds, and private benevolence did not
supply sufficient means to procure an adequate number of instructors. By
means of this instruction, even with its scanty staff of teachers, the college
in that age raised, not only a large body of devoted ministers, but a great
number of the ablest statesmen and lawyers of which America can boast,
and furnished professors to a great many colleges, west and south. [1] Witherspoon took four different departments, composition, taste, and criticism ;
chronology and history ; moral philosophy ; and divinity. Many of his
pupils have testified to the benefit which they derived from his instructions,
so sagacious, so stimulating and practically useful. In particular, James
Madison, perhaps the most philosophical of all the founders and framers
of the American constitution, acknowledges his obligations to the study of
moral philosophy under Witherspoon. " The increased attention paid to the
study of the nature and constitution of the human mind, and the improvements which had been introduced into this fundamental department of
knowledge by the philosophical inquiries of his own countrymen, constituted a marked and most important feature of Dr. Witherspoon's reforms.
Mr. Madison formed a taste for these inquiries, which entered deeply, as we
shall hereafter have occasion to remark, into the character and habits of
his mind, and gave to his political writings in after life a profound and
philosophic cast, which distinguished them eminently and favorably from
the production of the ablest of his contemporaries." (" Life and Times
of Madison," by William C. Rives.)

President Ashbel Green tells us, " The Berkeleyan system of metaphysics
was in repute in the college when he entered. The tutors were zealous

[1] " Princeton College during the Eighteenth Century," by Samuel D. Alexander.

believers in it, and waited on the president with some expectation of either confounding him, or making him a proselyte. They had mistaken their man. He first reasoned against the system, and then ridiculed it till he drove it out of the college. The writer has heard him state, that, before Reid or any other author of their views had published any theory on the ideal system, he wrote against it, and suggested the same trains of thought which they adopted, and that he published his essay in a Scotch magazine." He refers in his moral philosophy to the common-sense school of Scotland. "Some late writers have advanced, with great apparent reason, that there are certain first principles or dictates of common-sense, which are either simple perceptions or seen with intuitive evidence. These are the foundation of all reasoning, and, without them, to reason is a word without a meaning. They can no more be proved than you can prove an axiom in mathematical science. These authors of Scotland have lately produced and supported this opinion, to resolve at once all the refinement and metaphysical objections of some infidel writers. ("Moral Philosophy," sect. v.) His son-in-law, and his successor as president, Samuel Stanhope Smith, at one time inclined to Berkeleyanism, formally renounces idealism. "Whatever medium, in the opinion of these philosophers (Locke, Berkeley, and Hume), nature may employ to connect the object with the organ of sense, whether image or idea, or any other sensible phantasm, it is, beyond a doubt, the object itself, not its idea, which is discovered by the sense; any image or phantasm, in the case, being either unknown or unperceived, and at the time wholly unthought of. An idea is merely a conception of the fancy, or the reminiscence of the object." [1] From this date, the Scottish became the most influential philosophy in America.

His work on moral philosophy is not particularly profound or interesting. But I suppose we have only the skeleton of his course; and, as he illustrated it orally by his reading and wide observation of mankind, I believe it was useful and attractive. He discussed such authors as Leibnitz, Clarke, Hutcheson, Wollaston, Collins, Nettleton, Hume, Kames, Adam Smith, Reid, Balfour, Butler, Balguy, Beattie. He had vigorously opposed Hutcheson in Scotland, and he sees the logical result of his view of virtue in the systems of Hume and Home, who are criticised by him. He refers to the theory of his predecessor in office, Edwards, that "virtue consists in the love of being as such," but without approval. His own view is summed up in these words: "There is in the nature of things a difference between virtue and vice; and, however much virtue and happiness are connected by the divine law and in the event of things, we are made so as to feel towards them and conceive of them as distinct, — we have the simple perceptions of duty and interest." "The result of the whole is, that we ought to take the rule of duty from conscience, enlightened by reason, experience, and every way by which we can be supposed to learn the will of our Maker."

[1] Stanhope Smith's "Lectures on Moral and Political Philosophy." Stanhope Smith was the author of an "Essay on the Causes of the Variety of Complexion and Figure of the Human Species." He holds by the unity of the race, and accounts for the diversities by natural causes. It was first published, 1787, and ran through several editions.

But Witherspoon was a man of action, rather than reflection.   His administration of the college seems to have been successful.   Following the original theory of the American college, Princeton college was placed in a
village supposed to be away from the temptations of great cities.   " It
is not," Witherspoon says, " in the power of those who are in great
cities to keep the discipline with equal strictness where boys have so
many temptations to do evil, and can so easily and effectually conceal it
after it is done.   With us, they live all in college, under the inspection
of their masters ; and the village is so small that any irregularity is immediately and certainly discovered, and therefore easily corrected."   The
rules of government which he explained to the tutors are admirable. " Govern, govern always, but beware of governing too much.   Convince your
pupils, for you may convince them, that you would rather gratify than
thwart them ; that you wish to see them happy ; and desire to impose no
restraints but such as their real advantage, and the order and welfare of
the college, render indispensable.   Put a wide difference between youthful
follies and foibles, and those acts which manifest a malignant spirit or
intentional insubordination.   Do not even notice the former, except it be
by private advice.   Overlook them entirely, unless they occur in such a
public manner that it is known that you must have observed them.   Be
exceeding careful not to commit your own authority or that of the college,
in any case that cannot be carried through with equity.   But having pursued this system, then, in every instance in which there has been a manifest intention to offend or resist your authority, or that of the college, make
no compromise with it whatever : put it down absolutely and entirely.
Maintain the authority of the laws in their full extent, and fear no consequences."

But his influence was exerted and felt far beyond the college walls.   As
might have been expected from his love of liberty, and his impetuous spirit,
and the part he took in Scotland, he early threw himself into the struggle
for independence, and he was elected a representative in Congress for the
State of New Jersey, in 1776, and declared there the way by which he had
been led.   " We were contending for a restoration of certain privileges
under the government of Great Britain, and were praying for a reunion
with her.   But in the beginning of July, with the universal approbation of
all the States now united, we renounced this conviction, and declared ourselves free and independent."   His is one of the names — the most honored of any in America — attached to the Declaration of Independence,
and his portrait adorns Independence Hall.   I rather think that — if we
except Washington, Franklin, and perhaps half a dozen others — none had
so important an influence as Witherspoon in guiding the American Revolution.   It will be remembered that one of the decisive battles of the war
was fought at Princeton ; and, in 1783, the Congress sat for months in the
college, presided over by one of the trustees, and with Witherspoon as a
member.   When in Congress, he exerted himself to secure a firm, central
government, and a gold instead of a paper standard.   He retired from
Congress in 1783, to give himself to his college work.   He died, Nov.
15. 1794.

From the picture of him by the elder Peale in Princeton college, and the account given by Ashbel Green, we learn that " his stature was of middle size, with some tendency to corpulence. His limbs were well-proportioned, and his complexion was fair. His eyes were strongly indicative of intelligence. His eyebrows were large, hanging down at the ends next his temples, occasioned, probably, by a habit he had contracted of pulling them when he was under excitement." His whole air is that of a man of strong character ; and we see traces of his being naturally a man of strong passion, which,however, he was able to subdue.   Scotland did not allow him, what would have been for her good, to become a leader of men ; and Scotland's loss became America's gain.

————◆————

XXIV. — *JAMES BALFOUR.*

HE was a member of the Scotch bar, and one of the many Edinburgh lawyers who devoted themselves to philosophy.   He was one of the first to write against the ethical principles of Hume, which he did in his " Delineations of the Nature and Obligations of Morality," published anonymously, 1752 or 1753.   He sets out with the principle that private happiness must be the chief end and object of every man's pursuit ; shows how the good of others affords the highest happiness ; and then to sanction natural conscience he calls in the authority of God, who must approve of what promotes the greatest happiness.   This theory does not give morality a sufficiently deep foundation in the constitution of man or the character of God, and could not have stood against the assaults of Hume.   In 1754, he was appointed professor of moral philosophy in the university of Edinburgh, — the chair which David Hume had wished to fill some years before, — and continued to hold it till 1764, when he became professor of the law of nature and nations, and held the office till about 1779.   In 1768, he published a second work, written against Hume and Lord Kames and in defence of active power and liberty.   Like all enlightened opponents of the new scepticism, he felt it necessary to oppose the favorite theory of Locke, that all our ideas are derived from sensation and reflection.   " It may indeed be allowed that the first notions of things are given to the mind by means of some sensation or other ; but then it may also be true that after such notions are given the mind, by the exertion of some inherent power, may be able to discover some remarkable qualities of such things, and even things of a very different nature, which are not to be discovered merely by any sense whatever."   He published " Philosophical Dissertations," in 1782.

He was born in 1705, and died 1795.   His father was a merchant in Edinburgh, and his mother a daughter of Hamilton of Airdrie, from which family Sir William Hamilton was descended.   He seems to have received his education first in Edinburgh College, and then, like so many scholars of the preceding ages, at Leyden.

HE was the son of the minister of a parish, called the chapel of Garioch, in Aberdeenshire, and was born in 1728. In July, 1752, he was admitted professor of moral philosophy in Marischal College. In August, 1755, he submits in a printed paper an improved plan of education for the college. He argues powerfully against the established practice of teaching logic in the early years of the course. He recommends that the curriculum consist: First year, classics ; second year, history and elementary mathematics ; third year, natural philosophy, with belles-lettres and mathematics ; fourth year, pneumatology, or natural philosophy of spirit, including the doctrine of the nature, faculties, and states of the human mind, and natural theology ; moral philosophy, containing ethics, jurisprudence, and politics, — the study of these being accompanied with a perusal of some of the best ancient moralists ; logic, or the laws and rules of inventing, proving, retaining, and communicating knowledge ; and metaphysics. This is, in many respects, an enlightened course, but confines the attention of every student too exclusively to one department for the year, — whereas the mind works better with some variety, — and does not give a sufficient space to classics and English. This course was substantially adopted by the college, which thus came to differ from the other Scotch universities.

It is indicative of a strong desire on the part of an enlightened body of men to promote elegance and refinement in their country, that the Edinburgh Society for the Encouragement of Arts, Sciences, Manufactures, and Agriculture offered a premium for the best essay on " Taste," the phrase " taste " having come unfortunately into use as the translation of the French "goût." The prize was gained by Gerard, and the work was published in 1759, the publisher adding three dissertations by Voltaire, D'Alembert, and Montesquieu. Anxious to promote the objects of the above-named society, he offered through it a gold medal on style in composition. In the same year, he was chosen professor of divinity in Marischal, and, in 1773, he became professor of divinity in King's College, and his attention was thus called away from philosophy. In 1766, he published " Dissertations on Subjects relating to the Genius and Evidences of Christianity." Still cherishing his old tastes, he published, in 1774, an " Essay on Genius," meant to be the complement of his work on " Taste." He wrote also " Sermons," in two volumes ; " The Pastoral Care ; " and " The Evidences of the Christian Religion."

He is best known by his work on " Taste." He enlarges the number of senses or tastes far beyond what Hutcheson or any other has done, — illustrating the sense or taste of novelty, sublimity, beauty, imitation, harmony, oddity and ridicule, and virtue, and shows how they all enter into fine taste. He calls them internal or reflex senses, as distinguished from external senses. He does not enter upon a searching inquiry into their psychological nature, nor seek to determine what objective reality is implied in them : he contents himself with a graceful, pleasant exposition and illustration.

In his other philosophical work, he describes genius as the faculty of invention, treats of such interesting subjects as the influence of habit and passion on association, and quotes largely from the best writers of Greece and Rome, France and England; but shows little analytic or metaphysical acumen. By his lectures and works, he helped to create and foster a literary taste in the region of which Aberdeen claims to be the capital, and is believed to have had influence on the studies and teaching of Beattie. Beattie is said to allude to him, when he speaks of a person who "by two hours' application could fix a sermon in his mind so effectively as to be able to recite it in public without the change, omission, or transposition of a single word." He died in 1795.[1]

XXVI. — *THOMAS REID.*[2]

IF he was not the founder, he is the fit representative of the Scottish philosophy. He is in every respect, a Scotchman of the genuine type : shrewd, cautious, outwardly calm, and yet with a deep well of feeling within, and capable of enthusiasm ; not witty, but with a quiet vein of humor. And then he has the truly philosophic spirit : seeking truth modestly, humbly, diligently ; piercing beneath the surface to gaze on the true nature of things ; and not to be caught by sophistry, or misled by plausible representations. He has not the mathematical consecutiveness of Descartes, the speculative genius of Leibnitz, the sagacity of Locke, the *spirituel* of Berkeley, or the

[1] I may mention, as belonging to the same age, "An Essay on Virtue and Harmony, wherein a Reconciliation of the Various Accounts of Moral Obligation is attempted," by William Jameson, M.A. minister of Kerick, 1749. He shows that man is endowed with various senses, but especially with a moral sense ; and, "as several parts or strains of music and different musical instruments do compose a concert, so the various sorts of beauty, order, proportion, and harmony in the vegetable kingdom, in the animal, and in the intellectual system, constitute one universal harmony or concert : in that grand concert, every man is bound to perform his part in a proper key, as it were, or in just consonance with the whole which can only be done by the order and harmony of his affections, and the beauty and regularity of his actions." The scepticism of Hume cast aside these inquiries into senses and tastes, and led to the profounder philosophy of Reid.

[2] "Account of the Life and Writings of Thomas Reid," by Dugald Stewart ; "The Works of Thomas Reid," by Sir William Hamilton ; MS. letters in possession of the late Alexander Thomson of Banchory (used by Hamilton) ; Papers of Dr. Reid in possession of Francis Edmond of Aberdeen.

detective skill of Hume ; but he has a quality quite as valuable
as any of these, even in philosophy ; he has in perfection that
common-sense which he so commends, and this saves him
from the extreme positions into which these great men have
been tempted by the soaring nature of their inexorable logic.
" It is genius, and not the want of it, that adulterates philosophy." He looks steadily and inquires carefully into the subjects of which he is treating ; and if he does not go round them
he acknowledges that he has not done so ; and what he does see,
he sees clearly and describes honestly. " The labyrinth may
be too intricate, and the thread too fine to be traced through
all its windings ; but if we stop when we can trace it no farther,
and secure the ground we have gained, there is no harm done,
and a quicker eye may at times trace it farther." Speculative
youths are apt to feel that, because he is so sober, and makes
so little pretension, he cannot possibly be far-seeing or profound ; but this is at the time of life when they have risen
above taking a mother's counsel, and become wiser than their
fathers ; and, after following other and more showy lights
for a time, they may at last be obliged to acknowledge that
they have here the true light of the sun, which it is safer to
follow than that of the flashing meteor. M. Cousin, in his
preface to the last edition of his volume on the Scottish philosophy, declares that the true modern Socrates has not been
Locke, but Reid. " Kant," he says, " has commenced the German philosophy, but he has not governed it. It early escaped
him, to throw itself in very opposite directions. The name of
Kant rests only on the ruins of his doctrines. Reid has impressed on the Scottish mind a movement less grand, but this
movement has had no reactions." " Yes," he adds, " Reid is
a man of genius, and of a true and powerful originality ; so we
said in 1819, and so we say in 1857, after having held long converse with mighty systems, discovered their secret, and taken
their measure." There is profound truth in this ; but it is
scarcely correct to say that there have been no reactions
against Reid in Scotland. There was a reaction by Brown
against his indiscriminate admission of first principles. Again,
there is a reaction in the present day on the part of those who
dislike his appeal to consciousness as revealing to us a certain
amount of truth, and who deal, in consequence, solely with

historical sketches of philosophic systems, or who make the philosophy of the human mind a branch of physiology. Still Reid has continued to exercise a greater influence than any other metaphysician on the thought of his country. It is true, that in some respects he resembles Socrates ; but in others he differs from him quite as much as the Scotch mind differs from the Greek. Both have very much the same truth-loving spirit, the same homely sense, and contempt for pretension : but Socrates has vastly more subtlety and dialectic skill, and reaches the conclusion that truth cannot be found except in moral subjects ; whereas Reid firmly maintains and resolutely proclaims that settled truth can be attained by observation, in the kingdoms both of mind and matter. Reid's style will not please those who are seeking for flashes of genius, of wit or eloquence. But it always clearly expresses his ideas ; and some prefer his plain statements, his familiar idioms, commonly purely English, to the stateliness of Stewart, — who cannot express a commonplace thought except in a rounded period, — and the perpetual rhetoric of Brown.

Thomas Reid was born, April 26, 1710, at Strachan, which is situated about twenty miles from Aberdeen, on the banks of a lively mountain stream, which rises on the high Grampians, and flows down the hollows of their northern slope into the Dee. The place is rather tame, and must have been bleak enough in winter ; but it is quite a spot in which a thoughtful student might profitably pass the long summer vacations which the Scotch colleges allow, and have enjoyable rambles among the heath-clad and rocky mountains above him, including Clochnaben with the conspicuous stone on the top. His father, the Rev. Lewis Reid, was minister of the place for fifty years, and stood by the whig and reformation cause at the great crisis of the Revolution of 1688, when the people of that region, still under strong landlord influence, might have been readily swayed to the one side or the other. He was descended from a succession of presbyterian ministers in Banchory-Ternan on the Dee, who traced their descent from an old county family, and go as far back as the Reformation. His mother was Margaret Gregory of Kinnairdie in Banffshire, and belonged to the family of that name, which was so illustrious in Scotland during the whole of last century and the beginning

of this. On both sides of his house were persons who had
risen to eminence in literature and science. On his father's
side, Dugald Stewart mentions Thomas Reid, who, on finishing
his education at home, went to the continent, and maintained
public discussions in several universities, and afterwards collected his theses in a volume ; who published some Latin poems
to be found in the " Delitiæ Poetarum Scotorum ;" who
became Secretary in the Greek and Latin tongues to James I.,
and, along with Patrick Young, translated the works of that
monarch into Latin. A brother of his, Alexander Reid, was
physician to King Charles I., and published several books on
medicine ; and another brother, Adam, translated into English
Buchanan's " History of Scotland." On the side of the Gregorys
the subject of our memoir could claim as grand-uncle, James
Gregory, the inventor of the reflecting telescope, and as uncles
David Gregory, — Savilian professor of astronomy at Oxford,
and an intimate friend of Sir Isaac Newton's, — and two others,
professors of mathematics respectively at St. Andrews and
Edinburgh. Such a kinsmanship must have given a powerful
stimulus towards literature and science to a thoughtful youth
like Thomas Reid.

The boy was two years at the parish school of Kincardine
when the teacher foretold " that he would turn out to be a man
of good and well-wearing parts." He was then sent to Aberdeen to prosecute his classical studies. He entered Marischal
College, Aberdeen, in 1722, when he was only twelve years of
age. He was in the first Greek class taught by Dr. Thomas
Blackwell, afterwards principal, who took such pains to revive
the study of the Greek tongue in the north of Scotland ; and
the pupil seems to have caught somewhat of the spirit of his
master, for in after life he was known to recite in his class
demonstrations of Euclid in the Greek language. But his
special instructor was Dr. George Turnbull, who conducted
him and other thirty-nine pupils through a three years' course
in what was called philosophy.

He has left us in a letter written in 1779, an account of a
curious youthful experience.

" About the age of fourteen, I was almost every night, unhappy in my
sleep, from frightful dreams : sometimes hanging over a dreadful hemi-
sphere and just ready to drop down ; sometimes pursued for my life and

stopped by a wall, or by a sudden loss of all strength ; sometimes ready to be devoured by a wild beast. How long I was plagued with such dreams, I do not now recollect. I believe it was for a year or two at least ; and I think they had quite left me before I was fifteen. In those days, I was much given to what Mr. Addison, in one of his " Spectators," calls castle-building ; and, in my evening solitary walk, which was generally all the exercise I took, my thoughts would hurry me into some active scene, where I generally acquitted myself much to my own satisfaction ; and, in these scenes of imagination, I performed many a gallant exploit. At the same time, in my dreams, I found myself the most arrant coward that ever was. Not only my courage, but my strength, failed me in every danger ; and I often rose from my bed in the morning in such a panic that it took some time to get the better of it. I wished very much to be free of these uneasy dreams, which not only made me unhappy in sleep, but often left a disagreeable impression in my mind, for some part of the following day. I thought it was worth trying whether it was possible to recollect that it was all a dream, and that I was in no real danger. I often went to sleep with my mind as strongly impressed as I could with this thought, that I never in my lifetime was in any real danger, and that every fright I had was a dream. After many fruitless endeavors to recollect this when the danger appeared, I effected it at last, and have often, when I was sliding over a precipice into the abyss, recollected that it was all a dream, and boldly jumped down. The effect of this commonly was, that I immediately awoke. But I awoke calm and intrepid, which I thought a great acquisition. After this, my dreams were never very uneasy ; and, in a short time, I dreamed not at all. During all this time I was in perfect health : but whether my ceasing to dream was the effect of the recollection above mentioned, or of any change in the habit of my body, which is usual about that period of life, I cannot tell. I think it may more probably be imputed to the last. However, the fact was that, for at least forty years after, I dreamed none, to the best of my remembrance ; and, finding from the testimony of others that this is somewhat uncommon, I have often, as soon as I awoke, endeavored to recollect without being able to recollect any thing that passed in my sleep. For some years past, I can sometimes recollect some kind of dreaming thoughts, but so incoherent that I can make nothing of them. The only distinct dream I ever had since I was about sixteen, as far as I remember, was about two years ago. I had got my head blistered for a fall. A plaster, which was put on it after the blister, pained me excessively for a whole night. In the morning I slept a little, and dreamed very distinctly that I had fallen into the hands of a party of Indians, and was scalped. I am apt to think that, as there is a state of sleep and a state wherein we are awake, so there is an intermediate state which partakes of the other two. If a man peremptorily resolves to rise at an early hour for some interesting purpose, he will of himself awake at that hour. A sick-nurse gets the habit of sleeping in such a manner that she hears the least whisper of the sick person, and yet is refreshed by this kind of half sleep. The same is the case of a nurse who sleeps with a child in her arms. I have slept on horseback, but so as to preserve my balance ; and, if the horse stumbled, I could make the exertion necessary for saving me from a fall, as if I was awake. I hope the sciences at your good university are not in this state. Yet, from so many learned men so much at their ease, one would expect something more than we hear of."

He graduated in 1726 at the age of sixteen. His college life was prolonged by his being appointed librarian to the university, which office he continued to hold till 1736. Ever a student, and busied with solid work, he joined eagerly with his friend John Stewart, afterwards professor in Marischal College, in pursuing mathematical studies, specially the "Principia" of Newton. His life was varied by his taking with his friend Stewart an excursion into England, and visiting London, Oxford, and Cambridge. Through his relative David Gregory he got access to the house of Martin Folkes, where he met with "the most interesting objects which the metropolis had to offer to his curiosity. At Cambridge he saw Dr. Bentley,—who delighted him with his learning and amused him with his vanity,—and enjoyed repeatedly the conversation of the blind mathematician Saunderson, a phenomenon in the history of the human mind to which he has referred more than once in his philosophical speculations."

In 1737, he was presented by King's College, Aberdeen, to the living of New Machar,—a country parish about a dozen miles from Aberdeen, lying on the level agricultural land of the county, but with glorious views of the distant mountains towards the west. The circumstances connected with his settlement furnish a vivid picture of the age. By this time there was a keen antagonism between the Evangelical and the Moderate parties in the Church of Scotland and this was fiercely manifested on this occasion. In order to his being settled, the probationer or minister had not only to receive a presentation from the patron, but a "call" from the people, which, however, was by this time becoming a mere form, as the ecclesiastical courts falling under the influence of the patronage spirit contrived to avoid insisting on a *bona fide* concurrence from the members of the congregation. We have preserved "A Sermon preached before the Reverend the Presbytery of Aberdeen in the Church of New Machar, Feb. 10, 1737, at the Moderation of a Call to a Minister for that vacant Church, by Mr. John Bisset, Minister of the Gospel at Aberdeen." Mr. Bisset had formerly been minister of New Machar, and was known all over the north as a popular preacher, a defender of evangelical religion, and an opponent of patronage. In this discourse, which is full of stirring appeals, he warns the people against "the fear of man which bringeth a snare," against being intimidated by their landlords, and acting on the slavish principle, "I am for the man the laird is for." Expressing his affection for a people to whom he had been minister for twelve years, he reminds them that when he left them their landlords had persuaded them to take a minister who had fallen into fornication and absconded. He complains of persons not residing in the parish, or though residing in it not attending gospel ordinances, interfering to serve a friend, referring, it is supposed, to a near relative of Dr. Reid's. He asserts that the election of a minister is a Christian right, and that "the poor Christian in vile raiment may claim the same regard that is paid to him who wears the gay clothing, the gold ring, and the goodly apparel." "It is a poor and worthless story for any man to say, that you, the people, are tenants at will, and to improve this as if you were to have no will but theirs in the work of this day. Well may you reply that you are tenants at God's will, who can take them away with His stroke when they are thinking to have their wills of you. He exhorts them to trust in God and do what is right, and warns them that, even though they should by acting an unconscientious part secure an earthly habitation, yet they might soon be driven out of it." The appea produced a powerful effect. The people, having no hope of getting their rights protected by the church courts, adopted a mode of expressing their feelings characteristic of the times. The tradition is that, when their minister came to the place, men dressed in women's clothes, ducked him in a pond; and that, on the sabbath on which he preached his first sermon, an uncle of his who resided at Rosehill, two miles off, defended him on the pulpit stair with a drawn sword.

I am not sure that the sphere to which Reid was now appointed was the one exactly suited to him, or that he was the fittest man to preach the gospel of Christ to a country congregation, or indeed that the old Scotch theory of connecting the church and the colleges so closely was the best either for the church or the colleges. For the first seven years he was in the way of preaching the sermons of others, a practice very obnoxious to the people. The tradition is that on one occasion when at Fintray, three miles off, the lady of Sir ———— Forbes thanked him for preaching on the previous sabbath so excellent a sermon from Tillotson ; whereupon he denied in strong terms that he had taken a sermon from Tillotson. To his confusion he found, on retiring to his bedroom, a volume of Tillotson's on his table, lying open at the place where was the discourse he had preached. Ashamed, not of the fact of his preaching another man's sermons, but of his being supposed capable of uttering a falsehood, he hastened to inform the lady that he had taken the discourse not from Tillotson's published sermons, but from a packet which he had otherwise.[1]

But while thus obnoxious at his first settlement, he is said to have gradually won the good opinion of his parishioners by the propriety of his conduct, his conscientiousness, and his kindness. His popularity was increased when, in 1740, he married Elizabeth, — the daughter of his uncle Dr. George Reid, physician in London, — who endeared herself to the people by her kind offices to the sick and poor. There is reason to believe that in the later years of his ministry he became earnest in his Master's service. The tradition is that, in dispensing the sacrament of the supper, tears rolled from his eyes, when he spoke of the loveliness of the Saviour's character. The following dedication of himself to God is preserved in the manuscripts,[2] and lets us see more clearly than any thing that has been printed by Dugald Stewart the deep feeling that lay beneath that calm outward demeanor. It is dated March 30, 1746.

"O God: I desire humbly to supplicate thy Divine Majesty in behalf of my distressed wife, who is by thy hand brought very low, and in imminent danger of death, if thou, who alone dost wonders, do not in mercy interpose thy Almighty arm, and bring her back from the gates of death. I deserve justly, O Lord, that thou shouldst deprive me of the greatest comfort of my life, because I have not been so thankful to thee as I ought for giving me such a kind and affectionate wife. I have forgot thy goodness in bringing us happy together by an unforeseen and undesigned train of events, and blessing us with so much love and harmony of affections and so many of the

[1] One version is, that Tillotson had preached from Clarke, and that, in consequence, one of Clarke's sermons had been published among Tillotson's sermons, and that Reid had taken the sermon from Clarke, while the lady had read it in Tillotson. I have not found any confirmation of this.

[2] In possession of Francis Edmond.

comforts and conveniences of life. I have not been so careful as I ought to have been to stir her up to piety and Christian virtues. I have not taken that pains with my children and servants and relatives as I ought. Alas! I have been too negligent of my pastoral duty in my private devotions, too much given to the pleasures and satisfactions of this world, and too little influenced by thy promises and the hopes of a future state. I have employed my studies, reading, and conversation, rather to please myself than to edify myself and others. I have sinned greatly in neglecting many opportunities of making private applications to my flock and family in the affairs of their souls, and in using too slight preparation for my public exercises. I have thrown away too much of my time in sloth and sleep, and have not done so much for the relief of the poor and destitute as I might have done. The means that Providence has afforded me of correcting my evil inclinations I have abused to pamper and feed them, n various instances. For these and many other sins which have escaped my memory, thou mightst justly inflict so great a chastisement upon me, as to make my children motherless, and deprive me of my dear wife. O Lord, for thy mercy's sake, accept of my humble and penitent confession of these my offences, which I desire to acknowledge with shame and sorrow, and am resolved by thy grace to amend. If thou art pleased to hearken to the voice of my supplications, and grant my request in behalf of my dear wife in restoring her to health, I do promise and covenant through grace to turn from these backslidings, to express my thankfulness by a vigorous discharge of my duty as a Christian, a minister, and master of a family ; and by an alms of ten pounds sterling to the poor, in meal and money. Lord, pardon, if there is any thing in this over presumptuous, or unbecoming a humble, penitent sinner ; and, Lord, accept of what is sincerely designed as a new bond upon my soul to my duty, through Jesus Christ, my Lord and Saviour."

Stewart tells us that, " during his residence at New Machar, the greater part of his time was spent in the most intense study; more particularly in a careful examination of the laws of external perception, and of the other principles which form the groundwork of human knowledge. His chief relaxations were gardening and botany, to both of which pursuits he retained his attachment in old age." It was while he was minister, and at the mature age of thirty-eight, that he published in the " Transactions of the Royal Society of London," " An Essay on Quantity, occasioned by reading a Treatise in which Simple and Compound Ratios are applied to Virtue and Merit." Francis Hutcheson had spoken of the benevolence of an agent — which with him constitutes virtue — as "proportional to a fraction, having the moment of good for the numerator and the ability of the agent for denominator." I suspect that he meant this to be little more than an illustration, and did not seriously propose to apply mathematical demonstration to moral subjects. But Pitcairn and Cheyne had been applying mathematical reasoning to medicine ; and Reid thought it of importance to show what it is that renders a subject susceptible of mathematical demonstration. It is interesting to notice that the first publications both of Reid and Kant had a relation to mathematical subjects. But it was the publication of Hume's " Treatise of Human Nature" that first directed his intellectual abilities to independent philosophic research. In his " Essays on the Intellectual Powers," published in 1785, he says, " having long believed the prevailing doctrine of ideas, it came into my mind more than forty years ago to put the question, What evidence have I for this doctrine, that all the objects of my knowledge are ideas of my own mind ? From that time to the present, I have been candidly and impartially, as I think, seeking for the evidence of this principle ; but can find none, excepting the authority of philosophers." It is clear that the professors of King's College put one so employed in the fitting place, when, in 1752, they elected him professor of philosophy.

" Immediately on Dr. Reid's appointment to the place of one of the regents of King's College, he prevailed on his colleagues to make great improvements in their system of university education. The session was extended from five to seven months ; a humanity class was added, on a higher scale than had been taught previously ; and the teaching of the elements of Latin, by the professor of humanity, discontinued ; some of the small bursaries were united, and an account of these alterations was given to the public, in 1754. Dr. Reid was in favor of one professor teaching the whole or the greater part of the curriculum, and therefore did not follow the plan of confining the professors to separate branches, as had been done in Glasgow since 1727, and at Marischal College since 1723. The plan of a seven-months' session, after a trial of five years, was abandoned." [1]

In Aberdeen he was surrounded by an able body of colleagues in the two universities, by not a few thoughtful and accomplished men, ministers and professional men of the town and neighborhood ; and he had under him a succession

[1] MS. notes furnished me by Thomson of Banchory.

of shrewd students, whom he conducted, in a series of years, through all the higher branches. He managed to bring together the literary and scientific men by means of the famous "Aberdeen Philosophical Society," which he was the main instrument in founding, and which helped to call forth and combine what may be called the Aberdeen branch of the Scottish philosophy. To that society he contributed a series of papers containing most of the views which were afterwards embodied in the work which established his reputation, "An Inquiry into the Human Mind on the Principles of Common Sense." That work was published in 1764.

In the end of 1763, he was invited by the University of Glasgow to the professorship of moral philosophy there, and entered upon his duties the following year. In this new sphere he confined his instructions to the intellectual and active powers of man, and unfolded a system of ethics comprising some general views with respect to natural jurisprudence and the fundamental principles of politics ; he delivered, besides, a few lectures on rhetoric to an advanced class. We have here a sketch of him by his most distinguished pupil and biographer : "In his elocution and mode of instruction there was nothing peculiarly attractive. He seldom, if ever, indulged himself in the warmth of extempore discourse ; nor was his manner of reading calculated to increase the effect of what he had committed to writing. Such, however, was the simplicity and perspicuity of his style, such the gravity and authority of his character, and such the general interest of his young hearers in the doctrines which he taught, that, by the numerous audiences to which his instructions were addressed, he was heard, uniformly, with the most silent and respectful attention. On this subject I speak from personal knowledge, having had the good fortune during a considerable part of the winter of 1772 to be one of his pupils."

We have preserved letters[1] of his to his old Aberdeen friends, Dr. Andrew Skene and Dr. David Skene, which give us glimpses of the Glasgow college life of the period. — "Glasgow, Nov. 14, 1764. I must launch forth in the morning so as to be at the college (which is a walk of eight minutes), half an hour after seven o'clock, when I speak for an hour, without inter-

---

[1] MS. letters possessed by Thomson of Banchory.

ruption, to an audience of about a hundred. At eleven, I examine for an hour upon my morning prelection, but my audience is little more than a third part of what it was in the morning. In a week or two, for three days of the week, I have a second prelection at twelve, upon a different subject, when my audience will be made up of those who hear me in the morning, but do not attend at eleven. My hearers attend my class two years at least. The first session they attend the morning prelection and the time of examination at eleven; the second and subsequent years they attend the two prelections, but not the hour of examination. They pay fees for the first two years; and then they are *cives* of that class, and may attend gratis as many years as they please. Many attend the moral philosophy class four or five years, so that I have many preachers and students of divinity and law of considerable standing, before whom I stand in awe to speak without more preparation than I have leisure for. I have great inclination to attend some of the professors here, several of whom are very eminent in their way, but I cannot find much leisure. Much time is consumed in our college in business meetings, of which we have, commonly, four or five in the week. We have a literary society once a week, consisting of the masters and two or three more, where each of the members has a discourse once in the session. The professors of humanity, Greek, logic, and natural philosophy, have as many as I have, some of them more. All the other professors, except one, teach at least one hour a day, and we are no less than fourteen in number. The hours of the different professors are different, so far as can be, that the same student may attend two or three, or perhaps more, at the same time. Near a third part of our students are Irish. Thirty came over lately in one ship, besides those that went to Edinburgh. We have a good many English, and some foreigners. Many of the Irish, as well as Scotch, are poor and came up late to save money, so that we are not fully convened, though I have been teaching ever since the 10th of October. Those who pretend to know say that the number of students this year, when fully convened, will amount to 300. The masters live in good habits with one another, and manage their political differences with good manners, although with a good deal of intrigue and secret caballing when there is an election."

A year after we have another picture of his collegiate position. "Our college is considerably more crowded than it was last session. My class indeed is much the same as last year, but all the rest are better. I believe the number of our students of one kind or other may be between four and five hundred. But the College of Edinburgh is increased this year much more than we are. The professor, Ferguson, is indeed as far as I can judge a man of noble spirit, of very elegant manners, and has a very uncommon flow of eloquence. I hear he is about to publish, I do not know under what title, a natural history of man, exhibiting a view of him in the savage state, and in the several successive states of pasturage, agriculture, and commerce." "The most disagreeable thing in the teaching part is to have a great number of stupid Irish teagues who attend classes for two or three years, to qualify them for teaching schools or being dissenting teachers. I preach to these as St. Thomas did to the fishes. I do not know what pleasure he had in his audience; but I should have none in mine if there was not in it a mixture of reasonable creatures. I confess I think there is a smaller portion of these in my class this year than there was the last, although the number on the whole was not less. I have long been of opinion that in a right constituted college there ought to be two professors for each class, — one for the dunces, and another for those who have parts. The province of the former would not be the most agreeable; but perhaps it would require the greatest talents, and therefore ought to be accounted the post of honor. There is no part of my time more disagreeably spent than that which is spent in college meetings, of which we have often five or six a week." "These meetings are become more disagreeable by an evil spirit of party, that seems to put us in a ferment; and I am afraid will produce bad consequences." We have here glimpses of the evils arising from the college patronage being so largely vested in a limited self-elected body, who turned it to party and family ends. As to the roughness of the Irish *teagues* (colts) which seems partly to have amused, and partly to have alarmed him, the blame of it is partly to be charged on the college itself, which received these students too eagerly, and allowed them to graduate too easily after a shorter period of attendance than the Scottish youths. The presbyterian youth of

Ulster — shut out from Dublin University, owing to its sectarian character — received from Glasgow, if not a refined, a very useful education, which enabled them, as ministers, doctors, and teachers, to raise their province above the other districts of Ireland in industry and intelligence.

As it is interesting to notice the Aberdeen philosopher's view of the frolicsome Irish youth, so it is instructive to observe the estimate by the Aberdeen moderate of the Calvinistic religion of the land of the covenant. Writing to Aberdeen, July 13, 1765: "I think the common people here and in the neighborhood, greatly inferior to the common people with you. They are Bœotian in their understandings, fanatic in their religion, and clownish in their dress and manners. The clergy encourage this fanaticism too much, and find it the only way to popularity. I often hear a gospel here which you know nothing about; for you neither hear it from the pulpit nor will you find it in the Bible." Possibly this gospel was the very gospel of grace so valued by the people of the west of Scotland. It is possible, too, that at this time, when the contest between the refined moral system and the evangelical system was the closest and keenest, Dr. Reid may have been kept at a distance from the latter. In another letter he sees some of the more favorable features of the western character. "The common people have a gloom in their countenance which I am at a loss whether to ascribe to their religion or to the air and climate. There is certainly more of religion among the common people in this town than in Aberdeen, and although it has a gloomy enthusiastic cast, yet I think it makes them tame and sober. I have not heard either of a house or head broke, of a pocket pict [picked], or of any flagrant crime, since I came here. I have not heard any swearing in the streets, nor seen a man drunk (excepting, *inter nos*, one prof —— r), since I came here." The Aberdeen moderate is not prepossessed in favor of the west-country religion, but testifies in behalf of the west-country morality. He has an idea that the morality may somehow be connected with the religion; and possibly he might have seen more amiability and cheerfulness in the piety of the common people had he come in closer contact with it. It is significant that the drunk man is to be found in the class which had risen above the national faith. We shall have to look at a very different picture half a century later, when Chalmers begins his labors in Glasgow. By that time, under the moderate *régime*, both morality and religion have disappeared from the region (Drygate) in which Reid lived. The Glasgow professors may not have been directly responsible for the growing wickedness; but there was nothing in their teaching, moral or theological, adequate to the task of purifying the pollution coagulating all around them.

There are indications in these letters of the interest taken by Reid in every sort of scientific pursuit. He confidentially reports to Dr. David Skene Dr. Black's theory of heat before it was made known to the world. He is aiding a Turin professor of medicine who comes to Glasgow in his inquiries about the petrifaction of stones. He sends philosophical instruments to his friends in Aberdeen (Feb. 25, 1767). " For my part, if I could find a machine as proper for analyzing ideas, moral sentiments, and other materials belonging to the Fourth Kingdom, I believe I should find in my heart to bestow the money for it. I have the more use for a machine of this kind, because my alembic for performing these operations — I mean my cranium — has been a little out of order this winter by vertigo, which has made my studies go on heavily, though it has not hitherto interrupted my teaching."

Thus flowed along, quietly and honorably, the remaining days of Dr. Reid. He corresponded with Lord Kames and Dr. James Gregory on such subjects as liberty, cause, motives, and volition. The letters have been published. Many of them are controversial, but they are conducted in an admirable spirit. He wrote a number of papers of some value, apparently for the literary society of Glasgow. In particular, he has " Some Observations on the Modern System of Materialism," meaning by Materialism that advanced by Dr. Priestley in his " Disquisitions relating to Matter and Spirit" (1777), and " A free Discussion of the Doctrines of Materialism and Philosophical Necessity" (1777). This paper appears in no fewer than five forms, showing what pains he had taken with it. One or two of the forms look like mere notes or preparations, the other three are fully written out. It is of a thorough and searching character, distinguished for acuteness beyond almost any of his published writings, and written with great point and *naïveté*. He also wrote " Miscellaneous Reflections on Priestley's Account of Hartley's Theory of the Human Mind." He speaks with great fondness and respect of Hartley, but shows that his doctrines were unfounded hypotheses. He is severe upon Priestley's application of Hartley's theories, and examines the attempt to explain the memory, and the mental faculties generally, and the passions and volitions, by association.[1] But the principal work of his declining life consisted in writing his " Essays on the Intellectual Powers of Man," published in 1785, and the " Essays on the Active Powers," which appeared in 1788.

Underneath the calm, unpretentious demeanor, there was a deep fountain of devout feeling ready to burst out on certain occasions. Again we are told that, in dispensing the sacrament of the Lord's supper, he could not refer to the love of Christ without tears running down his eyes.[2] In the autumn of 1796, he had repeated strokes of palsy, and he died Oct. 7th. His daughter Mrs. Carmichael writes : " His piety and resignation never forsook him in times of deepest affliction, and in all his distress during his last illness. Such is the blessed effect of the power of religion, and of a conscience void of offence towards God and man."[3]

Turning now to the philosophy of Reid, we find it distinguished throughout by independence of thought and a love of truth. He admires the genius of those who were rulers in the world of speculation in his time, but he does not follow them. He might have been inclined to do so, but he was staggered by the consequences which had been drawn by Hume ; and this led him to review the philosophy that prevailed in his time, and which claimed as its authors the illustrious names of Descartes, Locke, and Berkeley. The consequence is, that his works, though expository throughout, have all along a polemical front, but always bearing a calm, a polite, and benignant aspect. We cannot understand his philosophy, and we cannot appreciate his originality, unless we bear this circumstance in mind, which, I may add, we are not likely to forget, as he is constantly referring to some one or other of these authors. He claims

[1] MS. papers of Dr. Reid, in possession of Francis Edmond, Esq.
[2] Life of Dr. McKinlay of Kilmarnock, prefixed to a volume of his " Sermons."
[3] MS. papers in possession of Francis Edmond.

credit in regard to two points, — one in examining and undermining the ideal theory of sense-perception, the other in establishing the doctrine of common sense. These are the topics
on which I mean chiefly to dwell in the exposition and criticism
of his two works.

His "Inquiry" is occupied almost exclusively with the
senses. It is one of the excellencies of his philosophy as compared with those that have gone before, and most of those
that have appeared since his time, that he so carefully inquired
into these original inlets of knowledge. In doing so, he shows
that he is acquainted with all that had been done in physiology
down to his time, and that he had been in the way of making
original observations. He goes over the senses one by one,
beginning with the simpler, smelling and tasting ; and going
on to the more complex, hearing, touch, and seeing. Under
smelling he announces a number of general principles applicable to all the senses, as in regard to sensation considered
absolutely, and the nature of judgment and belief. Under hearing he speaks of natural language ; and under touch, of natural
signs and primary qualities. He dilates at greatest length on
sight : discussing such topics as color, visible figure, extension,
the parallel motion of the eyes, squinting, and Berkeley's
theory of vision. He treats them physiologically, so far as
physiology could then carry him ; but he treats them also, which
so many later German and British psychologists do not, in the
light of the revelations of consciousness. He takes up the
same subject in the earlier parts of his "Essays."

"All philosophers, from Plato to Hume, agree in this that we
do not perceive external objects immediately, and that the
immediate object of perception must be some image present
to the mind." He shows that no solid proof has been advanced
of the existence of the ideas ; that they are a mere fiction
and hypothesis, contrived to solve the phenomena of the human
understanding ; that they do not at all answer this end ; and
that this hypothesis of ideas or images of things, in the mind
or in the sensorium, is the parent of foolish paradoxes.

Let us try to determine precisely his doctrine as to perception by the senses. Negatively : he denies, first, that we perceive
by means of ideas, in the mind or out of it, coming between the
mind and the material object perceived ; secondly, that we

reach a knowledge of the external object by means of reasoning ; and, thirdly, that, in order to the conception of any thing,
it is necessary to have some impression or idea in our minds
which resembles it, particularly setting himself against the
doctrine of Locke, that our ideas of the primary qualities are
resemblances of them. What he advances on these points
seems to me clear, full, and satisfactory. He has done special
service to philosophy by removing these confusing and trouble-
some intermediaries which were called *ideas*. It may be that
the great body of philosophers had not drawn out for their
own use such a doctrine of ideas as Reid exposes ; it may be
that some of them, if the question had been put to them, would
have denied that they held any such doctrine ; it may be, as
Hamilton has tried to show, that some few held a doctrine of
perception without ideas : but I believe that Reid was right
in holding that mental philosophers generally did bring in an
idea between the mind perceiving and the external object ; that
some objectified the internal thought, and confounded it with
the object perceived ; that others created an image in the
mind or in the brain ; and that some had not clearly settled
what they meant by the term they employed. I believe he is
right when he says generally, that " ideas being supposed to be
a shadowy kind of beings, intermediate between the thought
and the object of thought, sometimes seem to coalesce with the
thought, sometimes with the object of thought, and sometimes
to have a distinct existence of their own." I am sure that
the discussion in which he engaged has been of great utility
in compelling those philosophers who still use the word " idea " to
tell us what they mean by it, and of still greater utility in leading so many to abandon the use of the phrase altogether in
strictly philosophic investigations.

I am not to enter deeply into the interminable discussions
as to the sense in which the word " idea " has been used by
Descartes and Locke. Hamilton says that by the phrase Descartes " designated two very different things ; viz., the proximate
bodily antecedent and the mental consequence." (" Works," p.
273.) As to the meaning which Locke attached to the term, I
must content myself with referring to the discussions of Stewart,
Brown, and Hamilton. After reading these with care, I am convinced that the following observations of Reid are as just as

they are important : " Perhaps it was unfortunate for Mr. Locke
that he used the word idea so very frequently as to make it very
difficult to give the attention necessary to put it always to the
same meaning. And it appears evident that, in many places,
he means nothing more by it but the notion or conception we
have of any object of thought ; that is, the act of the mind in
conceiving it, and not the object conceived." But then he frequently uses it to signify " the images of external things in the
mind." " There is a third sense in which he uses the word not
unfrequently, — to signify objects of thought that are not in
the mind, but external." " Thus we see that the word idea has
three different meanings in the ' Essay ;' and the author seems
to have used it sometimes in one, sometimes in another, without
being aware of any change in the meaning. The reader slides
easily into the same fallacy, that meaning occurring most
readily to his mind which gives the best sense to what he
reads." It is specially true of Locke what Reid affirms generally : " The way in which philosophers speak of ideas seems
to imply that they are the only objects of perception " (p. 263).

The service which Reid has done to philosophy by banish-
ing these intermediaries between perception and its external
object cannot be over-estimated. He has also been successful in proving that it cannot be by a process of reasoning
that we reach the conception of, and belief in, the existence of
body. There is nothing in any organic affection of the nerves or
brain, nothing in the sensation in the mind, to entitle us to believe
in an extended resisting object. He also deserves great credit
for showing so clearly that the conceptions of the qualities of
matter are not to be supposed to have a resemblance to the
qualities themselves. Locke acknowledges as to the secondary
qualities of matter that the ideas are not to be regarded as
being like them ; but he still talked of ideas of the primary
qualities as being resemblances. This may have been little
else than loose language on the part of Locke, to indicate that
there was a correspondence or relation of some kind ; but it
was desirable to correct it, as it was fitted to convey a very
erroneous impression. In a later age, Hamilton exposed thoroughly the more general error that like can only influence like,
and that like can only be known by like. It is disheartening
to think how much of the energy of our greatest thinkers has

been spent in correcting errors which other great thinkers have introduced. It looks as if it were only by a continued struggle that truth is to gain a victory over error.

He has not been so successful in establishing a doctrine of his own as in opposing the errors of others. But his view of perception, whether we approve of it or not, can be understood by us. He maintains that there is first a sensation in the mind, and that this sensation suggests a perception. The word *suggestion* to denote the rise of a thought in the mind, was employed by earlier philosophers, but was adopted by Reid from Berkeley, who again took it from Locke. Reid maintains that "there are natural suggestions; particularly that sensation suggests the notion of present existence, and the belief that what we perceive or feel does now exist; that memory suggests the notion of past existence, and the belief that what we remember did exist in time past; and that our sensations and thoughts do also suggest the notion of a mind, and the belief of its existence and of its relation to our thoughts. By a like natural principle it is, that a beginning of existence, or any change in nature, suggests to us the notion of a cause and compels our belief in its existence. . . . And, in like manner, certain sensations of touch, by the constitution of our nature, suggest to us extension, solidity, and motion." ("Works," p. 111.) Closely connected or rather identical with this theory of suggestion is his doctrine of natural language and signs, — a phraseology also taken from Berkeley. He maintains that there are natural signs, "which, though we never had any notion or conception of the thing signified, do suggest it, or conjure it up, as it were by a natural kind of magic, and at once give us a conception and create a belief in it." He calls "our sensations signs of external objects." The operations are represented by him as "simple and original, and therefore inexplicable, acts of the mind."

The whole account seems to me unsatisfactory, nearly as much so as the ideal hypothesis. There is no evidence that sensation comes before perception. The two are thus distinguished by Reid: "When I smell a rose, there is in this operation both sensation and perception. The agreeable odor I feel, considered by itself, without relation to any external object, is merely a sensation." The quality in the rose which

produces the sensation "is the object perceived, and that act of
my mind by which I have the conviction and belief of this
quality is what I call perception." (310.) These two seem to
me to constitute one concrete act, and they can be separated
only by a process of abstraction. There is not first a sensation of a colored surface, and then a perception of it; but
we have the two at once. This does away with the necessity of signs and suggestions, which might be quite as trouble-
some intermediaries as ideas. It would be better to say that,
upon certain affections of sense being conveyed to the mind,
it *knows* (this is a better phrase than *conceive*, or than *believe
in*) at once the colored surface.

Hamilton, when he began to edit Reid, thought that Reid's
doctrine was the same as his own. But, as he advances, he sees
that it is not so; and he comes to doubt whether, after all, Reid
held the doctrine to which he himself adhered so tenaciously, —
that of immediate perception. Reid does, indeed, represent
perception as immediate; meaning that it is direct, and without a process of reasoning. Yet he tells us that, "although
there is no reasoning in perception, yet there are certain means
and instruments, which, by the appointment of nature, must intervene between the object and our perception of it; and by
these our perceptions are limited and regulated." Surely Hamilton himself will admit that there are such means in the action
of the senses, of the nerves, and the brain, without which
there can be no perception. Reid indeed calls in more of such
anterior processes than Hamilton does; in particular, he calls
in signs and suggestions, and makes sensation come before
perception. But, after all, the two agree in the main point.
While both allow, as all men do, that there are processes prior
to the perception, both agree that when the mind is perceiving,
it is perceiving not an idea, or even a sensation or suggestion,
but an external extended object.

On one point, however, and this not an unimportant one,
Reid and his commentator do differ; and that is as to what
should be represented as the object of perception. Locke
means by idea, "whatever is the object of the understanding
when it thinks." But the word *object*, in such a connection,
may be as ambiguous as *idea*. Reid speaks of the stars as the
objects before the mind when we look into the heavens. Ham-

ilton says that the object is the rays of light reaching the eye. He maintains that in perception the proper object is not a distant one, but is either the organism or the objects in contact with the organism. Physiological research seems to show that in this respect Hamilton is right. But still it is true that, whatever be the immediate object, the distant star, and not the rays of light, does become, always by an easy process of observation and inference, the main object contemplated. The two are agreed that the object is an external extended one ; is, in short, a natural object, and not an idea in the mind, or a modification of the mind.

Let us attend a little more carefully to the view which he gives of perception proper. "If, therefore, we attend to that act of our mind which we call the perception of an external object, we shall find in it these three things : First, some conception or notion of the object perceived ; secondly, a strong and irresistible conviction and belief of its present existence ; thirdly, that this conviction and belief are immediate, and not the effect of reasoning." (" Works," p. 258.) The two first of these he discovers by an analysis of the concrete act. They are not happily expressed. The better statement is, that in perception we know at once the object ; and this knowledge embraces what he calls the " notion " or " conception," — phrases which should be reserved for the abstract and general notions which are formed by a subsequent discursive process, — and also what he calls the conviction and belief, which latter phrase should be confined, I think, to the conviction which we have of objects not now present, to objects of faith as distinguished from objects of sight or sense generally. By giving this account we are saved from being obliged to represent such ideas as extension as concomitants of our perceptions. The correct statement is that, by sight and touch, — I believe by all the senses, — we know objects as extended ; and we can then separate, by abstraction, the extension from the other parts of our concrete cognition, and can also inquire what intuitive convictions are involved in it. Hamilton, venturing " a step beyond Reid and Stewart, no less than Kant " has fallen into the awkwardness of calling in both an *a priori* conception with Kant, and an *a posteriori* perception with Reid. (p. 126.) Our cognition of extension is just one experience, but involves certain intuitive convictions.

Reid, like Locke, draws the distinction between the primary and secondary qualities of matter ; but he grounds it on a different principle. According to Locke, primary qualities are "such as are utterly inseparable from the body in what state soever it be." ("Essay" II., 8.) According to Reid, "the distinction is this, that our senses give us a direct and a distinct notion of the primary qualities, and inform us what they are in themselves. But of the secondary our senses give us only a relative and obscure notion. They inform us only that they are qualities that affect us in a certain manner ; that is, produce in us a certain sensation : but, as to what they are in themselves, our senses leave us in the dark." He says more expressly : "Of some things, we know what they are in themselves : our conceptions of such things I call *direct*. Of other things, we know not what they are in themselves, but only that they have certain properties or attributes, or certain relations to other things : of these our conception is only *relative*." (p. 513.) Hamilton remarks that "by the expression, 'what they are in themselves,' in reference to the primary qualities, and of 'relative notion' in reference to the secondary, Reid cannot mean that the former are known to us *absolutely and in themselves* ; that is, *out of relation* to our cognitive faculties." (pp. 313, 314.) Certainly Reid was not dealing with such ideas as the absolute, and things "out of relation to our faculties :" these are phrases and distinctions belonging to a very different philosophy. He means that, when we look on a material object, we are led to believe it to be extended ; whereas, when we experience the sensation of heat, we simply know that there must be an external object causing it, without knowing what it is. When physical science shall have thrown farther light on the qualities of bodies, I should like to have the distinction between the primary and secondary qualities of bodies reviewed by a competent philosopher. For the present, the distinction, as drawn by Reid, seems to me to be upon the whole the best : "The notion we have of primary qualities is direct, and not relative only." Hamilton might have done well, in reference to his own theory of relativity, to ponder the statement of Reid : "A relative notion of a thing is, strictly speaking, no notion of the thing at all, but only of some relation which it bears to something else."

The substance of the "Essays on the Intellectual Powers of Man," was delivered annually, for more than twenty years, in lectures to his class in the University of Glasgow, and for several years before in Aberdeen. He commences with such topics as the explication of words, principles taken for granted, analogy, the proper means of knowing the operations of the mind, the difficulty of attending to the operations of the mind, on all of which he has remarks characterized by much sound sense and fitted to be eminently useful to those entering on the study of the human mind. He closes Essay I. with a classification of the mental powers : 1. The powers we have by means of our external senses ; 2. Memory ; 3. Conception ; 4. The power of resolving and analyzing complex objects, and compounding those that are simple ; 5. Judging ; 6. Reasoning ; 7. Taste ; 8. Moral perception ; and, last of all, consciousness. I may offer a few remarks on each of these.

Perception. After the full discussion in which we have been engaged in reviewing his "Inquiry," it is not needful to dwell on this subject. A large portion of Essay II. is occupied with a review of the "sentiments of philosophers about the perception of external objects," such as the Peripatetics, Malebranche, Descartes, Locke, Berkeley, Hume, Arnauld, and Leibnitz. His account of the opinions of these men is marked by great conscientiousness and candor: it is generally clear, often searching, always characterized by plain sense, at times superficial and mistaken. Hamilton has shown that Reid has fallen into gross blunders from not having mastered, as a whole, the higher speculative systems, such as those of Aristotle, Descartes, and Leibnitz. Hamilton's notes should always be read with Reid's exposition. These notes are as valuable for their logical acumen and erudition, as the text is for its independence and its homely sense.

Memory. His analysis of this power, which will be found to contain such elements as retention, phantasy, association, and recognition, is not at all searching. But he is successful in showing that it is an original faculty, and he has a number of useful, though somewhat superficial, remarks upon its mode of operation. He describes memory as giving us an immediate knowledge of things past, which leads to a very severe criticism by Hamilton, who remarks that an immediate knowl-

edge of things past is a contradiction. But Reid does not use
the word 'immediate' in the same rigid sense as Hamilton :
all that he means is that, in our recognition of the past, there
is no reasoning or any other discursive process. Hamilton
is right when he says that the immediate object before the
mind is a phantasm or representation in the mind ; but it is
also true that in memory we go intuitively, beyond the representation in the mind, to the past occurrence which it represents.
Reid says that "our notion of duration, as well as our belief
in it, is got by the faculty of memory." Whereon Hamilton
remarks that this is to make "time an empirical or generalized
notion," and then tells us that time is a necessary notion, arising on the occasion of experience. But Reid's doctrine is the
more correct of the two. In every act of memory we have the
remembrance of an event in time past, and have thus the idea
of time in the concrete, and get the idea of time in the abstract
by separating the time from the event ; and upon reflection we
discover that there are necessary convictions involved in our
belief in time. Reid's account of the idea of time, though not
exhaustive, is thus correct so far as it goes. By not calling in
a faculty of recognition, Hamilton has not been able to show
how we get the idea of time, and has been obliged with Kant
to make it some sort of *a priori* form.

Conception. Under this phrase he includes three things.
"They are either the conceptions of individual things, the creatures of God ; or they are conceptions of the meaning of general
words ; or they are the creatures of our own imagination." He
has sensible remarks as to each of these, but not a good nomenclature to indicate the distinctions. It is in this essay
that he treats of the train of thought in the mind, which he
does in a superficial manner, compared even with his predecessors Turnbull and Hutcheson.

Abstraction. He does not distinguish so carefully as he should
have done between the abstract and general notion. He has a
glimpse of the distinction between the comprehension and
extension of a general conception. "The species comprehends
all that is in the genus, and those attributes, likewise, which
distinguish that species from others belonging to the same
genus, and, the more subdivisions we make, the names of the
lower become still the more comprehensive in their significa-

tion, but the less extensive in their application to individuals."
(p. 391.) In regard to the subjects discussed by the nominal-
ists, realists, and conceptualists, he is a moderate conceptual-
ist, dwelling fondly on the necessity of observing the points
of resemblance in the objects placed in the group. He has
some good remarks on the formation of general notions, but
does not discover — what is, after all, the essential point — the
putting together in the class all the objects possessing the
common attribute, or attributes, fixed on. His realistic tendency is seen in the remark : "When I speak of general notions,
or general conceptions, I always mean things conceived, and
not the act of the mind in conceiving them." (p. 404.)

Judgment. Under this head we are introduced to the full
discussion of his favorite subject, common sense, which he says
means common judgment. "We ascribe to reason two offices,
or two degrees. The first is to judge of things self-evident ;
the second, to draw conclusions which are not self-evident
from those that are. The first of these is the province and the
sole province of common sense ; and therefore it coincides with
reason in its whole extent, and is only another name for one
branch or degree of reason." (p. 425.) He divides the principles
of common sense into two classes : — as they are contingent ;
or as they are necessary and immutable, whose contrary is impossible.

I. Principles of Common Sense relating to Contingent Truth.

1. The existence of every thing of which I am conscious.

2. The thoughts of which I am conscious are the thoughts
of a being which I call myself, my mind, my person.

3. Those things did really happen which I distinctly remember.

4. Our own personal identity and continued existence as far
back as we remember distinctly.

5. Those things do really exist which we distinctly perceive
by our senses, and are what we perceive them to be.

6. We have some degree of power over our actions, and the
determinations of our wills.

7. The natural faculties by which we distinguish truth from
error are not fallacious.

8. There is life and intelligence in our fellow-men with whom we converse.

9. That certain features of the countenance, sounds of the voice, and gestures of the body, indicate certain thoughts and dispositions of the mind.

10. There is a certain regard due to human testimony in matters of fact, and even to human authority in matters of opinion.

11. There are many events depending on the will of man in which there is a self-evident probability, greater or less according to circumstances.

12. In the phenomena of nature, what is to be will probably be like to what has been in similar circumstances.

II. Principles relating to Necessary Truths.

1. Grammatical ; as, that every adjective in a sentence must belong to some substantive expressed or understood.

2. Logical axioms ; such as, any contexture of words which does not make a proposition is neither true nor false.

3. Mathematical axioms.

4. Axioms in matters of taste.

5. First Principles in Morals ; as, that an unjust action has more demerit than an ungenerous one.

6. Metaphysical ; as that, —

> *a.* The qualities which we perceive by our senses must have a subject, which we call body; and that the thoughts we are conscious of must have a subject, which we call mind.
>
> *b.* Whatever begins to exist must have a cause which produced it.
>
> *c.* Design and intelligence in the cause may be inferred with certainty from marks or signs of it in the effect.

The first remark I have to make on this scheme is, that it may be doubted whether the distinction which he draws between contingent and necessary truths is so profound as he would represent it. The test of the latter is that "their contrary is impossible." But is it not true of all the truths of common sense when they are properly expressed, that their contrary or rather contradictory is impossible? Thus take the case of the intuitive conviction of our own existence. The conviction is not that I must have existed, but that " I do now exist ; " and of the contradictory of this, " I do not now exist," the conviction is as impossible as of the contradictory of the metaphysical principle of substance and quality, — namely, that this quality does not imply a substance.

Looking to the account as a whole, including the division and arrangement, it seems to me sufficiently crude. Some of the principles enumerated under the head of contingent truths have no claim to be regarded as original laws of reason ; such as the signification of sounds of the voice, and gestures of the body, the belief in human testimony, and the uniformity of nature. These seem rather to be the result of a gathered experience, to which we may be impelled by natural inclination ; and in all such cases the natural principle, which in the case of the uniformity of nature is the principle of cause and effect, should have been enunciated, and not the experiential rule. If these laws were principles of reason, there could be no exceptions to them : but every one knows that the sounds of the voice, and the expression of the countenance, and human testimony, may deceive ; and it is conceivable that the present order of things may be changed "as a vesture." I cannot see how, under the head of principles relating to necessary truth, he should include convictions relating to so artificial a product as language. It may be argued, I think, that the principle of design is a modification of the principle of causality ; that is, discovering design as an effect, we argue an intelligent cause. By his loose statements he exposed himself to the criticism of Priestley,[1] who

[1] "An Examination of Dr. Reid's 'Inquiry into the Human Mind, on the Principles of Common Sense,' Dr. Beattie's 'Essay on the Nature and Immutability of Truth,' and Dr. Oswald's 'Appeal to Common Sense in Behalf of Religion,'" by Joseph Priestley, 1774. Reid's work appears to him "an ingenious piece of sophistry." He wonders that none of the Scottish writers (except Beattie) refer to Hartley. "Something was done in this field by Descartes, very much by Mr. Locke, but most of all by Dr. Hartley, who has thrown more useful light on the theory of the mind than Newton did upon the theory of the natural world." "The evidence that any two properties are necessarily united is the constant observation of their union." Propositions and reasoning "are in fact nothing more than cases of association of ideas." "There are many opinions which we know to be acquired, and even founded on prejudice and mistake, which, however, the fullest correction that they are void of all real foundation cannot erase from the mind ; the groundless belief and expectation founded upon it being so closely connected with the idea of certain circumstances, that no men-

objects to our regard for testimony as being a principle of common sense. "It is a long time before a child hears any thing but truth, and therefore it can expect nothing else. The contrary would be absolutely miraculous." But while Reid may be justly charged with a defect of critical analysis, and of categorical expression, he has enunciated in a plain manner an immense body of important truth which can be shown to have the sanction of intuitive reason.

The question has been much discussed, Where did Reid get the phrase common sense? I believe it is not difficult to settle that question. The phrase was introduced formally into philosophy by Shaftesbury, who, however, shows that it was in use before. Reid has been charged with borrowing it without acknowledgment from Buffier, who certainly employs it in much the same sense as Reid.[1] But it might be argued with greater show of reason, but yet with no sufficient reason, that Buffier, who published his "First Truths" in 1717, took it from Shaftesbury or those who were familiar with the writings of Shaftesbury, which became known on the Continent at an early date. It is certain that by the time of Reid the phrase was in constant use.[2] Even Berkeley says that "since his revolt from metaphysical notions to the plain dictates of nature and com-

tal power of which we are possessed can separate them:" and he gives, as an example, our fear of ghosts. We see the commencement of the feud which culminated in John Stuart Mill's "Examination of Hamilton's Philosophy." But Priestley, like Mill, is obliged, unconsciously and surreptitiously, to call in first truths. "No man ever denied that there are self-evident truths, and that these must be assumed as the foundation of all our reasoning." "I never met with any person who did not acknowledge this." It is curious to find him saying that they "recommend particular positions as axioms, not as being founded on the perception of the agreement or disagreement of any ideas, which is the great doctrine of Mr. Locke, and which makes truth depend upon the necessary nature of things, to be *absolutely unchangeable and everlasting;* but merely some unaccountable instinctive persuasions depending on the arbitrary constitution of our natures."

[1] The translator of Buffier (1780) charges Reid with plagiarism. Dugald Stewart defends him ("Elements," vol. ii., pp. 63, 64); as does also Hamilton (Reid's "Collected Works," p. 789), who shows that Reid "only became acquainted with the treatise of Buffier after the publication of his own 'Inquiry;' for in his 'Account of Aristotle's Logic,' written and published some ten years subsequently to that work, he says, 'I have lately met with a very judicious treatise, written by Father Buffier.'"

[2] In "Scot's Magazine," February, 1847, was advertised "The Impartial Philosopher, or the Philosophy of Common Sense," by the Marquis d'Argens, in two volumes, 6s.

mon sense he found his understanding strangely enlightened."
(Preface to " Dialogues.")   In the previous age philosophy had
taken up a number of extreme positions, and those who were
not ready to adopt them, and yet were not prepared to refute
them by logic, were everywhere appealing to common sense.

Notwithstanding the able and learned defence of the phrase
by Hamilton, I look upon it as an unfortunate one.   The word
sense seems to associate the faculty with the bodily organism,
with which certainly it has no connection.   Still the term was
so frequently used by Locke, Shaftesbury, and Hutcheson, who
all talked not only of a bodily but an internal sense, while the
two latter called in a moral sense and a sense of beauty, that
it might, in accordance with established usage, be employed to
indicate that the sense common to all mankind is an original
inlet of knowledge, — an aspect often overlooked by those who
represent it as an *a priori* form or regulative principle.   By employing the word, Shaftesbury, Hutcheson, and Reid meant to
intimate that there are other sources of ideas besides the external and internal senses, sensation and reflection.   The fundamental objection to the phrase "common sense" is, that it is
ambiguous.   In saying so, I do not refer to the meaning attached
to it by Aristotle, who denoted by κοινὴ αἴσθησις the knowledge
imparted by the senses in common.   This continued, for long, to
be one of the meanings of the phrase in philosophy ; but by Reid's
time it was thus known only to scholars.   In the use which
Reid makes of it, there is a fatal ambiguity.   It is employed
to signify two very different things.   It denotes that combination of qualities which constitutes *good sense*, being, according
to an old saying, the most uncommon of all the senses.   This
valuable property is not common to all men, but is possessed
only by a certain number ; and there are others who can never
acquire it, and it is always the result of a number of gifts and
attainments, such as an originally sound judgment and a careful observation of mankind and the world.   In this signification
common sense is not to be the final appeal in philosophy, science, or any other department of investigation ; though in all it
may keep us from much error.   Practical sense, as it claimed to
be, long opposed the doctrine of there being an antipodes and of
the earth moving ; it spoke contemptuously in the first instance
of some of the greatest achievements of our world, the deeds

of philanthropists, and the sufferings of martyrs; it laughed at
the early poetry of Wordsworth and Tennyson. All that good
sense can do in science and philosophy is to guard us against
accepting any doctrine till it is settled by inductive proof.

But the phrase has another and a different signification in
the philosophical works, including Reid's, of last century. It
denotes the aggregate of original principles planted in the
minds of all, and in ordinary circumstances operating in the
minds of all. It is only in this last sense that it can be legitimately employed in overthrowing scepticism, or for any philosophic purpose. Reid seeks to take advantage of both these
meanings. He would show that the views he opposes, though
supported by men of high intellectual power,—such as Locke,
Berkeley, and Hume,—have the good sense of mankind against
them. It can easily be shown that he employs the phrase
once and again to designate sound practical judgment. He describes Newton's " Regulæ Philosophandi " as " maxims of common sense." (p. 97.) He is constantly opposing common sense
to reason and philosophy; whereas he admits elsewhere, using
the phrase in the other sense that " philosophy has no other
root but the principles of common sense." (p. 101.) This dex-
terous attempt to combine the two meanings, while perhaps
contributing to the immediate popularity of Reid, and still more
of Beattie, turned in the end against them (in the use of a two-
edged sword, one edge is apt to wound him who uses it) in the
estimation of philosophic thinkers, who, looking on the appeal
as only to vulgar judgment, which may be prejudice, have denied
the validity of the argument.

Hamilton has succeeded, so I think, in showing that the
argument as employed by Reid is valid in itself, and legitimately used against scepticism. His appeal is to principles in
our constitution which all are obliged to admit and act upon.
But an appeal in a loose way to a sense supposed to be in all
men may be very illusive. In order to its philosophical application, it must be shown that the principle is in all men as a
necessary principle; and this Reid has commonly done, though
there are cases, we have seen, in which he admits first principles too readily. But he should have done more: it is only
when we have carefully ascertained the precise nature of the
original perception, and expressed it in a law, that we are enti-

tled to employ it in constructing a philosophy or in opposing scepticism. As long as it is a mere loose appeal to an undetermined principle, the argument may be very illusive. At this point Reid has often failed, owing to a deficiency of logical power. What he calls in is commonly a genuine mental principle; but, owing to his not furnishing a rigid account of its nature and its laws, we may be in doubt whether the application which he makes of it is legitimate. The important work of Reid needs to be supplemented by an investigation, conducted in his own careful manner, of the precise nature of the principles of common sense, of their points of agreement and of difference, of their precise laws and varied modes of action.

It is not easy to determine to what the appeal is ultimately to be in the philosophy of Reid. It is to common sense: but in what signification? Because it is a sense? Or because it is so constituted as to discern objects and truth? Or because it is common to all men? Or because we must trust to it whether we will or no? It is not easy to ascertain what would be Reid's, or even Hamilton's, answers to these questions. There are frequent passages in which Reid's appeal seems to be to the constitution of our minds (Hamilton's ultimate test, like Kant's, seems to be necessity); for he says, we "cannot have a better reason for trusting consciousness, than that every man, while his mind is sound, is determined by the constitution of his nature, to give implicit belief to it." But some one may ask, Why should we trust our constitution? May not our constitution, common or individual, deceive us? Has Hume succeeded in showing that our constitution followed out in different ways leads to contradictions? To such questions Reid would have little else to say than that we *must* attend to these principles of common sense; and this would make his appeal to be, like that of Kant and Hamilton, to stern necessity. It is worthy of being stated that, in his manuscript papers,[1] an answer is attempted to some of these questions, and this of a more satisfactory kind than any thing I have noticed in his published writings. "As soon as this truth is understood, that two and two make four, I immediately assent to it; because God has given me the faculty of immediately discerning its truth, and if I had not this faculty, I would not perceive its truth. The truth

[1] In possession of Francis Edmond.

itself, therefore, does not depend on my constitution ; for it was
a truth before my existence, and will be a truth, although I were
annihilated : but my perception evidently depends on my constitution, and particularly upon my having, as a part of my
constitution, that faculty, whether you call it reason or common sense, by which I perceive or discern this truth." " The
truth of this proposition, that a lion is a ravenous beast, depends on the constitution of a lion, and upon nothing else."
In like manner, as to right and wrong, " although the rectitude
or depravity has a real existence in this case, yet it cannot be
discerned by a spectator who has not the faculty of discerning
objects of this kind." " Evidence is the sole and ultimate
ground of belief, and self-evidence is the strongest possible
ground of belief ; and he who desires reason for believing what
is self-evident knows not what he means." Any one who
would join into a consistent whole the various characteristics
referred to in this paper, and give each its exact place, will
advance a step beyond Reid, and, I may add, beyond Hamilton.
The question occurs, Why has he not placed these statements
in his published works ? Was it because he was not prepared
to reduce them to a rigid consistency, and was averse to utter
any thing which he could not stand by in every respect ?

It is also worthy of being noticed that, in one of the manuscripts, he shows that he had a glimpse of the distinction
between what Kant calls analytic and synthetic judgments.
The question is put, " Is there not a difference between the
evidence of some first principles and others ?" and he answers,
" There are various differences. This seems to be one, that, in
some first principles, the predicate of the proposition is evidently contained in the subject, as in this, two and three are
equal to five, a man has flesh and blood ; for, in these and the
like self-evident principles, the subject includes the predicate in
the very notion of it. There are other first principles in which
the predicate is not contained in the notion of the subject, as
when we affirm that a thing which begins to exist must have
a cause." This last is an example of what Kant calls synthetic judgments *a priori*. Reid, however, has not laid hold of
the distinction so firmly as Kant, nor did he see its importance,
and elaborate it so fully as the great German metaphysician.
It is interesting to notice these correspondences between the
Scottish and German opponents of Hume.

I do not mean to dwell on the remaining portion of the essays, which contain many sound remarks, but little that is fresh and novel.

Reasoning. This essay has nothing worthy of comment, except a vigorous attempt to show, as against Locke, that morality is not capable of demonstration.

Taste. He argues that "it implies an original faculty, and that it is in the moral and intellectual perfections of mind, and in its active powers, that beauty originally dwells." In a letter to Rev. Archibald Alison, he claims: "I am proud to think that I first, in clear and explicit terms, and in the cool blood of a philosopher, maintained that all the beauty and sublimity of objects of sense is derived from the expression they exhibit of things intellectual, which alone have original beauty." (p. 89.) Possibly this may be a pretty close approximation to the truth. It seems to me to be a more just and enlightened view than that presented by Alison, and those Scotch metaphysicians who refer beauty to the association of ideas capable of raising feeling.

Active Power in General. He argues resolutely, that we have an idea of active power, and examines the doctrines of Locke and Hume. It does not appear to him that there can be active power "in a subject which has no thought, no understanding, no will." He maintains that natural philosophy, even if brought to perfection, "does not discover the efficient cause of any one phenomenon in nature." He draws the distinction between efficient and physical causes. "A physical cause is not an agent. It does not act, but is acted on, and is passive as to its effect." (p. 74.) He holds that it is the business of natural philosophy, to discover physical cause. On this, Cousin remarks that "to pretend that all cause is necessarily endowed with will and thought, is to deny all natural cause." The human race believes in the reality of natural causes : it believes that the fire burns, that the fire is the cause of pain which we feel, &c. ; and, at the same time, according as it reflects, it attaches all natural causes to their common and supreme principle." When we discover a true physical cause, say that oxygen and hydrogen when joined in certain proportions, produce water, intuitive reason leads to believe that there is property, that is power, in the object ; that the physical cause is truly an efficient cause ; and that the effect follows from a power in the agents.

Will. He is a strenuous advocate of free-will. "Every man is conscious of a power to determine in things which he conceives to depend on his determination." He draws the distinction between desire and will. " The distinction is, that what we will must be an action, and our own action : what we desire may not be our own action ; it may be no action at all. The following statement is taken from the manuscripts : "I grant that all rational beings are influenced, and ought to be influenced, by motives. But the relation between a motive and the action is of a very different nature from the relation between an efficient cause and its effect. An efficient cause must be a being that exists, and has power to produce the effect. A motive is not a thing that exists. It is only a thing conceived in the mind of the agent. Motives supply liberty in the agent, otherwise they have no influence at all." Such statements may not go down to the depths of this deep subject, but they are worthy of being considered and weighed.

Principles of Action. By which he means "every thing that makes us to act." He divides them into mechanical, animal and rational. Under mechanical he includes instincts and habits. Under animal principles, appetites and desires, benevolent affections and passions. The rational embrace a regard to our good upon the whole, the notions of duty, rectitude, and moral obligation ; and, in treating of these, he offers observations on conscience, maintaining that it is both an active and intellectual power.

The Liberty of Moral Agents. He had entered on this subject in treating of the will. He now discusses it more fully, showing that man has a power over the determination of his own will, and that we have by our constitution a natural conviction or belief that we act freely.

Morals. If he delivered nothing more to his class than is contained in this essay, it must have been a very defective system of moral philosophy ; but there is no reason to believe that he published all the instruction he conveyed in college. What he does say is always weighty. He shows that there are first principles in morals, that an action deserving moral approbation must be done with the belief of its being morally good. "Hence it follows necessarily that the moral goodness which we ascribe to an action considered abstractly, and that which we ascribe to a person for doing that action, are not the same." He is careful to explain that "morality requires not only that a man should act according to his judgment, but that he should use the best means in his power that his judgment be according to truth," thus pointing to a standard above the judgment. He argues powerfully against Hume that justice is a natural, and not a mere artificial, virtue. He maintains that we draw the sentiments of justice from conscience. That these sentiments are not the effects of education or acquired habits we have the same reason to conclude, as that our perception of what is true, and what is false, is not the effect of education or acquired habits." "By the conscience we perceive a merit in honest conduct, and a demerit in dishonest, without regard to public utility." He is particularly successful in proving that a contract implies an obligation, independent of the beneficial or prejudicial consequences that may follow.

XXVII. — *THE ABERDEEN PHILOSOPHICAL SOCIETY.*[1]

THIS society deserves a special notice, as from it proceeded, directly or indirectly, the greater number of the works of the Aberdeen metaphysicians. The names of the members are worthy of being preserved, as they were all men of ability. The original members were Dr. John Gregory, Dr. David Skene, Mr. Robert Trail, Mr. George Campbell, Mr. John Stewart, and Mr. Thomas Reid. In 1758, were elected Mr. Charles Gordon, Mr. Alexander Gerard, Mr. John Farquhar (minister at Nigg), and Mr. John Kerr. In later years were elected Mr. James Beattie in 1760, Dr. George Skene in 1763, Mr. W. Ogilvy in 1763, Mr. James Dunbar in 1765, and Mr. William Traill in 1766. Dr. Reid was secretary for the first year. The society met twice a month, in the afternoon or evening, in a tavern in one or other of the towns. We are amused at the provision made by the philosophers for their bodily wants. There was an entertainment, the expense of which was not to exceed eighteen pence a head; the whole expense might be about ten shillings, of which one-half was for a bottle of

---

[1] Original minutes of the Society, kindly lent me by Francis Edmond; "Biographical Sketch of David Skene, M.D.," by Alexander Thomson of Banchory.

port, for punch and porter, the other half for the more solid eatables. It was a written rule, showing how anxious the grave men were to secure propriety, that "any member may take a glass at a by-table while the president is in the chair, but no health shall be drunk during that time." The meeting continued its sittings for three hours, there being room for free conversation half an hour before, and half an hour after, the president took or vacated the chair. The attendance may have averaged half a dozen. The first meeting was held Jan. 12, 1758. About 1772, the forfeits for non-attendance are getting heavy, and discontent is expressed. The minutes show a meeting so late as February, 1773, after which the society disappears.

The society was formed for the purpose of reading discourses or dissertations, and making observations on the subjects of them, and of discussing questions proposed and sanctioned. "The subjects of the discourses and questions shall be philosophical; all grammatical, historical, and philological discussions being conceived to be foreign to the design of this society [it is evident that they had no idea of the importance of philology]. And philosophical matters are understood to comprehend every principle of science, which may be deduced by just and lawful induction from the phenomena either of the human mind, or of the material world; all observations and experiments that may furnish materials for such inductions : the examination of false schemes of philosophy and false methods of philosophizing; the subserviency of philosophy to arts, the principles they borrow from it, and the means of carrying them to their perfection."

It is interesting to notice that so many of the speculations of the Aberdeen philosophers, afterwards given to the world in their published writings, were first laid before this society. Thus Dr. Reid, on May 24, 1758, intimates that the subject of his discourse at next meeting (June 13) is to be "The philosophy of the mind in general, and particularly on the perceptions we have by sight." In 1760, he gives an analysis of the senses, and a discourse on the sense of touch. On Jan. 26, 1762, he read a discourse at the laying down of the office of president, on "Euclid's definitions and axioms." On Oct. 11, 1762, Dr. Reid read a discourse, which the society approved of; but he declined inserting it, in regard he proposed soon to send it to the press, along with the other discourses he had read before the society.

Gerard, too, discourses on his own subjects, from 1758 to 1771, and reads a series of papers on genius, and a paper on the effect of the passions on the association of our ideas. Between 1761 and 1768, he inquires : "What is peculiar to those Operations of the Mind of which we can form some Ideas, and what distinguishes them from other Operations of the Mind of which we can form no Ideas ?" He writes on the Principles which determine our Degrees of Approbation in the Fine Arts ; upon the "Characters of Poetical Imagination ;" upon the "Difference between Common Sense and Reason ;" and he gives a series of papers on the "Universality and Immutability of the Moral Sentiment." From 1761 to 1767, Dr. Campbell reads papers on "Eloquence ;" on "The Relation of Eloquence to Logic ;" on "The Dependence of Eloquence on Grammar."

The other members take up cognate subjects. Traill takes " An Abstract of a Discourse of M. Rousseau, of the Sourse [so spelled] of the Inequality among Mankind." Mr. Gordon treats of " Memory and its Influence in forming Characters among Men ; " on the " Origin of Polytheism ; " on the Universal Belief in a Deity ; on the " Existence and Perfections of the Supreme Being ; " on " Language ; " and on the "Alphabet." Farquhar reads on the " Imagination," and a " Particular Providence." Dr. David Skene has a paper on " The Different Branches of Philosophy," particularly " The Study of the Nature and Philosophy of the Mind." Dr. Gregory discourses on " The Usefulness of Natural Philosophy ; " on The Prolongation of Human Life ; " " The Retardation of Old Age ; " and " The Foundation of Taste in Music." Mr. Ross takes up " The Use of the Leaves of Plants ; " and " The Methods of Classing Plants." Professor Stuart writes on the " Nature of Evidence ; " on " Mathematical Evidence ; " on the " Evidence of Experience ; " and " Moral Evidence." Dr. George Skene reads on " The Abuse of Mechanical Reasoning in Natural Philosophy." Mr. Traill discourses on " The Arrangement and Evidence of Mathematics ; " and Dunbar, on " The Union of King's and Marischal Colleges," on " The Equality of Mankind," and " The Influence of Place and Climate upon Human Affairs." Dr. David Skene has a paper on " Happiness." Surely there is proof here of great intellectual activity, and of the keen interest felt in a wide range of subjects.

Most of the topics discussed turn round the various departments of mental science and speculative philosophy. But it will be seen, from the list of questions propounded for discussion, that they travelled over other fields. Many of the discussions had a special reference to the new sceptical philosophy ; so that Reid could write to Hume, March 18, 1763: "Your friendly adversaries, Drs. Campbell and Gerard, as well as Dr. Gregory, return their compliments to you, respectfully. A little philosophical society here, of which all three are members, is much indebted to you for its entertainment. Your company would, although we are all good Christians, be more acceptable than that of Athanasius ; and since we cannot have you upon the bench, you are brought, oftener than any other man, to the bar ; accused and defended, with great zeal, but without bitterness. If you write no more in morals, politics, or metaphysics, I am afraid we shall be at a loss for subjects."

———◆———

XXVIII. — *JAMES OSWALD.*

PRIESTLEY speaking of "a set of pretended philosophers, of whom the most conspicuous and assuming is Reid," says of Oswald, that he wonders how his "performance should have excited any other feeling than that of contempt." "As to Dr. Oswald, whom I have treated with the least ceremony, the disgust his writings gave me was so great, that I could not possibly show him more respect." ("Examination of Dr. Reid's Inquiry.") Oswald's work is entitled " An Appeal to Common Sense in behalf of

Religion." The first volume appeared in 1766, and it reached a second edition in 1768. The second volume was published in 1772. He takes substantially the same line of defence as Reid; but the "Appeal" is less pointed, and is vastly looser than Reid's "Inquiry;" and one feels it a dreary task to go through its platitudes. He entrenches himself behind certain distinctions recognized in the age. "The distinction between the occasion and cause of a thing is too considerable to be overlooked in a philosophical inquiry. Sensation and reflection, do indeed give occasion to all our ideas, but do not therefore produce them. They may in our present state be considered as the *sine qua non* to our most rational and sublime conceptions, but are not therefore the powers by which we form them." He opposes Lord Kames, and blames him for resting morality on feeling, and Adam Smith for resting it on sympathy, whereas it should be represented as founded on common sense. "Common sense perceives and pronounces upon all primary truths with the same indubitable certainty with which we perceive and pronounce on objects of sense by our bodily organs." "By the discernment peculiar to rational beings we perceive all primary truths, in the same manner as we perceive objects of sense by our bodily organs." "Primary truths of religion and morality are as much objects of common sense as other primary truths." In the advertisement to the second volume, he mentions that some think that this Appeal ought to have set out with a definition of common sense; and he goes on to show that he does not mean by it common opinion, just or unjust. He calls it the simple authority of reason, or that capacity of pronouncing on obvious truth. "Reason requires our admitting primary truths on its authority, under the penalty of being convicted of folly and nonsense, if we do not." Oswald cannot be represented as grappling with the deeper problems of metaphysics, as, for example, with the question, whether the common sense is subjective or objective, or whether it is subjective in one sense, as it is in the mind, and objective in another sense, as the mind in many cases — not all, however — looks to external objects. He seems to me to be right when he combines two elements in moral apprehension : "we have a feeling, as well as perception, of moral excellence." Dr. Oswald was born in Dunnet, became minister there (1727), and at Methven (1750), and died in 1793.

XXIX. — *JAMES BEATTIE.*[1]

JAMES BEATTIE was born Oct. 25, 1735, at the north-east end of Lawrencekirk, a village in the heart of the *Howe of the Mearns* in Kincardineshire, where his father kept a retail shop, and rented a small farm in the neighborhood. He was educated,

[1] "An Account of the Life and Writings of Dr. Beattie," by Sir William Forbes.

as so many eminent Scotchmen have been, at his parish school,
and showed an early taste for reading, especially books of poetry.   In 1749, he entered Marischal College, Aberdeen, where
he competed for and received a bursary ; and there his classical
tastes were at once discovered by Dr. Blackwell, and there in
coming years he studied philosophy under Dr. Gerard.   In
1753, he was appointed schoolmaster of the parish of Fordoun
about six miles from his native place, in a hollow at the base of
the Grampians.   He had all along a taste for the beauties of
nature ; and his poetical genius was kindled, and may have been
partly guided into the direction which it took, by the peculiar
scenery of the country, where a fine rich plain stretches out
with a low range of hills overlooking the German Ocean on the
one side, and the lofty Grampians on the other.   The tradition
is, that at this period of his life he would saunter in the fields
or on the hills the livelong night, watching the aspects of the
sky and welcoming the approach of day, and that he was specially fond of wandering in a deep and finely wooded glen in
the neighborhood.   While at this place he secured friends
and patrons in the parish minister, in Lord Monboddo and
Lord Gardenstone.   The last named of these having seen some
pieces of his poetry in manuscript, and being in doubt whether
they were entirely the composition of so young a man, asked
him to translate a passage of Lucretius ; whereupon Beattie
retired into an adjoining wood, and produced a translation in a
very short time.   While a schoolmaster at Fordoun, he seems
to have attended divinity lectures during several winters at
Aberdeen, with a view to the gospel ministry ; but he soon
relinquished the pursuit.   In 1757, he stood a competitive
examination for the office of usher in the grammar-school of
Aberdeen, and was defeated ; but so satisfied were the judges
of his qualifications that, on the office falling vacant the following year, he was appointed to it without any farther examination.   In this more public position, his literary abilities became
known ; and, through the influential friends whom he had
acquired, he was installed professor of moral philosophy and
logic in Marischal College in 1760.   About this time he
became a member of the Aberdeen Club, and associated with
such men as Reid, Campbell, John Gregory, and Gerard.

As professor, he lectured and examined two or three hours

every day, from November to April, on pneumatology, embracing psychology and natural theology ; on speculative and practical ethics, economics, jurisprudence, politics, rhetoric, and logic, with readings in Cicero and others of the ancient philosophers. As a moral philosopher, he felt himself called to oppose the scepticism of which Hume was the champion. It appears from letters of Dr. John Gregory, published in Forbes's "Life of Beattie," that atheism and materialism were at that time in high fashion, and were spouted by many who used the name of Hume, but who had never read his works, and who were incapable of understanding them. Reid had for years been examining the foundations of philosophy, which Hume had been undermining, and published his "Inquiry" in 1764. Beattie followed in 1770, with the Essay on "The Nature and Immutability of Truth." This work was his principal study for four years : he wrote it three times over, and some parts of it oftener. It had so rapid a sale that, in 1771, a second edition was demanded ; and, shortly after, there were proposals to translate it into French, Dutch, and German. While engaged in these severer labors, he was all the while cherishing, what I suspect was to him the more congenial occupation, his taste for poetry. So early as 1766, he is laboring in the style and stanza of Spencer, at a poem in which he is to give an account of the birth, education, and adventures of one of the old minstrels. The First Book of the "Minstrel" was published anonymously in 1771, and a new edition of this Book and the Second Book, with his name attached, in 1774. Beattie, it may be acknowledged, stands higher as a poet than a philosopher. Some of his poems are in the first rank of their kind.   .

The personal incidents in his remaining life worthy of being recorded are not numerous. In 1767, he had married Miss Mary Dunn, who was inflicted with a tendency to mental disease, which broke out first in a distempered mind, and afterwards in insanity, which greatly distressed the kind husband, and compelled him at last to provide for her living separate from him. His quiet life was varied by several visits paid to London, where, as he became known by his works, he received considerable attention and was introduced to many eminent literary men. On two several occasions he had the honor of

an interview with George III., who had a great admiration of
the character and object of his works, and granted him a pen-
sion. The famous painter Sir Joshua Reynolds took a fine
portrait of him, with the " Essay on Truth " under his arm, and
above him a winged angelic being holding scales in one hand,
as if weighing truth, and with the other pushing three hideous
figures, supposed to represent Sophistry, Scepticism, and Folly
(Reynolds meant two of these to be Voltaire and Hume),[1] who
are shrinking away from the light of the sun, beaming from
the breast of the angel.

His defences of religion were highly esteemed by several of
the bishops and a number of the clergy of the Church of England, and he was offered a rich living if he would take orders in
that church. This he declined, not because he disapproved
of the doctrine or worship of the Episcopal Church, but he was
apprehensive that by accepting such preferment he " might
strengthen the hands of the gainsayer and give the world some
ground to believe that the love of the truth was not quite so
ardent or so pure as he had pretended." In 1773, Oxford
University conferred an honorary degree of LL.D. upon him.
The same year, he was offered the chair of moral philosophy in
Edinburgh, but declined, as he preferred Aberdeen as his sphere,
and was indisposed to go to a place where he would be in the
heart of those he had attacked. His declining days were em-
bittered by trials, which sank deep into his soul ; such as the
state of his wife, and the death first of one and then of the other
of his sons, one of them being a very promising young man,
called in early life to be his father's assistant in the college.[2]
We discover traces of irritation in his afflictions ; and one could
have wished to see him sustained not only by what he sincerely entertained, a belief in providence and in the word of
God, but in the peculiar doctrines of redemption and grace,
so specially fitted to give comfort in trouble. He died Oct. 5,
1802.

[1] This portrait was lately in possession of the Misses Glennie, his grandnieces,
in Aberdeen. A print of it is to be found in a few copies of Forbes' "Life of
Beattie."

[2] The father published "Miscellanies," by James Hay Beattie, A.M., in two
volumes, 1799. There are some verses worth preserving : —
        " And how Milton has glands in his brain
        That secreted the ' Paradise Lost.' "

In person he was of a middle size, with something of a slouch
in his gait ; and in his latter years he was inclined to corpu-
lency. He had dark eyes, and a mild and somewhat pensive
look. There is an account of his life and writings in a work
by Sir W. Forbes, in three volumes. It contains many of his
letters, which are full of criticisms of no great profundity, and
display at once the amiabilities and weaknesses of the author.

The following are the titles, with the dates, of his works : Poems (1760) ;
Essay on Truth (1770) ; Minstrel, B. I. (1771) ; B. II. (1774) ; on Poetry
and Music, on Laughter and Ludicrous Composition, on Classical Learning
(1776) ; Dissertations on Memory and Imagination, on Dreaming, on the
Theory of Language, on Fable and Romance, on the Attachments of Kindred,
on Illustrations of Sublimity (1783) ; Evidences of Christianity (1786) ;
Elements of Moral Science (1790–93). He has also Scotticisms, and original notes to an edition of Addison's papers.

His poems will ever hold a place among the classical writings of Great Britain. His " Minstrel " and his " Hermit " are
exquisite poems of their kind : simple, graceful, tender, and
leaving a peaceful and peace-giving impression on the mind ;
and therefore not likely to be appreciated by those whose
tastes were formed by the passionate and startling style of
poetry introduced in the next age by Byron, who was at school
in Aberdeen while Beattie was in his declining years. His
prose works do not exhibit much grasp or depth of thought,
but are characterized by much ease and elegance. In his
lectures he dwelt fondly on style (" Elements of Mental Science," part 10), and his remarks are clear and judicious, though
somewhat tame and commonplace, but not on that account the
less useful. His criticism of the " Pilgrim's Progress " may be
compared with that of Macaulay, written in a later age : " It was
written about a hundred and thirty years ago, while the author,
who had been a tinker, was in prison in Bedford, where he was
confined twelve years. Some false notions in theology may be
found in it ; and the style is vulgar, and savors of the author's
trade ; but the fable is ingenious and entertaining." He everywhere holds forth Addison as the model English writer. His
own style is without the idiom, the playfulness, the corrusca-
tions, the flexible windings by which the best papers of the
" Spectator " are characterized. In reading such a work as his
" Moral Science," we feel as if we were walking along a road
with pleasant grass and corn fields on either side, but without a

turn in it, and without a rock or stream, without a hill or valley. His papers on literary subjects are more attractive, as allowing free scope for his fine taste.

In his " Theory of Language " he argues strongly that speech is of divine origin. In his " Dissertation on the Imagination," which is very pleasantly written, he holds the theory, afterwards expanded by Alison, that the feeling of beauty arises from the association of ideas. He begins his " Elements of Moral Science " with psychology. He mentions the twofold division of the faculties into perception and volition, but says it is not accurate, and adds affections, approaching thus to the threefold division adopted by Kant and Hamilton. He mentions nine perceptive faculties : external sensation, consciousness, memory, imagination, dreaming, speech, abstraction, reason (judgment or understanding), conscience. I rather think he is right in giving speech a place among the native faculties, but we wonder to find dreaming there. His account of consciousness is loose and popular, but he avoids the error of Dugald Stewart in making it look merely at qualities, and of Kant in making it look merely at phenomena. " Of the things perceived by this faculty, the chief is the mind itself," &c. He has often valuable remarks on the faculties. Thus, under memory : " What we perceive by two senses at once has a good chance to be remembered. Hence, to read aloud slowly and with propriety, when one is accustomed to it, contributes greatly to remembrance ; and that which we write in a good hand, without contractions, with dark-colored ink, exactly pointed and spelled, in straight lines, with a moderate space between them, and properly subdivided into paragraphs as the subject may require, is better remembered than what we throw together in confusion. For by all these circumstances attention is fixed, and the writing, being better understood, makes a deeper impression. Those things, also, which are related in two or more respects are more easily remembered than such as are related in one respect only. Hence, by most people verse is more easily remembered than prose, because the words are related in measure as well as in sense ; and rhyme, than blank verse, because the words are related not only in sense and measure, but also by similar sounds at the end of the lines." Some will think that the students who listened to such prelections ranging over all the faculties, and touching on a great variety of topics, esthetical and moral, might be as much benefited as those who had to listen to the more scholastic discussions of the German universities. He says that "laughter is occasioned by an incongruity or unsuitableness of the parts that compose, or seem to compose, any complex idea or object."

The philosophical work by which Beattie was best known in his own day, and by which he is still known by students, is his " Essay on the Nature and Immutability of Truth, in Opposition to Sophistry and Scepticism." He quotes approvingly Reid's " Inquiry," and Campbell's " Philosophy of Rhetoric." In an edition published in 1776 he replies to some who had blamed him for borrowing some hints without acknowledgment from Dr. Price, Dr. Oswald, and Buffier. " I beg to say that I am to this hour totally unacquainted with that work of Dr. Price which is alluded to, and that when I published the first edition of the 'Essay on Truth' I was totally unacquainted with the writings of Buffier and Dr. Oswald. I had heard, indeed, that the French philosopher used the term 'common sense' in a way similar to that in which I use it ; but this was only hearsay, and I have since found that, though between his fundamental opinions and mine there is a striking resemblance, his application of that term is not entirely the same." All I have to remark on this statement is, that if he had not read those well-known works on the subject of which he was treating he ought to have done so.

The work is pleasantly and pointedly written, and it had an immediate and wide circulation. It wants the depth and shrewdness of Reid's "Inquiry," but on that account was better relished by many readers, such as George III. The book is, throughout, a popular, rather than a scientific one. His somewhat *ad captandum* appeals gained the ear of those who had never been troubled with doubts, but rather turned away those who wished to find the great sceptic met by an opponent worthy of him.

His object is, first, to trace the several kinds of evidence up to their first principles ; second, to show that his sentiments are in accordance with true philosophy and the principles of the most eminent philosophers ; and, third, to answer sceptical objections. He says it is difficult, perhaps impossible, to give a definition of truth ; but endeavors to give such a description of it as may make others understand what we mean by the word. He then tells us that he accounts " that to be truth which the constitution of human nature determines a man to believe, and that to be falsehood which the constitution of human nature determines man to disbelieve." This makes the ultimate appeal to lie to man's constitution ; and does not meet those who say that man's constitution may be an accretion of fortuitous agencies gathered in the course of ages, and may lead us into partial or total falsehood. According to this definition, there might be events without a cause in the constellation Orion, or at a " reasonable distance beyond," provided the constitution of the inhabitants there had been determined by a different experience. He then distinguishes between truth perceived intuitively and truth perceived in consequence of a proof, and enters upon a discussion as to the most appropriate terms to employ to designate these two kinds of truth. " We might call the one ' reason,' and the other ' reasoning ; ' but the similarity of the terms would frequently occasion both obscurity and harshness in the sound." Henceforward he seems to use the words "reason" and "reasoning" as synonymous, and uses " reason " in the sense of " reasoning." He is quite aware of the ambiguity in the phrase "common sense ; " but he is to use it to denote that " faculty by which we perceive self-evident truth," and then distinguishes between common sense and reason. This distinction between common sense and reason is no modern discovery, and he proceeds to quote Aristotle's account of axioms, principles, and common sentiments.

He starts the question, " By what criterion shall we know a sentiment of nature from a prejudice of education, a dictate of common sense from the fallacy of an inveterate opinion ? " It is clear that Reid must often have had that question before him, but does not give a very articulate reply. Beattie answers it clearly, and I believe judiciously. " He takes that for an ultimate principle which forces our belief by its own intrinsic evidence, and which cannot by any reasoning be rendered more evident." Here the main stress is laid, as I believe it ought, on self-evidence, while necessity comes in secondarily ; " it forces our belief by its own intrinsic evidence," a better account than that given by Leibnitz and Kant, who put necessity in the front.

He illustrates his views by mathematical evidence and the evidence of sense ; and shows that they agree, in both having the sanction of common sense.   He argues that analogy and testimony are principles of common sense ; but he is in evident difficulties when he is obliged to admit that both of these may deceive.   He draws a distinction between two kinds of truths, 'each intuitively certain.   " It is a character of some that their contraries are inconceivable ; such are the axioms of geometry. But of many other intuitive truths the contraries are inconceivable. ' I do feel a hard body,' ' I do not feel a hard body ; ' these propositions are equally conceivable."   If we would defend fundamental truth effectively, we must draw such distinctions ; but the main point here is to determine what we are led intuitively to believe in the different cases.   He shows convincingly, in opposition to Locke, that self-evidence is not confined to propositions.

He sustains these principles pretty satisfactorily ; but when he proceeds to apply them in a criticism of Berkeley and Hume, is not eminently successful.   He understands Berkeley, as he has been vulgarly understood, as denying the existence of matter ; whereas Berkeley is continually asserting that he believes firmly in the existence of matter ; only he regards it as having no existence, except as an idea, in a contemplative mind, — whereas our intuitive convictions represent it as having a reality, so far, independent of the mind contemplating it.   The consequence is, that Beattie's objections are felt by us as missing the point ; as when he argues that, if Berkeley's doctrine be true, we should not run out of the way of threatened danger.   He delights to point out some petty incongruities in Hume ; but we see at once that he is not able to meet him face to face, and to wrestle with him.   He acknowledges the superior abilities of Hume ; but thinks the sceptics unworthy of any kind of reserve or deference, and maintains that their reasonings were not only false but ridiculous, and that their talents as philosophers and logicians were absolutely contemptible.

WE are still in an age in which young men belonging to county families devoted themselves to the work of the ministry of the gospel. George Campbell was the son of the Rev. John Campbell, a minister in Aberdeen, and one of the Campbells of Westhall, who claimed to be cadets of the house of Argyll. He was educated at the grammar-school, Aberdeen, and at Marischal College ; and, being destined by his family to the law, he was apprenticed to a writer to the signet in Edinburgh. But he had a strong disposition towards the church, and he attended divinity lectures first in Edinburgh, and then in Marischal and in King's, Aberdeen. He was licensed to preach the gospel in 1746, and was settled as minister of Banchory-Ternan on the banks of the Dee in 1748. He was translated to a church in Aberdeen in 1757, and there (in 1758) became a member of the famous Philosophical Society, and contributed papers which were afterwards elaborated into volumes. In 1759, he was made principal of Marischal College, and every one felt that he was worthy of the office and fitted for it. In 1771, he was appointed professor of divinity in the same college, as successor to Gerard. In his opening lecture he says : " It is supposed that I am to teach you every thing connected with the study of divinity." " I am to teach you nothing ; but, by the grace of God, I will assist you to teach yourselves every thing." He now resigned his city charge ; but, as minister of Grayfriars, an office conjoined with the professorship, he preached every Sunday in one of the churches.

It is a curious coincidence that as Reid succeeded the Rev. John Bissett in Old Machar, so Campbell succeeded him in Aberdeen : the earnest evangelical giving way in both cases to the cultured moderate. From his entrance into Aberdeen he was much admired by the educated and refined. The story is that some one told Gerard that he must now look to his laurels, whereupon the old professor replied that the incomer was indolent, a remark which was reported to Campbell, who

[1] Life, by Rev. Dr. Keith. MS. Papers in possession of Andrew Farquharson of Whitehouse, kindly lent me.

profited by it, and became remarkable for his diligence. It is certain that in his later years he showed amazing industry in his literary pursuits. From time to time he gave to the press sermons characteristic of the age : calm, dignified, elegant, and moral, full of reverence, and carefully free from all extravagance and fanaticism. One feels as if he should have been a bishop delivering charges to his clergy, fitted to sustain the dignity of the Church of England. His speaking is thus described : " The closeness, the force, the condensed precision of his reasoning exceed the power of description. Not a single superfluous word was used, no weak or doubtful argument introduced."

But he gave to the world more elaborate works. Hume's influence was now beginning to be felt, and in 1763, Campbell publicly entered the lists against him, in "A Dissertation on Miracles." Before publishing the work, he transmitted through Dr. Blair a copy to Hume, who writes him in his usual pleasant manner, not entering into controversy, but stating how his own argument had occurred to him when a Jesuit was plying him with some "nonsensical miracle." In answering the sceptic, Campbell proposes to prove that testimony hath a natural and original influence on belief antecedent to experience. He may be right in saying that there is such a tendency, — I believe it to be hereditary in children ; but this can serve him very little in his argument, as it is not of the nature of a necessary principle, and he is obliged to admit that testimony often deceives, so that we are brought back, as Hume maintains, to experience. But he is more successful when he shows that experience can prove a miracle, and this notwithstanding that nature is uniform. "For this purpose I make the following supposition. I have lived for some years near a ferry. It consists with my knowledge that the passage-boat has a thousand times crossed the river, and as many times returned safe. An unknown man, whom I have just now met, tells me in a serious manner that it is lost, and affirms that he himself saw the passengers carried down the stream and the boat overwhelmed. No person who is influenced in his judgment of things, not by philosophical subtleties, but by common sense, a much surer guide, will hesitate to declare that in such a testimony I have probable evidence of the fact asserted." The last work published by him was " The

Four Gospels, translated from the Greek, with Preliminary Dissertations, and Notes Critical and Explanatory," 1789. The translation, though elegant, is not idiomatic ; but the dissertations show a fine critical spirit. After his death, his " Lectures on Ecclesiastical History," his " Lectures on Systematic Theology and Pulpit Eloquence," and his "Lectures on the Pastoral Character," were published. But in this work we have to look merely at the philosophical discussions in his work on the " Philosophy of Rhetoric," which was commenced at Banchory, and published in 1776.

We have seen all throughout this history that the Scottish metaphysicians following Shaftesbury were fond of speculating about beauty and taste, and that all the Scottish thinkers at this time were anxious to acquire an elegant style. Adam Smith for several years read lectures with great eclat on rhetoric and belles-lettres in Edinburgh, under the patronage of Lord Kames, and afterwards did the same in the class of logic in Glasgow University. Lord Kames himself discussed like subjects in his " Elements of Criticism." The elegant preacher Dr. Hugh Blair lectured on the subject in the university of Edinburgh, and his " Lectures on Rhetoric and Belles-lettres " is one of the most useful books ever published on the art of composition. These works were used for several ages, not only in Scotland, but even in England, and helped to make rhetoric a leading branch of study in all the American colleges. Among all the works, Campbell's " Philosophy of Rhetoric " is perhaps the most philosophical, or is, at least, the one in which there is the most frequent discussion of philosophic problems.[1]

He opens: " In speaking, there is always some end in view, or some effect which the speaker intends to produce on the hearer." The word *eloquence*, in its greatest latitude, denotes that art or talent by which the discourse is adapted to its end. In speaking of oratory suited to light and trivial matters, he endeavors to define wit. " It is the design of wit to excite in

---

[1] This may be the most appropriate place for referring to Ogilvie's " Philosophical and Critical Observations on the Nature, Character, and Various Species of Composition," 1774. The author was born 1737, became minister of Midmar in Aberdeenshire, and died in 1814. He was a miscellaneous writer in poetry and prose. In "The Theology of Plato compared with the Principles of Oriental and Grecian Philosophy," he treats of topics not usually discussed by the Scottish metaphysicians.

the mind an agreeable surprise, and that arising not from any thing marvellous in the subject, but solely from the imagery she employs, or the strange assemblage of related ideas presented to the mind." This end is effected in one or other of these three ways, — first, in debasing things pompous or seemingly grave;" "secondly, in aggrandizing things, little and frivolous ; thirdly, in setting ordinary objects by means not only remote, but apparently contrary, in a particular and uncommon point of view."

He enlarges, as most of the Scottish metaphysicians have done, on the different kinds of evidence. He begins with intuitive evidence, which, he says, is of different sorts. "One is that which results purely from intellection. Of this kind is the evidence of these propositions : 'One and four make five ;' 'things equal to the same thing are equal to one another ;' 'the whole is greater than a part ;' and, in brief, all in arithmetic and geometry. These are in effect but so many different expositions of our own general notions taken in different views." "But when the thing, though in effect coinciding, is considered under a different aspect, — when what is single in the subject is divided in the predicate, and conversely, or when what is a whole in the one is regarded as a part of something in the other, — such propositions lead to the discovery of innumerable and apparently remote relations." Under this head he also places, secondly, consciousness, "whence every man derives the perfect assurance which he hath of his own existence." He mentions, thirdly, common sense, giving to Buffier the credit of first noticing this principle as one of the genuine springs of our knowledge, whereas Shaftesbury had previously given it a special and important place. That he has not a definite idea of what common sense is as a philosophic principle, is evident from his stating that "in different persons it prevails in different degrees of strength," thus confounding the common principles of intelligence in all men with the sound sense possessed only by certain persons. He mentions a number of such principles, such as "whatever has a beginning has a cause ;" "when there is in the effect a manifest adjustment of the several parts to a certain end, there is intelligence ;" "the course of nature will be the same to-morrow that it is to-day." He tries to draw distinctions between different kinds of intuitive truth. Thus,

in regard to primary truths of the third class, " it may be urged
that it cannot be affirmed of them all at least, as it may be of
the axioms in mathematics, or the assurances we have from
consciousness, that the denial of them implies a contradiction."
It is necessary, I believe, to draw some such distinctions as
these between the various kinds of first truths ; some of them
seem to me to be of the nature of primitive cognitions, others
of primitive judgments.   But it is doubtful whether Campbell
has been able to enunciate the nature of the difference.   That
he has no clear ideas of the relation of our primary perceptions
to realities is evident from his statement.   " All the axioms in
mathematics are but the enunciations of certain properties in
our abstract notions, distinctly perceived by the mind, but have
no relation to any thing without themselves, and cannot be made
the foundation of any conclusion concerning actual existence ;"
as if the demonstrations of Archimedes as to conic sections
had not been found to apply to the elliptic orbits of the comets
as discovered by Kepler.

In speaking of deductive evidence, he distinguishes between
scientific and moral. 1. " The subject of the one is abstract, independent truth, or the unchangeable and necessary relation of
ideas ; that of the other, the real but often changeable and contingent connections that subsist among things actually existing." 2. Moral evidence admits degrees, demonstration doth not.
3. In the one there never can be any contrariety of proofs ;
in the other, there not only may be, but almost always is.
4. The one is simple, consisting of only one coherent series ;
whereas moral evidence is generally complicated, being in
reality a bundle of independent proofs.   Under moral reasoning he treats of experience, analogy, testimony, calculation of
chances, &c.   He discusses the nature and use of the scholastic art of syllogizing.   He has no idea of the syllogism being
merely an analysis of the process which passes through the
mind in all ratiocination.   His objections have been satisfactorily answered by Whately.

He has a very interesting chapter on the cause of that
pleasure which we receive from objects or representations that
excite pity and other painful feelings, criticising the explanations by others, and unfolding one of his own, which is rather
complicated.   We are not concerned to follow him when he en-

ters on style and elocution. Speaking of his philosophic ability,
I am inclined to place him next to Reid in the Aberdeen school.

When minister at Banchory, he married Miss Farquharson,
of Whitehouse, of whom "I can say with truth that I never
knew a more pious, more humane woman, or a woman of better
sense. She had an enlargement of sentiment not often to be
found in man (who have many advantages by education), and
very unlike the contracted notions of the party among whom
she had been bred. You will not mistake me, my dear; it is not
those of the Church of England I mean, — a society for which
I have a great respect, — but our Scotch nonjurors, who, though
they concur pretty much with the other in the ceremonial part,
differ widely in the spirit they infuse." This is an extract from
letters to his niece, Annie Richardson, who had gone to a
boarding-school at Durham. These letters are preserved in the
Farquharson manuscripts, and are very kindly. "You may depend upon it we do not forget our dear little niece who has
been so long with us, and whom we do and cannot help considering as one of ourselves, — as an essential part of our little
family." The advices given, though rather commonplace, are
not on that account the less useful. "Let it be an invariable
maxim with you, my dear, that no art will continue long to
have influence but what is founded on truth. Deceit and falsehood may sometimes serve a present turn, but never fail
sooner or later to be detected. An injury is done to the in-
tegrity of one's own mind by doing what is wrong, though it
should never be discovered; the discovery which commonly
follows injures one's character." His religious counsels are
characteristic: "In regard to religion, you are now at the time
of life when it specially claims your attention; and I shall at
present only observe to you that you ought to study to be possessed of the spirit of it, which consists truly in fearing God
and working righteousness; in other words, in loving God and
your neighbor; but avoid carefully an excessive attachment to
any particular form or mode of worship. The two extremes
to be guarded against are libertinism and bigotry. The former
consists in the want of a proper sense of religion; and the
latter in an inordinate attachment to forms, or to any of the
distinguishing badges of a particular sect or party."

In the Farquharson manuscripts there are letters from Dr. Douglas, of Windsor, from which we gather some glimpses of the times. "It appears that in Oxford and Cambridge the number of students [letter dated 1789] had greatly decreased in consequence of the little attention which many of the bishops of late years had paid to their degrees." He goes on to say: " The very great influx of young men from Scotland offering themselves as candidates for orders has been generally remarked. This did not use to be the case, and nothing perhaps will check it but a strictness which, in particular cases, will, I have no doubt, be dispensed with." It appears from these letters that he is in London in July, 1787, along with Dr. Beattie and his son, and that he is making arrangements about the publication of his "Dissertations." He spends a week with Dr. Douglas ; and had the honor of a little conversation with his Majesty no less than three different times, and once, which is still more, with the Queen. "It is not to be questioned, that, after such distinction, I feel myself a much greater man than when you knew me at Aberdeen."

In person he was below the middle size, with a mild and delicate expression. In conversation he was pleasant and agreeable, though at times falling into fits of absence. He resigned his professorship in 1795, and soon after his principalship. He died April 1, 1796.

———•———

XXXI. — *JAMES BURNETT (LORD MONBODDO).*

He was descended from an ancient family in Kincardineshire, and was born in October, 1714, at Monboddo, which is beautifully situated on the southern slope of the Grampians, and commands a view of the *Howe of the Mearns*, lying below it. He received the rudiments of his education at the parish school of Laurencekirk, which lies a few miles off, and studied the usual branches at King's College, Aberdeen, where he showed a taste for Greek literature, and graduated there in 1729. It was still the habit of Scottish youths who wished to have a high education to resort to Holland, and he went to Gröningen, where he continued three years studying civil law, and where, it is reported, in the society of some English gentlemen and French refugees, he contrived to get rid of his Scotch pronunciation, and to acquire an accurate knowledge of the French tongue. In 1738, he was admitted to the Scotch bar, where he rose to eminence by his learning and his shrewdness, and particularly distinguished himself in the famous Douglas case, and helped to gain the title and estates for his client. In 1767, he was raised to the bench by the title of Lord Monboddo. As a judge, he was painstaking and upright ; his decisions were sound, and supported by great erudition and acuteness. From time to time he rode up to London on horseback, and there mingled in the best literary circles, with such men as Murdoch, Armstrong, James Thomson, and Mallet, Markham, the Archbishop of York, Earl Stanhope, the first and second Earls of Mansfield, Lords Thurlow and Grantley, Bishops Horsley, Lowth, Porteous, Shipley, and Burgess, Sir John Pringle, Lewis, Scot, Seward, and Harris the author of " Hermes." While there, he showed himself at the levee and drawing-room at St. James, where the King took special notice of him.

He married a very lovely woman, Grace Farquharson, who died early, having had three children, a son and two daughters ; the son and one of the daughters were cut off, to the great distress of the father. The poet Burns, who received much attention from the judge, addressed a poem to that daughter, and says of her : " There has not been any thing nearly like her, in all the combinations of beauty, grace, and goodness the great Creator has formed, since Milton's Eve, on the first day of her existence." In the midst of his legal studies and his domestic afflictions he ever turned eagerly to metaphysical pursuits. In 1773, he published his elaborate work, "On the Origin and Progress of Language," and at various times from 1779 to 1799 his still larger work on " Ancient Metaphysics." At his country seat, he acted the farmer, lived on terms of pleasant familiarity with the people on his estate, was generously hospitable, and zealously promoted agriculture in his neighborhood. At this place he received Samuel Johnson on his Scottish tour. In Boswell's account of the intercourse of the two, Lord Monboddo appears in by no means a disadvantageous light. He died at his house in Edinburgh, May 26, 1799.

The eccentricities of his opinions and his conduct never interfered with his practical sagacity, or lowered him in the esteem and affection of the community. "His unbounded admiration of the customs, the literature, and the philosophy of the ancients strongly prepossessed him in favor of whatever was connected with such studies. In them, he supposed that he beheld all that was praiseworthy and excellent, while he looked on the moderns as a degenerate race, exhibiting only effeminacy and corruption. This attachment to ancient manners led him to imitate them, even in his amusements and habits of life. He was fond of athletic exercises in his youth, particularly fencing and fox-hunting, which tended to strengthen a constitution naturally healthy and robust. His general hour of rising in all seasons was six in the morning; and till a late period of his life he used the cold bath in the open air, even in the middle of winter. He took a light, early dinner, and a plentiful supper. The ancient practice of anointing, even, was not forgotten, though the lotion he used was not the oil of the ancients, but a saponaceous liquid composed of rose-water, olive oil, saline aromatic spirit, and Venice soap, which, when well mixed, resembled cream. This he applied at bedtime, before a large fire, after coming from a warm bath. His method of travelling was also in conformity to his partiality for ancient customs. A carriage, which was not in common use among the ancients, he considered as an engine of effeminacy and sloth; and to be dragged at the tail of a horse, instead of mounting upon his back, appeared to him to be a truly ludicrous degradation of the genuine dignity of human nature."[1] In Kames's Life it is said his "temper was affectionate, friendly, social. He was fond of convivial intercourse, and it was his daily custom to unbend himself amidst a select party of literary friends, whom he invited to an early supper. The entertainment itself partook of the costume of the ancients; it had all the variety and abundance of a principal meal; and the master of the feast crowned his wine, like Anacreon, with a garland of roses. His conversation, too, had a *race* and flavor peculiarly its own. It was nervous, sententious, and tinctured with genuine wit. His apothegms, or, as his favorite Greeks would rather term them, γνῶμαι, were singularly terse and for-

---

[1] Article, James Burnett, in the "Edinburgh Encyclopedia."

cible, and the grave manner in which he often conveyed the keenest irony, and the eloquence with which he supported his paradoxical theories, afforded the highest amusements of those truly Attic banquets which will be long remembered by all who had the pleasure of partaking in them."

I confess that I have felt a deep interest in reading the philosophical works of Lord Monboddo, — he is so unlike any other Scotch metaphysician, he is so unlike his age. As appearing among a body of inductive inquirers, and in the middle of the eighteenth century, he looks very much like a megatherium coming in upon us in the historical period. His society is not with the modern empiricists, not even with the Latins, but with Plato and the Neo-Platonists, with Aristotle and his commentators. As regards the higher Greek philosophy, he is the most erudite scholar that Scotland has produced, not excepting even Sir William Hamilton. His favorite author among the moderns is Cudworth, whom he characterizes as "more learned in the whole ancient philosophy, the older as well as the later, than any modern author I know." He speaks of Locke's Essay as "no other than a hasty collection of crude, undigested thoughts, by a man who thought and reasoned by himself upon subjects of the greatest difficulty and deepest speculation, without assistance of learning." He refers to Andrew Baxter, and charges the Newtonian astronomy with making the system of the heavens a mere machine; it supposes the universe had a beginning in time, contrary to all the ancients, who held that it "was an eternal emanation of an eternal being." It is mind that moves the celestial bodies, — mind moving simply and uniformly. He refers to Berkeley, and also to Hume, lately deceased, and says of the latter, that his chief argument arises from "confounding sensations and ideas." He refers also to Reid's "Inquiry," and I suppose that the rising Scottish school was before him when he speaks of it as an unsatisfactory philosophy, which would maintain that "the perception of every sensible object is necessarily accompanied with a belief of its existence; that is the constitution of our nature, and that we are to inquire no more about it." He holds it "to be impossible that intellect can believe any thing without a reason." He maintains that we do not form

ideas by nature. " We mistake habits of judging acquired by
experience for the natural perceptions of sense." He thinks
that by the eye we perceive objects first as double and in-
verted. His postulatum is that " the evidence of consciousness is infallible." " By consciousness, we know that we have
perceptions of sense." " In the perceptions of sense, every
man is conscious that he is passive, and that he is moved or
excited to sensation by some thing." Of all his contemporaries,
he is most thoroughly in sympathy with Mr. Harris, the author
of " Hermes," with whom he corresponded.

We may here give an extract-letter from Lord Monboddo
to Mr. Harris, in return for presentation copy of " Hermes."

" Edinburgh, Wednesday, 26 March, 1766. — As your works first introduced me to the Greek Philosophy, so this present you have now made me
has revived my taste for that study, which, though never quite extinguished,
had been lost for some time amid the hurry of law business. I fell on
greedily, as soon as the book was sent me, and began with the most philosophical part of your ' Hermes,' viz., the chapter upon General Ideas, which
you have explained most truly and philosophically, according to the dictates of that school to which, I confess, I have entirely addicted myself, — I
mean the school of Aristotle, for as to Plato, he speaks of them in such
mysterious and enigmatical terms, as if they had been a secret known only
to himself; and I remember he makes Hippias the Sophist, when he was
asked what the τὸ καλὸν was, answer, 'it was a fine virgin.' If philosophy was
in such a state in the days of Plato, as not to understand perfectly what is
the foundation of all science and knowledge among men, how much is it indebted to that wonderful man, Aristotle, who, besides his discoveries in
every branch of philosophy, has cleared the principles of it from that
obscurity which the enthusiasm and mystic genius of Plato had thrown
upon them ?

" I think I may, without the least suspicion of flattery, give to you the
praise which Cicero takes to himself, of teaching philosophy to speak a new
language ; for as he taught it to speak Latin, so you have taught it to speak
English. The language which Mr. Locke has put into her mouth is mere
stammering, and is, in my opinion, as contemptible as the matter which he
has made her utter. Mr. Hobbes I am not so well acquainted with ; but as
he is of the same heresy, that is, one of those who pretend to philosophize,
without the assistance of the ancients, I suppose he has succeeded as ill.
As for myself, I am meditating great things in the literary way, but I am
not sure that I will ever execute any thing. I have one work in view, which
I think would not make a bad second part, if it were executed, to your
' Hermes,' — I mean a work showing the origin and progress of this most
wonderful of all the arts of man, the art of speech. What set me upon this
train of thinking was the study of some most barbarous and imperfect languages, spoken in America, from grammars and dictionaries which I had

out of the King's Library, when I was last at Paris. Besides the curiosity of seeing the process of so wonderful an art, in tracing the progress of language, you at the same time trace the progress of the human understanding, and I think I have already collected materials from which a very good history of the human mind might be formed, — better, at least, than that which Mr. Locke has given us. This, if I had leisure, I would make part of a much greater work which I project, viz., a History of Man ; in which I would propose to trace him through the several stages of his existence ; for there is a progression of our species from a state little better than mere brutality to that most perfect state you describe in ancient Greece, which is really amazing, and peculiar to our species. But the business of a laborious profession will, I'm afraid, prevent me from executing this, and several other projects which I have had in my head. But with respect to you, being now eased of the care of public affairs, the world will certainly exact from you an account of your leisure ; especially as you have given them such pledges of your capacity to instruct and entertain them. You have done enough upon grammar. But I would have you do something upon logic, to show an ignorant age that the greatest discovery in science ever made by any one man is the discovery of the syllogism by Aristotle." [1]

He has two great philosophic works. The first is "Ancient Metaphysics, or the Science of Universals; with an Appendix containing an Examination of the Principles of Sir Isaac Newton's Philosophy." It is in six quarto volumes, averaging four hundred pages each. He treats first of metaphysics and then of man. The proper subject of metaphysics is "mind pure and separate from all matter." In nature, all is either body or mind or their accidents. There is not in the universe, so far as our knowledge extends, any body without mind ; they are never separated in the material world. "What is moved I call body, what moves is called mind." "Under mind in this definition I include, 1st, the rational and intellectual ; 2d, the animal life ; 3d, the principle in the vegetable by which it is nourished, grows, and produces its like, and which, therefore, is commonly called the vegetable life ; and 4th, the motive principle, which I understand to be in all bodies, even such as are thought to be inanimate." He says the Greek word ψυχή denotes the three first kinds ; the fourth, the motive, is not commonly in Greek called ψυχή, but Aristotle says it is ὥσπερ ψυχή. He makes moving or producing motion an essential property of mind. In respect of quality, motion applies to mind as well as body. By motion the whole business of nature above, below, and round about us is carried on. "It is impossible that any thing can be generated, come to maturity, or be extinguished without passing from one state to another. Now that passage is motion." He proves the immateriality of mind in general, (1) from the nature of motion, (2) from the nature of body, (3) from the nature of mind. He establishes the two first *a priori*, and the third by a demonstration *ex absurdo*. He has then *a posteriori* proof. " Sensation cannot be produced by a material cause ; reasoning and consciousness far less."

Coming to minds, he adopts the Aristotelean distinction between the gnostic and orective powers. The gnostic powers are sense, phantasy, and comparison. In sense, the mind is not conversant with the visible object itself, but with the image or εἴδωλον, as the Epicureans called it, thrown off from the object. The essential distinction between sense and phantasia is, that what we perceive by the sense is present and operating upon the sense, whereas the object of the imagination is not present. Phantasy is only of sensible objects. Memory is only of ideas, and belongs exclusively to man. " Brutes have no idea of time, or of first and last. Phantasy serves to them the purpose of memory." The object is painted on the brute's phantasia, but without any perception of the time when he first saw it. Sense and phantasy perceive particular things, — comparison, generals or ideas. He thinks that brutes possess the comparative faculty, and that here the mind of the brute acts without the assistance of the body. As to will, he reckons "all will as free, and, at the same time, it is necessary ; but of a necessity very different from material or physical." Much of this psychology is avowedly taken from Aristotle, but at the same time exhibits traces of shrewdness and independence, and, it has to be added, of eccentricity.

He criticises Locke's theory of the origin of ideas. He acknowledges no innate ideas, if we mean ideas present to the mind, and contemplated before they are excited by objects ; but they are there though " latent and unproductive," and are there even before our existence in this world. Nature, however, " has so ordained it, that they can only be excited by the impulse of objects upon our organs of sense." It should be noticed here, that notwithstanding the prominence given to it by

Locke, Lord Monboddo has no recognition of reflection or consciousness as a separate source of ideas.

He dwells with evident fondness on categories or universal forms. All things are to be known by their causes. The knowledge of first causes belongs to metaphysics. Every thing that is to be known falls under one or other of the categories. He shows that God must have ideas. Man is capable of forming ideas. Time is not a cause, but is a necessary adjunct or concomitant of the material world. If nothing existed, it is evident there could be no such thing as time. His definition of time does not make the subject much clearer, as it introduces the phrase duration, which needs explanation quite as much as time does: "it is the measure of the duration of things that exist in succession by the motion of the celestial bodies. Beings which suffer no change, neither in substance, qualities, nor energies, cannot be in time. Of this kind we conceive Divinity to be, and therefore he is not in time but in eternity." As to space, it is nothing actually, but it is something potentially; for it has the capacity of receiving body, "for which it furnishes room or place." Here it should be observed that room or place comes in to explain space, which is as clear as either room or place, — which are, in, fact embraced in it. "Space has not the capacity of becoming any thing, but only of receiving any thing."

He represents Aristotle as saying that the beauty of nature consists in final causes, without which we can conceive no beauty in any thing. In expounding his own views, he tells us that in a single object there may be truth, but no beauty. In order to give beauty to truth, there must be "a system, of which the mind, perceiving the union, is at the same time struck with that most agreeable of all perceptions which we call beauty. And the greater the variety there is in this system, the greater the number of parts, the more various their connections and dependencies upon one another, the greater the beauty, provided the mind can distinctly comprehend the several parts in one united view." There must be some truth here, though it may not be the whole truth.

In vols. iii. and iv. he treats of man. This is the only part of his book fitted to excite an interest in these times. "It is surprising," he says, "that so little inquiry has been made con-

cerning the natural history of our own species." He then
proceeds to divulge his own theory, which, in some respects, is
an anticipation of the Darwinian. He maintains that man was
at first a mere animal, that he walked on all fours, and that he
possessed a tail, of which we discover the rudiments. There
has been a progression in mankind from one stage to a higher ;
they erect themselves, they learn the use of their hands, and
they learn to swim. They lived first on natural fruits as they
presented themselves, and then learned hunting and fishing.
Men were for a time solitary, and then came to herd together.
He is not so trustworthy as Darwin in his facts : he tells us
that there is a whole nation of Esquimaux with only one leg ;
that the one-eyed cyclops of Homer is not a mere fiction ; that
in Ethiopia men have only one eye, and this in their foreheads ;
and he expresses his belief in mermaids.

But he detects far higher properties than the Darwinians
have yet done. Man's mind was at first immersed in matter ;
but, by exerting its native power, it can act without the assistance of body, and transports itself into that ideal world which
every man who believes in God must believe to be the archetype of this material world. But he insists that there has been
a great degeneracy in the race, of which Moses' account of the
fall of man is an allegorical version. Corruption of manners
begins in every nation among the better sort, and from them
descends to the people. He shows that there must be a total
reformation of manners and morals ; and, in doing so, he speaks
of the effeminacy which has arisen from the use of clothes.
But he is ever insisting on the difference between man and
brute. The actions of man proceed from opinion, but not the
actions of brutes. In the lower animals there is no consideration of means and ends. He finds one great difference in the
circumstance that man is dissatisfied, envies, and repines, which
the brute creatures never do.

In volume vi. he treats of the being of God. Nothing can
exist without a cause. A first cause, therefore, is necessary,
and he inquires into what must be the nature of the cause of
the world. The cause must be self-existent, — necessarily existent, eternal, and unchangeable Of this nature must be the
efficient cause of the world. But he agrees with Aristotle that
there must also have been a natural cause from all eternity. In

his work on language he represents the theology of Plato as more sublime than that of Aristotle.   The theology of Aristotle, so far as it goes, is a pure system of theism ; but it is defective in two great points.   First, the providence of God over all his works is not asserted ; on the contrary, God is represented as passing his whole time in contemplation.   Secondly, he does not make God the author of the material world, but only the mover ; he does not derive from Him even the minds that animate this world.

His work on " The Origin and Progress of Language," in six vols. 8vo., is less important.   Still, it contains some shrewd remarks.   By language he means the expression of the conceptions of the mind by articulate sounds.   He does not think that language is natural to man.   Men came to invent articulate sounds by the imitation of other animals.   A political state was necessary for the invention of language.   He had evidently some acquaintance with the affinities of the Teutonic, Persian, Greek, and Latin.   He represents the Hebrew, Phœnician, Syriac, and Chaldaic, as having also an affinity.   He believes that there may also be an affinity between the two groups.

He corrects a very common misapprehension of his day as to abstract and general ideas.   In his work on metaphysics : "Abstract ideas are different from general, though they be confounded by our modern philosophers ; an idea must be first abstracted from the particular object from which it exists before it can be generalized."   In his work on language, he shows that we may have a conception of a particular quality of any substance abstracted from its other qualities without averring such quality to belong to any other substance.   " In order to form the general idea, a separation or discrimination is necessary of these qualities one from another ; and this kind of abstraction I hold to be the first act of human intellect, and it is here the road parts betwixt us and the brute ; for the brute perceives the thing and perceives the perception in his memory just as the object is presented by nature — that is, with all its several sensible qualities united ; whereas the human intellect separates and discriminates and considers by itself the color, *e.g.*, without the figure, and the size without either."

HE was the son of Rev. Adam Ferguson, minister of the parish of Logrerait, Perthshire, and was born June 20, 1723. The Scottish ministers often belonged to good families in these times, and Carlyle describes Ferguson as the son of a Highland clergyman with good connections and a Highland pride and spirit. He received his early education partly from his father, partly at the parish school. We are ever discovering traces of the influence of the parish schools of Scotland in producing its great men. He afterwards went to the grammar school of Perth, where he excelled in classics and the composition of essays, which has always had a high place in Scotland, fostered by the very circumstance that boys had to unlearn the Scottish and learn the English tongue. Thence he resorted to the University of St. Andrews, where he graduated May 4, 1742, with a high reputation in classics, mathematics, and metaphysics. He now entered on the study of theology, first at St. Andrews, and then in Edinburgh, where he fell into the circle of Robertson, Blair, Wedderburn, and Carlyle, and joined them in forming a debating society. Before finishing his theological course, he was appointed deputy-chaplain of the Highland forty-second regiment, and was present at the battle of Fontenoy, where he went into action at the head of the attacking column with a drawn sword in his hand. His military career helped him afterwards to give accurate descriptions of battles in his "Roman History," and furnished him opportunities for studying human nature and politics. He never had any predilection for the clerical profession, and abandoned it altogether on the death of his father. After spending some time in Holland, as so many Scottish youths had done in the previous century, he returned to his old associates in Edinburgh, where he was appointed, in 1757, David Hume's successor as librarian and clerk in the Advocate's Library. He there became a member of the "Select Society" instituted

[1] Biographical Sketch of Adam Ferguson, LL.D., F.R.S.E, Professor of Moral Philosophy in the University of Edinburgh, by John Small, M.A., Librarian to the University. Read before the Philosophical Society of Edinburgh, April 18, 1864.

in 1754 by Allan Ramsay, and holding its meetings in one of the inner apartments of the library, for literary discussion, philosophical inquiry, and improvement in public speaking. Among its members were Hume, Robertson, Smith, John Home, Wilkie, Lord Hailes, Lord Monboddo, Sir John Dalrymple, and the elder Mr. Tytler, the men who constituted the bright literary constellation of their age and country. This society declined after a time, but was renewed in 1762, under the name (at the suggestion of Ferguson) of the " Poker Club." Ferguson became involved in the controversy stirred by his friend Home writing the play of Douglas, and published " The Morality of Stage Plays seriously Considered." He seems to have left the office of librarian rather abruptly, being allured by an offer to become tutor to the sons of Lord Bute. By the influence of his friends he was made professor of natural philosophy in the University of Edinburgh in 1759, and David Hume remarked : " Ferguson had more genius than any of them, as he had made himself so much master of a difficult science, viz., natural philosophy, which he had never studied but when at college, in three months, so as to be able to teach it." In 1760, he was elected to an office more congenial to him, that of professor of pneumatics and moral philosophy, as successor to Mr. Balfour, who took the chair of the law of nature and nations. In less than two years he published his " Essay on the History of Civil Society," a work on which he had been engaged for a considerable time. It was conceived in the manner of Montesquieu, but dwelt on elements at work in the formation of civil society which the French author had overlooked. Part I. treats of the " General Characteristics of Human Nature." Works on social economy proceed very much on the principle that man is mainly swayed by a desire to promote his own interests, and they furnish no analysis of the other interests which men look to. They do not consider that man has social and conscientious feelings, by which many are influenced quite as much as by self-love ; and that he is as often swayed by caprice, vanity, and passion, as by a cold-hearted selfishness. Ferguson perceived this. Mankind, we are told, are devoted to interest, and this in all commercial nations is undoubtedly true. But it does not follow that they are by their natural dispositions averse to society and mutual affec-

tion. Speaking of those who deny moral sentiment, he says
that they are fond of detecting the fraud by which moral restraints have been imposed ; "as if to censure a fraud were not
already to take a part on the side of morality." "The foreigner who believed that Othello on the stage was enraged for
the loss of his handkerchief was not more mistaken than the
reasoner who imputes any of the more vehement passions of
men to the impressions of mere profit or loss." So, after discussing the question of the state of nature, he treats of the
principles of self-preservation, of union among mankind, of
war and dissension, of intellectual powers, of moral sentiment,
of happiness, of national felicity. In unfolding these, he insists
that mankind should be studied in groups or in society. He
then traces these principles in the history of rude nations, of
policy and arts, the advancement of civil and commercial arts,
the decline of nations, corruption of political slavery. The
tone of the work is healthy and liberal, but is filled with common-place thought and observation. I find a sixth edition
published in 1793. After this it was not much heard of. The
French Revolution gave men more earnest questions to think
of. But these disquisitions, and still more effectively the publication of the "Wealth of Nations," in 1776, kindled a taste
for social inquiries in the University of Edinburgh and in the
capital of Scotland.

The smallness of his salary, only £100 a year, tempted him
to undertake the charge of the education of Charles, Earl of
Chesterfield, nephew to the earl who wrote on manners, and
he had the benefit of a continental tour with his pupil. He
waited upon Voltaire at Ferney, where, he tells us, "I encouraged every attempt at conversation, even jokes against
Moses, Adam, and Eve, and the rest of the prophets, till I
began to be considered as a person who, though true to my
own faith, had no ill-humor to the freedom of fancy in others."
His description is graphic : "I found the old man in a state of
perfect indifference to all authors except two sorts, — one, those
who wrote panegyrics, and those who wrote invectives on himself. There is a third kind, whose names he has been used to
repeat fifty or sixty years without knowing any thing of them,
—such as Locke, Boyle, Newton, &c. I forget his compet-
itors for fame, of whom he is always either silent or speaks

slightingly.   The fact is, that he reads little or none ; his mind
exists by reminiscence, and by doing over and over what it has
been used to do, — dictates tales, dissertations, and tragedies,
even the latter with all his elegance, though not with all his
former force.   His conversation is among the pleasantest I
ever met with.   He lets you forget the superiority which the
public opinion gives him, which is indeed greater than we conceive in this island."   In consequence of his absence, the town
council tried to turn Ferguson out of his office in Edinburgh,
but he resisted at law, and returned to his duties in 1775.

He had evidently a strong inclination to active life, which
might bring him into new scenes and situations favorable to
the study of character.   So in 1778 he was appointed secretary to the commissioners appointed to discuss and settle the
points in dispute between Great Britain and her American
colonies.   In New York the commissioners received a communication from Congress intimating that the only ground upon
which they could enter on a treaty would be an acknowledgment of the independence of the States and the withdrawal of
the British force from America.   So he returns the following
year to his professorial duties, which it is interesting to notice
were performed during his absence by his pupil, Dugald Stewart.   During these years he became involved in the controversy
about the authenticity of the " Poems of Ossian," taking, as
might be expected of a Highlander, the side of Mr. McPherson.
He also took an active part in the formation of the Royal Society of Edinburgh, which originated very much with Principal
Robertson, and was incorporated in 1783.   He had long been
engaged on the work by which he was best known in his own
day, " The History of the Progress and Termination of the
Roman Republic."   Avoiding the early and disputed period of
Roman history, and leaving the later period to Gibbon, he gives
a clear and judicious account of the time which elapsed between 240 A. U. C. and the death of Tiberius.   I am not sure
that we have a better account of the republic, published prior
to the investigations started by Niebuhr.

In 1766, he had published a short syllabus of his lectures, entitled " Analysis of Pneumatics and Moral Philosophy, for the
use of Students in the College of Edinburgh."   Using this as
a text-book, he lectured to his class without writing out what

he said. He claims, however, that he bestowed his utmost diligence in studying the subject, including the order in which it
was to be treated, and in preparing himself for every successive
step he was to make in his course, but to have no more in
writing than the heads or short notes from which he was to
speak, preparing himself, however, very diligently for every particular day's work. When his health gave way, in 1781, he
wrote out his course, and during his retirement corrected it for
the press and published it in 1792 : "Principles of Moral and Political Science ; being chiefly a retrospect of Lectures delivered
in the College of Edinburgh." He confesses that he is partial
to the Stoic philosophy, and acknowledges his obligations to
Shaftesbury, Montesquieu, Harris, and Hutcheson. The work
is divided into two parts, — the first relating to the fact of
man's progressive nature ; the second, to the principles of right,
or the foundations of judgment and choice. The sources of
knowledge are consciousness, perception, testimony, and inference. Consciousness is the first and most essential attribute
of the mind. To other animals, appetite continues to be the
sole motive to action ; and the animal in every moment of time
proceeds on the motive then present. But to man, the repeated
experience of gratification and crosses, like the detail of particulars in any other, is matter of generalization ; he collects
from thence the predicaments of good and evil, and is affected
towards any particular object according as he has referred it
to the one or the other. In unfolding his views, he has important remarks on the purposes served by abstraction. "The
abstract form of an operation is a physical law, and its application the constituent of physical science. The abstract form
and expression of what is excellent or good is a moral law and
principle of moral science." But "to whatever object we incline, or however we may have classed individual things in our
conception of what is good or evil, it is proper to remember in
this place that every effort of the mind is also individual and
particular, relating to an object in some particular and individual
situation." There is a hint here of a distinction between governing principles in their individual exercise and in their abstract form fashioned by the logical understanding, which
might have cleared up a vast amount of confused discussion,
had he carried it out. He adds : "The more general character

of man's inclinations or active dispositions is not a blind propensity to the use of means, but instinctive intimation of an
end for the attainment of which he is left to discover and to
choose by his own observations and experience the means
which may prove most effectual." He starts questions which
had been discussed by Aristotle, but which had been lost sight
of by modern moralists, as to the ends by which man is swayed,
and the importance in ethics of considering means and end,
and for this gets an occasional commendation from Sir W. Hamilton. Believing in the progression of man, he would set before
him no meaner end than the attainment of perfection, and
places in this the principle of moral approbation, and for this
he receives the commendation of M. Cousin. "We find in
his method the wisdom and circumspection of the Scottish
school, with something more masculine and decisive in its results. The principle of *perfection* is a new one, at once more
rational and comprehensive than benevolence and sympathy,
and which, in our view, places Ferguson as a moralist above
all his predecessors." He thinks that he embraces all moral
systems in his own, admitting, with Hobbes and Hume, the
power of self-interest or utility, Hutcheson's benevolence and
Smith's sympathy,—all helping progression, and tending towards
perfection. All this sounds very lofty, and contains important
truth, as we should all aim at our own perfection and that of
the race, but leaves the question unsettled, what is this perfection to be, — a perfection in felicity, as the final end, or a
perfection in moral good : and what is the nature and criterion
of moral good ?

Ferguson's style and manner are not so subdued as those of
the Scottish metaphysicians who preceded him. He has more
of a leaping mode of composition, as if he had an audience
before him, and is at times eloquent or magniloquent. I have
an idea that, as Dugald Stewart drew his philosophy mainly from
Reid, so he got his taste for social studies from Ferguson, who
may also have helped to give him a livelier style, — the academic dignity, however, being entirely Stewart's own.

In 1785, he resigned his professorial labors. He passed the
remainder of his life in retirement, residing in various places,
and living till 22d June, 1816. The following pen-and-ink
sketch of the old man by Lord Cockburn, in the " Memorials

of his Time," brings him vividly before us : "His hair was silky and white ; his eyes animated and light-blue ; his cheeks sprinkled with broken red, like autumnal apples, but fresh and healthy ; his lips thin, and the under one curled.   A severe paralytic attack had reduced his animal vitality, though it left no external appearance, and he required considerable artificial heat.   His raiment, therefore, consisted of half-boots, lined with fur ; cloth breeches ; a long cloth waistcoat, with capacious pockets ; a single-breasted coat ; a cloth greatcoat, also lined with fur ; and a felt hat, commonly tied by a ribbon below the chin.   His boots were black, but, with this exception, the whole coverings, including the hat, were of a quaker-gray color, or of a whitish-brown ; and he generally wore the furred greatcoat even within doors.   When he walked forth, he used a tall staff, which he commonly held at arm's-length out towards the right side ; and his two coats, each buttoned by only the upper button, flowed open below, and exposed the whole of his curious and venerable figure.   His gait and air were noble ; his gesture slow ; his look full of dignity and composed fire.   He looked like a philosopher from Lapland."   I never heard of his dining out except at his relation, Joseph Black's, where his son, Sir Adam (the friend of Scott), used to say "it was delightful to see the two rioting over a boiled turnip.   Domestically, he was kind, but anxious and peppery."   "He always locked the door of his study when he left it, and took the key in his pocket ; and no housemaid got in till the accumulation of dust and rubbish made it impossible to put the evil day off any longer, and then woe on the family."

XXXIII. — JAMES HUTTON.

He was the son of a merchant in Edinburgh, was born June 3, 1726, studied first in his native city, then in Leyden, where he took the degree of M.D., and devoted his life to agricultural pursuits and scientific investigations in chemistry, mineralogy, and specially in geology. He died March 26, 1797. He is best known as the author of a " Theory of the Earth," which was expounded in a clear and elegant manner by Playfair.   He accounts for the present condition of the earth by the operation of a central heat ; and there was long a contest between his theory and that of Werner, who explains the formation of strata by water ; geologists now find place for both agencies. It is not so generally known that he found much satisfaction in the pursuit of metaphysics, and is author of an elaborate work in three large quarto volumes, " An Investigation of the Principles of Knowledge, and of the Progress of Reason from Sense to Science and Philosophy." The work is full of awkwardly constructed sentences and of repetitions, and it is a weariness in the extreme to read it. Yet we are made to feel at times that these thoughts must be profound, if only we could understand them. He certainly speculates on recondite subjects, but does not throw much light on them. Knowledge is " considered as consisting first of external information ; secondly, of internal conception. In the first, mind is made to know no passion ; in the second, it is made to know no action." " Knowledge is no more the attribute of mind than mind is that of knowledge. We suppose that there is a substance called mind, and we then attribute knowledge to this substance ; but knowledge is the very thing which in this case subsists. Space and time are conceptions of the mind, founded upon activity and inactivity ; that is to say, upon the volition of the mind, whereby either on the one hand action is produced that is change, or on the other hand inaction is ordained wherein the powers of the mind are preserved in a state of attention to the idea then in view." In his view of matter, he expounds a dynamical theory which becomes an ideal theory, closely approaching that of Berkeley. " There is no inert matter subsisting with magnitude and figure ; but the external thing exists with moving and resisting powers." " Real solidity or impenetrability is truly a conception of our intellect, like that of equal lines and angles, but it is a supposition which nothing in nature authorizes us to make." " We deceive ourselves when we imagine that there is a subsisting independent of our thought, — an external thing, which is actually extended and necessarily figured." " Figure is a thing formed in the mind alone, or produced by the proper action of our thinking substance." He says it is wrong to suppose that magnitude and figure subsist without our mind. He tells us that his theory agrees with that of Berkeley in this, that " figure and magnitude are not real and absolute qualities in external things ; " but he holds that " there is truly an external existence as the cause of our knowledge," whereas Berkeley holds that there is no such external existence. We have here a view of matter very different from that of the Scottish school, who have commonly been inclined to the doctrine of Descartes. Metaphysical science will now have to set itself to determine what substantial truth there is in idealism, and, with the light of modern inquiries as to atoms, what truth there is in the dynamical theory of matter.

XXXIV. — *JOHN GREGORY.*[1]

THE Gregorys are about as illustrious a family as Scotland has produced. Chalmers, in his " Biographical Dictionary." reckons no fewer than sixteen who have held British professorships. The founder of the family was James Gregory, the inventor of the reflecting telescope which bears his name. He became professor of mathematics in St. Andrew's, where he died in 1675, at the early age of thirty-six. He had a son James, who became professor of medicine in King's College, Aberdeen, and founded the school of medicine there. John, who merits a passing notice in our pages, was the son of this gentleman. He was born at Aberdeen in 1724, was educated there, occupied successively the chairs of philosophy and medicine, and, along with Reid, instituted the famous literary society. To this society he read essays, which were methodized and published in 1764, under the title, "Comparative View of the State and Faculties of Man with those of the Animal World." He considers the condition of man in a state of society under three different aspects : (1) in a savage state, where he is distinguished by his corporeal powers ; (2) when the social affections and the heroic virtues appear ; (3) where men have the means of acquiring wealth, and seek refinement and luxury. In treating of these topics he offers many thoughtful reflections. He remarks that men of refined genius must live in a manner abstracted from the world, that hence they are liable to cherish envy and jealousy ; so there is perhaps less real friendship among authors than among the rest of mankind. "Certain it is, virtue, genius, beauty, wealth, power, and every natural advantage one can be possessed of, are usually mixed with some alloy, while disappointing the fond hopes of their raising the possessor to any uncommon degree of eminence, and even in some measure bring him down to the common level of his species." He dwells fondly on taste, and remarks, "wherever what is denominated a very correct taste is generally prevalent, genius and invention soon languish." In treating of religion, he exhibits the rising spirit of his age. "The articles of religious belief falling within the comprehension of mankind are few and simple, but have been erected by ingenious men into monstrous systems of metaphysical subtlety." "Speculative and controversial theology injure both the temper and affections." In the same year he removed to the wider field offered in Edinburgh, and became one of the ornaments of the brilliant literary circle there. Two years after he was appointed professor of the practice of medicine in the university, and was a very popular teacher. He published a number of medical works, and left behind him when he died in 1773 a work composed after he lost his wife, "A Father's Legacy to his Daughter." It is characterized by calm wisdom, often somewhat worldly, and for long had a large circulation. "Be ever cautious in

---

[1] Life, by Lord Woodhouselee, prefixed to his "Works" in four volumes ; "Literary and Characteristical Lives," by William Smellie.

displaying your good sense.   It will be thought you assume a superiority
over the rest of the company.   But if you happen to have any learning, keep
it a profound secret, especially from the men, who generally look with a
jealous and malignant eye on a woman of great parts and a cultivated understanding."

----◆----

XXXV. — *JAMES GREGORY.*

James Gregory, the third of this name, was the son and the successor in
the chair of medicine in Edinburgh of John Gregory.   He was born in
Aberdeen in 1753, and died in 1821.   For many years he stood at the head
of his profession as a physician in Edinburgh.   He published a number of
medical works.   His " Conspectus Medicinæ Theoreticæ," written in good
Latin, was long used as one of the works on which the candidates for medical degrees were examined.   He comes before us as author of " Philosophical and Literary Essays," dated Jan. 1st, 1790, and published 1792.   He
dedicates the work to Reid, and acknowledges that he had taken a principal
argument from one of Reid's observations in the essays on the " Intellectual Powers of Man."   The most important essay is " On the difference
between the Relation of Motive and Action and that of Cause in Physics,
on Physical and Mathematical Principles."   In an introduction in which he
is long in coming to the point, he dwells on the looseness and ambiguity of
the word "cause," and remarks that if " there should be occasion to attend
to the more minute or specific differences among the several things comprehended under the genus 'cause,' it would be highly expedient or rather
absolutely necessary to give to each of them a specific name, were it only an
addition to the generic name cause."   He has a glimpse of there being
more than one agent involved in cause.   " No substance is of itself a
physical cause ; this depends on its relation to some other substance, and
implies the tendency to change in the latter."   " The substance in which
the change is observed is considered as the subject, the other as the cause ;
and as change occurs generally in both or all of the substances so related,
though it be not always of the same kind in them all, it depends on the
circumstance of our attention being directed first and chiefly to one or other
of them, and on our opportunities of observing the changes that occur in
them, which of them we shall regard as the subject and which as the cause,
as in the example of the communication and the loss of motion, of mutual
gravitation, of the solution of salt and saturation of water, the melting of ice,
or the boiling of water and the absorption of heat."   This is a vague anticipation of the doctrine started in our day as to their being two or more
agents in all material causation, — a doctrine, I may add, not yet followed out
to its consequences in regard to mechanical, chemical, and physiological
action.   He insists that there is in mind a certain independent self-govern-
ing power which there is not in body ; in consequence of which there is a
great difference between the relation of motive and action and that of cause

and effect in physics ; and by means of which a person in all cases may at his own discretion act, either according to or in opposition to any motive or combination of motives applied to him ; while body in all cases irresistibly undergoes the change corresponding to the cause or combination of causes applied to it. " I propose to demonstrate the falsity and absurdity of the doctrine of necessity on mathematical principles, in mathematical form, partly by means of algebraic formulæ, partly with the help of diagrams," and he uses mathematical formulæ and others invented by himself. He endeavors to show by an indirect demonstration that the doctrine of necessity must be false, as it leads to false conclusions. He takes the case of a porter carrying a burden : " If a guinea should be offered for carrying it in the direction of A B, and half a guinea for carrying it in the direction A C, and let him be assured that if he can earn the guinea he cannot earn the half guinea, and that if he earn the half guinea he cannot earn the guinea ; will he go in the direction of A B or A C, or remain at rest in A ? " He answers, that if the principle on which the necessity is founded be true, he must move in the diagonal A D. " But as it must be acknowledged that the porter will not move in that direction, experience proving the fact, then it follows that the law of physical causes and that of motives do not coincide, and that the relation between motives and actions is not necessary as between physical causes and their effects." Dr. Crombie attacked Dr. Gregory's reasoning, Sir W. Hamilton says "with much acrimony and considerable acuteness." There subsequently appeared letters from Dr. James Gregory, of Edinburgh, in defence of his essay on the " Difference of the Relation between Motive and Action and that of Cause and Effect in Physics ; with Replies by the Rev. Alexander Crombie, LL.D." London : 1819. " It is much to be regretted that Dr. Gregory did not find leisure to complete his answer to Messrs Crombie, Priestley, and Co., of which five hundred and twelve pages have been printed, but are still unpublished." (Coll. Works of Reid, by Hamilton. p. 87.) We are reminded that the clearest defence by Reid of the doctrine of the freedom of the will is contained in letters to Dr. Gregory, and published in Hamilton's edition of his works. At a time when the Calvinistic faith of Scotland might have led theologians into perilous necessarian doctrines, it was of great moment to have the essential liberty of will (which Calvin never denied) defended by such philosophers as Reid and Gregory.

XXXVI. —*ALEXANDER CROMBIE.*

He was born in Aberdeen in 1760, and lived till 1842. He became a Presbyterian minister in London, and a schoolmaster at Highgate and afterwards at Greenwich. He wrote a number of educational works of value, as " Etymology and Syntax of the English Language," and " Gymnasium sive Symbola Critica." He has two philosophical works, — one on " Philosophical Necessity," dated Newington Green, 1793, and another on " Natural Theology," in 1829. In the preface to the first of these works, he tells us

that he was initiated in the principles of moral science by Dr. Beattie ; that
when he was a student in divinity the question was debated in a theological
society, " Is man a free or necessary agent ? " that he was then attached to
the libertarian system, and continued to be so till he read Priestley's " Illustrations ; " and that he was confirmed in the change of view by Hartley's
" Observations."   He answers Gregory's argument and illustration quoted
above : " This demonstration of the essayist's is founded in error.   It proceeds on the supposition that the two motives are not directly but indirectly
repugnant, which is obviously false ; any reconciliation between them being
absolutely impossible."   " If a guinea is offered to carry a letter ten miles
east, and another to carry a letter ten miles south ; and if I know I cannot
earn both ; if I know also that by taking any intermediate road I shall
receive nothing, — then my situation is precisely the same as if the directions, instead of being eastward and southward, had been to points diamet-
rically opposite."   He admits " that a necessarian, consistently with his
principles, cannot feel that remorse which is founded on the conviction that
he has acted immorally, and might have acted otherwise ; but by the law of
his nature he feels pain from that state of mind which is connected with a
vicious conduct."   " A necessarian should feel no remorse, no painful sentiment for any past action, as he knows it was necessary for general happiness."   The opponents of necessity argue that these are the logical
consequences of the system, in order to land it in a *reductio ad absurdum :*
but scarcely any of the defenders have allowed this.   It is evident that the
necessity he expounds is very different from that of Edwards.   His work
on " Natural Theology " is a clear and judicious one.   He argues that no
metaphysical argument such as Clarke's, and no metaphysical principle
such as Reid's common sense, can of itself prove the existence of God.
The question is : " Are or are there not conclusive proofs in the phenomena
of nature that they must be productions of an intelligent author ? "
" Wherever we find order and regularity obtaining, either uniformly or
in a vast majority of instances, where the possibilities of disorder are indefi-
nitely numerous, we are justified in inferring from this an intelligent cause."
He argues against materialism, and in favor of the immateriality of the
soul.

XXXVII. — *ARCHIBALD ARTHUR.*

He was born at Abbot's Inch in the parish of Renfrew in 1774, and died in
1797.   He became assistant and successor to Dr. Reid, in the chair of
moral philosophy, in Glasgow.   There is a posthumous volume by him,
entitled " Discourses on Theological and Literary Subjects," 1803, edited
by Professor Richardson, and containing an account of his life.   His views
do not seem profound or original, but his style is elegant, and he has some
good remarks on cause and effect, and on beauty.

XXXVIII. — *JOHN BRUCE.*

HE was born in 1744, and died in 1826. He published a little book for the use of his students, — " First Principles of Philosophy, by John Bruce, A.M., Professor of Philosophy in the University of Edinburgh." It reached a second edition in 1781. It consists of mere notes or heads. Logic has a wide enough field : — it is " the comprehensive science which explains the method of discovering and applying the laws of nature." He makes the sources of human knowledge to be sensation, understanding, and consciousness. He has another work, " Elements of the Science of Ethics, on the Principles of Natural Philosophy." He defines the moral faculty as " the power of perceiving the objects which regard the happiness or enjoyments of human nature." If we ask in what the physical law of gravitation consists, the answer is, in the uniformity of the effect in material nature. If we ask in what the moral law consists, the answer is, in the uniformity of the effect " that the observation of rights is the source of enjoyment." Mr. Bruce does not sound the depths of any subject of which he treats.

————•————

XXXIX. — *REVIEW OF THE CENTURY.*

By the close of the century, the fathers and elder sons of the family have passed away from the scene ; and we may be profited by taking a glance at the work they have done. The Scottish metaphysicians have had an influence on their country, partly by their writings, but still more by the instruction which they imparted in the colleges to numerous pupils, afterwards filling important offices in various walks of life, and scattered all over the land. I cannot do better here than quote from the chapter in which M. Cousin closes his criticism of Reid. "By his excellencies as well as his defects, Reid represents Scotland in philosophy." "It would be impossible to write a history of Scotland in the last half of the eighteenth century, without meeting everywhere in the numerous and remarkable productions of the Scotch genius of this epoch, the noble spirit which that genius has excited, and which, in its turn, has communicated to it a new force. In face of the authority of Hume, and despite the attacks of Priestley, the philosophy of common sense spread itself rapidly, from Aberdeen to Glasgow, and from Glasgow to Edinburgh ; it penetrates into the universities, among the clergy, into the bar, among men of letters and men of the world ; and, without producing a movement so vast as that of the German philosophy, it exercised an influence of the same kind within narrower limits." We have the testimony of a succession of eminent men, to the effect that the chairs of mental philosophy, taken along with the essay-writing which the professors holding these chairs demanded, exercised a greater influence than any others in the colleges ; and sent forth a body of youths capable of thinking, and of expressing their thoughts in a clear and orderly manner. From an old date, a reverence for the Roman law ; and, at a later date, the judicial training of many youths in Holland — had given a logical form to the pleadings at the Scottish bar, and the decisions of the bench : and now the philosophy widened the comprehension of the Edinburgh lawyers, and gave to their law papers a philosophical order scarcely to be found in those of England or Ireland.[1] The Scottish philosophy never attempted, as the German philosophy did (greatly to the injury of religion), to absorb theology into itself ; but keeping to its own field, that of inductive psychology, it allowed the students to follow their own convictions, evangelical or rationalistic, but training all to a habit of skilful arrangement and exposition. It enabled and it led the theological professors to dwell on the relation between the truths of God's Word, and the fundamental principles of human nature ; to lay a

[1] Not a few of the Edinburgh lawyers wrote philosophical treatises. Thus, "Essays, Moral and Divine," by Sir William Anstruther, of Anstruther, one of the Senators of the College of Justice, 1701. He treats of atheism, providence, learning and religion, trifling studies, stage-plays and romances, incarnation, Jesus Christ, and redemption of mankind. He opposes Locke with some ability, and shows that the idea of a Perfect Being is simple and innate, imprinted on our minds by God in our creation. Then in Sir George Mackenzie's (the bloody Mackenzie) "Works," two vols. folio, 1716, we have an essay on happiness. He shows that nothing without us, not even philosophy, can make us happy, that religion alone can do so. He treats of atheism, of moral gallantry, of the moral history of frugality. He begins with an address to fanatics. He would act the religious stoic, and holds that solitude is to be preferred to public employment. We have also, "Some Thoughts concerning Religion, Natural and Revealed, with Reflections on the Sources of Incredulity with regard to Religion," by Rt. Hon. Duncan Forbes, of Culloden, 1750.

deep and solid foundation for moral principle, to impart a moral tone to their teaching in divinity, and to expound, clearly and wisely, the arguments for the existence of God and the immortality of the soul.   In the pulpit, it produced a thoughtful style of address, of which English and Irish hearers were wont to complain, as requiring from them too great a strain of thought. It fostered a habit of reasoning and discussion among educated men generally ; and, through the ministers of religion and the parochial teachers, — not a few of whom were college bred, — it descended to the common people as a general intelligence and independence of spirit.

On literature the influence of the Scottish has not been so great as that of the German philosophy ; but still it has been considerable, and altogether beneficent.   All the professors paid great attention to style : they weeded out their Scotticisms with excessive care ; not a few of them were teachers of rhetoric ; they exacted essays on the subjects lectured on, and sent forth a body of pupils capable of writing clearly and easily. Every one who has read their writings notices a style common to the whole Aberdeen school : it consists of simple sentences without strength or genuine idiom, but always limpid, calm, and graceful.   It is worthy of being mentioned that, in the last quarter of the century, Edinburgh had a distinguished literary circle: embracing the historian Robertson ; the preacher Blair ; Mackenzie, the author of " The Man of Feeling ; " such scientific men as Hutton, Black, Playfair, the Monros (father and son), and Cullen with the Gregories ; and among them the metaphysicians, Hume, Smith, Ferguson, Monboddo, and Dugald Stewart, held a prominent place.

It has to be allowed that the original genius of Scotland was not called forth by the Scottish philosophy, nor, it may be added, by the Scottish colleges.   The truth is, it is not the province of colleges, or of education even, to produce originality : their function is to guide and refine it.   Robert Burns owed little to school training, and nothing to college learning ; still such a man, with so much profound sense mingling with lust and passion, could have appeared only in a state of society in which there was a large amount of intelligence.   His father was a thoughtful man, with a considerable amount of reading, and the mother's memory was filled with Scottish songs. After mingling in the literary circle of Edinburgh, he testifies that he had found as much intelligence and wit among the jolly bachelors of Tarbolton, as among the polished men of the capital.[1] It is to the credit of the Scottish metaphysicians, — such as Lord Monboddo, Ferguson, and Stewart, — that they paid the most delicate attention to the young poet when he came to Edinburgh in 1786. He strove to understand the Scottish metaphysics with

---

[1] Having, in my boyish days, often "kissed the cup to pass it by," among those who had drunk and been drunk with Burns, I am prepared to believe this: but I have to add, that though the sense and humor were strong and shrewd they were often coarse and sensual. Burns was reared in an age in which the uncompromising religion of the covenant was giving way, in the south-west of Scotland, to the milder religion or irreligion of the moderate type. He owed much to the sincere devoutness of his father; but, in spite of all that the literary admirers of Burns may say to the contrary, I am not sure that it was for the benefit of the son that the father, brought up in the more latitudinarian east coast of Scotland, attached himself to the New-Light party, as the youth was thereby thrown among those who had no depth of piety, and who rather rejoiced in the ebullitions against religion which he uttered in moments of passion, which he never meant to publish, and over which he lamented in his declining life. Burns ever held firmly by the great truths of natural religion, and had a profound reverence for the Bible, to which he turned fondly in his latter days : he seems often, always in times of impulse, to have prayed, and would rise from his prayers to write to Clarinda : "I have just been before the throne of my God, Clarinda ; according to my association of ideas [observe the Scotch metaphysics], my sentiments of love and friendship, I next devote myself to you." He declared, in the presence of the elegant Dr. Blair, that his favorite preacher in Edinburgh was the evangelical Dr. Walker. Burns lived in the age in which, contemporaneous with the declining piety, the two great vices of Scotland, intemperance and illicit intercourse of young men and women, descended to the common people. The evangelical ministers had not the courage to check in the bud the rising intemperance, and, in the second age of moderatism, many of the moderate clergy became the victims of it. The dwellings of the Scottish peasantry were wretched ; and courtship among the young people was concealed as if it were a crime, and driven out of the house into places of darkness, the summons to which is indicated in the line, "Whistle, and I'll come to you, my lad." The consequence was, coarse tastes among the small farmers' and cotters' daughters and servant girls, which neither the evangelicals nor the moral philosophers or clergy bred by them sought to refine. Cromek, speaking of Burns's visit to Edinburgh, says : "But a refined and accomplished woman was a thing almost new to him, and of which he had formed but a very inadequate idea." The evil was not lessened, but rather fomented, by the coarse mode of public ecclesiastical discipline which greatly chafed Burns when applied to him. I am convinced that the conduct and poetry of Burns helped greatly to foster the national vices. I speak what I know, as my boyish days were spent in the land of Burns, and I met with old men who knew Burns and the state of society in which he lived.

only imperfect success.[1] Alison's " Essay on Taste " made known to him the theory which refers beauty to association of ideas, and Burns yields his theoretical assent, while evidently doubting inwardly.   He writes : " That the martial clangor of a trumpet had something in it vastly more grand, heroic, and sublime, than the twingle-twangle of a jew's-harp ; that the delicate texture of a rose-twig, when the half-blown flower is heavy with the tears of dawn, was infinitely more beautiful and elegant than the upright stalk of the burdock, and that from something innate, and independent of all association of ideas, — these I had set down as irrefragable orthodox truths until perusing your book shook my faith."   It is an interesting circumstance that young Walter Scott met with Burns in Edinburgh, in the house of Adam Ferguson, and was struck with his dark, expressive eye, and with his combined humor and pathos.   Scott did not owe much more than Burns to the Scottish philosophy. But he was a pupil of Dugald Stewart's, and may have owed to him and his college training, that power of clear exposition and order by which his prose works are distinguished above those of most men of high imaginative genius.[2]

It may be interesting at this point to look across the channel, and inquire what philosophy was doing on the continent. I begin with that country which was the ancient ally of Scotland.   Both the Scotch and French philosophies professed to draw much from Locke ; but they seized on very different elements.   The Scotch followed him in his cautious spirit and

[1] I've sent you here, by Johnie Simson,
Twa sage philosophers to glimpse on : —
Smith wi' his sympathetic feeling,
And Reid to common sense appealing.
Philosophers have fought and wrangled,
And mickle Greek and Latin mangled,
Till, wi' their logic-jargon tired
And in the depth of science mired,
To common sense they now appeal,
That wives and wabsters see and feel.
It is curious to find Burns referring to the philosophy of Spinoza.

[2] In Stewart's class he wrote an essay on the "Manners and Customs of the Northern Nations," and the professor said, "the author of this paper shows much knowledge of his subject, and a great taste for such researches."   Scott became, before the close of the session, a frequent visitor in Mr. Stewart's family, and an affectionate intercourse was maintained between them through their after lives. (Lockhart's " Life of Scott.")

careful observation, but withstood from the beginning the rash
hypothesis which derived all our ideas from sensation and
reflection ; and they called in, besides the external and internal
senses, other senses as inlets, and in the end came to look
upon them as being exercises of reason.[1]   The French looked
exclusively at the other side of Locke's philosophy, at the experiential side, carrying Locke's theory a stage farther ; they
left out reflection, made little use of observation, betook
themselves to analysis, and exerted their ingenuity to derive
all ideas from sensation.   Condillac (born 1715, died 1786),
made all man's ideas, even the highest, such as cause and
moral good, transformed sensations.   Most of his works were
written for the purpose of helping to educate a prince of
Parma, and the author did not mean to undermine morality or religion.   But the logical consequences of error follow
it unrelentingly, and are apt to come out in practical issues
which the authors of it never contemplated.   If Condillac
did not see, those who came after him clearly perceived that
we could not, out of the mere materials supplied by the
senses, extract, by any mental chemistry, the idea of moral
obligation and of a spiritual God.   Helvetius expounded a
morality of self-interest ; Cabanis evolved all thought out of
organized matter, made the brain secrete thought as the liver
secretes bile ; D'Holbach showed that the issue was blank
atheism ; and licentious men and women were rejoicing in the
thought that they had got rid of duty, of mind, and of God.
The fruit of the whole was seen, not in the French Revolution,—
which was much needed, and would have come, with or without
the philosophy, — but in the direction which it took, and the
atrocities which it perpetrated, and which caused it, unlike the
English and American revolutions, to issue in a military des-
potism.   By the close of the century, this philosophy had gone
beyond ripeness to rottenness, and finer minds were turning
away from it, and seeking for something better.   The reaction
started by Laromiguierre, and carried on more effectively by
Royer Collard, and yet more so by his pupils Jouffroy and

---

[1] In " Dissertatio Philosophica Inauguralis de Analogia et Philosophia Prima,"
Feb. 23, 1739, Professor Cleghorn says : "Idea innata nulla est.   Aptitudo quædam innata menti inest qua ad ideas hasce, vulgo innatas dictas, percipiendas
approbandasque, quandocumque se obtulerit necessario dirigetur."

Cousin, turned eagerly, as we shall see, towards the well-grounded philosophy of Reid and Stewart.

In Germany, philosophy took a very different direction. Leibnitz had opposed Locke and his experiential method, and had imparted a speculative spirit and an ideal elevation to the German thinking ; and Wolf had labored to reduce the whole to logical forms. And now, as the offspring of the two, of idealism and formalism, the true German philosophy came forth from the brain of Emmanuel Kant, who was born 1724, died 1804, and published his great work, the " Kritik der reine Vernunft " in 1781, which took a considerably revised form in 1787. That philosophy was already taking firm hold of the German mind, and has not at this day lost its grasp, notwithstanding the efforts of Darwinism and materialism to loosen it. As it differed from the French, so it also differed from the Scotch. In a sense, indeed, Kant's philosophy was transplanted from the Scottish soil. Kant's grandfather named Cant, a saddler, emigrated from Scotland ;[1] and some think that he thence derived hereditarily his high conception of moral law : and he acknowledges that he was roused from his dogmatic slumbers by Hume's sceptical account of the relation of cause and effect. But Reid and Kant, though both opposed to Hume, took up very different lines of defence. In respect of method, Reid followed the inductive method, with self-consciousness as the instrument of observation ; whereas Kant inaugurated the critical method, as distinguished from the dogmatic method of Descartes on the one hand, and the empirical method of Locke on the other. The critical method takes upon itself to criticise all principles ; but it can do so only by other principles, —

[1] I have employed more time than I would like to tell any one, in searching after the Scottish ancestry of Kant, but without success. I find that the name Cant was not uncommon in Forfarshire in last century : it occurs on the tombstones in a number of churchyards. In a map of a piece of ground at the north end of Brechin, there is mention of its belonging successively to George Cant and Alexander Cant. There was a James Cant, weaver in Brechin, admitted to the guild in 1779. I have seen a deed in which George Scott sells, in 1799, to John Cant, tanner in Brechin, a piece of property on the east side of High Street. It had been bought in 1796 by the two, in a contract of copartnery for carrying on the business of manufacturing and selling of leather. As leather and saddlery are connected, I have at times favored the idea that Kant, the saddler, may have been descended from the same Cants as John Cant, the tanner, who it is understood came from Montrose to Brechin. It is proper to state that I have been assisted in these researches by D. D. Black, Esq., town clerk, Brechin.

avowed, or more frequently unavowed, — and the question is started: How are these other principles to be judged? by other principles, and these by other principles without end? Or, if we must stop somewhere, the question is, Where? and, Why there? Every German metaphysician plants himself on his own stand-point, which he says cannot be disputed: but his neighbor disputes it or selects another; and there is a perpetual criticism, and an endless building, but without an undisputed foundation. In one respect, indeed, the two, the Scotch and German philosophies, were alike: both stood up for principles which did not derive their authority from experience. But the Scottish metaphysicians discovered these by a careful inquiry into the operations of the human mind; Kant, by a process of logical discussion. On another point they differed: the Scottish metaphysicians make our primitive perceptions or intuitions look at realities; whereas Kant stands up for *a priori* principles, which regulate experience and have only a subjective validity. Having allowed idealism to enter, there was no means of arresting its career. As Kant had made time and space, substance and cause, mere forms in the mind, Fichte was only advancing a few steps farther on the same road when he made the whole universe a projection of the mind; and, in the succeeding age, Schelling made it an intellectual intuition, and Hegel a logical process. Even as the French sensationalism led to atheism, so the German idealism culminated in pantheism. Every one will allow that the German philosophy had a much more elevated character, and a much more elevating tendency, than the French. Its influence on the great body of the German people may not have been so great as that of the Scottish philosophy on the Scottish thought. On the other hand, its influence has been vastly greater on literature, to which it has imparted a high ideal character, as seen especially in the poetry of Germany, and of other countries which have borrowed from it.

DUGALD STEWART was born in the old college buildings, Edinburgh, on November 22, 1753. His father was Dr. Matthew Stewart, at one time minister at Roseneath, and afterwards successor to Maclaurin in the mathematical chair in Edinburgh, and still known as one of those British mathematicians, who were applying, with great skill and beauty, the geometrical method, while the continental mathematicians were far outstripping them by seizing on the more powerful instrument of the calculus. His mother was the daughter of an Edinburgh writer to the signet. He was thus connected on the part of his father (and also of his grandfather, who had been minister of Rothesay), with the Presbyterian ministry, and on the part of his mother with the Edinburgh lawyers, — the two classes which, next to the heritors, held the most influential position in Scotland.

Dugald was a feeble and delicate infant. He spent his boyish years partly in Edinburgh, and partly in the maternal mansion-house of Catrine, which I remember as being, when I paid pilgrimage thither many years ago, a whitewashed, broad-faced, common-place old house, situated very pleasantly in what Wordsworth calls expressively the "holms of bonnie Ayr," but unpleasantly near a cotton-mill and a thriving village, which, as they rose about 1792, destroyed to Stewart the charms of the place as a residence. Stewart entered, at the age of eight, the High School of Edinburgh, where he had, in the latter years of his attendance, Dr. Adam for his instructor, and where he was distinguished for the elegance of his translations, and early acquired that love for the prose and poetical works of ancient Rome which continued with him through life. He entered Edinburgh College in the session 1765–66 ; that is, in his thirteenth year. I remember that Bacon, David Hume, Adam Smith, Thomas Reid, and many other original-minded men, entered college about the same age ; and I am strengthened in the conviction that, in order to

1 "The Collected Works of Dugald Stewart, edited by Sir William Hamilton, Bart., with a Memoir of Dugald Stewart, by John Veitch."

the production of fresh and independent thought, it is of advantage to have the drilling in the ordinary elements all over at a comparatively early age, and then allow the mind, already well stocked with general knowledge, to turn its undivided energies to its favorite and evidently predestinated field ; and that the modern English plan of continuing the routine discipline in classics or mathematics till the age of twenty-two, while well fitted to produce good technical scholars, is not so well calculated to raise up great reformers in method and execution. What the Scottish colleges have to deplore is not so much the juvenility of the entrants — though this has been carried to excess — as the total want of a provision for bringing to a point, for carrying on, for consolidating and condensing the scattered education which has been so well begun in the several classes. But to return to the college youth, we find him attending, among other classes, that of logic under Stevenson, for two sessions ; that of moral philosophy under Adam Ferguson ; that of natural philosophy under Russell : and from all of these he received a stimulus and a bent which swayed him at the crisis of his being, and abode with him during the whole of his life.

After finishing his course in Edinburgh, he went to Glasgow in 1771, partly by the advice of Ferguson, that he might be under Dr. Thomas Reid, and partly with the view of being sent to Oxford on the Snell foundation, which has been of use to many students of Glasgow, but has in some respects been rather injurious to the college ; as it has led many to ascribe to it the mere reflected glory of being a training-school to higher institutions, whereas Glasgow should assert of itself that it is prepared to give as high an education as can be had in any university in the world. The youth seems at this time to have had thoughts of entering the Church of England ; and if he had gone south, he would no doubt, in that event, have discharged the duties of the episcopal office with great propriety and dignity. But a destiny better suited to his peculiar character and gifts was awaiting him. In the autumn of 1772 — that is, when he was at the age of nineteen — he became substitute for his father in the chair of mathematics in Edinburgh. It is precisely such an office as this, a tutorship or assistant professorship, that the Scottish colleges should provide for their more promising students ; an office not to be reserved for sons or personal friends of professors, but to be thrown open to public competition. This is the one thing needful to the Scottish universities, to enable them to complete the education which they commence so well, and to raise a body of learned youths, ready to compete with the tutors and fellows of Oxford and Cambridge. In 1775, Mr. Stewart was elected assistant and successor to his father ; in 1778, on Professor Adam Ferguson going to America as secretary to a commission, he, upon a week's notice, lectured for him on morals ; and, in 1785, Ferguson having resigned, Stewart was appointed to the office for which he was so specially fitted, — to the chair of moral philosophy in the university of Edinburgh.

We pause in the narrative, in order to look at the circumstances which combined to influence the youth, to determine his career, and to fit him for the good work which he performed. First we have a mind, not certainly of bright original, genius, or of great intellectual force, but with a blending of harmonious qualities, a capacity for inward reflection, and a disposition toward it, a fine taste, and consummate judgment. From his youth he breathed the air of a college. He was early introduced to Roman literature, and made it his model. Stevenson used Wynne's " Abridgment of Locke's Essay " as a text-book, and from it the student may have caught the fresh and observational spirit which Locke had awakened, while, at the same time, he was kept from what Cousin describes as the common defect of the British philosophy — being "insular " — by the other text-books employed, namely, the " Elementa Philosophiæ " of Heineccius, and the " Determinationes Ontologicæ " of De Vries ; works which discussed, in a more abstract and scholastic method, the questions agitated on the continent posterior to the publication of the philosophy of Descartes. A still greater influence was exercised over the youth by Ferguson, who, with no great metaphysical ability, but in an altogether Roman and in a somewhat pagan manner, discussed, with great majesty and sweep, the topics — of which the pupil was ever after so fond — lying between mental science on the one hand, and jurisprudence on the other. From his own father, and through his own academical teaching, he acquired a taste for the geometrical method, so well fitted to

give clearness and coherency to thought, and to teach caution
in deduction. He thus became one of those metaphysicians
(and they are not few) who have been mathematicians likewise,
in this respect resembling (not to go back to Thales, Pythagoras, and Plato, in ancient times) Descartes, Leibnitz, Samuel
Clarke, Reid, and Kant. In the class of natural philosophy he
was introduced to the Newtonian physics, which had been taught
at an early date in Scotland, and caught an enthusiastic affection for the inductive method and for Bacon, which continued
with him through life, and is his characteristic among metaphysicians. But the teacher influencing him most, and, indeed,
determining his whole philosophic career, was Thomas Reid,
who, in a homely manner, but with unsurpassed shrewdness,
and great independence and originality, was unfolding the
principles of common sense, and thus laying a foundation for
philosophy, while he undermined the scepticism of Hume.
Stewart has found in Reid the model instructor, and it may
be added that Reid has found in Stewart the model disciple.
This whole course was an excellent training for a metaphysician : it would have been perfect if, along with his knowledge
of natural philosophy, his somewhat dull apprehension had
been whetted by an acquaintance — such as that of Locke in
an earlier, and that of Brown in a later age — with the more
fugitive and complicated phenomena of the physiology of the
body ; and if, in addition, his over-cautious temper had been
raised heavenward by an intimacy with the lofty spirit of Plato,
or, better still, by an appreciation of the deep theological discussions which had collected around them so much of the
English and Scottish speculative intellect of the two preceding
centuries.

Like every other man not altogether self-contained, Stewart
must have felt the spirit of his age, which, as coming in from
every quarter, like air and sunshine, commonly exercises a
greater influence on young men than individual teachers can
possibly do through the special channels open to them. Hume
had stirred the thoughts of thinkers to their greatest depths ;
and this was now the age in which Hume had to be met.
Stewart was born fourteen years after the publication of the
great sceptical work of modern times, the " Treatise on
Human Nature ; " and two years after the publication of the

work from which all modern utilitarianism has sprung, the " Inquiry concerning the Principles of Morals." At the time when the youth was forming his convictions, Hume was living in Edinburgh, and the centre of an influence radiating round the man, who was a mixture of the lively, good-natured animal and of the intellectual giant, but with a terrible want of the high moral and spiritual. The original disposition of Stewart did not tempt him to daring speculation ; his domestic training must have prepossessed him against infidelity ; and he had been placed, in Glasgow, under the only opponent worthy of Hume, who had appeared ; and so these earthquake shocks just made him look round for a means of settling fast the foundations of the temple of knowledge.

Locke's philosophy had been the reigning one for the last age or two. Mr. Veitch speaks of the " tradition of sensation-alism, which the Scottish universities during the first half of the century, and up to the time of Reid, had in general dispensed in Scotland." This statement is too sweeping : for, first, Locke had given as high a place to reflection as to sensation ; and, secondly, he had given a high office to intuition ; while, thirdly, Locke's philosophy had not been received in Scotland without modification, or in its worst aspects, as it had been in France. Stewart, like Reid, entertained a high admiration of Locke, and was unwilling to separate from him, but he saw at the same time the defects of Locke, and that there were fundamental laws in the mind which Locke had overlooked, or only incidentally noticed. In Glasgow he must have felt the influence left behind by a train of eminent men. There Hutcheson had been the founder of the genuine Scottish school. In Glasgow, too, Adam Smith had expounded those original views which he afterwards published in his " Theory of Moral Sentiments" and his "Wealth of Nations." In order to estimate the character of the age, it must also be taken into account that there was a strong expectation that results were to follow, from the application of inductive science, to mental phenomena, similar to those which had flowed from its application to physics. Turnbull's aim was to " apply himself to the study of the human mind, in the same way as to that of the human body, or to any other part of natural philosophy." Catching this spirit, Reid was even now employing it to discover

principles deeper than any that had been systematically noticed by Locke, by Hutcheson, or any Scottish philosopher.
To this same noble work Stewart now devoted himself; but
seeking, meanwhile, to combine with the profound philosophy
of Reid a literary excellence like that of Hume and Smith.

And this leads us to notice that we cannot form any thing
like an adequate idea of the influences which combined to
mould the character of Stewart, who cultivated literature as
eagerly as he did philosophy, without taking into account that
he lived in an age of great literary revival in Scotland. The
union between Scotland and England being now compacted, it
was seen that the old Scottish dialect must gradually disappear; and ambitious youths were anxious to get rid of their
northern idioms, and even grave seniors, including noblemen
and dignified doctors, like Robertson (as we learn from Lord
Campbell's " Life of Loughborough"), had formed a society, in
order to be delivered from their Scottish pronunciation. A
company of authors had sprung up, determined to assert their
place among the classical writers of England; and this had
been already allowed to Hume, to Robertson and Smith, and
was being allowed to Beattie. Stewart had, no doubt, an ambition to take his place among the classical writers of Scotland.

While pursuing his studies at Glasgow, he read a paper on
" Dreaming " before a literary society in connection with the
university; and he subsequently read the same paper to a similar society in Edinburgh. The theory here started was afterwards embodied in his " Elements," and contains certainly not
the whole truth on this mysterious subject, but still *a* truth,
namely, that in dreaming the will is in abeyance, and the mind
follows a spontaneous train. In the Edinburgh society he also
read papers on " Taste," on " Cause and Effect," and " Scepticism." The fact that such topics were discussed is a sign of
the spirit which prevailed among the youth of Scotland at that
time. It is worthy of being noticed that at Glasgow he boarded
in the same house with Mr. Alison, who afterwards, in his essay
on " Taste," carried out the theory which had been started by
Beattie in his " Dissertation on Imagination," as to the feeling of beauty being produced by the association of ideas.

Quitting his course of training, we may now view him as
delivering his professorial lectures in the class-room in Edin-

burgh. By far the liveliest account of him is by Lord Cockburn. It is worthy of being read again by those who may have seen it before.

" He was about the middle size, weakly limbed, and with an appearance of feebleness which gave an air of delicacy to his gait and structure. His forehead was large and bald ; his eyebrows bushy ; his eyes gray and intelligent, and capable of conveying any emotion from indignation to pity, from serene sense to hearty humor, in which they were powerfully aided by his lips, which, though rather large perhaps, were flexible and expressive. The voice was singularly pleasing ; and, as he managed it, a slight burr only made its tones softer. His ear both for music and for speech was exquisite ; and he was the finest reader I have ever heard. His gesture was simple and elegant, though not free from a tinge of professional formality, and his whole manner that of an academical gentleman. . . . He lectured standing, from notes which, with their successive additions, must, I suppose, at last have been nearly as full as his spoken words. His lecturing manner was professorial, but gentlemanlike, calm and expository, but rising into greatness, or softening into tenderness, whenever his subject required it. A slight asthmatic tendency made him often clear his throat ; and such was my admiration of the whole exhibition, that Macvey Napier told him not long ago that I had said there was eloquence in his very spitting. ' Then,' said he, ' I am glad there was at least one thing in which I had no competitor.' . . . To me, his lectures were like the opening of the heavens. I felt that I had a soul. His noble views, unfolded in glorious sentences, elevated me into a higher world."

There were hearers who felt that there was a want in his expositions, and there are readers still who feel in the same way. Ardent youths, like Brown and Chalmers, looked on him as timid and over-cautious. Chalmers wrote in 1801 : " I attend his lectures regularly. I must confess I have been rather disappointed. I never heard a single discussion of Stewart's which made up one masterly and comprehensive whole. His lectures seem to me to be made up of detached hints and incomplete outlines, and he almost uniformly avoids every subject which involves any difficult discussion." Chalmers lived to proclaim him the highest of academic moralists. Still there was ground, in appearance and in reality, for the early criticism. In his writings he adopts the plan which Dr. Robertson took credit for introducing, that of throwing a great deal of his matter into notes and illustrations. This method, carried to the extent to which it has been done by Robertson, Stewart, and M'Crie, is a radically defective one, as it interrupts the flow of the discourse, and, with this, the interest in and comprehension of the whole. He has a most sensitive aversion to all such bold speculations as Leibnitz indulged in, and is jealous of all such consecutive deductions as Descartes and Kant have drawn out. He has no ability for sharp analysis, and he looks on a high abstraction with as great terror as some men do on ghosts. He studiously avoids close discussion, and flinches from controversy; he seems afraid of fighting with an opponent, lest it should exhibit him in no seemly attitudes. Seldom does he venture on a bold assertion, and, when he does, he takes shelter immediately after behind an authority. Determined to sustain his dignity and keep up his flow of language, he often takes rounded sentences and paragraphs to bring out what a more direct mind would have expressed in a single clinching clause, or even by an expressive epithet. Often does the eager, ingenuous youth, in reading his pages, wish that he would but lay aside ceremony for a very little, and speak out frankly and heartily.

Still we should form a very unjust opinion of Stewart, if, in consequence of weaknesses, we thought him devoid of originality, independence, or profundity. We certainly do not claim for him the sagacity of Locke, or the speculative genius of Leibnitz, or a power of generalizing details equal to Adam Smith, or the shrewdness of Reid, or the logical grasp of Kant and Hamilton, and I admit that he was inferior to all these men in originality; but he has admirable qualities of his own,— in soundness of judgment he is more to be trusted than any of them; and, if he is without some of their excellencies, he is also without some of their faults. He has no such rash and unmeasured diatribes as Locke's assault on innate ideas; no such extravagances as the monadical theory of Leibnitz; no such wasting of ingenuity as Smith's theory in his " Moral Sentiments ;" he does not commit such gross misapprehensions in scholarship as Reid does; and he never allows any logic to conduct h,m to such preposterous conclusions as Kant and Hamilton landed themselves in, when they declared causation to be a law of thought and not of things. I have noticed that in many cases Stewart hides his originality as carefully as others boast of theirs. Often have I found, after going the round of philosophers in seeking light on some abstruse subject, that, on turning to Stewart, his doctrine is, after all, the most profound, as it is the most judicious.

I do not mean to enter into the details of his remaining life. In 1783, he married a Miss Bannatyne of Glasgow, who died in 1787, leaving an only child, afterwards Colonel Stewart. He spent the summers of 1788 and 1789 on the Continent. In the appendix to the Memoir, there is a selection from the letters which he wrote to his friends at home. Though written in the midst of instructive scenes, and on the eve of great events, they are excessively general and common-place, and display no shrewdness of observation. In 1790, he married a daughter of Lord Cranston, a lady of high accomplishments, fascinating manners, and literary tastes. His house now became the resort of the best society of Edinburgh, and he himself the centre and bond of an accomplished circle, at a time when the metropolis of Scotland in the winter months was the residence of many of the principal Scottish families, and of persons of high literary and scientific eminence. The weekly reunions in his house, which happily blended the aristocracies of rank and letters, bringing together the peer and the unfriended scholar, were for many years the source of an influence that most beneficially affected the society of the capital. His influence was extended by his receiving into his house, as boarders, young men chiefly of rank and fortune. In his classes of moral philosophy and of political economy, he had under him a greater body of young men who afterwards distinguished themselves, than any other teacher that I can think of. Among them we have to place Lord Brougham, Lord Palmerston, Lord John Russell, Francis Horner, Lord Lansdowne, Francis Jeffrey, Walter Scott, Sydney Smith, Thomas Brown, Thomas Chalmers, James Mill, Archibald Alison, and many others who have risen to great eminence in politics, in literature, or philosophy; and most of these have acknowledged the good which they derived from his lectures, while some of them have carried out in practical measures the principles which he inculcated. He seems, in particular, to have kindled a fine enthusiasm in the breast of Francis Horner, who ever speaks of him in terms of loftiest admiration, and, though cut off in early life, lived long enough to exhibit the high moral aims which he had imbibed from the lessons of Stewart.

It was in 1792 that the first volume of his "Elements" was published. In 1793, appeared his "Outlines of Moral Philosophy," containing an epitome of the doctrines expanded in his larger writings. His other works appeared after successive intervals : his Account of Adam Smith in 1793, of Robertson in 1796, and of Reid in 1802 ; his "Philosophical Essays" in 1810 ; the second volume of his "Elements" in 1814 ; the first part of his Dissertation, in 1815, and the second in 1821 ; the third volume of his "Elements" in 1827 ; and the "Active and Moral Powers" in 1828. The lectures on Political Economy, were not published till 1856.

In 1805, he threw himself, with more eagerness than he was wont to display in public matters, into the controversy which arose about the appointment of Leslie — a man of high scientific eminence, but with a great deal of the gross animal in his nature — to the chair of mathematics. He wrote a pamphlet on the subject, and appeared in the General Assembly of the Church of Scotland, as a Presbyterian elder, to aid the evangelical party, who, under the leadership of Sir Henry Moncreiff, were no way inclined to join the moderate party in their attempt to keep out a distinguished man, because he entertained certain views on the subject of physical causation, and to retain the college chairs for themselves. In his speech on the occasion, Stewart does let out feeling for once, and it is mingled pride and scorn. "After having discharged for more than thirty years (not, I trust, without discredit to myself) the important duties of my academical station, I flatter myself that the House does not think it incumbent on me to descend to philosophical controversies with such antagonists. Such of the members, at least, as I have the honor to be known to, will not, I am confident, easily allow themselves to be persuaded that I would have committed myself rashly and wantonly on a question in which the highest interests of mankind are involved." In delivering the speech from which the above is an extract, he was called to order, and, not being accustomed to such handling, he sat down abruptly. The motion of Sir Henry Moncreiff was carried by a majority, which occasioned great joy to the Edinburgh Liberals, and helped to sever the connection between the universities and the church.

In 1806, the Whig party, being in power, procured for him a sinecure office, entitled the writership of the "Edinburgh Gazette," with a salary of 300*l.* a year. In 1809, he was in a precarious state of health, much aggravated by the death of a son by his second wife, and he asked Dr. Thomas Brown to lecture for him. In 1810, Brown, being strongly recommended to the Town Council by Stewart, was appointed conjoint professor, and henceforth discharged all the duties of the office. Brown never attacked Stewart, but he openly assailed Reid ; and we suppose the intimacy between Stewart and Brown henceforth could not have been great. Stewart delivered his ultimate estimate of Brown in a note appended to the third volume of the "Elements." There is evidently keen feeling underlying it ; but the criticism is, on the whole, a fair and just one. Stewart now lived, till the close of his life, at Kinniel House, Linlith-gowshire, — a residence placed at his service by the Duke of Hamilton. Henceforth he was chiefly employed in maturing and arranging the philosophical works which he published. The details given of this part of his life are scanty and uninstructive. In 1820, he came forth to support Sir James Mackintosh as successor to Brown ; and when Sir James declined the office, Stewart recommended Sir William Hamilton, who seems ever afterwards to have cherished a feeling of gratitude towards Stewart. The election fell on Professor Wilson, who, while the fittest man living for the chair of rhetoric and belles-lettres, had no special qualifications for a chair of philosophy.

In 1822, Mr. Stewart had a stroke of paralysis, from which, however, he partially recovered. Mrs. Stewart describes him, in 1824, as troubled with a difficulty of speech, and a tremor in his hand, as walking two or three hours every day, as cheerful in his spirits, his mind as acute as ever, and as amusing himself with reading on his favorite pursuits, and with the classics. He had just given to the world his work on the "Active Powers," and was on a visit to a friend in Edinburgh, when he died on 11th June, 1828. He was buried in the family vault in the Canongate. There is a monument in honor of him on the Calton Hill ; but the fittest memorial of him is to be found, first, in his pupils, who have done a good work in their day, and now in his writings, which may do a good work for ages to come.

His collected works have been edited by Sir William Hamilton. The editor has not enriched it with such notes as he has appended to his edition of Reid, — notes distinguished for the very qualities which Reid was deficient in, extensive scholarship and rigid analysis. Sir William Hamilton, in undertaking the work, stipulated that Mr. Stewart's writings should be published without note or comment. I rather think that Hamilton had not such a sympathy with the elegant and cautious disciple as with the shrewd and original master. Besides, elaborate notes to Stewart must have been very much a repetition of his notes to Reid. In this edition Hamilton is tempted at times to depart from his rule: he does give us a note or comment when the subject is a favorite one, such as the freedom of the will; and often must he have laid a restraint on himself, in not pruning or amending to a greater extent. But the value of this edition consists in its being complete, in its having references supplied, and one index after another, and in its containing additions from Stewart's manuscripts, and these often of great value, both in themselves and as illustrating Stewart's philosophy. Sir William Hamilton was cut off before the edition was completed, but Mr. Veitch has carried on the work in the same manner and spirit. Having said so much of this fine edition, we must protest against the occasional translation of the language and views of Stewart into those of Hamilton, in places where it is purported to give us Stewart himself. Thus, in index, vol. iv., p. 408, Stewart is represented as, in a place referred to, discussing the question as to whether some of our notions be not "native or *a priori,*" but, on looking up the page, no such language is used; and the same remark holds good of vol. v., p. 474, where Stewart is spoken of as describing our notions both of matter and mind as merely "phenomenal," a view thoroughly Kantian and Hamiltonian, and not sanctioned by Stewart. I must be allowed, also, to disapprove of the liberty taken with the "Outlines of Moral Philosophy," which is cut up into three parts, and appears in three distinct volumes. This is the most condensed and direct of all Stewart's writings: it contains an abridgment of his whole doctrines; it is one of the best text-books ever written, and it should have appeared in its unity, as Stewart left it.

I do not propose to criticise these ten massive volumes of his works. This would be a heavy work to my readers : it would almost be equivalent to a criticism of all modern philosophy. Nevertheless, I must touch on some topics of an interesting and important kind, as discussed by Stewart, and again discussed by later writers on mental science.

The first volume of the collected works contains the " Dissertation on the Progress of Metaphysical and Ethical Philosophy." I look upon it as the finest of the dissertations in the " Encyclopædia Britannica " ; and this is no mean praise, when we consider the number of eminent men who have written for that work. I regard it, indeed, as, upon the whole, the best dissertation which ever appeared in a philosophical serial. As a history of modern philosophy, especially of British philosophy, it has not been superseded, and, I believe, never will be set aside. It is pre-eminent for its fine literary taste, its high moral tone, its general accuracy, its comprehensiveness of survey, and its ripeness of wisdom. When we read it, we feel as if we were breathing a pure and healthy atmosphere, and that the whole spirit of the work is cheering, as being so full of hope in the progress of knowledge. Its critical strictures are ever candid, generally mild, very often just, and always worthy of being noted and pondered. The work is particularly pleasing in the account given of those who have contributed by their literary works to diffuse a taste for metaphysical studies, such as Montaigne, Bayle, Fontenelle, and Addison. It should be admitted that the author has scarcely done justice to Grotius, and failed to fathom the depth of such minds as Leibnitz and Jonathan Edwards. I agree, moreover, with those who regret that he should ever have been tempted to enter on a criticism of Kant, whose works he knew only from translations and imperfect compends.

The next three volumes contain the " Elements of the Philosophy of the Human Mind," and are introduced by a portion of the " Outlines of Moral Philosophy." In the first volume of the " Elements " and in the opening of the second, he spreads out before us a classification of the intellectual powers, — as perception, attention, conception, abstraction, association of ideas, memory, imagination, and reason. The list is at once defective and redundant. Stewart acknowledges self-consciousness, which is an inseparable concomitant of all the present operations of the mind, to be a separate attribute ; and in this he seems to be right, inasmuch as it looks at a special object, namely, self in the existing state, and gives us a distinct class of ideas, namely, the qualities of self, such as thinking and feeling. Yet it is curious that, while he gives it half a page in his "Outlines," it has no separate place in the "Elements." It is also a singular circumstance that Reid dismisses it in the same summary way. An inductive observation, with an analysis of the precise knowledge given us by self-consciousness, would give a solid foundation for the doctrine of human personality, and clear away the greater part of the confusion and error lingering in the metaphysics of our day. Nor is there any proper account given in the "Elements" of that important group of faculties which discover relations among the objects known by sense-perception and consciousness. The omission of this class of attributes has led him into a meagre nominalism, very unlike the general spirit of his philosophy. He restricts the word conception to the mere imaging power of the mind, and even to the picturing of bodily objects, as if we could not represent mental objects as well, as, for example, ourselves or others in joy or sorrow. In a later age, Hamilton has confined the term in an opposite direction to the logical or general notion. Stewart's classification is also redundant. Attention is not a separate faculty, but is an exercise of will, — roused, it may be, by feeling, and fixing the mind on a present object. He does not seem to know what to make of reason as a distinct faculty ; and, as defined by him, it ought to include abstraction, which is certainly a rational exercise. But, if the work is defective in logical grasp, it excels in its descriptions of concrete operations, and in its explanations and elucidations of phenomena presenting themselves in real life. All his works are replete with those "intermediate axioms" which Bacon commends as most useful of all, as being removed equally from the lowest axioms, which differ but little from particulars, and from the highest and most general, which are notional, abstract, and of no weight ; whereas the "intermediate are true, solid, full of life, and upon them depend the business and fortune of mankind." The fine reflection and lofty eloquence of Stewart come out most pleasingly and instructively in all those passages in which he treats of association and imagination.

On one important point, discussed frequently in the "Elements," the school of Reid and Stewart was led into error by their excessive caution, and by being awed so much by the authority of Locke. Reid maintained in a loose way, that we do not know substance, but qualities ; and Stewart wrought this view into a system. We are not, he says, properly speaking, conscious of self or the existence of self : we are conscious merely of a sensation or some other quality, which, by *a subsequent suggestion of the understanding*, leads to a belief in that which exercises the quality. — (" Phil. Essays," p. 58, etc.) This I must regard as a radically defective doctrine. We do not know intuitively a quality of self apart from self ; we know both in one primitive, concrete act, and it is only by a subsequent operation that we separate in thought the quality which may change in its action from the self or substance which abideth. Descartes erred I think, when he represented the mental process as being " *cogito, ergo sum :* " the primitive cognition is of the *ego cogitans.* But I look on Stewart as equally erring when he says, that there is first a sensation and then a belief in self. In a later age, Sir William Hamilton connected the *qualitative* theory of Stewart with the *phenomenal* theory of Kant. In doing so he was guilty, I must take the liberty of saying, of a great and inexcusable blunder. Stewart would have repudiated the phenomenal theory of Kant as at all identical with his own. Stewart, no doubt, speaks of the phenomena of the mind ; but he means by phenomena not, as Kant did, *appearances*, but individual *facts* to be referred to a law ; and qualities with him were *realities.* But, legitimately or illegitimately, Hamilton identifying the qualitative theory with the phenomenal, deduces from them a system of relativity, which ended in nihilism, or at least in nescience. I am glad to notice that Mr. Mansel, notwithstanding his great and just admiration of Hamilton, has emancipated himself from this fundamental error. He proclaims, "I am immediately conscious of myself, seeing and hearing, willing and thinking." — (" Proleg. Logica," p. 129 ; also Art. *Metaph.* in " Encyc. Brit."). I have sometimes thought that, if Stewart had foreseen all the logical consequences to be deduced from his views, he would have fallen

19

back on the same common-sense doctrine. I regret that Mr. Mansel has not gone a step farther, and placed our cognition of matter on the same footing in this respect as our knowledge of mind. I am sure, at least, that this would be altogether in the spirit of Reid and Stewart. I maintain that, just as by self-consciousness we know self as exercising such and such a quality, say thinking or feeling, so, by sense-perception, we know a body as extended and exercising power or energy. This is the simplest doctrine: it seems to be the only one consistent with consciousness, and is the proper doctrine of natural realism as distinguished from an artificial system of relativity.

In the second volume of the " Elements," after a feeble and chiefly verbal disquisition on reason, he proceeds to treat of the "fundamental laws of belief." I reckon the phrase a very happy one, and a great improvement on "common sense," which labors under the disadvantage of being ambiguous; inasmuch as it usually denotes that unbought, untaught sagacity, which is found only in certain men, and which others can never acquire, whereas it can be admitted into philosophical discussion only when it denotes principles which are regulating the minds of all. I have a remark to make as to the place in which he discusses these fundamental laws. It is after he has gone over the greater number of the faculties, and he seems to treat them as involved in reason. And I acknowledge that there may be some advantages in first going over the faculties and then speaking of these fundamental laws. But we must guard against the idea that these principles are not involved in the faculties which he has previously gone over; such as, perception, abstraction, and memory. The "fundamental laws" are not to be regarded as different from the faculties: they are, in fact, the necessary laws of the faculties, and guiding their exercise. These laws work in all minds, infant and mature, sane and insane. M. Morel was asked to examine a prisoner who seemed to be deranged, and he asked him how old he was; to which the prisoner replied: "245 francs, 35 centimes, 124 carriages," etc. To the same question, more distinctly asked, he replied,: "5 metres, 75 centimetres." When asked how long he had been deranged, he answered: "Cats, always cats." M. Morel at once declared his madness to be simulated, and states : " In their extreme aberrations, in their most furious delirium, madmen do not confound what it is impossible for the most extravagant logic to confound. There is no madman who loses the idea of cause, of substance, of existence." (See " Psychol. Journal," Oct. 1857.)

Stewart's doctrine of causation seems to me to be deficient and inadequate. He is altogether right in calling it a fundamental law of belief, which necessitates the mind to rise from an effect to a cause. But he does not seem to observe all that is involved in the cause. He gives in too far to Hume on this subject, and prepares the way for Brown's theory. He does not see, in particular, that causation springs from power being in the substance or substances which act as the cause, and that we intuitively discover power to be in substances both mental and material. His distinction between efficient and physical cause is of a superficial and confused character. It may be all true that, in looking at physical action, we may not know intuitively where the full efficiency resides, whether in the physical object alone or in mind (the divine) acting in it ; but we are certain that there is an efficiency somewhere in some substance. I am by no means sure that he is right in limiting power in the sense of efficiency to mental action. I agree here with the criticisms of Cousin (as indeed I agree with most of the criticisms of Cousin on the Scottish school) where he says that, while our first idea of cause may be derived from our own voluntary action, we are at the same time intuitively led to ascribe potency to other objects also ; and that Reid and Stewart, in denying that we discover efficiency in body, are acting contrary to their own principles of common sense, and in contradiction to the universal opinion of the human race, which is, that fire burns and light shines. (See Cousin, " Phil. Ecoss.," p. 437, ed. 1857.) Stewart has also failed, as it appears to me, to give the proper account of the intuition which regulates and underlies our investigations of nature. This is not, as he represents it, a belief in the uniformity of nature ; a belief which appears to me to be the result of experience, which experience, as it discovers the rule, may also announce the exceptions. The child does not believe, nor does the savage believe, nature to be uniform. The underlying beliefs, which carry us on in our investigations of nature are those of identity, of being, of substance and quality, of cause and effect. Hence it is quite possible to prove a miracle which may not be in conformity with the uniformity of nature, but is quite compatible, as Brown has shown, with our intuitive belief in causation ; for when creature power fails we can believe in creative.

It is in the second volume of the " Elements " that we find the logical disquisitions of Stewart. He has utterly failed in his strictures on Aristotle's logic. The school of Locke, and the school of Condillac, and the school of Reid, have all failed in constructing a logic of inference which can stand a sifting examination. The Aristotelian analysis of reasoning stands at this moment untouched in its radical positions. The objections of Campbell and Stewart have been answered by Whately, who shows that the syllogism is not a new or peculiar mode of reasoning, but an analytic of the process which passes through the mind when it reasons. In giving an adherence to the Aristotelian analysis, I admit that improvements were wrought in it by that school of logicians which has sprung from Kant, and of which Hamilton was the leader in Great Britain, followed by such eminent men as Mansel, Thomson, and Spalding. But their improvements ought not to be admitted till the formal logicians thoroughly deliver their exposition of the laws of thought from all that false Kantian metaphysics which represents thought as giving to the objects a "form" which is not in the objects themselves. Besides, I cannot allow logic to be an *a priori* science except under an explanation : I admit that the laws of thought operate in the mind prior to all experience ; but I maintain that they can be discovered by us only *a posteriori*, and by a generalization of their individual actings.

But while we may thus expect a perfected universal logic, treating of the laws of thought as laws of thought, — not independent of objects, but whatever be the objects, — I hope there will grow up alongside a particular logic, which will be a more practically useful logic, to consider the laws of thought as directed to particular classes of objects, and to treat of such topics as demonstrative and probable evidence, induction, and analogy. In regard to this latter logic, Stewart must ever be referred to as an authority. So far, indeed, as the theory of definitions and axioms is concerned, I prefer very much the view of Whewell, as developed in his " Philosophy of the Inductive Sciences." But, in regard to induction, I believe that Stewart's account of it is, upon the whole, the best which appeared from the time of Bacon down to his own age. Since his time, we have two great works, which have left every other far behind, — that of Whewell and that of Mr. John Stuart Mill. Not that I regard either of these as perfect. Dr. Whewell has exaggerated the place of the mental element, and has expressed it in most unfortunate phraseology, such as "fundamental ideas" and "conceptions," terms which have been used in twenty different significations, and are used by him to denote that the mind superinduces on the facts something not in the facts, whereas the mental power merely discovers what is in the facts. Mr. Mill, on the other hand, has overlooked the mental element altogether, and denies all necessary and universal truth. We may hope, in future years, to have a perfect inductive logic by a judicious combination of these two works ; but this can be done only by a man of the same high intellectual stature as Whewell and Mill, and this will seldom be met with. It is to be regretted that, since the days of Stewart, there is not a single Scotchman who has presented a work on induction, of any name or value.[1] In regard to analogy, the discoveries as to the typical forms of animals and plants and evolution will enable logicians to give a far more comprehensive and yet more stringent view of reasoning from analogy than has been done by Stewart, by Whewell, or by Mill.

The third volume of the " Elements " treats of certain concrete and practical matters, which Stewart was peculiarly qualified to discuss, and which bring out some of the finer qualities of his mind. All his disquisitions had tended to become verbal ; and here he treats expressly of language, which he does with fine discernment, but falls into a great blunder in regard to

---

[1] It is an interesting circumstance that, perhaps, the fairest estimate which we have of Bacon and the inductive system is by a German, Kuno Fischer, in his " Francis Bacon of Verulam " (translated by Oxenford). He errs, however, after the usual German mode of theorizing, in connecting Bacon with such men as Hobbes and Hume, the former of whom never professed to follow the Baconian method, and the latter of whom formed a very low estimate of Bacon, and has been most effectively met by Reid and Stewart, who professedly and really adopted the inductive system. This has been shown by Remusat, in his pleasantly written and judicious work, " Bacon : Sa Vie, son Temps, sa Philosophie ; " where there is a just estimate of Bacon's general philosophy, and some good remarks on the metaphysical points involved in induction.

Sanscrit, which he represents as of comparatively late origin, and analogous to mediæval Latin, whereas it has a literature reaching back at least twelve hundred years before Christ. He has some interesting, though by no means profound, remarks on the sympathetic affections. But by far the finest parts of the volume are those in which he treats of the varieties of intellectual character, and of the peculiarities of the metaphysician, the mathematician, the poet, and the sexes. Thus, of the mere metaphysician, he says, that, "he cannot easily submit to the task of examining details, or of ascertaining facts, and is apt to seize on a few *data* as first principles, following them out boldly to their remotest consequences, and afterwards employing his ingenuity to reconcile, by means of false refinements, his theoretical assumptions with the exceptions which seem to contradict them." He shows that the metaphysician is safe from the checks met with in physics, "where speculative mistakes are contradicted by facts which strike our senses." Again, of mathematics, he says, " that, while they increase the faculty of reasoning or deduction, they give no employment to the other powers of the understanding concerned in the investigation of truth." He adds : " I have never met a mere mathematician who was not credulous to excess."

In the same volume he discusses cautiously and judiciously the comparison between the faculties of man and brutes. I suspect, however, that the theory has not yet been devised — it has certainly not been published — which is fitted to give a satisfactory account of the relation of the brute to the human faculties. I suppose that Bonnet is right when he says that we shall never be able to understand the nature of brute instinct, till we are in the dog's head without being the dog. It is certain that we have at this moment nothing deserving of the name of science on this subject. I have sometimes thought that the modern doctrine of homologues and analogues, if extended and modified to suit the new object, might supply the key to enable us to express some of the facts. Certain of the brute qualities are merely analogous to those of man (as the wing of a butterfly is analogous to that of a bird) ; others are homologues, but inferior in degree ; while there are qualities in man different in kind from any in the brute. Aristotle called brute instincts, μιμήματα τῆς ἀνθρωπίνης ζωῆς. They would be more accurately described as anticipations or types of the coming archetype.

The volume closes with an account of James Mitchell, a boy born blind and dumb.

The "Philosophical Essays" are an episode in his system as a whole, even as his numerous notes and illustrations are episodes in the individual volumes. I am tempted, in looking at them, to take up two of the subjects discussed, as a deep interest still collects around them, and the questions agitated cannot yet be regarded as settled.

Every careful reader of Locke's "Essay" must have observed two elements running through all his philosophy, — the one, a sensational, or rather to do justice to Locke, who ever refers to reflection as a separate source of ideas, an experiential element, and the other a rational. In the opening of the "Essay" he denies innate ideas apparently in every sense, and affirms that the materials of all our ideas are derived from sensation and reflection; but, as he advances, his language is, that by these sources ideas are "suggested and furnished to the mind" (the language adopted by Reid and Stewart); he calls in faculties with high functions to work on the materials; speaks of ideas which are "creatures and inventions of the understanding;" appeals to "natural law" and the "principles of common reason;" and in the Fourth Book gives a very high, or rather deep, place to intuition; says we have an intuitive knowledge of our own existence; speaks of the "mind perceiving truth as the eye doth light, only by being directed toward it;" declares that, in the "discovery of and assent to these truths, there is no use of the discursive faculty, no need of reasoning, but they are known by a superior and higher degree of evidence," and talks even of a "necessary connection of ideas." It unfortunately happened that in France, to which Locke was introduced by Voltaire and the encyclopedists, they took the sensational element alone, and the effect on thought and on morality was most disastrous. Unfortunately, too, Locke has become known in Germany, chiefly through France, and hence we find him, all over the Continent, described both by friends and foes as a sensationalist; and the charge has been re-echoed in Great Britain by Sir William Hamilton and Dr. Morell. Yet it is quite certain that Locke has an intellectual as well as a sensational side.[1] I have,

---

[1] The intellectual side has been brought out to view by Henry Rogers, Professor Bowen of Harvard, and Professor Webb of Dublin.

in a careful perusal of the "Essay," mainly for this very end, discovered in every book, and in the majority even of the chapters, both sides of the shield; but I confess that I have not been able to discover the line that joins them. I do not think that Stewart's remarks on this subject are exhaustive or decisive: he is evidently wrong in supposing that Locke identified reflection with the reason which discovers truth, but his strictures are always candid and sometimes just.

In the "Philosophical Essays," Stewart has many fine observations on taste and beauty. On this subject he was favorably disposed towards the theory of his friend Mr. Alison, and he ascribes more than he should have done to the association of ideas. But he never gave his adhesion to this hypothesis as a full explanation of the phenomena. "If there was nothing," he says, "originally and intrinsically pleasing or beautiful, the associating principle would have no materials on which it could operate." The theory of association was never favorably received by artists, and has been abandoned by all metaphysicians. The tendency now is to return to the deeper views which had been expounded long ago by Plato, and, I may add, by Augustine. I find that Stewart refers to the doctrine of Augustine, who "represents beauty as consisting in that relation of the parts of a whole to each other which constitutes its unity;" and all that he has to say of it is: "The theory certainly is not of great value, but the attempt is curious." The æsthetical writers of our age would be inclined to say of it that there is more truth in it than in all the speculations of Alison, Stewart, Jeffrey, and Brown. It may be safely said that, while earnest inquirers have had pleasant glimpses of beauty, to no one has she revealed her full charms. When such writers as Cousin, Ruskin, and Macvicar dwell so much on unity, harmony, proportion, I am tempted to ask them: Does then the feeling of beauty not arise till we have discovered such qualities as proportion, unity, and harmony? And if they answer in the affirmative, then I venture to show them that they are themselves holding a sort of association theory; for they affirm that the beautiful object does not excite emotion till, as a sign, it calls forth certain ideas, — I suspect of truth and goodness. I am not quite sure that we can go the length of this school, when they speak of beauty as a quality necessary, immutable, eternal, like truth and moral good, and connect it so essentially with the very nature of God. There are sounds and colors and proportions felt to be beautiful by us, but which may not be appreciated by other intelligences, and which are so relished by us, simply because of the peculiarities of our human organization and constitution. I acknowledge that, when we follow these colors and sounds and proportions sufficiently far, we come invariably to mathematical ratios and relations ; but we are now, be it observed, in the region of immutable truth. Other kinds of beauty, arising from the contemplation of happiness and feeling, land us in the moral good, which is also necessary and eternal. I have sometimes thought that beauty is a gorgeous robe spread over certain portions of the true and the good, to recommend them to our regards and cluster our affections round them. Our æsthetic emotions being thus roused, the association of ideas comes in merely as a secondary agent to prolong and intensify the feeling.

The two volumes on the " Philosophy of the Active and Moral Powers " were published by Stewart immediately before his death. The leading ideas unfolded in them had been given, in an epitomized form, in the " Outlines," published many years before. They are somewhat too bulky for all the matter they contain, and they want somewhat of the freshness of his earlier works ; but they are characterized by profound wisdom, by a high moral tone, by a stately eloquence, and the felicitous application of general principles to the elucidation of practical points. He begins with the instinctive principles of action, which he classifies as appetites, desires, and affections. The arrangement is good in some respects, but is by no means exhaustive. As the next step in advance in this department of mental science, an attempt must be made to give a classification of man's motive principles, or of the ends by which man may be swayed in desire and action. Among these will fall to be placed, first of all pleasure and pain ; that is, man has a natural disposition to take to pleasure and avoid pain. But this is far from being the sole motive principle in man's mind. There are many others. There is, for example, the tendency of every native faculty to act, and this irrespective of pleasure or pain. Again, there are particular natural appetencies, which look to ends of their own, towards (to use the lan-

guage of Butler) particular external things of which the mind
hath always a particular idea or perception, towards these things
themselves, such as knowledge, power, fame, and this independent of the pleasure to be derived from them. Higher than
all, and claiming to be higher, is the moral motive, or obligation
to do right. A classification of these motive principles, even
though only approximately correct, would serve most important
purposes in philosophy generally, and more especially in ethics
and all the social sciences. Very low and inadequate views
have been taken of these motive principles of humanity, especially by those who represent man as capable of being
swayed only by the prospect of securing pleasure or avoiding pain. It should never be forgotten, that the emotive part
of man's nature may be excited by a great many other objects
as well as pleasure and pain, by all the objects, indeed, which
are addressed to the motive principles of man. It is the apprehension of objects as about to gratify the motive principles
of the mind — whatever they be — which stirs up the emotions.
Thus, the apprehension of a coming object, which is to gratify
a motive principle, excites hope, which is strong in proportion
to the strength of the apprehension, and the strength of the
particular motive principle ; while the apprehension of a coming
object, which is to disappoint this motive principle, stirs up
fear. It is strange that Stewart nowhere treats of the emotions in his " Philosophy of the Active Powers."

Stewart's view of the moral power in man, and of moral good,
seems to me to be substantially correct. In treating of these
subjects, he avows his obligations to Butler and Price. His
doctrine has been adopted, with some modifications, which are
improvements, by Cousin. Stewart and Cousin are the most
elevated of all the moralists who treat of ethics on grounds
independent of the Word of God. I am convinced that they
never could have given so pure a morality, had they not lived
in the midst of light shed abroad on our earth by a supernatural religion. I have always felt it to be a strange circumstance, that Stewart and Cousin, in giving so high a view of the
moral faculty, are never led to acknowledge that it condemns
the possessor ; and after presenting moral good in so rigid a
form, are not constrained to acknowledge that the moral law
has not been kept by man. Taking their own high principles

along with them, neither could have looked within, without discovering sin to be quite as much a reality as virtue. Stewart
could not have gone out of his dwelling in the old College or
the Canongate, nor could Cousin have gone out of his chambers in the Sorbonne, without being obliged to observe how far
man and woman have fallen beneath the ideal picture which
they have drawn in their lectures. At the very time when the
Scottish metaphysicians were discoursing so beautifully of
moral virtue, there was a population springing up around their
very colleges in Edinburgh and Glasgow, sunk in vice and
degradation, which appalled the good men of the next age —
the age of Chalmers — to contemplate, which the men of this
age know not how to grapple with, and which is not to be arrested by any remedy which the mere philosophic moralists
have propounded. I acknowledge most fully, that Stewart's
lectures and writings have tended, directly or indirectly, to
carry several important measures which are calculated to elevate the condition of mankind, such as reform in the legislature, prison improvement, and the abolition of tests and
of restrictions on commerce. But the institutions which aim
at lessening the sin and misery of the outcast and degraded —
such as missions, ragged schools, and reformatories, — have
proceeded from very different influences ; and a philosophy
embracing the facts which they contemplate, must dive deeper
into human nature, and probe its actual condition more faithfully, than the academic moralists of Scotland ever ventured
to do.

It is very evident that the Scottish academic metaphysicians
of last century, while they pay a dignified respect to Christianity, have not identified themselves with its profound peculiarities. Without meaning to excuse this deficiency, I may
yet affirm that some incidental advantages have sprung from
this *reticence.* It was certainly better that they should have
kept at a respectful distance from Christianity, than that they
should have approached it only, like the great German metaphysical systems, to set all its truths in rigid philosophic framework, or to absorb them all within themselves, as by a devouring flame. But the peculiar advantage arising from their
method consists in this, that they have, by induction, established a body of ethical truth on grounds independent of re-

vealed religion; and this can now be appealed to in all defences of Christianity, and as an evidence of the need of something which philosophy is incompetent to supply. Divines can now found on those great truths which the Scottish philosophers have established, as to there being a distinct moral faculty and an immutable moral law, and then press on those whose conscience tells them that they have broken that law, to embrace the provision which revelation has made to meet the wants of humanity.

The space which I have occupied with the "Mental and Moral Philosophy" precludes me from entering on the two volumes of "Political Economy," published partly from manuscripts left by Stewart himself, and partly from notes by pupils. The views expounded will scarcely be regarded as much advancing the science in the present day; but they did good service when delivered for twenty years in lectures. They are still worthy of being looked at on special topics; they may form an interesting chapter in the history of the literature of political economy, and they illustrate the character of Stewart's intellect and philosophy.

An estimate of the influence which has been exercised by Stewart may form an appropriate close to this article.

In Scotland, he increased the reputation of the Edinburgh University. Horner speaks of "many young Englishmen who had come to Edinburgh to finish their education," and not a few of these had been attracted by Stewart. He has had a greater influence than perhaps any other, in diffusing throughout Scotland a taste for mental and moral science. I have referred to the power exercised on him by Reid; but, if Stewart owed much to Reid, Reid owed nearly as much to his grateful pupil, who finished and adorned the work of his master, and by his classical taste has recommended the common-sense philosophy to many who would have turned away with disdain from the simpler manner of Reid. And here I am tempted to give utterance to the feeling, that Reid has been peculiarly fortunate in those who have attached themselves to his school. If Stewart helped to introduce Reid to polite society, Sir William Hamilton, by his unmatched logic and vast erudition, has compelled philosophers to give him — notwithstanding the somewhat untechnical character of his writings — a place in their

privileged circle.   By his expositions of Reid, and his own independent labors, Mr. Stewart aided in throwing back a tide
of scepticism : — which had appeared in France in the previous
century ; in England toward the beginning of the eighteenth
century, on the back of the licentious reigns of Charles II. and
James II. ; and, in Scotland, about the middle of that century.
This tide came to a height about the time of the French Revolution, and it was one of the avowed aims of Stewart, " to stem
the inundation of sceptical, or rather atheistical, publications
which were imported from the Continent."   Nor is it to be
forgotten, that Stewart, directly by his lectures and indirectly
by his pupils, contributed as much as any man of his age, to
diffuse throughout Scotland a taste for elegant literature, and
enlarged and liberal opinions in politics.

As to England, Sir J. Mackintosh, writing to Stewart in
1802, speaks of the want of any thing which he could call purely
philosophical thinking ; and Horner, in 1804, declares, that the
highest names in the estimation of those in the metropolis,
who felt any interest in speculative pursuits, were Hobbes and
Hartley.   Such works as the " Moral Philosophy " of Paley, were
fitted to lower still farther, rather than elevate, this taste.   It
was altogether, then, for the benefit of English thought, that
Stewart did become gradually known in South Britain, where
his elegant style, his crowning good sense, and the moderation
of his opinions, recommended him to many who had imbibed as
great an aversion to Scotch metaphysics as ever George III. had.
There are still Englishmen who abhor the infidelity of Hume,
and who despise the plainness of Reid, who suspect the rhetoric of Brown, and are frightened by the bristling nomenclature
and logical distinctions of Hamilton, but who are attracted by
the writings of Stewart, which are felt to be as pleasing and
as regular as their own rich fields bounded by hedge-rows.   In
England he has so far been of use in creating a philosophical
spirit, where none existed before, and in checking the utilitarianism of Paley.   He is also entitled to a share of the credit
of the great measures of reform, which such pupils as Horner,
Brougham, Lord John Russell, Palmerston, Jeffrey, and Lansdowne carried in Parliament.   Perhaps these eminent men
have never estimated the amount of wholesome impulse which
they received in early life from the prelections and lofty character of the Edinburgh professor.

In France the influence of Reid and Stewart has been considerable, and has been of the most beneficial character. In that country, Locke's philosophy, unfortunately introduced by Voltaire and accepted in its worst side, had wrought only mischief, partly by its drawing away the attention of thinkers from the more spiritual philosophy of Descartes, and partly by its tempting a set of speculators to derive all men's ideas from sensation, and to deny the existence of all ideas which could not be derived from this source, — such as the idea of moral good, of infinity, and of God. This wretched philosophy — if philosophy it can be called — was one of the fatal powers which operated to give an evil issue to the Revolution, and prevented good from coming out of it. After sensationalism — which used, but only to abuse, the name of Locke — had reigned for more than half a century, there appeared a reaction led on by M. Royer Collard, who began in 1811 to lecture at the Normal School. It is a most interesting circumstance, that, in conducting this war against the debasing systems which prevailed, he betook himself to the philosophy of Reid and Stewart. Exercising a considerable influence in himself, Royer Collard has had a more extended sway through his pupils, especially Victor Cousin and Theodore Jouffroy. In the course of years, the works of Reid were translated into French, with an admirable historical and critical introduction, by Jouffroy. So early as 1808, the first volume of Stewart's " Elements " was translated into French by M. Prevost of Geneva ; and, at a later date, M. Peisse, has translated the other two volumes of the same work. Stewart's " Outlines " were translated into the same tongue by Jouffroy, who has prefixed a preface of great judgment and acuteness. It thus appears, that the great reaction in favor of sound philosophy, commenced by Royer Collard and conducted by Cousin and Jouffroy, has made large and profitable use of the Scottish school, and rejoices to acknowledge its obligations to Scotland. No doubt, it has also called in aid from other quarters. Cousin has been indebted to the school of Kant, as well as to the school of Reid, and has derived some of his favorite principles immediately from the great metaphysician of his own country, Descartes ; and he has besides carefully examined the human mind, in an inductive manner ; and he has been able to give a unity to these materials, because he is possessed of great original genius, acuteness, and comprehensiveness of mind. I am sometimes inclined to think, however, that he has got the most precious element in his eclectic system from the school of Scotland. I have been greatly gratified to observe, that, after he had been drawn aside for a time from his attachment to the Scottish philosophy, by a later affection for German transcendentalism (this is very visible in his course of lectures delivered in 1828 and 1829), he returned in his later years to his first love, — and this at a time when Scotland was rather forsaking the inductive method, and turning its regards towards the *a priori* method of Germany.

I feel proud, I confess, of the eulogiums which have been pronounced on Scotland, not only by Cousin, but by Jouffroy and Remusat. But these philosophers have scarcely seen, after all, wherein lies the peculiar strength of the Scottish nation. This is not to be found in its systems of moral philosophy, but in its religion, of which the high moral tone of its philosophy is but a reflection, which would soon wax dim and vanish were the original light extinguished ; — nay, in remembering that Kant was descended from Scottish parentage, I have sometimes thought that his high moral precepts may be also a reflection from the same light. Often, I should think, when M. Cousin looked around him on these scenes of revolution through which France has passed, must he have seen that his country needs something deeper and more influential than any system of moral science, even though it should be as pure and elevated as that which he inculcated.

In Germany Stewart has been little known, and has exercised no power for good or for evil. The only English philosopher familiarly referred to in that country is Locke, and even he is known, I suspect, more through his French consequences than from the study of his work. The German professors speak of him, under the name of Lockè, as the representative of sensationalism, overlooking the constant reference which he makes to reflection as a separate source of ideas, and to the lengthened account which he gives of intuition, — a much juster account, in some respects, of its function than that given by Kant or Schelling. The great English ethical writer, Butler, who has established for ever the great truth of the supremacy of conscience in the human constitution, is either altogether unknown in Germany, or referred to by such writers as Tholuck only to show that he is not understood or appreciated. The only Scottish metaphysician thoroughly known in Germany is David Hume. Reid is occasionally spoken of, only to be disparaged in his system and its results. Stewart is scarcely ever named. I must be allowed to regret this. Such a body of carefully inducted fundamental truth as we have in the philosophy of Reid and Stewart is precisely what was and is needed · to preserve thought from the extravagances of the transcendental schools in the last age, and now, in the natural recoil which has taken place, since 1848, from the tide of materialism which is setting in so strongly, and with no means or method of meeting it. The philosophy of Germany must ever go by oscillations, by actions and reactions, till the critical method of Kant is abandoned, and the inductive method is used to determine the rule and law of those *a priori* principles of which so much use is made, while there has been so little careful inquiry into their precise nature and mode of operation.

This may be the proper place for referring to the relation in which Stewart stood toward Kant. I have already expressed my regret that Stewart should have entered on a criticism of Kant without a deeper acquaintance with his system. No doubt it might be retorted, that the criticisms of Stewart upon Kant are not more ignorant and foolish than those of the disciples of Kant upon Reid; but it is better to admit that Stewart committed a blunder in his review of the Kantian system. Some have supposed that, if he had known more of Kant, he would have formed a totally different opinion of his philosophy. And I admit that a further acquaintance with Kant's works would have raised Kant in his estimation; would have kept him from describing his nomenclature as "jargon," and his philosophy as "incomprehensible," from affirming that Kant has "thrown no new light on the laws of the intellectual world;" would have shown him many curious points of correspondence between the views of Kant and the profoundest of his own doctrines, and have enabled him, when he did depart from Kant, to give fair and valid reasons, and thus to help in what must be one of the tasks of philosophy in this age, — the work of taking from Kant what is good and true, and casting away

what is evil, because false.   While I admit all this, I am convinced at the same time that Stewart would never have given
an adhesion to the peculiarities of Kantism.   He would have
said, " My method of induction is better than your method of criticism, and my account of the intuitive convictions of the mind is
correct when I represent them as fundamental laws of thought
and belief ; whereas you are giving a wrong account of them
when you represent them as *a priori* forms imposing on the objects in all cognition something which is not in the objects."   I
cannot conceive him, in any circumstances, allowing to Kant (as
Hamilton unfortunately did) that space and time and causation
are laws of thought and not of things, and may have merely a
subjective existence.   His caution, his good sense, and his
careful observation, would have prevented him from ever falling
into a system of nescience such as that to which the relentless
logic of Hamilton has carried him, founding, I acknowledge,
on premises which Stewart as well as Kant had furnished.
He would have adhered, after knowing all, to his decision :
" We are irresistibly led to ascribe to the thing itself (space) an
existence independent of the will of any being."   It is an "incomprehensible doctrine which denies the objective reality of
time."   " That space is neither a *substance*, nor an *accident*, nor
a *relation*, may be safely granted ; but it does not follow from
this that it is nothing objective."   " Our first idea of space or
extension seems to be formed by abstracting this attribute from
the other qualities of matter.   The idea of space, however, in
whatever manner formed, is manifestly accompanied with an
irresistible conviction that space is necessarily existent, and
that its annihilation is impossible," etc.   He adds, " To call
this proposition in question, is to open a door to universal
scepticism."   (" Diss.," pp. 596, 597.)

The great work which the school of Reid has done consists
in its careful investigation, in the inductive manner first, of the
faculties of the mind ; and, secondly, and more particularly, of
man's primary and intuitive convictions.   For this they ought
to be honored in all time.   Kant did a work similar to this last,
but in a different manner.   Rejecting (as Reid had done) the
combined dogmatic and deductive method of Descartes, he
introduced the critical method, affirming that reason can criticise itself, and proceeding to criticise reason by a kind of

logical process of a most unsatisfactory kind. Criticism has succeeded criticism, each new critic taking a new standing-point,
or advancing a step farther, till Hegel's system became the
reductio ad absurdum of the whole method of procedure inaugurated by Kant. I admit that Kant was right in affirming that
a priori principles should be examined before they are assumed
in philosophical investigation. We are not at liberty to assume
a first truth till we have shown it to be a first truth ; and we
have no right to use it in argument or deduction till we have
determined its precise nature and law ; but this is to be done,
I maintain, in the inductive manner, with its accompanying
analysis and exclusions. The Scottish school commenced this
work, but they do not profess to have completed it. Stewart
everywhere proclaims that it is to be done by the combined
efforts of successive inquirers, pursuing the same method for
ages.

Reid and Stewart nowhere profess to give a full list, or even
a rigid classification, of the intuitive convictions of the mind.
All that they affirm is, that those principles which they have
seized for the purpose of meeting the scepticism of Hume, are
and must be intuitive. They do not even pretend to give a
full account of these, or to express them in their ultimate form.
They vacillate in the account which they give of them, and in
the nomenclature which they employ to denote them. They
draw no definite distinction between cognitions, beliefs, and
judgments. They treat of the faculties, and also of the principles of common sense, but they do not tell us how the two
stand related to each other. And here I may be permitted to
observe, that I look on these fundamental laws as being the
necessary laws of the faculties regulating all their exercises,
but not as laws or principles before the consciousness ; and
they are to be reflexly discovered as general laws only by the
induction of their individual acts. Reid and Stewart do not
even tell us what are the tests by which their presence may
be detected : these I hold to be, first, as Aristotle and Locke
have shown, self-evidence ; and, second, as Leibnitz and Kant
have shown, necessity and universality. Such defects as these
they were quite willing to confess in that spirit of modesty
which was one of their highest characteristics ; and to any one
complaining that they had not settled every point, they would,

as it were, say, Go on in the path which we have opened ; we are sure that there is more truth yet to be discovered, and rejoice we must and will if you succeed where we have failed and raise a little higher that fabric of which we have laid the foundation.

———◆———

XLI. —*WILLIAM LAWRENCE BROWN.*

IN 1785, Mr. Burnett, a merchant in Aberdeen, bequeathed certain sums to be expended at intervals of forty years in the shape of two premiums for the best works furnishing "evidence that there is a Being, all powerful, wise, and good, by whom every thing exists : and particularly to obviate difficulties regarding the wisdom and goodness of the Deity ; and this, in the first place, from considerations independent of written revelation, and, in the second place, from the revelation of the Lord Jesus, and from the whole to point out inferences most necessary for and useful to mankind." This endowment has not called forth any one great work ; but, on each of the two occasions on which it has been competed for, it has been the means of publishing two excellent treatises. On the first competition, the first prize was awarded to Principal Brown of Aberdeen, and the second to the Rev. John Bird Sumner, afterwards Archbishop of Canterbury.

Dr. Brown was born at Utrecht, 1755, and became minister of the Scotch church there. He removed to Scotland in 1795, became professor of divinity in Aberdeen, and afterwards principal of Marischal College. He lived till 1830. When in Holland he wrote an " Essay on the Folly of Scepticism." His Burnett Prize Essay, "On the Existence of a Supreme Creator," was given to the world in 1816. The work did not produce much impression in its own age, and is now all but forgotten. People wonder that so large a sum (upwards of £1,200) did not call forth a more brilliant production ; but the truth is, that money cannot produce an original work, which can come only from the spontaneous thoughts of the man of genius, that prize essays are commonly respectably good and nothing more. and, while they may serve a good purpose in their own day, are seldom valued as a legacy by posterity. The book is in many respects the perfection of a prize essay. It conforms rigidly to the conditions imposed by the donor ; it is supremely judicious ; it did not startle the judges by any eccentricity or even novelty, and certainly not by any profundity ; and altogether is a clear and able defence of natural and revealed religion. It interests us to notice that the principles of the Scottish philosophy are here employed to support the great truths relating to the being of God and the destiny of man.

XLII. — ARCHIBALD ALISON.

HE was born in Edinburgh in 1757, studied at Glasgow University, went thence to Oxford, where he matriculated in Baliol College. Taking orders in the Church of England in 1784, he received several preferments ; such as, a prebendal stall in Salisbury, and the perpetual curacy of Kenley in Shropshire. He married a daughter of John Gregory, and thus became more closely identified with Edinburgh, where he continued usually to reside, and where he discharged the duties of an Episcopal clergyman in the Cowgate chapel from the year 1800 down to the time of his death in 1839. He was distinguished for his excessive politeness. He published a volume of sermons, which had the good fortune (or the bad, for the "Edinburgh" had never a great reputation as a critic of sermons) to get a laudatory notice in the Edinburgh Review, where they were compared to the "Oraisons Funèbres" of Bossuet, and it was said of them : " We do not know any sermons so pleasing or so likely to be popular, and do good to those who are pleased with them. All the feelings are generous and gentle, all the sentiments liberal, and all the general views just and ennobling." But the work which lives is " Essays on the Nature and Principles of Taste," which was published in 1790, but seems to have passed very much out of sight till the booksellers in 1810 told him that there was a wish expressed for the second edition, which was reviewed by Francis Jeffrey in 1811, and afterwards had an extensive circulation in various countries.

The arrangement and manner of the work are admirable. The style is distinguished by infinite grace, and is worthy of being compared to that of Addison : — indeed I am not sure if we have a more beautiful specimen of the last-century manner of composition, moulded on the " Spectator," on the French classics, and the wits of Queen Anne. Every word is appropriate, and is in its appropriate place ; and the sentences glide along like a silvery stream. The descriptions of natural scenery, which are very numerous, are singularly felicitous and graceful : that word *graceful* ever comes up when we would describe his manner. He does not seem to have had an equal opportunity of studying beauty in the fine arts, in architecture, statuary, and painting, though the allusions to the universally known models of these are always appreciative and discriminating.

Drawing a distinction, very essential in all such inquiries, he would investigate, first, the nature of those qualities that produce the emotions of taste, and then that faculty by which the emotions are received. This distinction, clearly announced, is not thoroughly carried out. In the body of the work, in inquiring into the faculty raising the emotions, he makes the remark, that they are not " the objects of immediate observation," and that they are often obscured under the number of qualities with which they are accidentally combined. He does not seem to have expounded his views as to the faculty. He opposes the theories which have uniformly taken for granted the simplicity of the emotion, and especially those which have made it a sense or senses. He endeavors to show that it has no resemblance to a sense, and that it is finally to be resolved into the more general principles of our constitution. He shows that " it is not, in fact, a simple but a complex emotion : that it involves in all cases, first, the production of some simple emotion or the exercise of some moral affection ; and, secondly, the consequent excitement of a peculiar exercise of the imagination ; that these concomitant effects are distinguishable and very often distinguished in our experience ; and that the peculiar pleasure of the beautiful or sublime is only felt when these two effects are conjoined, and the complex emotions produced."

In entering on his " Analysis," he proceeds on the philosophic principle, that we should consider the effects before we proceed to determine the cause. So he is to begin with considering the effect produced on the mind when the emotions of beauty or sublimity are felt, and then go on to investigate the causes which are productive of it, or, in other words, the sources of the beautiful and sublime in nature.

I. " When any object either of sublimity or beauty is presented to the mind, I believe man is conscious of a train of thought being immediately awakened in his imagination analogous to the character or expression of the original object. The simple perception of the object, we frequently find, is insufficient to excite these emotions, unless it is accompanied with this operation of mind ; unless, according to common expression, our imagination is seized and our fancy busied in the pursuit of all those trains of thought which are allied to this character or expression. Thus, when we feel either the beauty or sublimity of natural scenery, the gay lustre of a morning in spring, or the mild radiance of a summer evening, the savage majesty of a wintry storm, or the wild magnificence of a tempestuous ocean, — we are conscious of a variety of images in our minds very different from those which the objects themselves can present to the eye. Trains of pleasing or of solemn thought arise spontaneously within our minds : our hearts swell with emotions of which the objects before us afford no adequate cause." The state of mind most favorable to the emotions of taste is one in which the imagination is free and unembarrassed ; and the feeling is not interfered with by any thing which interrupts the flow, is not interfered with in particular by the intrusion of criticism. He shows that the exercise of imagination and the feeling of beauty is increased by association, especially that of resemblance, and enters upon the field which had been so cultivated by Beattie. He remarks very truly how an acquaintance with poetry in our earlier years has a powerful influence in increasing our sensibility to the beauties of nature.

He then gives an analysis of the peculiar exercise of the imagination. There is, in all cases, the indulgence of a train of thought. But then, every train of thought does not raise emotions of beauty ; and so he investigates the nature of those trains of thought that are produced by object of sublimity and beauty, and their difference from those ordinary trains which are unaccompanied with such pleasure. This difference consists in two things : first, in the nature of the ideas or conceptions which compose such trains ; and, secondly, in the nature of the law of their succession. Some ideas are fitted to raise emotions : these he calls " ideas of emotions ; " and the train of thought which produces beauty is in all cases composed of ideas capable of exciting some affection or emotion." Thus, the ideas suggested by the scenery of spring are ideas productive of emotions of cheerfulness, of gladness, and of tenderness. The images suggested by the prospect of ruins are images belonging to pity, to melancholy, to admiration. The ideas in the same manner awakened by the view of the ocean in a storm are ideas of power, of majesty, and of terror. But farther the ideas themselves must have some general principle of connection, subsisting through the whole extent of the train, giving them a certain and definite character, and a conformity to that peculiar emotion which first excited them. It appears, that " in every operation of taste, there are thus two different faculties employed ; viz., some affection or emotion raised, and the imagination excited to a train of thought corresponding to this emotion. The peculiar pleasure which attends and which constitutes the emotions of taste, may naturally be considered as composed of the pleasures which separately attend the exercise of those faculties, or, in other words, as produced by the union of pleasing emotion with the pleasure which by the constitution of our nature is annexed to the exercise of the imagination." Our consciousness testifies that there is truth and very important truth in all this. Every form of beauty in nature and art, music for instance, raises a train of ideas which are accompanied with emotions all of a certain kind. While he has brought before us a body of facts, it may be doubted whether he has seen himself, or exposed to the view of others, the whole of the mental phenomena. The question arises, What starts the train? and a farther question follows, What gives the unity and harmony to the train ? An answer to these questions, or rather to this question, — for the questions are one, — may disclose to our view an objective beauty and sublimity very much overlooked by Alison, and the supporters of the association theory.

II. It is proper to state that Alison does speak in the second and longest essay of the beauty and sublimity of the material world. He treats of the beauty of sound, color, form, motion, and of the human countenance and form. He says matter in itself is unfitted to produce any kind of emotion, and can raise an emotion of beauty only by an association with other qualities, and " as being either the signs or expressions of such qualities as are fitted by the constitution of our nature to produce emotion." To those who consider sounds simply as sounds they have no beauty. There is surely an oversight here : for music has in itself a beauty which can be mathematically expressed ; but then the feeling of beauty is prolonged and intensified by the train of emotional ideas which is set a going. Alison traces the associations raised by sounds. The sublimity of thunder is founded on awe and some degree of

terror.   Sounds are no longer sublime when they do not
awaken such feelings.   " There is nothing more common than
for people who are afraid of thunder to mistake some very common and indifferent sound for it ; as, the rumbling of a cart, or
the rattling of a carriage.   While their mistake continues, they
feel the sound as sublime : the moment they are undeceived,
they are the first to laugh at their terror and to ridicule the
sound which occasioned it.   Children, at first, are as much
alarmed at the thunder of the stage as at real thunder.   Whenever they find that it is only a deception, they amuse themselves by mimicking it."   He represents the real power of
music as consisting in its imitation of those signs of emotion
or passion which take place in the human voice.

In respect of colors, he holds that they are not beautiful,
except as " expressive to us of pleasing or interesting qualities."
He is successful in showing that there is a beauty of color
arising from association of color, as in dress for instance : but
science announces that there is a harmony of colors, as of com-
plementary colors, that is, of colors making up the white beam,
which is beautiful physiologically.   He maintains that "the
beauty of forms arises altogether from the associations we connect with them," or the qualities of which they are expressive
to us.   Sublimity of forms arises from their suggesting ideas
of danger or power, or from their magnitude.   Among natural
objects, angular forms are associated with hardness, strength,
or durability, suggesting force ; and winding forms, with free-
will, fineness, delicacy, ease.   He labors to prove that proportion, as in architecture, is felt to be beautiful, because expressive
of fitness.   Æsthetic science maintains in opposition that there
are certain proportions in length and composition which to our
eye have a beauty in themselves.   As to motion, it is felt to be
beautiful, because associated with power.   Rapid motion in a
straight line is simply expressive of great power.   Slow motion
in curves is expressive of gentle power, united with ease, freedom, and playfulness.

He dwells at length on the different sources of the beauty
or sublimity of the countenance of man.   It arises, first, from
physical beauty, or the beauty of certain colors and forms considered simply as forms or colors ; secondly, from the beauty of
expression and character, or that habitual form of features and

color of complexion which, from experience, we consider as significant of those habitual dispositions of the human mind which we love or approve or admire ; thirdly, from the beauty of emotion, or the expression of certain local or temporary affections of mind which we approve or love or admire.   Each of these species of beauty will be perfect when the composition of the countenance is such as to preserve, pure and unmingled, the expression which it predominantly conveys ; and when no feature or color is admitted but which is subservient to the unity of this expression.   The last or highest degree of beauty or sublimity of the human countenance will alone be attained when *all* these expressions are united : when the physical beauty corresponds to the characteristic ; when the beauty of temporary emotion harmonizes with the beauty of character ; and when all fall upon the heart of the spectator as one whole, in which matter, in all its most exquisite forms, is only felt as the sign of one great or amiable character of mind."

In criticising this theory, I am prepared to admit that the ingenious author has seized and unfolded to our view a large body of truth which had never been so fully developed before. He is surely right in saying that there is a train of ideas in all those operations of mind in which we contemplate what is called beautiful and sublime : it is so, as we listen to music, grave or gay ; as we gaze at a waterfall, or into the starry vault of heaven. It is also certain that all these ideas are emotional : that is, accompanied with emotion ; and that the ideas and emotions are all of a connected kind, and thus produce the one effect.   On these points his views seem to me to be just, and they are to a great extent original.   It should farther be allowed that in all this there is the influence of association of ideas, regulated by such principles as contiguity and resemblance : this had been shown fully before his time by Hutcheson, by Beattie, and others of the Scottish school.   But is this all ?   It seems as if we needed, besides, both a start to the movement and a principle of connection to make it proceed in one direction.   In music there are sounds which produce a pleasant sensation : these are regulated, as has been known since the time of Pythagoras, by mathematical relations.   This pleasant sensation gives the impulse to the train of emotional thought, it sustains it, and gives to it a congruity.   Again, it has been shown that there are melodious and harmonious colors, which are pleasing to the eye ; and these set out the mind on a pleasant train of association, and keep it on the one tract.   Attempts have been made, since the days of Plato, to discover forms which are essentially beautiful ; and these have so far been successful.   There are proportions and there are curves which are adapted to the laws of light on the one hand, and to our sensory organs on the other.   Are not these the roots from which our associated ideas and emotions spring ?   Are not the objects possessing them entitled to be called beautiful and sublime ?

While there is a beauty of sound, color, and form to act as the root of the feeling, it is to be allowed to Alison that there is a train of ideas and feelings which constitutes, as it were, the growing trunk.   But, as Alison has shown, it is not every train of idea, nor even every train of emotional idea, that is fitted to raise emotions which are beautiful or sublime.   There is need of a bond of connection to raise the proper kind of ideas, and to make them flow in one direction, so as to produce a uniform result.   The objective sound, color, form, proportion, expression, must not only start the association, but must so far guide it along a consistent line ; make the ideas and feelings, for instance, which are raised as we stand gazing on a lovely countenance or a lofty waterfall, all to be of a sort and to contribute to one emotional result.

There are two grand oversights in the explanations of Alison : he overlooks the moving power which starts the train, and the guiding rails which direct it.   This leaves a very great gap in his theory : he has no objective ground for beauty ; and this has set against it both artists and scientific investigators, who are apt to turn away from it with unbelief or with scorn, saying that they are not to be taken in by this illusory picture, for they are sure that beauty is a reality in the thing itself.   It is the business of science, by its own methods, to investigate the precise objective nature of sounds, colors, and forms ; and there is ground for believing that the laws involved will at last be enunciated in mathematical expressions.

But there is a higher element than all this in beauty ; an element seen by Plato and by those who have so far caught his spirit, — such as, Augustine, Cousin, MacVicar, and Ruskin, — but commonly overlooked by men of science and the upholders of the association theory. The mere sensations or perceptions called forth by the presence of harmonious sounds, colors, and proportional forms, is not the main ingredient in the lovely and the grand. Beauty, after all, lies essentially in the ideas evoked. I hold by an association theory on this subject. But the ideas entitled to be called æsthetic should be of mind, and the higher forms of mind, intellectual and moral. There was, therefore, grand truth in the speculation of Plato, that beauty consists in the bounding of the waste, in the formation of order out of chaos ; or, in other words, in harmony and proportion. There was truth in the theory of Augustine, that beauty consists in order and design ; and in that of Hutcheson, that it consists in unity with variety. Alison had, at times, a glimpse of this truth, but then lost sight of it. He speaks with favor of the doctrine held by Reid, that matter is not beautiful in itself, but derives its beauty from the expression of mind ; he holds it true, so far as the qualities of matter are immediate signs of the powers or capacities of mind, and in so far as they are signs of those affections or dispositions of mind which we love, or with which we are formed to sympathize. He thus sums up his views : " The conclusion, therefore, in which I wish to rest is, that the beauty and sublimity which is felt in the various appearances of matter are finally to be ascribed to their expression of mind ; or to their being, either directly or indirectly, the signs of those qualities of mind, which are fitted, by the constitution of our nature, to affect us with pleasing or interesting emotion." There is a singular mixture of truth and error in this statement : truth, in tracing all beauty and sublimity to the expression of mind ; but error, in placing it in qualities which raise emotion according to our constitution. Beauty and sublimity are not the same as the true and the good ; but they are the expression and the signs of the true and the good, suggested by the objects that evidently participate in them.

XLIII. — *GEORGE JARDINE.*

ALL throughout the seventeenth century, there was a strong reaction in Great Britain against Aristotle, scholasticism, and formal logic generally. College youths everywhere were protesting against the syllogism, moods and figures, and reduction. Unfortunately, logic — in Glasgow, Edinburgh, and Saint Andrews, — came in the second year of the college course ; and youths of fifteen or sixteen groaned under the yoke, and longed for something more fascinating and less arduous. The professor who did most to gratify this taste was Jardine, professor of logic and rhetoric in the university of Glasgow.

For several sessions after his appointment, he followed the established method, giving the usual course of logic and metaphysics, though he says, " every day more and more convinced me that something was wrong in the system of instruction ; that the subjects on which I lectured were not adapted to the age, the capacity, and the previous attainments of my pupils." " To require the regular attendance of very young men two hours every day during a session of six or seven months, on lectures which they could not understand, and in which, of course, they could take no interest, had a direct tendency to produce habits of negligence, indifference, and inattention, which, it is well known, frequently terminate in a positive aversion to study of every description. The change from the animated perusal of the Greek and Roman classics to the unfathomable depths of logic and metaphysics was far too abrupt." The fault evidently lay, not in having logic as a required branch of study, and not in requiring it to be thoroughly learned, but in bringing it in too early in the course, and in not having in the second year a course on English literature and composition. Jardine did give a course of formal logic, but it was very much pressed into a corner. His text-book, " Quædam ex Logicæ Compendiis Selectæ," is a meagre abridgment carrying the student among the bones of the study, without clothing them with life, and fitted to leave the impression that the branch is as useless as it is dry. He enlarged with much deeper interest on the human mind generally, and the various faculties : on language, on taste, on beauty, on criticism, — showing no originality or grasp of intellect, but furnishing a course of great utility to young students, and felt to be interesting and stimulating.

His views were expounded in his " Outlines of Philosophical Education, illustrated by the Method of Teaching the Logic Class in the University of Glasgow." The work is still worthy of being looked into by all who would study what the Germans call " Pedagogic." He points out the advantages of the lecturing system. " While listening to a discourse delivered with some degree of animation, the mind of the student is necessarily more awakened, and feels a more powerful demand made upon its energies, than when perusing a printed volume." " In a class-room, a sympathetic feeling pervades the whole ; the glow of zeal and an expression of curiosity

are perceived in almost every countenance; all the faculties of the mind
are exerted ; and powers unused before are awakened into life and activity."
But he insists that the lecturing be accompanied with regular examinations.
The teacher " will not examine the class in any stated order, but occasionally
call upon the same individual at two successive hours, or even twice in one
hour ; and, as a check upon open negligence, he may sometimes select such
as appear the least attentive, and thereby expose their idleness to their
fellow-students." But the most important part of his work is that in which
he explains his views as to themes for composition, recommending that
some be presented as fitted to enable the student to form clear and accurate
notions and to express his thoughts, others to give a power of analysis and
classification, a third to exercise and strengthen the reasoning faculties,
and a fourth to encourage processes of investigation. Under this fourth
head, he suggests as a theme, " There was fine linen in Egypt in the time
of Moses," and would have the student thence determine the state of Egypt
as to government, science, and art.

Professor Jardine was born at Wandal, in the upper ward of Lanark-
shire, in 1742. He was educated at Glasgow College, and became a licentiate of the Church of Scotland. In 1771, he became tutor to two sons
of Baron Mure, and travelled with them in France. On his return in 1773,
he was an unsuccessful candidate for the chair of humanity in Glasgow;
but, in 1774, he was appointed assistant and successor to Mr. Clow, professor of logic and rhetoric. In 1824, he retired from the teaching of
logic, and died in 1827. His pupils acknowledged their deep obligations
to him in interesting them in study and imparting to them a power of writing the English language. But certainly he did not advance the science
of logic, or help to promote the study of it among young men. Francis
Jeffrey, who was fond of expressing his gratitude to him, may be taken as
the representative pupil produced by him, capable of thinking and expressing himself clearly and ably on every subject, but not diving into the
depths of any subject. It required all the ability and energy of Sir William
Hamilton to bring back Scottish youths to the scientific study of logic.

XLIV. — *THOMAS BROWN*.[1]

In regard to the younger years of Thomas Brown, it is enough
to mention, that he was born at Kirkmabreck, in the stewartry
of Kirkcudbright, in January, 1778; that his father, who was
minister of that place, died soon after, when the family removed to Edinburgh; that he there received the rudiments

[1] "Account of the Life and Writings of Thomas Brown, M.D." (1825), by
David Welsh. Shorter Memoir by same prefixed to Brown's " Lectures."

of his education from his mother; that, in his seventh year, he went to London, under the protection of a maternal uncle, and attended successively schools at Camberwell, Chiswick, and Kensington, down to the time of the death of his uncle, in 1792, when he returned to Edinburgh, to reside with his mother and sisters, and begin his collegiate course in the university. He is described as a precocious child, and we can believe it. He was precocious all his life, and in every thing. We have to regret that he did not take sufficient pains to secure that the flower which blossomed so beautifully should be followed by corresponding fruit. We can credit his biographer, when he tells us that he learned the alphabet at a single lesson; but I suspect that there must have been the prompting of some theological friend preceding the reply which he gave, when he was only between four and five, to an inquiring lady, that he was seeking out the differences in the narratives of the evangelists. At school he was distinguished by the gentleness of his nature and the delicacy of his feelings; by the quickness of his parts, and particularly by the readiness of his memory; by his skill in recitation, and his love of miscellaneous reading, especially of works of imagination. Nor is it to be forgotten that he also gave promise of his genius for poetry, by verses which one of his masters got published, perhaps unfortunately for the youth, in a magazine. He read with a pencil in his hand, with which he made marks; and, in the end, he had no pleasure in reading a book which was not his own. He began his collegiate course in Edinburgh by the study of logic under Finlayson; and having, in the summer of 1793, paid a visit to Liverpool, Currie, the biographer of Burns, introduced him to the first volume of Stewart's "Elements." The following winter he attended Stewart's course of lectures, and had the courage to wait on the professor, so renowned for his academic dignity, and read to him observations on one of his theories. Mr. Stewart listened patiently, and then read to the youth a letter which he had received from M. Prevost of Geneva, containing the very same objections. This was followed by an invitation to the house of the professor, who, however, declined on this, as he did on all other occasions, to enter into controversy. It is but justice to Stewart to say, that he continued to take a paternal interest in the progress of his pupil, till the revolt of Brown against the whole school of Reid cooled their friendship, and loosened the bonds which connected them.   In 1796 he is studying law, which, however, he soon abandoned for medicine, and attended the medical classes from 1798 till 1803.   At college, he received instructions from such eminent professors as Stewart, Robison, Playfair, and Black, and was stimulated by intercourse with college friends, such as Erskine, Brougham, Reddie, Leyden, Horner, Jeffrey, and Sidney Smith, — all precocious and ambitious like himself, and who, in the "Academy of Sciences," debated on topics far beyond their years and their knowledge.

It was when Brown was at college, that Erasmus Darwin's "Zoonomia" was published.   The work is filled with premature theories as to life and mind, and proceeds on the method, as Brown calls it, of "hypothetical reasoning," — a method, I may remark, carried still further, but with a more carefully observed body of facts to support it, by his illustrious grandson, Charles Darwin.   Brown read it at the age of eighteen, was irritated by its materialistic tendency, and scribbles notes upon it ; these ripen into a volume by the time he is nineteen, and were published by the time he was twenty, — "Observations on the Zoonomia of Erasmus Darwin, M. D."   Brown was an excellent physiologist for his day ; but both the original work and the reply proceed on principles now regarded as antiquated. But Brown's criticism is a remarkable example of intellectual precocity.   In the midst of physiological discussions, most of the metaphysical ideas which he developed in future years are to be found here in the bud.   He considers the phenomena of the mind as mental states, speaks of them as "feelings," delights to trace them in their succession, and so dwells much on suggestion, and approaches towards the theory of general notions, and the theory of causation, expounded in his subsequent works.   It should be added, that the book committed him prematurely to principles which he was indisposed to review in his riper years.   It appears from a letter to Darwin, that, at the age of nineteen, he had a theory of mind which he is systematizing.

Out of the "Academy of Sciences" arose, as is well known, the "Edinburgh Review," in the second number of which there was a review, by Brown, of Viller's "Philosophie de

Kant." The article is characterized by acuteness, especially when it points out the inconsistency of Kant in admitting that matter has a reality, and yet denying this of space and time, in behoof of the existence of which we have the very same kind of evidence. But the whole review is a blunder, quite as much as the reviews of Byron and Wordsworth in the same periodical. He has no appreciation of the profundity of Kant's philosophy, and no anticipation of the effects which it was to produce, not only on German but on British thinking. Immersed as he was in medical studies, fond of French literature, and tending towards a French sensationalism, he did not relish a system which aimed at showing how much there is in the mind independent of outward impression. The effects likely to be produced on one who had never read Kant, and who took his views of him from that article, are expressed by Dr. Currie : " I shall trouble myself no more with *transcendentalism ;* I consider it a philosophical hallucination." It is a curious instance of retribution, that, in the succeeding age, Brown's philosophy declined before systems which have borrowed their main principles from the philosophy of Kant, and deal as largely with *à priori* "forms," "categories," and "ideas," as Brown did with "sensations," "suggestions," and "feelings."

We feel less interest than he did himself in two volumes of poetry, which he published shortly after taking his medical degree in 1803. His next publication was a more important one. The chair of mathematics in Edinburgh was vacant, and Leslie was a candidate. The city ministers attached to the court party wished to reserve it for themselves, and urged that Leslie was incapacitated, inasmuch as he had expressed approbation of Hume's doctrine of causation. It was on this occasion that Brown wrote his " Inquiry into the Relation of Cause and Effect," — at first a comparatively small treatise, but swollen, in the third edition (of 1818), into a very ponderous one It is divided into four parts, — the first, on the import of the relation ; the second, on the sources of the illusion with respect to it ; the third, on the circumstances in which the belief arises ; and the fourth, a review of Hume's theory. The work is full of repetitions, and the style, though always clear, is often cumbrous, and wants that vivacity and eloquence which so distinguish his posthumous lectures. It is characterized by great ingenuity and power of analysis. He has dispelled for ever a large amount of confusion which had collected around the relation ; and, in particular, he has shown that there is no link coming *between* the cause and its effect. " The *substances* that exist in a train of phenomena are still, and must always be, the whole constituents of the train." If the cause be A and the effect B, there is not a third thing *x* necessary in order to A being followed by B. He agrees with Hume, in representing the relation as consisting merely in invariable antecedence and consequence. In this he has been guilty of a glaring oversight. It may be all true, that there is nothing coming *between* the cause and its effect, and yet there may be, what he has inexcusably overlooked, a power or property in the substances acting as the cause to produce the effect. He calls in substances, we have seen. " The cause must always be a substance existing in a certain state, and the effect, too, a substance existing in a certain state ; " — he does not see that in material action there are substances two or more in the cause, and substances two or more in the effect. But he fails to enquire what is involved in substances, and the qualities of substance, and does not discover that power is involved in substance and properties. It is but justice to Brown to add, that, in one very important particular, he differs from Hume ; that is, in regard to the mental principle which leads us to believe in the relation. This, according to Hume, is mere custom ; whereas, according to Brown, it is an irresistible intuitive belief. By this doctrine, he attached himself to the school of Reid, and saved his system from a sceptical tendency, with which it cannot be justly charged. This irresistible belief, he shows, constrains us to believe that the universe, as an effect, must have had a cause. It is to be regretted that he did not inquire a little more carefully into the nature of this intuitive belief which he is obliged to call in, when he would have found that it constrains us to believe not only in the invariability of the relation but in the potency of the substances operating as causes to produce their effects.

We are not concerned to follow him in his medical career, in which he became the associate of the famous Dr. Gregory in 1806. We are approaching a more momentous epoch in his life. Dugald Stewart being in a declining state of health,

Brown lectured for him during a part of sessions 1808–9 and 1809–10; and, in the summer of 1810, Stewart having expressed a desire to this effect, Brown was chosen his colleague, and, from that time, discharged the whole duties of the office of Professor of Moral Philosophy.

Even those who have never seen him can form a pretty lively image of him at this time, when his talents have reached all the maturity of which they are capable, and his reputation is at its height. In person, he is about the middle size; his features are regular, and in the expression of his countenance, and especially of his eye, there is a combination of sweetness and calm reflection. His manner and address are somewhat too fastidious, not to say finical and feminine, for a philosopher; but the youths who wait on his lectures are disposed to overlook this, when they fall under the influence of his gentleness, so fitted to win, and of the authority which he has to command. Expectation was on the tiptoe, and he fully met and gratified it. His amiable look, his fine elocution, his acuteness and ingenuity, his skill in reducing a complex subject into a few elements, his show of originality and independence, the seeming comprehensiveness of his system, and, above all, his fertility of illustration, and the glow, like that of stained glass, in which he set forth his refined speculations, did more than delight his youthful audience, — it entranced them; and, in their ecstasies, they declared that he was superior to all the philosophers who had gone before him, and, in particular, that he had completely superseded Reid, and they gave him great credit, in that he generously refrained from attacking and overwhelming Stewart. He had every quality fitted to make him a favorite with students. His eloquence would have been felt to be too elaborate by a younger audience, and regarded as too artificial and sentimental by an older audience, but exactly suited the tastes of youths between sixteen and twenty. A course so eminently popular among students had not, I rather think, been delivered in any previous age in the University of Edinburgh, and has not, in a later age, been surpassed in the fervor excited by Chalmers or Wilson. In the last age you would have met, in Edinburgh and all over Scotland, with ministers and lawyers who fell into raptures when they spoke of his lectures, and assured the younger generation that in comparison with him Wilson

was no philosopher, and Hamilton a stiff pedant. It should
be added, that, when the students attending him were asked
what they had got, not a few could answer only by exclamations
of admiration, " How fine !" " How beautiful !" " How ingenious !" In those large classes in the Scottish colleges which
are taught exclusively by written lectures, large numbers, including the dull, the idly inclined, and the pleasure-loving, are
apt to pass through without receiving much benefit, — unless,
indeed, the professor be a very systematic examiner and laborious exacter of written exercises ; and this, I rather think,
Brown was not. As he left the impression on his students,
that there was little wisdom in the past, and that his own system was perfect, he did not create a spirit of philosophic reading such as Hamilton evoked in select minds in a later age.
But all felt the glow of his spirit, had a fine literary taste awakened by his poetical bursts, had their acuteness sharpened by
his fine analysis, went away with a high idea of the spirituality
of the soul, and retained through life a lively recollection of
his sketches of the operations of the human mind. This, I
venture to affirm, is a more wholesome result than what was
substituted for psychology in the succeeding age, — *à priori*
discussions derived from Germany, or demonstrated idealisms
spun out by an exercise of human ingenuity.

His biographer tells us that, on his appointment to the chair,
he had retired into the country in order that fresh air and exercise might strengthen him for his labors, and that, when the
session opened, he had only the few lectures of the previous
winters ; but such was the fervor of his genius and the readiness of his pen, that he generally commenced the composition
of a lecture after tea and had it ready for delivery next day by
noon, and that nearly the whole of the lectures contained in
the first three of the four-volumed edition were written the first
year of his professorship, and the whole of the remaining next
session. Nor does he appear to have rewritten any portion of
them, or to have been disposed to review his judgments, or
make up what was defective in his philosophic reading. He
seems to have wasted his life in sending forth volume after volume of poetry, which is, doubtless, beautifully and artistically
composed, after the model of the English poets of the eighteenth century, but its pictures are without individuality, and

they fail to call forth hearty feeling.   Far more genuine poetical power comes out incidentally in some of the bursts in
his philosophic lectures than in whole volumes of his elaborate versification.

   The incidents of his remaining life are few, but are sufficient
to bring out the lineaments of his character.   His chief enjoyments lay in his study, in taking a quiet walk in some solitary
place, where he would watch the smoke curling from a cottage
chimney, or the dew illuminated with sunshine on the grass,
and in the society of his family and a few friends.   Never had
a mother a more devoted son, or sisters a more affectionate
brother.   In his disposition there is great gentleness, with a
tendency to sentimentality : — thus, on the occasion of his last
visit to his native place, he is thrown into a flood of sensibility,
which, when it is related in future years to Chalmers, on his
happening to be in the place, the sturdier Scotch divine was
thrown into a fit of merriment.   We perceive that he is fond
of fame and sensitive of blame, but seeking to cherish both as
a secret flame ; and that he is by no means inclined to allow
any one to offer him counsel.   In 1819, he prepared his
" Physiology of the Mind," as a text-book for his students, and
put it into the press the following winter.   By the Christmas
of that year he was rather unwell ; in spring he removed for
the benefit of his health to London, and died at Brompton in
April, 1820.   His remains were deposited in the churchyard
of his native place, beside those of his father and mother.

   His lectures were published shortly after his death, and excited an interest wherever the English language is spoken,
quite equal to that awakened by the living lecturer among the
students of Edinburgh.   They continued for twenty years to
have a popularity in the British dominions and in the United
States greater than any philosophical work ever enjoyed before.
During these years most students were introduced to metaphysics by the perusal of them, and attractive beyond measure
did they find them to be.   The writer of this article would give
much to have revived within him the enthusiasm which he felt
when he first read them.   They had never, however, a great
reputation on the Continent, where the sensational school
thought he had not gone sufficiently far in analysis ; where
those fighting with the sensational school did not feel that he

was capable of yielding them any aid ; and where the transcendental school, in particular, blamed him for not rendering a sufficiently deep account of some of the profoundest ideas which the mind of man can entertain, such as those of space, time, and infinity.   His reputation was at its greatest height from 1830 to 1835, from which date it began to decline, partly because it was seen that his analyses were too ingenious, and his omissions many and great ; and partly because new schools were engaging the philosophic mind ; and, in particular, the school of Coleridge, the school of Cousin, and the school of Hamilton.   Coleridge was superseding him by views derived from Germany, which he had long been inculcating, regarding the distinction between the understanding and the reason ; Cousin, by a brilliant eclectic system, which professedly drew largely from Reid and Kant ; and Hamilton, by a searching review of Brown's theory of perception, and by his own metaphysical views promulgated in his lectures and his published writings.   The result of all this was a recoil of feeling in which Brown was as much undervalued as he had at one time been overrated.   In the midst of these laudations and condemnations, Brown's psychological system has never been completely reviewed.   Now that he has passed through a period of undeserved popularity, and a period of unmerited disparagement, the public should be prepared to listen with candor to an impartial criticism.

The psychology of Brown may be summarily described as a combination of the Scottish philosophy of Reid and Stewart, and of the analyses by Condillac, Destutt de Tracy, and the higher philosophers of the sensational school of France, together with views of the association of ideas derived from a prevailing British school.   To Reid and Stewart he was indebted more than he was willing to allow, and it would have been better for his ultimate reputation had he imbibed more of their spirit, and adhered more closely to their principles. He admits everywhere with them the existence of principles of irresistible belief ; for example, he comes to such a principle when he is discussing the beliefs in our personal identity, and in the invariability of the relation between cause and effect.   But acknowledging, as he does, the existence of intuitive principles, he makes no inquiry into their nature and laws

and force, or the relation in which they stand to the faculties.
In this respect, so far from being an advance on Reid and
Stewart, he is rather a retrogression.   His method is as much
that of Condillac, Destutt de Tracy, and the ideologists of
France, as that of Reid and Stewart.   He is infected with the
besetting sin of metaphysicians, — that of trusting to analyses
instead of patient observation ; and, like the French school,
his analysis is exercised in reducing the phenomena of the
mind to as few powers as possible, and this he succeeds in
doing by omitting some of the most characteristic peculiarities
of the phenomena.   His classification of the faculties bears a
general resemblance to that of M. de Tracy, the metaphysician of the sensational school.   The Frenchman's division of
the faculties is — sensibility, memory, judgment, and desire ;
Brown's is —sensation, simple and relative suggestion, and
emotion.

In estimating the influences exercised from without on
Brown, we must further take into account, that ever since the
days of Hartley there had been a great propensity in Britain to
magnify the power and importance of the association of ideas.
Not only habit but most of our conceptions and beliefs had
been referred to it : Beattie and Alison, followed by Jeffrey,
ascribed to it our ideas of beauty ; and, in a later age, Sir
James Mackintosh carried this tendency the greatest length,
and helped to bring about a reaction, by tracing our very idea
of virtue to this source.   It is evident that Brown felt this influence largely.   Our intelligence is resolved by him into simple and relative suggestion.   There is a flagrant and inexcusable oversight here.   All that association, or, as he designates
it, suggestion, can explain, is the order of the succession of our
mental states ; it can render no account of the character of the
states themselves.   It might show, for example, in what circumstances a notion of any kind arises, say our notion of time,
or space, or extension, but cannot explain the nature of the
notion itself.

But it will be necessary to enter a little more minutely into
the system of Brown.   From the affection which I bear to his
memory, and remembering that his views have never been used
by himself or others to undermine any of the great principles
of morality, I would begin with his excellences.

1. In specifying these, I am inclined to mention, first, his lofty views of man's spiritual being. He everywhere draws the distinction between mind and body very decidedly. In this respect, he is a true follower of the school of Descartes and Reid, and is vastly superior to some who, while blaming Locke and Brown for holding views tending to sensationalism, or even materialism, do yet assure us that the essential distinction between mind and matter is now broken down.

2. I have already referred to the circumstance, that Brown stands up resolutely for intuitive principles, and in this respect is a genuine disciple of the Scottish school. He calls them by the very name which some prefer as most expressive, — " beliefs ; " and employs the test which Leibnitz and Kant have been so lauded as introducing into philosophy. He everywhere characterizes them as "irresistible," — a phrase pointing to the same quality as "necessary," — the term used by the German metaphysicians. No one, not even Cousin, has demonstrated, in a more effective manner, that our belief in cause and effect is not derived from experience. " When we say, then, that B will follow A to-morrow, because A was followed by B to-day, we do not prove that the future will resemble the past, but we take for granted that the future is to resemble the past. We have only to ask ourselves why we believe in this similarity of sequence ; and our very inability of stating any ground of inference may convince us that the belief, which it is impossible for us not to feel [observe the appeal to necessity, but it is an appeal to a necessity of feeling], is the result of some other principle of reasoning." ("Cause and Effect," P. iii.) " In ascribing the belief of efficiency to such a principle, we place it, then, on a foundation as strong as that on which we suppose our belief of an external world, and even of our own identity, to rest. What daring atheist is he, who has ever truly disbelieved the existence of himself and others ? For it is he alone who can say, with corresponding argument, that he is an atheist, because there is no relation of cause and effect." " The just analysis, then, which reduces our expectation of similarity in the future trains of events to intuition, we may safely admit, without any fear of losing a single argument for the existence of God." By this doctrine he has separated himself for ever from sensationalists, and given great trouble to those clas-

sifiers of philosophic systems who insist, contrary to the whole history of British philosophy, that all systems must either be sensational or ideal. It is quite obvious that such men as Butler, Brown, and Chalmers, cannot be included in either of the artificial compartments, and hence one ground of their neglect by the system-builders of our age.

3. His account of sensation is characterized by fine analysis : in particular, his discrimination of the sensations commonly ascribed to touch, and his separation of the muscular sense from the sense of touch proper. About this very time Charles Bell was establishing the distinction of the nerves of sensation and motion. " I was finally enabled," says Sir Charles, "to show that the muscles had two classes of nerves ; that on exciting one of these the muscles contracted, that on exciting the other no action took place. The nerve which had no power to make the muscle contract was found to be a nerve of sensation." Contemporaneously, Brown was arguing, on psychological grounds, that by the muscular sense we get knowledge which cannot be had from mere feeling or touch. " The feeling of resistance is, I conceive, to be ascribed not to our organ of touch but to our muscular frame." Hamilton, by his vast erudition, has been able (note appended to Reid's works) to detect anticipations of these views ; but they were not so clearly stated, and they were not conclusively demonstrated. Brown started, and carried a certain length, those inquiries regarding the variety of sensations commonly ascribed to touch, which have ever since had a place in psychological treatises.

4. Nor must we omit his ingenious and felicitous mode of illustrating the succession of our mental states, called by him "suggestion," to intimate that there is no connection in the nature of things between the ideas, and not "association," which might leave the impression that there was a *nexus* joining them. He is particularly successful in showing how by association the various ideas and, he adds, feelings blend, and, as it were, coalesce. He has called attention to an important phenomenon, which has been little noticed ever since he brought it out to view, and which he himself did not see the significance of. " In our mental sequences, the one feeling which precedes and induces another feeling does not necessarily on that account give place to it ; but may continue in

that virtual sense of combination, as applied to the phenomena of the mind, of which I have often spoken, to coexist with the new feeling which it excites, outlasting it, perhaps, and many other feelings to which, during its permanence, it may have given rise. I pointed out to you how important this circumstance in our mental constitution is to us in various ways: to our intellectual acquirements, since without it there would be no continued meditation, but only a hurrying confusion of image after image, in wilder irregularity than in the wildest of our dreams; and to our virtue and happiness, since, by allowing the coexistence and condensation of various feelings in one complex emotion, it furnishes the chief source of those moral affections which it is at once our happiness to feel and our virtue to obey." He has here got a glimpse of a great truth, which needs to be developed more fully than it has yet been; it is the power of a motive principle, and of a strong purpose and resolution abiding in the mind to sway the train of thoughts and feelings. Had he followed out his own hint, it would have led him to discover deep springs of action directing the flow of suggestions.

While he illustrates the laws of suggestion under the three Aristotelian heads of contiguity, resemblance, and contrast, he intimates his belief that they may all be reduced to a finer kind of contiguity. As the latest speculations have not yet got down to the depths of this subject, it may be useful to know the hints thrown out by Brown, who seems to me to be so far on the right track, but not to have reached the highest fountain from which the stream issues: —

" All suggestion, as I conceive, may, if our analysis be sufficiently minute, be found to depend on prior existence, or at least on such immediate proximity as is itself very probably a modification of coexistence." He begins with resemblance: " if a portrait be faithfully painted, the effect which it produces on the eye that perceives it is the same, or very nearly the same, as the effect produced on the eye by similar light reflected from the living object; and we might therefore almost as justly say, that when any individual is seen by us repeatedly he suggests himself by resemblance, as that he is thus suggested by his portrait." This surely comes very close to Hamilton's principle, that resembling objects, so far as they are alike, are the same, and to his law of repetition or identity. The following brings us quite as near his law of redintegration : " In many other cases, in which the resemblance is less complete, its operation may, even without such refinement of analysis as that to which I have alluded, be very obviously brought under the influence of contiguity. Thus, as the drapery forms

so important a part of the complex perception of the human figure, the
costume of any period may recall to us some distinguished person of that
time. A ruff like that worn by Queen Elizabeth brings before us the sovereign
herself, though the person who wears the ruff may have no other circumstance of resemblance : because the ruff and the general appearance of
Queen Elizabeth, having formed one complex whole in our mind, it is necessary only that one part of the complexity should be recalled — as the
ruff in the case supposed — to bring back all the other parts by the mere
principle of contiguity. The instance of drapery, which is but an adjunct
or accidental circumstance of the person, may be easily extended to other
instances, in which the resemblance is in parts of the real and permanent
figure." " In this manner, by analyzing every complex whole, and tracing,
in the variety of its composition, that particular part in which the actual
similarity consists, — and which may therefore be supposed to introduce the
other parts that have formerly coexisted with it, — we might be able to
reduce every case of suggestion from direct resemblance — to the influence
of mere contiguity." " By the application of a similar refined analysis to
other tribes of associations, even to those of contrast, we may perhaps
find that it would be possible to reduce these also to the same comprehensive influence of mere proximity as the single principle on which all suggestion is founded." I am far from holding that this analysis into parts
of the concrete idea starting the suggestion, furnishes a complete solution
of the difficulties connected with fixing on one ultimate law ; but it seems
to set us on the right track.

He gives us a somewhat crude, but still important, classification of what he calls the secondary laws of suggestion,
which induce one associate conception rather than another.
He mentions longer or shorter continuance ; more or less liveliness ; more or less frequently present ; more or less purity
from the mixture of other feelings ; differences of original
constitution ; differences of temporary emotion ; changes in
the state of the body; and general tendencies produced by
prior habits. Had this arrangement been presented by another
he would have proceeded to reduce it to simpler elements.

5. His distribution of the relations which the mind can
discover is worthy of being looked at : they are —

I. COEXISTENCE.
1. Position.
2. Resemblance or Difference.
3. Degree.
4. Proportion.
5. Comprehension (whole and parts).

II. SUCCESSION.
6. Casual Priority.
7. Causal Priority.

This classification is worthy of being placed along side that of Locke and Hume. It may be compared with Kant's " Categories of the Understanding ;" but it should be observed that the German metaphysician makes his categories forms imposed by the mind on things, whereas the Scotch psychologist simply gives to the mind the power of discerning the relations in things. The arrangement of Brown is superior to that of Hamilton, to be afterwards discussed, and vastly more comprehensive and just than that of those later physiological psychologists who reduce the relations which the mind can perceive to the single one of resemblance and difference, thus restricting the powers of intelligence within far narrower limits than have been assigned by nature, and all to make it somewhat easier to account for the whole on materialistic principles.

6. His biographer declares his account of the general notion to be a great advance on all that had been proposed by previous philosophers. Brown states the process to be the following : " We perceive two or more objects, — this is one state of the mind. We are struck with the feeling of their resemblance in certain respects, — this is a second state of the mind. We then, in the third stage, give a name to these circumstances of felt resemblance, a name which is, of course, applied afterwards only where this relation of similarity is felt." He has here seized some of the characteristic steps in the process of forming the general notion. He is right in giving a prominent place to the discovery of resemblance, but he should have called it a perception of resemblance, and not a *feeling* of resemblance, — language which seems to ascribe the whole to the emotive rather than the cognitive part of our nature. And he has missed, after all, the essential, the consummating step,—the placing of the objects under a head or in a class which embraces all the objects possessing the resembling qualities, to which class thus formed the name is given. He has a searching review of nominalism, which he charges with overlooking the resemblance. He asks, " Why do I class together certain objects, and exclude certain others from the class which I have formed ?" He shows that the infant must reason before it has acquired language. " He has already calculated distances long before he knew the use of a single word expressive of distance. "

7. He has some fine remarks on beauty. He separates from

Alison, who resolves it into the general feelings of our nature, and argues resolutely that there is an original and unresolvable class of feelings excited by the beautiful. He remarks that in the emotion of beauty, "by a sort of reflex transfer to the object which excited it, we identify or combine our agreeable feeling with the very conception of the object, whether present or absent." He is able to come to the conclusion : " It is mind alone that is the living fountain of beauty, because it is the mind which, by reflection from itself, embodies in the object or spreads over it its own delight." He overlooks, however, the objective beauty arising from the harmony of sounds and colors, and from proportion and harmony.

8. Some place higher than any of his other excellencies his eloquent exposition of the emotions,— an exposition which called forth the laudations both of Stewart and Chalmers, the latter of whom wrote a preface to that part of his lectures which treats of the feelings. He is particularly successful in showing that man is not by his nature and constitution a selfish being, but is possessed of social and benevolent affections. His lectures on the emotions are radiant all over with poetry, and will repay a careful reading much better than many of the scholastic discussions or anatomical descriptions which are furnished in some of the chairs of mental science.

9. It would be injustice not to add that he has some very splendid illustrations of natural theism, fitted at once to refine and elevate the soul. I have never heard of any youth being inclined towards scepticism or pantheism, or becoming prejudiced against Christian truth, in consequence of attending or reading the lectures of Brown. In note E, appended to his work on " Cause and Effect," he has a powerful argument in favor of the possibility of a miracle, showing that it is not inconsistent with the intuitive law of cause and effect. " There is no violation of a law of nature, but there is a new consequent of a new antecedent."

Over against these excellencies I have to place certain grave deficiencies and errors.

1. I take exception to the account which he gives of the very object and end of mental science. According to him, it is to analyze the complex into the simple, and discover the laws of the succession of our mental states. There is a great

and obvious oversight here.   The grand business of the science of the human mind is to observe the nature of our mental states, with the view of co-ordinating them and rising to the discovery of the laws which they obey and the faculties from which they proceed.   Taking this view, analysis becomes a subordinate though of course an important instrument ; and we have to seek to discover the faculties which determine the nature of the states as well as the laws of their succession.

2. In his analysis he often misses the main element of the concrete or complex phenomena.   In referring ideas to sensation he neglects to consider how much is involved in body occupying space, and how much in body exercising property; and in the account of memory he fails to discover how much is implied in recognizing the event remembered as having happened in time past, — that is, he omits the idea of time.   Often, too, when he has accomplished an analysis of a complex state, does he forget the elements, and reminds us of the boy who imagines that he has annihilated a piece of paper when he has burnt it, forgetting that the elements are to be found in the smoke and in the ashes.   It is by a most deceitful decomposition — it is by missing the very *differentia* of the phenomena — that he is able to derive all our intellectual ideas from sensation and simple and relative suggestion.

3. He grants that there are intuitive principles of belief in the mind ; but he has never so much as attempted an induction of them, or an exposition of their nature and of the laws which regulate them, or a classification of them.   In this respect he must be regarded as falling behind his predecessors in the school, and behind Hamilton, who succeeded him in the estimation of students of mental science.   The intelligent reader is greatly disappointed to find him, after he has shown so forcibly that there is an intuition involved in our belief in personal identity and in causation, immediately dropping these intuitions and inquiring no more into their nature.   He takes great credit for reducing the faculties and principles enumerated by Reid to a much smaller number ; but if we gather up all the elements which he is obliged to bring in, we shall find the list to be as large as that of Reid or Stewart.

4. Thus he represents consciousness as merely a general term for all the states and affections of mind ; and then, in order to account for our belief in the sameness of self, he is obliged to call in a special instinct. "We believe our identity, as one mind, in our feelings of to-day and our feelings of yesterday, as indubitably as we believe that the fire which burned yesterday would in the same circumstances burn us to-day, — not from reasoning, but from a principle of instinct and irresistible belief, such as gives to reasoning itself all its validity." It is this irresistible belief, involved in the very nature of consciousness, this belief in self and the identity of self, which makes consciousness — I mean self-consciousness (and not a vague consciousness) — a separate faculty. This faculty is a source to us of a separate set of cognitions and ideas, the knowledge of self and of the states of self, — such as thinking, feeling, resolving.

5. According to Brown, in perception through the senses we look immediately on a sensation in the mind, and not on any thing out of the mind. Hamilton has severely criticised this doctrine. Hamilton had a discriminately searching classification of the forms which ideal sense-perception had assumed, and he makes Brown's theory one of the forms of idealism. But the truth is, Brown's doctrine can scarcely be called idealism. It might be appropriately called inferentialism. It is the same substantially as that of Destutt de Tracy and the French ideologists, who, maintaining the existence of body, argued that infants reach a knowledge of it by a process of inference. The argument is unfolded by Brown at great length and with much ingenuity. The mind can never perceive any thing directly but the sensation, but then this sensation as a phenomenon must have a cause. He argues this on the principle, perceived to be intuitively certain, that every effect has a cause. The sensation then must have a cause ; but then it has not, like some other of our mental states and affections, — such as our sentiments and perceptions of duty, — a cause within the mind itself ; it must therefore have a cause without the mind, and this cause is matter. It is clear as to this inference, that it will be acknowledged frankly only by those who look on causation as an intuitive conviction. If belief in causation be merely experimental, it is doubtful whether

we should ever discover the law to be universal, for by far the greater number of our sensations would be phenomena of which we could discover no cause. We might group the phenomena in some way, but we should not be able to say logically whether they have a cause or not. But leaving this, as perhaps only a doubtful point, we can affirm confidently that even if, by such a process, we could infer that these sensations have a cause, it must be an unknown cause, a cause of which we have no experience. But matter seems to be something known. We certainly have an idea of extension, or rather of something extended — I would add, a belief in an extended substance. Our belief is not in an unknown cause, but in a known existence,— known as existing and extended. But we never could reach the belief, we never could reach even the idea of space which we certainly have, by any logical process proceeding on the existence of a sensation. From a sensation, which is unextended, we cannot rise to the idea of an extended thing. Logically and consequentially, Brown's theory of the cognition of matter prepared the way for that of J. S. Mill, who makes our idea of body to be of a mere possibility of sensations.

6. He overlooks some of the distinguishing attributes of the reproductive powers of the mind. Conception, memory, and imagination are merely exercises of simple suggestion. He does not give the phantasy or imaging power a separate place. " Memory is not a distinct intellectual faculty, but is merely conception or suggestion combined with the feeling of a particular relation, — the relation to which we give the name of priority." Observe what confusion of things we have here : memory is a " suggestion," but implies a " relation," which is represented as a " feeling ; " and " priority," implying the idea of time past, present, and future, comes in so quietly that we are not expected to notice it, though it is one of the most profound of our ideas. In imagination, he overlooks that high intellectual power which binds the scattered images in a unity, often of a very grand character. A simplification gained by overlooking these characteristic qualities is altogether illusive.

7. In his account of the faculties of relative suggestion, he mixes up two things which ought to be carefully distinguished, — the suggestion, which is a mere law of the succession

of our ideas, and comparison, by which we discover the relations of things. He cannot make these one by calling them by the one name of relative suggestion.

8. He has discovered an important element in the process of reasoning. He sees that in reasoning there is the explication of what is involved in the conceptions ; but he does not notice the laws of comprehension and extension involved in drawing one conception from another or others.

9. He has a fine exposition of the emotions, dividing them according to the principle of time, — as immediate, retrospective, and prospective ; but he overlooks two essential elements. One is, the idea or phantasm as the basis of the emotion. We cannot have a feeling towards a mother unless we have an idea of her. He is guilty of a greater oversight : he has taken no notice of those springs of action or motive principles, dwelt on by Stewart, — such as the love of self, of our neighbor, of society, of power, — which call forth and guide the emotions in certain channels.

10. He does not distinguish between our emotions on the one hand and the wishes and volitions on the other, — a distinction always drawn in one form or other by our highest moralists, and strongly insisted on by Kant and his school in Germany. Surely there is a difference in kind between such an emotion as that of hope or fear on the one hand and a purpose or determination to act on the other. With Brown, will is merely the prevailing desire, and desire an emotion.

11. His view of the moral faculty is very defective. It is represented by him as a mere class of emotions. He calls them " emotions of approbation and disapprobation." The very epithets employed by him, "approbation" and "disapprobation," might have shown that judgment is involved. Conscience is not only an emotive, it is a cognitive power, revealing to us what ought and ought not to be done. Dr. Chalmers shows that he has overlooked the great truth brought out by Butler, that conscience is a power in the mind, not simply co-ordinate with the others, but authoritative and supreme, claiming subjection from all the voluntary powers. Nor ought it to be omitted that he does not bring out fully that the moral faculty declares man to be a sinner. He thus constructed an ethical system, and delivered it in Edinburgh, — which some-

times claims to be the metropolis of evangelical theology, — without a reference to redemption or grace. No teachers ever inculcated a purer moral system than Reid, Stewart, or Brown ; but they do not seem willing to look at the fact that man falls infinitely beneath the purity of the moral law. They give us lofty views of the moral power in man, but forget to tell that this power condemns him. Taking up the demonstrations of the Scottish metaphysicians in regard to the conscience, an inquiry should be made, — How are they affected by the circumstance that man is a sinner? This was the grand topic started by Chalmers, and by which he effected a reconciliation between the philosophy and the theology of Scotland.

12. He has not been able to give an adequate account of some of the profoundest ideas which the mind of man entertains ; such as, that of personal identity, of power in substances, of infinity and moral good. The tendency of his philosophy was counteracted in the next age by Coleridge, Cousin, and Hamilton, drawing largely from German sources.

XLV. — *FRANCIS JEFFREY.*[1]

Francis Jeffrey was not specially a metaphysician, but he studied metaphysics and wrote upon them, and so deserves a passing notice. He was the son of a depute clerk of the Court of Session, and was born on a " flat " in Charles Street, Edinburgh, October 23, 1773. At the age of eight, he entered (in an intensely excited state) the high school, at that time presided over by Dr. Adam, a scholar and a man of character ; and at fourteen he entered Glasgow College with some idea of getting an Oxford exhibition, and there he was under Jardine, the professor of logic and rhetoric, of whom he says : " It is to him and his most judicious instruction I owe my taste for letters, and any literary distinction I may since have been enabled to attain." A fellow-student, afterwards Principal Macfarlan of Glasgow, reports of him that in the first year " he exhibited nothing remarkable,

---

[1] " Life of Francis Jeffrey," by Lord Cockburn.

except a degree of quickness, bordering, as some thought, on pet-
ulance ;" and another fellow-student, afterwards Principal Haldane of St. Andrews, describes him as a little black creature
whom he had not observed, but was noticed by him as haranguing
some boys on the college green against voting for Adam
Smith as lord rector, and who was opposed by young Jeffrey
because he was the candidate of the professors.   In the second
year he broke upon them very brilliantly as one of the most acute
and fluent speakers, his favorite subjects being criticism and
metaphysics.   While at college he was most diligent in writing,
in a terribly illegible hand, whole volumes of notes of his
professors' lectures, mixed with remarks of his own, and innumerable essays, most of them of a critical character.   Francis
Jeffrey was absolutely destined to be a critic.   Any one might
have seen this in these restless eyes, ever scintillating, and
might have argued it from his quick and clear apprehension,
from his searching spirit and his sound judgment on all subjects
not requiring wide comprehension or original genius.   On leaving Glasgow, he went home to the "dear, retired, adored little
window" of his Lawnmarket garret, and again scribbled papers,
sixty of which remained in the time of his biographer.   Jeffrey
was the genuine product of the lecture-hearing, essay-writing,
debating-society privileges of the Scottish colleges.   In 1791
he went up to Oxford, the instruction in which, as requiring
quiet study and no writing, he did not enjoy so much as that of
Glasgow, and he describes his fellow-students as "pedants, cox-
combs, and strangers."   He eagerly sought when in England
to get rid of his Scotch pronunciation, and succeeded in acquiring a clipped and affected English.   At the end of the
academic year, he went back to Scotland, where he got into the
heart of a body of clever and ambitious youths.   His peculiar talents were specially called forth by the "Speculative
Society," which had been instituted in 1764, and which reached
its highest reputation at the time he attended it ; and there he
had to wrestle with such men as Francis Horner, Henry
Brougham, Lord Lansdowne, and David Boyle, afterwards president of the Court of Session ; and Henry Cockburn tells us how
enraptured he was with speeches by him on national character,
by Horner on the immortality of the soul, and Brougham on the
power of Russia.   I doubt much whether any of them threw

much light on these subjects ; but they discussed them ably, and to the great delight of the aspiring youths of Edinburgh. His business consisted in attending law lectures, and his amusement in writing thousands of lines of poetry, the moon being the special object of his admiration among natural beauties. His ambition then was, " I should like, therefore, to be the rival of Smith and Hume." He joined conscientiously and eagerly the Whig party, which included such men as James Gibson (afterwards Sir James Gibson Craig), the Rev. Sir Henry Wellwood Moncreiff, John Allen, John Thomson in the medical profession, and Dugald Stewart and John Playfair in the college ; and in doing so he knowingly cut himself off from all hope of receiving government patronage.

We now come to the most important event in his life, — the establishment of the " Edinburgh Review," the first number of which appeared in October, 1802. The account is given by Sydney Smith : " One day we happened to meet on the eighth or ninth story or flat [it was actually the third, but the whole party wished to make their descriptions lively and telling] in Buccleuch Place, the elevated residence of the then Mr. Jeffrey. I proposed we should set up a Review : this was acceded to with acclamation. I was appointed editor (not formally), and remained long enough in Edinburgh to edit the first number." The most influential writers were Jeffrey, Smith,[1] Brougham, and Horner ; but the ruling spirit and the guiding hand was Jeffrey, who now found the sphere for which he was fitted by native taste and capacity, and for which he had been prepared by his whole training in reading miscellaneously and writing systematically, and in his legal learning. Horner describes him at this period, " when the genius of that little man was almost unknown to all but his most intimate acquaintances. His manner is not at first pleasing ; but, what is worse, it is of that cast which almost irresistibly impresses upon strangers the idea of levity and superficial talents. Yet there is not any man whose real character is so much the reverse. He has, indeed, a very sportive

[1] I am afraid we cannot claim Sydney Smith (born 1771, died 1845) as one of the Scotch metaphysicians as he was not a Scotchman : he merely resided for a time in Edinburgh. But his "Lectures on Moral Philosophy," delivered in London, 1804–6, and published in a volume (1850), is drawn from the Scottish philosophy, especially from Stewart, and is a remarkably clear, lively, and judicious work.

and playful fancy ; but it is accompanied with an extensive and varied information, and a readiness of apprehension almost intuitive, with judicious and calm discernment, with a profound and penetrating understanding."

The starting of the "Edinburgh Review," with its blue and yellow cover, undoubtedly constituted an era in the history of literature.   There had been magazines and even reviews, such as the earlier " Edinburgh Review," but none of the same comprehensive, independent, and fearless character.   Hitherto literary periodicals had been very much the organs of booksellers ; but these bold youths undertook to make the publisher their mere agent, and required him to pay decently for the articles.   In the first number seven articles were written by Smith, four by Horner, four commonly ascribed to Brougham, and five by Jeffrey.   None of the writers were learned, in the proper sense of the term ; none of them were engaged in profound investigations : but they were all well informed men, and possessed of brilliant talents, if not of genius.   They wrote quickly, easily, clearly, pungently, with quite as much information as their readers wished.   The early writers did little fitted to advance science, or the higher forms of literary genius ; but they cut down pretension of every kind unmercifully, and they were ever in favor of good taste and good sense.   They have left nothing permanent themselves ; but they produced a mighty influence on their own age and through it on the succeeding age.   They failed to discover the rising genius of Byron ; they did not appreciate Wordsworth ; they did not encourage the study of Goethe,[1] and of the great German writers ; they ridi-

---

[1] Thus of Wordsworth's "Excursion" Jeffrey says : "This will never do." "It is longer, weaker, and tamer than any of Mr. Wordsworth's other productions." Of Goethe's " Wilhelm Meister " he says : "To us it certainly appears, after the most deliberate consideration, to be eminently absurd, puerile, incongruous, vulgar, and affected ; and, though redeemed by considerable powers of invention and some traits of vivacity, to be so far from perfection as to be almost from beginning to end one flagrant offence against every principle of taste and every rule of composition."   How different the estimate formed by Thomas Carlyle of the second period of the Edinburgh Review !   The late Lord Ashburton shortly after the decease of his lady, who was a great admirer of Carlyle, did the author of this work the honor of applying to him to explain what Carlyle could mean by an advice which he gave.   "I inquired of him," said his Lordship, "what I could do to form my character, and make myself what I ought to be. 'Read " Wilhelm Meister,"' said he.   So I read ' Wilhelm Meister ' and went back to my counsellor, saying that I had read the book and admired it, but could

culed missionary effort when it appeared in the churches, and proclaimed that heathen nations must be civilized before they can be Christianized, — as if to teach men that they have a soul were not the most potent means of awakening thought and thereby starting civilization. But the "Review" promoted a healthy tone of writing and a liberal spirit in politics, and helped more than any other literary organ to effect a reform in the legislature. From this time forth, Francis Jeffrey became the terror of all authors about to publish, and of all bigoted Tory politicians. While thus an object of dread to strangers, he seems to have been loved by all who knew him. He was editor of the " Review" for twenty-seven years, and wrote two hundred and sixty-one articles. He published a selection from these in 1843.

Though obnoxious to the government of the day, and without political or family patronage, and not a favorite with some of the old writers to the signet who had the means of sending cases to him or keeping them back, he rose steadily at the bar, and in the course of years stood in the first rank. He was well read in law, was particularly fitted to discuss questions of right and equity, was clear and philosophical in his arrangement, ingenious in his arguments, fluent in utterance, tasteful in language, ready at reply, poignant in repartee, and sharp in his strokes of wit. Judges came to appreciate his legal ability, juries liked his point and life, and church courts enjoyed his ingenious defences of bad causes, which he was often called to defend.

We are now arrived at the second great literary epoch of the capital of Scotland. In the first, that of the last half of the previous century, had appeared a number of grave and thinking men, each striking out a path for himself. This second consisted of a brilliant circle of writers, critics, and talkers. They formed a club of which Scott, Jeffrey, Stewart, Playfair, Sydney Smith, Brougham, the " Man of Feeling," Cockburn,

not discover any thing in it fitted to accomplish the end I have in view. 'Read " Wilhelm Meister," ' said the great man, ' a second time.' Now I have read it a second time without getting what I wish. I now come to you to see if you can tell me what Carlyle can mean." I told him he must go to the oracle himself to find out what he meant : but I added that I believed that neither Goethe nor Carlyle, though eminent literary geniuses, knew of, or could direct him to, what might effect the good end his Lordship had in view.

Horner, Alison, and Thomas Brown were members. In this circle, the two most eminent men were Walter Scott, the poet and reputed novelist, and Francis Jeffrey, the critic. " Edinburgh was at that time, to a far greater extent than it is now the resort of the families of the gentry, who used to leave their country residences and enjoy the gayety and the fashion which their presence tended to promote. Many of the curious characters and habits of the preceding age — the last purely Scotch age that Scotland was destined to see—still lingered among us." After this time the ambitious youths of Scotland trooped to London, and left Edinburgh as specially a lawyers' city, relieved by a healthy mixture of university professors, of eminent doctors, and high-class teachers. When Jeffrey's professional income became large, he had as his residence Craigcrook, three miles northwest of Edinburgh, on the eastern slope of the Corstorphine Hill, and he lived there thirty-four seasons. Thither a select but miscellaneous band of visitors resorted on the Saturday afternoons " The Craigcrook party began to assemble about three, each taking to his own enjoyment. The bowling-green was sure to have its matches in which the host joined with skill and keenness ; the garden had its loiterers ; the wall, not forgetting the wall of yellow roses, their worshippers ; the hill its prospect-seekers. The banquet that followed was generous ; the wines never spared, but rather too various ; mirth unrestrained except by propriety ; the talk always good, but never ambitious, and those listening in no disrepute."

As he had promoted the cause of parliamentary reform so steadily and consistently, there was an appropriateness in his being sent to the House of Commons, where he spoke in behalf of the Reform Bill, and, after the Reform Bill passed, in his being the representative of the city of Edinburgh. One of the great speeches in behalf of the bill was by him, and he carried through the Scotch Reform Bill and the Borough Reform measure. Still his career in Parliament was not eminently successful. I remember that, when he was first sent to St. Stephen's, the question was eagerly discussed in Edinburgh, whether their great literary critic was likely to prove a parliamentary statesman and orator, when Chalmers decided, " he wants momentum." He retired from the House of Commons in 1834, and became a judge, his decisions being always wise and weighty. In partic-

ular he defended the ancient rights and the independence of
the church of Scotland in a very able paper, showing that he
had a very clear apprehension of the distinction between the
spiritual and temporal powers.   When between four and five
hundred ministers threw up their livings rather than submit to
have the spiritual privileges of the church and the liberties of
the people trampled on, he exclaimed : " I am proud of my country."   He died January, 1850, giving so far as is known no religious sign either in life or in death.

In his " Contributions to the Edinburgh Review," he has a
number of articles on metaphysical subjects.   He has a long review, afterwards republished in the " Encyclopædia Britannica,"
of Alison on Taste.   He argues against the notion of beauty
being a simple sensation, or the object of a separate and peculiar faculty, and urges the difference of tastes as a proof of this :
an analogous argument might show that there was no faculty to
discern truth or moral good.   He also opposes the idea of
beauty being a real property of objects.   He then expounds his
own theory.   " In our opinion, then, our sense of beauty depends entirely on our previous experience of simpler pleasures
or emotions, and consists in the *suggestion* of agreeable or interesting sensations with which we had formerly been made familiar
by the direct and intelligible agency of our common sensibilities ;
and that vast variety of objects to which we give the name of
beautiful become entitled to that appellation, merely because
they all possess the power of recalling or reflecting those sensations of which they have been the accompaniments, or with which
they have been associated in our imagination by any other
more casual bond of connection."   This theory differs slightly
from that of Alison ; but is not an improvement of it, and is liable
to the same objections.   In one point, he seems to have the
advantage of the author he reviews.   Jeffrey holds the perception of beauty " to be, in most cases, quite instantaneous, and
altogether as immediate as the perception of the external qualities of the object to which it is ascribed."   I believe that Alison is right when he says that there is a flow of imagination ; but
then there must be something to start it, and this something — be
it a color, a form, a sound, a harmony — raises a feeling at once,
and is entitled to be called beautiful.   He maintains that objects are sublime or beautiful when, along with other qualities

they act as "natural signs and perpetual concomitants of pleasurable sensations, or, at any rate, of some lively feeling or emotion in ourselves, or in some other sentient beings." I am inclined to think that beautiful objects act as signs, but they do so by suggesting ideas of the true and the good.

He has a review of Priestley, and in it examines materialism. He shows that "the qualities of matter are perceived, but perception cannot be perceived." "If the eye and the ear, with their delicate structures and fine sensibility, are but vehicles and apparatus, why should the attenuated and unknown tissues of the cerebral nerves be supposed to be any thing else?" "Their proposition is, not that motion produces sensation, — which might be as well in the mind as in the body, — but that sensation *is* motion, and that all the phenomena of thought and perception are intelligently accounted for by saying that they are certain little shakings in the pulpy part of the brain." "There may be little shakings in the brain for any thing we know, and there may even be shakings of a different kind accompanying every act of thought or perception; but that the shakings themselves *are* the thought or perception we are so far from admitting that we find it absolutely impossible to comprehend what is meant by the assertion."

He has a review of Stewart's "Life of Reid" and of Stewart's "Philosophical Essays." He writes in the most laudatory terms of both, and of the Scotch philosophy generally. But he ventures to criticise them, and blames Reid for multiplying without necessity the number of original principles and affections : he sees no reason for admitting a principle of credulity or a principle of veracity in human nature, or for interpreting natural signs. He commends his exemplary diligence and success in subverting the ideal system, but adds: "We must confess that we have not been able to perceive how the destruction of the ideal can be held as a demonstration of the real existence of matter," — as if Reid had ever claimed that it did so, or as if he had not expressly rested our belief on body on the principle of common sense. He labors to show that mental science cannot bring with it any solid issues, and represents "the lofty estimate which Mr. Stewart has made of the *practical* of his favorite study as one of those splendid visions by which men of genius have been so often misled in the enthusiastic pursuit of

science and virtue."   No doubt psychology cannot directly add
to our animal comforts, as chemistry can, but surely when we
know approximately and *provisionally* (which is all we know
in chemistry) the laws of the senses, of memory, of association,
imagination, judgment, reasoning, feeling, and conscience, we
may get *practical* benefits of another kind in being better able
to regulate our own minds and influence the minds of others.
On one point he seems rather to have the advantage of Stewart.   In his review of Stewart's " Life and Writings of Reid,"
he maintains that it is principally by· *experiment*, and not by
mere observation, that those splendid improvements have been
made which have erected so vast a trophy to the prospective
genius of Bacon."   Stewart replied, in his " Philosophical Essays " and "Dissertation," showing that experiment is a species
of observation and that mind can be and has been experimented
on : " Hardly any experiment can be imagined which has not
already been tried by the hand of nature."   But Jeffrey has
a truth which, however, he has not elaborated successfully.
The physical investigator has much more accurate tests than
the mental philosopher in the means which modern science has
provided for weighing and measuring the results ; and this, I
apprehend, is the main reason for the fact that there is less disputing about physical than mental laws.   On the other hand,
we have more immediate, constant, and familiar access to our
thoughts and feelings than we have to any facts of natural philosophy ; and thus our knowledge of mind, scientific and practical, may, without being so much observed by the vulgar, be as
useful as our knowledge of physics, as it may at all times be
restraining and constraining us, though unconsciously, and
enabling us to sway the minds and actions of others.

" I WAS born," he tells us, " at Aldowrie, on the banks of Loch Ness within seven miles of the town of Inverness, in Scotland, on the 26th of October, 1765." His father was a subaltern and younger brother, possessed of a small family property, and his mother was pressed with many anxieties ; but she and the whole female kindred combined to lavish kindness upon the child and possibly fondled him too much. In 1775, he was sent to the school at Fortrose. The boarding mistress was very pious and orthodox, and at times rebuked the usher who was suspected of some heretical opinions. He betook himself early to reading thoughtful works, some of them beyond his years, such as Burnet on the Thirty-Nine Articles, and he formed opinions of his own, and became a warm advocate for free-will.

" About the same time," he says, " I read the old translation (called Dryden's) of Plutarch's ' Lives ' and Echard's ' Roman History.' I well remember that the perusal of the last led me into a ridiculous habit, from which I shall never be totally free. I used to fancy myself emperor of Constantinople. I distributed offices and provinces amongst my school-fellows ; I loaded my favorites with dignity and power, and I often made the objects of my dislike feel the weight of my imperial resentment. I carried on the series of political events in solitude for several hours ; I resumed them, and continued them from day to day for months. Ever since, I have been more prone to building castles in the air than most others. My castle-building has always been of a singular kind. It was not the anticipation of a sanguine disposition, expecting extraordinary success in its pursuits. My disposition is not sanguine, and my visions have generally regarded things as much unconnected with my ordinary pursuits and as little to be expected as the crown of Constantinople at the school of Fortrose. These fancies, indeed, have never amounted to conviction, or, in other words, they have never influenced my actions ; but I must confess that they have often been as steady and of as regular recurrence as conviction itself, and that they have sometimes created a little faint expectation, — a state of mind in which my wonder that they should be realized would not be so great as it rationally ought to be. The indulgence of this dreaming propensity produces good and bad consequences. It produces indolence, improvidence, cheerfulness ; a study is its favorite scene ; and I have no doubt that many a man, surrounded by piles of folios and apparently engaged in the most profound researches, is in reality often employed in distributing the offices and provinces of the empire of Constantinople."

---

[1] "Memoirs of the Life of the Right Honorable Sir James Mackintosh," edited by his son, Robert James Mackintosh.

The instruction he received at school was loose and far from accurate. "Whatever I have done beyond has been since added by my own irregular reading.   But no subsequent circumstance could make up for that invaluable habit of vigorous and methodical industry which the indulgence and irregularity of my school life prevented me from acquiring, and of which I have painfully felt the want in every part of my life." In 1780 he went to college at Aberdeen. "I bought and read three or four books this first winter, which were very much out of the course of boys of fifteen anywhere, but most of all at Aberdeen.   Among them was Priestley's "Institutes of Natural and Revealed Religion," and Beattie's "Essay on Truth," which confirmed my disposition to metaphysical inquiries, and Warburton's "Divine Legation," which delighted me more than any book I had yet read, and which perhaps tainted my mind with a fondness for the twilight of historical hypothesis, but which certainly inspired me with that passion for investigating the history of opinions which has influenced my reading through life. At the college he formed an intimacy with a most engaging and promising youth, Robert Hall, who afterwards became the most brilliant preacher of his age.   "His society and conversation had a great influence on my mind ; our controversies were almost unceasing.   We lived in the same house, and we were both very disputatious.   He led me to the perusal of Jonathan Edwards's book on Free Will, which Dr. Priestley had pointed out before. I am sorry that I never got the other works of that most extraordinary man, who, in a metaphysical age or country, would certainly have been deemed as much the boast of America as his great countryman Franklin." In their joint studies the two youths read much of Xenophon and Herodotus and more of Plato ; and so well was this known — exciting admiration in some, in others envy — that it was not unusual, as they went along, for their class-fellows to point at them and say: "There go Plato and Herodotus."   But the arena in which they met most frequently was that of morals and metaphysics.   "After having sharpened their weapons by reading, they often repaired to the spacious sands upon the sea-shore, and still more frequently to the picturesque scenery on the banks of the Don above the old town, to discuss with eagerness the various subjects to which their attention had been directed.   There was scarcely an important position in Berkeley's "Minute Philosopher," or Butler's "Analogy," or in Edwards on the Will, over which they had not thus debated with the utmost intensity. Night after night, nay month after month, for two seasons, they met only to study or dispute, yet no unkindly feeling ensued." (Gregory's "Memoir of Robert Hall.")

In 1784 he entered on the study of medicine, and was under the famous Dr. Cullen, but attached himself to the fancies of John Brown, author of the Brunonian system, which had its little day. At Edinburgh he became a member of the famous Speculative Society, which did so much to stimulate the intellectual life of young men. He is able to testify of Edinburgh University, "that it is not easy to conceive a university where industry was more general, where reading was more fashionable, and where indolence and ignorance were more disreputable. Every mind was in a state of fermentation. The direction of mental activity will not indeed be universally approved. It certainly was very much, though not exclusively, pointed towards metaphysical inquiries." To the "Royal Physical Society," he read a paper on the instincts and dispositions of animals, and showed that animals had memory, imagination, and reason in different degrees ; declining to enter on the difficult question : " To what circumstance are we to attribute the intellectual superiority of man over other animals ? " He took his medical degree with credit, but it does not appear that he ever had the taste for the patient observation of physiological facts which would have made him eminent in the profession. It is quite clear that, while a hard student, he mingled freely in the excesses for which the Edinburgh lawyers and students were noted at that period. It is proper to add that, when in Edinburgh, he attended the lectures of Dugald Stewart, with whom he carried on an occasional correspondence through life.

He was now seized with the disposition attributed to his countrymen of going south when they have to seek a settlement for life, and he went to London in the spring of 1788. There he meant to follow the medical profession, but he was easily turned aside from it. He became deeply interested in the politics of the time, which took their direction from the revolt of the American colonies, and from the fermentation preceding the revolutionary outburst in France. He listened eagerly to the orations of Burke and Sheridan; and became a speaker himself in one of the numerous political societies of the period. He was led by his social dispositions to mingle in the society that was open to him. "His company was sought after, and few were the occupations which induced him willingly to decline a pleasant invitation." Feeling a difficulty in sustaining himself, he sold his little highland estate, and bravely entered into the state of matrimony. He now betook himself to the study of the law, and, had he kept to it steadily, would undoubtedly have risen to great eminence in certain departments of it requiring thought and lofty eloquence. But an opportunity now presented itself to call forth his special gifts, and enable him at once to rise to distinction.

About this time there was a wide difference of opinion in England in regard to the tendency and influence of the French Revolution. Young minds of a liberal tendency were strongly impressed with the need of political reformation in France. But, as the revolution advanced, not a few who at first favored it became alarmed at the infidelity and the cruel excesses. Burke, in particular, denounced the whole movement in language of extraordinary power and eloquence in his "Reflections." But multitudes were not disposed to abandon the hope which they cherished. Many were the replies to Burke, but they were all feeble compared with that now issued, in April, 1791, — the "Vindiciæ Gallicæ," by Mackintosh. The work has not the magnificent glow of Burke; but it is philosophical and eloquent, and had a rapid and wide circulation. At a later date, when some Frenchmen at Paris complimented him on the "Vindiciæ Gallicæ," he replied: " Messieurs, vous m'avez si bien réfuté."

In 1795 he was called to the bar, and gradually acquired a considerable practice. But his native tendency was still toward speculation, and in 1799 he delivered a course of thirty-nine "Lectures on the Law of Nature and Nations." This work does not exhaust the grand topic of which it treats; but it was a most important contribution to the science of natural and international law, and furnished ample evidence of the eminently philosophical mind of the author. " The foundation of moral government and its tests he examined at great length and with much acuteness; he entered into a question which, many years after, received from him almost as much elucidation as can be

hoped, — the relation of conscience and utility as the guides
of moral conduct ; he showed the vanity of every system that
would sacrifice the particular affections to general benevolence ;
the origin and use of rules and of habits to the moral being." Parr
wrote him a characteristic letter : " You dog, nobody can do it
better ; nobody I say, — not Hume, not Adam Smith, not Burke,
not Dugald Stewart ; and the only exception I can think of is
Lord Bacon. Yet, you dog, I hate you, for you want decision.
O Jimmy ! feel your own powers, assert your dignity, out upon
vanity and cherish pride." In writing to Dugald Stewart about the
state of philosophical opinion at this time (1802), he says : " One
might give a just account of the state of learning at Paris, by
saying that the mathematical and physical sciences were very
actively and successfully cultivated, polite literature neglected,
erudition extinct, and that moral and political speculation were
discountenanced by the government and had ceased to interest
the public." " Germany is metaphysically mad. France has
made some poor efforts which have ended in little more than
the substitution of the word ideology for metaphysics."

His next great effort was his defence of M. Peltier, an
emigrant royalist, for a libel on Napoleon Bonaparte, at that
time first consul of France. His oration is regarded by some
as one of the most eminent displays of forensic eloquence which
modern times have produced. But he has now to consider two
very important points, — one is how he is to execute what he intends to make his life-work, and the other is how is he to get a living
suited to his tastes and habits. He has all along been cherishing
ambitious literary projects, not always very clearly defined,
but pointing towards a great work on moral philosophy and a
history of England or certain eras of it. But these schemes
could not very well be carried into execution by one who had to
toil at the bar. And then he was fond of society, and had not
sufficient moral restraint to curb expenditure. In these circumstances he was led to accept (1804) the office of Recorder of
Bombay, which was handsomely offered by the tory government, and he became Sir James Mackintosh. He thought he
would now be able to undertake and complete, as he expressed
it, " my intended work on morals and politics, which I consider
as the final cause of my existence." But his hopes were not
realized. He had not sufficient decision to contend with the re-

laxing influence of the climate. " Our climate may be endured :
but I feel that, by its constant though silent operation, existence is rendered less joyous and even less comfortable.   I see
around me no extraordinary prevalence of disease, but I see no
vigorous cheerful health." He longed for letters from England
and wrote letters to his friends which are full of thought.
" Philosophy is my trade, though I have hitherto been but a
poor workman, I observe you touch me with the spur once or
twice about my book on morals ; I felt it gall me, for I have not
begun ; and I shall not make any promises to you till I can say
that it is well begun : but I tell you what has either really or
apparently to myself retarded me ; it was the restless desire of
thoroughly mastering the *accursed* German philosophy." " It is
vain to despise them.   Their opinions will, on account of their
number and novelty, occupy more pages in the history of philosophy than those of us humble disciples of Locke and Hartley.
Besides, their abilities are not really contemptible.   It seems to
me that I am bound not only to combat these new adversaries,
but to explain the principle and ground of their hostility, which
is in itself a most curious confutation in detail."

He discharges the duties of his office, and instituted the Literary Society at Bombay and had a plan for forming a comparative vocabulary of Indian languages, read a great number and
variety of books, and often writes critiques upon them, some
of them distinguished by great ability and worthy of being preserved in a more permanent form than in the memoir written by
his son. In philosophy, he reads Reinhold, Tiedemann, and says :
" I shall begin with Descartes' ' Meditations ' and ' Objections,'
Spinoza, Hobbes on ' Human Nature,' Berkeley's ' Principles'
and ' Dialogues,' Hume on ' Human Nature,' then Kant."
" The German philosophy, under its present leader Schelling, has
reached a degree of darkness in comparison of which Kant
was noonday.   Kant, indeed, perplexed all Europe ; but he is
now disdainfully rejected by his countrymen as a superficial
and popular writer " ! While engaged in this reading, he says :
" My nature would have been better consulted, if I had been
placed in a quieter situation, where speculation might have been
my business, and visions of the fair and good my chief recre-
ation." I venture to affirm that, if he had been placed in
such a position, he would not have remained in it a month. He

remembers the feelings and projects of his youth, when "my most ardent ambition was to have been a professor of moral philosophy." He writes to Dugald Stewart: "I am now employed in attempting to throw into order some speculations, on the origin of our notions of space and time, of poor Tom Wedgwood." "I am very desirous of seeing what you say on the theory of ethics. I am now employed on what the Germans have said on that subject. They agree with you in rejecting the doctrine of personal or public interest, and in considering the moral principle as an ultimate law. I own to you that I am not a whit more being a Kantian than I was before; yet I think much more highly of Kant's philosophical genius than I did when I less comprehended his writings." He reads one hundred pages of Fichte's Lectures on "The Characteristic Features of the present Age," "a very ingenious book with most striking parts." "Finished Fichte, — a book, certainly, of extraordinary merit, but so mysterious and dogmatical as to be often unintelligible and often offensive. Read one hundred pages of Kieswetter's 'Introduction to the Kantian Philosophy.' It is the first clear book on this subject which I have seen." I have given so many extracts from his journal and letters, because they exhibit so vividly the process through which in that age many a young mind had to pass, in trying to cross from the British to the German philosophy.

Thus did he pass eight years of his life. He returned to England in 1812; and, as his opinions had undergone considerable modification since he wrote against Burke, he had flattering political offers from Perceval and Canning. But he conscientiously stuck by his whig friends and whig principles. He was soon in the whirl of London society, the charms of which he could not resist. He and Madame de Staël became for a season the most brilliant conversers in the literary and political circles. "She treats me as the person whom she most delights to honor: I am generally ordered with her to dinner, as one orders beans and bacon; I have in consequence dined with her at the houses of nearly all the cabinet ministers." Through the influence of his whig friends, he became M. P. for the County of Nairn, and in the House of Commons promoted every liberal measure, and, from time to time, made speeches of a very high order, — in thought, expression, in tone, far above the

ordinary level of statesmen. He also wrote miscellaneous articles in the "Edinburgh Review." But what of his cherished
work? He had not formally abandoned it. But he had not the
courage to resist the pleasures of society, and the excitement
of politics, and devote himself to what he knew to be his
proper sphere.

Two opportunities presented themselves for returning to his
favorite philosophic pursuits. In 1818 he was appointed professor of law and general politics in the college instituted for
the education of the civil servants of the East India Company
at Haileybury. There he treated of moral science, dividing it
into ethics and jurisprudence ; and of law, civil, criminal, and
constitutional. He did not commit his lectures to writing, and
nothing is preserved of them but the barest outline. Another
opportunity, and the last, presented itself. On the death of
Thomas Brown in May, 1820, he was offered the chair of moral
philosophy, in the university of Edinburgh. It was the very
place for him. He would have been one of the three mighty
men in the capital of Scotland, the others being Walter
Scott and Francis Jeffrey. He would have been constrained
to complete his philosophical reading, and thoroughly work
out his system, and might have left works worthy of being
ranked with those of Reid, Stewart, and Hamilton, though not
equal to the first and last of these in originality. But he is
sucked back into the amenities of London society and the agi-
tations of politics.

He was the favorite of every society he entered, by his good-
nature, his urbanity, his extensive knowledge, his keen sense
of the ludicrous, his pleasant humor, his good-natured wit,
and his profound wisdom. As a parliamentary orator, he was
thoughtful, always thoughtful ; and thoughtful hearers were
pleased to notice that he was evidently thinking as he spoke.
His speeches had also the charm of elegant diction and brilliant illustration. But for popular effect they were too candid,
and wanted coarseness, invective, satire, and passion. His
whig friends never made him a member of the cabinet, and
Sir James Scarlet commented : " There is a certain degree of
merit which is more convenient for reward than the highest."
The students of Glasgow University paid him an appropriate
honor when they elected him lord rector. At length he set

himself vigorously to write a history of England. The work
is calm, candid, full of fine generalizations and analyses of character ; but wants liveliness of narrative, and a searching detec-
tion of motives, especially bad motives, — he was too charitable,
or, rather, too genial, to believe in human wickedness. His
greatest work might have been a " History of the Revolution
in England," as he had such a sympathy with the wisdom and
moderation of the event ; but he left the book unfinished. He
was persuaded with some difficulty to write a " Dissertation of
the Progress of Ethical Philosophy," for a new edition of the
" Encyclopædia Britannica." He took an active part in promoting Catholic emancipation and the Reform Bill. He was now
evidently hastening to fulfil the grand work which he had allotted to himself. But he was seized with illness ere he completed it. He had not identified himself much with the religion
of Jesus in his life, but he turned to it at his dying hours. His
son reports : " He would speak of God with more reverence
and awe than I have almost ever met with." " Our Lord
Jesus was very frequently the subject of his thoughts ; he
seemed often perplexed and unable to comprehend much of
his history. He once said to me : ' It is a great mystery to me,
— I cannot understand it.' " " His difficulty lay in the account
given of the manner in which he became the Saviour of men."
" I said to him at one time : ' Jesus Christ loves you ;' he answered slowly and pausing between each word : ' Jesus Christ
— love — the same thing.' After a long silence, he said : ' I
believe — ' We said, in a voice of inquiry : ' In God ?' He
answered : ' In Jesus.' He spoke but once more after this."

We have very imperfect means of knowing what his philosophy would have been had he fully formed it. We can judge of
it only by the skeleton of his lectures at Haileybury, preserved
in the Memoir, and by his historical and critical dissertation in
the Encyclopædia. He has a clear idea of the end to be served
by ethical science : " Not what *is*, but what *ought to be.* Here
a new world opens on the mind : the word, the idea, *ought* has
no resemblance to any object of natural science ; no more than
colors to sound, not so much. Both are phenomena. The
question by what rules the voluntary actions of men ought to
be governed. This important word *ought*, which represents no
fact, is yet intelligible to all mankind ; a correspondent term in

every language, — the terms 'right,' 'wrong,' 'moral,' 'immoral,' 'duty,' 'crime,' 'virtue,' 'vice,' 'merit,' 'demerit,' distinguished and contrasted." He has evidently kept three ends before him in his "Dissertation:" The progress of the science, especially during the two previous centuries ; a critical examination of the more eminent ethical writers ; and an exposition of his own views. These three ends are not kept separate, but run through the whole work. We may first take a cursory view of the historical exposition, and then critically examine his own theory.

He has a retrospect of ancient ethics. His sketches are not equal to those of Adam Smith in his "Theory of Moral Sentiments," but are worthy of being placed near them. They are not very erudite or very profound, but they are by no means superficial. He can sketch admirably the practical tendency of a philosophic system such as that of the Stoics. He has then a retrospect of scholastic ethics. It could scarcely be expected of a whig that he should have much reverence for mediæval times ; but, in his treatment of the schoolmen, he is appreciative in the highest degree of their excellencies. It is evident that he has not that thorough acquaintance with their discussions and individual opinions which later research on the part of historians of philosophy and of the church might have enabled him to attain. He enters on a more congenial theme when he comes to modern times.

He begins with Grotius and Hobbes, of both of whom he has a high admiration, but remarks of Hobbes' system, that "a theory of man which comprehends in its explanations neither the social affections nor the moral sentiments must be owned to be sufficiently defective." He then enters on the controversies concerning the moral faculties and social affections, and gives a critical exposition of Cumberland, Cudworth, Clarke, Shaftesbury, Bossuet, Fenelon, Leibnitz, Malebranche, Edwards, and Buffier. He has formed a higher estimate of the merits of Edwards than most Europeans, whether British or German. He had studied the "Treatise on the Will" when a student in Aberdeen, and he favors the view taken by Edwards that virtue consists in love to being as being, according as being has claims on it. But whence the claims of being ? An answer to this question must bring us, whether we wish or no, to an ethical principle guiding the direction and flow of the affection. The discussion by Edwards is certainly a very profound one, and he brings out deep truths of which Mackintosh did not discover the importance.

He goes on to men who are represented as laying the foundations of a more just theory of ethics ; that is, as approaching nearer the theory of Mackintosh. He gives just and valuable accounts of the systems of Butler, Hutcheson, Berkeley, Hume, Smith, Price, Hartley, Tucker, Paley, Bentham, Stewart, and Brown. He perhaps, exaggerates the originality of Butler, who was much indebted to Shaftesbury, but passed far beyond him in maintaining the supremacy of conscience. "In these sermons he has taught truths more capable of being exactly distinguished from the doctrines of his predecessors, more satisfactorily established by him, more comprehensively applied to particulars, more rationally connected with each other, and, therefore, more worthy of the name of discovery, than any with which we are acquainted ; if we ought not, with some hesitation, to accept the first steps of Grecian philosophy towards a theory of morals." Mackintosh does not seem to be aware that, lofty as was Berkeley's idealism in its moral tone, his ethical system is based on pleasure as the ultimate good. " Sensual pleasure is the *summum bonum*. This is the great principle of morality. This once rightly understood, all the doctrines, even the severest of the gospels, may clearly be demonstrated. Sensual pleasures, *quâ* pleasure, is good and desirable by a wise man. But if it be contemptible, 'tis not *quâ* pleasure, but *quâ* pain, or (which is the same thing) of loss of greater pleasure." (" Berkeley's Works, by Fraser, vol. iv. 457). He has a great admiration of Hartley, but points out his defects. "The work of Dr. Hartley entitled 'Observations on Man' is distinguished by an uncommon union of originality with modesty in unfolding a simple and fruitful principle of human nature. It is disfigured by the absurd affectation of mathematical forms then prevalent ; and it is encumbered by a mass of physiological speculations, groundless, or at best uncertain." He was particularly struck with the shrewdness and graphic though homely illustrations of Tucker, who was always a great favorite with him. He criticises Bentham at considerable length. He blames him, in particular, for maintaining that, " because the principle of utility forms a necessary part of every moral theory, it ought therefore to be the chief motive of human conduct." But he has not seized on the fundamental defect in Bentham's theory, for he himself has so far given in to it by reckoning tendency to produce happiness as the constituent of virtue. As setting so high a value on the social affections, he was specially offended with Mr. James Mill, who " derives the whole theory of government from the single fact that every man pursues his interest when he knows it."

Altogether, these sketches have not the calm wisdom nor some of the other admirable qualities of those drawn by Dugald Stewart, who had evidently devoted his life to the study, and contemplated the subject on all sides. But they are often searching, generally just, and always candid, sympathetic, and comprehensive.

He criticises the ethical writers, as we might expect, by a standard of his own, which is ever cropping out, and at the close of his dissertation he expounds his own theory. He insists, very properly, on a distinction being drawn between the inquiry into right and wrong, and into the mental power which discerns them. In answer to the first, he maintains that virtue consists in beneficial tendency, and to the second that it consists of a class of feelings gendered by association. In both these points, he goes a step in the descending progress beyond Brown, who makes moral good a simple unresolvable quality, and the feeling of moral approbation an original one. I propose to consider both these points in the reverse order to that which he follows.

(1). He lays down the principle that morality is not affected by the way in which we explain the rise of the moral emotion, whether we trace it to moral reason, to an original feeling, or to association. I am not prepared to give in to this. If it is to be ascribed with Brown to mere feeling, it will always be competent to argue that the distinction between good and evil depends on human temperament, and does not imply an original, a necessary, and eternal distinction between good and evil. If it is regarded with Mackintosh, as a mere feeling gendered by association, then it is simply the product of circumstances, and may shift with circumstances. It is vain on this theory to appeal, as Mackintosh would wish to do, to conscience as having authority, and supreme authority ; it has merely the authority of association, and cannot claim the authority of God, or even of our essential constitution.   I rather think that Mackintosh would have shrunk from his doctrine, had he foreseen how physiologists, by means of heredity and undesigned natural selection, manufacture moral feeling out of animal sensations. The authority of conscience depends on the source from which it is derived.

According to Brown, conscience is a mere class of feelings, and Mackintosh follows him.   But Mackintosh makes the feelings to be gendered by association.   In order to support this theory, he is obliged to give to association a larger power than was given to it even by Brown.   He corrects " the erroneous but prevalent notion, that the law of association produces only such a close union of thought as gives one the power of reviving the other ; " and insists that " it forms them into a new compound, in which the properties of the component parts are no longer discoverable, and which may itself become a substantive principle of human nature.   They supposed the condition, produced by its power, to resemble that of material substances in a state of mechanical diffusion ; whereas, in reality, it may be better likened to a chemical combination of the same substances from which a totally new product arises " (Sect. VII).   But what does he mean by association ?   I suppose merely the succession of ideas.   The laws of the association of ideas are merely the laws of their succession.   It is quite a straining of the word to give association the power of creating a new idea.   We place oxygen and hydrogen in a certain relation to each other, and water is the product ; and the water possesses properties not discernible in the elements separately.   But chemists do not ascribe this to the mere *association* of the two : they derive it from the properties of the oxygen and the hydrogen.   In like manner when a new idea springs up, we are not to attribute it to the association of feelings, but to a property of the feelings, — a property proceeding from a power actual or potential.   We have thus to go back to a power deeper and more fundamental, and to get a source of ideas, not in mere association, but in the *intellectus ipse* of Leibnitz, or in the feelings themselves ; and this is the moral power.

(2). If we thus prove that there is an original moral faculty of the nature of moral perception, discerning between good and evil, we are in a position to settle the further question : Whether virtue can be resolved into benevolence ? Mackintosh stands up for the existence and authority of conscience as a class of feelings. He holds that our business is to follow conscience, even when we do not see the consequences of the acts we perform. But what is the common quality in the acts which conscience approves of ? He maintains that, in the last resort, it is beneficial tendency which distinguishes virtuous acts, and dispositions from those which we call vicious. He allows that the virtuous man may not see the beneficial consequences of the acts he performs, that the man who speaks truth may never think that to speak truth leads to happiness : he does it simply because it is right. Still, if we inquire into it, it will be found that beneficial tendency is the essential quality in virtuous acts. I dispute this statement, appealing to conscience as the arbiter. For conscience affirms that justice, that veracity, that candor, are good, quite as much so as benevolence itself, and it is difficult, I believe impossible, to resolve justice and the virtues embraced under it, such as veracity and the love of truth, into benevolence.

Altogether Sir James Mackintosh never fulfilled the expectations that were formed by Robert Hall and his other friends. He went from medicine to law, and from law to politics ; and with first-rate intellectual powers, failed to reach the highest positions in any one of these departments. He was without firmness of purpose to resist temptation and concentrate his energies on what he acknowledged to be his life-work, and so was at the mercy of circumstances, and attained the highest eminence only as a *talker* in the best social circles of London, where he had a perpetual stimulus to excel. If he had only had the courage to devote himself to what he knew to be his forte, but which could not bring him immediate fame ; had he read systematically, instead of discursively, and made himself as well acquainted with the higher forms of the Greek and German philosophy, as he did with the later forms and of British philosophy,— he might have ranked with the highest thinkers of his age. As it is he has left us little that will endure beyond these able and candid sketches of ethical writers.

XLVII. — *HENRY (LORD) BROUGHAM.*[1]

LORD BROUGHAM was born in Scotland, was the son of a Scotch mother, was trained in the Scotch metaphysics, and employed them with advantage in his work on natural theology, and was swayed by them, often unconsciously, in his addresses at scientific associations, in his speeches, his sketches of statesmen and philosophers, and in his legal opinions and decisions which, when they relate to moral themes, are evidently founded on sound ethical principles, caught from Stewart and the Scottish professors. We are therefore entitled to claim him as belonging to the fraternity.

He was born in Edinburgh, September, 1779. His father was Henry Brougham, of Brougham Hall, Westmoreland, who came to Edinburgh after the death of his first wife, and there married Eleanor Lyme, a niece of Principal Robertson, the historian. He was educated at the high school of Edinburgh, where he early showed his great capacity and his power of application. At the university he devoted himself closely and systematically to higher learning, and at times took excessive fits of study. If tradition speaks true, he had also fits of drinking, from the visible effects of which he was kept by his strong mind and bodily constitution. He attended Dugald Stewart's lectures; and we see traces of a happy influence produced on his restless temper by the calm, moral wisdom of that true philosopher and great teacher. But he was specially addicted to physical and mathematical studies, and profited greatly by the instructions of Playfair, Black, and Robison. "Great as was the pleasure and solid advantage of studying under such men as Playfair and Stewart, the gratification of attending one of Black's last courses exceeded all I ever enjoyed." At a very early age, from sixteen to twenty, he had papers on optics and porisms inserted in the " Philosophical Transactions " of Edinburgh. He acquired at this time an immense body of information which he turned to profitable use as a pleader and a statesman, and which greatly increased his usefulness. No doubt his admirers ascribed to him, and he probably ascribed to himself, a larger amount of learning than he really possessed : still he had attained and mastered a vast amount of real knowledge. He continued all his life an ardent and laborious student ; and he had laid, in his college days, a solid foundation on which to build his acquirements.

He became, as we might expect, a stirring member of the Speculative Society, which at that time embraced, among its younger members, Jeffrey, Horner, Murray, Moncreiff, Miller, Loch, Adam, Cockburn, Jardine, Charles (afterwards Lord) Kinnaird, Lord Webb Seymour, and at a somewhat later date the two Grants, Glenelg and his brother Sir Robert. "After the day's work we would adjourn to the Apollo Club, where the orgies were more of the 'high jinks' than of the calm or philosophical debating order, or to Johnny Dow's, celebrated for oysters. Sometimes, if not generally, these nocturnal meetings had endings that in no small de-

---

[1] The Life and Times of Henry Lord Brougham, written by himself.

gree disturbed the tranquillity of the good town of Edinburgh." He became a member of the Society of Advocates in 1800, and in 1808 he was called to the bar at Lincoln's Inn, London. The profession was at first distasteful to him in the highest degree, but he soon got reconciled to it when it brought him into scenes of excitement, as when he became counsellor to the Princess Caroline, and earned such fame by his defence of her.

There would be no propriety in our entering into the details of his London life, where he espoused the liberal side in politics, became member of parliament, and compelled all men to acknowledge at once that he was a debater of extraordinary power. His eloquence was of a very marked kind, — full, elaborate, yet pointed and telling. His sentences were complex, often taking in a mighty sweep of arguments and facts ; and people wondered how he was ever to get out of the labyrinth in which he had involved himself, but in the end he always came out perspicuous. His clear arrangement of a difficult subject, the fulness of his information, gained the judgment, while his massive language made the whole argument come down with the power of a sledge-hammer. His speeches did resemble thunder quite as much as those of any modern orator ; and if Demosthenes " fulmined " over Greece, Brougham " fulmined " over Westminster Hall and St. Stephen's, and popular meetings all over England. His sarcasm was very biting and his invective terrific, and the effect was increased by a nervous curl of the lip, resembling the snarl of a dog. He had every quality of a great orator except tenderness and pathos.

He was a powerful (the most powerful in his day) advocate of every measure of reform, political and social. He uttered the most withering denunciations of slavery ; he advocated law reform, and parliamentary reform, and took a deep interest in education and in all social questions, — becoming president of the Social Science Congress. But perhaps his greatest work was the formation of the Society for the Diffusion of Useful Knowledge, which did so much to extend a knowledge of literature and science and promote reading among the people.

His vast powers, however, were greatly marred by certain weaknesses. He was impelled by a fiery intellect to constant labor, and was often busy when he might have carried his point more effectively by retiring. He was intensely fond of popular applause, — partly through his sympathy with mankind, and often sought fame in quarters where he got only infamy. All this wrought in him a restlessness and an inequality of temper ; and his party, even his friends, complained that they could not trust him. When the Whigs carried the Reform Bill he was made Lord Chancellor, — unfortunately for himself, for he had not all the qualities necessary to make a dignified and a wise supreme judge in a great country with such complicated interests. His predecessor, Lord Eldon, had hesitated and delayed in his judgments, so that there was an immense accumulation of undecided cases ; and Brougham cleared them all off in an amazingly brief time. Many of his decisions were reckoned rash by the wisest lawyers ; but his opinions in all cases involving equity — in which he had been instructed by his ethical training in Edinburgh — will ever be reckoned of great value. As he had excessive self-will and little prudence, his colleagues were in a constant state of alarm as to what he might do next. They felt that he was dragging the Great Seal through the dirt in a tour which he took through Scotland, receiving congratulations from quarters which did not add to his dignity.[1] At one of his meetings he boasted that he would write that evening to his sovereign, King William, telling him how great was the honor which had been conferred on him. His colleagues took advantage of the occasion to ,part with him, and henceforth he held a somewhat ambiguous position in political life ; cast off by the liberals and not willing to join the tories, notwithstanding his excessive admiration of the Duke of Wellington and Lord Lyndhurst. Still he led a useful life, helping on every educational cause, such as Mechanics' Institutes and the London University.

He was elected, as so many eminent men have been, lord rector of Glasgow University, and delivered, in 1825, a very able and elaborate defence of learning ; but declared that man is no more responsible for his belief than for the color of his skin. He may have imagined that the supporters of Calvinism would not frown on such a doctrine ; but he was immediately met by Chalmers, Wardlaw, and a host of others, who could not stand such a perversion of the doctrine of necessity, and who showed that the will had much to do with the formation of opinions, for which man, therefore, was responsible, if not to his neighbors, at least to God.

Prompted by a boundless ambition and activity of mind, he threw himself into an infinite number and variety of works, in no one of which, except oratory, did he reach the highest eminence. He continued to cultivate science, physical and mathematical, but had not leisure nor patience to widen the boundaries of any one department. He wrote innumerable articles and papers, especially sketches of statesmen and philosophers. These are always able, candid, kindly, but are deficient in delicate appreciation of character and motive. In his later years he employed a portion of his time in writing an autobiography.

He had been all along an able defender of the great truths of natural religion. He had spoken with reverence of the scriptures, and delighted to show that the theology of nature had sustained revelation. But it was only in his later days that he seemed thoroughly to bow down before God. It is believed that he was much affected by a change which had taken place in the character of Lord Lyndhurst, whose clear and sharp intellect he so much admired. Certain it is that in old age he gave forth utterances which show that he was thoroughly penetrated with the importance of divine realities. He spent a good deal of his later life at Cannes, and died there May 9, 1868.

I believe that there is a philosophy underlying most of the criticisms,

---

[1] He was to be received at Brechin in the parish church. He separated from those who were to conduct him, and came to the door in tartan trews, and was refused entrance by an old sergeant who had charge of the admission. "Do not you know," thundered his lordship, "that an order of mine could hang you on that lamp-post?" To which the sergeant replied that he knew nothing as to what the person addressing him could do, but he knew that it was his duty not to allow any one to enter at that door without an express order.

and even the orations, of Brougham. His metaphysical principles especially appear in his " Discourse on Natural Theology," prefixed to his
edition of Paley, a work executed when he held the Great Seal of England.
This discourse professes to be logical, but does not throw much light on
the method of inquiry, or on the nexus of the parts of the theistic argument. He professes to proceed throughout on the method of Bacon,
of whom he entertained, as all the Scottish metaphysicians did, a high
admiration. He maintains that natural theology "is strictly a branch of
inductive theology, formed and supported by the same kind of reasoning
upon which the physical and psychological sciences are founded." He
argues that "the two inquiries, that into the nature and constitution of the
universe and that into the evidence of design which it displays, are to a
large extent identical." Turning to psychology, he expresses his wonder
that writers in modern times have confined themselves to the proofs afforded
by the visible and sensible works of nature, while the evidence furnished
by the mind and its operations has been neglected. "The structure of
the mind, in every way in which we can regard it, affords evidence of the
most skilful contrivance. All that adapts it so admirably to the operations
which it performs, all its faculties, are plainly means working to an end."
He refers in proof to the processes involved in reasoning, association, habit,
memory, and to the feelings and affections so adapted to their end. In
speaking of habit, he gives a powerful description of what no doubt was
his own experience as a speaker. "A practised orator will declaim in
measured and in various periods ; will weave his discourse into one texture ;
form parentheses within parentheses ; excite the passions or move to laughter ; take a turn in his discourse from an accidental interruption, making it
the topic of his rhetoric for five minutes to come, and pursuing in like manner the new illustrations to which it gives rise ; mould his diction with a
view to attain or to shun an epigrammatic point, or an illiteration, or a
discord ; and all this with so much assured reliance on his own powers, and
with such perfect ease to himself, that he will even plan the next sentence
while he is pronouncing off-hand the one he is engaged with, adapting each
to the other, and shall look forward to the topic which is to follow, and fit
in the close of the one he is handling to be its introducer ; nor will any
auditor be able to discover the least difference between all this and the portion of his speech he has got by heart or mark the transition from the one
to the other." I do believe that there is proof of design in the structure of
a mind that is capable of bringing forth such products ; but to ascribe all
this to habit while there are a great many other principles involved, argues
a defective power of mental analysis on the part of our author. He thinks
to the ordinary argument an addition of great importance remains to be
made. "The whole reasoning proceeds necessarily upon the assumption
that there exists a being or thing separate from and independent of matter
and conscious of its own existence, which we call mind." So he sets himself against materialism.

He sets no great value on the argument *a priori*, and examines it, not
very powerfully, in the form in which it is put by Clarke. He admits, however, that, after we have, by the argument *a posteriori*, "satisfied ourselves

of the existence of the intelligent cause, we naturally connect with this cause those impressions which we have derived from the contemplation of infinite space and endless duration, and hence we clothe with the attributes of immensity and eternity the awful Being whose existence has been proved by a more vigorous process of investigation." Brougham, it is evident, was ignorant of the terrible criticism to which the theistic argument had been subjected half a century before by Kant, with whose philosophy he seems to have been utterly unacquainted. He does not see clearly what Kant had proven, that the *a priori* principle of cause and effect is involved in the argument from design. We look on design as an effect, and infer a designer as a cause, on the principle that every effect has a cause. At the same time he treats of cause and effect. "Whence do we derive it? I apprehend only from our consciousness. We feel that we have a will and a power; that we can move a limb, and effect, by our own powers excited after our own volition, a change upon external objects. Now from this consciousness we derive the idea of power, and we transfer this idea and the relation on which it is founded, between our own will and the change produced, to the relations between events wholly external to ourselves, assuming them to be connected as we feel our volition and our movements are mutually connected. If it be said that this idea by no means involves that of necessary connection, nothing can be more certain. The whole is a question of fact, — of contingent truth." This statement is exposed to criticism. Whence this transference of what we feel, or rather the legitimate application of it, to the objective world? If there be not a necessary principle involved, how are we entitled to argue that world-making, of which we have no experience, implies a world-maker. He argues in behalf of the immortality of the soul, and that it is quite possible to prove a miracle. It has to be added that he has some papers on instinct, on which he throws no great light, as he had not caught the idea that instinct is the beginning of intelligence, and that it is capable, within a limited degree, of being cultivated and made hereditary.

XLVIII. — *JAMES MYLNE.*

IT is a curious circumstance that systems of philosophy so like each other should have been formed, simultaneously in the end of last century, and propounded at the beginning of this, by three men so different in temperament as James Mylne of Glasgow, Thomas Brown of Edinburgh, and James Mill of London. But the phenomenon can be explained. They could not have borrowed from each other, but they felt a common influence. All felt that Hume had undermined a great many received principles, that Hartley had resolved into association many operations of the mind before referred to independent faculties; all three, but especially Mylne and

Brown, were acquainted with the analyses of Condillac, De Tutt Tracy, and the ideologists of France ; and all lived under the reaction against the excessive multiplication of first principles by Reid and Stewart. Of the three, Brown had the greatest genius and the keenest analytical power ; Mill, of London, the greatest tenacity of purpose, of consistency, and in the end of influence : but, Mylne, of Glasgow, had quite as much of searching ability as either of the others.   He died without publishing any philosophic work ; but for upwards of forty years he delivered to large classes in Glasgow a course of lectures which set many minds a working. There was nothing attractive, certainly nothing stimulating, in his manner, his language, or his system ; but the author of this work remembers him, as he lectured every winter morning at half-past seven in the dingy old class-room in Glasgow College, as the very embodiment and personification of wisdom, which had viewed a subject on all sides and looked it through and through.

He was the son of the Rev. James Mylne, of Kinnaird, near Dundee ; was born in the same shire as James Mill of London ; was licensed to preach in 1779 ; was soon after ordained as deputy chaplain of 83d Foot ; and admitted minister of the Abbey Church, Paisley, in 1783. He was appointed professor of philosophy in Glasgow College in 1797, resigned on the 3d and died on the 21st of September, 1839. His business was to preach or provide preachers for the students in the college chapel. The students felt his preaching and that of his substitutes to be cold, and regarded him as secretly a rationalist or a Socinian. After the revival of evangelical faith in the city of Glasgow under Chalmers, loud complaints were uttered as to the doctrine taught in the college chapel.

Opposed to the national creed of Scotland, and an adherent of liberal principles, he was regarded as a dangerous man by the government of the day. On Sunday, March 26, 1815, news came of the escape of Bonaparte from Elba, and in the chapel he happened to give out the paraphrase used in the Scotch worship, " Behold, he comes ! your leader comes ! " and it was interpreted as a welcome to the restored emperor, and he was subjected to a prosecution by the Lord Advocate. He answered with spirit in a pamphlet, " Statement of the Facts connected with a Precognition taken in the College on March 30 and 31, 1815." He speaks of Bonaparte as "a man whom he had long regarded with sentiments of the deepest abhorrence and detestation, not only as the disturber of the peace and happiness of nations, but as the greatest enemy to the civil and political liberties of mankind."

His philosophy was a sufficiently simple one : he made it very clear, and he saw no difficulties. There are three, and only three, faculties of the mind, — sensation, memory, and judgment. With certain explanations he adopts the principle " nihil in intellectu quod non prius fuerit in sensu." He sees that it may be necessary to have a separation of the senses usually represented as touch, — one sense to receive sensations from solids, and another from such qualities as heat. He does not get rid of memory so readily as Brown and Mill. He opposes the theory of the French philosophers who affirm that memory is a mere modification of former impressions, and from Hume who makes conceptions differ merely in degrees from sensation. The eye, indeed, after long looking at a bright object, when shut retains the brightness; but this, he argues, is a proof that memory is not a sensation, for frequently, at the very time the spectrum, as it is called, remains in the eye, we can remember that it is not the same. He is obliged to make judgment a separate faculty; but then it consists merely in perceiving the difference of feelings. He starts the question, whether our ideas are images of external objects, and answers that external objects are rather pictures of our sensations. He distinguishes between ideas and sensations. An idea is a feeling in the mind which it has distinguished and recognized as different from the other feelings, and a feeling becomes an idea as soon as this distinction is made.

It seems to him easy to explain all the operations of the mind by these three faculties. He accounts for attention by showing that some of our sensations and feelings are more strong and lively than others. He thinks the laws of association may be reduced to two, — contiguity and (taking the hint from Stewart) relationship. As most of our perceptions are furnished in combinations, no wonder that they are again brought together before the mind in combination. But the associations of relationship are much more numerous than those of contiguity. Abstraction is nothing more than the attention directed in a particular way. He explains the peculiarity of habit by the circumstance that, by the frequent repetition of an action, we become acquainted with all the means necessary towards its accomplishment. This is surely not the whole truth, for habit is often carried on without any exercise of will; but there may be some truth in his idea that there may be volitions which are not remembered. Feelings are nothing but modifications of sensation, — the effect of sensations. Conscience is a decision of the judgment, accompanied in many cases by strong and vivid emotions. Desire is the conception of an object as good, as absent, and as attainable. He succeeds in this cool way to account for all the deeper and higher acts and ideas of the mind; but it is by simply overlooking their peculiar and distinguishing properties.

He dwells at length on principles of action. The ultimate principle is a desire to secure pleasure and avoid pain. He traces the intellectual operation of conception in all affections and passions, following out the Stoic resolution of passion as developed by the representative of Stoicism in Cicero's "Tusculan Disputations" (lib. iv.),[1] and by which they thought that passion might be brought thoroughly under the control of judgment by a proper regulation of the conception. The Stoic moralists and Mylne did service to philosophy by giving the proper place to the idea or conception; but then he does not see that the conception must be of something appetible or inappetible, derived from a spring of action in the heart or will. He has a good division of the affections into: 1. Those in which the object of them is regarded as in possession, including joy and all its modifications; 2. Those in which the object is absent, though attainable: this produces desire; 3. Those in which the object either already attained, or about to be attained, is produced by ourselves, which produces self-satisfaction;

---

[1] Lætitia autem et libido in bonorum opinione versatur, &c.

4. Those in which the agency of others is concerned, giving rise to affection and esteem.

He held firmly by the doctrine of philosophical necessity in its sternest and most unrelenting form. Altogether, he had much of the character of an old Stoic philosopher, but without those lofty ideas about following nature and the will and decree of God which elevated the systems of Zeno, Cleanthes, Epictetus, and Marcus Aurelius.

———◆———

XLIX. — *JOHN YOUNG.*[1]

Two pupils of Professor Mylne's created and sustained for a number of years a strong taste for mental science in the Irish province of Ulster, from which the founder of the Scottish philosophy had come. These were professors in the Belfast College, which imparted a high and useful education to the young men of the north-east of Ireland for a considerable number of years, and till it gave way to Queen's College, Belfast. One of these was John Young, professor of moral philosophy, and the other William Cairns, professor of logic and belles-lettres.

John Young was the son of a seceder elder, and was born in Rutherglen in the neighborhood of Glasgow in 1781. He early showed, in the midst of business pursuits, a taste for reading of a high order, for composition, and for spouting. He had difficulties in getting a learned education ; but he taught a school, became a clerk in a bleach-field in the neighborhood, and then in a mercantile house in Glasgow ; and struggled on, as many a Scotch youth has done, till in 1808, at the age of twenty-seven, he became a student in the University of Glasgow, where he distinguished himself in the classes of logic and moral philosophy, taught by Professors Jardine and Mylne, and took an active part in the college societies, where he displayed, as was thought, extraordinary eloquence. He next attended the divinity hall in the university, and, losing his faith in the stern principles of the seceders, had his thoughts directed towards the ministry in the established church. But his destination was fixed when, in 1815, the spirited inhabitants of Belfast set up the Belfast Academical Institution, embracing a college. Mr. Young, on the recommendation of the Glasgow professors, was appointed professor of moral philosophy.

Belfast was at that time a much smaller place than it is now, but a place of great enterprise ; and among its merchants, its flax spinners, its linen manufacturers, and its ministers of religion, it had a body, if not of very refined yet of very intelligent men, many of them inclined to the Unitarian, or non-subscribing faith ; and these men desired to have a good education

[1] "Lectures on Intellectual Philosophy, by the late John Young, with a Memoir of the Author, edited by William Cairns."

for their sons, and were proud of the pleasant, the accomplished, and public-spirited man who now came to live among them. His manners were genial ; he had acquired a very varied knowledge ; he was a ready and instructive talker and an eloquent speaker. The consequence was that he became a favorite in the best society of the place, and, it is to be added, spent too much of his time in dining out, and in entertaining the citizens by his humor and his sparkling conversation.

But he was an able and a most successful teacher, expounding his views with great clearness and fire, and creating a taste for the study, even among the mercantile classes, but especially among the ministers of religion, subscribing and non-subscribing, in Ulster. His lectures were at first carefully written out ; but, as years rolled on, he became less dependent on his papers, and expanded like a flood on his favorite topics, and had difficulty in compressing his superabundant matter in the limited course allowed him. He collected for the college a vast number of books published from the time of Locke down to his own day in mental philosophy : these were subsequently bought by the Queen's College. He continued a popular and useful member of society and of his college down to his death, March 9, 1829. His lectures were edited by his colleague, Dr. Cairns, and published in 1834. These published lectures scarcely do justice to him, as they are taken from his manuscripts written in the early years of his college life, and do not contain the oral illustrations and emendations which he was accustomed to pour forth from day to day in his class-room.

At the basis of his whole system, we discover the threefold division of the intellectual faculties by Mylne into sensation, memory, and judgment. Yet his lectures were of a more quickening and comprehensive character than those of his preceptor. We discover, too, that as Dr. Brown's views were given to the world, Professor Young grafted many of the living buds of that ingenious analyst on the old and drier stock. He is obliged like Stewart, and unlike Mylne, — who used to speak of that "undescribed and undescribable faculty of the mind" denominated common sense, — to call in fundamental laws of belief, and places among these causation and personal identity. "Experience itself does not reveal to reason the relation of cause and effect." "Cause is not that only which in a particular instance precedes a change ; but that which, in similar circumstances, we believe must always have been followed by a similar change, and will always be so followed in future : our belief in the relation of cause and effect thus presents us with a universal truth." "The belief is irresistible and is derived from an instinctive principle in our nature." He says "another important idea connected with the fundamental laws of belief is that of personal identity." "If we ask why each of us believes in his own identity, or regards the feelings which he formerly experienced as belonging to the same person which he now calls himself, does not the very statement of the question show its absurdity ? Is it not obvious that, even in the casual expressions which we employ, we take the fact for granted by the use of the pronouns, I and he ? It is to be referred, therefore, to a primary law of our nature."

He dwells fondly on the senses, in the operation of which he took a keen interest.   He holds that, in perception, there is involved sensation, memory, and judgment.   There are sensations ; they are remembered ; and then a judgment pronounced that the sensations must have a cause, which cause is body.   "All our sensations are connected with the conviction of certain external things as their cause; and things which are independent of us, because we cannot command their existence by our volition."   "We not only believe that, in the act of perception, we are conscious of knowing two different things, matter and mind, which are at the moment distinct ; but we believe that they are permanently distinct and independent."   It is not very clear to me how he reaches this result.   He seems to refer it, like Reid and Hamilton, to an original belief.   "The belief is of the same kind and rests on the same grounds with our belief in the permanence of the laws of nature." (Lect. L.)   I believe the principle he appeals to, is that of cause and effect, and he holds that we are bound by our very constitution to believe that every effect has a cause.   This might entitle him to argue, by this instinctive principle of causation, that our sensations, having no cause within the mind, must have a cause without the mind : if indeed we could in such circumstances rise to the idea of a without.   But he knows that what a cause is we must learn from experience : and from a sensation, which is unextended, we could never reach the idea of any thing extended.   But our idea of body is of something extended ; and we never can reach this except by some original perception as is maintained by Reid and Hamilton.   He is thus in all the difficulties of the inferential theory, in the illogical process of arguing from something unextended within to an extended existence without.

He argues powerfully that our knowledge of motion is prior to our knowledge of extension, and that, in motion, there is implied time and the observation of the succession of our thoughts.

——◆——

L. — *WILLIAM CAIRNS.*

THE Belfast College was modelled on the Scotch colleges, and was meant to give a liberal education to a large body of students.   Dr. Cairns was the professor of logic and belles-lettres.   He was born in Calton, in the suburbs of Glasgow, about 1780-85.   His father was so anxious he should be a scholar that he carried him in his arms to his first school.   He received his higher education in the grammar-school and the college of Glasgow, took license as a preacher in connection with the secession church about 1804, and was ordained a minister in Johnshaven in 1806.   From his known intellectual ability, he was appointed professor of Belfast in 1815, and continued to give instruction there till his death in 1848.   His knowledge of English and classics was extensive, his taste pure and highly refined, and his reading and elocution of a high order.   He was greatly respected by all for his talents and accomplishments ; he endeared himself to his friends, and was greatly beloved in his family circle. He took great pains in instructing his pupils in the art of English composition, and helped to produce a fine taste among the ministers of religion and the educated men of Ulster. His nature was too sensitive, and the younger pupils took advantage of this infirmity to irritate him and disturb the class. In his later days the institution with which he was connected was greatly disquieted by disputes between the Trinitarians, who composed the great body of the people, and the Unitarians, who had the chief control of the school and college ; and Dr. Cairns was often in great perplexity, as he was a man of liberal spirit on the one hand, and a firm supporter of evangelical religion on the other. The breach was not healed till the institution of Queen's College, in 1849.

He published an elaborate treatise on " Moral Freedom," 1844. It is not easy to give an analysis of it : in fact it is not easy to understand it. He starts with the very defective view, for which the teaching of Mylne of Glasgow had prepared him, that all the mental phenomena consist of sensations and ideas, a doctrine which James Mill of London was contemporaneously turning to a very different purpose. He finds a difficulty in rearing his loftier view of man's spiritual nature on such a basis. He dwells fondly on a principle of particular reference and comparative survey as the highest intellectual exercises, carrying us upward to volition, motive, and moral freedom. He is resolute in claiming for man an essential freedom ; and opposes Edwards and those divines who, as Chalmers, were connecting the philosophical doctrine of necessity with the Scripture doctrine of predestination. He regards it as a contracted view to indentify moral freedom and freedom of will. He finds moral freedom not in mere volition, but in the great influential principle of comparative survey. He unfolds, not very clearly, a whole theory of human nature. The truth in his system seems to be, that more is involved in moral freedom than mere volition , that the whole soul, including the intellect, is involved in it ; and that a preferential feeling, as he calls it, is an essential part of it, — pointing to the fact that there may be preference or choice not amounting to full volition, but implying responsibility. He shows that the freedom he advocates may be compatible with divine foreknowledge.

----•----

LI. — *JAMES MILL.*[1]

THE author, as he writes this article, has before him a photograph of a house which stood at Upper North Water Bridge, on the south side of the North Esk River, which there divides Angus from Mearns, and flows into the German Ocean a few miles below. The house consists of two apartments " a but and a ben," with possibly a closet, and a lower addition at one end

[1] " Autobiography by John Stuart Mill ; " " Personal Life of George Grote," by Mrs. Grote ; &c.

for a workshop. Here, a hundred years ago, lived a shoemaker, named James Mill, with several men under him; he was also a crofter farming some acres of land. His wife was Isabel Fenton, said to have been a woman of superior manners and intelligence, the daughter of a farmer who was out in the "forty-five" on the pretender's side. In this house on April 6, 1773, was born James Mill, destined to exercise such an influence on thought. He was one of a family of three, having a brother William, who died young; and a sister Marjory, who married William Greig, who succeeded to her father's trade and left descendants in the district. He seems to have been educated at the school of his native parish, Logie-Pert. His abilities were discovered by his minister, Rev. Dr. Peter, of Logie-Pert, and by Rev. James Foote,[1] of Fettercairn, some miles off, where was the family seat of Sir John Stuart, to whose notice Dr. Foote introduced him; and he was sent to the university of Edinburgh, his son says, "at the expense of a fund established by Lady Jane Stuart [the wife of Sir John Stuart], and some other ladies for educating young men for the ministry." In the university of Edinburgh, he pursued the usual course in arts and theology, and attended the lectures of Dugald Stewart. We have no account of his student's life or his preacher's life;[2] for he became a licentiate of the Church of Scotland. "For a few years he was a private tutor in various families in Scotland, among others that of the Marquis of Tweeddale." He expected, it is said, to receive a presentation to the parish church of Craig, which, however, was given to Dr. James Brewster, brother to (the afterwards) Sir David Brewster. People may speculate as to what sort of minister in faith and practice he would have become, had he been settled in that country parish of farmers and fishers.

We may believe that at no time had the ministry of the gospel any particular charm for him. In the year 1800, he went to London, where it is said that he preached in the Presbyterian churches. But he soon devoted himself to literature and author-

[1] I had this from a son of Dr. Foote, Archibald Foote, Esq., manufacturer, Montrose, to whom John Stuart Mill applied to get information about his father, who does not seem to have been very communicative to his family about his parentage or younger years.

[2] It is said that he published two sermons under the name of James Miln or Milne.

ship. We do not know to which of the two strong parties in
the church of Scotland he had attached himself, whether to the
moderate or rationalistic, — which Burns and most literary men
favored, — or to the evangelical, to which Dr. Peter and Mr.
James Foote belonged. It is not uncommon for Scotchmen, when
they bury themselves in London, to lose their religious faith,
which is so sustained by public opinion — as Mill would have said
by association of ideas — in their native land. With his usual reticence he has not furnished us with any account of the struggle
which must have passed in his mind when he abandoned his
belief, not only in the Bible, but in the very existence of God
and providence. Such a record would have given us a deeper
insight into the depths of human nature than all his refined
metaphysical analyses. If he ever belonged sincerely to the
evangelical party, there must have been a tremendous revulsion
of feeling in the change. If he belonged to the moderates, he
had little to abandon beyond the doctrines of natural religion.

He married — it is curious that the son never refers to the
lady — not long after his settlement in London, and when he had
no resource but the precarious one of writing in periodicals.
He must have had a hard struggle in these times, but he
bore it resolutely. A writer in the "Edinburgh Review" (July,
1873) describes him. "In appearance he was strikingly like
the portraits of Charles XII. of Sweden, with a lofty forehead, a
keen and cutting face. His powers of conversation were extraordinary; but, both in his family and among his disciples, he
was to the last degree tyrannical, arbitrary, and impatient of contradiction." "He was a harsh husband and a stern father." The
first great literary work planned by him was the "History of
British India," which he commenced and completed in about
ten years, and published in 1817-18. In 1819 the Court of Di-
rectors of the India Company appointed him to the high post of
assistant examiner of India correspondence, and he held this
office till within four years of his death. He wrote articles in
the "Encyclopædia Britannica," on government, education,
jurisprudence, law of nations, liberty of the press, colonies,
and prison discipline. He was also a contributor to the "Westminster Review," and the "London Review," which after a few
months was merged in the "London and Westminster." In
1821-22 he published his "Elements of Political Economy;" in

1829 his "Analysis of the Human Mind;" and in 1835 the " Fragment on Mackintosh," being the last work before his death, which took place 23d June, 1836.

For the last fifteen or twenty years of his life he was an important member of a thinking and writing circle, he himself being the centre of a smaller circle within that circle. In morals and politics he attached himself to Bentham, at that time obnoxious in the extreme to many, but adored by a select few. " Mr. Bentham, " says Mrs. Grote, " being a man of easy fortune, kept a good table, and took pleasure in receiving guests at his board, though never more than one at a time. To this one guest he would talk fluently, yet not caring to listen in his turn." James Mill was often the one guest so highly favored. " Bentham lived in Queen's Square Place, Westminster, close to the residence of Mill and his family, and his house was lent to the historian of India." Acquainted with mental science (at that time not studied in London), through his training in Scottish philosophy, and his reading of Hartley, he became the leader in metaphysical thought in the metropolis. He had qualities which fitted him to influence young men. He was earnest ; he was clear ; he was strongly impressed with the evils of the past and present ; he spoke authoritatively and dogmatically, and with contempt of those who opposed him, and facile minds bent before him. We have a friendly picture of him drawn by Mrs. Grote as he began to exercise a powerful influence over her husband. " Before many months the ascendancy of James Mill's powerful mind over his younger companion made itself apparent. George Grote began by admiring the wisdom, the acuteness, the depths of Mill's intellectual character. Presently he found himself inthralled in the circle of Mill's speculations ; and, after a year or two of intimate commerce, there existed but little difference, in point of opinion, between master and pupil. Mr. Mill had the strongest convictions as to the superior advantages of democratic government over the monarchical or the aristocratic ; and with these he mingled a scorn and hatred of the ruling classes which amounted to positive fanaticism. Coupled with this aversion to aristocratic influence (to which influence he invariably ascribed most of the defects and abuses prevalent in the administration of public affairs), Mr. Mill entertained a profound prejudice against the Established Church, and, of course, a corresponding dislike to its ministers. These two vehement currents of antipathy came to be gradually shared by George Grote, in proportion as his veneration of Mr. Mill took deeper and deeper root. Although his own nature was of a gentle, charitable, humane quality, his fine intellect was worked upon by the inexorable teacher with so much persuasive power that George Grote found himself inoculated, as it were, with the conclusions of the former almost without a choice, since the subtle reasonings of Mr. Mill appeared to his logical mind to admit of no refutation. And thus it came to pass that, starting from acquired convictions, George Grote adopted the next phase ; viz., the antipathies of his teacher,— antipathies which colored his mind through the whole period of his ripe meridian age, and may be said to have inspired and directed many of the important actions of life. Originating in an earnest feeling for the public good, these currents gradually assumed the force and sanction of duties, prompting George Grote to a systematic course both of study, opinion, action, and self-denial, in which he was urgently encouraged by the master-spirit of James Mill, to that gentleman's latest breath in 1836. This able dogmatist exercised considerable influence over other young men of that day as well as over Grote. He was indeed a propagandist of a high order, equally master of the pen and of speech. Moreover, he possessed the faculty of kindling in his auditors the generous impulses towards the popular side both in politics and social theories ; leading them at the same time to regard the cultivation of individual affections and sympathies as destructive of lofty aims and indubitably hurtful to the mental character." Mr. Grote says in 1819 : " I have met Mill often at his (Ricord's) house, and hope to derive great pleasure and instruction from his acquaintance, as he is a very profound-thinking man and seems well disposed to communicate, as well as clear and intelligible in his manner. His mind has indeed all that cynicism and asperity which belong to the Benthamian school ; and what I chiefly dislike in him is the readiness and seeming preference with which he dwells on the faults and defects of others, even of the greatest of men. But it is so very rarely that a man of any depth comes across my path, that I shall almost assuredly cultivate his acquaintance a good deal farther." We have a less favorable picture in an article in the " Edinburgh Review" (July, 1873),

which says of the son : " His fine and loving temper was con
stantly struggling against the imperious dictates of his master,
who had taught him to regard, as Mr. Grote tells us, the cultivation
of individual affections and sympathies as destructive of lofty
aims, and hurtful to the mental character.   In the course of
years several young men devoted to the study of metaphysics
and mental philosophy were accustomed to meet twice a week
at Mr. Grote's in the city, at half-past eight in the morning,
for an hour or two.   Jeremy Bentham was regarded by them as
a kind of deity, whose utterances were closely watched and
reverently received.   James Mill was their prophet, who exercised uncontrolled sway over their minds."   Mrs. Grote
gives an account of the men and their studies.   " They
read Mr. Mill's last work, " The Analysis of the Phenomena of the Human Mind," Hartley " On Man," Dutrieux's
" Logic," Whately's works, &c., discussing as they proceeded.
Mr. John Stuart Mill, Mr. Charles Buller, Mr. Eyton Tooke, (son
of Mr. Thomas Tooke), Mr. John Arthur Roebuck, Mr. G. H.
Graham, Mr. Grant, and Mr. W. G. Prescott formed part of
their class."

He now became a leader of opinion, and imparted his own
character to a whole school.   His intellect was clear, but not
comprehensive ; was strong, but one-sided.   He saw what he
wished to see, and did not go round the object to view the
other side.   Hence he was not troubled with uncertainties or
doubts, and he laid down his opinions coolly and dogmatically,
wondering how every man did not see as he did, and bearing
no contradiction.   The school of which he was a leader — or,
rather, I believe, *the* leader — came to be called " Philosophical
Radicalism," or sometimes the " Westminster Review " school,
from that review being its organ.   It was founded on Utilitarianism in morals and on sensational empiricism in philosophy ;
and Mill gave it its earnestness, its narrowness, its exclusiveness, and its fanaticism.   The school had at first the general
sentiment against them ; but they persevered, and came in a
few years to exercise a potent influence, which is felt at this
day, in consequence mainly of the able men, then young, but
now old or deceased, who became attached to it.

He has left us no account of the religious crisis through
which he passed, but his son has told us the results which he

reached: "The turning point of his mind on the subject was reading Butler's 'Analogy.' That work, of which he always continued to speak with respect, kept him, as he said, for some considerable time a believer in the divine authority of Christianity, by proving to him that, whatever are the difficulties in believing that the Old and New Testaments proceed from, or record the acts of, a perfectly wise and good Being, the same and still greater difficulties stand in the way of the belief that a Being of such a character can have been the Maker of the universe. He considered Butler's argument as conclusive against the only opponents for whom it was intended. Those who admit an omnipotent as well as perfectly just and benevolent Maker and Ruler of such a world as this can say little against Christianity but what can, with at least equal force, be retorted against themselves. Finding, therefore, no halting place in deism, he remained in a state of perplexity, until, doubtless after many struggles, he yielded to the conviction that, concerning the origin of things, nothing whatever can be known. This is the only correct statement of his opinion; for dogmatic atheism he looked upon as absurd, as most of those whom the world has considered atheists have always done." "He found it impossible to believe that a world so full of evil was the work of an Author combining infinite power with perfect goodness and righteousness." He saw, what natural religion shuts its eyes to, that there were manifold evils in the world; so say the Scriptures, and tell us how they sprang up, and point to the remedy,—a remedy which Mr. Mill was not prepared to adopt, and so was left without any relief from the dark prospect. We do not wonder in these circumstances that "he thought human life a poor thing at best, after the freshness of youth and of unsatisfied curiosity had gone by."

He was thoroughly discontented with the education commonly given to the young. "In psychology his fundamental doctrine was the formation of all human character by circumstances, through the universal principle of association, and the consequent unlimited possibility of improving the moral and intellectual condition of mankind by education." So he took the education of his oldest son into his own hand. At three he taught him Greek; and by the age of eight the boy had read "the whole of Herodotus, of Xenophon's 'Cyropædia' and

'Memorials of Socrates,' some of the 'Lives of the Philosophers' by Diogenes Laertius, part of 'Isocrates ad Demonicum' and 'Ad Nicoclem.'" At the age of nine he had read the first six Dialogues of Plato, from the "Euthyphron" to the "Theætetus" inclusive. He was made to begin Latin in his eighth year; and from his eighth to his twelfth year he read the "Bucolics" of Virgil and the first six books of the "Æneid," all Horace except the "Epodes," the "Fables" of Phædrus, the first five books of Livy, with the remainder of the first decade, all Sallust, a considerable part of Ovid's "Metamorphoses," some plays of Terence, two or three books of Lucretius, several of the orations of Cicero and of his writings on oratory and his "Letters to Atticus;" and this while he was adding largely to his Greek and devouring elaborate volumes of history. At the age of twelve he entered on the study of logic, beginning with the "Analytics" of Aristotle. Everybody feels that it was a dangerous thing to lay such a load on the mind of one so young; and that there was an imminent risk either of his brain being overworked or of his being turned into a pedant. The success of the trial proves that a boy of good ability may learn much more by systematic teaching than most people imagine. In the morning walks with the father the boy was induced to give an account of what he had read the day before.

There were surely great oversights in this training, as, for instance, in not allowing him to mingle with other boys, and in restraining natural emotions. "For passionate emotions of all sorts, and for every thing that has been said or written in exaltation of them, he expressed the greatest contempt. He regarded them as a form of madness. The intense was with him a byword of scornful disapprobation." In respect of religion the son says: "I am thus one of the very few examples of one who has not thrown off religious belief, but never had it: I grew up in a negative state with regard to it." The father "looked forward to a considerable increase of freedom in the relations between the sexes, though without pretending to define exactly what would be or ought to be the precise conditions of that freedom." A writer in the "Quarterly" (July, 1873) says: "He was full of what we should call the fanaticism of Malthusianism; to such a degree that he risked his own fairly earned repu-

tation with decent people, and involved in the like discreditable
danger the youth of his son, by running a Malay muck against
what he called the superstitions of the nursery with regard to
sexual relations, and giving the impulse to a sort of shameless
propaganda of prescriptions for artificially checking population.
We should not even have alluded to this grave offence against
decency, on the part of the elder and younger Mill, had it
not been forced on our notice by recent events." The result
was what might have been expected. We can understand
how the son's natural feelings, so repressed, should have been
ready to flow forth towards a lady who entered thoroughly into
his peculiar views on all subjects, and that he did not seek to
restrain these feelings, and had no compunctions of conscience,
though that lady was married to another man. I believe we can
see the result of the training in a younger son, represented as an
engaging youth, who went to a warm climate for his health,
and when there insisted on the physician telling him whether
there was any hope of his recovery, and, on receiving an unfa-
vorable reply, went and shot himself to avoid a lingering death.[1]

The work with which we have to do, is his "Analysis of the
Human Mind." The title indicates the aim of the treatise. It
is not an inductive observation of facts ; it is not a classification
of facts in a cautious and careful manner : it is a determined
attempt to resolve the complex phenomena of the mind into as
few elements as possible. Mental analysis, called by Whewell
the decomposition of facts, is undoubtedly a necessary agent in
all investigation : but it should be kept as a subordinate instrument ; and it requires to be preceded, accompanied, and verified
throughout, by a microscopic and conscientious inspection of
facts, with particular attention to residuary phenomena and apparent exceptions ; if this is neglected the whole process may
lead to most fallacious results. Thomas Brown had proceeded
very much in the method of analysis, and accomplished a great
many feats in the way of decompounding the faculties enumerated by Reid and Stewart ; and, encouraged by his success, Mill
advances a great way further on the same route. Brown had
stood up resolutely for the existence and validity of intuition,

---

[1] I had this from the late John Pim, of Belfast, who was at the place at the
time. I would not have referred to it had the suicide been the result of a mental
derangement : it was the logical consequence of the philosophic training.

maintaining in particular that we have an intuitive belief in cause and effect ; had allotted a place, though an inadequate one, to judgment, under the name of "relative suggestion ;" had poured forth a most eloquent exposition of the emotions, and defended the great truths of natural religion, including the existence of the deity and the immortality of the soul. Mill resolves all mental exercises into sensations and ideas, with laws of association connecting and combining them ; and has left himself avowedly no religious belief whatever.

Dugald Stewart's teaching seems to have exercised little influence on his mind except to suggest the order in which he takes up his topics. I suspect he derived more from Hume than from Stewart. With Hume there is nothing in the mind but impressions and ideas ; with Mill, only sensations and ideas ; and both undermine our belief in the reality either of mind or body. He took advantage of all that has been done, in illustrating the influence of association, by Hutcheson, Smith, Hume, Beattie, Alison, and Brown, and accounted by it for principles which these men reckoned original. He had also profoundly studied Hartley (" Observations on Man "), who had accounted for our complex mental feelings by sensations, ideas of sensations and association, connecting the whole with a theory of nerve vibrations, which Mill, following the Scottish school, abandoned.

Following the sensational school of France and Brown, he calls all the exercises of the mind "feelings." He begins with sensations, and goes over (Chap. I.) smell, hearing, sight, taste, touch, carefully separating from touch as Brown had done, and as Mr. Bain has since done, the feeling of resistance, extension, and figure, which he refers to muscular sensation ; he also dwells fondly, as Mr. Bain has done, on the sensations of disorganization in the alimentary canal. He then treats of idea (Chap. II.) ; and now " we have two classes of feelings, one which exists when the object of sense is present, another that exists after the object of sense has ceased to be present. The one class of feelings I call sensations ; the other class of feelings I call ideas." At this stage we wonder where or how he has got objects of sense with nothing but sensations and ideas. " As we say sensation, we might also say ideation :" "sensation would in that case be a general name for one part of our constitution, ideation for another." It is clear that Mill's analysis has been the main book, or the only book on mental science, carefully studied by a certain class of London physiologists, — such as Carpenter, Huxley, and Maudesley, — who seldom rise above the contemplation of sensations and sensations reproduced. Verily it is an easy way of enunciating and unfolding all the varied processes of the mind to represent them as feelings, and put them under two heads, sensations and ideas ; the ideas being copies of sensations, so that he is able to say : " There is nothing in the mind but sensations and copies of sensations." There is no room left for knowledge of objects or belief in objects, internal and external, no judgment or reasoning, no perception of moral good and evil. It is a more inadequate resolution than that of Condillac, who called in a sort of alchemical power, and spoke of " transformed sensations." Mr. Grote writes to the younger Mill: " It has always rankled in my thoughts that so grand and powerful a mind as he should have left behind it such insufficient traces in the estimation of successors." I do not wonder that such a meagre exposition should not have carried with it the highest minds of the age, which turned more eagerly towards the German speculators, and towards Coleridge, Cousin, and Hamilton. But his book has had its influence over the school to which he belonged, including Mr. Grote, and over certain physiologists, who, if they have only sensations and copies of sensations to account for, are tempted to imagine that they can explain them all by organic processes. His son, John Stuart, and Mr. Bain, have been greatly swayed by the elder Mill, but have clearly perceived the enormous defects of the analysis, which they have sought to rectify in the valuable edition of the work published in 1869 ; the fundamental defects however remain, and the corrections admit principles which these authors have not dared to avow or to carry out, as they involve so many other mental operations beyond sensations and ideas.

In Chap. III. he goes on to his favorite subject, association of ideas. Ideas have a synchronous and a successive order. When sensations have occurred synchronically, the ideas also spring up synchronically," and thus he fashions many of our complex ideas, as of a violin with a certain figure and tone. He resolves the ideas of successive associations into the one

law of contiguity. This resolution has been criticised by
Hamilton (" Reid's Collected Works " Note D. . . . § 2), and
also by his son (Note to Chap. III.), who endeavor to show that
the suggestion of similars cannot be thus accounted for, which
they certainly cannot be unless we call in some intermediate
processes.   He shows how, by these associations, we get certain complex ideas, as the ideas of metals from the separate
ideas of several sensations, — color, hardness, extension, weight.
In illustrating this point, he says, that " philosophy has ascertained that we draw nothing from the eye whatever but sensations of color."   In opposition to this, Hamilton has demonstrated that, if we perceive color, we must also perceive the line
that separates one color from another (Met. Lect. 27).   The
result he has reached is summed up : " We have seen first that
we have sensations ; secondly, that we have ideas, the copies
of these sensations ; thirdly, that those ideas are sometimes
simple, the copies of one sensation ; sometimes complex, the
copies of several sensations so combined as to appear not several ideas but one idea ; and, fourthly, that we have trains of
these ideas, or one succeeding another without end."

He turns to naming (Chap. IV.), and treats of the various
parts of speech, but throws little light on them. He goes on
to explain the various processes of the mind, beginning with
consciousness (Chap. V.).   " To say I feel a sensation, is merely
to say I feel a feeling, which is an impropriety of speech ;
and to say I am conscious of a feeling is merely to say that I
feel it.   To have a feeling is to be conscious, and to be con
scious is to have a feeling."   " In the very word ' feeling ' all that
is implied in the word ' consciousness ' is involved."   There is a
palpable oversight here. When I feel a sensation it is of a sensitive organ as affected, and knowledge is involved in this.
To be conscious is to know self as feeling or in some other
state.   " When I smell a rose, I am conscious."   True, but I
am conscious not of the rose, but of self as having the sensation.   In explaining consciousness, he overlooks the very
peculiarity of the thing to be explained.

He then (Chap. V., VI., VII., VIII., IX.) treats of conception,
imagination, classification, abstraction.   " Conception applies
only to ideas and to ideas only in a state of combination.   It
is a general name, including the several classes of complex

ideas." But the question arises, What intellectual bond combines things generally? and we have no satisfactory answer. He thus misses one of the most important capacities of our mental nature. "An imagination is the name of a train;" but what combines so many scattered things into one image, often so grand? He has a long disquisition on classification. "The word 'man,' we shall say, is first applied to an individual; it is first associated with the idea of that individual, and acquires the power of calling up the idea of him; it is next applied to another individual, and acquires the power of calling up the idea of him, so of another and another, till it has become associated with an infinite number, and has acquired the power of calling up an indefinite number of these ideas indifferently." "It is association that forms the ideas of an indefinite number of individuals into one complex idea." Here again he has explained every thing by overlooking the *differentia* of the process,—the resemblance between the individuals; the perception of the resemblances; the placing the resembling objects into a class of which so many predications may be made; and, as might be expected, he has no idea that there is such a thing as classes in nature. By taking a superficial view, he is able to throw ridicule on the theory of ideas by Plato, by Philo, by Cudworth, and Harris, in which there is no doubt much mysticism, but also much truth, which it should be the business of a correct analysis to bring out to view. The father thus set his son to what he is so fond of in his "Logic" and other works,—the exposure of the error of looking on concepts as if they were individual existences. True, universals are not the same as singulars, yet they may have a reality which we should try to seize: some of them *ante rem*, in the Divine mind arranging classes in nature; *in re*, in the common attributes which join the objects in the class; and *post rem*, in the concepts formed by the mind, and performing most important functions in thought. Both Mr. Grote and Mr. John Stuart Mill in their notes have tried to improve Mill's doctrine of generification, but have left it, and their own doctrine as well, in a most unsatisfactory state. Abstract terms "are simply the concrete terms with the connotation dropped," whereon his son annotates. "This seems a very indirect and circuitous mode of making us understand what an abstract name signifies. Instead of aiming

directly at the mark, it goes round it. It tells us that one
name signifies a part of what another name signifies, leaving
us to infer that part." Neither father nor son has seen that
abstraction in all cases implies a high exercise of judgment or
comparison, in which we perceive the relation of a part to a
whole, a process which is the basis of so many other intellectual exercises.

He turns (Chap. X.) to memory, which has so puzzled the
son, who says : "Our belief in the veracity of memory is evidently ultimate : no reason can be given for it which does not
presuppose the belief and assume it to be well grounded."
The subject presents no difficulties to the father. He acknowledges that in memory there is not only the idea of the thing
remembered ; there is also the idea of my having seen it : and
he shows that this implies "the idea of my present self, the
remembering self ; and the idea of my past self, the remembered or witnessing self ?" But where has he got self ? Where
a past self ? He brings in, without attempting to explain
them, *self*, and *time present*, and *past*, which are not sensations nor copies of sensations. All that is done is "to
run over a number of states of consciousness called up by the
association." There is here, as in so many other cases, simply
the shutting of the eye to the main element in memory, the
recognition of an object as having been before the mind in
time past : in which there is involved, first, belief, and, secondly, time in the concrete, from which the mind forms the
idea of time in the abstract.

There follows (Chap. XI.) an elaborate discussion of belief,
which both his son and Mr. Bain have been seeking to amend
without success ; because their own views, starting from those
of the older Mill, are radically defective. In all belief, as it
appears to me, there is a conviction of the reality of the object
believed in. When the object is present, I would be disposed
to call this knowledge ; but, if any one calls it belief, the question
between him and me would be simply a verbal one, provided
he acknowledges the existence of a conviction. In other cases
the conviction or belief is the result of judgment or reasoning.
Let us now look at the account given by Mill. "A sensation
is a feeling, but a sensation and a belief of it is the same thing.
The observation applies equally to ideas. When I say I have

the idea of the sun, I express the same thing exactly as when I
say that I believe I have it. The feeling is one: the names
only are different." Here again the resolution is accomplished
so dexterously, because the main elements of the thing resolved are not noticed. In a sensation I have not only a feeling, but a belief in the existence of a sentient organ. To have
a belief in the existence of the sun is something more than
merely to have an idea of the sun. The belief, be it intuitive,
or be it derivative, is a different thing from the sensation and
the idea, and should have a separate place in every system of
psychology.

It is at this place that he develops most fully the principle
for which he has received such praise from his son, — the principle of inseparable association. "In every instance of belief,
there is indissoluble association of the ideas," and he defies
any one to show that there is any other ingredient. But, surely,
there is often belief without any inseparable association : thus
I may believe that a friend is dead, though in time past all my
associations have been of him as alive. But, even in cases of
indissoluble association, the belief is different from the association. One of the grand defects of the whole theory consists in
accounting by association of ideas for what is assuredly a
different process, for judgment, for judgment proceeding on a
knowledge of things. At no other point do we see so clearly
the tendency of the whole school to degrade the dignity and
undermine the trustworthiness of the human intellect.

By this indissoluble association he can account easily for our
belief in causation. "I hear words in the street, — *event;* some
one of course is making them, — *antecedent.* My house is
broken and my goods are gone, — *event;* a thief has taken them,
— *antecedent.* This is that remarkable case of association in
which the association is inseparable." "We cannot think
[in the sense of having an idea] of the one without thinking of
the other." Once more the essential element is left out ; we
not only have an idea, we judge, decide, and believe ; and when
we judge, decide, and believe, that everywhere, at all times,
and for ever, an event has and must have a cause, the process
seems to me to be justifiable, but to involve an intuitive principle. Mr. John Stuart Mill is only following out the principles
advocated by his father, when he holds that there may be worlds

in which two and two make five, and in which there may be an
effect without a cause. In another subject James Mill has
led his son to a point where the father has stopped, while the
son has gone on. "In my belief, then, of the existence of an
object, there is included the belief that, in such and such circumstances, I should have such and such sensations. Is there
any thing more?" "I not only believe that I shall see St.
Paul's church-yard, but I believe that I should see it if I were
in St. Paul's church-yard this instant." This is on the very verge
of the son's definition of body and of mind. We see how needful
it is to examine the fundamental assumptions of a philosophy
which has culminated in such results, and is undermining our
belief in the reality of things.

In Chap. XII. we have a short and feeble account of ratiocination, in which he proceeds on the syllogistic analysis without comprehending the principles involved in it. He takes as
his example, "All men are animals. Kings are men. Therefore kings are animals;" and he shows that in all this there is
only association, and the belief which is part of it. In the proposition "kings are men," the belief is merely the recognition that
the individuals named kings are part of the many of whom men
is the common name. "Kings" is associated with "all men,"
"all men" with "animals;" "kings," therefore, with animals.
The account of evidence, in the short chapter which succeeds,
is merely a summation of what had gone before, and is exceedingly meagre.

He now turns (Chap. XIV.) to "names requiring particular
explanations," and explains, according to his theory of sensations and ideas, such profound subjects as relations, numbers,
time, motion, identity. Mr. Bain represents him as here "endeavoring to express the most fundamental fact of consciousness,
the necessity of change or transition from one state to another,
in order to our being conscious. He approaches very near to,
without exactly touching, the inference, that all consciousness,
all sensation, all knowledge, must be of *doubles*," as if we could
not have a sensation of pain till there is a change into pleasure,
or of pleasure till we have also pain. This is to reverse the
natural process in which we have first the individuals, and thus
and then discover relations between them, — it may be, many
and varied, according to the knowledge we previously have of

the individuals. According to Mill, that a feeling of red and a feeling of blue is "different and known to be so, are not two things but one and the same thing ;" thus doing away with all relation, in fact with all comparison and judgment, and reasoning as founded on comparison. "Space is a mere abstract term formed by dropping the connotation. Linear extension is the idea of a line, the connotation dropped ; that is, the idea of resisting dropped." We ask what is the line? Infinite is the concrete term, here denoting line : drop the connotation, and you have infinity, the abstract." It is a convenient but certainly a most fallacious way of reducing realities to nonentities. Time is "pastness, presentness, and futureness" joined by association ; but he can render no account of pastness, presentness, and futureness. The idea of motion and the idea of extension are the same. Identity is merely the name of a certain case of belief. " Reflection (Chap. XV.) is nothing ; but consciousness is the having the sensations and ideas :" most people would say it is a knowledge of self, as having an idea, a sensation, or some other mental exercise.

He treats from Chap. XVI.–XXII. of the active powers of the mind, or the powers which excite to action. All throughout, he gains a delusive simplicity, simply by overlooking an element, commonly the main element, in the phenomenon. Desire is the same thing as the idea of a pleasure, "and the number of our desires is the same with that of our pleasurable sensations ; the number of our aversions, the same with that of our painful sensations." I hold that desire is something superadded to mere sensation, and indicating a higher capacity, and that we may and ought to desire many things beside mere sensations of pleasure. He then proceeds to show us in the way the Scottish metaphysicians had done, from Hutcheson and Turnbull downwards ; how the desire of pleasure gives rise to other impulses, which may by association become ends, and not mere means ; such as, wealth, power, dignity, friendship, kindness, family, country, party, mankind. "A man looks upon his child as a cause to him of future pains and pleasures, much more certain than any other person ;" and thus gathers round it a whole host of associations that constitute parental love. All this I admit will mingle with and strengthen family affection ; but in the heart of the affection there is a natu-

ral love on the part of parents for their children.   In accounting for the love of beauty, he takes advantage of Alison's theory,
a theory not favored by those who have discovered mathematical
relations in beautiful forms.   The following quotation will enable us to understand what he means by motives : "As every
pleasure is worth having, — for otherwise it would not be a pleasure, — the idea of every pleasure associated with that of an
action of ours as the cause is a motive ; that is, leads to the
action.   But every motive does not produce the action. The
reason is, the existence of other motives which prevent it.   A
man is tempted to commit adultery with the wife of his friend :
the composition of the motive is obvious.   He does not obey
the motive.   Why ?   He obeys other motives which are stronger.
Though pleasures are associated with the immoral act, pains
are associated with it also ; the pains of the injured husband,
the pains of the injured wife, the moral indignation of mankind, the future reproaches of his own mind.   Some men obey
the first rather than the second motive.   The reason is obvious.
In them the association of the act with the pleasure is, from
habit, unduly strong : the association of the act with the pains
is, from want of habit, unduly weak.   This is a case of education."
I believe that if men were trained to think that chastity has no
other foundation than Mr. Mill has given it, the husband would
be little attended to when he claimed to be injured, and the wife
would cease to believe that she had injured any one, and the
moral indignation of mankind would disappear ; thus perilous
would it be to remove morality from its foundation in moral
principle, and place it on the shifting sand of association.

We are prepared for his analysis of the moral sense.   "It is
interesting here to observe by what a potent call we are summoned to virtue.   Of all that we enjoy more is derived from
those acts of other men on which we bestow the name ' virtue,' than from any other cause.   Our own virtue is the principal
cause why other men reciprocate the acts of virtue towards us :
with the idea of our own acts of virtue there are naturally associated the ideas of all the immense advantages we derive from
the virtuous acts of our fellow-creatures.   When this association
is formed in due strength, which it is the main business of a
good education to effect, the motive of virtue becomes para-
mount in the human breast."   By all means let us try to collect

good associations round virtuous acts; but, as the centre and bond of the whole, let us have the principle that virtuous acts should be done because they are right. Discard this restraint, and attractive associations will be sure to gather round vice. He tells us (" Fragment on Mackintosh "), that his analysis of virtue into the love of pleasure and association does not lessen the influence of the motive. "Gratitude remains gratitude, resentment remains resentment, generosity, generosity in the mind of him who feels them, after analysis, the same as before." Yes in the mind of him "who feels them;" but the feeling may be undermined, and remorse for sin be quieted.

He closes the work with a discussion as to will and intention. Will is the peculiar state of mind or consciousness by which action is preceded. He treats of its influence over the actions of the body, and over the actions of the mind. He shows that sensations and ideas are the true antecedents of the bodily actions, and so he does not need to call in a separate capacity called the will. He then turns to the power which the mind seems to possess over its associations. He proves, as Brown and others had done, that we cannot will an absent idea before us, — for to will it is already to have it; and the recalling is always a process of association. He does not see that, by a stern act of will, we can detain a present thought, and thus gather around it a whole host of associations. He speaks of ends, but has no idea of the way in which ends spring up and influence the mind. He takes no notice of the essential freedom belonging to the will, and thus leaves no ground on which to rear the doctrine of human responsibility.

LII. — *JOHN BALLANTYNE.*[1]

HE was born at Piteddie, parish of Kinghorn, Fifeshire, May 8, 1778, and received his early education in the village school of Lochgelly. He matriculated in the university of Edinburgh in 1795, and seems there to have enjoyed the privilege of sitting under the instructions of Dugald Stewart. His parents belonged to the church of Scotland, but from conscientious

[1] " Recollections of Rev. John Ballantyne," an address delivered at a *soirée* on opening the new United Presbyterian Church, Stonehaven, by Rev. John Longmuir, Aberdeen, 1862.

motives, and from perceiving the want of religion in the students intending
for the ministry in that body, he joined the burgher branch of the seceders,
and attended their theological hall, where his metaphysical abilities were
noticed by his professor Dr. Lawson. After being licensed to preach the
gospel, he taught schools at Lochgelly, and at Colinsburgh. In 1805, he
was settled as minister in the shire of Kincardine, at Stonehaven, a somewhat exposed place on the German ocean, but made interesting by bold
rocks in the neighborhood, and a grand old ruined castle where the covenanters had been imprisoned. There he ministered to a small congregation
of fifty members, and specially exerted himself in establishing sabbath
schools, at that time very much unknown in the district. He lived a shy
and retired life, cheerful in his own home, but not much known beyond,
except by a few who noticed him taking his solitary walk daily along the
links of Cowie, with tall and well-proportioned frame, and high capacious
forehead, pondering, they supposed, some deep ecclesiastical or philosophic
subject. In 1824, he published anonymously, "A Comparison of Established and Dissenting Churches by a Dissenter," and, in 1830, an enlarged
edition of the same with his name prefixed. This work may be regarded
as starting the voluntary controversy, which was carried on vigorously by
the religious body to which he belonged, for years agitated Scotland from
one end of it to the other, in the course of time spread into England,
and, directly or indirectly, has been followed by far-reaching results, that
have not yet exhausted themselves. There is reason to believe that he
foresaw the consequences ; he told his friend, Mr. Longmuir, that he expected to see him out of the established church and a dissenting minister
like himself.

But he was also speculating on other topics. In 1828, he published
"An Examination of the Human Mind." It should be interesting to any
one who has had to contend with adverse circumstances to contemplate
this man in his quiet seceder manse on that bare coast, and among a people
who appreciated his piety and devotedness, but had no comprehension of
his philosophy, devoting himself so earnestly to the original study of the
human mind. He could have been swayed by no inferior hope in the shape
of an expected chair in one of the Scottish colleges ; for these, while open to
persons adhering really or nominally to established-church Presbyterianism
and Episcopacy were practically closed to a dissenting minister. This was
doubtless one of the rankling causes that prompted the seceders to espouse
the voluntary side so eagerly. They felt, in an age which was moving on
towards the reform bill, that they had a title to complain of being consigned
to an inferior position : it should be added that they felt that they had to
abandon their strict covenanting principles, which were seen to be exclusive. Nor was this man or his book likely to get a favorable hearing from
the literary or metaphysical readers in Scotland, where the influential
thinkers were James Mylne and Thomas Brown, to whose philosophy he
was entirely opposed ; and, as to England, it felt little interest in such inquiries. The work, though clearly written, has no such literary beauties as
drew many towards the writings of Stewart and Brown, and it had some
difficulty in getting into notice. There is no evidence that any of the pro-

fessors in the chairs of mental science took any interest in it, or were disposed to lift the author out of his obscurity. Nevertheless there were some in his own religious communion, and beyond it, who perceived the merit of the work, which is distinguished for its independence, and its rising above the philosophy of his time. "A gentleman," says Mr. Longmuir, "eminent both for his wealth and literary distinction, (the late Mr. Douglas of Cavers?) having seen the manuscript, and been informed of the limited means of the author, kindly offered to run the risk of its publication; but Mr. Ballantyne, having found that he had accumulated sufficient means to publish it himself, gratefully declined the generous offer. Some time after, a considerable sum of money was sent by the same gentleman, and placed entirely at Mr. Ballantyne's disposal. Instead of applying it, however, to the publication of his book, he paid it over for the benefit of the missionary operations that his presbytery was then promoting." A disparaging notice of his work appeared in "The Edinburgh Literary Journal," a periodical long since consigned to oblivion, but he was not moved by it: he had done his work, and left it to speak for itself. Thus lived, and thus died, Nov. 5, 1830, one who was, above all things, resolute in maintaining his independence, both of action and thinking, — independence not of God, but of man.

He finds it necessary to criticise Dr. Brown, and has anticipated some of the objections, afterwards propounded more formally by Hamilton. "The system of Dr. Brown certainly discovers great ingenuity, and is expounded with great eloquence; but it appears to betray a want of that persevering diligence and scrupulous caution, without which metaphysical inquiries are in a great measure unavailing." He begins with a discussion of the sensitive principle." He distinguishes between sensations and ideas of sensation. "The sensations and ideas of extension, as far as can be ascertained, are suggested at the very same instant," where, it may be observed, that he uses the very objectionable word "suggest." "Almost the whole of the body, whether external or internal, is sensitive; and an impression on every sensitive part, whether occasioned by an external or internal influence, is accompanied with a sensation." "It is also accompanied, I imagine, with an idea of extension corresponding to the form and magnitude of the impression." "We always find that an impression on the organ of taste is accompanied not only with a sensation, but with an idea of the part of the organ affected." "It is highly probable that the organ of smell also affords ideas of extension." "The sense of hearing seems to be governed by the same laws." Locke taught that we get our ideas of extension solely from sight and touch. Ballantyne maintains that we have them from all the senses, because by all the senses we have "an idea of the part of the organ affected," here anticipating favorite positions of Hamilton and the physiologist Müller.

He criticises the doctrine of Brown, that by the eye we discern only color, not in so clinching a manner as Hamilton, but in a like spirit. "Some indeed contend that sight affords only sensations of color, and no idea of extension at all; but this opinion has never been established by adequate evidence and appears to be incompatible with not a few phenomena. At any rate, in the present state of our knowledge, we certainly have by sight ideas of extension and ideas of greater or smaller portions of it, other things being equal, according to the impression on the organ, and are bound, therefore, to regard this as an ultimate principle, till it be traced to one more general. This, so far as I know, has never yet been done, and I am utterly unable to perceive how it can be done."

" We never but find that an impression on a sensitive organ is accompanied with an idea of duration, as well as with a sensation and an idea of extension." " Every impression, besides suggesting a sensation and an idea of extension, suggests in connection with them an idea of a portion of duration corresponding to the duration of the impression." And here he has again to criticise Brown, and by anticipation Mill. " There are no doubt many analogies between duration and extension ; but to assume that they are literally one and the same thing, as Dr. Brown most evidently does, is one of the most unwarrantable assumptions that ever was hazarded." " That doctrine is, that duration and extension are substantially one and the same thing, and that a cubical foot, or a cubical yard, is not essentially different from an hour or a day." The sensations and ideas of extension " will give rise to the notion of length of duration as occurring in different points of duration, and of course as occurring in succession ; but, unless length of duration be the same thing with length of extension, they can evidently give us no manner of notion of this latter species of length at all."

He has a very elaborate inquiry into the associative principle, " a branch of our constitution still involved in considerable obscurity." As I believe him to be right in affirming that at this point there are many unsettled questions, and as his observations are original and independent, I will quote from him at considerable length. He shows that ideas suggest each other, not according to relation among their objects, but among the ideas themselves. He dwells on what he calls the law of precedence. " One idea acquires power to suggest another by immediately preceding it," using the word "power" in the sense in which it is commonly used in physical inquiries. It follows, (1.) " If one idea acquire power to suggest another by immediately preceding it, the greater the number of ideas that it immediately precedes, the greater the number it will acquire the power of suggesting." (2.) If one idea acquire power to suggest others by immediately preceding them, the more frequently it precedes, the greater power it must acquire to suggest them. He thus explains the circumstance that, when we meet with a person whom we have formerly seen only in one particular place, there is usually, to our recollection, a very distinct idea of that place ; but when we meet with a person whom we have seen in a great many different places, there is seldom recalled an idea of any of them. (3.) If an idea acquire power to suggest others by immediately preceding them, the greater the number of ideas that immediately precede any others, the greater will be their power when they recur to suggest these ideas. (4.) If an idea acquire power to suggest another by immediately preceding it, the more vivid the idea that precedes any other, the greater will be its power when it recurs in a state equally vivid to suggest it.

He says that the law of contiguity in point of time is really three laws, —

that "an idea will acquire power to suggest another by immediately preceding it, by existing at the same with it, and by immediately following it.
The first of these laws is that of precedence, and into it he resolves all the
others.   Thus he resolves the law of coexistence into precedence.   " Let
A and B be two ideas which coexist for two sensible points of time, then
A, while existing in the first point, precedes B while B is existing in the
second ; and B, while existing in the first point, precedes A while A is
existing in the second point."   Proceeding on the principle that the greater
the number of ideas that coexist with any other, the greater the number
afterwards suggested by it, he explains how the longer an idea continues in
the mind, the more readily will it afterwards recur ; how the more frequently
it has been in the mind, it will come up the more readily ; how the longer it
continues, it will be the more likely to recur ; and how the more frequently
it has been in the mind, it will be the more likely to continue.   He resolves
in the same way the law of contiguity in place, and the law of cause and
effect ; and affirms that the idea of cause has no power, independently of the
law of precedence, to suggest the idea of an effect.   He tries hard to explain
in the same way the law of similarity.   " Yesterday I saw a winged animal,
to-day a winged animal of the same species."   "When I yesterday saw
the first animal, I obtained ideas of its peculiar qualities, and likewise of
those common to it with all the individuals of the species to which it belonged.   To-day, when I saw the other animal, I also obtained ideas of its
peculiar properties, and of those common to it with all the species to which
it belonged, that is, along with the ideas of the peculiar properties of the
second animal, I obtained a number of ideas which coexisted with those of
the peculiar properties of the first.   According to the doctrine of coexistence, formerly explained, they would suggest ideas of the peculiar properties
of the first.   When they do so, I have ideas both of the common and of the
peculiar properties of the first animal ; in other words, I have an idea of
the first animal itself, for that idea can be nothing but the aggregate of the
ideas of its common and peculiar properties."   He explains the law of contrast by showing that, in every case where contrasted ideas suggest one
another, it will be found that there is a considerable degree of similarity
along with the contrast.   He accounts by the same law of precedence for the
secondary laws of Brown.   Some of these resolutions seem to me over
subtle, but they are worthy of consideration by those who would sound the
depths of the subject.

He treats at length of the voluntary principle, and offers many judicious
remarks.   He criticises Stewart's doctrine of power, according to which
" the author of nature has bestowed on matter no powers at all, of course
never preserves its powers in being, nor even employs them in accomplishing his purposes, as there are no powers to be exercised.   In the second
volume (Part II.), he treats of moral law, of right, jurisprudence, and politics,
somewhat after the manner of Stewart, with considerable sweep of style,
but no great power of metaphysical analysis.

HITHERTO there has been a severance, at times an opposition, if not avowed yet felt, between the Scottish philosophy and the Scottish theology. The one had magnified human nature, and tended to produce a legal, self-righteous spirit; whereas the other humbled man and exalted God, enjoining such graces as faith, humility, and penitence. But there never was any real opposition between the facts gathered by the one and the truths taken out of God's Word by the other. The metaphysicians had shown that there is such a faculty in man as the conscience; and the conscience proclaims that man is a sinner, while the Bible provides a forgiveness for the sinner in a way which honors the moral law. The reconciliation between the philosophy and the religion was effected by Thomas Chalmers, who has had greater influence in moulding the religious belief and character of his countrymen than any one since the greatest Scotchman, John Knox.

He was born at Anstruther, in the "East Neuk" of Fife, and was the son of a reputable merchant there. In his boyish days he had to suffer not a little from a nurse and from a teacher who ruled by the rod; but he was "joyous, vigorous, and humorous." He manifested his natural character from an early age, being eager and impetuous in pursuing his favorite ends. He was not a very diligent pupil, but was a leader in fun and frolic. At the age of twelve he entered the University of St. Andrews, which about that time had such pupils as John (afterwards Sir John) Leslie, James Mylne, and John (afterwards Chief Justice) Campbell. He is described as "enthusiastic and persevering in every thing he undertook, giving his whole mind to it, and often pursuing some favorite and even, as we thought, some foolish idea, whilst we were talking around him and perhaps laughing at his abstraction, or breaking in upon his cogitations and pronouncing him the next thing to mad;[2] and then he would good-naturedly join in the merriment with

[1] "Memoir of Thomas Chalmers," by William Hanna.

[2] In fact, "Daft Tam Chalmers" was a phrase applied to him by those who could not discern his greatness in the bud.

his common affectionate expression 'very well, my good lads.'"
It was in 1793 that he was awakened intellectually, and became
excited with and absorbed in geometry, for which he had a
strong taste and talent.

"St. Andrews," he tells us in after years, "was at this time
overrun with moderatism, under the chilling influence of which
we inhaled not a distaste only, but a positive contempt, for all
that is properly and peculiarly gospel ; insomuch that our confidence was nearly as entire in the sufficiency of natural theology as in the sufficiency of natural science." He has left it
on record that he profited by the debating societies of the college. At this time he studied Godwin's "Political Justice,"
and was staggered by Mirabaud's "System of Nature." His
friend, Professor Duncan, tells us that "he studied Edwards
on Free Will with such ardor that he seemed to regard nothing
else, could scarcely talk of any thing else, and one was almost
afraid of his mind losing its balance." His favorite study,
however, continued to be mathematics, towards which, as the
science of quantity, he had a strong predilection, as shown in
his propensity to count his steps as he walked. Still, even at
this time, he had aspirations after something higher. One
common expression in his college prayers was : "Oh! give us
some steady object for our mind to rest on." "I remember
when a student of divinity, and long ere I could relish evangelical sentiment, I spent nearly a twelvemonth in a sort of mental Elysium, and the one idea which ministered to my soul all
its rapture, was the magnificence of the godhead and the universal subordination of all things to the one great principle for
which he evolved and was supporting creation. I should like
to be impressed over again, but with such a view of the Deity
as coalesced and was in harmony with the doctrine of the New
Testament."

He was licensed to preach the gospel in 1799. His brother
writes : "We are at some pains in adjusting his dress, manner,
&c. ; but he does not seem to pay any great regard to himself."
Mathematical studies continue to engross his attention. He
spent a winter in Edinburgh, studied under Robison, for whom
he entertained a profound reverence, and Stewart, and devoted
himself to chemistry and moral philosophy. Of Stewart he
says : "I have obtained a much clearer idea than I ever had of

the distinctive character of Reid's philosophy. I think it tends to a useless multiplication of principles, and shrinks even from an appearance of simplicity." He was ordained minister at Kilmany, in his native county, in 1803. He still contrived to teach mathematics and chemistry in St. Andrews, — a divided work from which he would have shrunk in later years, when he attained a higher idea of the importance of the ministerial office. In 1806, Napoleon Bonaparte issued his famous Berlin decree, shutting continental ports to British goods. Chalmers had all along a predilection for political economy: he was convinced that Great Britain had resources which made it independent of any other country, and in 1807 he published "An Inquiry into the Extent and Stability of National Resources."

We are now approaching the crisis of his life. In 1818 he was required to write an article for the " Edinburgh Encyclopædia," at that time under the editorship of Dr. Brewster, on the " Evidences of Christianity ;" and he had to study the Christian religion and the proof which can be adduced in its favor more carefully and earnestly than he had ever done before. Meanwhile there occurred a number of deaths among his relatives, and he was deeply affected. He now felt himself called on to strive after a pure and heavenly morality. " March 17, 1810, — I have this day completed my thirtieth year ; and, upon a review of the last fifteen years of my life, I am obliged to acknowledge that at least two-thirds of that time have been uselessly or idly spent, sometimes to while away an evening in parish gossip or engaging in a game at cards." A change has evidently come over him : he did not yet open it fully, but he made allusions to it. "I find that principle and reflection afford a feeble support against the visitations of melancholy." He was subjected to a period of confinement, and was led to read Wilberforce's " Practical View." " The conviction was now wrought in him that he had been attempting an impossibility ; that he had been trying to compound elements which would not amalgamate ; that it must be either on his own merits wholly or on Christ's merits wholly he must lean." He now betook himself in earnest to the study of the Bible. A visible change appeared in him. He became more diligent in the visitation of his parish, and his sermons had a power over his people such as they never had before.

One so able, so earnest, must take an active part in the affairs of his country and of his age. He sets out with an excessive admiration of the parochial system of Scotland, not just as an end in itself, but as fitted to accomplish the ends which his great heart cherished. It seemed to him to provide every thing which the good and the elevation of a country required. It secured a school in every parish, and a minister to preach to and to visit every man and woman, and a body of assistant elders to watch over the morals of the community. It provided, too, for the wants of the poor by a voluntary relief which did not interfere with their spirit of independence. The whole system bulked in magnificent proportions before his splendid imagination. No doubt he saw that the church was not realizing this pattern : he knew that there were ministers around him who were not fulfilling these high ends. But then the church, by the exercise of the high prerogatives given it by Christ, could restrain the evils of patronage, and carry out thoroughly the original design of the Church of Scotland. He did not foresee the difficulties he would have to meet in carrying out his grand ideal, — difficulties arising from the State, which did not wish too zealous and too powerful a Church, and on the part of the people, who were jealous of too strong an ecclesiastical organization.

He was called to Glasgow in 1815, and there labored with all his might to put his idea in execution, first in the Tron Church and then in St. John's Church, — built expressly for him. He preached as no man in Glasgow had ever preached before. He visited from house to house, and thus became aware of, and hastened to proclaim to all men, the awfully degraded condition to which Glasgow, and, as was soon discovered by others, to which all the great cities in Scotland and England had been reduced. The world, as well it might, was startled and awed by the scene disclosed. The philosophers had made no inquiry into the subject, and had no remedy for the evil. The refined city ministers were satisfied with preaching well-composed sermons, moral or evangelical, to the better classes. The dissenters ministered zealously to their own select congregations, but were not able for the Herculean task of cleansing the impurity which had been accumulating for ages. But the evils must be remedied. So he set about erecting chapels, and

called on the paternal government to endow them. But he met
with opposition from statesmen not willing to tax the community for the benefit of one sect, and from dissenters who believed that their own method of spreading the gospel was the
better. The voluntary question was started, and he threw himself into the fight, and defended religious establishments on the
ground that man, being carnal, would not seek for spiritual
things, which could not, therefore, be left to the ordinary political principle of demand and supply, — thereby, as some of us
think, overlooking the power in the living converted members
of the church, who are more likely than the State to supply what
is wanted to the careless and the outcast. He certainly did
not estimate, as he ought to have done, the enmity of the
world toward the church, — an enmity which met him at every
point. But he persevered manfully, never losing sight of his
grand aim. His course may seem an inconsistent one to a
superficial observer ; but there was a unity given to it by
the end which he pursued as steadfastly as the sun moves in
the heavens above the winds and clouds of the earth. He must
have the glorious gospel of Jesus Christ preached to every creature, and he supported the Established Church as fitted to accomplish this end, at the same time holding resolutely by the
spiritual independence of the church as given it by Christ, and
as necessary to enable it to fulfil its grand ends. And when he
found that the church he so loved was interfered with in carrying out its designs, he went on bravely to the disruption of
1843, and amidst convulsions led on an exodus towards a land
which he saw before him, but into which he could scarcely be
said to enter. Ere he departed in 1847, he had by his wisdom
established a sustentation fund for the benefit of the ministers of religion, which he hoped would secure the stability and
other benefits of an established church without its temptations. He lived to see churches multiplied by means of the
secession far beyond his most sanguine expectations ; but he
did not live to see such a union among churches as is fitted to
secure the grand end which he kept ever before him, — the
spread of the gospel in all the destitute and depraved districts
of the land.

I regard Chalmers as the greatest preacher which Scotland
has produced. Those who have heard him can never forget

the impression he produced.   As he spoke, he stood firm upon
his legs, and looked with a broad, honest face on his audience.
At first there was a flabbiness, a sort of cheesiness, about his
look and a blankness in his expression ; but he uttered a clear,
broad, emphatic sentence, and gained the attention of his
hearers ; and as he advanced he was evidently interested himself and thoroughly interested the congregation ; and soon he
became absorbed as did all who listened to him ; and in the
end there was mind and heart manifested in every member and
in every action (often uncouth) of his body, and the people
were carried along to the close by a torrent which they could
not resist, and to which they enthusiastically yielded.   His
pronunciation was Scotch, — provincially Scotch. His style was
not pure, not classical, was scarcely English ; but it was his
own, as is Thomas Carlyle's.   It was clear, manly, broad, and
massive.   But when he spoke no one ever thought of his manner
or language : everybody was so carried along by his earnestness
and his matter.   He commonly began by a clear enunciation
of some philosophic or moral principle of great practical moment, and then proceeded to unfold and illustrate it.   He did
not turn aside himself and he did not distract his hearers by
the introduction of a variety of topics ; he keeps to his one
principle, but he presents it under a vast variety of aspects, all
contributing towards the one impression.   He is marching up
a hill, and he takes us with him ; he often lingers by the way
and gives us glorious retrospects of the ground we have trav-
ersed and glorious prospects of the heights to which he is to
conduct us, and he carries us at last to a lofty height with a
magnificent scene spread all around.   The result is that he has
gained our convictions : he has done more, we are ready, by
the impulse he has given, to execute what he proposes.   At the
close, as we feel that he has forgot himself, so we forget ourselves, and forget him as a speaker in an admiration of the
truth he has expounded or an eager desire to perform what he
has inculcated.   What he has said has become incorporated
with us, like food to strengthen us and go with us.   He
has planted a principle in the heads and hearts of his hearers
to continue there for ever, to send out roots downward and
stems and branches upward.   The consequence was, that, if he
was not the most intellectual or emotional speaker of his age,

he was the most practically influential, spreading his power over the length and breadth of Scotland.

Even in the most active operations, and the keenest controversies thereby excited, he retained his academic and philosophic tastes. He delivered in 1815–16 his "Astronomical Discourses," which drew on week-days the busiest Glasgow merchants from their offices and warerooms. In these discourses he obviates the prepossession apt to be created and fostered in intelligent and refined minds by the Scripture doctrine of the Son of God dying for man, and he does so by showing how great care God takes of the most minute objects and events. In most of his sermons he proceeds upon and unfolds some important philosophic principle. In his "Mercantile Discourses" he lays down the moral principles of business transactions, and shows how a rigid attention to them would restrain injurious speculation and promote a healthy trade. In those on "Human Depravity," he proves that there may be the deepest sinfulness in hearts which yet have many amiabilities. In his "Commentary on the Epistle to the Romans," he is not always able to enter into the thoughts of the apostle, or follow him in his subtle transitions ; but he powerfully defends the grand doctrines of revelation by showing that they are sustained by a profound philosophy. His doctrine, drawn from Scripture, is substantially that of the old Scotch divines from Knox downwards : but every one feels that it is pervaded by a new and fresh spirit ; it has less of a stern aspect ; it is tolerant ; it is catholic. The stream has descended from the stern rocks of the sixteenth, and is sweeping along amid the fertility of the nineteenth, century.

I never met any man who had so large a veneration for all that is great and good. It was primarily a veneration of God, and derivatively for all excellence. He had a profound reverence for royalty, for greatness, for rank and station ; was essentially a conservatist in politics ; and felt very keenly when by his unflinching adherence to principle he seemed to be separating the upper classes from the Church of Scotland. Without being a hero-worshipper, for he worshipped God only, he had a great admiration of intellectual greatness, at least when it was associated with humility. He never wearied to dilate on the greatness of Sir Isaac Newton, and often introduced him somewhat inappropriately. Jonathan Edwards he admired for his profound metaphysical ability and his consuming piety ; and he employed the arguments of that great man on behalf of philosophical necessity to support, what is a different thing, the Scripture doctrine of predestination. But the author from whom he derived most, and who again was indebted to him for eloquent expositions of his philosophy, was Bishop Butler. He was vastly impressed with his enlarged views and with his cautious, practical wisdom ; and learned from him the habit of connecting nature and revelation.

With such tastes and aims we can conceive that he would look with a favorable predilection towards the occupation of an academic position. So in 1823 he accepted the call to become professor of moral philosophy in the University of St. Andrews. Here he exercised a very great influence in attracting students, in exciting a prodigious enthusiasm among them, and in setting them forth with high purposes to noble works. He gained the position of highest influence when he was appointed in 1827 to the chair of theology in the University of Edinburgh. I am not sure that Scotland has ever had a higher instructor than Chalmers, in respect of all the qualities that go to constitute a successful teacher. He was always well prepared : he was as orderly as a mathematician could be ; even his very prayers were often written out. He was a very methodical examiner on his text-books and his lectures, having his very questions ready, but departing from his prepared queries when circumstances required. As a lecturer he did more than delight his audience : he entranced them. They gazed upon him ; and at times had difficulty in taking notes, they were so moved and elevated. He did not carry on his students very rapidly or over much ground ; but he made them thorough masters of the subject, and imparted an impulse which led them to enter fields of their own. He was particularly interesting and successful when he was expatiating in the border country which lies between theology and philosophy. His course of moral philosophy in St. Andrews, and that on natural theology in Edinburgh, were particularly relished by all students capable of appreciating high truth. He expatiated with great delight on the analogies between natural and revealed religion. His special lectures on the "Evidences of Christianity" were not so eminently successful, though they were very valuable. In his early and immature work on the " Evidences," he was particularly anxious to make the whole proof inductive, and missed some of those great principles of our moral nature, which, however, he afterwards expanded so fully and so effectively in the work as it took its later forms. The student feels that he is deficient in scholarship, and that he gives us metaphysics when he should have presented us with history. In his theology proper, it is evident that he is not specially an exegete. No one would reckon him a high authority in the exposition of a passage of Scripture. But he presents the great truths of the Bible in noble and attractive forms. His creed is essentially Calvinistic ; that is, he holds by the same views as Calvin drew out of the Scriptures ; but they appear with a more humane and benignant aspect, and with a more thorough conformity to the principles of man's nature.

In his philosophical works he unfolds and enforces a number of very important principles, not, it may be, absolutely original, but still fresh and independent in his statement and illustration of them, and setting aside error on the one side or other. His " Sketches of Moral and Mental Philosophy " cannot be said to be a full work on ethics, but it enforces great truths in a very impressive and eloquent way. He draws the distinction between mental and moral philosophy : the one has to do with *quid est*, and the other with *quid oportet*. He holds by the distinction between will and desire, maintaining that the former may be moral or immoral, whereas the latter is not. It seems to me that he has scarcely hit on the essential ethical distinction, which is not between will and desire, but between emotion and will ; the latter of which may embrace not only volition, but wishes ; in short, every thing optative, every thing in which is choice. He treats of the emotions, and shows that there is always a conception (the better expression is phantasm) involved in them. He dwells on the command which the will has over the emotions and of the morality of the emotions. Nothing is either virtuous or vicious unless the voluntary in some way intermingles with it ; but then the will has influence over a vast number of the operations of the mind. " It may be very true that the will has as little to do with that pathological law by which the sight of distress awakens in my

bosom an emotion of pity, as with that other pathological law
by which the sight of a red object impresses on my retina the
sensation peculiar to that color ; yet the will, though not the
proximate, may have been the remote, and so the real cause
both of the emotion and sensation notwithstanding. It may
have been at the bidding of my will that, instead of hiding myself from my own flesh, I visited a scene of wretchedness, and
entered within the confines, as it were, of the pathological influence, in virtue of which, after that the spectacle of suffering was seen, the compassion was unavoidable." He has
very just remarks, propounded with great eloquence, on the
final cause of the emotions.

His views on natural theology appeared first in the " Bridge-
water Treatise," on " The Adaptation of External Nature to
the Moral and Intellectual Constitution of Man." The feeling
of admiration excited was mingled with disappointment. The
bulk was too great for the matter, and the work had the appearance of a hasty recooking of his old thoughts which were
grand in themselves, but were not formed into a duly proportioned whole. His arguments and his illustrations have a much
better form given them in his subsequently published work, —
" Natural Theology." He begins with a discussion of the *à
priori* argument for the existence of God, and examines Samuel
Clarke's " Demonstration." He objects that Clarke would make
the test of a logical and mathematical truth to be also the test
of a physical necessity in the existent state of actual nature,
and that he confounds a logical with a physical impossibility. He turns to the *à posteriori* argument, but is obliged,
without his being aware of it, to call in an *à priori* principle.
" The doctrine of innate ideas in the mind is totally different
from the doctrine of innate tendencies in the mind, which tendencies may be undeveloped till the excitement of some occasion have manifested or brought them forth." He proceeds, as
every one must, in constructing the argument from design, on
the principle of cause and effect, but identifies that principle
with what is surely a different thing, — with the expectation of a
uniformity in the succession of events. At this point he draws
the distinction, which has been accepted by J. S. Mill, and has
ever since been identified with Chalmers's name, between the
laws of matter and the collocations of matter. It is from the

collocations of matter rather than the laws of matter that he draws his argument for the divine existence. The distinction seems to be deep in the constitution of things, but might be better represented, perhaps, as the distinction between the properties of matter and the dispositions of matter, these dispositions manifesting design, and consequently intelligence.

He is most successful when he is arguing from the constitution of the human mind. He dwells with great fondness and force on the supremacy of conscience and the inherent pleasure of virtuous and the misery of vicious affections, and gives a powerful exposition of the law of habit. He has a clear, masterly, and eloquent exposition of Leibnitz's theory of the origin of evil, not positively adopting it, but using it as an hypothesis to obviate objections. Here and elsewhere he unfolds a very favorite principle, that hypotheses may be advanced in theology to answer objections even when they do not establish positive truth. The logical meaning of this principle is, that the hypothesis sets aside the unlimited major premise necessary to establish the infidel objection. He seeks to answer the objection to prayer drawn from the uniformity and fixed character of the laws of nature by showing that we can trace the agencies of nature only a little way back, and that interferences may take place in that outer region which lies beyond the ken of man. It may be replied that, by just inference, we can trace the agencies far beyond the immediate inspection of man, and that we find them everywhere uniform. It might be wiser in these circumstances to trace up both the prayer and its answer to the pre-established harmony of things appointed by God. He closes his work by showing that natural theology is as useful in exhibiting man's needs, and thus preparing him to receive the remedial complement supplied by the Bible, as even in the positive truths which it has established.

We have seen in the cases of Stewart, Brown, and Mackintosh what difficulties those trained in the Scottish metaphysics had in comprehending the German philosophy and accepting the truth. Hamilton, we shall find, labored to combine the two. Chalmers, meanwhile, was engrossed with philanthropic work; he did not understand the German language, and it was not till the last year of his life, when he got a little lull in 1847 after the disruption storm, that he became acquainted with the

German philosophy, to which he was introduced by Mr. J. D. Morell's well-written and interesting work, " An Historical and Critical View of the Speculative Philosophy of Europe in the Nineteenth Century." He entered on the study with a youthful enthusiasm, and reviewed the work in the " North British Review." " It is long since any work has made its appearance before a public in a state of greater expectancy and readiness for its lessons." With a mind of singular openness and candor, he is ready to receive whatever truth Kant and the Germans may offer. He confesses his gratification on finding, "amid all these conflicting systems and speculations, that our theology is safe." He rejoices to find profound points of agreement between Reid and Kant, and is willing to take the truth in either form. " Now, for comparing the Scottish and German philosophies, whether as it respects their similarities or their differences, it is of importance to mark how these primary beliefs of Dr. Reid are at one with the primitive judgments of Kant, or with his forms of the understanding. They may have been the better named by the latter of these two philosophers ; he may have probed more deeply into their foundations, or, rather, perhaps, into their method of development ; he may have constructed a fuller and more accurate list of them, and, without pronouncing on his scheme for their application, or by which he would bring his categories to bear on the objects of the external world, it might be fully conceded that, altogether, he has enlarged and in some respects amended the philosophy of Dr. Reid. Yet let us not, because of the altered nomenclature, or of the new garb that has been thrown over them, overlook the substantial identity, and that, in respect of almost all, between the principles of the Scottish school and those from which Kant has earned his chief reputation." It is clear that he was not sufficiently far advanced in his knowledge of Kant and of the German philosophy to discover that there was a subtle scepticism in the philosophy which made the forms of the reason merely subjective ; whereas Reid gave them an objective validity, an external validity when they related to external objects.

With great shrewdness he seizes on an incipient error, which has since grown into a formidable error. " We demur to the proposed substitution of Mr. Morell for Dr. Reid's account of perception, that it is altogether an act of the mind. He affirms that the very essence of perception consists in the felt relation between mind and matter. And what we affirm is, that matter might be perceived, and, with the strongest sense and conviction in the mind of its reality, when the mind itself is altogether out of the reckoning." " It is not more necessary to be conscious of the mind in the business of perceiving than to be conscious of the eye in the business of seeing." " We can perceive without thinking of the mind, as we can perceive without thinking of the eye ; " and he complains of the " undue mixing up of the subjective with the objective, in which chiefly it is that the erratic movements of the German philosophy have taken rise." He here opposes at the entrance that doctrine of relativity which was developed by Hamilton, and has been applied by Herbert Spencer.

He also makes good use of the distinction, as drawn by M. Cousin, between the spontaneous and the reflex exercises of the human understanding. " We have long been in the habit of recognizing these under the title of the mind's direct and reflex processes, and we shall continue so to name them." " Though it be only by looking inwardly or looking back upon ourselves that we take cognizance of our various beliefs, these beliefs must be formed so as to exist ere they can be recognized, or reflected on." So he blames Mr. Morell for constantly " mixing up consciousness and the facts of consciousness," and M. Cousin for finding the ground of our belief in an external world in a subjective act. " He looks for it, and imagines that he has got his first hold of it among the reflections of the psychological tablet within, whereas, if it is to be had at all, spontaneous as it is, it will be the primary act of looking direct on that radiance that cometh from the object of contemplation without." In following this train of thought he comes near to, and yet does not reach, a distinction on which I set great value, — the distinction between our primitive apperceptions or intuitions as they spontaneously act and as they are generalized into maxims, axioms, or fundamental truths by the metaphysician. Considered under the first aspect, they act whether we observe them or no, and act best when, like the physiological processes of breathing, they are not noticed, and they cannot in any circumstances be supposed to err ; whereas under the other aspect they are the result of a discursive process of abstraction and generalization, in which there may be much error, by our adding to, or taking from, or mutilating the spontaneous process in the reflex account given of it by those who would put what is concrete and individual into a universal form.

This was one of the last compositions of Thomas Chalmers, who was found dead in his bed on the morning of May 31, 1847. His soul was transparently ready for the new truth to be disclosed to him in heaven, where what he saw as through a glass darkly on earth, appeared to him face to face.

LIV. — *JOHN ABERCROMBIE.*

Can mental science be made popular and practical? It is certainly desirable that it should become so. It is of moment that the great body of educated men and women, in knowing something of history and physics, should also be acquainted with the laws of their own mind, and this though they have no predilection for the abstruse discussions of metaphysics. We have admirable compends of physical science made comprehensible to the common understanding. If we are to preserve the intelligent mind of the country from falling under the influence of the advancing materialism, we should have like expositions of mental and moral investigation for the use of upper schools, male and female, and the reading population who have not the advantage of a collegiate education. We have such works in Abercrombie's "Intellectual Powers" (1830) and his "Philosophy of the Moral Feelings" (1833). He proceeds throughout on the method of Reid, and his treatises summarize some of the best results of the philosophy of Scotland. They are also valuable for the admirably reported cases illustrative of the influence of mind on body and body on mind. Nor is it to be omitted that there runs through all his works a vein of evangelical piety, decisive and outspoken without being offensive.

He was the son of a minister of the Church of Scotland, and was born at Aberdeen in 1780. He studied medicine in the University of Edinburgh, and became, after the death of Dr. Gregory, the most eminent Scotch physician of his time, being distinguished for his great skill and judgment. He wrote a number of medical works, treating of the brain, spinal cord, and of disease. He died in 1844.

In his "Intellectual Powers," he begins with stating what he regards as the object of science: it is to observe facts and trace their relations. He here treats of cause and effect, which he confounds with the uniformity of nature. He makes our belief in it an original instinct, but awkwardly brings observation and inference as involved in it. He distinguishes, in the manner of Reid and Stewart, between physical and efficient cause, regarding the former as the only object of philosophic inquiry. He opposes materialism, but not very effectively. He then treats of the faculties of the mind arranging them : sensation and perception, consciousness and reflection, memory, abstraction, imagination, reason or judgment. Under the last he treats of first truths. But by far the most interesting and useful parts of his works are those in which he treats of the practical application of metaphysical subjects, as, for instance, of the laws of investigation, of fallacies, attention. He is in his own field when he is illustrating dreaming, somnambulism spectral illusions, and insanity. He makes a most useful application of the whole to the study of medicine. His statement of cases may always be depended on for its accuracy. I may give a few examples. He says of Dr. Leyden that he could repeat correctly a long act of parliament, or any similar document, after having once read it. When he was on one occasion congratulated by a friend on his remarkable power in this respect, he replied that, instead of an advantage, it was often a source of great inconvenience. This he explained by saying that when he wished to recollect a particular point in any thing which he had read, he could do it only by repeating to himself the whole from the commencement till he reached the point which he wished to recall. Again, "a distinguished theatrical performer, in consequence of the sudden illness of another actor, had occasion to prepare himself in a few hours' notice for a part which was entirely new to him, and the part was long and rather difficult. He acquired it in a very short time, and went through it with perfect accuracy, but immediately after the performance forgot it to such a degree that, though he performed the character for several days in succession, he was obliged every day to study it anew. Characters which he had acquired in a more deliberate manner he never forgets, but can perform them at any time without a moment's preparation. When questioned respecting the mental process which he employed the first time he performed this part, he says that he lost sight entirely of the audience, and seemed to have nothing before him but the pages of the book from which he had learned, and that if any thing had occurred to stop this illusion, he should have stopped instantly." I may give another instance. "A lady, in the last stage of chronic disease, was carried from London to a lodging in the country ; there her infant daughter was taken to visit her, and, after a short interview, carried back to town. The lady died a few days after, and the daughter grew up without any recollection of her till she was of mature age. At this time she happened to be taken into the room in which her mother died without knowing it to have been so. She started on entering it, and, when a friend who was along with her asked the cause of her agitation, replied : ' I have a distinct impression of having been in this room before, and that a lady who lay in that room, and seemed very ill, leaned over me and wept.' "

The work on the " Moral Feelings " does not seem to me so valuable, and this because he cannot, in treating of such a subject, have so many of those cases which he as a medical man had so carefully noted. But it is characterized by a fine spirit, and it has a useful tendency. He has some important remarks on the " Analogy between first Truths or Intuitive Principles of Belief in Intellectual and Moral Science." " In applying to these important articles of belief the name of first truths or primary principles of moral conviction, I do not mean to ascribe to them any thing of the nature of innate ideas. I mean only that they come with a rapid or instantaneous conviction, entirely distinct from what we call a process of reasoning in every well-regulated mind, when it is directed by the most simple course of reflection to the phenomena of nature without and to the moral feelings of which it is conscious within." In his analysis of man as a moral being, he includes : 1. The desires, the affections, and self-love ; 2. The will : 3. Moral principle or conscience ; 4. The moral relation of man towards the Deity. The discussion of these subjects is not very deep or original, but it is commonly correct and always useful.

----◆----

LV. — *DAVID WELSH.* [1]

At the time we have now reached there was a strong reaction against moderatism and rationalism, and a tendency to return to the simple faith of the Bible ; and a reconciliation of Scotch philosophy and evangelism was openly proclaimed. Ministers from the pulpit, and theologians in the divinity halls, were employing the principles of the mind and of morality to support the peculiar truths of Christianity. If there be a moral law, it points to a law-giver. If that law be immutable and unbending, it shows that man is a sinner ; it points to the need of an atonement, and requires such evangelical graces as humility, faith, and repentance. We have a fine exemplification of this union of philosophy and evangelism in Dr. David Welsh.

He belonged to a " God-fearing " family residing in that somewhat bare but romantic sheep country in which the rivers Clyde, Tweed, and Annan rise. He was born Dec. 11, 1793, was educated first by a private tutor, next at the parish school of Moffat, then at the high school of Edinburgh, and thence went to the university. There he fell, in 1808–9, under the attractive influence of Dr. Brown, " who admitted him to much and intimate intercourse, directed him in his private studies, discussed with him the subjects of his reading, and aided in cultivating his taste for polite literature." When in the university he devoted himself carefully to composition, and afterwards recommended the habit to his pupils. " I cannot conceive it possible for a young man to think very closely or profoundly upon any subject if he does not commit his thoughts to paper. A confused idea, a kind of half comprehension, a partial glimpse of any subject, will satisfy every person — I mean every young person — who has not to make an immediate use of his information upon that subject. But if you have to write upon the subject, an indefinite conception will not suffice : the current of your thoughts is arrested ; you are compelled calmly and deliberately to revolve and to consider, and the consequence necessarily must be that you arrive at clear and comprehensive views."

1 " Memoir of Dr. Welsh," by Alexander Dunlop, Esq., prefixed to his Sermons.

He was licensed to preach in 1816, but in these days of patronage did not get a church till 1821, when he was settled in Crossmichael, a peaceful country parish among the hills of Galloway.   There he was a much beloved and respected pastor for six years, and there he wrote his life of Dr. Brown.   In 1827 he became minister of St. David's, Glasgow, and was soon very influential as a preacher.   "His delivery wanted some of those outward graces which often gloss over defect in matter.   He was far from fluent; and indeed he preached apparently with effort.   In conse- quence of the weakness of his chest, there was often a straining in the getting out his words, which was at times painful to the listener; though it added to, rather than detracted from, the earnestness with which his dis- courses were delivered."   He gathered a large congregation of thoughtful people, including not a few students of Glasgow University, who were de- lighted with his clear, chaste language, his fine reflection, and his warm piety.   He was a noble example of a philosopher, teaching, not philosophy, but the doctrines of the cross, always in a philosophic manner and spirit. In 1831 he was elected professor of church history in the university of Edinburgh, where he was a conscientious, careful teacher, and a discerner and patron of young men of promise.   He did not take a very prominent part in church politics, but was a consistent opponent of church patronage, and a firm supporter of popular rights and the spiritual independence of the church.   He was moderator of the general assembly of the Church of Scot- land in 1842, which passed a solemn "claim, declaration, and protest against the encroachment of the civil courts."   In 1843 he had to preach at the opening of the assembly. and took as his text, "Let every one be fully persuaded in his own mind;" and delivered a sermon, through which there runs a vein of fine philosophy.   After reading the protest he headed the imposing procession of ministers, who marched through the streets of Edin- burgh to the Canonmills Hall.   In the Free Church of Scotland he especially interested himself in the cause of education.   He died April 24, 1845.

In his life of Brown we have a very interesting account of the man, and an able abstract of his philosophy.   He gives a full and fair statement of the favorite tenets of Brown, and defends them from objections which have been taken to them.   He dwells with fondness on the additions which Brown is regarded as making to philosophy by his theory of causation, by his analysis of the faculties, by his account of suggestion simple and rela- tive, and specially of generalization.   As might be expected of one who had felt the fascination and enjoyed the eloquence of his master, he over-esti- mates his merits.   "In the philosophic love of truth, and in the patient investigation of it, Dr. Brown may be pronounced as at least equal, and in subtlety of intellect and powers of analysis as superior, to any metaphysician that ever existed.   Or if there ever was any philosopher who might dispute with him the palm for any one of these qualities, of this at least I am cer- tain, — that no one ever combined them all in equal perfection."

It was hoped by many that Dr. Welsh would write a philosophic work of his own.   But he became "fully convinced of the substantial truth of the doctrines originally published by Dr. Gall."   He is careful to explain: "The cerebral organs are not the mind, nor is any state of these organs the mind.

The mind we believe to be a simple and indivisible substance." In a sketchy article in an early number of the " North British Review," of which he was editor at the time, he showed that he was able to grapple with the deeper problems of the day. We see in all his sermons and papers an underlying philosophy gendered by the study of the Scottish school. But his energy was directed to preaching, to lecturing on church history, and to philanthropic objects.

———◆———

LVI. — *JOHN WILSON.*[1]

At the end of last century, Paisley had a considerable body of high-class citizens who made money and benefited their town by turning cotton into gauze and other useful products. John Wilson was the son of one of these, and was born in 1785 in by no means a poetical spot in a dingy court at the head of the High Street. We can believe that the boy was "as beautiful and animated a creature as ever played in the sunshine." He received his education first in his native town, and then at the manse of Mearns, — a bare, wild upland district. fitted to call forth a sense of freedom, but with nothing grand or romantic in its scenery. On the death of his father he entered as a student in Glasgow University, and continued there till 1803. In future years he acknowledged in " Blackwood " his obligations to Jardine as "a person who, by the singular felicity of his tact in watching youthful minds, had done more good to a whole host of individuals, and gifted individuals too. than their utmost gratitude could ultimately repay. They spoke of him as a kind, intellectual father, to whom they were proud of acknowledging the eternal obligations of their intellectual being." He indulged freely in dinners, balls, and parties ; but Glasgow College made its students work, and Wilson was an ardent student. He began to keep a diary, and we have an entry : " Prize for the best specimens of the Socratic mode of reasoning given out in the logic." " Got the first prize in the logic class." Prizes have always been numerous. often not very discriminating in their subjects, in Glasgow College, and he records : " Prizes distributed ; got three of them." .

In all his youthful days he luxuriated in fishing and field sports, and nobody could match him at " hop, step, and jump." At an early age. when the " Edinburgh Review " was ridiculing Wordsworth. Wilson was seized with an admiration of him, and wrote him : " In all your poems you have adhered to natural feelings, and described what comes within the range of every one's observation. It is from following this plan that, in my estimation, you have surpassed every poet both of ancient and modern times." Yet he ventures to hint a fault. " No feeling, no state of mind, ought, in my mind, to become the subject of poetry that does not please."

[1] "Christopher North. A Memoir of John Wilson, by his daughter, Mrs. Gordon."

In 1803 he entered, as a gentleman commoner, Magdalen College, Oxford, and participated ardently both in the high studies and in the boating and physical sports. Here he began a common-place book, which was doubtless of great use to him : " In the following pages I propose to make such remarks upon the various subjects of polite literature as have been suggested to my mind during the course of my studies by the perusal of writers on the different branches of human knowledge : reflections upon law, history, philosophy, theology, and poetry, will be classed under separate heads." " With regard to the department of poetry, original verses of my own composition will be frequently introduced." " Should any reflections upon men and authors occur in my mind, even with regard to the general characters of mankind, or the particular dispositions of acquaintances and friends, they shall be written down as they occur, without any embellishment. In short, this common-place book, or whatever else it may be called, will contain, so far as it goes, a faithful representation of the state of my mind, both in its moments of study and retirement."

At the close of his Oxford life he passed, in 1806, a brilliant examination. " Sotheby was there, and declared it was worth while coming from London to hear him translate a Greek chorus." On leaving college, having, as he believed, an independent fortune, he betook himself to the Lake country of England, and purchased Elleray, within nine miles of Wordsworth, and henceforth may be regarded as one of the Lake poets. He now divided his activities between poetry and rural sports, and "had a small fleet on Windermere." By 1810 he had written as many poems " as will make a volume of 400 pages," of which the principal was " The Isle of Palms," descriptive of sea and island scenery, with a love story. In 1811 he was married to Miss Penny. A few years later he lost suddenly the fortune which his father had laid up for him so industriously. He bore the trial manfully, but had to remove to Edinburgh to the home of his mother, and he became an advocate. He did not acquire a large practice at the bar, and had time to write novels and poems, which were noticed favorably in the " Edinburgh Review."

Jeffrey asked him to write for the " Edinburgh," and he furnished an article on Byron. But Wilson was destined to occupy a place of his own. " Blackwood's Magazine " was started in 1817 by others, but did not become a power till it came under the control of Wilson. He was never formal editor. Blackwood retained the management in his own hand : and, knowing that literary men were commonly both needy and dilatory, he kept them to punctuality by not remunerating them till they produced the articles, and then paying them handsomely. But the winds and the sails were given to the vessel by Wilson, and " Blackwood " immediately became the best literary magazine of its day.

So that city of Edinburgh is still maintaining its high literary reputation. In Jeffrey they have a representative of the talent, and in Scott, with Wilson in an inferior degree, representatives of the genius of their country. The " blue and yellow " is the organ of the one and old " ebony " of the other. The one favors taste and judgment : the other originality and literary beauty. The one is seeking to improve things, has no great reverence for the wisdom of the ancients, looks forward to the future, and is considerably cool and indifferent towards religion : the other likes things as they are, has a profound reverence for old customs and feudal castles, and speaks highly of the forms of religion as established by law and custom.

"Blackwood's Magazine" is the great work of Wilson. His tales are full of sentiment too ; much in the manner of Mackenzie, — so much so as to be at times cloying as treacle. He professes to describe the trials and sorrows of the poor ; but it is clear that he paints them as one who, with a warm heart, has viewed them at a distance, and who has never truly become one of them. His poor are certainly not the Scotch poor, with their deep feeling, which oppresses them all the more that it cannot get an outlet except in brief and restrained phrases, showing that they are repressing what should be allowed to flow out. His poetry is certainly beautiful in imagery and expression, but has too redundant foliage in proportion to the stem and branches which support it, and often wants a healthy air and a manly bearing. But the whole soul of Wilson comes out in the "Noctes Ambrosianæ." We have here an extravaganza full of all excellencies and defects, of fun and frolic, wit and humor, fancies and imaginations, shrewd wisdom and ingenious nonsense, of offensively personal comment and genuine pathos, of drinking, swearing, morality, and religion, — which, however, always smells of the whiskey punch of the tavern. The whole is a sort of rhapsody which reads like an inspiration, but breathing more of the soil of earth than the air of heaven. It is a waste newly turned up, and yielding an exuberance of seeds and trees, flowers and fruit ; but with weeds and chills and fevers.

In 1820, when Brown died, there was a keen struggle for the chair of moral philosophy. Sir James Mackintosh might have had it, but could not resist the temptations of politics and London society. The contest lay between Wilson and Sir William Hamilton known already as a scholar, but not as an author. The town council was unreformed : the tories had the political power of the city ; they were annoyed by the attacks of Jeffrey and jealous of the growing liberal spirit fostered by the philosophical professors of the University. So Wilson was started and warmly supported by the government. Scott, the literary genius of Edinburgh, threw himself thoroughly into the canvass for Wilson, who received the appointment. Every one felt that Scottish metaphysics had suffered a reverse : but some rejoiced at this, as feeling that the Scottish colleges were too exclusively metaphysical, and introduced students to philosophy at too early an age, and they expected Wilson to give an impulse to literary culture.

We have a record in the "Memoir" of the attempts of the literary man and the poet to produce a course of lectures on philosophy. He would commence with some attractive and eloquent introductory lectures of a "popular though philosophical character, so as to make a good impression at first on his students and also on the public," and so he proposes to give eight or ten lectures on the moral systems of ancient Greece. Then he is to have six or more lectures on the physical nature of man. And now the difficulties meet him. Must he tread in the steps of Reid and Stewart,

" which to avoid would be of great importance " ? " Surely," he says, " we may contrive to write with more spirit and effect than either of them : with less formality, less caution ; for Stewart seems terrified to place one foot before another."   Then he would branch forth on taste and genius, which he was glad to find had been treated of by the Scotch moralists.   Then comes the moral nature, the affections, and conscience, or whatever name that faculty may be called ; and he anticipates that the passions and affections will furnish fine ground for description.   Then there is the will and all its problems ; " but here I am also in the dark."   One more lecture on man's spiritual nature will make fifty-eight in all.   " I would fain hope that something different from the common metaphysical lectures will produce itself out of this plan."   Then he would treat of duties to God and man ; of virtues and vices, — in all, 108 lectures.   Such was his projected plan. In later years he modified it, giving more time to the moral faculty, on which he did not throw any light.

He was never very systematic in his course.   He enlarged on subjects suited to him, and was always poetical, often eloquent.   The writer of this article remembers the impression left as he passed one day into his class-room.   The students received him with applause. — I believe they always did so ; and he advanced in a rapid, genial manner, fresh as if he had just come from the Highlands or Lake country.   He produced a roll of papers, some of them apparently backs of letters.   I could not discover where he was in his course, but I soon found myself carried along pleasantly but irresistibly by a glowing description of faith, of its swaying and elevating influence.   On another occasion I found him enlarging on the place which association has in forming our imaginations.   I am not able to give his theory, but it seemed to me at the time fresh and original.   His pupils felt that it was a stimulating thing to be under such a man.   " One indubitable advantage," says Mr. Hill Burton, " was possessed by all Professor Wilson's students who had ' eyes to see and ears to hear,' viz., the advantage of beholding closely the workings of a great and generous mind swayed by the noblest and sincerest impulses, and of listening to the eloquent utterances of a voice which, reprobating every form of meanness and duplicity, was ever raised to its loftiest pitch in recommendation of high-souled honor, truth, virtue, disinterested love, and melting charity." Another pupil, Mr. A. Taylor Innes, describes him : " His appearance in his class-room it is far easier to remember than forget.   He strode into it with the professor's gown hanging loosely on his arms, took a comprehensive look over the mob of young faces, laid down his watch so as to be out of the reach of his sledge-hammer fist, glanced at the notes of his lecture (generally written on the most wonderful scraps of paper), and then, to the bewilderment of those who had never heard him before, looked long and earnestly out of the north window towards the spire of the old Town Kirk, until, having at last got his idea, he faced round and uttered it with eye and hand and voice and soul and spirit, and bore the class along with him.   As he spoke, the bright blue eye looked with a strange gaze into vacancy, sometimes sparkling with a coming joke, sometimes darkening before a rush of indignant eloquence, the tremulous upper lip curving with every wave of thought or hint or passion, and the golden-gray hair floating on the old man's shoulders." He had no philosophy himself, and so could not impart it to his pupils. But at times he made a profound remark, as when, in the "Noctes," he says: "Honesty is the best policy, but it is only the honest man who will discover this." Hamilton, who was ardently attached to the man praises his metaphysical acuteness as shown in a review of Brown's theory of cause and effect in "Blackwood" for 1837.

But his true merit consisted in creating a literary taste among his students. He was not a very rigid examiner or exacter of essays, and idle students passed through his class without much severe study. But he read conscientiously the papers given in to him, and was a discerning critic, particularly appreciative of excellence. The more ambitious youths cherished secretly or avowedly the idea that they might be asked by him to write a communication to dear old North for "Blackwood;" but Wilson had to consult the tastes of his readers, and their hopes had often to be disappointed.

Thus did he pass his rather lengthened life, ever looking after the magazine with which he identified himself, lecturing all winter to his students, taking excursions in the summer, and very often dining in company in the evening where the wine and the wit flowed freely, and where he was always the favorite. In 1850 his health began to break down. He retained his universal sympathy all along. His ruling passion was strong in death. "It was an affecting sight to see him busy, nay quite absorbed, with the fishing tackle scattered about his bed where he lay propped up with pillows." "How neatly he picked out each elegantly dressed fly from its little bunch, drawing it out with trembling hand along the white coverlet, and then replacing it in his pocket-book; he would tell ever and anon of the streams he used to fish in of old." The prospect of death produced more solemn feelings, and he betook himself to the Bible, "for is not all human nature and all human life shadowed forth in these pages?" The tender and anxious question which he asked concerning Robert Burns, "Did he read his Bible?" may, perhaps, by some be asked about himself. On a little table near his bedside his Bible lay during his whole illness, and was read morning and evening regularly. His servant also read it frequently to him. Thus departed John Wilson, April 2, 1853.

HE is the most learned of all the Scottish metaphysicians. Not that the Scottish school ought to be described, as it has sometimes been, as ignorant. Hutcheson was a man of learning, as well as of accomplishment, and visibly experienced great delight in quoting the Greek and Roman philosophers, as he walked up and down in his class-room in Glasgow. Adam Smith had vast stores of information ; and the ground-plan which he has left of departments of ancient philosophy, and the sketch of the sects which he has given in his "Moral Sentiments," show that he was more competent, had he devoted his attention to the subject, than any man of his age to write a history of philoso phy. Hume had extensive philosophic, as well as historical, knowledge ; but he was so accustomed to twist it to perverse uses, that we cannot trust his candor or accuracy. Reid was pre-eminently a well-informed man. His first printed paper was on quantity. He taught in Aberdeen College, according to the system of rotation which continued even to his day, natural as well as moral philosophy ; and continued, even in his old age, to be well read on all topics of general interest. Beattie and Campbell were respectable scholars, as well as elegant writers ; and the former was reckoned at Oxford, and by the English clergy, as the great expounder, in his day, of sound philosophy. Lord Monboddo was deeply versed in the Greek and Roman philosophies, and in spite of all his paradoxes has often given excellent accounts of their systems. Dugald Stewart was a mathematician as well as a metaphysician ; and, if not of very varied, was of very correct, and, altogether, of very competent, ripe, and trustworthy scholarship. Brown was certainly not widely or extensively read in philosophy ; but, besides a knowledge of medicine, he had an acquaintance with Roman and with modern French literature. Sir James Mackintosh was familiar with men and manners, was learned in all social questions,

[1] Article by Thomas Spencer Baynes in "Edinburgh Essays" by members of the University of Edinburgh ; "Memoir of Sir William Hamilton" by John Veitch.

and had a general, though certainly not a very minute or correct, knowledge of philosophic systems. But, for scholarship,
in the technical sense of the term, and, in particular, for the
scholarship of philosophy, they were all inferior to Hamilton, who
was equal to any of them in the knowledge of Greek and Roman
systems, and of the earlier philosophies of modern Europe ; and
vastly above them in a comprehensive acquaintance with all
schools ; and standing alone in his knowledge of the more philosophic fathers, such as Tertullian and Augustine ; of the more
illustrious schoolmen, such as Thomas Aquinas and Scotus ; of
the writers of the Revival, such as the elder Scaliger ; and of
the ponderous systems of Kant, and the schools which ramified
from him in Germany.

When he was alive, he could always be pointed to as redeem-
ing Scotland from the reproach of being without high scholarship. Oxford had no man to put on the same level. Germany
had not a profounder scholar, or one whose judgment in a disputed point could be so relied on. Nor was his the scholarship
of mere words : he knew the history of terms, but it was because
he was familiar with the history of opinions. In reading his
account, for example, of the different meanings which the word
" idea" has had, and of the views taken of sense-perception, one
feels that his learning is quite equalled by his power of discrimination. No man has ever done more in clearing the literature
of philosophy of common-place mistakes, of thefts and impost-
ures. He has shown all of us how dangerous it is to quote
without consulting the original, or to adopt, without examination,
the common traditions in philosophy ; that those who borrow at
second hand will be found out ; and that those who steal, without acknowledgment, will, sooner or later, be detected and
exposed. He experiences a delight in stripping modern authors
of their borrowed feathers, and of pursuing stolen goods from
one literary thief to another, and giving them back to their
original owner. For years to come, ordinary authors will seem
learned by drawing from his stores. In incidental discussions,
in foot-notes, and notes on foot-notes, he has scattered nuts
which it will take many a scholar many a day to gather and to
crack. It will be long before the rays which shine from him
will be so scattered and diffused through philosophic literature —
as the sunbeams are through the atmosphere — that they shall

become common property, and men shall cease to distinguish the focus from which they have come.

The only other decided lineament of his character that I shall mention is his logical power, including therein all such exercises as abstraction, generalization, division, definition, formal judgment, and deduction. In this respect he may be placed alongside of those who have been most distinguished for this faculty ; such as, Aristotle, Saint Thomas, Descartes, Spinoza, Samuel Clarke, Kant, and Hegel. In directing his thoughts to a subject, he proceeds to divide, distribute, define, and arrange, very much in the manner of Aristotle : take, as an example, his masterly analysis of the primary qualities of matter. He pursues much the same method, in giving the history of opinions, as on the subjects of the principles of common sense and perception. No man ever displayed such admirable examples of Porphyry's tree, reaching from the *summum genus* to the *infima species*. It is quite clear that, had he lived in the days of the schoolmen, he would have ranked with the greatest of them, — with Albertus Magnus, Thomas Aquinas, Duns Scotus, and Abelard, — and would have been handed down to future generations by such an epithet as Doctor Criticus, Doctor Doctissimus, or Doctor Indomitabilis.

Here, however, his strength is his weakness. He attempts far too much by logical differentiation and formalization. No man purposes now to proceed in physical investigation by logical dissection, as was done by Aristotle and the schoolmen. I have at times looked into the old compends of physical science which were used in the colleges down even to an age after the time of Newton. Ingenious they were beyond measure, and perfect in form far beyond what Herschel or Faraday have attempted. I am convinced that logical operations can do nearly as little in the mental as they have done in the material sciences. I admit that Sir William Hamilton had deeply observed the operations of the mind, and that his lectures contribute more largely to psychology than any work published in his day. But his induction is too much subordinated to logical arrangement and critical rules. His system will be found, when fully unfolded, to have a completeness such as Reid and Stewart did not pretend to, but it is effected by a logical analysis and synthesis, and much that he has built up will require to be taken down.

We may compare him with the Scotch metaphysician who had the greatest reputation when Hamilton determined to claim a place for himself. Brown and Hamilton are alike in the fame which they attained, in the influence which they exercised over young and ardent spirits, in the interest which they excited in the study of the human mind, and in their success in upholding the reputation of the Scottish colleges for metaphysical pursuits: each had an ambition to be independent, to appear original and establish a system of his own; both were possessed of large powers of ingenuity and acuteness, and delighted to reduce the compound into elements; and each, we may add, had a considerable acquaintance with the physiology of the senses: but in nearly all other respects they widely diverge, and their points of contrast are more marked than their points of correspondence. They differed even in their natural disposition. The one was amiable, gentle, somewhat effeminate, and sensitive, and not much addicted to criticism; the other, as became the descendant of a covenanting hero, was manly, intrepid, resolute, — at times passionate, — and abounding in critical strictures, even on those whom he most admires. As to their manner of expounding their views, there could not be a stronger contrast. Both have their attractions; but the one pleases by the changing hues of his fancy and the glow of his sentiment, whereas the other stimulates our intellectual activity by the sharpness of his discussions, and the variety and aptness of his erudition. The one abounds in illustrations, and excites himself into eloquence and his readers into enthusiasm: the other is brief and curt; seldom giving us a concrete example; restraining all emotion, except it be passion at times; never deigning to warm the students by a flash of rhetoric; and presenting only the naked truth, that it may allure by its own charms. If we lose the meaning of the one, it is in a blaze of light, in a cloud of words, or in repeated repetitions: the quickest thinkers are not always sure that they understand the other, because of the brevity of his style, and the compression of his matter; and his admirers are found poring over his notes, as the ancients did over the responses of their oracles. The one helps us up the hill, by many a winding in his path, and allows us many a retrospect, when we might become weary, and where the view is most expanded; whereas the other conducts us straight up the steep ascent, and, though he knows all the paths by which others have mounted, he ever holds directly on ; and if there be not a path made for him, he will clear one for himself.   Both were eminently successful lecturers : but the one called forth an admiration of himself in the minds of his whole class ; whereas the other succeeded in rousing the energies of select minds, in setting them forth on curious research, and in sharpening them for logical dissection. One feels, in reading Brown, as if he were filled and satisfied ; but sometimes, as he finds in the digestion, the food has been far from substantial : whereas we are forced to complain, in regard to Hamilton, that he gives us the condensed essence, which the stomach feels great difficulty in mastering.   The one never coins a new technical word, when the phrases in current use among the British and French philosophers of the previous century will serve his purpose ; the other delights to stamp his thoughts with a nomenclature of his own, derived from the scholastics or the Germans, or fashioned out of the Greek tongue : and so the one feels soft as a bird of delicate plumage, whereas the other is bristling all over with sharp points like a porcupine. The works of the one remind us of Versailles, with its paintings, its woods, its fountains,— all somewhat artificial, but beautiful withal ; those of the other are ruled and squared like the pyramids, and look as if they were as lofty, and must be as enduring.

Both were extensive readers : but the reading of the one was in the Latin classics, and the works of the well-known authors of England and France in the last century ; whereas the other ranged over all ancient literature, and over the philosophic systems of all ages and countries ; delighted supremely in writings which had never been read since the age in which they were penned ; troubled many a librarian to shake the dust from volumes which no other man had ever asked for ; and must, we should think, have gratified the dead, grieving in their graves over neglect, by showing them that they were yet remembered.   The one delights to show how superior he is to Reid, to Stewart, to the Schoolmen, to the Stagyrite ; the other rejoices to prove his superior learning by claiming for old, forgotten philosophers the doctrines attributed to modern authors, and by demonstrating how much we owe to the scholastic ages and to Aristotle.

Both departed so far from the true Scottish school : but the one went over to France for refinement and sentiment, the other to Germany for abstractions and erudition.   If Brown is a mixture of the Scottish and French schools, Hamilton is a union of the schools of Reid and Kant.   Brown thought that Reid's influence was too high, and had a secret desire to undermine him and Stewart with him ; Hamilton thought that Brown was over-rated, and makes no scruple in avowing that he labors to strip him of the false glory in which he was enveloped ; and he took up Reid at the time he was being decried in Scotland, and allowed no man — but himself — to censure the common-sense philosopher.   Brown had no sense of the merits of Kant, and did his best (along with Stewart) to keep him unknown for an age in Scotland ; Hamilton was smitten with a deep admiration of the great German metaphysician, helped to introduce him to the knowledge of Scottish thinkers, was caught in his logical network, and was never able thoroughly to extricate himself.

As to their method of investigation, both employ analysis as their chief instrument, but the one uses a retort and proceeds by a sort of chemical composition, while the other employs a lens and works by logical division.   In comparison with Reid and Stewart, both erred by excess of decomposition and overlooked essential parts of the phenomenon ; but the object of the one was to resolve all mental states into as few powers as possible, whereas the aim of the other was to divide and subdivide a whole into parts, which he again distributes into compartments of a framework provided for them.   The one has added to the body of philosophy mainly by his acute analyses of concrete phenomena and by his illuminated illustrations of psychological laws ; the other by his vast erudition, which enabled him to dispose under heads the opinions of all philosophers, and by his skill in arranging the facts of consciousness by means of logical division and distribution.

Brown acquired a wide reputation at an early date ; but, like those showy members of the female sex who have many admirers but few who make proposals of union, he has had scarcely any professing to follow him throughout.   His most distinguished pupil, Dr. Welsh, was possessed of a fine philosophic spirit, but abandoned Scotch metaphysics for phrenology and for theological and ecclesiastical studies.   Several eminent men, not pupils, have been influenced by Brown. Payne's work on Mental and Moral Science is drawn largely from his lectures. Isaac Taylor, in his " Elements of Thought," has adopted some of his peculiarities. Chalmers had to prepare his lectures on moral philosophy when Brown's name was blazing high in Scotland, and, feeling an intense admiration of his eloquence and of the purity of his ethical system, has followed him perhaps further than he should have done, but has been kept from following him in several most important points by his attachment to Reid and Butler. John Stuart Mill has got the very defective metaphysics which underlies and weakens much of his logic from his father, James Mill, from Brown, and from Comte. Still, Brown has no school and few professed disciples. It is different with Hamilton. His influence, if not so extensive — to use a favorite distinction of his own — has been more comprehensive. His articles in the " Edinburgh Review " were above the comprehension, and still further above the tastes, of the great body even of metaphysical students in Great Britain when they appeared between 1829 and 1833. But they were tanslated by M. Peisse into the French language, and there were penetrating minds in Britain, America, and the Continent which speedily discovered the learning and capacity of one who could write such dissertations. By the force of his genius he raised up a body of pupils ready to defend him and to propagate his influence. He has had a school and disciples, as the Greek philosophers had in ancient times, and as such men as Descartès, Leibnitz, and Kant have had in modern times. His pupils employ his distinctions and delight in his nomenclature : their speech everywhere " bewrayeth " them. Some of them, it is true, remind us of a modern soldier in mediæval coat of mail, and move very cumbrously under the ponderous armor of their master ; but, as a whole, they constituted an able and influential school of abstract philosophy. Some of them seem incapable of looking on any subject except through the well-cut lenses which Hamilton has provided for them ; others seem dissatisfied with his negative conclusions, and with his rejection *à la Kant* of final cause as a proof of the divine existence, but they do not seem to have the courage to examine and separate the truth from the error in that doctrine of relativity on which his whole system is founded.

While Hamilton has thus been establishing a school and acquiring an authority, it has not been without protest. In saying so, I do not refer to the criticisms of his attacks on the character and doctrines of Luther, which have been repelled by Archdeacon Hare and others, but to opposition offered to his philosophic principles. There has been a general dissent even by disciples, such as Mansel, from his doctrine of causation, and, if this tenet is undermined, his elaborate scheme of systematized "Conditions of the Thinkable" is laid in ruins. Dr. Calderwood has opposed his negative doctrine of the infinite. Others, not pupils, have expressed doubts of his whole theory of relativity. Ulrici, in the leading philosophic journal of Germany, "Zeitschrift für Philosophie" (1855), has charged him with departing in his method from the standpoint of Scotland, with giving in to the critical method of Kant, and ploughing with the German heifer, and alleges that he or his school must advance with Germany. As the unkindest cut of all, Mr. Ferrier, who was supported by Hamilton in the competition for the moral philosophy chair in Edinburgh when Professor Wilson retired, and with whom Hamilton (as he assured the writer of this article) was long in the habit of consulting, published the "Institutes of Metaphysic," which is a complete revolt against the whole Scottish philosophy; and Kant was not more annoyed with the idealism of Fichte than Hamilton was with the "Object *plus* Subject" of Ferrier. There has been an able review of him from the stand-point of Hegel by Mr. Sterling. But the most formidable attack was made on him in 1865 by John Stuart Mill in his "Examination of the Philosophy of Sir William Hamilton." The physiological psychologists and materialists of the present day are seeking to turn away the attention from him.

William Hamilton was born in the dingy Professors' Court of Glasgow College, March 8, 1791. He was the son of Dr. Thomas Hamilton, professor of anatomy and natural history in that college, and, it is worthy of being noted, physician to the family of Thomas Reid. He was the lineal descendant of Sir Robert Hamilton, the not very wise commander of the Covenanters at Drumclog, and through him, of the Hamiltons of Preston, who claim to be descended from the second son of the progenitor of the Duke of Hamilton; and he succeeded in establishing his claim to the title of Sir William Hamilton. Having lost his father in early life, he was boarded for some time with the Rev. Dr. Summers, the parish minister at Mid Calder, and was afterwards sent to a school at Bromley, where he was taught classics in the thorough old English style. He entered the University of Glasgow in 1803, attended three winters, and there studied logic under Jardine, and moral philosophy under Mylne, standing at the head of his class in both departments, by the votes of his fellow-students — the method of determining honors at that time when competitive examinations had not been exalted into so exclusive a place. By this time he had become an irregular, but most insatiable devourer and also an eager collector of books — in the end his library amounted to nearly ten thousand volumes. In 1807 he was sent up on the Snell foundation to Oxford, and entered Balliol College. Here he took his share in the boating and other gymnastic exercises, but entered with far more eagerness into the study of Aristotle, the favorite of Oxford at that time. " His manner of reading was characteristic. He had his table, chairs, and generally his floor strewed with books ; and you might find him in the midst of this confusion studying with his foot on a chair, poising one great folio on his knee, with another in his hand. His mode of ' tearing out the entrails of a book,' as he termed it, was remarkable. A perusal of the preface, table of contents, and index, and a glance at those parts which were new to him, which were few, were all that was necessary." The paper which he gave in at his examination for the degree was preserved as being singular : —

" Divinity : Aristotle's Philosophy of Man.

" Theoretical : De Anima, &c.

" Practical — Moral — Ethic : Nic., Mag., Cic. Op. Ph. Domestic : Œcon. Civil : De Republ.

" Instrumental : Logic : Organon. Rhetoric : Ars. Rhet., Cic. Op. Rhet. Poetic : De Poetica, Pindar, Æschylus."

" He allowed himself to be examined on more than four times the number of philosophical and didactic books ever wont to be taken up even for the highest honors ; and those, likewise, authors far more abstruse than had previously been attempted in the schools ; while at the same time he was examined in more than any ordinary complement of merely

classical works." In 1812 he went to Edinburgh, and in the
following year, he became an advocate. He lived in the house
of his mother, and married an estimable lady, Miss Janet Mar-
shall, a niece of his mother's. In 1820, when Brown died, he
became a candidate for his chair, and had the support of
Dugald Stewart, who was greatly impressed with his learning
and philosophical ability. He was not particularly successful
at the bar, and every one rejoiced when, in 1821, he was
appointed professor of universal history by the faculty of advocates, the patrons of the chair. His class was not a large one;
but he studied and expounded rare and profound subjects.
About this time phrenology, as expounded by George Combe,
was favored by a considerable body of people in Edinburgh; and
Hamilton set himself determinedly against it. He conducted
numerous experiments with his own hands, sawing open skulls,
dissecting and testing the weight of brains: he is said to
have weighed one thousand brains belonging to above fifty
species of animals. In 1827, he published in the " Edinburgh
Review," his famous article on Cousin and the philosophy of
the conditioned. This was followed in 1830 by an article on
perception, and on Reid and Brown; and in 1833 by an article on Whately and on logic. In 1836 he was appointed
professor of logic and metaphysics in the University of Edinburgh, in opposition to Isaac Taylor, supported by the religious
public, and George Combe, supported by the phrenologists.
He has now a large class of students, numbering from perhaps
one hundred and twenty to one hundred and fifty, and he prepared for them the courses of lectures in logic and metaphysics,
which he, or his assistants for him, delivered each successive
session, till his decease. Having occasion to prelect on Reid,
his labors led, in 1856, to his edition of Reid's " Collected Works,
with Notes and Dissertations," which was left unfinished by
him, but had additions made to it after his death by papers
which he had written. In 1852 the articles in the " Edinburgh "
were republished in the " Discussions on Philosophy," with
large additions on university education, including his vehement and senseless diatribe against mathematics. Some years
before his death he had a stroke of paralysis, which partially
affected his speech and his power of using his pen, and his
lectures had to be read in part or in whole by an assistant,

while his lady acted as his amanuensis. A second attack carried him off, after a few days' illness, May 6, 1856.

Mr. George Moir describes his person: "The massive though well-cut features, the firm compressed mouth, and the eagle-looking eye, of which the whole pupil was visible, created a feeling akin to awe. But in proportion to this apparent sternness was the charm of his smile and of his whole manner when animated." Though a most devoted reader, he never liked composition, and commonly wrote under pressure. There were stories told in Edinburgh of the nervous agitation into which he wrought himself when he had to prepare his lectures for his class. His style was always clear and clinching, but gives evidence that the writer composed painfully and elaborately, and was unwilling to waste a single unnecessary word. His temper was keen and vehement, but never mean or vindictive. When he could not carry his purposes, he might break off in a passion. He was appointed secretary to the college senatus, and there he had a great many projects for elevating the university scholarship, and often came into collision with his colleagues.

Of all thinkers Hamilton is the least disposed to call any man master; still there were forces operating upon him and making his native tendencies take the particular direction which they did. I am convinced that a wholesome tone was given to his mind by the philosophy of Reid, the metaphysician of his native college, and who died six years after Hamilton was born. Had he been trained exclusively in Oxford, he might have spent his powers in mere notes and comments on others, and we should have been without his profound original observations. Had he been reared in Germany, his speculative spirit might have wasted itself in a hopelessly entangled dialectic, like that of Hegel. To Glasgow and to Reid he owes his disposition to appeal, even in the midst of his most abstract disquisitions, to consciousness and to facts. To Oxford we may trace his classical scholarship and his love of Aristotle, the favorite for long ages with technical Oxonian tutors. We only wish that he had been led to drink as deep into Plato as he did into Aristotle: it would have widened his sympathies, and rubbed off some acute angles of his mind, and made his philosophy less cold and negative. A third master mind exercised as great a power over him as either Reid or Aristotle. In prosecuting his researches, he was necessarily led beyond the narrow scholarship of Britain into the wide field of German learning, and while ranging there could not but observe that there was a constant reference to the name of Kant. The logical power of the author of the "Critic of Pure Reason" at once seized his kindred mind, and he eagerly took hold of his critical method, and adopted many — I think far too many — of his distinctions. Kant exercised as great an influence over him as even Reid did. His whole philosophy turns round those topics which were discussed in Kant's great work; and he can never get out of those "forms" in which Kant set all our ideas so methodically, nor lose sight of those terrible antinomies, or contradictions of reason which Kant expounded, in order to show that the laws of pure reason can have no application to objects, and which Hegel gloried in and was employing as the ground principle of his philosophy. From Kant he got the principle that the mind begins with phenomena instead of things, and builds thereon by forms or laws of thought; and it was as he pondered on the sphinx enigmas of Kant and Hegel, that he evolved his famous axiom about all positive thought lying in the proper conditioning of one or other of two contradictory propositions, one or other of which must, by the rule of excluded middle, be void. Fortunately he fell in, at the same time, with the less hard and more genial writings of Jacobi, who taught him that there was a faith element as well as a rational element in the human mind; but, unfortunately, Jacobi thought that faith was opposed to reason, and had no distinct views as to the nature of faith, or as to the harmony between faith and reason. To this source we may trace those appeals which Hamilton is ever making to faith, but without specifying what faith is. To his legal studies we may refer somewhat of his dry manner and his disputatious spirit. His readings in connection with the chair of history enabled him to realize the precise condition of the ages in which the opinions of philosophers were given forth. The catholic views which his extensive reading led him to adopt set him in determined opposition to the miserably narrow sensational school of France, and to Professor Mylne, of Glasgow, and Dr. Thomas Brown, who had given way too much to that school. The lofty spiritual views which he had caught from Reid and Kant set him against materialism; and his medical studies, to which his father's profession may have directed him, enabled him to meet phrenology, and to give an admirable account of the physiology of the senses. Such was the course of training which he had gone through when he was asked to write a review of Cousin, and found himself face to face with the philosophy of the absolute.

In contemplating these two eminent philosophers, — Hamilton and Cousin, — then brought into collision, it is difficult to say whether one is most struck with their resemblances or their differences. They are alike in respect of the fulness and the general accuracy of their scholarship. Both are alike distinguished for their historical knowledge and critical power. Even here, however, we may observe a contrast, — Cousin being the more universal in his sympathies, and Hamilton being the more discriminating and the more minutely accurate in his acquaintance with rare and obscure authors. Both, perhaps, might have had some of their views expanded, if, along with their scholarship, they had entered more thoroughly into the inductive spirit of modern physical researches. But the age of universal knowledge is past, and it is vain to expect that any human capacity will contain all learning. Both are original, vigorous, and independent thinkers; and both are distinguished by a catholic spirit in philosophy: but the one is more Platonic, and the other more Aristotelian, in his tastes and habits. The one delights to show wherein he agrees with all others, the other is more addicted to show wherein he differs from all others. Both are clear writers: but the one is distinguished by the eloquence of his composition and the felicity of his illustrations; the other, by the accuracy and expressiveness of his, at times, harsh nomenclature. Cousin is, undoubtedly, the man of finest genius and most refined taste; the other appears to me to have been the man of coolest and most penetrating intellect. The one makes every subject of which he treats irridescent by the play of his fancy; the other bands it into a structure of great solidity by the rigidity of his logic. Both were admirers of the German as well as the Scottish schools of philosophy; but Cousin's predilections were at one time more towards the former, and of a later date he became more attached to the latter; whereas Hamilton started more in the Scottish spirit, and swung latterly towards the German method. The two came into collision when the Scotchman reviewed the Frenchman in the "Edinburgh Review." But when Hamilton became a candidate for the chair of moral philosophy in Edinburgh he received powerful and generous aid from his rival; and when Hamilton published his edition of Reid, he dedicated it to M. Victor Cousin.

The writer of this article has a very vivid recollection of Sir William in happening to pass into his class-room a year or two after his appointment. There was an evident manliness in his person and his whole manner and address. His features were marked, he had an eye of a very deep lustre, and his expression was eminently intellectual. He read his lecture in a clear, emphatic manner, without show, pretension, or affectation of any kind. His nomenclature sounded harsh and uncouth to one unacquainted with it, but his enunciations were all perspicuous and explicit. The class was a large one, numbering I should suppose 150. At the opening there was a furious scribbling, visible and audible, by all the students in their note-books; but I observed that, as the lecture proceeded, one after another was left behind, and, when it was half through, at least one-third had ceased to take notes, and had evidently lost their interest in, or comprehension of, the subject. Unfortunately for the Scottish colleges, unfortunately for the youth attending them, students enter the logic class in the second year of their course, when the majority are not ripe for it. A course of lectures, like that given by Jardine of Glasgow, might be fit for such a class, but not a rigid course like that of Hamilton, who did, indeed, make his thoughts as clear as such profound thoughts could be made, but could not bring them down to the comprehension of a promiscuous class, of which many are under seventeen, and some under sixteen, or even fifteen years of age. But even among second year students there were every year a larger or less number who rejoiced to find that he first awakened independent thought within them, and who were ready to acknowledge ever afterwards that they owed more to him than to any other professor, or to all the other professors under whom they studied.

In his examinations he expected a sort of recitation of his lectures from the students. He also encouraged his pupils to submit to voluntary examinations on private studies undertaken by them. He prescribed essays on subjects lectured on, and in these essays he allowed great latitude in the expression of opinions, and some of his students, out of a spirit of independence or contradiction, would at times take up the defence of Dr. Brown, and were not discouraged. All students of high intellectual power, and especially those of a metaphysical taste, received a stimulus of a very lofty kind from his lectures, and these examinations and essays. I suspect that some of the duller and idler passed through the class without getting much benefit. In his whole intercourse with young men there was great courtesy and kindness, and a readiness to appreciate talent and independent thinking wherever he found it. For a number of years before his death, Sir William was oppressed with infirmities, and had to employ an assistant ; and it was characteristic of him that he was in the habit of selecting for the office some one of those who had been his more distinguished students. We may now look at his metaphysics and his logic.

Metaphysics. The first of the volumes is on philosophy generally and on mental philosophy in particular. He begins by recommending the study, gives the definitions, unfolds the divisions, explains the terms with amazing erudition and unsurpassed logical precision, and dwells largely on consciousness, its laws and conditions. The reading of this volume will prove as bracing to the mind as a run up a hill of a morning on a botanical or geological excursion is to the body. We especially recommend the study of it to those whose pursuits are usually of a different character, as, for example, to those who are dissipating their minds by light literature, or whose attention has been directed exclusively to physical facts, and who have thus been cultivating one set of the faculties which God has given them, to the neglect of others, and have thus been putting their mental frame out of proper shape and proportion, — as the fisher, by strengthening his chest and arms in rowing, leaves his lower extremities thin and slender. There is a fine healthy tone about his defence of the liberal as against the more lucrative sciences, which latter Schelling called *Brodwissenchaften,*

which Hamilton wittily translates, *the bread and butter sciences.*
He quotes with approbation the well-known sentiment of Les-
sing, " Did the Almighty, holding in his right hand *Truth,* and
in his left *Search after Truth,* deign to tender me the one
I might prefer, — in all humility, but without hesitation, I
would request Search after Truth." But we should concur in
such statements as these only with two important explanations
or qualifications ; the one is, that the search be after truth,
which we must value when we find it ; and the other is, that it
be after attainable and useful truth. It has been the great
error and sin of speculative philosophy that it has been expend-
ing its strength in building in one age ingenious theories
which the next age takes down. I maintain that such activity
wastes the energy without increasing the strength. He who
thus fights is like one beating the air, and his exertion ends,
not in satisfaction, but in weariness and restlessness. The
admirable test of Bacon here comes in to restrain all such useless speculation, viz., that we are to try them by their fruits.
Had this been the proper place we could have shown that
Bacon's doctrine on this subject has often been misunderstood.
He does not say that science is to be valued for its fruits, but it
is to be tested by its fruits ; just as faith, which, however, is of
value in itself, is to be tried by the good works to which it
leads. Thus limited and thus understood, there is profound
wisdom in the caution of Bacon, which will not discourage an
inductive inquiry into the human mind, its laws and fundamental principles, but will lay a restraint on the profitless metaphysical theories which have run to seed prematurely in
Germany, where thinkers are sick of them, and are now being
blown into our country and scattered over it like the down of
thistles.

This volume is full of brief and sententious maxims. Take
the following as examples : —

" It is ever the contest that pleases us, and not the victory. Thus it is in
play ; thus it is in hunting ; thus it is in the search after truth ; thus it is in
life. The past does not interest, the present does not satisfy, the future
alone is the object which engages us." " What man holds of matter does
not make up his personality. They are his, not he ; man is not an organism, — he is an intelligence served by organs." " I do not mean to assert
that all materialists deny or actually disbelieve a God. For in very many
cases this would be at once an unmerited compliment to their reasoning,

and an unmerited reproach to their faith." "Wonder has been contemptuously called the daughter of ignorance; true, but wonder we should add is the mother of knowledge." "Woe to the revolutionist who is not himself a creature of the revolution! If he anticipate he is lost, for it requires what no individual can supply, a long and powerful counter-sympathy in a nation to untwine the ties of custom which bind a people to the established and the old."

The following is his tabular view of the distribution of philosophy:—

Mind or Con-scious-ness.	Facts, — Phænomenology, Empirical Psychology,	Cognitions. Feelings. Conative Powers (Will and Desire).	
	Laws, — Nomology, Rational Psychology,	Cognitions, — Logic. Feelings, — Aesthetic.	
		Conative Powers,	Moral Philosophy. Political Philosophy.
	Results, — Ontology, Inferential Psychology,	Being of God. Immortality of the Soul, &c.	

I set little value on this division. The same topics would require to be discussed under more than one head. In his lectures Sir William has taken up only one of the three grand general groups, viz., Empirical Psychology, and even this he has discussed only in part. A portion of the second group is treated of in his lectures on logic. On the others he never entered.

It will be seen from the above table that he followed Kant in giving a threefold distribution of the mental faculties into the Cognitive, the Emotive, and the Conative. This is an improvement on the old division by Aristotle into the cognitive and motive, or of that of the schoolmen into the understanding and the will. Still it is not complete and exhaustive. He is obliged to include the imagination in the first head, and yet it can scarcely be called a cognitive power, though, of course, it implies a previous cognition. The conscience comes in under the conative powers; but, in fact, the conscience partakes of the nature both of a cognitive and conative power. It is one of the defects of the arrangement that it does not allot a clearly separate place to the conscience.

The following is his division of the cognitive powers:—

I.	Presentative,	External=Perception. Internal=Self-Consciousness.
II.	Conservative, =	Memory
III.	Reproductive. =	Without Will=Suggestion. With Will=Reminiscence.
IV.	Representative. =	Imagination.
V.	Elaborative, =	Comparison. — Faculty of Relations.
VI.	Regulative, =	Reason, — Common Sense.

The account of the cognitive powers in the first 332 pages of the second volume, down to the regulative powers, not included, will be regarded in the end, if I do not mistake, as the most valuable part of Sir William Hamilton's metaphysics. His pupils will probably fix on the very part I have designedly excepted, viz., the regulative faculties, as being the most important. Farther on in this article I mean to show that he has greatly misapprehended the nature of these regulative powers. Meanwhile let us look at the account which he has given of the other mental faculties.

1. Like the Scotch metaphysicians he paid great attention to the Senses. His views were first given to the world in his article in the "Edinburgh Review," republished in the Discussions, and have been expanded in his notes on Reid and in his class lectures. He has a famous arrangement of the various forms which have been taken by the ideal theory of sense-perception. Realists are either natural, who maintain that we know the external thing directly; or hypothetical (cosmothetic idealists), who suppose that there is a real world not directly known. Idealists are absolute or presentative, who suppose that there is only the idea; or cosmothetic or representative (hypothetical realists) who hold that we know the external thing by a representation. The possible forms of the representative hypothesis are three: (1.) The representative object not a modification of mind, but an extra-mental object, physical or hyperphysical; (2.) The representative object a modification of mind, dependent for its apprehension, but not for its existence, on an act of consciousness, say an idea in the mind, as was held apparently by Locke; (3.) The representative object a modification of mind, non-existent out of consciousness, the idea and its perception only different relations of an act (state) really identical; the view taken by Arnauld and Brown. The distinctions thus drawn are of great importance, and should be kept steadily in view in judging of theories. But his divisions do not embrace all cases. Dr. Brown does not hold by the ideal, but the causal or inferential, theory; and Hamilton has missed the mark in his criticism of him.

I am inclined to agree with him that our original perceptions are probably of our organism, or of objects in immediate contact with it. This doctrine seems to have been expounded simultaneously by Hamilton ; by Saisset, the French metaphysician ; and by John Müller, the physiologist. On one small point I would differ from Hamilton. Our original perceptions through the eye do not seem to me to be points of light, but of a colored surface affecting our organism, but at what distance we cannot say till experience comes to our aid. But the doctrine identified with his name is that of immediate perception. He intended to take the same view as Reid did, and, when he began to edit Reid's works, he thought that their opinions were the same. But, as he advances, he sees that they differ ; and he ends by doubting whether Reid was after all a realist. Reid's doctrine is, that there is first an organic affection ; then a sensation in the mind ; and, thirdly, a perception suggested by an unreasoning and instinctive process. Hamilton's doctrine is, that, following the organic affection, there is simultaneously a sensation and perception, the one being strong as the other is weak, and *vice versa ;* that is, when the sensation is lively the perception is faint, and when the perception is prominent the impression is feeble. Both, however, agree in the main point, that the process is intuitive and that there is no reasoning involved. Hamilton's doctrine is specially that of *immediate* perception ; that is, of perception without a medium.

It is objected to Hamilton's theory, that he overlooks the numerous intermediate processes revealed by physiology. In vision there are the rays of light ; the reflection and refraction of them, the picture on the retina, an action along the optic nerve to the seat of sensation, an action thence we know not how to the brain, an action in the cells which constitute the gray matter surrounding the brain, and then, or perhaps not even then, but only after some farther steps, the perception of the object, say a tree, from which the rays of light come. How it is asked can perception be immediate, when all these media are evidently implied ? To this the followers of Hamilton might reply, that he never thought of disputing the existence of steps between the external object and the percipient mind, which, when it comes into exercise, contemplates the tree, and not an image or representation of it in the mind, in the body or out of the body. But the objection may now take a somewhat different form. It may be urged that, after all, we do not see the tree, and it will be asked, What do we perceive intuitively? Certainly not the brain cells, or the influence transmitted to them, or the action of the sensorium, or even the image on the retina, or the coats and humors of the eye, or the vibrations that constitute the light. What, then, do we perceive? Hamilton allowed that it was not the distant tree ; for he adopted the Berkleian theory of vision, and held that we are immediately percipient of distance by the eye. What, then, do we see immediately? Hamilton was helped here by another doctrine of his, that the mind may be said to be indiscriminately in the brain and in the whole nervous apparatus, so long as it keeps up its connection with the centre; and by the further doctrine that our primary perceptions are of our bodily frame and of objects in contact with it. In taste, smell, and hearing, we perceive the palate, nostrils, ear ; in feeling, our extended frame ; and by the muscular sense an extra-organic object resisting our energy. The proper account is, that in sense-perception, when formed, we perceive our frame as affected or objects affecting the frame. I am ready to allow as many processes as the physiologist can prove to exist in the nervous system and brain prior to perception. But I hold that perception is a mental and not a bodily act. We hold further that nervous action, and brain action and cellular, do not constitute perception, which is knowledge. I assert that, while there may be bodily antecedents, they are not properly the causes of perception or any proper mental act, such as the perception of beauty or of moral excellence. I may add that I have no objections to find them represented as the occasions or conditions of sense-perception, not therefore of our higher mental acts. If we hold, as I hold, that in creature action all causes are concauses, that is composed of more than one agent, then the brain action may be an agent, a necessary but inferior agent, in producing perception, — the main agency being a capacity of the mind. I am inclined to go a step further, and to allow that the defenders of natural realism might admit for the sake of argument, and admit out and out if proven, that there is a process of reasoning in every perceptive operation, even in such an operation as perceiving snow as a colored surface — just as all admit that there is inference when we place that snow on a mountain top at a distance. But still they will insist that when mind perceives matter, it perceives it as out of itself, and as extended; that it cannot infer this from a nervous action, or from an unextended sensation or impression within the mind; and that the perception of an external, extended object, be it in the body or beyond the body, must be immediate, intuitive, and original.

2. Sir William Hamilton has been much lauded for the view which he has given of Consciousness. In this I cannot concur. He avows that he uses consciousness in two distinct senses or applications. First, he has a general consciousness treated of largely in the first volume. This he tells us cannot be defined. (Vol. I. p. 158.) "But it comprehends all the modifications, — all the phenomena of the thinking subject." (p. 183.) "Knowledge and belief are both contained under consciousness." (p. 191.) Again, "consciousness is co-extensive with our cognitive faculties." "Our special faculties of knowledge are only modifications of consciousness." (p. 207.) He shows that consciousness implies discrimination, judgment, and memory. (p. 202–206.) This is wide enough: still he imposes a limit; for consciousness "is an immediate not a mediate knowledge." (p. 202.) Already, as it seems to me, inconsistencies are beginning to creep in; for he had told us first that consciousness includes "all the phenomena of the thinking subject;" now he so limits it as to exclude "mediate knowledge," which is surely a modification of the thinking subject. Consciousness is represented as including belief; and yet it must exclude all those beliefs in which the object is not immediately before us. He stoutly maintains what no one will deny, that this general consciousness is not a special faculty; but when he comes to draw out a list of faculties in the second volume, he includes among them a special faculty, which he calls consciousness, but to which, for distinction's sake, he prefixes self, and designates it self-consciousness. It is the office of this special faculty to "afford us a knowledge of the phenomena of our minds." (Vol. II. p. 192.) He justifies himself in drawing a distinction between sense-perception and self-consciousness on the ground that, "though the immediate knowledge of matter and of mind are still only modifications of consciousness, yet that their discrimination as subaltern faculties is both allowable and convenient."

Such is the doctrine and such the nomenclature of Hamilton

on this subject. I confess that I have great doubts of the propriety of applying the phrase "consciousness," both in this general and specific way. In the first sense "consciousness constitutes, or is co-extensive with all our faculties of knowledge," and he speaks of our being endowed with a faculty of cognition or consciousness, in general (Vol. II. p. 10), and says that "consciousness may be regarded as the general faculty of knowledge." Now it is certainly desirable to have a word to denote our faculties of knowledge, or of immediate knowledge ; but why not call them knowing powers, or cognitive powers, and their exercise or energy, knowledge or cognition, and then the word "consciousness" would be reserved unambiguously for the cognizance which the mind takes of self in its particular states. The word (from *con scio* to know together with) seems the appropriate one to denote that knowledge of self which co-exists with all our other knowledge of things material or things spiritual ; and indeed with all our other mental exercises, such as feelings and volitions. It is certainly in this sense that the term is employed by Hutcheson, by Reid, by Stewart, by Royer-Collard ; and all Hamilton's vehement criticisms of these men are inapplicable and powerless, for this very obvious reason, that they use the word consciousness as he uses self-consciousness, acknowledged by him to be a special faculty. It is an inevitable result of using the phrases in two senses, a wider and a straiter, that we are ever in danger of passing inadvertently from the one meaning to the other, and making affirmations in the one sense which are true only in the other. I rather think that Hamilton himself has not escaped this error, and the confusion thence arising. He is ever appealing to consciousness, as Locke did to idea, and Brown did to suggestion ; but we are not always sure in which of the senses, whether in both, or in one, or in which one. He is ever ascribing powers to consciousness, which he would have explained, or modified, or limited, if the distinction had been kept steadily in view. Thus he is often announcing that consciousness is the universal condition of intelligence ; if this is meant of the general consciousness, it can mean no more than this, that man must have knowing powers in order to know ; if meant of the special consciousness, it is not true ; it is rather true that there must be some mental exercise as a condition of the knowledge of self. He calls the principles of common sense the facts of consciousness, emphatically ; whereas these principles, as principles, are not before the consciousness as principles at all. The individual manifestations are of course before the consciousness (though not more so than any other mental exercise), but not the principles themselves, which are derived from the individual exercises, by a reflex process of abstraction and generalization. He speaks everywhere as if we must ever be conscious at one and the same time of subject and object, — meaning external object ; whereas we may be conscious of the subject-mind thinking about some state of self present or absent. His *quondam* friend, Professor Ferrier, carried the doctrine a step farther, and maintained that a knowledge of self is a condition of all knowledge of not self, whereas it is merely a fact that the one co-exists with the other in one concrete act, in which we know not self to be different from self, and independent of self.

3. The Conservative, Reproductive, and Representative faculties might all have been included, I think, under one head, with subdivisions. The account which he gives of this group is upon the whole the best which we have in our language. Still there are oversights in it. Thus, in order to make the analysis complete, I should have had the recognitive power, or that which recognizes the object recalled as having been before the mind *in time past.* Had he given this power a separate place, he would have seen more clearly than he does how the idea of time arises. Along with the mere representative power he should have mentioned the compounding or grouping power of imagination, which combines the scattered images into one new whole. He refers at times to man's native power of using signs ; why not specify a symbolic power, enabling man to think by signs standing for notions.

In explaining the nature of the conservative or retentive faculty, and elsewhere, he has unfolded some peculiar views which I consider to be as correct as they are profound, but he carries them to a length which I am not prepared to allow. What is the state of an idea when not falling at the time under consciousness ? This is a question which has often been put. Thus having seen the Crystal Palace of 1851, the question is put, — what place has that idea in my mind, when

I am not precisely thinking about the object? Is it dead or simply dormant? We must of course answer that the idea can have no existence as an idea, when not before the consciousness. Still it must have some sort of existence. There exists in the mind a power to reproduce it according to the laws of association. The writer of this article having had occasion, years ago, to pass over the plains of Lombardy, is not therefore always imaging them, but he has the power of recalling them, and finds that they are recalled every time he hears of the jealousies between Austria and Italy. It is a great truth that the mind is ever acquiring potency, is ever laying up power. We have something analogous in the physical world. Thus a power coming from the sun in the geological age of the coal-measures was laid up in the plant, went down into the strata of the ground, and comes up now in our coals ready to supply us with comfortable heat in our rooms, and with tremendous mechanical force for our steam-engines. This is the doctrine of all the physicists of our day. But there is a similar laying up of power in the mind, of intellectual, and we may add, of moral or immoral power. Aristotle had certainly a glimpse of some such doctrine, and spoke of a *dunamis*, an *entelecheia*, and an *energeia*; the first denoting the original capacity, the second the capacity in complete readiness to act, and the third the capacity in act or operation. Modern mechanical science is enunciating this doctrine in a more definite form, and distinguishing between capacity and potential energy and actual energy. Sir William Hamilton, taking the hint from Aristotle, has adopted the views of the German Schmid (who again had certain speculations of Leibnitz before him), who declares that the energy of mind which has once been cannot readily be conceived as abolished, and that "the problem most difficult of solution is not how a mental activity endures, but how it ever vanishes." (Vol. II. p. 212.)

So far I can concur; but when he maintains that there are in the mind, acts, energies, and operations, of which it is not conscious, I hesitate and draw back. His doctrine on this subject is founded on the views of Leibnitz, as to there being perceptions below consciousness. The class of facts on which he rests his opinion seem to me to be misapprehended.

"When we hear the distant murmur of the sea, what are the constituents of this total perception of which we are conscious?" He answers that the murmur is a sum made up of parts, and that if the noise of each wave made no impression on our sense, the noise of the sea as the result of these impressions could not be realized. "But the noise of each several wave at the distance, we suppose, is inaudible; we must, however, admit that they produce a certain modification beyond consciousness, on the percipient object." (Vol. I. p. 351.) He speaks of our perception of a forest as made up of impressions left by each leaf, which impressions are below consciousness. There is an entire misinterpretation of the facts in these statements, and this according to Hamilton's own theory of the object intuitively perceived. The mind is not immediately cognizant of the sound of the sea or of its several waves; nor of the trees of the forest and their several leaves. All that it knows intuitively is an affection of the organism as affected by the sound or sight. The impression made by the distant object is on the organism, and when the impression is sufficiently strong on the organism, the mind is called into exercise, and from the organic affections *argues* or *infers* the external and distant cause. Thus there is no proof of a mental operation of which we are unconscious.

He explains by these supposed unconscious acts a class of mental phenomena with which every one who has ever reflected on the operations of his own mind is familiar. The merchant walks in a brown study from his house to his place of business; there must have been many mental acts performed on the way, but they are now all gone. The question is, were they ever before the consciousness? Hamilton maintains that they never were; Dugald Stewart maintains that they were for the time, but that the mind cannot recall them. Notwithstanding all the acute remarks of Hamilton, I adhere to the theory of Stewart. I do so on the general principle that in devising a theory to explain a set of phenomena we should never call in a class of facts, of whose existence we have no other proof, when we can account for the whole by an order of facts known to exist on independent evidence. Hamilton says: "When suddenly awakened during sleep (and to ascertain the fact I have caused myself to be roused at different seasons of the night), I have always been able to observe that I was in the middle of a dream ;" but adds, "that he was often scarcely certain of more than the fact that he was not awakened from an unconscious state, and that we are often not able to recollect our dreams." He gives, as the peculiarity of somnambulism, that we have no recollection when we awake of what has occurred during its continuance. (Vol. I. p. 320–322.) Every one will admit that we are often conscious of states at the time, which we either cannot remember at all, or (what will equally serve our purpose) more probably cannot remember, except for a very brief period after we have experienced them. We have thus an established order of facts competent to explain the whole phenomenon without resorting to a Leibnitzian doctrine, which has been applied by certain later German pantheists to show how existence may rise gradually from deadness to life, and from unconsciousness to consciousness.

Under the head of the reproductive faculties he has two profound lectures on the Association of Ideas. In the close of his edition of Reid there is a learned disquisition on the well-known passage of Aristotle, in which he gives, with his usual brevity, a classification of laws which regulate the train of our thoughts. Hamilton so interprets that passage as to make Aristotle announce one generic law and three special ones. I am unwilling to set my authority against so accurate a scholar as Hamilton ; but I have often looked into that passage, and can find no evidence of Aristotle having resolved all into one law. In the same note Hamilton had begun to expound his own theory, but broke off, and closed the book in the middle of a sentence. Most readers will feel that the account given in these lectures, though somewhat fuller, is far too brief, and illustrated by too few examples to be easily understood. His pupils could not be more profitably employed than in fully unfolding the doctrine of their master on this subject, and applying it to explain the well-known phenomena. He thinks that the whole facts can be explained by one great law, which he calls the law of redintegration, which he finds incidentally expressed by Augustine. This law may be thus enounced, — "Those thoughts suggest each other which had previously constituted parts of the same entire or total act of cognition." (Vol. II. p. 238.) He again quotes Schmid : " Thus the supreme law of association, — that activities excite each other in proportion as they have previously belonged as parts to one whole activity, — is explained from the still more universal principle of the unity of all our mental energies in general." (p. 241.) I am inclined to look on this as, on the whole, the most philosophical account which has been given of the law of association. It at once explains the cases of simple repetition in which one link of a chain of ideas which had previously passed through the mind, being caught, all the rest come after ; as when we have got the first line of a poem committed to memory, and the others follow in order. It easily explains, too, all cases in which we have had a variety of objects before us in one concrete act, — thus if we have passed along a particular road, with a certain person, observing the mountain or river in front, and talking on certain objects, — we find that when any one of these recurs it is apt to suggest the others. It is thus if we have often heard in youth the cry of a particular animal, goose or grouse, turkey or curlew, the cry will ever bring up afresh the scenes of our childhood. It is more doubtful whether the law can explain a third class of cases when it is not the same which suggests the same, but an object suggests another object which has never been individually associated with it, but is like it, or is otherwise correlated with it ; as when the conqueror Alexander suggests Julius Cæsar or Bonaparte. It needs an explanation to show how the law can cover such a case, which, however, I rather think it can, though I am by no means inclined to admit the explanations of the Hamiltonians proceeding on their narrow and peculiar view of correlates.

4. This leads us to refer to the next faculty, — the Elaborative, equal to Comparison, — that is the Faculty of Relations. The phrase elaborative is an expressive epithet, but is not a good special denomination, as there is elaboration in other exercises as well as in this. Comparison, or the correlative faculties, or the faculties of relation, is the better epithet. Under this head he has some learned and acute remarks on the abstract and the general notion, and on language, and is terribly severe, as usual, on Dr. Thomas Brown. I am of opinion that Brown's views on this subject are, in one or two points, more enlarged than those of Hamilton himself, who has over-

looked essential elements. " In so far," he says, " as two objects
resemble each other, the notion we have of them is identical,
and, therefore, to us, the objects may be considered as the
same." (Vol. II. pp. 294.) I cannot give my adherence to
this doctrine of the identity of resembling objects. Altogether
his account of the relations which the mind can discover is
narrow and exclusive.   He specifies first the judgment virtually
pronounced in an act of perception of the *non-ego,* or an act
of self-consciousness of the *ego ;* then secondly the something
of which we are conscious and of which the predicate existence
is twofold, the *ego* and the *non-ego ;* thirdly, the recognition
of the multiplicity of the co-existent or successive phenomena,
and the judgment in regard to their resemblance or dissimilar-
ity ; fourthly, the comparison of the phenomena 'with the
native notion of substance ; fifthly, the collection of successive phenomena under the native notion of causation.   He
might have seen a much broader and more comprehensive account of the relations which the mind can perceive in Locke's
" Essay " (B. II. c. 28); in Hume's " Treatise on Human Nature "
(B. I. p. i. § 5) ; or in Brown's Lectures (Lect. xlv.)   I am surprised he has never made a reference to such relations — on
which the mind so often dwells — as those of space, time,
quantity, properties of objects, cause and effect, and moral
good.

5. We have now only to consider, and in doing so have to
discuss, the Regulative Faculties of the mind.   I like the phrase
regulative, only we must dissociate it from the peculiar sense in
which it is used by Kant (from whom Hamilton has borrowed
it), who supposes that the mind in judging of objects imposes
on them a relation not in the objects themselves.   The epithet
expresses that such principles as substance and quality, cause
and effect, are " the laws by which the mind is governed in
its operations " (Vol. II., p. 15), which laws I may add — but
Hamilton would not — are not before the consciousness as
principles when we exercise them.   In calling them faculties,
he acknowledges that he uses the word in a peculiar signification.   (p. 347.)   The truth is Hamilton does not see the relation in which they stand to the faculties : they are not separate
faculties, but are involved in all the faculties, being, in fact,
the necessary laws which spontaneously and unconsciously

guide their exercise.   His treatment of this subject in a more
elaborate manner, in the " Conditions of the Thinkable Systematized, or the Alphabet of Human Thought," appended to
the Discussions, and in a somewhat more popular manner in his
Lectures, was probably regarded by himself, and is certainly
regarded by his admiring pupils, as the most important contribution made by him to philosophy.   On the other hand, I look
on the system as being, on the whole, a failure.   He has
labored to combine the philosophies of Reid and Kant ; but we
see everywhere the chinks at the line of junction.   The principles
of common sense looking at objective truth, will not join on to
the empty forms which imply and guarantee no reality.   In
the construction of his philosophy of the relative or conditioned,
as he calls it, he has expended an immense amount of logical
ability ; but he has lost himself in Kantian distinctions, giving
in to Kant's theory as to space and time, making them, and
also cause and effect, merely subjective laws of thought and
not of things ; and the system which he has reared is an artificial one, in which the flaws and oversights and rents are
quite as evident as the great skill which he has shown in its
erection.   I dispute three of his fundamental and favorite
positions.

(1.) I dispute his theory of relativity.   I acknowledge that
there is a sense in which human knowledge is relative.   There
is a sense in which all thinkers, except those of the extravagant
schools of Schelling and Hegel, hold a doctrine of relativity ;
but this is not the same as that elaborated by Hamilton :
" From what has been said you will be able to understand
what is meant by the proposition that all our knowledge is
only relative.   It is relative, — first, because existence is not
cognizable absolutely and in itself, but only in special modes ;
second, because these modes can be known only if they stand in
a certain relation to our faculties ; and, thirdly, because the
modes thus relative to our faculties are presented to, and known
by, the mind only under modifications determined by these
faculties themselves." (Vol. I., p. 148.)

In these three general propositions, and in the several
clauses, there are an immense number and variety of assertions
wrapped up : to some I assent, from others I as decidedly
dissent.   I acknowledge, first, that things are known to us

only so far as we have the capacity to know them ; in this sense, indeed, even the divine knowledge is relative. I acknowledge, secondly, that we do not know all things ; nay, that we do not know all about any one thing. Herein human knowledge differs from the divine : but the word relative is not the phrase to attach to human knowledge ; in order to point out the difference, it would be better to say that man's knowledge is partial or finite as distinguished from perfect or absolute. I may admit, thirdly, that man discovers external objects under a relation to himself and his cognitive mind. So much, then, I freely allow. But, on the other hand, I demur, first, to the statement that we do not know existence in itself, or, as he expresses it elsewhere in Kantian phraseology, that we do not know the thing in itself (Ding an sich). I do not like the language : it is ambiguous. I doubt whether there be such a thing as " existence in itself ; " and, of course, what does not exist cannot be known. If he mean to assert that we do not know things as existing, I deny the statement. Every thing we know, we know as existing ; not only so, but we know the thing itself, — not all about the thing, but so much of the very thing itself. Then I demur secondly, to the statement, which is thoroughly Kantian, that the mind in cognition adds elements of its own : as he expresses it elsewhere, " Suppose that the total object of consciousness in perception = 12 ; and suppose that the external reality contributes 6, the material sense 3, and the mind 3 ; this may enable you to form some rude conjecture of the nature of the object of perception." (Vol. II., p. 129.) I allow that sensations, feelings, impressions associate themselves with our knowledge : but every man of sound sense knows how to distinguish between them , and it is surely the business of the philosopher not to confound them, but to point out the essential difference. To suppose that in perception, or cognition proper, the mind adds any thing, is a doctrine fraught with perilous consequences ; for, if it adds one thing, why not two things, or ten things, or all things, till we are landed in absolute idealism, or, what is nearly allied to it, in absolute scepticism ?

The defective nature of the whole Hamiltonian philosophy comes out in its results. Comparing his philosophy with that of Germany he says : " Extremes meet. In one respect both coincide, for both agree that the knowledge of nothing is the principle or the consummation of all true philosophy, ' *Scire nihil, — studium quo nos lætamur utrique.*' But the one doctrine openly maintaining that the nothing must yield every thing, is a philosophic omniscience, whereas the other holding, that nothing can yield nothing, is a philosophic nescience. In other words : the doctrine of the unconditioned is a philosophy confessing relative ignorance, but professing absolute knowledge ; while the doctrine of the conditioned, is a philosophy professing relative knowledge, but confessing absolute ignorance." (Dis. p. 609.) Surely this is a pitiable enough conclusion to such an elaborate process. A mountain labors, and something infinitely less than the mouse emerges.

I suspect that Sir William Hamilton was wont to meet all such objections, and try to escape from such a whirlpool as that in which Ferrier would engulf him, by taking refuge in belief, — in faith. And I am thoroughly persuaded of the sincerity of his faith, philosophic and religious. But it is unsatisfactory, it is unphilosophic, to allow that cognition and intelligence may lead to nihilism, and then resort to faith to save us from the consequences. Surely there is faith involved in the exercises of intelligence ; there is faith (philosophical) involved, when from a seen effect we look up to an unseen cause. I am sure that human intelligence does not lead to absolute knowledge, but as little does it lead to scepticism or to nothing. Of this I am further sure, that the same criticism which pretends to demonstrate that intelligence ends in absolute ignorance, will soon — probably in the immediately succeeding age — go on to show with the same success, that our beliefs are not to be trusted.

The same doctrine of relativity carried out led him to deny that there could be any valid argument in behalf of the divine existence, except the moral one. I acknowledge that the moral argument, properly enunciated, is the most satisfactory of all. I admit that the argument from order and adaptation (the physico-theological) can prove no more, than that there is a living being of vast power and wisdom, presiding over the universe ; but this it can do by the aid of the law of cause and effect properly interpreted. The proof that this Being is infinite must be derived from the mental intuition in regard to the infinite. Hamilton has deprived himself of the power of using the arguments from our belief in causation and infinity by what I regard as a defective and mutilated account of both these intuitions. He has nowhere stated the moral argument which he trusts in. I suspect that the criticism which cuts down the argument from intelligence, needs only to be carried a step further to undermine the argument from our moral nature. This process has actually taken place in Germany, and I have no desire to see it repeated among metaphysical youths in this country. It is on this account, mainly, that I have been so anxious to point out the gross defects in the account given by Hamilton of our necessary convictions.

(2.) I dispute his doctrine of causation. It is so lamentably defective in the view taken of the nature of cause, and so perversely mistaken in the theory grounded on this view, that several of his most distinguished disciples have been obliged to abandon it. The following is his account of effect and cause: " An effect is nothing more than the sum or complement of all the partial causes, the concurrence of which constitutes its existence." I remember no eminent philosopher who has given so inadequate a view of what constitutes cause. It leaves out the main element, — the power in the substance, or, more frequently, substances, acting as the cause to produce the effect. It leads him to represent the effect as an emanation from previously existing elements, a doctrine which he turns to no pantheistic use, but which has, undoubtedly, a pantheistic tendency. Taking such a view it is no wonder that he should represent creation as inconceivable; for the only creation which he can conceive, according to his theory, is not a creation of a new substance by God, but a creation out of God. Thus defective is his view of cause in itself. His view of the internal principle, which leads us, when we discover an effect to look for a cause is equally inadequate. According to him it is a mere *impotence* to conceive that there should not be something out of which this effect is formed; and, to complete the insufficiency of his theory, he makes even this a law of thought and not of things. Surely all this is in complete opposition to the consciousness to which he so often appeals. Our conviction as to cause is not a powerlessness, but a power ; not an inability, but an ability. It is an intuitive and necessary belief that this effect, and every other effect, must have a cause in something with power to produce it.

(3.) I dispute his theory as to our conviction of infinity. "We are," he says, "altogether unable to conceive space as bounded — as finite ; that is, as a whole beyond which there is no farther space." "On the other hand, we are equally power-less to realize in thought the possibility of the opposite contra-dictory : we cannot conceive space infinite or without limits." (Vol. II., p. 369, 370.) The seeming contradiction here arises from the double sense in which the word " conceive " is used. In the second of these counter propositions the word is used in the sense of imaging or representing in consciousness, as when the mind's eye pictures a fish or a mermaid. In this signification we cannot have an idea or notion of the infinite. But the thinking, judging, believing power of the mind is not the same as the imaging power. The mind can think of the class fish, or even of the imaginary class mermaid, while it can-not picture the class. Now, in the first of the opposed proposi-tions the word "conceive" is taken in the sense of thinking, deciding, being convinced. We picture space as bounded, but we cannot think, judge, or believe it to be bounded. When thus explained all appearance of contradiction disappears — indeed all the contradictions which the Kantians, Hegelians, and Hamiltonians are so fond of discovering between our intuitive convictions, will vanish if we but carefully inquire into the nature of these convictions. Both propositions, when rightly understood, are true, and there is no contradiction. They stand thus : — " We cannot image space as without bounds :" "we cannot think that it has bounds or believe that it has bounds." The former may well be represented as a creature impotency ; the latter is, most assuredly, a creature potency, — is one of the most elevated and elevating convictions of which the mind is possessed, — and is a conviction of which it can never be shorn.

It will be seen from these remarks that I refuse my adhe-rence to his peculiar theory of relativity, and to his maxim that " positive thought lies in the limitation or conditioning of one or other of two opposite extremes, neither of which, as unconditioned, can be realized to the mind as possible, and yet

of which, as contradictions, one or other must, by the fundamental laws of thought, be recognized as necessary." (Reid's
" Works," p. 743.)   It fails as to causation and as to infinity, and
he has left no formal application of it to substance and quality,
where, as Kant showed, there is no such infinite *regressus*, as
in infinite time and space or cause.   He would have found
himself in still greater difficulties had he ventured elaborately
to apply his theory to moral good.   As I believe him to
have been on the wrong track, I scarcely regret that he has
not completed his system and given us a doctrine of rational
psychology or ontology.   Indeed I have no faith whatever in a
metaphysics which pretends to do any more than determine,
in an inductive manner, the laws and faculties of the mind,
and, in doing so, to ascertain, formalize, and express the fundamental principles of cognition, belief, judgment, and moral
good.   The study of logic began to revive from the time that
Archbishop Whately constrained it to keep to a defined province.
The study of metaphysics would be greatly promoted if the
science would only learn to be a little more humble and less
pretending, and confine itself to that which is attainable.

Logic.   We may now look at his work on Logic, which is a
very elaborate one, and contains very able discussions and
learned notes.   It proceeds upon a very thorough acquaintance
with Aristotle and his commentators, with the schoolmen and
the logical writers of the seventeenth century ; but was directly
suggested by the Kantian criticism and amendment of logic, and
by the works of such men as Esser, Fries, Krug, and Drobisch,
who carried out the principles of the great German metaphysician.   Just as the " Port Royal Logic " has all the excellencies
and defects of the philosophy of Descartes, so the logic of
Hamilton has the combined truth and error of the metaphysics
of Kant.   It should be added, that his analytic, so far drawn
from German sources in some of its fundamental views, is,
after all, Hamilton's own, in the way in which it is wrought
out and applied.   Logic is defined as " the science of the
laws of thought as thought."   It is represented to be an *à
priori* science.   "It considers the laws of thought proper as
contained *à priori* in the nature of pure intelligence."   He
does not state, and evidently does not see, that these laws
of thought, while not the laws of the objects of thought,

are laws of thought as employed about objects, and can be discovered not *à priori*, but simply by an observation of the workings of thought.

He reviewed the not very philosophical but very shrewd and useful work of Whately, in the " Edinburgh Review " for 1833, criticising it with terrible severity, and giving indications of his own views. He was already cogitating his system, he expounded it to his class after he became professor, and he gave it to the public in "An Essay toward a new Analytic of Logical Forms," being that which gained the prize proposed by Sir William Hamilton, in the year 1846, for the best exposition of the new doctrine propounded in his lectures, with an historical appendix, by Thomas Spencer Baynes. It would require a treatise as elaborate as Hamilton's two volumes to state and examine it in detail, but I may notice some of the fundamental points.

The Concept. It proceeds on the distinction between the extension and comprehension of a term or notion. He makes no pretensions to the discovery of this principle. He knew that it was stated in the " Port Royal Logic," and that it was taught in Glasgow University by Hutcheson. Professor Baynes has shown in his translation of the " Port Royal Logic " that there were anticipations of it in earlier works. Hamilton carries out the distinction more thoroughly than it had ever been before. " The comprehension of a concept is nothing more than the sum or complement of the distinguishing characters or attributes of which the concept is made up ; and the extension of a concept is nothing more than the sum or complement of the objects themselves, whose resembling characters were abstracted to constitute the concept." (Vol. I., p. 148.) If we except his exposition of this distinction, he does not seem to me to throw much light, otherwise, on the first part of logic, — the part as it appears to me which has most need to be cleared up. He draws no distinction between the general notion and the abstract notion, but treats of both under the one designation, concept. But surely there is a distinction between two such notions as "animal" on the one hand, embracing an indefinite number of objects, and "life," which has not a complement of objects, but is only an attribute of objects.

Judgment. He claims originality chiefly for his doctrine of the thorough quantification of the predicate. "Touching the principle of an explicitly quantified predicate, I had by 1833 become convinced of the necessity to extend and correct the logical doctrine on this point." "Before 1840 I had become convinced that it was necessary to extend the principle equally to negatives." (Vol. II., p. 209.) This doctrine, as Professor Baynes shows, had been partially anticipated, but had never been fully carried out. I am inclined to admit that the credit, if there be any credit, in the thorough quantification of the predicate belongs to Hamilton. But I set no value on the supposed improvement. It proceeds on the simple logical postulate, " to state explicitly what is thought implicitly." I admit the principle, but deny that it requires the predicate to be universally quantified. When we say "the dog barks," we make the predication, without inquiring in thought whether there are or are not other dogs that bark, whether dogs are all or only some barking animals. When we say " man is rational," we do not determine whether or no there are other creatures that are rational ; whether, for example, angels may be called rational, whether men are " all " or only " some " rational. As the predicate is not always or even commonly quantified in spontaneous thought, so we do not require always to quantify it in the logical enunciation. At the same time, it is of importance to be able to quantify it on demand, and thus to see reflectively what is involved in every proposition.

In carrying out his principle, he adds to the four classes of propositions acknowledged in the received logic A, E, I, O, other four, —

    U. Common salt is chloride of sodium.
    Y. Some stars are all the planets.
    η. No birds are some animals.
    ω. Some common salt is not some chloride of sodium.

I do regard it as of moment to place in a distinct class those propositions which assert the equivalence of subject and predicate (U). But the others seem to me to be converted or rather perverted forms that never do present themselves in spontaneous thought : in which we say instead "all the planets are stars," and " some animals are not birds," and that " chloride of sodium in this cellar is not the same as chloride of sodium in that salt-cellar."

It is one of the supposed advantages of his analytic that it reduces the conversion of propositions from three species to one, — that of simple conversion. This holds true after we have converted the proposition into the form in which Hamilton has put it. When we say, "The bird sings," which is the form in spontaneous thought, Hamilton insists that logically it is, "The bird is some singing animal;" and after we have thus converted it once, the second conversion follows simply, "Some singing animals are birds." But there is nothing saved by requiring us to put every proposition in a form so different from that which it assumes in spontaneous thought.

Hamilton has done service to logic by unfolding more fully than had been done before what Kant called "syllogisms of the understanding," and which he calls immediate inferences, that is, inferences without a middle term, as when, from the proposition "All men have a conscience," we infer that some men have a conscience. He includes very properly under this head every form of conversion and opposition ; and it has been shown by him and others that it includes other immediate inferences which it is important to spread out to view. But instead of placing them under reasoning, they might be allowed to remain where conversion and opposition have usually been placed, in the second part of logic.

Reasoning. It is an alleged advantage of his analytic that it is "the revocation of two terms of a proposition to their true relation ; a proposition being always an equation of its subject and predicate." So he says the proposition all men are mortal, means "all men = some mortal." That in some propositions the subject and predicate are equivalent may be allowed ; and in such cases there may be no impropriety in using the mathematical equation, though generally it is better to allow mathematicians to keep their own symbols, as in their science they have a definite meaning, a meaning in regard to quantity ; and if we introduce symbols into logic, let us introduce new symbols appropriated to the ideas. Human thought is employed about a great many other objects as well as quantity. When we say, "Virtue leads to happiness," we are not uttering a quantitative

statement, " Virtue $=$ some things that lead to happiness ; "
but primarily an attributive assertion, that virtue has the attribute of leading to happiness, and by implication in extension,
" among the things that lead to happiness is virtue."

The new analytic claims that it reduces all the general laws
of categorical syllogisms to a single canon.   But what is that
canon ?   I confess I have difficulty in finding it.   Mr. Baynes
states it : " A syllogism is the product of that act of mediate
comparison " by which we recognized that two notions stand to
each other in the relation of whole and part, through the recognition that these notions severally stand in the same relation
to a third.   This canon is vague enough till it is explained
what is meant by the relation of whole and parts.   There is
valid ratiocination where the relationship does not seem that
of whole and parts.

> Chloride of sodium is not common salt ;
> Pepper is not chloride of sodium ;
> Therefore pepper is not common salt.

In many cases the relation is one of whole and parts.   But
of what kind of whole ?   Hamilton says that it is first one of
comprehension, and complains that logicians have overlooked
it.   Thus (Vol. I., p. 272) : —

> Every morally responsible agent is a free agent ;
> Man is a morally responsible agent ;
> Therefore man is a free agent, —

which is thus explained : The notion man comprehends in it
the notion responsible agent ; but the notion responsible agent
comprehends in it the notion free agent ; therefore, on the
principle that a part of a part is a part of a whole, the notion
man also comprehends in it the notion free agent.

But it is clear to me that in every one of these propositions
there is generalization or extension implied.   We have " every
responsible agent," " every man," and in the class of " free
agents," or " some free agents."   I acknowledge that there is
also comprehension involved, for all extension involves comprehension.   But the uppermost thought seems to me to be in
extension : Man is in the class responsible ; which again is in the
class free agent ; consequently man is in the class free agent.
Unless our knowledge of attributes is such as to enable us

thus to form classes, the reasoning is not valid; and the best form in which to bring out the principle involved is, —

All responsible agents are free agents;
But man is a responsible agent;
Therefore he is a free agent.

But if this be so, then we are back to the *dictum*, "Whatever is true of a class is true of all the members of the class." But as all extension involves comprehension, it is of moment to be able on demand to put reasoning in the form of comprehension.

It is urged in favor of the practical value of the analytic, that it makes figure unessential and reduction unnecessary. But it enlarges the number of legitimate moods, making them 36 under each figure, or in all 108, — a number which is apt to frighten the student.

He vacillates in his account of hypotheticals and disjunctives. His final opinion is given (Vol. II., 370–378 — "Hypotheticals (conjunctive and disjunctive), April 30, 1849"). "These syllogisms appear to be only modifications or corruptions of certain immediate inferences, for they have only two terms, and obtain a third proposition only by placing the general rule of inference (stating, of course, the possible alternatives), disguised, it is true, as the major premises."

He had divided logic into pure and modified, and he treats of the latter in Vol. II. He doubts whether there can be a modified logic; and is ever striving to impart to what he says under that head a rigidly technical form. The remarks which he throws out are often characterized by much intellectual ability, and some of them are of great value. But most of the topics discussed do not admit of so formal a treatment as he would give them. His account of the Baconian induction is a failure. The truth is, he never appreciated or understood the method pursued in the physical sciences.

The appendix contains a miscellaneous but very valuable set of papers on logical subjects. I doubt much whether Hamilton's system of logic will ever as a whole be adopted by our colleges. We have, however, two admirable text-books founded on it: — Thomson's "Outline of the Laws of Thought" and Bowen's "Logic." It will be acknowledged by all, that the discussions he has raised have done more to clear up unsettled points in formal logic than any work published since the days of Kant. These discussions will be looked at by writers on logic in all coming ages.

In parting with this great man, now gone from our world, it is most satisfactory to notice what was the professed aim of all his philosophy,— it was to point out the limits to human thought, and thereby to teach man the lesson of intellectual humility. It is instructive to find that this has been the aim of not a few of the most profound philosophers with which our world has been honored. The truth is, it is always the smallest minds which are most apt to be swollen with the wind engendered by their own vanity. The intellects which have gone out with greatest power to the farthest limits are those which feel most keenly the barriers by which man's capacity is bounded. The minds that have set out on the widest excursions, and which have taken the boldest flights, are those which know best that there is a wider region beyond, which is altogether inaccessible to man. It was the peculiarly wise man of the Hebrews who said, " No man can find out the work that God maketh from the beginning to the end." The Greek sage by emphasis declared that if he excelled others it was only in this, that he knew that he knew nothing. It was the avowed object of the sagacious Locke to teach man the length of his tether,— which, we may remark, those feel most who attempt to get away from it. Reid labored to restrain the pride of philosophy, and to bring men back to a common sense in respect of which the peasant and philosopher are alike. It was the design of Kant's great work to show how little the speculative reason can accomplish. And now we have Sir William Hamilton showing within what narrow limits the thought of man is restrained ; and the metaphysician, *par excellence*, of Oxford has, in the Bampton lectures, employed this philosophy to lay a restraint on the rational theology of Britain, and the speculative theology which is coming like a fog from the German Ocean. It is pleasant to think that Sir William Hamilton ever professed to bow with reverence before the revelations of the Bible, and takes delight in stating it to be the result of all his investigations, " that no difficulty emerges in theology which had not previously emerged in philosophy." In one of the letters which the author of this article has had from him he proceeds on the great Bible doctrines of grace ; and from all I know of him personally, I am prepared to believe in the account which I have heard from what I reckon competent authority, that the prayer which came from him at his dying hour was, " God be merciful to me, a sinner." It is most instructive to perceive the publican and the philosopher thus made to stand on the same level before the all-righteous Judge.

LVIII. — *THE METAPHYSICS OF THE FUTURE.*

WHAT are we to make in these times of metaphysics ? It is quite clear that this kind of investigation has lost, I suspect for ever, the position once allowed it, when it stood at the head of all secular knowledge, and claimed to be equal, or all but equal, in rank to theology itself. " Time was," says Kant, " when she was the queen of all the sciences ; and if we take the will for the deed, she certainly deserves, so far as regards the high importance of her object-matter, this title of honor. Now it is the fashion to heap contempt and scorn upon her ; and the matron mourns forlorn and forsaken like Hecuba." Some seem inclined to treat her very much as they treat those *de jure* sovereigns wandering over Europe whom no country will take as *de facto* sovereigns, — that is, they give her all outward honor, but no authority ; others are prepared to set aside her claims very summarily. The multitudes who set value on nothing but what can be counted in money never allow themselves to speak of metaphysics except with a sneer. The ever-increasing number of persons who read, but who are indisposed to think, complain that philosophy is not so interesting as the new novel, or the pictorial history, which is quite as exciting and quite as untrue as the novel. The physicist, who has kept a register of the heat of the atmosphere at nine o'clock in the morning for the last five years, and the naturalist, who has discovered a plant or insect, distinguished from all hitherto known species by an additional spot, cannot conceal their contempt for a department of inquiry which deals with objects which can neither be seen nor handled, neither weighed nor measured.

In the face of all this scorn I boldly affirm that mental philosophy is not exploded, and that it never will be exploded. Whatever men may profess or affect, they cannot, in fact, do without it. It often happens that a profession of contempt for all metaphysics, as being futile and unintelligible, is often an introduction to a discussion which is metaphysical without the parties knowing it (just as the person in the French play had spoken prose all his life without being aware of it) ; and of such metaphysics it will commonly be found that they are futile and unintelligible enough. Often is Aristotle denounced in language borrowed from himself, and the schoolmen are disparaged by those who are all the while using distinctions which they have cut with sharp chisel in the rock, never to be effaced. There are persons speaking with contempt of Plato, Descartes, Locke, and all the metaphysicians, who are taking advantage of the great truths which they have discovered. Perhaps these individuals are telling you very solemnly that they prefer the *practical* to the *theoretical*, or that they care little for the *form* if they have the *matter*, and are profoundly ignorant that they are all the while using distinctions introduced by the Stagyrite, and elaborated into their present shape by the scholastics. But surely, they will tell you, the discovery of a new *species* of an old *genus* is a more important event than all your philosophic discoveries ; and they will be surprised to learn that we owe the introduction of the phrases genus and species to Plato or to Socrates. Or perhaps they boast that they can have *ideas* without the aid of the philosophers, forgetting that Plato gave us the word *idea*, while Descartes and Locke brought it to its present signification. "Ah, but," says our novel reader, eager to discover whether the heroine so sad and forlorn in the second volume is to fall in with her lover, and be married to him before the close of the third, "metaphysics are *associated* in my mind with a dreary desert without and a headache within ; " and is quite unaware that he is able so to express himself, because philosophers have explained that ideas are associated. I could easily show that in our very sermons from the pulpit, and orations in the senate, and pleadings at the bar, principles are ever and anon appealed to which have come from the heads of our deepest thinkers in ages long gone by, and who may now be forgotten by all but a few antiquarians in philosophy. Our very natural science, in the hands of such men as Faraday and Mayer, is ever touching on the borders of metaphysics, and compelling our physicists to rest on certain fundamental convictions as to extension and force. The truth is, in very proportion as material science advances, do thinking minds feel the need of something to go down deeper and mount up higher than the senses can do ; of some means of settling those questions which the mind is ever putting in regard to the soul, and the relation of the universe to God ; and of a foundation on which the understanding can ultimately and confidently repose.

II. Metaphysics may have now to take a new start by taking advantage of physiological research. The Scottish school has never been slow to profit by the discoveries of science as to the brain, the nerves, the senses. From the first, and all along, they embraced and used all that was established in regard to the eye not being originally percipient of distance, to the distinction between the nerves of sensation, and to the reflex system in the human body ; and they set themselves against premature and rash hypotheses by Hartley, by Erasmus Darwin, and by the phrenologists. But physiology in its natural and necessary progress is coming nearer and closer to the line which divides mind from matter, and in these circumstances mental science has both to watch and profit by the investigations which are being so diligently pursued.

First, metaphysics must restrain the rash inferences of mere physiologists, as Reid did the vibration theory of Hartley, as Brown did the hypotheses of Darwin as to life, and as Hamilton did the pretended science of craniology. They must make the whole educated community know, believe, and realize, that such physical actions as attraction, repulsion, and motion are one set of phenomena, and perception, reasoning, desire, and moral discernment another and a very different set of phenomena. We can trace so far into the brain what takes place when the mother sees her son thrown out from a boat on the wild waves ; we can follow the rays of light through the eye on to the retina, to the sensorium, possibly on to the gray matter in the periphery of the brain ; and in the end physiology may throw some light on the whole cerebral action. But in the end, as at the beginning, we are in the domain of matter and motion ; we have only the same action as takes place in the brain of the dog as it looks on. But when the mother's affection rises up, when she forgets herself in thinking of her boy, when she uses expedients for rescuing him, when she resolves to plunge into the water and buffets the billows till she clasps her boy and lavishes her affection on him, we are in a region beyond that reached by the physiologist, — a region which I believe he can never reach ; and it is of importance to tell him so. But the psychologist can reach that region by consciousness, and ought diligently to explore it. Whatever be the pretensions it makes, physiology has hitherto thrown little light on purely mental phenomena, and none whatever on higher mental action, such as ratiocination, the idea of the good, and resistance to temptation.

Secondly, the metaphysician must enter the physiological field. He must, if he can, conduct researches ; he must at least master the ascertained facts. He must not give up the study of the nervous system and brain to those who cannot comprehend any thing beyond what can be made patent to the senses or disclosed to the microscope. I do cherish the hope that physiological psychology may in the end be rewarded by valuable discoveries. Light may be thrown on purely mental action by the fact that sensory action travels to the brain at the rate of 144.32 feet in the second, and from the brain at the rate of 108.24 ; that the movement is slowest in the case of the sense of sight and quickest in touch ; and by what is alleged by Donders that a thought requires $\frac{1}{216}$ of a second. There are mental actions which cannot well be explained by mental laws, such as the rise of certain states and the association of certain states ; the rise, for instance, and the association of cheerful thoughts in the time of health, and of gloomy thoughts when we are laboring under derangement of the stomach. There may here be latent processes which do not fall under consciousness, but may be detected by the microscope or chemical analysis. By such researches the results reached by the psychologist may be so far modified on the one hand and considerably widened on the other. But all such investigations should be conducted by those who can understand and appreciate the peculiar nature of mental phenomena, and allow them their full and legitimate space. No physiologist can talk of,

or so much as refer to, mental action without speaking of feelings, affections, thoughts, fancies, imaginations, desires, purposes, resolves ; but no eye, no mechanical instrument, can
detect these. They cannot be weighed in the balance or
measured by the line. There is a division of the mental faculties commonly adopted in the present day into the senses and
the intellect, the emotions and the will ; but this distribution is
suggested by the inward sense, and could never be discovered
by an inspection of the compartments of the brain.

III. Metaphysics will now require to determine by the aid of
physical science what truth there is in idealism. All is not
real that may seem or be declared to be so. The sky is not a
vault ; color is produced on the visual organism by vibration
in a medium ; the pleasure is not in the musical sounds. To
save realism we are obliged to draw distinctions, say with
Aristotle, between common and proper percepts, or with Locke
and the Scottish school, between the primary and secondary
qualities of matter. But I have a strong conviction that all
such distinctions may only be partially correct, and are only
provisionally applicable. But as physical and physiological
science make farther progress, we may ascertain the exact
truth, and find that it clears up many obscure points. As the
facts are ascertained, metaphysics should take them up, and,
combining our intuitive perceptions with them, may determine
precisely what we are entitled to affirm of matter. In the end
some of the statements of the Scottish school as to the precise
nature of the external reality may be modified or even set
aside. But the great truths propounded by such men as Hamilton will only be established, and seen to rest on a basis which
can never be moved. It will be acknowledged that there is an
external thing independent of mind, and that this is extended,
and has a passive potency. However much we may refine it,
enough will be left of matter to undermine Berkleianism and
every form of idealism.

IV. Metaphysics may be able to give a more accurate expression of fundamental truth. It is one of the peculiar excellencies of the Scottish school that they stand up for first truths
which cannot be proven on the one hand nor set aside on the
other. They are not just agreed as to the form which they should
take, or the language in which they should be expressed. Mr.

J. S. Mill and Mr. Herbert Spencer think that they can account for all or many of these by the association of ideas or heredity. But neither of these thinkers is so bold as to maintain that he has done away with all fundamental truth. It can be shown that Mr. Mill is for ever appealing to truths which he assumes and regards himself as entitled to assume. (See "Examination of the Philosophy of J. S. Mill.") Mr. Spencer falls back on a law of necessity which testifies to a great unknown, which he allots as a territory to faith and to religion. I do not admit that he has given a proper expression to the fundamental verity or fundamental verities which he assumes. He starts on the principle of relativity, as expounded by Hamilton and Mansel, the authoritative metaphysicians when he began to speculate. I do not admit that the known logically or metaphysically implies the unknown. I am sure that his followers will leave behind them as they advance this unknown region of faith. Following out his own method, they will account for it all by circumstances working from generation to generation. But as Mill and Spencer have not been able to get rid of first truths, so no others will, and this whether they avow it or no. All processes must conduct to something ultimate. Thought requires a final resting-place, which will be found self-evident, necessary, universal. The age demands that the whole subject be rediscussed, with the view of determining what are the first, the last, and the everlasting principles of thought and truth. Some of those defended by the Scottish metaphysicians may be derivative, but they will be found to imply a root from which they are sprung.

APPENDIX.

APPENDIX.

―――

Art. I. *Extracts from MS. Letters of Francis Hutcheson to the Rev. Thomas Drennan, Minister of First Presbyterian (non-subscribing) Congregation, Belfast; lent me by his grandson, Dr. Drennan.* (*See p. 64.*)

Glasgow, Jan. 31, 1737. — I am glad your present situation is agreeable to you. I must insist on your promise of a visit whenever you find honest Mr. Haliday (Mr. Drennan's colleague) in good health, so that he could take the whole burden for a month or six weeks. Robert Simson, with you and Charles Moor, would be wondrous happy till three in a morning; I would be with you from five to ten. I can write you little news. Our college is very well this year as to numbers and quality of scholars, but the younger classes are less numerous as people here grow less set on a college education for lads designed for business. . . . I must tell you a shameful story of our college. My letter I wrote from Dublin stopped Clotworthy O'Neal getting his degree upon his first application. He got some folks in this country who are tools of the court to recommend the matter to our principal. He made a compliment of twenty guineas to the college library, and the principal watched an opportunity when there was a thin meeting, but his tools all present, and carried to him a degree in ——; that too, only an honorary one, and declared so in the diploma without any certificate for his learning or manners. My dissent is entered in the books, and four more masters decline signing it."

April 17, 1738. — Robert Simson, if he were not indolent beyond imagination, could in a fortnight's application finish another book which would surprise the connoisseurs. About November last, I sent a manuscript to Will Bruce chiefly for his and Mr. Abernethy's perusal. He showed it to the Bishop of Derry, who, it seems, is much pleased with it, and promises me a long epistle soon. I heartily wish you had seen it, but it did not get to Dublin till February, and was in the bishop's hands till the beginning of this month. I believe Will is perusing it now. I am not expecting it back again speedily. During our college session I get nothing done, but if I get them back during our vacation, with remarks of my friends, I shall endeavor to put the last hand to them. If I can get leisure next month, I shall endeavor to send you such a letter as I once gave you an imperfect promise of, if my hand be not gone out of use. We have at last got a minister in Glasgow to my taste. As I know your laziness, I really wish you and he could interchange sermons now and then. I am surprised to find some people of very good sense, laymen more than clergy, here not a little pleased with some of the notions of the foreign mystics; they have raised my curiosity of late to look into these books. I shall, sometime or other, let you know the result of my reading that way. I am persuaded their warm imaginations would make them moving preachers. I am going to read Madame Bourignon when I have leisure. You'll make Sam Haliday laugh heartily by telling him this particular. My most hearty respects to him.

Glasgow, March 5, 1738-39. — I had yours of the 26th of February on Friday, and could not answer sooner. I had resolved, when I first read yours, to have wrote you in the negative, being in as much hurry at present as I have been this session by many letters of business as well as by my ordinary work. I have got on my hands almost the whole paternal care of my old pupil Lord Kilmarnock's three sons here. But upon reading over your letter this morning, with the deepest concern for that worthy, friendly, generous man, I could not refuse you altogether what you desire; though I concluded it must be either an unreasonable diffidence in yourself or an unjust value your friendship makes you put upon what comes from me, that occasions such requests. I shall be forced to work in starts, with many interruptions, which never succeeds right with me; and beseech you be as busy as you can in some scheme of your own, and don't take any sudden interrupted attempts of mine as fit for all the purposes you say are expected by friends on this occasion. I hint to you my plan that you may work upon it, and be the readier to patch up a right thing out of the two : — "A consideration of what sort of life is most worthy and best suited to a being capable of such high endowments, and improvements, and actions destined to an immortal existence, and yet subjected for a certain space to a mortal existence in this world, and then without drawing a character, leaving it to the audience to recollect how much of this appeared in our friend's life."

I hope Jack Smith has sent down to your town a "Serious Address to the Kirk of Scotland," lately published in London; it has run like lightning here, and is producing some effect; the author is unknown; he wrote with anger and contempt of the Kirk and Confession; but it has a set of objections against the Confession which I imagine few will have the brow to answer.

I really suffer with you heartily in the loss of your worthy friend; you will miss him exceedingly, and so will your cause.

A worthy lad in this town, one Robert Foulis, out of a true public spirit, undertook to reprint for the populace an old excellent book, "A Persuasive to Mutual Love and Charity," wrote by White, Oliver Cromwell's chaplain; it is a divine old-fashioned thing. Some are cast off in better paper, sold at 9*d.* in marble paper; the coarse ones are sold at 5*d.* in blue paper, and at 4*d.* to booksellers. I wish your booksellers would commission a parcel of both sorts. There has been some whimsical buffoonery about my heresy, of which I will send you a copy.

Glasgow, June 1, 1741.[1] — Our countrymen very generally have such an affectation of being men and gentlemen immediately, and of despising every thing in Scotland, that they neglect a great deal of good, wise instruction they might have here. I am truly mortified with a vanity and foppery prevailing among our countrymen beyond what I see in others; and a softness and sauntering forsooth which makes them incapable of any hearty drudgery at books. We had five or six young gentlemen from Edinburgh, men of fortune and fine genius at my class, and studying law; our Irishmen thought them poor book-worms.

Glasgow, June 15, 1741. — The wretched turn their minds take is to the silly manliness of taverns. . . . I shall not leave Glasgow except about three weeks in July for this whole vacation, but have more avocations by too numerous an acquaintance than you can imagine. In short, Tom, I find old age not in gray hairs and other trifles, but in an incapacity of mind for such close thinking or composition as I once had, and have pretty much dropped the thoughts of some great designs I had once sketched out. In running over my papers I am quite

---

[1] In this letter, and in several of those that follow, there is a great deal said about a young man named Robert Haliday, who is studying at Glasgow, and about whom Hutcheson is very anxious.

dissatisfied with method, style, matter, and some reasonings, though I don't repent my labor, as by it and the thoughts suggested by friends,—a multitude of which I had from W. Bruce and Synge, and still more in number from some excellent friends here,—I am fitter for my business ; but, as to composing in order, I am quite bewildered, and am adding confusedly to a confused book all valuable remarks in a farrago, to refresh my memory in my class lectures on several subjects. You'll find the like. Pray lay up a good stock of sermons. You would see a noble one by one of my Scotch intimates, who sees all I do, Mr. Leechman.

Glasgow, April 12, 1742. You are such a lazy wretch that I should never write you more. Not one word of answer to my congratulatory epistle you got six weeks before you were married. Not one word of godly admonitions about spending an evening with friends at the Welshes Head, and other pious sentiments about the vanity and folly of staying at home in the evenings.

Glasgow, May 31, 1742. — The bearer, Mr. Hay, takes over some copies of a new translation of Antoninus, the greater half of which, and more, was my amusement last summer for the sake of a singular worthy soul, one Foulis ; but I don't let my name appear in it, nor indeed have I told it to any here but the man concerned : I hope you'll like it. The rest was done by a very ingenious lad, one Moore. Pray try your critical faculties in finding what parts I did, and what he did. I did not translate books in suite ; but I one or two, and he one or two. I hope if you like it that it may sell pretty well with you about Belfast. I am sure it is doing a public good to diffuse the sentiments ; and, if you knew Foulis, you would think he well deserved all encouragement.

Date cut off. — Having this opportunity, I must trouble you with a small affair. Upon conversation with Mr. Brown, who came lately from Ireland, along with Mr. Alexander Haliday, about the circumstances of some ministers, very worthy men, in your presbytery, it occurred to me that a little liberality could not be better exercised than among them. I am concerned that in my prosperous circumstances I did not think of it sooner. If you have any little contributions made towards such as are more distressed than the rest, you may mark me as a subscriber for 5*l*. per annum, and take the above ten pounds as my payment for the two years past. Alexander Young will advance it immediately, as I wrote him lately that I would probably draw such a bill, without telling him the purposes. I think it altogether proper you should not mention my name to your brethren, but conceal it. I am already called New Light here. I don't value it for myself, but I see it hurts some ministers here, who are most intimate with me. I have been these ten days in great hurry and perplexity, as I have for that time foreseen the death of our professor, who died last Wednesday, and some of my colleagues join me in laboring for Mr. Leechman to succeed. We are not yet certain of the event, but have good hopes. If he succeeds, it will put a new face upon theology in Scotland. I am extremely concerned for your divisions in Belfast. I find they talk of Jack Maxwell of Armagh or young Kennedy. The talents of this latter I know not, but believe he has a very honest heart. Jack Maxwell is an ingenious, lively fellow, for any thing I could discover. That presbytery will miss him much. Pray write me now sometimes. I am sorry the event in your family made some hints in my last so seasonable. But your son is now as well as if he had lived sixty years a Plato or a Cæsar, or if he is not, life is scarce worth spending under such a Providence : we should all long ὕδωρ καὶ γαῖα γίνεσθαι.

Glasgow, August 5, 1743. — I have had two letters of late from Mr. Mussenden; one about five weeks ago, with an invitation to Mr. Leechman to succeed Dr. Kilpatrick. Leechman was then just upon his marriage. I concluded the matter

quite impracticable, and returned an answer to that purpose ; and, upon conversing, Leechman found I was not then mistaken. He was lately very ill treated by
our judges in a discretionary augmentation he applied for, which they could have
given with full consent of parties. His wife is not so averse to removal as formerly. Indeed the difficulty is with himself. You never knew a better, sweeter
man, — of excellent literature, and, except his air and a little roughness of voice,
the best preacher imaginable. You could not get a greater blessing among you of
that kind. As I have heard nothing from other hands, I want fuller information.
Are the people generally hearty for Leechman upon the character they hear? Is
there no other worthy man on the field? Unless these points be cleared, he will take
no steps. I remember one Millan, an assistant. Pray is he to be continued, and
no way affronted or neglected in this design? Leechman is well as he is, and
happy, though preaching to a pack of horse-copers and smugglers of the rudest
sort. He would do nothing hard or disagreeable to any worthy man, and has no
desire of change. But if the field be clear, it were *peccare in publica commoda* not
to force him out of that obscure hole where he is so much lost. He was the man
I wished in the first place to be our professor of theology. . . . I have no news
but that we expect immediately from Robert Simson a piece of amazing geometry,
reinventing two books of Appollonius, and he has a third almost ready. He
is the best geometer in the world, reinventing old books, of which Pappius preserves only a general account of the subjects.

Glasgow, Sept. 20, 1743. — I had the favor of yours by Mr. Blow, but could
not return an answer by him, being much employed in promoting the affair you
wrote about. I had also very urgent letters from Messrs. Mairs and Duchals to
the same purpose. 'Tis very difficult to persuade a modest worthy man who is
tolerably settled, to adventure upon a new scene of affairs among strangers. I
shall use my utmost endeavors to prevail upon him as I have been doing for some
time past. I am sorry I cannot give you great hopes of success , but I don't yet
so despair as to quit solicitation, as he is exceedingly moved with the affection
and generosity of that people. My most humble and hearty respects to your
brethren of your presbytery, whom I shall always remember with the greatest
esteem and affection.

Glasgow, Feb. 20, 1743-44. — I am not a little surprised that I have not heard
from you these four months past, though there were some of my letters which any
other person would have thought required an answer. I could tell you a good
deal of news upon the unexpected election of a professor of divinity, and the
furious indignation of our zealots ; but you deserve no news from anybody. We
have our own concern about the settlement in Belfast, but we are to expect no
accounts from you of any thing. Pray tell Mrs. Haliday her son is doing very
well. . . . I was never more honored than since our late professor's death. Our
hearty respects to Mrs. Drennan, and sympathy on the loss of her boys. ·

> Dicimus autem hos quoque felices qui ferre incommoda vitæ
> Nec jactare jugum vita dedicere magistra.

Glasgow, April 16, 1746. — Our public news of the 15th from Edinburgh was,
that the duke had passed the Spey, that 2,000 rebels on the banks fled precipi-
tately upon his pointing his cannon at them. They may reassemble, and, as they
are very cunning, may have some artifice to surprise ; but I cannot but hope they
are dispersing, and their chiefs making their escape. You have heard no doubt
of our taking from them the "Hazard" sloop they had taken at Montrose. She
returned from France with 150 men and arms and ammunition, and had landed
them ; but Lord Rea very boldly attacked them with a smaller number, and took

them all prisoners with 13,000*l.* sterling. The same man-of-war took another of their ships, with arms and ammunitions, which had seized twelve small merchant-men in Orkneys for their use. The duke has endeared himself to some of his very enemies by his good sense and humanity, void of all state or pride.

I had this day a letter from a presbytery of Pennsylvania, of a very good turn, regretting their want of proper ministers and books, expecting some assistance here; it was of a very old date of October last. I shall speak to some wise men here, but would as soon speak to the Roman conclave as our presbytery. The Pennsylvanians regret the want of true literature; that Whitfield has promoted a contempt of it among his followers, and bewailing some wretched contentions among themselves. The only help to be expected from you is sending some wise men if possible. I shall send them my best advice about books and philosophy, and hope to be employed to buy them books cheaper here than they are to be got anywhere. I long for a fuller letter about all your chat and news. I am in a great deal of private distresses about Jo Wilson and his sister, — the latter in the utmost danger, the other scarce recovered from death, my wife too very tender ; but by a set of most intricate business, upon which the soul of this college depends, and all may be ruined by the want of one vote, I cannot leave this till after the 26th of June, and we go to Dublin first.

ART. II. *Questions proposed in the Philosophical Society in Aberdeen* (*see p.* 227).

1. President. — Whether the greatest part of the matter that composes the bodies of vegetables and animals is not air or some substance that is mixed with the air and floats in it. Handled, Feb. 8.

2. Dr. Skene. — What are the proper characters of enthusiasm and super-stition, and their natural effects upon the human mind ? Handled, Jan. 25.

3. Mr. Trail. — What are the proper methods of determining the sun's par-allax by the transit of Venus over his disk in 1761 ? Handled, April 12.

4. Mr. Campbell. — What is the cause of that pleasure we have from repre-sentations or objects which excite pity or other painful feelings ? Handled, Feb. 8.

5. What is the true cause of the ascent, suspension, and fall of vapors in the atmosphere ? Mr. Stewart. Handled, Feb. 22.

6. Mr. Reid. — Whether some part of that food of plants which is contained in the air is not absorbed by the earth, and in the form a watery fluid conveyed into the vessels of plants. And whether any thing can enter into the vessels of plants that is not perfectly soluble in water. Handled, March 8.

7. President. — Is there a standard of taste in the fine arts and in polite writ-ing; and how is that standard to be ascertained ? Handled, March 22, and May 10.

8. Dr. Skene. — How far human actions are free or necessary. Handled, May 24, and June 14.

9. How far the motion of the earth and of light accounts for the aberration of the fixed stars. Mr. Trail. Handled, April 12.

10. Mr. Campbell. — Can the generation of worms in the bodies of animals be accounted for on the common principles of generation. Handled, June 28.

11. Is the human soul confined to any part of the human body ; and, if so, to what part ? Mr. Stewart. Handled, June 28.

12. Mr. Reid. — Are the objects of the human mind properly divided into impressions and ideas ? And must every idea be a copy of a preceding impression. Handled, July 13 and 26.

Jan. 25, no questions. Feb. 8, 22. March 8, none.

March 22, 1758.

13. Mr. Gordon. — What is the origin of polytheism ? Handled, Aug. 10.

14. Mr. Gerard. — What are the proper subjects of demonstrative reasoning ? Handled, Aug. 23, and Sept. 13.

April 12.

15. Mr. Farquhar. — Upon what the characters of men chiefly depend ? Nov. 15.

16. What is the apparent figure of the heavens, and what are the causes of it ? Humanist, Nov. 15.

17. Whether justice be a natural or artificial virtue. Nov. 22.

April 22.

18. Mr. Farquhar. — In the perfection of what faculty does genius consist ? Or if in a combination of faculties what are they ? Superseded, because the subject of Mr. Gerard's discourses.

19. What are the parts of the body so connected with the several faculties of the mind that the destruction of those parts brings on a destruction of the exercise of those faculties. Dec. 13.

20. Dr. Gregorie. — What are the plants that enrich a soil and what are those that impoverish it, and what are the causes of their enriching it, and impoverishing it ? Feb. 11, 1759.

21. Dr. Skene. — Wherein does happiness consist ? March 28.

22. Whether the ideas of mixed modes are to be considered as the mere creatures of the mind, or are formed after patterns, as well as the ideas of the substances whereof they are modes. Mr. Trail, Feb. 11, 1759.

23. Mr. Campbell. — Whether matter has a separate and permanent existence. The nature of contrariety. May 30.

24. Mr. Stewart. — Whether the sense of hearing may not be asserted by act, in like manner as that of seeing is by optical glasses. April 11.

25. Mr. Reid. — Whether mankind with regard to morals always was and is the same. June 12.

26. In what cases and for what causes is lime a proper manure ? Mr. Thos. Gordon. July 24, and Aug. 14.

27. Mr. Gerard. — What is the origin of civil government ? June 26.

28. Mr. Farquhar. — What is the foundation of moral obligation ? Sept. 26.

29. Mr. Ross. — How can it be accounted for that an inflammable spirit is obtained from regenerated tartar (vinegar saturated with chalk or saccharum saturne by distillation) ? Or how comes it about that vinegar is restored to the state of an ardent spirit by being distilled with fixed alkali, chalk, or lead ? Oct. 16, 1759.

30. Dr. Gregorie. — Whether the Socratic method of instruction or that of prelection is preferable. Jan. 8, 1760.

31. How far the ancient method of education in public seminaries from earliest infancy was preferable or inferior to the modern practice. By Dr. Skene, Nov. 27, 1759.

32. Mr. Trail. — What is the Agrian law which will conduce most to the populousness of a nation ? Or what is the maximum of estates fittest for that purpose ?

33. Whether education in public schools or by private tutors be preferable. Principal Campbell, Dec. 11, 1759, and Feb. 26, 1760.

34. Mr. Stewart. — Whether the time allotted for teaching Greek in the universities of Scotland be not too short, and, if so, what would be the proper remedy. Feb. 26, 1760.

35. Mr. Reid. — Whether it is proper to educate children without instilling principles into them of any kind whatsoever. April 1, 1760.

36. Mr. Gordon. — Whether there be not, in the very nature of our teaching societies, a tendency to stop farther advancement in those branches of learning which they profess. And, if it is so, what is the best remedy. June 24, and July 9, 1760.

37. Prof. Gerard. — In what manner the general course of education may be conducted so as it may answer best as a preparation for the different businesses of life. Aug. 12, 1760.

38. What is the best method for training to the practice of virtue? Mr. Farquhar. Dec. 9, 1760.

39. What are the natural consequences of high national debt; and whether, upon the whole, it be a benefit to a nation or not? Dr. Gregorie. Jan. 13, 1761.

40. Whether paper credit be beneficial to a nation or not. Dr. Skene, Feb. 24.

41. What is the cause of the apparent color of the heavens? Or what is properly the object to which that color can be attributed? Principal Campbell, March 10.

42. Whether the idea of cause and effect include in it any thing more than their constant conjunction. And, if so, what it is that it includes. Prof. Stewart. March 10th and 31st.

43. Mr. Trail. — Whether the substituting of machines instead of men's labor, in order to lessen the expense of labor, contributes to the populousness of a country. Feb. 24.

44. Mr. Reid. — Whether moral character consists in affections, wherein the will is not concerned; or in fixed habitual and constant purposes. April 15.

45. Mr. Gordon. — Whether slavery be in all cases inconsistent with good government. Nov. 24.

46. Mr. Gerard. — Whether there be any such affection in human nature as universal benevolence. Dec. 8.

47. Mr. Farquhar. — Whether in writing history it be proper to mix moral and political reflexions or to draw characters. Dec. 8.

48. Whence does man derive the authority which he assumes over the brutes, and how far does this authority extend? Mr. Beattie. Dec. 22, 1761.

49. What are the best expedients for preventing an extravagant rise of servants' wages, and for obliging them to bestow their labor where agriculture and manufactures require it. Jan. 12, 1762. Occasional question.

50. Doctor Gregorie. — What are the good and bad effects of the provision for the poor by poor's rates, infirmaries, hospitals, and the like? Feb. 9.

51. Doctor Skene. — Whether the determination by unanimity or a majority injuries is most equitable. March 9.

52. Doctor Campbell. — How far human laws can justly make alterations on what seems to be founded on the principles of the law of nature. March 23.

53. Mr. Stewart. — Whether human laws be binding on the consciences of men. April 16.

54. Mr. Reid. — Whether by the encouragement of proper laws the number of births in Great Britain might not be nearly doubled or at least greatly increased. June 8.

55. Mr. Thomas Gordon. — Whether the current coin of the nation ought not to be debased by alloy or raised in its value, so as there shall be no profit made by exporting it. Dec. 14.

56. Doctor Gerard. — Whether it be best that courts of law and courts of equity were different, or that the same court had the power of determining either according to law or equity as circumstances require. Feb 22, 1763.

57. Mr. Farquhar. — Whether justice is most effectually promoted in civil and criminal courts where the judges are numerous or where they are few. March 22.

58. Mr. Beattie. — What are the advantages and disadvantages of an extensive commerce? March 22.

59. Dr. Gregory. — Whether the art of medicine, as it has been practised, has contributed to the advantage of mankind. July 12.

60. Dr. Skene. — Whether in the same person opposite passions and affections, such as love and hatred, resentment of injuries and benefits, always subsist in an equal degree of strength. Oct. 10.

61. Dr. Campbell. — Whether any animals besides men and domestic animals are liable to diseases, the decay of nature and accidental hurts excepted ; and if they are not, whether there is any thing in the domestic life which can account for such diseases as men and domestic animals are obnoxious to. May 10.

62. Mr. Stewart. — Whether or not there be a real foundation for the distinction betwixt precepts or counsels in matters of morality. Dec. 13.

63. Dr. Reid. — Whether every action deserving moral approbation must be done from a persuasion of its being morally good. Nov. 22, 1763.

64. Mr. Thomas Gordon. — How far the profession of a soldier of fortune is defensible *in foro conscientiæ.* Jan. 24, 1764.

65. Dr. Gerard. — Whether eloquence be useful or pernicious. Feb. 28, 1764.

66. Mr. Farquhar. — What is the origin of the blacks? March 13, 1764.

67. Mr. Beattie. — What is that quality in objects that makes them provoke laughter? March 27.

68. Dr. George Skene. — Whether are men become degenerate in point of size and strength, or has the modern method of living increased the number of diseases or altered their nature? April 9.

69. Mr. William Ogilvy. — Whether curiosity be not the most powerful motive to study in the mind of youth and that which acts most uniformly. Nov. 27.

70. Dr. Gregory. — What are the distinguishing characteristics of wit and humor? May 8.

71. Dr. David Skene. — Whether brutes have souls ; or, if they have, wherein do they differ from the human? Nov. 15.

72. Dr. Campbell. — Whether the manner of living of parents affects the genius or intellectual abilities of the children. Jan. 22, 1765.

73. Mr. Stuart. — Whether the idea of an infinitely perfect Being be a good argument for his existence. June 11, 1765.

74. Dr. Reid. — Wherein does the nature of a promise consist, and whence does its obligation arise? March 12, 1765.

75. Mr. Thomas Gordon. — Whether there is any degeneracy of genius in the moderns. March 26, 1765.

76. Dr. Gerard. — Whether children do not take more after the mother than the father, and if they do, what are the causes of it? Aug. 13, 1765.

77. Mr. Farquhar. — Whether would the end of religion be most effectually promoted by a regular civil establishment for the support of the clergy, or by leaving their support to the voluntary contributions of the people? Nov. 12.

78. What is the difference between common sense and reason? Dec. 10, 1765.

79. Dr. George Skene. — Is light a body whose particles are thrown off with great velocity from the luminous body, or is it a *tremulous* motion excited and propagated through a subtle medium analogous to the tremors of flies which occasion sound? Dec. 9, 1766.

80. Mr. William Ogilvie. — Suppose a legislator were to form an establishment of clergy, on what principles ought he to proceed in order to render it most effectual for promoting religion and morality without favoring superstition? Nov. 11, 1766.

81. Mr. Dunbar. — Whether the considerations of good policy may not sometimes justify the laying of a restraint upon population in a state.

82. Dr. David Skene. — What are the advantages which mankind peculiarly derive from the use of speech? March 13, 1766.

83. Dr. Campbel. — Whether it is possible that the language of any people should continue invariably the same, and if not, from what causes the variations arise. Oct. 13, 1766.

84. Mr. Thomas Gordon. — Whether in science it ought to be an aim to increase or to diminish the number of first principles. June 10, 1766.

85. Dr. Gerard. — Whether any form of government can be perpetual. Dec. 9, 1766.

86. Mr. Farquhar. — Whether the observation of the unities of time and place are essentially requisite to the perfection of dramatic performances. Jan. 27, 1767.

87. Mr. Beattie. — Whether the different opinions and different practices which prevail in different nations be an objection to the universality of the virtuous sentiment. Feb. 24, 1767.

88. Dr. George Skene. — Whether the opportunities of acquiring a learned education may not be too much in the power of the commonalty either for the advancement of learning or the good of the state.

89. Mr. Ogilvy. — How does it appear to be equitable that the subjects of the state should be taxed in proportion to their respective fortunes and not equally over head or by any other rule? March 24, 1767.

90. Mr. Trail. — In what sense may virtue be said to consist in acting agreeably to nature, and vice in deviating from it?

91. Dr. David Skene. — If mankind are considered in respect of rank and fortune, in what class may we expect to find the virtuous principle most prevalent? June 9, 1767.

92. Dr. Campbel. — Whether the Greek language remained invariably the same so long as is commonly thought, and to what causes the duration which it had ought to be ascribed. Nov. 10, 1767.

93. Mr. Gordon. — What is the province and use of metaphysics? Dec. 8, 1767.

94. Dr. Gerard. — Whether poetry can be justly reckoned an imitative art; and, if it can, in what respects? Jan. 26, 1768.

95. Mr. Farquhar. — Whether the maintaining an esoteric and exoteric doctrine, as was practised by the ancients, is reconcilable to the principles of virtue.

96. Mr. Beattie. — Whether that superiority of understanding by which the inhabitants of Europe and of the countries immediately adjoining imagine themselves to be distinguished may not easily be accounted for without supposing the rest of mankind of an inferior species.

97. Dr. George Skene. — Whether the aim of a public teacher ought to be to adapt his instructions to the capacities of the duller part of his audience or to forward the ingenious.

98. Mr. Ogilvie. — What is that in the manners of any nation which exhibits it justly to the appellations of civilized or barbarous?

99. Mr. Dunbar. — What are the characteristics of polished language? and how is the comparative excellency of different languages to be estimated?

100. Mr. Trail. — How far may the inequalities of astronomical refraction be remedied by the thermometer and barometer?

101. Dr. David Skene. — Whether the late proceedings with respect to a favorite of the mob be an evidence of the corruption or of the improvement of our constitution.

102. Principal Campbel. — What is the proper notion of civil liberty? Oct. 24, 1769.

103. Mr. Gordon. — How far the facts relating to the burning of the Roman ships in the harbor of Syracuse be reconcilable to the laws of reflection and refraction of light. Nov. 1769.

104. Dr. Gerard. — Whether any account can be given of the causes why great geniuses have arisen at the periods which have been most remarkable for them, and why they have frequently arisen in clusters. Dec. 12, 1769.

105. Mr. Beattie. — Whether the use of translations can ever supersede the necessity of studying the Greek and Roman authors in the original languages. May 8, 1770.

106. Dr. George Skene. — What is the difference between pressure and momentum; and how are they to be compared? Nov. 27, 1770.

107. Mr. Ogilvy. — Whether there may be any reason to believe that the friendships of this life may continue after death.

108. Mr. Dunbar. — Whether the increasing the number of British peers tends to enlarge or diminish the power of the crown. March 27, 1770.

109. Mr. Trail. — What are the *desiderata* in mathematics? June 12, 1770.

110. Occasional question proposed by Mr. Beattie. — Whether it be not for the advantage of mankind as moral beings that the evidence of a future state is rather a high probability than an absolute certainty. Oct. 9, 1769.

111. Dr. David Skene. — What are the advantages and disadvantages arising from the different arrangements of words which obtain in the antient and modern languages?

112. Principal Campbel. — What is the best method of teaching a foreign or dead language?

113. Mr. Gordon. — How are *vis inertiæ* and weight to be distinguished, and in what do they agree?'

114. 'Dr. Gerard. — Whether national characters depend upon physical or moral causes, or whether they are influenced by both. Feb. 26, 1771.

115. Mr. Beattie. — Does it imply any absurdity or any thing inconsistent with the divine perfections to suppose that evil, both physical and moral, must be permitted to take place in a state of moral probation? March 26, 1771.

116. Dr. George Skene.

117. Mr. Ogilvy. — Is there any injustice done to an impressed man, when he is punished according to the articles of war? March 12, 1771.

118. Mr. Dunbar. — How are the proceedings of instinct to be distinguished from reason or sagacity in animals? Feb. 11, 1772.

119. Mr. Trail. — What is the cause of the color of the heavenly bodies? Feb. 25, 1772.

119. Dr. Campbel. — What are the advantages and disadvantages arising from the different arrangements of words which obtain in the ancient and modern languages?

120. Mr. Gordon. — How far is an expensive taste of living connected with corruption of manners and the ruin of a nation?

121. Dr. Gerard. — What are the ways in which watering operates in improving land? March 24, 1772.

122. Dr. Beattie. — How far is versification essential to poetry?

123. Dr. George Skene.

124. Mr. Ogilvy. — By what circumstances has slavery been so moderated as to become supportable to so many nations of mankind?

125. Mr. Dunbar.

126. Mr. Trail. — Does Dr. Halley's theory of evaporation sufficiently account for the constant influx into the Mediterranean at the Straits of Gibraltar?

———•———

Art. III. *MSS. Papers by Dr. Reid, lent me by Francis Edmund, Esq., Aberdeen (see pp.* 192, 223.)

I. *Some Observations on the modern System of Materialism.* This paper is in no fewer than five forms, showing what pains he took with it. One or two of the forms were notes or preparations, the other three fully written out as if to be read before a society.

By the modern system of materialism he means that advanced by Dr. Priestley in his "Disquisitions relating to Matter and Spirit," 1777, and "Free Discussion of the Doctrines of Materialism and Philosophical Necessity," 1777. The paper is of a thorough and searching character, distinguished for acuteness beyond almost any of the published writings of Reid, and written with great point and naïveté. It looks as if designed for publication. Chap. I. *Of the Connection of this System with other philosophical Opinions.* Here he describes the views entertained of substance by eminent men, criticising ably the defective views of Locke. Chap. II. *Of Newton's Rules of philosophizing,* showing that he had profoundly studied Newton. He gives fair explanations of Newton's rules. He shows that Priestley does not follow these rules. Chap. III. *Of the Solidity or Impenetrability of Matter,* showing there is an ambiguity in the meaning of the word solidity, and that Priestley has not succeeded in showing that matter is not solid or impenetrable. Chap. IV. *Of the Inertia of Matter,* showing that Priestley does not follow Newton. The whole is the result of much reading and reflection.

II. *Miscellaneous Reflections on Priestley's account of Hartley's Theory of the Human Mind.* He shows that Hartley's views were unfounded hypotheses, but speaks with great fondness and respect of Hartley. He is very severe upon Priestley's employment of Hartley's theories, particularly upon his attempt to explain every mental faculty by association. He refers to Aristotle's views of association. He shows that association cannot account for memory, which was explained by the vividness of the ideas. "Every man knows what memory is, and every man knows what is meant by vividness of ideas or conceptions, and their power of suggesting one another; and when we know and understand what each of these things is we can be at no loss to know whether they are one and the same. Let every man judge for himself whether memory is a certain degree of vividness in ideas, and of a certain degree of strength in their power of suggesting one another. To me they appear to be things quite of a different nature; and I could as easily believe that a hat is a pair of shoes as that memory is a certain degree of vividness in ideas and of strength in their association." "A malefactor that is going to be hanged has a cluster of very vivid ideas, and very strongly associated, of what he is about to suffer, but it is not the object of remembrance but of foresight;" or, "It appears evident, therefore, that something more than association of ideas is required to produce memory, and consequently that association is not of itself sufficient to explain or account for memory." He shows that association cannot account for judgment; "for if there is a power in the mind of comparing ideas and of perceiving certain relations between them, such as those of universal concurrence and perfect coincidence, this power is not that of association; for it is evident that ideas may be associated with any degree of strength without being compared, without perception of any relation between them." He shows in much the same way that association cannot account for the passions and volition. He shows in the same paper that Priestley's attempt to get Locke's ideas of reflection from sensation utterly fails. Priestley had said, "got by abstraction." "We would be glad to be informed by Dr. Priestley whether a man, when he thinks, is not conscious of his thoughts? Whether he has not the power of reflecting upon his own thoughts and making them an object of thought," &c.

III. *On Liberty or Necessity.* "The liberty of the will is a phrase similar to that of the liberty of speech. The last signifies not a power inherent in speech, but a power in the man to speak this or that. In like manner, the liberty of the will signifies not a power inherent in the will, but a power in man to will this or that." "This power is given by his Maker; and, at his pleasure whose gift it is, it may be enlarged or diminished, continued or withdrawn. No power in the creature can be independent of the Creator. The hook is in its nose; he can give it line as far as he sees fit, and when he pleases can restrain it or turn it whithersoever he will. Let this be always understood when we ascribe liberty to man or to any created being. Supposing it therefore to be true that man is a free agent, it may be true at the same time that his liberty may be impugned or lost by disorder of body or of mind, as in melancholy or in madness; it may be impaired or lost by vicious habits; it may in particular cases be restrained by divine interposition." He explains cause and effect, native and active power, liberty and necessity, standing up for efficient cause. In a fragmentary paper upon the same subject, perhaps a continuation: "I grant that all rational beings are influenced and ought to be influenced by motives. But the relation between a motive and the action is of a very different nature from the relation between an efficient cause and its effect. An efficient cause must be a being that exists and has power to produce the effect. A motive is not a thing that exists. It is only a thing conceived in the mind of the agent, and is what the schoolmen called an *ens rationis*, and therefore cannot possibly be the efficient cause of any thing. It may influence to action, but it cannot act. It is like advice or persuasion, which may have an influence of the same kind with that of motives; but they leave the man still at liberty and indeed suppose liberty. For in vain is advice given if the person be not at liberty either to follow or reject it. In like manner, motives suppose liberty in the agent, otherwise they have no influence at all."

IV. *Of Constitution.* Apparently a very old paper, not written with care for the press. "Every thing that is made must have some constitution,—some fabric, make, or nature,—from which all its qualities, appearances, powers, and operations do result." "It is one thing to say such a truth depends upon my constitution;

it is another thing to say that my perception of that truth depends on my constitution, and these two things ought most carefully to be distinguished." "My perception of every self-evident truth depends upon my constitution, and is the immediate effect of my constitution, and of that truth being presented to my mind. As soon as this truth is understood that two and two make four, I immediately assent to it, because God has given me the faculty of discerning immediately its truth, and if I had not this faculty I would not perceive this truth; but it would be a true proposition still, although I did not perceive its truth. The truth itself therefore does not depend upon my constitution, for it was a truth before I had an existence, and will be a truth, although I were annihilate; but my perception of it evidently depends upon my constitution, and particularly upon my having as a part of my constitution that faculty (whether you call it reason or common sense) by which I perceive or discover this truth." "If it should farther be inquired how far the truth of self-evident propositions depends on the constitution of the being that perceives them, the answer to this question is no less easy and obvious. As every truth expresses some attribute of a thing, or some relation between two or more things, the truth depends on the nature of the thing whose attribute is expressed. The truth of this proposition, that a lion is a ravenous beast, depends upon the constitution of a lion, and upon nothing else. The truth of this proposition, that the sun is greater than the moon, depends upon the magnitude of the sun and moon, and upon nothing else." In like manner as to right and wrong. "Although the rectitude or depravity has a real existence in the agent in this case, yet it cannot be discerned by a spectator who has not the faculty of discerning objects of this kind." "Why do I believe first principles?" "One philosopher says, Because I am so constituted that I must believe them. This, say some, is the only possible reason that can be given for the belief of first principles. But, say others, this is a very bad reason; it makes truth a vague thing which depends on constitution. Is not this the ancient sceptical system of Heraclitus, that man is the measure of truth, that what is true to one man may be false to another? How shall we judge of this controversy? Answer, This question admits of two meanings. 1. For what reason do you believe first principles? 2. To what cause is your belief of first principles to be ascribed?" "To first, evidence is the sole and ultimate ground of belief, and self-evidence is the strongest possible ground of belief, and he who desires a reason for believing what is self-evident knows not what he means." To the second the answer is not so satisfactory. It is, "that belief is a simple and original operation of the mind which always accompanies a thing we call evidence." "If it should be asked, what this evidence is which so imperiously commands belief, I confess I cannot define it." "If it should farther be asked, what is the cause of our perceiving evidence in first principles, to this I can give no other answer but that God has given us the faculty of judgment or common sense." The paper closes thus: "Q. Is there not a difference between the evidence of some first principles and others? A. There are various differences perhaps. This seems to be one, that, in some first principles, the predicate of the proposition is evidently contained in the subject: it is in this, two and three are equal to five; a man has flesh and blood. In these and the like self-evident principles, the subject includes the predicate in the very notion of it. There are other first principles in which the predicate is not contained in the notion of the subject; as, where we affirm that a thing which begins to exist must have a cause. Here the beginning of existence and causation are really different notions, nor does the first include the last. Again, when I affirm that the body which I see and feel really exists, existence is not included in the notion of a body. I can have the notion of it as distinct when it is annihilate. The truth of principles of the first kind is only perceiving some part of the definition of a thing to belong to it, and such propositions are indeed of very little use : they may justly, as Mr. Locke observes, be called trifling propositions. One general maxim may include all first principles of this kind ; viz., Whatever is contained in the definition of a thing may be predicated of it. But in reality the definition sufficiently supplies the place of such axioms. That the sides of a square are equal, that all the radii of a circle are equal, these do not deserve the name of axioms ; for they are included in the definitions of a square and of a circle. Of the same kind are these propositions that an effect must have a cause, that a son must have a father. There is nothing affirmed in such propositions but what is contained in the definition or in the notion of the terms. There are other first principles wherein the predicate is not contained in the definition or notion of the subject. Of this kind is every proposition which affirms the real existence of any thing. Existence is not included in the notion of any thing. I " — here the paper abruptly closes. The paper is the dimmest and yellowest of all : looks old. Query : when written ? The whole paper 11 pages.

V. *On the Axioms of Euclid.* " It seems no man pretends to define sum or difference, or what it is to be greater or less. There are therefore some terms that frequently enter into mathematical reasoning, so simple as not to admit of mathematical definition. The mathematical axioms ought to be employed about these and only about these."

VI. *On the Muscular Motion in the Human Body.* A paper worthy of constituting a chapter in " Paley's Natural Theology," showing a thorough knowledge of mechanical principles, and of the physiology of his time.

VII. *Some Thoughts on the Utopian System.* In this paper he seems to amuse himself with describing the advantages of a community without private property.

VIII. *An Essay on Quantity.* Royal Society of London, Oct., 1748, and published in works. — " P. S. When this essay was wrote in 1748, I knew so little of the history of the controversy about the force of moving bodies, as to think that the British mathematicians only opposed the notion of Leibnitz, and that all the foreign mathematicians adopted it. The fact is, the British and French are of one side ; the Germans, Dutch, and Italians of the other. I find likewise that Desaguliers, in the second volume of his course of ' Experimental Philosophy,' published in 1744, is of the opinion that the parties in dispute put different meanings upon the word force, and that in reality both are in the right when well understood."

INDEX.

31

www.ingramcontent.com/pod-product-compliance
Lightning Source LLC
Chambersburg PA
CBHW032017110726
47901CB00004B/1115